THE CIVIL COURT PRACTICE

2011

FORMS

LexisNexis®

Members of the LexisNexis Group worldwide

United Kingdom	LexisNexis, a Division of Reed Elsevier (UK) Ltd, Halsbury House, 35 Chancery Lane, LONDON, WC2A 1EL, and London House, 20–22 East London Street, Edinburgh EH7 4BQ
Australia	LexisNexis Butterworths, CHATSWOOD, New South Wales
Austria	LexisNexis Verlag ARD Orac GmbH & Co KG, VIENNA
Benelux	LexisNexis Benelux, Amsterdam
Canada	LexisNexis Canada, MARKHAM, Ontario
China	LexisNexis China, BEIJING and SHANGHAI
France	LexisNexis SA, PARIS
Germany	LexisNexis GmbH, Dusseldorf
Hong Kong	LexisNexis Hong Kong, HONG KONG
India	LexisNexis India, NEW DELHI
Italy	Giuffrè Editore, MILAN
Japan	LexisNexis Japan, TOKYO
Malaysia	Malayan Law Journal Sdn Bhd, KUALA LUMPUR
New Zealand	LexisNexis NZ Ltd, WELLINGTON
Poland	Wydawnictwo Prawnicze LexisNexis Sp, WARSAW
Singapore	LexisNexis Singapore, SINGAPORE
South Africa	LexisNexis Butterworths, DURBAN
USA	LexisNexis, DAYTON, Ohio

Published by LexisNexis Butterworths

A CIP Catalogue record for this book is available from the British Library.

ISBN for Forms supplement:

ISBN 978-1-4057-6028-7

9 781405 760287

ISBN for the set:

ISBN 978-1-4057-5581-8

9 781405 755818

ISBN for this volume: 978 1 4057 6028 7
ISBN for complete set of volumes: 978 1 4057 5581 8

Typeset by Columns Design Ltd, Reading England
Printed and bound in Great Britain by CPI William Clowes Ltd, Beccles, NR34 7TL

Visit LexisNexis UK at www.lexisnexis.co.uk

CIVIL COURT PRACTICE 2011
FORMS

INTRODUCTION

This supplement gathers together all the available forms referred to in the Practice Direction which supplements Part 4 of the Civil Procedure Rules, together with some additional miscellaneous forms. The Practice Direction to Part 4 of the Civil Procedure Rules was amended with effect from December 2002, changing the order in which forms are presented. These changes are reflected in this supplement.

Part 4 itself provides that:

> "(1) The forms set out in a practice direction shall be used in the cases to which they apply.
> (2) A form may be varied by the court or by a party if the variation is required by the circumstances of a particular case.
> (3) A form must not be varied so as to leave out any information or guidance which the form gives to the recipient.
> (4) Where these Rules require a form to be sent by the court or by a party for another party to use, it must be sent without any variation except such as is required by the circumstances of the particular case.
> (5) Where the court or a party produces a form shown in a practice direction with the words 'Royal Arms', the form must include a replica of the Royal Arms at the head of the first page."

The text of the Practice Direction is set out in Volume 1, para **CPR PD 4**. Please refer to the text for guidance on the way that the Practice Direction requires the forms to be used and their derivation.

The Index seeks to set out the forms by reference to their subject matter so that the practitioner who wishes to find a form relating to, for instance, "Charging Orders" will be referred to all the Forms relating to that topic by turning to that entry.

It should be remembered that there are only some forms which must be used or which are, in the old parlance, "prescribed".

The most important of the compulsory forms are:

1 the claim form: Form N1 (see **CPR PD 7A**, para 3.1);
2 the claim form for use under the alternative procedure in Part 8: Form N208 (see **CPR PD 7A**, para. 3.1);
3 Part 20 claim form: Form N211 (see **CPR PD 20**, para 3); and
4 an appellant's notice: Form N161 (see **CPR PD 52**, para 5.1).

The most important of the forms which "should" (as opposed to "must") be used are:

1 form of acknowledgment of service: (if one is used) Form N9 (see **CPR 10** and **CPR PD 10**, para 2);

2 form of acknowledgment of service in respect of a claim under Part 8: Form N210 (see **CPR PD 8A**, para 3.2);
3 notice of acceptance of a payment into court: Form N243 (see **CPR 36** and **CPR PD 36**, para 8.1);
4 list of documents: Form N265 (see **CPR PD 31**, para 3.1).

The "N" forms in Table 1 to the Practice Direction are those which are referred to in and are required to be used by various Practice Directions. They were originally set out in "Civil Procedure Rules, Practice Directions, Pre-Action Protocols and Forms" HMSO – as periodically amended. They are generally to be used in the form in which they appear in that publication (which is the form in which they are reproduced in this supplement).

The "No." forms (formerly prescribed by the RSC) and the "PF" forms (previously the "Practice Forms") are those which are most easily amenable to variation, as permitted by CPR 4(2), in order to meet the circumstances of the case. The provisions of CPR 4(3) ("A form must not be varied so as to leave out any information or guidance which the form gives to the recipient") must, however, always be borne in mind. They have been drafted to ensure that they contain all the information required by the Rules.

The Editors and Publishers believe that setting out all the forms in a single volume will assist practitioners and litigants alike. They would welcome any comments from subscribers, which should be sent to greenbook@lexisnexis.co.uk. For the latest civil procedure updates please see www.greenbook.co.uk.

March 2005
John Leslie
A Master of the Supreme Court, Queen's Bench Division

USER'S GUIDE TO THE CIVIL COURT PRACTICE 2011 FORMS SUPPLEMENT

The Forms supplement is supplied as part of the full subscription to *The Civil Court Practice 2011*. The forms in this supplement can also be found in the FORMS section of your 2011 CD-ROM.

The contents of this supplement are based on the three tables of forms listed in **CPR PD 4**. The forms may be modified as specified in the text of Practice Direction 4. See Volume 1, para **CPR PD 4**.

Subscribers should note that the forms marked by an asterisk in the lists below are now generated by the county courts' computer system. Therefore, these forms do not necessarily represent the final copy a litigant would receive.

Practice Direction 4 retains some of the old county court forms. Many of these old forms referred to N200 which provided a general title for proceedings under the County Court Rules. The old Form N200 is now obsolete and where the italic heading "General Title" is shown on the forms, practitioners should insert the names and description of parties, details of the relevant court and the case or claim number. A number of the old forms have not been revised since the Civil Procedure Rules came into force and practitioners may need to adapt the terminology accordingly (eg "in private" for "in chambers", "claim form" for "originating application"). In addition, some of the statutory references are now out of date and reference to the current statute should be made in accordance with the Interpretation Act 1978.

TABLE OF CONTENTS

Table 1

Table 2

Table 3

Claim Form

Click here to clear your data after printing

In the	
	for court use only
Claim No.	
Issue date	

Claimant

SEAL

Defendant(s)

Brief details of claim

Value

Defendant's name and address

	£
Amount claimed	
Court fee	
Solicitor's costs	
Total amount	

The court office at

is open between 10 am and 4 pm Monday to Friday. When corresponding with the court, please address forms or letters to the Court Manager and quote the claim number.

N1 Claim form (CPR Part 7) (01.02)

Printed on behalf of The Court Service

Claim No.	

Does, or will, your claim include any issues under the Human Rights Act 1998? ☐ Yes ☐ No

Particulars of Claim (attached)(to follow)

Statement of Truth
*(I believe)(The Claimant believes) that the facts stated in these particulars of claim are true.
* I am duly authorised by the claimant to sign this statement

Full name ______________________________

Name of claimant's solicitor's firm ______________________________

signed ____________________ position or office held ____________________
*(Claimant)(Litigation friend)(Claimant's solicitor) (if signing on behalf of firm or company)
delete as appropriate

Claimant's or claimant's solicitor's address to which documents or payments should be sent if different from overleaf including (if appropriate) details of DX, fax or e-mail.

Notes for claimant on completing a claim form

Before you begin completing the claim form

- You must think about whether alternative dispute resolution (ADR) is a better way to reach an agreement before going to court. The leaflet 'Making a claim? - Some questions to ask yourself' explains more about ADR and how you can attempt to settle your claim.
- Please read all of these guidance notes. The notes follow the order in which information is required on the form.
- If you are filling in the claim form by hand, please use black ink and write in block capitals.
- Copy the completed claim form and the defendant's notes for guidance so that you have one copy for yourself, one copy for the court and one copy for each defendant. Send or take the forms to the court office with the appropriate fee. The court will tell you how much this is.
- Court staff can help you fill in the claim form and give information about procedure once it has been issued. But they cannot give legal advice. If you need legal advice, for example, about the likely success of your claim or the evidence you need to prove it, you should contact a solicitor or a Citizens Advice Bureau.

Further information may be obtained from the court in a series of free leaflets.

Notes on completing the claim form

Heading

You must fill in the heading of the form to indicate the name of the court where you want the claim to be issued.

The claimant and defendant

As the person issuing the claim, you are called the 'claimant'; the person you are suing is called the 'defendant'. Claimants who are under 18 years old (unless otherwise permitted by the court) and patients within the meaning of the Mental Health Act 1983, must have a litigation friend to issue and conduct court proceedings on their behalf. Court staff will tell you more about what you need to do if this applies to you.

Providing information about yourself and the defendant

full address including postcode

You should provide the full address including postcode for yourself and the defendant. The postcode for any address in the United Kingdom may be obtained free from the Royal Mail Address Management Guide, or their website at www.royalmail.com.

If an address does not have a postcode you will need to ask the judge for permission to serve the claim with this information missing. There is no additional fee for this, but if you omit a postcode and fail to ask permission of the judge the court will not allow your claim to be served on the defendant until you supply the missing postcode or a judge permits service without it.

You must provide the following information about yourself and the defendant according to the capacity in which you are suing and in which the defendant is being sued.

When suing or being sued as:-

an individual:

You must enter his or her full unabbreviated name where known, including their first name and any middle name, their last name and the title by which she or he is known (i.e. Mr., Mrs., Ms., Dr., etc.) and residential address (including postcode and telephone number). Where the defendant is a proprietor of a business, a partner in a firm or an individual sued in the name of a club or other unincorporated association, the address for service should be the usual or last known place of residence or principal place of business of the company, firm or club or other unincorporated association.

Where the individual is:

trading under another name

you must enter his or her full unabbreviated name where known, and the title by which he or she is known and the full name under which he or she is trading, e.g. 'Mr. John Smith trading as Smith's Groceries'.

suing or being sued in a representative capacity

you must say what that capacity is e.g. 'Mr Joe Bloggs as the representative of Mrs Sharon Bloggs (deceased)'.

suing or being sued in the name of a club or other unincorporated association

add the words 'suing/sued on behalf of' followed by the name of the club or other unincorporated association.

an unincorporated business - a firm

In the case of a partnership (other than a limited liability partnership) you must enter the full name of the business followed by the suffix 'a firm'.

Enter the name of the firm followed by the words 'a firm' e.g. 'Bandbox - a firm' and an address including postcode for service. This may either be one of the partners residential addresses or the principal or last known place of business of the firm.

N1A Notes for claimant (04.06) HMCS

a company registered in England and Wales or a Limited Liability Partnership
In the case of a registered company or limited liability partnership, you must enter the full name of the company or partnership followed by the appropriate suffix, i.e. Ltd, Plc, LLP. You must provide an address, including postcode which is either the company's registered office or any place of business in England and Wales that has a real, or the most, connection with the claim e.g. a shop where goods were bought.

a corporation (other than a company)
enter the full name of the corporation and any suffix if appropriate and the address including postcode in England and Wales which is either its principal office or any other place where the corporation carries on activities and which has a real connection with the claim.

an overseas company (defined by s744 of the Companies Act 1985)
You must enter the company's full name and any suffix if appropriate and address including postcode. The address must either be the registered address under s691 of the Act or the address of the place of business having a real, or the most, connection with the claim.

under 18 write '(a child by Mr Joe Bloggs his litigation friend)' after the name. If the child is conducting proceedings on their own behalf write '(a child)' after the child's name.

a patient within the meaning of the Mental Health Act 1983 write '(by Mr Joe Bloggs his litigation friend)' after the patient's name.

Brief details of claim
You must set out under **this** heading:
- a concise statement of the nature of your claim
- the remedy you are seeking e.g. payment of money;

Value
If you are claiming a **fixed amount of money** (a 'specified amount') write the amount in the box at the bottom right-hand corner of the claim form against 'amount claimed'.

If you are not claiming a fixed amount of money (an 'unspecified amount') under 'Value' write "I expect to recover" followed by whichever of the following applies to your claim:
- 'not more than £5,000' **or**
- 'more than £5,000 but not more than £15,000' **or**
- 'more than £15,000'

If you are **not able** to put a value on your claim, write 'I cannot say how much I expect to recover'.

Personal injuries
If your claim is for 'not more than £5,000' and includes a claim for personal injuries, you must also write 'My claim includes a claim for personal injuries and the amount I expect to recover as damages for pain, suffering and loss of amenity is' followed by either:
- 'not more than £1,000' **or**
- 'more than £1,000'

Housing disrepair
If your claim is for 'not more than £5,000' and includes a claim for housing disrepair relating to residential premises, you must also write 'My claim includes a claim against my landlord for housing disrepair relating to residential premises. The cost of the repairs or other work is estimated to be' followed by either:
- 'not more than £1,000' **or**
- 'more than £1,000'

If within this claim, you are making a claim for other damages, you must also write:

'I expect to recover as damages' followed by either:
- 'not more than £1,000' **or**
- 'more than £1,000'

Defendant's name and address
Enter in this box the title, full names, address and postcode of the defendant receiving the claim form (ie. one claim form for each defendant). If the defendant is to be served outside England and Wales, you may need to obtain the court's permission.

Particulars of claim
You must set out under this heading:
- a concise statement of the facts on which you rely
- a statement (if applicable) to the effect that you are seeking aggravated damages or exemplary damages
- details of any interest which you are claiming
- any other matters required for your type of claim as set out in the relevant practice direction

Statement of truth
This must be signed by you,or by your solicitor or your litigation friend, if appropriate.

Where the claimant is a registered company or a corporation the claim must be signed by either the director, treasurer, secretary, chief executive, manager or other officer of the company or (in the case of a corporation) the mayor, chairman, president or town clerk.

Address for documents
Insert in this box the address at which you wish to receive documents and/or payments, if different from the address you have already given under the heading 'Claimant'. The address must be in England or Wales. If you are willing to accept service by DX, fax or e-mail, add details.

Notes for defendant on replying to the claim form

Please read these notes carefully - they will help you decide what to do about this claim. Further information may be obtained from the court in a series of free leaflets

- If this claim form was received with the particulars of claim completed or attached, you must reply within 14 days of the date it was served on you. If the words 'particulars of claim to follow' are written in the particulars of claim box, you should not reply until after you are served with the particulars of claim (which should be no more than 14 days after you received the claim form). If the claim was sent by post, the date of service is taken as the second business day after posting (see post mark). If the claim form was delivered or left at your address the date of deemed service will be the second business day (see CPR rule 6.17) after delivery.
- You may either:
  - pay the total amount i.e. the amount claimed, the court fee, and solicitor's costs (if any)
  - admit that you owe all or part of the claim and ask for time to pay, or
  - dispute the claim
- If you do not reply, judgment may be entered against you.
- The notes below tell you what to do.
- The response pack will tell you which forms to use for your reply. (The pack will accompany the particulars of claim if they are served after the claim form).
- Court staff can help you complete the forms of reply and tell you about court procedures. But they cannot give legal advice. If you need legal advice, for example about the likely success of disputing the claim, you should contact a solicitor or a Citizens Advice Bureau immediately.

Registration of Judgments: If this claim results in a judgment against you, details will be entered in a public register, the Register of Judgments, Orders and Fines. They will then be passed to credit reference agencies which will then supply them to credit grantors and others seeking information on your financial standing. **This will make it difficult for you to get credit.** A list of credit reference agencies is available from Registry Trust Ltd, 173/175 Cleveland Street, London W1T 6QR.

Costs and Interest: Additional costs and interest may be added to the amount claimed on the front of the claim form if judgment is entered against you. In a county court, if judgment is for £5,000 or more, or is in respect of a debt which attracts contractual or statutory interest for late payment, the claimant may be entitled to further interest.

Your response and what happens next

How to pay

Do not bring any payments to the court - they will not be accepted.

When making payments to the claimant, quote the claimant's reference (if any) and the claim number.

Make sure that you keep records and can account for any payments made. Proof may be required if there is any disagreement. It is not safe to send cash unless you use registered post.

Admitting the Claim

Claim for specified amount

If you admit all the claim, take or send the money, including the court fee, any interest and costs, to the claimant at the address given for payment on the claim form, within 14 days.

If you admit all the claim and you are asking for time to pay, complete Form N9A and send it to the claimant at the address given for payment on the claim form, within 14 days. The claimant will decide whether to accept your proposal for payment. If it is accepted, the claimant may request the court to enter judgment against you and you will be sent an order to pay. If your offer is not accepted, the court will decide how you should pay.

If you admit only part of the claim, complete Form N9A and Form N9B (see 'Disputing the Claim' overleaf) and send them to the court within 14 days. The claimant will decide whether to accept your part admission. If it is accepted, the claimant may request the court to enter judgment against you and the court will send you an order to pay. If your part admission is not accepted, the case will proceed as a defended claim.

Claim for unspecified amount

If you admit liability for the whole claim but do not make an offer to satisfy the claim, complete Form N9C and send it to the court within 14 days. A copy will be sent to the claimant who may request the court to enter judgment against you for an amount to be decided by the court, and costs. The court will enter judgment and refer the court file to a judge for directions for management of the case. You and the claimant will be sent a copy of the court's order.

If you admit liability for the claim and offer an amount of money to satisfy the claim, complete Form N9C and send it to the court within 14 days. The claimant will be sent a copy and asked if the

N1C Notes for defendant (10.08)

offer is acceptable. The claimant must reply to the court within 14 days and send you a copy. If a reply is not received, the claim will be stayed. If the amount you have offered is **accepted** -

- the claimant may request the court to enter judgment against you for that amount.
- if you have requested time to pay which is not accepted by the claimant, the rate of payment will be decided by the court.

If your offer in satisfaction is **not accepted** -

- the claimant may request the court to enter judgment against you for an amount to be decided by the court, and costs; and
- the court will enter judgment and refer the court file to a judge for directions for management of the case. You and the claimant will be sent a copy of the court's order.

Disputing the claim

If you are being sued as an individual for a specified amount of money and you dispute the claim, the claim may be transferred to a local court i.e. the one nearest to or where you live or carry on business if different from the court where the claim was issued.

If you need longer than 14 days to prepare your defence or to contest the court's jurisdiction to try the claim, complete the Acknowledgment of Service form and send it to the court within 14 days. This will allow you 28 days from the date of service of the particulars of claim to file your defence or make an application to contest the court's jurisdiction. The court will tell the claimant that your Acknowledgment of Service has been received.

If the case proceeds as a defended claim, you and the claimant will be sent an Allocation Questionnaire. You will be told the date by which it must be returned to the court. The information you give on the form will help a judge decide whether your case should be dealt with in the small claims track, fast track or multi-track. After a judge has considered the completed questionnaires, you will be sent a notice of allocation setting out the judge's decision. The notice will tell you the track to which the claim has been allocated and what you have to do to prepare for the hearing or trial. **Leaflets telling you more about the tracks are available from the court office.**

Claim for specified amount

If you wish to dispute the full amount claimed or wish to claim against the claimant (a counterclaim), complete Form N9B and send it to the court within 14 days.

If you admit part of the claim, complete the Defence Form N9B and the Admission Form N9A and send them both to the court within 14 days. The claimant will decide whether to accept your part admission in satisfaction of the claim (see under 'Admitting the Claim - specified amount'). If the claimant does not accept the amount you have admitted, the case will proceed as a defended claim.

If you dispute the claim because you have already paid it, complete Form N9B and send it to the court within 14 days. The claimant will have to decide whether to proceed with the claim or withdraw it and notify the court and you within 28 days. If the claimant wishes to proceed, the case will proceed as a defended claim.

Claim for unspecified amount/return of goods/ non-money claims

If you dispute the claim or wish to claim against the claimant (counterclaim), complete Form N9D and send it to the court within 14 days.

Personal injuries claims:

If the claim is for personal injuries and the claimant has attached a medical report to the particulars of claim, in your defence you should state whether you:

- agree with the report **or**
- dispute all or part of the report **and** give your reasons for doing so **or**
- neither agree nor dispute the report **or** have no knowledge of the report

Where you have obtained your own medical report, you should attach it to your defence.

If the claim is for personal injuries and the claimant has attached a schedule of past and future expenses and losses, in your defence you must state which of the items you:

- agree **or**
- dispute **and** supply alternative figures where appropriate **or**
- neither agree nor dispute or have no knowledge of.

Address where notices can be sent

This must be either your solicitor's address, your own residential or business address in the United Kingdom or (if you live elsewhere) some other address within the United Kingdom.

Statement of truth

This must be signed by you, by your solicitor or your litigation friend, as appropriate.

Where the defendant is **a registered company or a corporation** the response must be signed by either the director, treasurer, secretary, chief executive, manager or other officer of the company **or** (in the case of a corporation) the mayor, chairman, president or town clerk.

Notes for defendant on replying to the claim form (Consumer Credit Act claim)

Please read these notes carefully - they will help you decide what to do about this claim. You will have received a notice of hearing telling you when and where to come to court with the claim form. A leaflet is available from the court office about what happens when you come to a court hearing.

- You must reply to the claim form within 14 days of the date it was served on you. If the claim form was
  - sent by post, the date of service is taken as the second day after posting (see post mark)
  - delivered or left at your address, the date of service will be the day after it was delivered
  - handed to you personally, the date of service will be the day it was given to you
- You may either
  - pay the amount claimed
  - admit liability for the claim and offer to make payments to keep the goods
  - dispute the claim
- If you do not reply or attend the hearing, judgment may be entered against you.
- The notes below tell you what to do .
- Court staff can help you complete the forms of reply and tell you about court procedure. But they cannot give legal advice. If you need legal advice, for example about the likely success of disputing the claim, you should contact a solicitor or a Citizens Advice Bureau immediately.

Registration of Judgments: If this claim results in a judgment against you, details will be entered in a public register, the Register of Judgments, Orders and Fines. They will then be passed to credit reference agencies which will then supply them to credit grantors and others seeking information on your financial standing. **This will make it difficult for you to get credit.** A list of credit reference agencies is available from Registry Trust Ltd, 173/175 Cleveland Street, London W1T 6QR.

Costs and Interest: Additional costs and interest may be added to the amount claimed on the front of the claim form if judgment is entered against you. In a county court, if judgment is for £5,000 or more, or is in respect of a debt which attracts contractual or statutory interest for late payment, the claimant may be entitled to further interest.

Your response and what happens next

How to pay

Do not bring any payments to the court - they will not be accepted.

When making payments to the claimant, quote the claimant's reference (if any) and the claim number.

Make sure that you keep records and can account for any payments made. Proof may be required if there is any disagreement. It is not safe to send cash unless you use registered post.

Admitting the Claim

If you admit liability for the claim and offer to make payments in order to keep the goods. Complete Form N9C and send it to the court within 14 days. **Remember** to keep a copy for yourself. The court will send a copy of your admission to the claimant and ask if your offer is acceptable.

If the claimant **accepts your offer** and asks the court to enter judgment before the date of the hearing, you will be sent a copy of the judgment and need not come to the hearing. If you do not hear from the court it is in your interests to attend the hearing.

If your offer is **not accepted**, you should attend the hearing. The court will treat your admission as evidence so remember to bring a copy of your admission with you to the hearing.

Disputing the claim

If you dispute the claim or wish to claim against the claimant (counterclaim), complete Form N9D and send it to the court within 14 days. **Remember** to keep a copy for yourself and to bring it with you to the hearing. The court will send a copy of your defence to the claimant. At the hearing the court may make a final order or judgment in the claim. If the court agrees that you have a valid defence (or counterclaim), it will tell you and the claimant what to do to prepare for a future hearing. If you send your defence to the court after the 14 days has expired, and you want to rely on it at the hearing, the court may take your failure to file it on time into account when deciding what order to make in respect of costs.

Statement of truth

This must be signed by you, by your solicitor or your litigation friend, as appropriate.

Where the defendant is **a registered company or a corporation** the response must be signed by either the director, treasurer, secretary, chief executive, manager or other officer of the company **or** (in the case of a corporation) the mayor, chairman, president or town clerk.

N1(FD) Consumer Credit Act claim (04.06) HMCS

Click here to reset form | Click here to print form

Claim Form
(probate claim)

In the	
Claim No.	

In the estate of deceased (Probate)

SEAL

Claimant(s)

Defendant(s)

Brief details of claim

Defendant's name and address

Court fee	
Solicitor's costs	To be assessed

Issue date	

N2 Claim form probate (10.07)

Claim No.

Does, or will, your claim include any issues under the Human Rights Act 1998? ☐ Yes ☐ No

Particulars of Claim (attached)(to follow)

Statement of Truth

*(I believe)(The claimant believes) that the facts stated in this claim form are true.
* I am duly authorised by the claimant to sign this statement.

signed ______________________ date ______________________

*(Claimant)(Litigation friend *(where claimant is a child or a protected party)*)(Claimant's solicitor)
**delete as appropriate*

Full name ______________________

Name of claimant's solicitor's firm ______________________

position or office held ______________________
(if signing on behalf of a company)

Claimant's or claimant's solicitor's address to which documents should be sent if different from overleaf including (if appropriate) details of DX, fax or e-mail.

Click here to print form

Probate Claim
Notes for claimant on completing a claim form

Please read all these guidance notes before you begin completing the claim form. The notes follow the order in which information is required on it.

Court staff can help you fill in the claim form and give information about procedure once it has been issued. But they cannot give you legal advice. If you need legal advice, for example about the likely success of your claim, you should contact a solicitor or a Citizens Advice Bureau.

If you are filling in the claim form by hand, please use black ink and write in block capitals.

The claim form and all subsequent court documents relating to the probate claim must be marked at the top:

'In the estate of [name] deceased (Probate)'

Copy the completed claim form and the defendant's notes for guidance so that you have one copy for yourself, one copy for the court and one copy for each defendant. Send or take the forms to the court office with the appropriate fee. The court will tell you how much this is.

You must fill in the heading of the form to indicate the court where you want the claim to be issued. In London, you can issue your claim at the Royal Courts of Justice. The heading will be:

'In the High Court of Justice Chancery Division'

Outside London, you can only issue your claim in Birmingham, Bristol, Cardiff, Leeds, Liverpool, Manchester, Newcastle upon Tyne or Preston. This will be either in the District Registries; the heading will be :

'In the High Court of Justice Chancery Division District Registry'

or

in the county court; the heading will be:

'In the County Court'

As the person issuing the claim, you are called the 'claimant'; the person you are suing is called the 'defendant'.

Claimants who are under 18 years old or persons who lack capacity to conduct proceedings within the meaning of the Mental Capacity Act 2005 (ie. protected parties), must have a litigation friend to issue and conduct court proceedings on their behalf. Court staff will tell you more about what you need to do if this applies to you.

You must provide the following information about yourself and the defendant according to the capacity in which you are claiming and in which the defendant is being sued. When claiming or being sued as:-

An individual

All known forenames and surnames, whether Mr, Mrs, Miss, Ms or other (e.g. Dr.) and residential address (including postcode, telephone and fax number or e-mail address) in the United Kingdom.

Where the individual is
Under 18 write '(a child by "Mr Joe Bloggs" his litigation friend)' after the child's name. If the child is conducting proceedings on their own behalf write '(a child)' after the child's name.

A person who lacks capacity within the meaning of the Mental Capacity Act 2005 to conduct proceedings (ie. protected parties) write '(by "Mr Joe Bloggs" his litigation friend)' after the protected party's name.

Where your claim seeks revocation of a grant of probate or letters of administration, every person who is entitled to, or claims to be entitled to, administer the estate under the grant, must be made a party to the claim.

Claim form
- The claim form must contain a statement of the nature of the interest of the claimant and of each defendant in the estate.
- If you dispute another party's interest in the estate you must state this and set out your reasons.
- If you contend that
  - at the time when a will was executed the testator did not know of and approve its contents,
  - a will was not duly executed; or
  - at the time of the execution of a will the testator was not of sound mind, memory and understanding; or
  - the execution of a will was obtained by undue influence or fraud,

you must set out the contention specifically and give particulars of the facts and matters relied upon.

Statement of truth
This must be signed by you, by your solicitor or your litigation friend as appropriate. Proceedings for contempt of court may be brought against a person who signs a statement of truth without an honest belief in its truth.

N2A Notes for claimant on completing a claim form (10.08)

Address for documents
Insert in this box the address at which you wish to receive documents if different from the address you have already given under the heading 'Claimant'. The address must be in the United Kingdom.

If you are willing to accept service by DX, fax or e-mail, add details.

Documents to be filed

You must file any testamentary document of the deceased person which you have in your possession or control with your claim form.

A testamentary document means a will, a draft of a will, written instructions for a will made by or at the request of, or under the instructions of the testator and any documents purporting to be evidence of the contents, or to be a copy, of a will which is alleged to have been lost or destroyed.

In addition you must file written evidence about the documents which should be in the form annexed to the Practice Direction to Part 57. It must be signed by you personally (and not your solicitor) or by your litigation friend.

You may only file your claim form without the testamentary documents or evidence about them if the court gives permission. It will normally do this only in cases of urgency. For example, where you wish to apply for the immediate appointment of an administrator pending the determination of your claim and it is not possible to obtain the documents immediately.

If the court gives permission it will expect you to give an undertaking to lodge the documents by a specific date.

Inspection of testamentary documents
Except with the permission of the court, no party is allowed to inspect the testamentary documents or written evidence lodged or filed by another party until they have lodged their testamentary documents and filed their evidence.

Probate Claim
Notes for the defendant

Please read these notes carefully they will help you decide what to do about this claim. If you need legal advice, you should contact a solicitor or Citizens Advice Bureau immediately.

You have 28 days from the date on which you were served with particulars of claim in which to respond. Particulars of claim may be contained in the claim form itself or served separately. You should respond by completing and returning the acknowledgment of service enclosed with this claim form.

Court staff can help you complete the form and tell you about procedures but they cannot give you legal advice.

Responding to this claim

Acknowledgment of Service

Whether or not you wish to defend the claim, you must file an acknowledgment of service. The period for filing the acknowledgment of service is:

- if you have been served with a claim form which states that particulars of claim are to follow, within 28 days after you have been served with the particulars of claim;
- in any other case, 28 days after you have been served with the claim form.

Defence/Counterclaim

If you wish to defend the claim you must file a defence (and or a counterclaim). The period for filing it (them) is the same as the period for filing an acknowledgment of service set out above.

N2B Notes for the defendant (10.01)

Failure to acknowledge service

If you fail to acknowledge service, the claimant may, after the time for acknowledging has expired, ask the court to proceed with the claim.

Documents to be filed with the acknowledgment of service

When you file your acknowledgment of service with the court you must also lodge any testamentary documents of the deceased person that are in your possession and control.

A testamentary document means a will, a draft of a will, written instructions for a will made by or at the request of, or under the instructions of the testator and any documents purporting to be evidence of the contents, or to be a copy, of a will which is alleged to have been lost or destroyed.

In addition you must file written evidence about the documents which should be in the form annexed to the Practice Direction to Part 57. It must be signed by you personally (and not your solicitor) or by your litigation friend.

Non inspection of testamentary documents

A party is not, unless the court gives permission, allowed to inspect the testamentary documents or written evidence lodged or filed by any other party until they have lodged their testamentary documents and filed their evidence.

Counterclaim

If you believe that you have a claim or are entitled to a remedy relating to the grant of probate of the will, or letters of administration of the estate of the deceased person, you must serve a counterclaim.

If the claimant fails to serve particulars of claim within the time allowed, you may ask the court's permission to serve your counterclaim. If permission is granted, the claim will then proceed as if your counterclaim were the particulars of claim.

Click here to reset form | Click here to print form

Acknowledgment of service
(probate claim)

In the

Claim No.

Claimant(s)

Defendant(s)

In the estate of deceased (Probate)

You should read the 'notes for the defendant' attached to the claim form before you complete this form.

Tick the appropriate box

☐ I intend to defend this claim and attach my defence (and counterclaim).

☐ I **do not** intend to defend this claim.

Testamentary documents of the deceased

☐ Testamentary documents are described in the attached witness statement or affidavit. [The documents are also attached for lodging].

☐ I do not know of any testamentary documents - see attached witness statement or affidavit.

Revocation of existing Grant

Do not complete this part unless the claimant is seeking revocation of a grant of probate or letters of administration, and the grant has not already been lodged in court.

☐ I do not have the [probate] [letters of administration] under my control.

☐ I do have the grant of [probate] [letters of administration] under my control. [I am lodging it with this acknowledgment of service.]

Signed

(Defendant)(Defendant's Solicitor)
(Litigation friend *(where defendant is a child or a protected party)*)

Position or office held (if signing on behalf of a company)

This acknowledgment is filed on behalf of the *_____ Defendant, whose date of birth is D D M M Y Y Y Y
*(*Please state whether 1st, 2nd, 3rd etc. as appropriate)*

Address to which documents about this claim should be sent

	if applicable	
	fax no.	
	DX no.	
	e-mail	
Tel. no. Postcode	ref no.	

N3 Acknowledgment of service (10.07)

Claim form for possession of property

In the	
Claim No.	

Claimant
(name(s) and address(es))

SEAL

Defendant(s)
(name(s) and address(es))

The claimant is claiming possession of :

which (includes) (does not include) residential property. Full particulars of the claim are attached.
(The claimant is also making a claim for money).

This claim will be heard on: 20 at am/pm

at

At the hearing
- The court will consider whether or not you must leave the property and, if so, when.
- It will take into account information the claimant provides and any you provide.

What you should do
- Get help and advice immediately from a solicitor or an advice agency.
- Help yourself and the court by **filling in the defence form** and **coming to the hearing** to make sure the court knows all the facts.

Defendant's name and address for service

Court fee	£
Solicitor's costs	£
Total amount	£

Issue date	

N5 Claim form for possession of property (08.05) HMCS

Claim No.

Grounds for possession
The claim for possession is made on the following ground(s):

- ☐ rent arrears
- ☐ other breach of tenancy
- ☐ forfeiture of the lease
- ☐ mortgage arrears
- ☐ other breach of the mortgage
- ☐ trespass
- ☐ other *(please specify)* ....

Anti-social behaviour
The claimant is alleging:

- ☐ actual or threatened anti-social behaviour
- ☐ actual or threatened use of the property for unlawful purposes

Is the claimant claiming demotion of tenancy? ☐ Yes ☐ No

Is the claimant claiming an order suspending the right to buy? ☐ Yes ☐ No

See full details in the attached particulars of claim

Does, or will, the claim include any issues under the Human Rights Act 1998? ☐ Yes ☐ No

Statement of Truth
*(I believe)(The claimant believes) that the facts stated in this claim form are true.
* I am duly authorised by the claimant to sign this statement.

signed date ....
*(Claimant)(Litigation friend *(where the claimant is a child or a patient)*)(Claimant's solicitor)
**delete as appropriate*

Full name ....

Name of claimant's solicitor's firm

position or office held ....
(if signing on behalf of firm or company)

Claimant's or claimant's solicitor's address to which documents or payments should be sent if different from overleaf.

Postcode

if applicable

Ref. no.
fax no.
DX no.
e-mail
Tel. no.

Claim form for relief against forfeiture

In the	
Claim No.	

Claimant
(name(s) and address(es))

SEAL

Defendant(s)
(name(s) and address(es))

The claimant is interested in the lease dated 20 , of the property:

The defendant, as the person entitled to the reversion on the lease, on 20 , forfeited or served notice of intention to forfeit the lease.

The claimant seeks relief from that forfeiture so that the lease can continue.

Full particulars of the claim are [overleaf][attached].

The claim will be heard on: 20 at am/pm

at

Defendant's name and address for service

Court fee	£
Solicitor's costs	£
Total amount	£

Issue date	

N5A Claim form for relief against forfeiture (10.01)

The Court Service Publications Branch

Claim No.	

Particulars of Claim [are attached]

Statement of Truth

*(I believe)(The claimant believes) that the facts stated in this claim form are true.
* I am duly authorised by the claimant to sign this statement.

signed ______________________ date ______________________

*(Claimant)(Litigation friend *(where the claimant is a child or a patient)*)(Claimant's solicitor)
**delete as appropriate*

Full name ______________________

Name of claimant's solicitor's firm ______________________

position or office held ______________________
(if signing on behalf of firm or company)

Claimant's or claimant's solicitor's address to which documents should be sent if different from overleaf.

Postcode

if applicable	
Ref. no.	
fax no.	
DX no.	
e-mail	
Tel. no.	

Click here to reset form | Click here to print form

Claim form for possession of property
(accelerated procedure)
(assured shorthold tenancy)

In the	
Claim No.	

Claimant
(name(s) and address(es))

SEAL

Defendant(s)
(name(s) and address(es))

The claimant is claiming possession of:

for the reasons given in the following pages.
[The claimant is also asking for an order that you pay the costs of the claim.]

IMPORTANT - TO THE DEFENDANT(S)

This claim means that the court will decide whether or not you have to leave the premises and, if so, when. There will not normally be a court hearing. You must act immediately.

Get help and advice from an advice agency or a solicitor.
Read all the pages of this form and the papers delivered with it.
Fill in the defence form and return it **within 14 days** of receiving this form.

The notes on the last page of this form tell you more about what you can do.

Defendant's name and address for service

Court fee	£
Solicitor's costs	£
Total amount	£

Issue date	

N5B Claim form for property (accelerated procedure)(assured shorthold tenancy) (04.10)

Claim No.	

If you are a registered social landlord or a private registered provider of social housing claiming possession of premises let under a demoted assured shorthold tenancy, you should complete **only** sections 1, 2, and 7 to 12. Please see Notes for the claimant in Form N5C.	If you are not claiming possession of premises let under a demoted tenancy **do not** complete **section 2** but complete all other sections as appropriate. Please see Notes for the claimant in Form N5C.

1. The claimant seeks an order that the defendant(s) give possession of

("the premises") which is a dwelling house [part of a dwellinghouse].

2. On the 20 , the County Court made a demotion order. A copy of the most recent (assured) (secure) tenancy agreement marked 'A' and a copy of the demotion order marked 'B' is attached to this claim form. The defendant was previously (an assured) (a secure) tenant.

3. On , the claimant entered into a written tenancy agreement with the defendant(s). A copy of it, marked 'A' is attached to this claim form. The tenancy did not immediately follow an assured tenancy which was not an assured shorthold tenancy.
[One or more subsequent written tenancy agreements have been entered into. A copy of the most recent one, made on , marked 'A1', is also attached to this claim form.]

4. Both the [first] tenancy and the agreement for it were made on or after 28th February 1997.

a) No notice was served on the defendant stating that the tenancy would not be, or continue to be, an assured shorthold tenancy.

b) There is no provision in the tenancy agreement which states that it is not an assured shorthold tenancy.

c) The "agricultural worker condition" defined in Schedule 3 to the Housing Act 1988 is not fulfilled with respect to the property.

(or)

5. Both the [first] tenancy and the agreement for it were made on or after 15 January 1989.

a) The [first] tenancy agreement was for a fixed term of not less than six months.

b) There was no power for the landlord to end the tenancy earlier than six months after it began.

c) On the 19 (before the tenancy began) a notice in writing, stating that the tenancy was to be an assured shorthold tenancy, was served on the defendant(s). It was served by:

d) Attached to this claim form is a copy of that notice marked 'B' [and proof of service marked 'B1'].

6. Whenever a new tenancy agreement has replaced the first tenancy agreement or has replaced a replacement tenancy agreement,

a) it has been of the same, or substantially the same, premises, and

b) the landlord and tenant were the same people at the start of the replacement tenancy as the landlord and tenant at the end of the tenancy which it replaced.

Claim No.	

7. On the 20 , a notice in writing, saying that possession of the premises was required, was served upon the defendant(s). It was served by:

The notice expired on the 20 .
Attached to this claim form is a copy of that notice marked 'C' [and proof of service marked 'C1'].

8.
(a). The property is (or is part of) a House in Multiple Occupation and is required to be licensed under part 2 of the Housing Act 2004 and has a valid licence. Attached to this claim form is a copy of that licence marked 'D'. If the licence application is outstanding with the local housing authority, evidence of the application (including an application made under Section 346 of the Housing Act 1985) should be attached.

OR

(b) The property is required to be licensed under part 3 of the Housing Act and has a valid licence. Attached to this claim form is a copy of that licence marked 'D'. If the licence application is outstanding with the local housing authority, evidence of the application should be attached.

OR

(c) The property is not required to be licenced under part 2 or 3 of the Housing Act 2004.

9. The following section must be completed in all cases *(delete as appropriate)*

(a) a money deposit was received on or after 6 April 2007 ☐ Yes ☐ No

(b) If Yes, at the date of service of the Section 21 Notice:

(i) The deposit was held under a Tenancy Deposit Scheme (TDS) authorised under Part 6 of the Housing Act 2004

(ii) The initial requirements of the TDS had been complied with in relation to the deposit.

(iii) The claimant had given the defendant and anyone who paid the deposit on behalf of the defendant the prescribed information in relation to the deposit and the operation of the TDS

(c) The claimant received a deposit in the form of property on or after 6 April 2007 ☐ Yes ☐ No

(d) If Yes, at the date of service of the section 21 Notice that property had been returned to the person from whom it was received.

10. *(any further information, continue on separate sheet if necessary)*

Claim No.	

11. If the defendant(s) seek(s) postponement of possession on the grounds of exceptional hardship, the claimant is content that the request be considered without a hearing.

12. The claimant asks the court

to order that the defendant(s) deliver up possession of the property.

[to order the defendant(s) to pay the costs of this claim.]

13. Statement of Truth

*(I believe)(The claimant believes) that the facts stated in this claim form (and any attached sheets) are true.
* I am duly authorised by the claimant to sign this statement.

signed .... date ....

(Claimant)(Litigation friend(where claimant is a child or a protected party)*)(Claimant's solicitor)
**delete as appropriate*

Full name ....

Name of claimant's solicitor's firm ....

position or office held ....
(if signing on behalf of firm or company)

Claimant's or claimant's solicitor's address to which documents should be sent if different from that on the front page.

Postcode

	if applicable
Ref. no.	
fax no.	
DX no.	
e-mail	
Tel. no.	

Notes for the defendant

The claimant has used the accelerated procedure because it is said you have an assured shorthold tenancy or demoted assured shorthold tenancy. If so, the court is not allowed to consider whether it is reasonable or fair to make the order for possession. Therefore, if what is written in the claim form and in the defence form make it clear that the claimant is entitled to possession, the court will make the order without fixing a hearing.

The claimant cannot use the procedure if you have a tenancy of the whole, or part of a property that is required to be licensed under parts 2 or 3 of the Housing Act 2004, unless the local authority has granted a licence for the property or an application has been made to it for one. The claimant has given a declaration as to whether he requires (or does not require) a licence on the claim form.

You can check with your local authority whether a licence has been granted or an application for a licence has been received. Your authority maintains a public register of licensed properties which is available for inspection during normal working hours.

From 6 April 2007, the claimant cannot use the procedure if a deposit that has been taken for the tenancy has not been protected under sections 212 to 213 of the Housing Act 2004.

If you think there are reasons why the court should not make a possession order, you should consider getting advice from a solicitor or an advice agency immediately. If you dispute the claim, fill in the defence form and return it to the court office within 14 days of receiving the claim form. If you cannot give exact dates in your defence form, give them as nearly as you can. Make it clear that the dates you give are approximate. The judge can only take account of legally valid reasons.

You may qualify for assistance from Community Legal Service Fund (CLSF) to meet some or all of your legal costs. Ask about the CLSF at any county court office or any information or help point which displays this logo.

Community Legal Service

Court staff can only help you complete the defence form and tell you about court procedures. They cannot give legal advice.

If the court makes a possession order without a hearing, you will be entitled to apply, within 14 days of receiving the order, for it to be reconsidered. The application would have to show some good legal reason for varying or revoking the order.

Normally, if the court makes a possession order, it will tell you to leave the premises within 14 days. The judge can allow up to 42 days but only if satisfied that leaving within 14 days would cause you hardship which is exceptional (that is, worse than would usually be suffered by someone having to leave within 14 days). If you believe there are exceptional circumstances in your case, fill in section 11 of the defence form and return it to the court office. Usually, an order for possession in 14 days will still be made but a hearing will be fixed within the 14 day period. The judge will decide at the hearing whether or not to extend the period.

If the court orders you to pay the claimant's costs, normally the order requires payment within 14 days. If you would be unable to pay in that time, fill in section 12 of the defence form and give details of your means.

If you use the defence form, you must sign the Statement of Truth. Proceedings for contempt of court may be brought against a person who signs a Statement of Truth without an honest belief in its truth.

Send documents for the court to the court office at

Telephone:
Fax:

Please address all correspondence to "The Court Manager".

CERTIFICATE OF SERVICE

(completed on court copy only)

I certify that the claim form of which this is a true copy was served by me on

____

by posting it to the defendant(s) on

____

at the address stated on the first page of the claim form.

OR

The claim form has not been served for the following reasons:

Officer of the Court

Notes for the claimant (accelerated procedure)

These notes are not part of the claim form and need not be returned to the court. They are for guidance only in completing the claim form. They are not a full statement of the law, nor are they a substitute for legal advice. You can only use the accelerated possession procedure if you can make the statements printed in the claim form (as explained below) and attach the documents which it requires. If in doubt, take legal advice. You cannot ask for any other order than for possession and costs.
For example, you cannot ask for an order for payment of rent arrears.

Completing the claim form

- Write legibly in black ink.
- Fill in the full names and addresses, including postcode of the claimant and the defendant(s) and the full address of the premises on the front page.
- The statement must be made by the claimant, the claimant's litigation friend (if the claimant is a child or protected party) or the claimant's solicitor. If the claimant is a company or corporation, a person holding a senior position may sign on its behalf. The statement may not be signed by, for example, the claimant's managing agent.

The numbered notes below relate to similarly numbered sections in the claim form.

If you are a registered social landlord or a private registered provider of social housing claiming possession of premises let under a demoted assured shorthold tenancy, you should complete only sections 1, 2 and 7 to 12. Otherwise complete all sections as appropriate.

1. If the premises of which you seek possession are part of a building, identify the part (e.g. 'Flat 3' or 'rooms 6 and 7').

2. You must attach to the claim form a copy of the most recent tenancy agreement and a copy of the demotion order relating to that tenancy.

3. Give the date of the first written tenancy agreement. If there has been more than one, give also the date of the most recent - otherwise delete the words in square brackets. Attach a copy (of each), marking them 'A' (and 'A1').

4. Complete this section and delete section 5 if the tenancy (and any agreement for it) was made on or after 28th February 1997. Delete the word 'first' if it does not apply. If the property was let to an agricultural worker in connection with his employment, you may need to take appropriate advice before making this statement.

5. Complete this section and delete section 4 if the tenancy (or the agreement for it) was made before 15th January 1989. Delete the word 'first' if it does not apply. A copy of the notice served at the start of the tenancy must be attached, if this section applies. Mark it 'B'. Say how and by whom the notice was served. If you did not serve the notice yourself, attach documentary proof of service, if you can (e.g. a receipted copy), marking it 'B1'. If the defendant does not admit receiving the notice, the judge may fix a hearing so that evidence can be given.

6. Delete this section if there has been only the one tenancy.

7. The date on which the notice requires possession to be given must be at least two months after it was served. The notice must not require possession before the end of any current fixed term tenancy. In the case of a periodic tenancy, the date specified in the notice after which possession is required must be the last day of a period of the tenancy. If the tenancy agreement provides for notice to end it, this notice must comply with that provision. A copy of the notice must be attached. Mark it 'C'. Say how and by whom the notice was served. See note 5 above as to proof of service.

8. Delete the two options that do not apply.

9. If you have received a deposit on or after 6 April 2007, the judge cannot make a possession order if you have not complied with section 213 of the Housing Act 2004 and any Section 21 Notice you have served while you have not complied will be invalid. This section is for you to indicate whether you have complied. The court will usually also require evidence of compliance.

10. Set out the further evidence (if any) you wish the judge to take into account. Attach any documents referred to, marking them 'D1', 'D2' and so on.

11. With the exception of premises let on a demoted assured shorthold tenancy, the judge cannot make an order for possession to take effect before six months after the start of the (first) tenancy. Other than that, if an order for possession is made it will usually require the defendant to leave in 14 days unless the judge accepts that this would cause the defendant exceptional hardship. In that case, the judge may allow up to 6 weeks, but will not do so without fixing a hearing which you can attend, unless you indicate that you are content that the defendant's request be dealt with in your absence. Delete this section if you do want a hearing fixed if the defendant makes that request. If a hearing is fixed, the judge may order one party to pay the other's costs of attending.

12. If you do not seek an order for costs, delete the request.

13. The statement of truth must be signed. Proceedings for contempt of court may be brought against a person who signs a statement of truth without an honest belief in its truth. Unless a solicitor is acting for you, you must give the address of your residence or place of business (or, if you do not have such an address in England and Wales, some address within England and Wales where documents may be sent to you). If you agree that the court and the defendant(s) may communicate with you by Document Exchange, telephone, facsimile or email, complete the details.

N5C Notes for the claimant (accelerated procedure) (04.10)

Claim form for demotion of tenancy/ suspension of right to buy

In the	
Claim No.	

Claimant
(name(s) and address(es))

SEAL

Defendant(s)
(name(s) and address(es))

The claimant is claiming a:

☐ demotion order

☐ suspension order

in relation to the tenancy of:

which is a residential property. Full particulars of the claim are attached.

This claim will be heard on: 20 at am/pm

at

At the hearing the court will consider:

- whether you have or a person residing in or visting the property has, engaged or threatened to engage in anti-social behaviour; or used or threatened to use the property for unlawful purposes; and
- whether it is reasonable to make the order

What you should do

- Get help and advice immediately from a solicitor or an advice agency.
- Help yourself and the court by **filling in the defence form** and **coming to the hearing** to make sure the court knows all the facts.

Defendant's name and address for service

Court fee	£
Solicitor's costs	£
Total amount	£

Issue date	

N6 Claim form for demotion of tenancy/suspension of right to buy (08.05)

HMCS

Claim No.	

The claimant is alleging:

☐ actual or threatened anti-social behaviour

☐ use or threatened use of the property for unlawful purposes

Does, or will, the claim include any issues under the Human Rights Act 1998? ☐ Yes ☐ No

Statement of Truth

*(I believe)(The claimant believes) that the facts stated in this claim form are true.
* I am duly authorised by the claimant to sign this statement.

signed .... date ....

*(Claimant)(Claimant's solicitor)

**delete as appropriate*

Full name ....

Name of claimant's solicitor's firm ....

position or office held ____________________

(if an authorised signatory not acting as a solicitor)

Claimant's or claimant's solicitor's address to which documents or payments should be sent if different from overleaf.

	Postcode

if applicable	
Ref. no.	
fax no.	
DX no.	
e-mail	
Tel. no.	

Notes for defendant - mortgaged residential premises

The claimant has asked the court to make an order that you give up possession of the premises mentioned in the claim form. You should note that no-one can evict you from the property unless the court says that they can; the court will not make a decision before the hearing date. What you do may affect the court's decision. You should therefore take action immediately. These notes explain in more detail what you can do.

You should:
- get help and advice immediately from a solicitor or advice agency (see 'Getting help' below);
- fill in the attached defence form and return it to the court within 14 days of receiving the claim form;
- attend the hearing, even if you have agreed about repayment of any arrears with your mortgage lender.

What will happen at the hearing?

A judge will decide whether or not to make an order for possession. In making this decision, the judge will take account of the information provided by the claimant. The judge will also take account of any information you provide, such as details of your personal and financial circumstances, any proposal you have made to pay off any arrears, and any dispute you have about the amount owing. But the judge can only take the information into account if you provide it. Fill in these details on the defence form and attend the hearing. It is in your best interests to do both.

What kind of orders can the judge make?

The judge can:
- decide not to make an order
- make an order for possession but suspend it. This means that you will not have to give up possession so long as you can pay off any arrears in a reasonable time (the judge will decide how long) and pay the instalments as well;
- make a possession order for some future date to allow you time to move out or find somewhere else to live; or
- make an order that you give up possession a very short time ahead.
- if the loan agreement is 'regulated' (see paragraph 4 of the particulars of claim) the judge can make other orders which may help you.

Getting help

You should get help and advice immediately from a solicitor or an advice agency. This is particularly important whether or not you disagree with the claim. You may qualify for assistance from the Community Legal

N7 Notes for defendant - mortgaged residential premises (04.06) HMCS

Service Fund (CLSF) to meet some or all of your legal costs. Ask about the CLSF at any county court office or any information or help point which displays this logo. Court staff can only help you complete the defence form and tell you about court procedures. **They cannot give legal advice.**

Replying to the claim

Although you should normally fill in the defence form and return it to the court within 14 days, the court will accept your defence at any time before, or even at, the hearing. You should note, however, that if you do return the form after the 14-day period, the court may order you to pay any costs caused by the delay.

Regulated consumer credit agreements

If you intend to apply to the court to consider or change the terms of your agreement, you should get advice immediately.

Paying any arrears

The court cannot accept payments. If you want to pay all or part of any arrears, send them to the claimant at the address for payment shown on the claim form, quoting the claimant's reference number, if one is given. Make sure you get receipts for all payments made. Proof may be required if there is any disagreement. Make sure you include on your defence form details of any payments you have made since the claim was issued, saying how much was paid, to whom and when.

Enforcement of a possession order

Where the court makes a possession order, the claimant can ask a bailiff or enforcement officer to evict you if:

- you do not give up possession on the date given in the order for possession; or
- you do not make payments in accordance with the suspended order for possession.

If your circumstances change after the possession order is made, you may apply to the court for the order to be varied. Use application form N244, which is available from any court office. You may have to pay a fee to make the application.

Registration of judgments

If a county court makes a money judgment (e.g. for the balance due under the mortgage) your name and address will be entered in the Register of Judgments, Orders and Fines if the claimant has to take steps to enforce the judgment. This may make it difficult for you to obtain credit.

Notes for defendant - rented residential premises claim

The claimant has asked the court to make an order that you give up possession of the premises mentioned in the claim form. You should note that no-one can evict you from the premises unless the court says that they can; the court will not make a decision before the hearing date. What you do may affect the court's decision. You should therefore take action immediately. These notes explain in more detail what you can do.

You should:

- get help and advice immediately from a solicitor or advice agency (see 'Getting help' below);
- fill in the attached defence form and return it to the court within 14 days of receiving the claim form;
- attend the hearing, even if you have agreed about repayment of any arrears with your landlord.

What will happen at the hearing?

A judge will decide whether or not to make an order for possession. In making this decision, the judge will take account of the information provided by the claimant. The judge will also take account of any information you provide, such as details of your personal and financial circumstances, any proposal you have made to pay off any arrears, and any dispute you have about the amount owing. But the judge can only take the information into account if you provide it. Fill in these details in the defence form and attend the hearing. It is in your best interests to do both.

What kind of orders can the judge make?

Depending on the type of your tenancy the judge may:

- decide not to make an order for possession;
- make an order for possession but suspend it. This means that you will not have to give up possession so long as you can pay off any arrears in a reasonable time (the judge will decide how long) and pay the rent as well;
- make a possession order for some future date to allow you time to move out or find somewhere else to live; or
- make an order that you give up possession a very short time ahead.

If the claimant is claiming **demotion of tenancy** or a **suspension order** (see paragraph 11 of the particulars of claim), the judge can make a demotion or suspension order **instead** of a possession order. A demotion order means that your current tenancy will be replaced with a demoted tenancy. During the period of demotion (usually 12 months) you will lose a number of rights you currently enjoy under the tenancy. If the court makes a demotion order, this will not mean that you have to leave your home but it will be much easier to evict you in the future.

If the court makes a suspension order it would mean that you could not exercise your right to buy the premises during the period of suspension.

Getting help

You should get help and advice immediately from a solicitor or an advice agency. This is particularly important whether or not you disagree with the claim since these notes cannot cover every different type of tenancy. You may qualify for assistance from the Community Legal Service Fund (CLSF) to meet some or all of your legal costs. Ask about the CLSF at any county court office or any information or help point which displays this logo. Court staff can only help you complete the defence form and tell you about court procedures. **They cannot give legal advice.**

Replying to the claim

Although you should normally fill in the defence form and return it to the court within 14 days, the court will accept your defence at any time before, or even at, the hearing. You should note, however, that if you do return the form after the 14-day period, the court may order you to pay any costs caused by the delay.

Paying any arrears

The court cannot accept payments. If you want to pay all or part of any arrears, send them to the claimant at the address for payment shown on the claim form, quoting the claimant's reference number, if one is given. Make sure you have a receipt for all payments made. Proof may be required if there is any disagreement. Make sure you include on your defence form details of any payments you have made since the claim was issued, saying how much was paid, to whom and when.

Enforcement of a possession order

Where the court makes a possession order, the claimant can ask a bailiff or enforcement officer to evict you if:

- you do not give up possession on the date given in the order for possession; or
- you do not make payments in accordance with the suspended order for possession.

If your circumstances change after a possession order is made, you may apply to the court for the order to be varied. Use application form N244 which is available from any court office. You may have to pay a fee to make the application.

Registration of judgments

If a county court makes a money judgment (e.g. for rent arrears and costs) your name and address will be entered in the Register of Judgments, Orders and Fines if the claimant has to take steps to enforce the judgment. This may make it difficult for you to obtain credit.

Notes for defendant - forfeiture of the lease (residential premises)

The claimant has asked the court to make an order that you lose (forfeit) the lease of the premises mentioned in the claim form. You should note that no one can evict you from the premises unless the court says that they can. What you do may affect the court's decision. You should therefore take action immediately. These notes apply when the only ground relied on is rent arrears. They explain in more detail what you can do.

You should:

- If you can, pay all the unpaid rent and costs, including any rent which has become due since the claim was issued. **(See 'Paying the arrears' below).**
- If you cannot pay, get help and advice immediately from a solicitor or advice agency **(see 'Getting help' below)** and;
- Fill in the attached defence form and return it to the court within 14 days of receiving the claim form, and;
- Attend the hearing.

Paying the arrears:

If you pay all the arrears and costs and any rent due before the hearing, the claim will cease, the lease will continue unaffected and the hearing will be cancelled. Remember that you must include in your payments any rent which has become due since the claim was issued. The daily rate of rent is given at paragraph 2(c) of the particulars of claim. You should add this amount for each day that has passed since the claim was issued to the arrears and costs already due. The date of issue is on the front of the claim form.

You should make your payment at least **5 clear days** before the hearing. Make sure you get dated receipts. If you pay by cheque, the hearing will **not** be cancelled unless it has cleared.

What will happen at the hearing?

The judge will take into account information provided by the claimant. The judge will also take into account any information you provide, such as, details of your personal and financial circumstances, any proposal you have made to pay off any arrears, and any dispute you have about the amount owing. But the judge can only take the information into account if you provide it. Fill in the defence form and attend the hearing. It is in your best interests to do both.

What kind of orders can the judge make?

The judge can:

- refuse to make an order for forfeiture; or
- adjourn the claim to another day;
- suspend forfeiture of the lease on the condition that you pay the arrears and costs together with the current rent at a time and rate which the court will decide;
- make an order that you leave the premises.

Getting help

You should get help and advice immediately from a solicitor or an advice agency. This is particularly important whether or not you disagree with the claim. You may qualify for assistance from the Community Legal Service Fund (CLSF) to meet some or all of your legal costs. Ask about CLSF at any county court office or any information or help point which displays this logo. Court staff can only help you complete the defence form and tell you about court procedures. **They cannot give legal advice.**

Community Legal Service

Enforcement of a forfeiture order

Where the court makes a forfeiture order, the claimant can ask a bailiff or Enforcement Officer to evict you if:

- you do not pay all the rent and costs by the given date in the order;
- you do not give up possession of the premises by the date given in the order;
- you do not make payments in accordance with the suspended order.

If your circumstances change after a possession order is made, you may apply to the court for the order to be varied. Use application form N244 which is available from any court office. You may have to pay a fee to make the application.

Registration of judgments

If a county court makes a money judgment (e.g. for rent arrears and costs), your name and address will be entered in the Register of Judgments, Orders and Fines if the claimant has to take steps to enforce the judgment. This may make it difficult for you to obtain credit.

Notes for defendant - demotion/suspension claim

Demotion claims

The claimant (your landlord) has asked the court to make an order that will end your tenancy for the premises mentioned in the claim form and replace it with a demoted tenancy on the grounds that you, or a person residing in or visiting the premises, have used or threatened to use anti-social behaviour or use the premises for unlawful purposes. If the court makes a demotion order, this will **not** mean you have to leave your home but it will be much easier to evict you in the future.

You should note that your landlord cannot end your existing tenancy unless the court says that he can; the court will not make a decision before the hearing date. What you do may affect the court's decision. You should therefore take action immediately. These notes explain in more detail what you can do:

You should:

- get help and advice immediately from a solicitor or advice agency (see 'Getting help' below);
- fill in the attached defence form and return it to the court within 14 days of receiving the claim form;
- attend the hearing

What is the effect of a demotion order?

If you currently hold a secure tenancy and the court decides to grant a demotion order, this will end your secure tenancy and so you will lose a number of the rights you currently enjoy. This will include removing your right to buy your home and the right to exchange your home with another tenant.

If you currently hold an assured tenancy and the court decides to grant a demotion order, the terms of your tenancy will become an assured short-hold tenancy. This will remove a number of the tenancy rights you currently enjoy, during the demotion period.

The period of demotion will be for 12 months but may be extended if your landlord serves notice to seek possession of your property during this time.

If at the end of the demotion period your landlord is satisfied with the conduct of your tenancy and has not served notice to seek possession of your property then, depending on the tenancy you currently hold, your tenancy will become either:

- a secure tenancy if your landlord is a local authority or housing action trust; or
- if your landlord is a registered social landlord or a private registered provider of social housing an ordinary assured tenancy.

Suspension claims

If the claimant is claiming a suspension order (see claim form), and the court makes such an order, it would mean that during the period of suspension you could not exercise your right to buy the premises. The court decides the length of the suspension. On the application of the claimant, the court may make an order extending the period of suspension on the grounds of anti-social behaviour which has arisen since the making of the suspension order.

Getting help

Community Legal Service

You should get help and advice immediately from a solicitor or an advice agency. This is particularly important whether or not you disagree with the claim. You may qualify for assistance from the Community Legal Service Fund (CLSF) to meet some or all of your legal costs. Ask about the CLSF at any county court office or any information or help point which displays this logo. Court staff can only help you complete the defence form and tell you about court procedures. They cannot give legal advice.

Replying to the claim

Although you should normally fill in the defence form and return it to the court within 14 days, the court will accept your defence at any time before, or even at, the hearing. You should note, however, that if you do return the form after the 14-day period, the court may order you to pay any costs caused by the delay.

Registration of judgment

If a county court makes a money judgment (e.g. for costs) your name and address will be entered in the Register of County Court Judgments if the claimant has to take steps to enforce the judgment. This may make it difficult for you to obtain credit.

N7D Notes for defendant – demotion claim (04.10)

Response pack

You should read the 'notes for defendant' attached to the claim form which will tell you when and where to send the forms

Included in this pack are:

- either **Admission Form N9A** (if the claim is for a specified amount)
  or Admission Form N9C (if the claim is for an unspecified amount or is not a claim for money)
- either **Defence and Counterclaim Form N9B** (if the claim is for a specified amount)
  or Defence and Counterclaim Form N9D (if the claim is for an unspecified amount or is not a claim for money)
- **Acknowledgment of service** (see below)

	Complete
If you admit the claim or the amount claimed and/or you want time to pay	the admission form
If you admit part of the claim	the admission form and the defence form
If you dispute the whole claim or wish to make a claim (a counterclaim) against the claimant	the defence form
If you need 28 days (rather than 14) from the date of service to prepare your defence, or wish to contest the court's jurisdiction	the acknowledgment of service
If you do nothing, judgment may be entered against you	

Acknowledgment of service

Defendant's full name if different from the name given on the claim form

Name of court	
Claim No.	
Claimant (including ref.)	
Defendant	

Address to which documents about this claim should be sent (including reference if appropriate)

Postcode

If applicable	
Telephone no.	
Fax no.	
DX no.	
Your ref.	

E-mail

Tick the appropriate box

1. I intend to defend all of this claim ☐
2. I intend to defend part of this claim ☐
3. I intend to contest jurisdiction ☐

(My) (Defendant's) date of birth is __/__/____

If you file an acknowledgment of service but do not file a defence within 28 days of the date of service of the claim form, or particulars of claim if served separately, judgment may be entered against you.

If you do not file an application to dispute the jurisdiction of the court within 14 days of the date of filing this acknowledgment of service, it will be assumed that you accept the court's jurisdiction and judgment may be entered against you.

If served outside the jurisdiction see CPR rule 6.35 and 6.37(5).

Signed

(Defendant) (Defendant's solicitor) (Litigation friend)

Position or office held (if signing on behalf of firm or company)

Date __/__/____

The court office at

is open between 10 am and 4 pm Monday to Friday. When corresponding with the court, please address forms or letters to the Court Manager and quote the claim number.

N9 Response pack (10.08)

n9_1008.indd 1 23/09/2008 14:28:

Admission (specified amount)

- You have a limited number of days to complete and return this form
- Before completing this form, please read the notes for guidance attached to the claim form

When to fill in this form

Only fill in this form if:

- you are admitting all of the claim **and** you are asking for time to pay; or
- you are admitting part of the claim. (You should also complete form N9B)

How to fill in this form

- Tick the correct boxes and give as much information as you can. **Then sign and date the form.** If necessary provide details on a separate sheet, add the claim number and attach it to this form.
- Make your offer of payment in box 11 on the back of this form. **If you make no offer the claimant will decide how much and when you should pay.**
- If you are not an individual, you should ensure that you provide sufficient details about the assets and liabilities of your firm, company or corporation to support any offer of payment made in box 11.
- You can get help to complete this form at **any** county court office or Citizens Advice Bureau.

Where to send this form

- **If you admit the claim in full**
  Send the completed form to the address shown on the claim form as one to which documents should be sent.
- **If you admit only part of the claim**
  Send the form **to the court** at the address given on the claim form, together with the defence form (N9B).

How much of the claim do you admit?

☐ I admit the full amount claimed as shown on the claim form **or**

☐ I admit the amount of £

Name of court	
Claim No.	
Claimant (including ref.)	
Defendant	

1 Personal details

Surname

Forename

☐ Mr ☐ Mrs ☐ Miss ☐ Ms

☐ Married ☐ Single ☐ Other *(specify)*

Date of birth D D M M Y Y Y Y

Address

Postcode

Tel. no.

2 Dependants *(people you look after financially)*

Number of children in each age group

under 11 ☐ 11-15 ☐ 16-17 ☐ 18 & over ☐

Other dependants *(give details)*

3 Employment

☐ **I am employed as a**
My employer is

Jobs other than main job *(give details)*

☐ **I am self employed as a**

Annual turnover is........................ £

☐ **I am not** in arrears with my national insurance contributions, income tax and VAT

☐ **I am** in arrears and I owe.......... £

Give details of:
(a) contracts and other work in hand
(b) any sums due for work done

☐ **I have been unemployed for** years months

☐ **I am a pensioner**

4 Bank account and savings

☐ **I have a bank account**

☐ The account is in credit by........ £

☐ The account is overdrawn by.... £

☐ **I have a savings or building society account**

The amount in the account is......... £

5 Residence

I live in ☐ my own house ☐ lodgings
☐ my jointly owned house ☐ council accommodation
☐ rented accommodation

6 Income

My usual take home pay *(including overtime, commission, bonuses etc)*	£ per
Income support	£ per
Child benefit(s)	£ per
Other state benefit(s)	£ per
My pension(s)	£ per
Others living in my home give me	£ per
Other income *(give details below)*	
	£ per
	£ per
	£ per
Total income	**£ per**

8 Priority debts

(This section is for arrears only. Do not include regular expenses listed in box 7.)

Rent arrears	£ per
Mortgage arrears	£ per
Council tax/Community Charge arrears	£ per
Water charges arrears	£ per
Fuel debts: Gas	£ per
Electricity	£ per
Other	£ per
Maintenance arrears	£ per
Others *(give details below)*	
	£ per
	£ per
Total priority debts	**£ per**

7 Expenses

(Do not include any payments made by other members of the household out of their own income)

I have regular expenses as follows:

Mortgage *(including second mortgage)*	£ per
Rent	£ per
Council tax	£ per
Gas	£ per
Electricity	£ per
Water charges	£ per
TV rental and licence	£ per
HP repayments	£ per
Mail order	£ per
Housekeeping, food, school meals	£ per
Travelling expenses	£ per
Children's clothing	£ per
Maintenance payments	£ per
Others *(not court orders or credit debts listed in boxes 9 and 10)*	
	£ per
	£ per
	£ per
Total expenses	**£ per**

9 Court orders

Court	Claim No.	£	per

Total court order instalments **£ per**

Of the payments above, I am behind with payments to *(please list)*

10 Credit debts

Loans and credit card debts *(please list)*

	£ per
	£ per
	£ per

Of the payments above, I am behind with payments to *(please list)*

11 Offer of payment

☐ I can pay the amount admitted on

or

☐ I can pay by monthly instalments of £

If you cannot pay immediately, please give brief reasons below

12 Declaration

I declare that the details I have given above are true to the best of my knowledge

Signed

Date

Position or office held (if signing on behalf of firm or company)

Click here to reset form | Click here to print form

Defence and Counterclaim (specified amount)

- Fill in this form if you wish to dispute all or part of the claim and/or make a claim against the claimant (counterclaim).
- You have a limited number of days to complete and return this form to the court.
- Before completing this form, please read the notes for guidance attached to the claim form.
- Please ensure that all boxes at the top right of this form are completed. You can obtain the correct names and number from the claim form. The court cannot trace your case without this information.

How to fill in this form

- Complete sections 1 and 2. Tick the correct boxes and give the other details asked for.
- Set out your defence in section 3. If necessary continue on a separate piece of paper making sure that the claim number is clearly shown on it. In your defence you must state which allegations in the particulars of claim you deny and your reasons for doing so. **If you fail to deny an allegation it may be taken that you admit it.**
- If you dispute only some of the allegations you must
  - specify which you admit and which you deny; and
  - give your own version of events if different from the claimant's.

Name of court	
Claim No.	
Claimant (including ref.)	
Defendant	

- If you wish to make a claim against the claimant (a counterclaim) complete section 4.
- Complete and sign section 5 before sending this form to the court. Keep a copy of the claim form and this form.

Need help with your legal problems?
Community legal advice is a free confidential service, funded by legal aid. They can help you find the information and advice you need by putting you in touch with relevant agencies, helplines or local advice services. And if you are eligible for legal aid, the service can offer specialist legal advice over the telephone in cases involving: debt; housing; employment; benefits; and education.
Call **0845 345 4 345** or **www.communitylegaladvice.org.uk**

1. How much of the claim do you dispute?

☐ I dispute the full amount claimed as shown on the claim form.

or

☐ I admit the amount of £

If you dispute only part of the claim you must **either**:

- pay the amount admitted to the person named at the address for payment on the claim form (see How to Pay in the notes on the back of, or attached to, the claim form). Then send this defence to the court

or

- complete the admission form **and** this defence form and send them to the court.

☐ I paid the amount admitted on __/__/____

or

☐ I enclose the completed form of admission *(go to section 2)*

2. Do you dispute this claim because you have already paid it? *Tick whichever applies*

☐ **No** *(go to section 3)*

☐ **Yes** I paid £ ______ to the claimant on __/__/____ *(before the claim form was issued)*

Give details of where and how you paid it in the box below *(then go to section 5)*

3. Defence (If you need to continue on a separate sheet put the claim number in the top right hand corner.)

(continue over the page)

N9B Defence and Counterclaim (specified amount) (04.08)

Claim No.	

Defence (continued)

4. If you wish to make a claim against the claimant (a counterclaim)

- To start your counterclaim, you will have to pay a fee. Court staff can tell you how much you have t
- You may not be able to make a counterclaim where the claimant is the Crown (e.g. a Government Department). Ask at your local county court office for further information.

If your claim is for a specific sum of money, how much are you claiming? £

I enclose the counterclaim fee of £

My claim is for *(please specify nature of claim)*

What are your reasons for making the counterclaim?
If you need to continue on a separate sheet put the claim number in the top right hand corner.

5. Signed - To be signed by you or by your solicitor or litigation friend.

*(I believe) (The defendant believes) that the facts stated in this form are true.
*I am duly authorised by the defendant to sign this statement.

**delete as appropriate*

Position or office held
(If signing on behalf of firm or company)

Date / /

Defendant's date of birth, if an individual / /

Give an address to which notices about this case can be sent to you

Postcode

	If applicable
Telephone no.	
Fax no.	
DX no.	

E-mail

Admission (unspecified amount, non-money and return of goods claims)

- Before completing this form please read the notes for guidance attached to the claim form. If necessary provide details on a separate sheet, add the claim number and attach it to this form.
- If you are not an individual, you should ensure that you provide sufficient details about the assets and liabilities of your firm, company or corporation to support any offer of payment made.

In the	
Claim No.	
Claimant (including ref)	
Defendant	

In non-money claims only

☐ I admit liability for the whole claim (Complete section 11)

In return of goods cases only

Are the goods still in your possession?

☐ Yes ☐ No

Part A Response to claim *(tick one box only)*

☐ I admit liability for the whole claim but want the court to decide the amount I should pay / value of the goods

OR

☐ I admit liability for the claim and offer to pay ______ in satisfaction of the claim

(Complete part B and sections 1 - 11)

Part B How are you going to pay the amount you have admitted? *(tick one box only)*

☐ I offer to pay on (date) ______

OR

☐ I cannot pay the amount immediately because *(state reason)*

______

AND

I offer to pay by instalments of £ ______ per (week)(month)

starting *(date)* ______

1 Personal details

Surname ______

Forename ______

☐ Mr ☐ Mrs ☐ Miss ☐ Ms

☐ Married ☐ Single ☐ Other *(specify)* ______

Date of birth D D M M Y Y Y Y

Address ______

Postcode ______

Tel. no. ______

2 Dependants *(people you look after financially)*

Number of children in each age group

under 11 ☐ 11-15 ☐ 16-17 ☐ 18 & over ☐

Other dependants *(give details)* ______

3 Employment

☐ **I am employed as a** ______

My employer is ______

Jobs other than main job *(give details)* ______

☐ **I am self employed as a** ______

Annual turnover is........................ £ ______

☐ **I am not** in arrears with my national insurance contributions, income tax and VAT

☐ **I am** in arrears and I owe.......... £ ______

Give details of:

(a) contracts and other work in hand ______

(b) any sums due for work done ______

☐ **I have been unemployed for** ______ years ______ months

☐ **I am a pensioner**

4 Bank account and savings

☐ **I have a bank account**

☐ The account is in credit by........ £ ______

☐ The account is overdrawn by.... £ ______

☐ **I have a savings or building society account**

The amount in the account is......... £ ______

5 Residence

I live in

☐ my own property ☐ lodgings

☐ jointly owned house ☐ rented property

☐ council accommodation

N9C Admission (unspecified amount and non-money claims) (04.06) HMCS

6 Income

My usual take home pay *(including overtime, commission, bonuses etc)*	£	per
Income support	£	per
Child benefit(s)	£	per
Other state benefit(s)	£	per
My pension(s)	£	per
Others living in my home give me	£	per
Other income *(give details below)*		
	£	per
	£	per
	£	per
Total income	**£**	**per**

7 Expenses

(Do not include any payments made by other members of the household out of their own income)

I have regular expenses as follows:

Mortgage *(including second mortgage)*	£	per
Rent	£	per
Council tax	£	per
Gas	£	per
Electricity	£	per
Water charges	£	per
TV rental and licence	£	per
HP repayments	£	per
Mail order	£	per
Housekeeping, food, school meals	£	per
Travelling expenses	£	per
Children's clothing	£	per
Maintenance payments	£	per
Others *(not court orders or credit debts listed in sections 9 and 10)*		
	£	per
	£	per
	£	per
Total expenses	**£**	**per**

8 Priority debts

(This section is for arrears only. Do not include regular expenses listed in section 7)

Rent arrears	£	per
Mortgage arrears	£	per
Council tax/Community Charge arrears	£	per
Water charges arrears	£	per
Fuel debts: Gas	£	per
Electricity	£	per
Other	£	per
Maintenance arrears	£	per
Others *(give details below)*		
	£	per
	£	per
Total priority debts	**£**	**per**

9 Court orders

Court	Claim No.	£	per
Total court order instalments		**£**	**per**

Of the payments above, I am behind with payments to *(please list)*

10 Credit debts

Loans and credit card debts *(please list)*

	£	per
	£	per
	£	per

Of the payments above, I am behind with payments to *(please list)*

11 Declaration

I declare that the details I have given above are true to the best of my knowledge

Signed

Position or office held
(if signing on behalf of firm or company)

Date

Click here to reset form | Click here to print form

Defence and Counterclaim
(unspecified amount, non-money and return of goods claims)

Name of court	
Claim No.	
Claimant (including ref.)	
Defendant	

- Fill in this form if you wish to dispute all or part of the claim and/or make a claim against the claimant (a counterclaim)
- You have a limited number of days to complete and return this form to the court.
- Before completing this form, please read the notes for guidance attached to the claim form.
- Please ensure that all the boxes at the top right of this form are completed. You can obtain the correct names and number from the claim form. The court cannot trace your case without this information.

How to fill in this form

- Set out your defence in section 1. If necessary continue on a separate piece of paper making sure that the claim number is clearly shown on it. In your defence you must state which allegations in the particulars of claim you deny and your reasons for doing so. If you fail to deny an allegation it may be taken that you admit it.
- If you dispute only some of the allegations you must
  - specify which you admit and which you deny; and
  - give your own version of events if different from the claimant's.
- If the claim is for money and you dispute the claimant's statement of value, you must say why and if possible give your own statement of value.

- If you wish to make a claim against the claimant (a counterclaim) complete section 2.
- Complete and sign section 3 before returning this form.

Where to send this form

- send or take this form immediately to the court at the address given on the claim form.
- Keep a copy of the claim form and the defence form.

Need help with your legal problems?

Community legal advice is a free confidential service, funded by legal aid. They can help you find the information and advice you need by putting you in touch with relevant agencies, helplines or local advice services. And if you are eligible for legal aid, the service can offer specialist legal advice over the telephone in cases involving: debt; housing; employment; benefits; and education

Call **0845 345 4 345** or **www.communitylegaladvice.org.uk**

1. Defence

(continue over the page)

N9D Defence and Counterclaim (unspecified amount, non-money and return of goods claims) (04.08)

Claim No.	

Defence (continued)

2. If you wish to make a claim against the claimant (a counterclaim)

- To start your counterclaim, you will have to pay a fee. Court staff can tell you how much you have t
- You may not be able to make a counterclaim where the claimant is the Crown (e.g. a Government Department). Ask at your local county court office for further information.

If your claim is for a specific sum of money, how much are you claiming? £

I enclose the counterclaim fee of £

My claim is for *(please specify nature of claim)*

What are your reasons for making the counterclaim?
If you need to continue on a separate sheet put the claim number in the top right hand corner.

3. Signed - To be signed by you or by your solicitor or litigation friend.

*(I believe) (The defendant believes) that the facts stated in this form are true.
*I am duly authorised by the defendant to sign this statement.

**delete as appropriate*

Position or office held
(If signing on behalf of firm or company)

Date / /

Defendant's date of birth, if an individual / /

Give an address to which notices about this case can be sent to you

Postcode

	If applicable
Telephone no.	
Fax no.	
DX no	

E-mail

Notice that Acknowledgment of Service has been filed

In the	
Claim No.	
Claimant (including ref)	
Defendant (including ref)	
Date	

To the [Claimant]['s Solicitor]

The defendant filed an Acknowledgment of Service on

The defendant responded to the claim indicating an intention to [defend all of the claim.][defend part of the claim.][contest the court's jurisdiction.]

The defendant has 28 days from the date of service of the claim form with particulars of claim, or of the particulars of claim, to file [a defence.][an application to contest the court's jurisdiction.]

[The defendant's name has been corrected to read .]

[The defendant has given the following address for service of documents:]

[The acknowledgment was filed by the solicitors acting for the defendant who have given the following name and address for service of documents: .]

The court office at

is open between 10 am and 4 pm Monday to Friday. When corresponding with the court, please address forms or letters to the Court Manager and quote the claim number

N10 Notice that Acknowledgment of Service has been Filed

Click here to reset form | Click here to print form

Defence form

In the

Claim No.

Claimant

Defendant(s)

I dispute the claimant's claim because:-

Statement of Truth

*(I believe)(The defendant(s) believe(s)) that the facts stated in this defence form (and any continuation sheets) are true.

* I am duly authorised by the defendant(s) to sign this reply form.

signed ______________________ date ______________________

(Defendant(s))(Litigation friend(where the defendant is a child or a protected party)*)(Defendant's solicitor)

**delete as appropriate*

Defendant's date of birth D D M M Y Y Y Y

Full name ....

Name of defendant's solicitor's firm ....

position or office held ....

(if signing on behalf of firm or company)

Defendant's or defendant's solicitor's address to which documents should be sent.

Postcode

if applicable	
Ref. no.	
fax no.	
DX no.	
e-mail	
Tel. no.	

N11 Defence form (12.07)

Click here to reset form | Click here to print form

Defence form

(accelerated possession procedure)
(assured shorthold tenancy)

Name of court	Claim No.
Name of Claimant	
Name of Defendant(s)	

To the Defendant

Please read the notes on the back page of the claim form before completing this form.

Some of the questions in this form refer to numbered sections in the claim form. You will find it helpful to have that open as you answer them.

Please note that if section 2 of the claim form has been completed because you are a tenant of premises let under a demoted assured shorthold tenancy, you need only answer questions 1 and 6 to 12.

In all cases you **must** complete and sign the statement of truth.

Please write clearly and in black ink. If there is not enough room for an answer, continue on the last page.

1. Are you the tenant(s) named in the tenancy agreement, marked 'A' (or 'A1'), attached to the claim form? ☐ Yes ☐ No

Does that tenancy agreement (or do both) set out the present terms of your tenancy (except for any changes in the rent or the length of the tenancy)? ☐ Yes ☐ No

If No, say what terms have changed and what the changes are:

2. Do you agree the date, in section 3 of the claim form, when the claimant says the tenancy began? ☐ Yes ☐ No

If No, on what date did it begin? ☐☐/☐☐/☐☐☐☐

3. If the claimant has completed section 4 of the claim form, do you agree with what is said there? ☐ Yes ☐ No

If No, what do you disagree with and why?

N11B Defence form (accelerated possession procedure)(assured shorthold tenancy) (04.10)

4. If the claimant has completed section 5 of the claim form, did you receive the notice (a copy of which is attached to the claim form and marked 'B') and, if so, when?

☐ Yes ☐ No

If Yes, give date ☐☐/☐☐/☐☐☐☐

Do you agree with the rest of what is said in section 5?
If No, what do you disagree with and why?

☐ Yes ☐ No

5. If the claimant has not deleted section 6 of the claim form, do you agree that what is said there is correct?

☐ Yes ☐ No

If No, what do you disagree with and why?

6. Did you receive the notice referred to in section 7 of the claim form, (a copy of which is attached to the claim form and marked 'C') and, if so, when?

☐ Yes ☐ No

If Yes, give date ☐☐/☐☐/☐☐☐☐

7. Do you agree that what is said in section 8 of the claim form is correct?

☐ Yes ☐ No

8. Do you agree that what is said in section 9 of the claim form is correct?
If No, what do you disagree with and why?

☐ Yes ☐ No

9. If the claimant has put any additional information in section 10 of the claim form, do you agree that what is said there is correct?

☐ Yes ☐ No

If No, what do you disagree with and why?

10. If there is some other reason, not covered above, why you say the claimant is not entitled to recover possession of the property, please explain it here.

Postponement of possession

11. Are you asking the court, if it makes a possession order, to allow you longer than 14 days to leave the premises because you would suffer exceptional hardship? ☐ Yes ☐ No

If Yes, explain why the hardship you would suffer would be exceptional.

Say how long you wish to be allowed to remain in the premises. (The court cannot allow more than 42 days after the order is made.) up to .... 20......

Payment of costs

12. If the court orders you to pay the claimant's costs, do you ask it to allow you more than 14 days to pay? ☐ Yes ☐ No

If Yes, give details of your means *(continue onto last page if necessary)*

Statement of Truth

*(I believe)(The defendant(s) believe(s)) that the facts stated in this defence form (and any attached sheets) are true.

* I am duly authorised by the defendant(s) to sign this statement.

signed .... date ....

(Defendant)(Litigation friend(where defendant is a child or a patient)*)(Defendant's solicitor)

**delete as appropriate*

Defendant's date of birth | D | D | M | M | Y | Y | Y | Y |

Full name ....

Name of defendant's solicitor's firm ....

position or office held ....
(if signing on behalf of firm or company)

Defendant's or defendant's solicitor's address to which documents should be sent.

Postcode

if applicable	
Ref. no.	
fax no.	
DX no.	
e-mail	
Tel. no.	

Claim No.

Additional Information

(Include the number of the section which is being continued or to which the information relates)

Signed .... Date ....

(Continue on a separate sheet if necessary, remembering to sign and date it and heading it with the Claim Number)

Defence form
(demotion of tenancy)
(suspension of right to buy)

Name of court	Claim No.
Name of Claimant	
Name of Defendant	
Date of hearing	

Personal details
Please give your:

Forename(s)

Surname

Address *(if different from the address on the claim form)*

Post code

(Demotion claims only)

Did you receive the notice from the claimant referred to at paragraph 9 of the particulars of claim? ☐ Yes ☐ No

If Yes, when: / / DD/MM/YY

Disputing the claim
Do you agree with what is said about your conduct or use of the property? ☐ Yes ☐ No

If No, set out your reasons below:

(Continue overleaf)

(Use additional sheets if necessary)

Statement of Truth
*(I believe)(The defendant(s) believe(s)) that the facts stated in this defence form are true.
* I am duly authorised by the defendant(s) to sign this statement.

signed date

*(Defendant)(Litigation friend *(where defendant is a child or a patient)*)(Defendant's solicitor)
**delete as appropriate*

Full name

Name of defendant's solicitor's firm

position or office held
(if signing on behalf of firm or company)

Defence form
(mortgaged residential premises)

Name of court	Claim No.
Name of Claimant	
Name of Defendant	
Date of hearing	

Personal details

1. Please give your:

Title ☐ Mr ☐ Mrs ☐ Miss ☐ Ms ☐ Other

First name(s) in full

Last name

Date of birth D D | M M | Y Y Y Y

Address *(if different from the address on the claim form)*

Postcode

Disputing the claim

2. Do you agree with what is said about the property and the mortgage agreement in the particulars of claim? ☐ Yes ☐ No

If No, set out your reasons below:

3. Do you agree that there are arrears of mortgage repayments as stated in the particulars of claim? ☐ Yes ☐ No

If No, state how much the arrears are: £________ ☐ None

N11M Defence form (mortgaged residential premises) (04.06) HMCS

4. If the particulars of claim give any reasons for possession other than arrears of mortgage repayments, do you agree with what is said? ☐ Yes ☐ No

If No, give details below:

(Only answer these questions if the loan secured by the mortgage (or part of it) is a regulated consumer credit agreement)

5. Do you want the court to consider whether or not the terms of your original loan agreement are fair? ☐ Yes ☐ No

6. Do you intend to apply to the court for an order changing the terms of your loan agreement (a time order)? ☐ Yes ☐ No

Arrears

7. Have you paid any money to your mortgage lender since the claim was issued? ☐ Yes ☐ No

If Yes, state how much you have paid and when: £ date ....

8. Have you come to any agreement with your mortgage lender about repaying the arrears since the claim was issued? ☐ Yes ☐ No

I have agreed to pay £.................. each (week)(month).

9. If you have not reached an agreement with your mortgage lender, do you want the court to consider allowing you to pay the arrears by instalments? ☐ Yes ☐ No

10. How much can you afford to pay in addition to the current instalments? £.................. per (week)(month)

About yourself

State benefits

11. Are you receiving Income Support? ☐ Yes ☐ No

12. Have you applied for Income Support? ☐ Yes ☐ No

If Yes, when did you apply? ....

13. Does the Department of Social Security pay your mortgage interest? ☐ Yes ☐ No

Dependants (people you look after financially)

14. Have you any dependant children? ☐ Yes ☐ No

If Yes, give the number in each age group below:

☐ under 11 ☐ 11-15 ☐ 16-17 ☐ 18 and over

Other dependants

15. Give details of any other dependants for whom you are financially responsible:

Other residents

16. Give details of any other people living at the premises for whom you are not financially responsible:

Money you receive		Weekly	Monthly
17. Usual take-home pay or income if self-employed *including overtime, commission, bonuses*	£	☐	☐
Job Seekers allowance	£....................	☐	☐
Pension	£....................	☐	☐
Child benefit	£	☐	☐
Other benefits and allowances	£....................	☐	☐
Others living in my home give me	£....................	☐	☐
I am paid maintenance for myself (or children) of	£....................	☐	☐
Other income	£....................	☐	☐
Total income	**£**....................	☐	☐

Bank accounts and savings

18. Do you have a current bank or building society account? ☐ Yes ☐ No

If Yes, is it

☐ in credit? If so, by how much? £........

☐ overdrawn? If so, by how much? £........

19. Do you have a savings or deposit account? ☐ Yes ☐ No

If Yes,what is the balance? £........

Money you pay out

20. Do you have to pay any court orders or fines? ☐ Yes ☐ No

Court	Claim/Case number	Balance owing	Instalments paid
		Total instalments paid £	per month

21. Give details if you are in arrears with any of the court payments or fines:

22. Do you have any loan or credit debts? ☐ Yes ☐ No

Loan/credit from	Balance owing	Instalments paid
	Total instalments paid £	per month

23. Give details if you are in arrears with any loan / credit repayments:

Regular expenses
(Do not include any payments made by other members of the household out of their own income)

24. What regular expenses do you have?
(List below)

		Weekly	Monthly
Council tax	£__________	☐	☐
Gas	£__________	☐	☐
Electricity	£__________	☐	☐
Water charges	£__________	☐	☐
TV rental & licence	£__________	☐	☐
Telephone	£__________	☐	☐
Credit repayments	£__________	☐	☐
Mail order	£__________	☐	☐
Housekeeping, food, school meals	£__________	☐	☐
Travelling expenses	£__________	☐	☐
Clothing	£__________	☐	☐
Maintenance payments	£__________	☐	☐
Other mortgages	£__________	☐	☐
Other	£__________	☐	☐
Total expenses	£__________	☐	☐

Priority debts

25. This section is for arrears only. Do not include regular expenses listed at Question 24.

		Weekly	Monthly
Council tax arrears	£__________	☐	☐
Water charges arrears	£__________	☐	☐
Gas account	£__________	☐	☐
Electricity account	£__________	☐	☐
Maintenance arrears	£__________	☐	☐
Others (give details below)			
	£__________	☐	☐
	£__________	☐	☐
	£	☐	☐

26. If an order for possession were to be made, would you have somewhere else to live? ☐ Yes ☐ No

If Yes, say when you would be able to move in: ....

27. Give details of any events or circumstances which have led to your being in arrears with your mortgage (for example divorce, separation, redundancy, bereavement, illness, bankruptcy). If you believe you would suffer exceptional hardship by being ordered to leave the property immediately, say why.

Statement of Truth

*(I believe)(The defendant believes) that the facts stated in this defence form are true.
* I am duly authorised by the defendant to sign this statement.

signed .... date ....

*(Defendant)(Litigation friend(where defendant is a child or a patient))(Defendant's solicitor)

**delete as appropriate*

Full name ....

Name of defendant's solicitor's firm ....

position or office held ....

(if signing on behalf of firm or company)

Click here to reset form | Click here to print form

Defence form
(rented residential premises)

Name of court	Claim No.
Name of Claimant	
Name of Defendant	
Date of hearing	

Personal details

1. Please give your:

Title ☐ Mr ☐ Mrs ☐ Miss ☐ Ms ☐ Other

First name(s) in full

Last name

Date of birth D D M M Y Y Y Y

Address *(if different from the address on the claim form)*

Postcode

Disputing the claim

2. Do you agree with what is said about the premises and the tenancy agreement? ☐ Yes ☐ No

If No, set out your reasons below:

Did you receive the notice from the claimant referred to at paragraph 6 of the particulars of claim? ☐ Yes ☐ No

3. If Yes, when: ....

N11R Defence form (rented residential premises) (04.06) HMCS

4. Do you agree that there are arrears of rent as stated in the particulars of claim? ☐ Yes ☐ No

If No, state how much the arrears are: £.................. ☐ None

5. If the particulars of claim give any reasons for possession other than rent arrears, do you agree with what is said? ☐ Yes ☐ No

If No, give details below:

6. Do you have a money or other claim (a counterclaim) against your landlord? ☐ Yes ☐ No

If Yes, give details:

Arrears

7. Have you paid any money to your landlord since the claim was issued? ☐ Yes ☐ No

If Yes, state how much you have paid and when: £.................. date ....

8. Have you come to any agreement with your landlord about repaying the arrears since the claim was issued? ☐ Yes ☐ No

I have agreed to pay £__________ each (week)(month)

9. If you have not reached an agreement with your landlord, do you want the court to consider allowing you to pay the arrears by instalments? ☐ Yes ☐ No

10. How much can you afford to pay in addition to the current rent? £.................. per (week)(month)

About yourself

State benefits

11. Are you receiving Income Support? ☐ Yes ☐ No

12. Have you applied for Income Support? ☐ Yes ☐ No

If Yes, when did you apply? ....

13. Are you receiving housing benefit? ☐ Yes ☐ No

If Yes, how much are you receiving? £.................. per (week)(month)

14. Have you applied for housing benefit? ☐ Yes ☐ No

If Yes, when did you apply? ....

15. Is the housing benefit paid ☐ to you ☐ to your landlord

Dependants *(people you look after financially)*

16. Have you any dependant children? ☐ Yes ☐ No

If Yes, give the number in each age group below:

☐ under 11 ☐ 11-15 ☐ 16-17 ☐ 18 and over

Other dependants

17. Give details of any other dependants for whom you are financially responsible:

Other residents

18. Give details of any other people living at the premises for whom you are not financially responsible:

Money you receive

			Weekly	Monthly
19.	Usual take-home pay or income if self-employed *including overtime, commission, bonuses*	£	☐	☐
	Job Seekers allowance	£	☐	☐
	Pension	£	☐	☐
	Child benefit	£	☐	☐
	Other benefits and allowances	£	☐	☐
	Others living in my home give me	£	☐	☐
	I am paid maintenance for myself (or children) of	£	☐	☐
	Other income	£	☐	☐
	Total income	£	☐	☐

Bank accounts and savings

20. Do you have a current bank or building society account? ☐ Yes ☐ No

If Yes, is it

☐ in credit? If so, by how much? £________

☐ overdrawn? If so, by how much? £________

21. Do you have a savings or deposit account? ☐ Yes ☐ No

If Yes, what is the balance? £________

Money you pay out

22. Do you have to pay any court orders or fines?

Court	Claim/Case number	Balance owing	Instalments paid
		Total Instalments paid £	per month

23. Give details if you are in arrears with any of the court payments or fines:

24. Do you have any loan or credit debts? ☐ Yes ☐ No

Loan/credit from	Balance owing	Instalments paid
	Total Instalments £	per month

25. Give details if you are in arrears with any loan / credit repayments:

Regular expenses

(Do not include any payments made by other members of the household out of their own income)

26. What regular expenses do you have?
(List below)

		Weekly	Monthly
Council tax	£....................	☐	☐
Gas	£....................	☐	☐
Electricity	£....................	☐	☐
Water charges	£....................	☐	☐
TV rental & licence	£....................	☐	☐
Telephone	£....................	☐	☐
Credit repayments	£....................	☐	☐
Mail order	£....................	☐	☐
Housekeeping, food, school meals	£....................	☐	☐
Travelling expenses	£....................	☐	☐
Clothing	£....................	☐	☐
Maintenance payments	£....................	☐	☐
Other	£....................	☐	☐
Total expenses	£....................	☐	☐

Priority debts

27. This section is for **arrears** only. **Do not** include regular expenses listed at Question 26.

		Weekly	Monthly
Council tax arrears	£________	☐	☐
Water charges arrears	£________	☐	☐
Gas account	£________	☐	☐
Electricity account	£________	☐	☐
Maintenance arrears	£________	☐	☐
Others *(give details below)*			
	£________	☐	☐
	£________	☐	☐
	£________	☐	☐

28. If an order for possession were to be made, would you have somewhere else to live? ☐ Yes ☐ No

If Yes, say when you would be able to move in: ________________

29. Give details of any events or circumstances which have led to your being in arrears of rent *(for example divorce, separation, redundancy, bereavement, illness, bankruptcy)* or any other particular circumstances affecting your case. If there are any reasons why the date any possession order takes effect should be delayed, give them here. If you believe you would suffer exceptional hardship by being ordered to leave the property immediately, say why.

You need only answer question 30 if the claim form includes a claim for demotion or suspension of right to buy.

30. Do you agree with what is said about your conduct or use of the property? ☐ Yes ☐ No

If No, set out your reasons below:

Statement of Truth

*(I believe)(The defendant(s) believe(s)) that the facts stated in this defence form are true.
* I am duly authorised by the defendant(s) to sign this statement.

signed ______________________ date ______________________

(Defendant)(Litigation friend(where defendant is a child or a patient)*)(Defendant's solicitor)

**delete as appropriate*

Full name ______________________

Name of defendant's solicitor's firm ______________________

position or office held ______________________
(if signing on behalf of firm or company)

Click here to print form

Click here to reset form | Click here to print form

Acknowledgment of service
(arbitration claim)

Name of court	
Claim No.	
Claimant (including ref)	
Defendant	

You should read the 'notes for defendant' attached to the claim form which will tell you how to complete this form, and when and where to send it.

Tick and complete sections A - D as appropriate.
In all cases you must complete sections E and F

Section A

☐ I **do not** intend to contest this claim

Section B

☐ I intend to contest this claim

Give brief details of any different remedy you are seeking.

Section C

☐ I intend to dispute the court's jurisdiction

(Please note, any application must be filed within 14 days of the date on which you file this acknowledgment of service)

The court office at

When corresponding with the court, please address forms or letters to the Court Manager and quote the claim number.

N15 Acknowledgment of Service (arbitration) (10.08)

Claim No.

Section D

☐ I intend to rely on written evidence

My written evidence:

☐ is filed with this form

☐ will be filed and served within 21 days after the date by which I am required to file this acknowledgment of service.

Section E

Full name of defendant filing this acknowledgment ____________________

Section F

Signed
(To be signed by you or by your solicitor)

*(I believe) (The defendant believes) that the facts stated in this form are true.

*I am duly authorised by the defendant to sign this statement.

**delete as appropriate*

Position or office held

(if signing on behalf of firm or company)

Date

Give an address in the United Kingdom to which notices about this case can be sent to you.

	If applicable	
	Telephone no.	
	Fax no.	

Injunction Order

Between .... Claimant

and .... Defendant

In the	
County Court	
Claim No.	
Claimant's Ref.	
Defendant Ref.	
For completion by the court **Issued on**	

Seal

If you do not obey this order you will be guilty of contempt of court and you may be sent to prison.

[1] The name of the person the order is directed to

On the of 20 the court considered an application for an injunction

The Court ordered that[1]

[2] The terms of any orders requiring acts to be done. Delete if no mandatory order is made.

must[2]

[3] Enter time (and place) as ordered

on or before[3]

[4] The terms of the injunction order. If the defendant is a limited company delete the words in brackets and insert "whether by its servants, agents, officers or otherwise"

[and] is forbidden (whether by himself or by instructing or encouraging or permitting any other person)[4] from

This order will remain in force until the of 20 at o'clock unless before then it is revoked by a further order of the court

[5] The terms of any orders, costs etc.

[6] State the clause numbers to which the power of arrest relates

It is further ordered that[5]

(i) A power of arrest be attached to clauses [ ] above[6]

(ii) The applicant do pay the costs of the application

[Notice of further hearing

The court will re-consider the application and whether the order should continue at a further hearing at:

on the day of 20 at o'clock

[7] Use when order is temporary and made without notice; otherwise delete.

If you do not attend at the time shown the court may make an injunction order in your absence.

You are entitled to apply to the court to re-consider the order before that day][7]

If you do not understand anything in this order you should go to a Solicitor, Legal Advice Centre or a Citizens' Advice Bureau

The court office at

is open between 10 am and 4 pm Monday to Friday. When corresponding with the court, please address forms or letters to the Court Manager and quote the claim number.

N16 General form of injunction for interim application or originating application (04.07)

Injunction Order - Record of Hearing

Claim No. ....

On .... the .... day of 20

Before (H Honour)(District) judge ....

The court was sitting at ....

....

The ☐ **Claimant** **(Name)** ....

was ☐ represented by Counsel

☐ represented by a Solicitor

☐ in person

The ☐ **Defendant** **(Name)** ....

was ☐ represented by Counsel

☐ represented by a Solicitor

☐ in person

☐ did not appear having been given notice of this hearing

☐ not given notice of this hearing

The court read the written evidence of

☐ the Claimant (sworn)(signed) on ....

☐ the Defendant (sworn)(signed) on ....

And of .... (sworn)(signed) on ....

....

The court heard spoken evidence on oath from

....

....

The Claimant gave an undertaking (through his counsel or solicitor) promising to pay any damages ordered by the court if it later decides that the Defendant has suffered loss or damages as a result of this order*

*Delete this paragraph if the court does not require the undertaking

Signed .... Dated ....

(Judges Clerk)

N16 General form of injunction for interim application or originating application

FORM N16(1) GENERAL FORM OF INJUNCTION (FORMAL PARTS ONLY)

Injunction Order

In the	
County Court	
Claim No.	
Claimant	
Defendant	
Claimant's Ref.	

For completion by the court
Issued on

Seal

Between .... **Claimant / Applicant / Petitioner**

and .... **Defendant / Respondent**

To (1)

of (2)

(1) The name of the person the order is directed to

(2) The address of the person the order is directed to

(3) The terms of any restraining order are to be preceeded by the words "is forbidden whether by himself or by instructing or encouraging any other person" or if the defendant is a limited company "by its servants, agents, officers or otherwise"

If you do not obey this order you will be guilty of contempt of court and you may be sent to prison

On the of [19][20] the court considered an application for an injunction

The Court ordered that (1)

(3)

If you do not understand anything in this order you should go to a Solicitor, Legal Advice Centre or a Citizens' Advice Bureau

The court office at

is open between 10 am and 4 pm Monday to Friday. When corresponding with the court, please address forms or letters to the Court Manager and quote the claim number.

N16(1) General form of injunction for interlocutory application or originating application
(Formal Parts - See complete N16 for wording of operating clauses)

Injunction Order - Record of Hearing **Claim No.** ....

On ....the .... day of ....[19][20]......
Before (H Honour) (District) Judge ....
The court was sitting at ....
....

The ☐ **Claimant** ☐ **Applicant** ☐ **Petitioner** **(Name)**...
was ☐ represented by Counsel
☐ represented by a Solicitor
☐ in person
The ☐ **Defendant** ☐ **Respondent** **(Name)**...
was ☐ represented by Counsel
☐ represented by a Solicitor
☐ in person
☐ did not appear having been given notice of this hearing
☐ not given notice of this hearing

The court read the affidavit(s) of
☐ the Claimant/Applicant/Petitioner sworn on ....
☐ the Defendant/Respondent sworn on ....
And of..sworn on ....
....

The court heard spoken evidence on oath from
....
....

The Claimant(Applicant/Petitioner) gave an undertaking (through his counsel or solicitor) promising to pay any damages ordered by the court if it later decides that the Defendant/Respondent has suffered loss or damage as a result of this order*

**Delete this paragraph if the court does not require the undertaking*

Signed ______________________________ Dated ______________________________
(Judges Clerk)

N16(1) (Formal Parts - See complete N16 for wording of operative clauses)

Application for Injunction (General Form)

Name of court	Claim No.
Claimant's Name and Ref.	
Defendant's Name and Ref.	

Notes on completion

Tick which boxes apply and specify the legislation where appropriate

(1) Enter the full name of the person making the application

(2) Enter the full name of the person the injunction is to be directed to

(3) Set out any proposed orders requiring acts to be done. Delete if no mandatory order is sought.

(4) Set out here the proposed terms of the injunction order (if the defendant is a limited company delete the wording in brackets and insert 'whether by its servants, agents, officers or otherwise').

(5) Set out here any further terms asked for including provision for costs

(6) Enter the names of all persons who have sworn affidavits or signed statements in support of this application

(7) Enter the names and addresses of all persons upon whom it is intended to serve this application

(8) Enter the full name and address for service and delete as required

☐ By application in pending proceedings

☐ Under Statutory provision ______________________

☐ This application is made under Part 8 of the Civil Procedure Rules

Seal

This application raises issues under the Human Rights Act 1998 ☐ Yes ☐ No

The Claimant(1)

applies to the court for an injunction order in the following terms:

The Defendant(2)

must(3)

The Defendant

be forbidden (whether by himself or by instructing or encouraging or permitting any other person)(4)

And that(5)

The grounds of this application are set out in the written evidence of(6) sworn (signed) on

This written evidence is served with this application.

This application is to be served upon(7)

This application is led by(8)

(the Solicitors for) the Claimant (Applicant/Petitioner)

whose address for service is

Signed Dated

* Name and address of the person application is directed to

To*

of

This section to be completed by the court

This application will be heard by the (District) Judge

at

on the day of 20 at o'clock

If you do not attend at the time shown the court may make an injunction order in your absence

If you do not fully understand this application you should go to a Solicitor, Legal Advice Centre or a Citizens' Advice Bureau

The court ofce at

is open between 10am and 4pm Mon - Fri. When corresponding with the court, please address all forms and letters to the Court Manager and quote the claim number.

N16A General form of application for injunction (04.07)

Judgment for Claimant
(amount to be decided by the court)

In the	
Claim No.	
Claimant (including ref)	
Defendant (including ref)	
Date	

To the [Claimant][Defendant]['s Solicitor]

[No [acknowledgment of service] [defence] having been filed] [The defendant having admitted liability][The defendant having admitted liability and offered an amount in settlement which the claimant has not accepted], it is ordered that the defendant must pay the claimant an amount which the court will decide, and costs. To prepare for the hearing

[Master][District Judge] orders that:

[You should attend the court at [am][pm] on the of

at

when the court will make its decision.]

The court office at

is open between 10 am and 4 pm Monday to Friday. When corresponding with the court, please address forms or letters to the Court Manager and quote the claim number.

N17

Limited civil restraint order

Name of court	
Claim No.	
Name of Claimant	
Name of Defendant	
Date of issue	

Enter name and address of person against whom the order is made

SEAL

You must obey the directions contained in this order. If you do not you will be guilty of contempt of court and you may be sent to prison.

SECTION 1

Date of order

Name of Judge

Name of person against whom order is made

The judge has considered an application by the ☐ Claimant ☐ Defendant

OR

The court has considered, of its own initiative ☐

AND

Upon hearing

Upon reading

And has found that the above named person has made two or more applications in these proceeding which are totally without merit.

SECTION 2

The Order

It is ordered that you be restrained from making any further application in these proceedings without first obtaining the permission of

Name of Judge

OR

If unavailable

It is further ordered

☐ **This order will remain in effect for the duration of these proceedings**

OR

☐ until

N19 Limited civil restraint order (08.04)

1. If you wish to apply for permission-

   (a) to make **an application** in these proceeding; **OR**

   (b) to make an application to **amend or discharge** this order,

   you must first serve notice of your application on the other party. The notice must set out the nature and grounds of the application and provide the other party with at least 7 days within which to respond. You must then apply for permission of the judge identified in the order. The application for permission must be made in writing and must include the other party's written response, if any, to the notice served. The application will be determined without a hearing.

2. If you repeatedly make applications for permission under 1 above which are totally without merit, the court may direct that if you make anyfurther application for permission which is totally without merit, the decision to dismiss the application will be final and there will be no right of appeal, unless the judge who refused permission grants permission to appeal.

3. Any application for permission to appeal a refusal of an application under 1 above must be made in writing and will be determined thout a hearing.

SECTION 3

Costs

☐ There is no order for costs

☐ It is ordered that you pay costs. The sum you must pay is ________

You must pay on or before ________

and send payment to the ☐ Claimant ☐ Defendant

Note

If you attempt to make a further application in these proceedings without first obtaining permission of the judge named in the order above, your application will automatically be dismissed without the judge having to make any further order and without the need for the other party to respond to it.	If this order was made in your absence, you may make an application to set aside, vary or stay the order. An application must be made within the period specified in the order or, where no period is specified, not more than 7 days after service of this order on you. You do not require permission of the court to make such an application.	If you do not understand anything in this order you should go to a Solicitor, Legal Advice Centre or a Citizens' Advice Bureau.

2

Extended civil restraint order

Name of court	
Claim No.	
Name of Claimant	
Name of Defendant	
Date of issue	

Enter name and address of person against whom the order is made

SEAL

You must obey the directions contained in this order. If you do not you will be guilty of contempt of court and you may be sent to prison.

SECTION 1

Date of order

Name of Judge

Name of person against whom order is made

The judge has considered an application by the ☐ Claimant ☐ Defendant

OR

The court has considered, of its own initiative ☐

AND

Upon hearing

Upon reading

And has found that the above named person has persistently issued claims or made applications which are totally without merit.

SECTION 2

The Order

It is ordered that you be restrained from issuing claims or making applications in any court specified below concerning any matter involving or relating to or touching upon or leading to the proceedings in which this order is made without first obtaining the permission of

Name of Judge

OR

If unavailable

☐ Court of Appeal

☐ The High Court

☐ County Court(s)

☐ Any county court

☐ Any court

N19A Extended civil restraint order (08.04)

1

It is further ordered

This order will remain in effect until

1. If you wish to apply for permission-

   (a) to make **an application** in these proceedings; **OR**

   (b) to make an application to **amend or discharge** this order,

   you must first serve notice of our application on the other party. The notice must set out the nature and grounds of the application and provide the other party with at least 7 day within which to respond. You must then apply for permission of the judge identified in the order. The application for permission must be made in writing and must include the other party's written response, if any, to the notice served. The application will be determined without a hearing.
2. If you repeatedly make applications for permission under 1 above which are totally without merit, the court may direct that if you make any further application for permission which is totally without merit, the decision to dismiss the application will be final and there will be no right of appeal, unless the judge who refused permission grants permission to appeal.
3. Any application for permission to appeal a refusal of an application under 1 above must be made in writing and will be determined thout a hearing.

SECTION 3

Costs

☐ There is no order for costs

☐ It is ordered that you pay costs. The sum you must pay is

You must pay on or before

and send payment to the ☐ Claimant ☐ Defendant

Note

If you attempt to make a further application in these proceedings without first obtaining permission of the judge named in the order above, your application will automatically be dismissed without the judge having to make any further order and without the need for the other party to respond to it.

If this order was made in your absence, you may make an application to set aside, vary or stay the order. An application must be made within the period specified in the order or, where no period is specified, not more than 7 days after service of this order on you. You do not require permission of the court to make such an application.

If you do not understand anything in this order you should go to a Solicitor, Legal Advice Centre or a Citizens' Advice Bureau.

General civil restraint order

Name of court	
Claim No.	
Name of Claimant	
Name of Defendant	
Date of issue	

Enter name and address of person against whom the order is made

SEAL

You must obey the directions contained in this order. If you do not you will be guilty of contempt of court and you may be sent to prison.

SECTION 1

Date of order

Name of Judge

Name of person against whom order is made

The judge has considered an application by the ☐ Claimant ☐ Defendant

OR

The court has considered, of its own initiative ☐

AND

Upon hearing

Upon reading

And has found that, despite the existence of an extended civil restraint order, the above named person persists in issuing claims or making applications which are totally without merit.

SECTION 2

The Order

It is ordered that you be restrained from issuing any claim or making any application in any court specified below without first obtaining the permission of

Name of Judge

OR

If unavailable

☐ Court of Appeal

☐ The High Court

☐ County Court(s)

☐ Any county court

☐ Any court

N19B General civil restraint order (08.04) 1

It is further ordered [ ]

This order will remain in effect until

1. If you wish to apply for permission-

   (a) to make **an application** in these proceedings; **OR**

   (b) to make an application to **amend or discharge** this order,

   you must first serve notice of your application on the other party. The notice must set out the nature and grounds of the application and provide the other party with at least 7 days within which to respond. You must then apply for permission of the judge identified in the order. The application for permission must be made in writing and must include the other party's written response, if any, to the notice served. The application will be determined without a hearing.
2. If you repeatedly make applications for permission under 1 above which are totally without merit, the court may direct that if you make any further application for permission which is totally without merit, the decision to dismiss the application will be final and there will be no right of appeal, unless the judge who refused permission grants permission to appeal.
3. Any application for permission to appeal a refusal of an application under 1 above must be made in writing and will be determined without a hearing.

SECTION 3

Costs

☐ There is no order for costs

☐ It is ordered that you pay costs. The sum you must pay is [ ]

You must pay on or before [ ]

and send payment to the ☐ Claimant ☐ Defendant

Note

If you attempt to make a further application in these proceedings without first obtaining permission of the judge named in the order above, your application will automatically be dismissed without the judge having to make any further order and without the need for the other party to respond to it.

If this order was made in your absence, you may make an application to set aside, vary or stay the order. An application must be made within the period specified in the order or, where no period is specified, not more than 7 days after service of this order on you. You do not require permission of the court to make such an application.

If you do not understand anything in this order you should go to a Solicitor, Legal Advice Centre or a Citizens' Advice Bureau.

Witness Summons

In the	
Claim No.	
Claimant (including ref)	
Defendant (including ref)	
Issued on	

To

You are summoned to attend at *(court address)*

on of at (am)(pm)

(and each following day of the hearing until the court tells you that you are no longer required.)

☐ to give evidence in respect of the above claim

☐ to produce the following document(s) *(give details)*

The sum of £ is paid or offered to you with this summons. This is to cover your travelling expenses to and from court and includes an amount by way of compensation for loss of time.

This summons was issued on the application of the claimant (defendant) or the claimant's (defendant's) solicitor whose name, address and reference number is:

Do not ignore this summons

If you were offered money for travel expenses and compensation for loss of time, at the time it was served on you, you must –

- attend court on the date and time shown and/or produce documents as required by the summons; and
- take an oath or affirm as required for the purposes of answering questions about your evidence or the documents you have been asked to produce.

If you do not comply with this summons you will be liable, in county court proceedings, to a fine. In the High Court, disobedience of a witness summons is a contempt of court and you may be fined or imprisoned for contempt. You may also be liable to pay any wasted costs that arise because of your non-compliance.

If you wish to set aside or vary this witness summons, you may make an application to the court that issued it.

The court office at

is open between 10 am and 4 pm Monday to Friday. When corresponding with the court, please address forms or letters to the Court Manager and quote the claim number.

N20 Witness Summons (09.02) *Printed on behalf of The Court Service*

Certificate of service

Claim No.	

I certify that the summons of which this is a true copy, was served by posting to ______________________________

(the witness) on ______________________ at the address stated on the summons in accordance with the request of the applicant or his solicitor.

I enclosed a P.O. for £ for the witness's expenses and compensation for loss of time.

Signed ________________________
Officer of the Court

Order for Examination of Deponent (before the hearing)

In the	
Claim No.	
Claimant (including ref)	
Defendant (including ref)	
Date	

To

Upon the application of the [claimant][defendant],[Master][District Judge]
has **ordered you to attend**

at [am][pm] on of

at

to be examined on oath.

[and] to produce the following document(s)]

[£ to cover your travelling expenses to and from the place of examination and compensation for your loss of time is attached]

[Sum to be offered or handed to deponent £ for travelling expenses to and from the place of examination (and compensation for loss of time)]

Do not ignore this order

If you were offered money for travel expenses and compensation for loss of time at the time it was served on you and you

- fail to attend or produce documents as required by the order: or
- refuse to take an oath or affirm for the purpose of the examination or to answer any lawful question or produce any document at the examination

you may be liable to fine and may in addition be ordered to pay any costs resulting from your failure to attend or refusal to take an oath or affirm.

The court office at

is open between 10 am and 4 pm Monday to Friday. When corresponding with the court, please address forms or letters to the Court Manager and quote the claim number.

N21 Order for Examination of Deponent (before the hearing)

General Form of Judgment or Order

In the	
Claim No.	
Claimant (including ref)	
Defendant (including ref)	

To [Claimant] [Defendant] ['s Solicitor]

SEAL

Note: If judgment is for £5,000 or more, or is in respect of a debt which attracts contractual or statutory interest for late payment, the claimant may be entitled to further interest

The court office at

is open between 10 am and 4 pm [4.30pm]Monday to Friday. When corresponding with the court, please address forms or letters to the Court Manager and quote the case number.

N24 -w3 General form of judgment or order (4.99)

Order for possession

In the

Claim No.

Claimant

Defendant(s)

On 20 ,

sitting at

heard

SEAL

and the court orders that

1. The defendant give the claimant possession of

   on or before 20 .

2. The defendant pay the claimant £ for
   [and £ per day from 20 , until possession of the property is given to the claimant.]

3. The defendant pay the claimant's costs of £
   [The defendant pay the claimant's costs, within 14 days after they are assessed [and in the meantime pay the claimant £ on account of those costs].]
   [The claimant's costs will be added to the amount owing under the mortgage.]

4. The defendant pay the total amount of £ to the claimant [on or before 20][by instalments of £ per , the first instalment to be paid to the claimant on or before 20]

To the defendant

The court has **ordered you to leave** the property by the date stated in paragraph 1 above.
If you do not do so, the claimant can ask the court, without a further hearing, to authorise a bailiff or Sheriff to evict you. (In that case, you can apply to the court to stay the eviction; a judge will decide if there are grounds for doing so.)

(If detailed assessment of costs is ordered)
The claimant will send you a copy of the bill of costs with a notice telling you what to do if you object to the amount. If you do object, the claimant will ask the court to fix a hearing to assess the amount.

(If there is an order to pay money - paragraph 2,3 or 4)
Payments should be made to the claimant, not to the court. If you need more information about making payments, you should contact the claimant.

Ref.

(If there is an order to pay money, made in a county court)
If you do not pay the money owed when it is due and the claimant has to take steps to enforce payment, the order will be registered in the Register of County Court Judgments. This may make it difficult for you to get credit. Further information about registration is available in a leaflet which you can get from any county court office.

N26 Order for possession

Order for possession
(accelerated procedure)
(assured shorthold
tenancy)

In the

County Court

Claim No.

Claimant

Defendant(s)

On the 20 ,

SEAL

sitting at

read the written evidence of the claimant (and the defendant)

and the court orders that

1. The defendant give the claimant possession of

   on or before 20 .

2. The defendant pay the claimant's costs of £ [on or before 20]
   [by instalments of £ per the first payment to be made on or before 20].

[3. The date for possession may be varied when the judge considers the defendant's request to postpone it.]

Note: This order was made without a hearing. Within 14 days of its being served, either party may apply for it to be set aside or varied.

To the defendant
The court has **ordered you to leave** the premises by the date stated in paragraph 1 above. (If notice is attached of a hearing to consider your request to remain longer, the date you must leave may be varied at that hearing.)
If you do not leave by the date fixed by the court, the claimant can ask the court, without a further hearing, to authorise a bailiff to evict you.

(If there is an order to pay costs)
Payments should be made to the claimant, not to the court. If you need more information about making payments, you should contact the claimant.
If you do not pay the money owed when it is due and the claimant takes steps to enforce payment, the order will be registered in the Register of County Court Judgments. This may make it difficult for you to get credit. Further information about registration is available in a leaflet which you can get from any county court office.

Ref.

N26A Order for possession (accelerated procedure)(assured shorthold tenancy)

Order for possession on forfeiture
(for rent arrears)

In the

Claim No.

Claimant

Defendant(s)

On 20 ,

sitting at

heard

SEAL

and the court orders that

1. The defendant give the claimant possession of
on or before 20 .
2. The defendant pay the claimant £ , for and £ per day from 20 until possession is given to the claimant or payment is made under paragraph 5 below.
3. The defendant pay the claimant's costs of £
[The defendant pay the claimant's costs, within 14 days after they are assessed [and in the meantime pay the claimant £ on account of those costs]
4. The defendant pay the total of the sums mentioned above to the claimant [on or before 20 .][by instalments of £ per , the first instalment to be paid to the claimant on or before 20 .]
5. If the defendant pays the claimant the sums mentioned above on or before 20 this order **shall have no effect** and **the lease will continue.**

To the defendant

The court has **ordered you to leave** the property by the date stated in paragraph 1 above. However that order **will not take effect if you pay** the arrears of rent, any use and occupation charge, and costs by the date stated above. Payment should be made to the claimant, not to the court. If you need more information about making payment, you should contact the claimant.

If you do not make the payment or leave the property, the claimant can ask the court, without a further hearing, to authorise a bailiff or Sheriff to evict you. In that case, you can apply to the court to stay the eviction; a judge will decide if there are grounds for doing so.

(If detailed assessment of costs is ordered)
The claimant will send you a copy of the bill of costs with a notice telling you what to do if you object to the amount. If you do object, the claimant will ask the court to fix a hearing to assess the amount.

Ref.

(If there is an order to pay money, made in a county court)
If you do not pay the money owed when it is due and the claimant takes steps to enforce payment, the order will be registered in the Register of County Court Judgments. This may make it difficult for you to get credit. Further information about registration is available in a leaflet which you can get from any county court office

N27 Order for possession on forfeiture (for rent arrears)

Order for possession on forfeiture
(for rent arrears)
(suspended)

In the

Claim No.

Claimant

Defendant(s)

On 20 ,

sitting at

heard

SEAL

and the court orders that

1. The defendant give the claimant possession of
on or before 20 .
2. The defendant pay the claimant £ , for
and £ per day from 20 , until possession is given to the claimant.
3. The defendant pay the claimant's costs of £
4. The defendant pay the total of the sums mentioned above, to the claimant on or before 20 .
5. The orders for possession and for payment of the amounts for unpaid rent and use and occupation [and costs] are **not to be enforced** and **the lease will continue** so long as the defendant pays the claimant the unpaid rent [and costs, totalling] £ by the payments set out below **in addition to the current rent.**

Payments required
[£ on or before 20 and]
£ per , the first payment being made on or before 20 .

To the defendant

The court has ordered that **unless you pay the arrears** [and costs] by at least the payments set out above **in addition to your current** rent, you must leave the property.
Payments should be made to the claimant, not to the court.
If you need more information about making payments, you should contact the claimant.

If you do not make the payments or leave the property, the claimant can ask the court, without a further hearing, to authorise a bailiff or Sheriff to evict you. (In that case, you can apply to the court to stay the eviction; a judge will decide if there are grounds for doing so.)

(If there is an order to pay money, made in a county court)
If you do not pay the money owed when it is due and the claimant takes steps to enforce payment, the order will be registered in the Register of County Court Judgments. This may make it difficult for you to get credit. Further information about registration is available in a leaflet which you can get from any county court office.

Ref.

N27(2) Order for possession on forfeiture (for rent arrears suspended)

Order for possession (rented premises) (suspended)

In the

Claim No.

Claimant

Defendant(s)

SEAL

On 20 ,

sitting at

heard

and the court orders that

1. The defendant give the claimant possession of

   on or before 20 .
2. The defendant pay the claimant £ for
3. The defendant pay the claimant's costs of the claim £ .
4. The defendant pay the total of £ to the claimant on or before 20 .
5. This order is not to be enforced so long as the defendant pays the claimant the rent arrears and the amount for use and occupation [and costs, totalling] £ by the payments set out below **in addition to the current rent.**

Payments required
[£ on or before 20 and]
£ per , the first payment being made on or before 20 .

To the defendant

The court has ordered that **unless you pay the arrears** and costs at the rate set out above **in addition to your current rent,** you must leave the premises.
Payments should be made to the claimant, not to the court. If you need more information about making payments, you should contact the claimant.

If you do not make the payments or leave the premises, the claimant can ask the court, without a further hearing, to authorise a bailiff or Sheriff to evict you. (In that case, you can apply to the court to stay the eviction; a judge will decide if there are grounds for doing so.)

(If there is an order to pay money, made in a county court)
If you do not pay the money owed when it is due and the claimant takes steps to enforce payment, the order will be registered in the Register of County Court Judgments. This may make it difficult for you to get credit. Further information about registration is available in a leaflet which you can get from any county court office.

Ref.

N28 Order for possession (rented premises)(suspended)

Order for possession
(rented premises)
(postponed)

Name of court	Claim No.
Name of Claimant	
Name of Defendant(s)	

On 20 ,

sitting at

heard

SEAL

and the court orders that

1. The defendant is to give up possession of [address] to the claimant.
2. The date on which the defendant is to give up possession of the property to the claimant is postponed to a date to be fixed by the court on an application by the claimant. The defendant's tenancy of the property will continue until that date.
3. The defendant must pay the claimant £[_____] for rent arrears and £[_____] for costs. The total judgment debt is £[_____] to be paid by instalments as specified in paragraph 4 below.
4. The claimant shall not be entitled to make an application for a date to be fixed for the giving up of possession and the termination of the defendant's tenancy so long as the defendant pays the claimant the current rent together with instalments of £[_____] [per week] towards the judgment debt.
5. The first payment of the current rent and the instalment must be made on or before [date].
6. Any application to fix the date on which the defendant is to give up possession may be determined on the papers without a hearing (unless the district judge considers that such a hearing is necessary)
7. This order shall cease to be enforceable when the total judgment debt is satisfied.

To the defendant

The court has ordered that **unless you pay the arrears** and costs at the rate set out above **in addition to your current rent,** you must leave the premises.

Payments should be made to the claimant, not to the court. If you need more information about making payments, you should contact the claimant.

If you do not make the payments or leave the premises, the claimant can ask the court, **without a further hearing,** to fix a date for you to leave the premises and if you do not do so, to authorise a bailiff or High Court Enforcement Officer to evict you. (You can apply to the court to stay the eviction; a judge will decide if there are grounds for doing so.)

(If there is an order to pay money)
If you do not pay the money owed when it is due and the claimant takes steps to enforce payment, the order will be registered in the Register of Judgments, Orders and Fines. This may make it difficult for you to get credit. Further information about registration is available in a leaflet which you can get from any court office.

Ref.

Need help with your problem?
Contact CLS Direct, a free government-funded confidential advice service. 0845 345 4345 www.clsdirect.org.uk

N28A Order for possession (rented premises)(postponed) (05.06)

Judgment for Claimant
(in default)

In the High Court of Justice	
Division District Registry	
Claim No.	
Claimant (including ref)	
Defendant (including ref)	
Date	

To [Claimant][Defendant]['s Solicitor]

Seal

To the Defendant

You have not replied to the claim form.

It is therefore ordered that you must pay the claimant £ for debt [and interest to date of judgment] and £ for costs [less £ which you have already paid]

You must pay to the claimant a total of £

[by instalments of £ per [week][month]

[the first payment to reach the claimant] by [and on or before this date each [week][month until the debt has been paid]

Warning

If you ignore this order your goods may be removed and sold, or other enforcement proceedings may be taken against you. If this happens further costs will be added. If your circumstances change and you cannot pay, ask at the court office what you can do.

Notes for the defendant

If you did reply to the claim form and believe judgment has been entered wrongly in default, you may apply to the court office giving your reasons why the judgment should be set aside. An application form is available for you to use and you will need to pay a fee. A hearing may be arranged and you will be told when and where it will take place. If you live in, or carry on business in, another court's area, the claim may be transferred to that court.

Address for payment

How to pay

- **Payment(s) must be made to the person named at the address for payment, giving the claimant's reference and claim number**
- **DO NOT bring or send payments to the court - they will not be accepted**
- You should allow at least 4 days for your payment to reach the claimant or his representative
- Make sure that you keep records and can account for all payments made. Proof may be required if there is any disagreement. It is not safe to send cash unless you use registered post

The court office at
is open between 10 am and 4.30 pm Monday to Friday. When corresponding with the court, please address forms or letters to the Court Manager and quote the claim number

N30 (HC)

Judgment for Claimant (in default)

In the County Court	
Claim No.	
Claimant (including ref)	
Defendant (including ref)	
Date	

To [Claimant] [Defendant] ['s Solicitor]

Seal

To the Defendant

You have not replied to the claim form.

It is therefore ordered that you must pay the claimant £ for debt [and interest to date of judgment] and £ for costs [less £ which you have already paid]

You must pay to the claimant a total of £

[by instalments of £ per [week][month]

[the first payment to reach the claimant] by [and on or before this date each [week][month] until the debt has been paid]

Warning

If you ignore this order your goods may be removed and sold, or other enforcement proceedings may be taken against you. If this happens further costs will be added. If your circumstances change and you cannot pay, ask at the court office what you can do.

Notes for the defendant

If you did reply to the claim form and believe judgment has been entered wrongly in default, you may apply to the court office giving your reasons why the judgment should be set aside. An application form is available for you to use and you will need to pay a fee. A hearing may be arranged and you will be told when and where it will take place. If you live in, or carry on business in, another court's area, the claim may be transferred to that court.

Address for payment

This judgment has been registered on the Register of County Court Judgments. This may make it difficult for you to get credit. **If you pay in full within one month** you can ask the court to cancel the entry on the Register. You will need to give proof of payment. You can (for a fee) also obtain a Certificate of Cancellation from the court. If you pay the debt in full after one month you can ask the court to mark the entry on the Register as satisfied and (for a fee) obtain a Certificate of Satisfaction to prove that the debt has been paid.

If judgment is for £5,000 or more, or is in respect of a debt which attracts contractual or statutory interest for late payment, the claimant may be entitled to further interest.

How to pay

- **Payment(s) must be made to the person named at the address for payment, giving the claimant's reference and claim number**
- **DO NOT bring or send payments to the court - they will not be accepted**
- You should allow at least 4 days for your payment to reach the claimant or his representative
- Make sure that you keep records and can account for all payments made. Proof may be required if there is any disagreement. It is not safe to send cash unless you use registered post
- Leaflets on registered judgments, how to pay and what to do if you cannot pay are available from the court

The court office at

is open between 10 am and 4 pm Monday to Friday. When corresponding with the court, please address forms or letters to the Court Manager and quote the claim number.

N30

Judgment for Claimant (acceptance)

In the High Court of Justice	
	Division District Registry
Claim No.	
Claimant (including ref.)	
Defendant (including ref.)	
Date	

To [Claimant][Defendant]['s Solicitor]

To the Defendant

You have made an offer of payment which the claimant has accepted.

It is therefore ordered that you must pay the claimant £ for debt [and interest to date of judgment] and £ for costs.

You must pay to the claimant a total of £

[by instalments of £ per [week][month]

[the first payment to reach the claimant] by [and on or before this date each [week][month] until the debt has been paid]

Warning

If you ignore this order your goods may be removed and sold, or other enforcement proceedings may be taken against you. If this happens further cost will be added. If your circumstances change and you cannot pay, ask at the court office what you can do.

Note to the defendant

If the payments are not what you offered, you should write at once to the court pointing this out.

How to pay

- **Payment(s) must be made to the person named at the address for payment, giving the claimant's reference and claim number**
- **DO NOT bring or send payments to the court - they will not be accepted**
- You should allow at least 4 days for your payment to reach the claimant or his representative.
- Make sure that you keep records and can account for all payments made. Proof may be required if there is any disagreement. It is not safe to send cash unless you use registered post.

Address for payment

The court office at
is open between 10 am and 4 pm Monday to Friday. When corresponding with the court, please address forms or letters to the Court Manager and quote the claim number.

N30(1)HC

Judgment for Claimant (acceptance)

In the	
County Court	
Claim No.	
Claimant (including Ref)	
Defendant (including Ref)	
Date	

To [Claimant][Defendant]['s Solicitor]

Seal

To the Defendant

You have made an offer of payment which the claimant has accepted.

It is therefore ordered that you must pay the claimant £ for debt [and interest to date of judgment] and £ for costs.

You must pay to the claimant a total of £

[by instalments of £ per [week][month]

[the first payment to reach the claimant] [and on or before this date each [week][month] until the debt has been paid]

Warning

If you ignore this order your goods may be removed and sold, or other enforcement proceedings may be taken against you. If this happens further cost will be added. If your circumstances change and you cannot pay, ask at the court office what you can do.

Notes to defendant

If the payments are not what you offered, you should write at once to the court pointing this out.

This judgment has been recorded on the Register of County Court Judgments. This may make it difficult for you to get credit. **If you pay in full within one month you can ask the court to cancel the entry on the Register.** You will need to give proof of payment. You can (for a fee) also obtain a Certificate of Cancellation from the court. If you pay the debt in full after one month you can ask the court to mark the entry on the Register as satisfied and (for a fee) obtain a Certificate of Satisfaction to prove that the debt has been paid.

Address for payment

If judgment is for £5,000 or more, or is in respect of a debt which attracts contractual or statutory interest for late payment, the claimant may be entitled to further interest.

How to pay

- **Payment(s) must be made to the person named at the address for payment, giving the claimant's reference and claim number**
- **DO NOT bring or send payments to the court - they will not be accepted**
- You should allow at least 4 days for your payment to reach the claimant or his representative.
- Make sure that you keep records and can account for all payments made. Proof may be required if there is any disagreement. It is not safe to send cash unless you use registered post.
- Leaflets on registered judgments, how to pay and what to do if you cannot pay are available from the court.

The court office at
is open between 10 am and 4 pm Monday to Friday. When corresponding with the court, please address forms or letters to the Court Manager and quote the claim number.

N30(1)

Judgment for Claimant
(after determination)

In the High Court of Justice	
	Division District Registry
Claim No.	
Claimant (including ref)	
Defendant (including ref)	
Date	

To [Claimant][Defendant]['s Solicitor]

SEAL

To the Defendant

The claimant has objected to the rate of payment you offered.

The court has therefore decided the rate at which you should pay. You must pay the claimant £ for debt [and interest to date of judgment] and £ for costs [less £ which you have already paid]

You must pay to the claimant a total of £

[by instalments of £ per [week][month]

[the first payment to reach the claimant] by [and on or before this date each [week][month] until the debt has been paid]

Warning

If you ignore this order your goods may be removed and sold, or other enforcement proceedings may be taken against you. If this happens further cost will be added. If your circumstances change and you cannot pay, ask at the court office what you can do.

Note to claimant and defendant

Either of you may object to the rate of payment fixed. You must apply to the court with your reasons within 16 days. The 16 days runs from the date on the envelope in which the judgment was posted. A form is available from the court. A hearing may be arranged and you will be told when and where it will take place. If you live in, or carry on business in, another court's area, the claim may be transferred to that court.

Address for payment

How to pay

- **Payment(s) must be made to the person named at the address for payment, giving the claimant's reference and claim number**
- **DO NOT bring or send payments to the court - they will not be accepted**
  You should allow at least 4 days for your payment to reach the claimant or his representative.
  Make sure that you keep records and can account for all payments made. Proof may be required if there is any disagreement. It is not safe to send cash unless you use registered post.

The court office at

is open between 10 am and 4.30 pm Monday to Friday. When corresponding with the court, please address forms or letters to the Court Manager and quote the claim number.

N30(2)(HC)

FORM N30(2) JUDGMENT FOR CLAIMANT (AFTER DETERMINATION CC)

Judgment for Claimant
(after determination)

In the	
County Court	
Claim No.	
Claimant (including ref)	
Defendant (including ref)	
Date	

To [Claimant][Defendant]['s Solicitor]

the Defendant

SEAL

The claimant has objected to the rate of payment you offered.

The court has therefore decided the rate at which you should pay. You must pay the claimant £ for debt [and interest to date of judgment] and £ for costs [less £ which you have already paid]

You must pay to the claimant a total of £

[by instalments of £ per [week][month]

[the first payment to reach the claimant] by [and on or before this date each [week] [month] until the debt has been paid]

Warning

If you ignore this order your goods may be removed and sold, or other enforcement proceedings may be taken against you. If this happens further costs will be added. If your circumstances change and you cannot pay, ask at the court office what you can do.

Note to claimant and defendant

Either of you may object to the rate of payment fixed. You must apply to the court with your reasons within 16 days. The 16 days runs from the date on the envelope in which the judgment was posted. A form is available from the court. A hearing may be arranged and you will be told when and where it will take place. If you live in another court's area, the claim may be transferred to that court.

If judgment is for £5,000 or more, or is in respect of a debt which attracts contractual or statutory interest for late payment, the claimant may be entitled to further interest.

Address for payment

Note to the defendant

This judgment has been registered on the Register of County Court Judgments. This may make it difficult for you to get credit. **If you pay in full within one month you can ask the court to cancel the entry on the Register.** You will need to give proof of payment. You can (for a fee) also obtain a Certificate of Cancellation from the court. If you pay the debt in full after one month you can ask the court to mark the entry on the Register as satisfied and (for a fee) obtain a Certificate of Satisfaction to prove that the debt has been paid.

How to pay

- **Payment(s) must be made to the person named at the address for payment, giving the claimant's reference and claim number**
- **DO NOT bring or send payments to the court - they will not be accepted**
- You should allow at least 4 days for your payment to reach the claimant or his representative.
- Make sure that you keep records and can account for all payments made. Proof may be required if there is any disagreement. It is not safe to send cash unless you use registered post.
- Leaflets on registered judgments, how to pay and what to do if you cannot pay are available from the court.

The court office at

is open between 10 am and 4 pm Monday to Friday. When corresponding with the court, please address forms or letters to the Court Manager and quote the claim number.

N30(2)

Judgment for Claimant
(after re-determination)

In the High Court of Justice	
	Division District Registry
Claim No.	
Claimant (including ref)	
Defendant (including ref)	
Date	

To [Claimant][Defendant][’s Solicitor]

Seal

) the Defendant

[Master][District Judge] has considered the [claimant’s][defendant’s] application to change the rate of payment decided by the court and has ordered that you must pay the claimant £ for debt [and interest to date of judgment] and £ for costs.

You must pay to the claimant a total of £

[by instalments of £ per [week][month]

[the first payment to reach the claimant] by [and on or before this date each [week][month] until the debt has been paid]

Warning

If you ignore this order your goods may be removed and sold, or other enforcement proceedings may be taken against you. If this happens further costs will be added. If your circumstances change and you cannot pay, ask at the court office what you can do.

Address for payment

How to pay

- ☐ **Payment(s) must be made to the person named at the address for payment, giving the claimant’s reference and claim number**
- ☐ **DO NOT bring or send payments to the court - they will not be accepted**
- ☐ You should allow at least 4 days for your payment to reach the claimant or his representative.
- ☐ Make sure that you keep records and can account for all payments made. Proof may be required if there is any disagreement. It is not safe to send cash unless you use registered post.

e court office at

›pen between 10 am and 4.30 pm Monday to Friday. When corresponding with the court, please address forms or letters to the Court Manager and quote the case number.

0 (3) HC

Judgment for Claimant
(after re-determination)

In the	
County Court	
Claim No.	
Claimant (including ref.)	
Defendant (including ref.)	
Date	

To [Claimant][Defendant]['s Solicitor]

Seal

To the Defendant

District Judge has considered the [claimant's][defendant's] application to change the rate of payment decided by the court and has ordered that you must pay the claimant £ for debt [and interest to date of judgment] and £ for costs.

You must pay to the claimant a total of £

[by instalments of £ per [week][month]

[the first payment to reach the claimant] by [and on or before this date each [week][month] until the debt has been paid]

Warning

If you ignore this order your goods may be removed and sold, or other enforcement proceedings may be taken against you. If this happens further costs will be added. If your circumstances change and you cannot pay, ask at the court office what you can do.

Note to the defendant

This judgment has been recorded on the Register of County Court Judgments. This may make it difficult for you to get credit. **If you pay in full within one month you can ask the court to cancel the entry on the Register.** You will need to give proof of payment. You can (for a fee) also obtain a Certificate of Cancellation from the court. If you pay the debt in full after one month you can ask the court to mark the entry on the Register as satisfied and (for a fee) obtain a Certificate of Satisfaction to prove that the debt has been paid.

If judgment is for £5,000 or more, or is in respect of a debt which attracts contractual or statutory interest for late payment, the claimant may be entitled to further interest.

Address for payment

How to pay

- ☐ **Payment(s) must be made to the person named at the address for payment, giving the claimant's reference and claim number**
- ☐ **DO NOT bring or send payments to the court - they will not be accepted**
- ☐ You should allow at least 4 days for your payment to reach the claimant or his representative.
- ☐ Make sure that you keep records and can account for all payments made. Proof may be required if there is any disagreement. It is not safe to send cash unless you use registered post.
- ☐ Leaflets on registered judgments, how to pay and what to do if you cannot pay are available from the court.

The court office at

is open between 10 am and 4 pm Monday to Friday. When corresponding with the court, please address forms or letters to the Court Manager and quote the case number.

N30 (3)

Order for possession (Suspended)
(mortgaged property)

In the	
County Court	
Claim No. *Always quote this*	
Claimant's Ref.	
Defendant's Ref.	

Claimant

Defendant(s)

Seal

District Judge
of

orders that the defendant(s) give the claimant possession of
on the

(1) Delete if no money judgment

(1)**The court adjudges** that the defendant(s) pay the claimant £ , which is the amount currently outstanding under the mortgage, on the

The court orders that the order (and judgment) be **suspended** and be not enforced so long as the defendant(s) pay to the claimant the arrears due under the mortgage of £ by the payments set out below **in addition to** the regular mortgage payments that fall due from time to time; and be discharged when those arrears have been paid.

Payments in respect of arrears

Complete and delete as necessary

£ on or before the
£ per calendar month; the first such payment being made on or before the
(for months and then £ per calendar month)

Delete or insert any additional orders made

The court orders that

The court orders that the claimant's costs of this action

Complete and delete as necessary

be taxed by the court on Scale and be added to the amount owing under the mortgage
assessed at the sum of £ be paid by the defendant(s) on or before the

Dated:

To the defendant(s)

This means that, unless you pay the arrears under the mortgage by at least the payments set out above **in addition to your normal payments,** you must leave the property on the date stated above.

If you do not make those payments or leave the property, the claimant will be able to ask the court bailiff to evict you.

Payments should be made to the claimant at the place where you would normally pay your monthly repayments. If you need more information about making payments you should contact the plaintiff. The court cannot accept any payments.

Delete if no order for assessment

The claimant's costs are to be assessed, that is looked at by a judge to decide if they are reasonable. You will be sent a copy of the claimant's bill and will be able to object to any amounts in it. The judge will decide if your objections are valid.

Plaintiff's/Solicitor's address

Note

Delete if no money judgement or order for payment of costs

If you do not pay the money owed when it is due and the claimant takes steps to enforce payment, the order will be registered in the Register of County Court Judgments. **This may make it difficult for you to get credit.** Further information about registration is available in a leaflet which you can get from any county court office.

The court office at

is open between 10 am and 4 pm. When writing to the court, please address forms or letters to the Court Manager and quote the claim number.

N31 Order for possession (possession suspended mortgaged property) (9.98)

Judgment for Delivery of Goods

In the	
Claim No.	
Claimant's Ref.	
Defendant's Ref.	

Claimant

Seal

To the Defendant

The court has decided that the claimant recover from you the following goods of the claimant wrongly kept by you, namely:

of the value of £ [and also the sum of £ for damages for the detention of the goods,] and £ for costs

District Judge [master] ordered

[that you return the goods to the claimant or pay £ , their value, to reach the claimant by]

[that you return the goods to the claimant by . And also that you pay (£ damage and) £ for costs to reach the claimant by].

Dated

Important Notice

If you ignore this order your goods may be removed and sold, or other enforcement proceedings may be taken against you. If this happens further costs will be added. If your circumstances change and you cannot pay, ask at the court office what you can do.

Address for payment

Note to the defendant

This judgment has been registered on the Register of County Court Judgments. This may make it difficult for you to get credit. **If you pay in full within one month** you can ask the court to cancel the entry on the Register. You will need to give proof of payment. You can (for a fee) also obtain a Certificate of Cancellation from the court. If you pay the debt in full after one month you can ask the court to mark the entry on the Register as satisfied and (for a fee) obtain a Certificate of Satisfaction to prove that the debt has been paid.

How to pay

- **Payment(s) must be made to the person named at the address for payment, giving the claimant's reference and claim number**
- **DO NOT bring or send payments to the court - they will not be accepted**
- You should allow at least 4 days for your payment to reach the claimant or his representative
- Make sure that you keep records and can account for all payments made. Proof may be required if there is any disagreement. It is not safe to send cash unless you use registered post
- Leaflets on registered judgments, how to pay and what to do if you cannot pay are available from the court

The court office at

is open between 10 am and 4 pm Monday to Friday. When corresponding with the court, please address forms or letters to the Court Manager and quote the case number.
N32

Judgment for Delivery of Goods

In the	
Claim No.	
Claimant's Ref.	
Defendant's Ref.	

Claimant

Defendant

Seal

delete
lated"
gments
under
Hire -
ise Act
1965

r as the
may be

) insert
of hirer

specify
e goods
hich the
decides
ve been
letained

District Judge **ordered** that, the defendant having failed to comply with the terms of a (regulated)(1) hire - purchase agreement (or regulated conditional sale agreement) dated the day of [19][20]
made between the claimant and the defendant(s)(2)
the claimant recovers against the defendant(3) (4)
the following goods of the claimant, being goods subject to the agreement and wrongfully kept by the defendant, namely:

and recovers against the defendant the sum of £ for costs (or his costs of this action to be assessed)

District Judge **has ordered** that the defendant do return the goods to the claimant by

And that the defendant pays the sum of £ for costs (or an amount of the costs when assessed) to the claimant by (or within 14 days of assessment)
(or by instalments of £ for every calendar month, the first instalment to reach the claimant by

Dated

Important Notice

To the defendant

If you do not pay in accordance with this order your goods may be removed and sold or other enforcement proceedings may be taken against you.

If judgment is for £5000 or more the claimant is entitled to interest.

This judgment has been registered in the Register of County Court Judgments. **This may make it difficult for you to get credit. If you pay in full within one month** you can ask the court to cancel the entry on the Register. You will need to give proof of payment. You can (for a fee) also obtain a Certificate of Cancellation from the court. If you pay the debt in full after one month you can ask the court to mark the entry on the Register as satisfied and (for a fee) obtain a Certificate of Satisfaction to prove that the debt has been paid.

Address for Payment

How to Pay

- **PAYMENT(S) MUST BE MADE to the person named at the address for payment quoting their reference and the court case number.**
- **DO NOT bring or send payments to the court. THEY WILL NOT BE ACCEPTED.**
- You should allow at least 4 days for your payment to reach the claimant or his representative.
- Make sure that you keep records and can account for all payments made. Proof may be required if there is any disagreement. It is not safe to send cash unless you use registered post.
- A leaflet giving further advice about payment can be obtained from the court.
- If you need more information you should contact the claimant or his representative.

The court office at

is open between 10 am and 4 pm Monday to Friday. When corresponding with the court, please address forms to the Court Manager and quote the claim number.

N32(1)HP/ CCA Judgment for delivery of goods

Judgment for Delivery of Goods (suspended)

Claimant

Defendant

In the

Court

Claim No.

Claimant's Ref.

Defendants's Ref.

Seal

District Judge **has ordered that**, the defendant having failed to comply with the terms of a (regulated)(1) hire - purchase agreement (or regulated conditional sale agreement) dated the day of [19][20]
made between the claimant and the defendant(s)(2)
the claimant do recover against the defendant(3)
the following goods of the claimant, being goods subject to the agreement and wrongfully detained by the defendant, namely:(4)

and do recover against the defendant the sum of £ for costs (or his costs of this action to be assessed)

District Judge **has ordered** that unless the defendant(s) fulfill the conditions of the suspension, the defendant(3) do return the goods to the claimant by

And that the operation of this order be suspended on condition that the unpaid balance of the hire - purchase price, namely £ , is paid to the claimant by instalments of £ for every calendar month, the first instalment to reach the claimant by
(5)

And that the terms of the above - mentioned agreement be modified in the following respects:
no sum except the above - mentioned instalments shall be payable to the claimant in respect of the agreement during the suspension
(6)

And also that the defendant do pay the sum of £ for costs (or the amount of the costs when assessed) to the claimant by instalments of £ for every calender month, the first instalment to be paid one calender month after the last instalment of the hire - purchase price is paid

(1) delete "regulated" for judgments made under the Hire - Purchase Act 1965

(2) or as the case may be

(3) insert name of hirer

(4) specify the goods which the court decides have been detained

(5) add any further conditions imposed by the court

(6) state any other respects in which the agreement is to be modified

Dated

To the defendant

If you do not pay in accordance with this order your goods may be removed and sold or other enforcement proceedings may be taken against you. If circumstances change and you cannot pay, ask at the court office about what you can do.

Take Notice

This judgment has been registered in the Register of County Court Judgments. **This may make it difficult for you to get credit. If you pay in full within one month** you can ask the court to cancel the entry on the Register. You will need to give proof of payment. You can (for a fee) also obtain a Certificate of Cancellation from the court. If you pay the debt in full after one month you can ask the court to mark the entry on the Register as satisfied and (for a fee) obtain a Certificate of Satisfaction to prove that the debt has been paid.

Address for Payment

How to Pay

- **PAYMENT(S) MUST BE MADE to the person named at the address for payment quoting their reference and the court case number.**
- **DO NOT bring or send payments to the court.THEY WILL NOT BE ACCEPTED.**
- You should allow at least 4 days for your payment to reach the claimant or his representative.
- Make sure that you keep records and can account for all payments made. Proof may be required if there is any disagreement. It is not safe to send cash unless you use registered post.
- A leaflet giving further advice about payment can be obtained from the court.
- If you need more information you should contact the claimant or his representative.

The court office at

is open between 10 am and 4 pm Monday to Friday. When corresponding with the court, please address forms to the Court Manager and quote the claim number.

N32(2)HP/ CCA Judgment for delivery of goods

Judgment for Delivery of Goods

In the	
Claim No.	
Claimant's Ref	

seal

Claimant

Defendant

(1) delete "regulated" for judgments made under the Hire-Purchase Act 1965

(2) or as the case may be

(3) insert name or hirer

(4) specify the goods which the court decides have been detained

(5) specify the remainder of the goods to which the agreement relates

District Judge ordered that, the defendant having failed to comply with the terms of a (regulated)[1] hire purchase agreement (or regulated conditional sale agreement) dated the day of [19][20]

made between the claimant and the defendant(s) [2]
the claimant do recover against the defendant [3]
the following goods of the claimant, being goods subject to the agreement and wrongfully detained by the defendant, namely: [4]

and do recover against the defendant the sum of £ for costs (or his costs to be assessed on scale)

District Judge has ordered that the defendant do return the goods to the claimant by

And that the defendant pay the sum of £ for costs (or the amount of the costs when assessed) to the claimant by (or within 14 days of assessment)
(or by instalments of £ for every calender month, the first instalment to reach the claimant by
And that the claimant's title to the following goods be transferred to the defendant.[5]

Dated

To the defendant

If you do not pay in accordance with this order your goods may be removed and sold or other enforcement proceedings may be taken against you. If your circumstances change and you cannot pay, ask at the court office about what you can do.

Address for payment

Important Notice

This judgment has been registered in the Register of County Court Judgments This may make it difficult for you to get credit. **If you pay in full one within one month** you can ask the court to cancel the entry on the Register. You will need to give proof of payment. You can (for a fee) also obtain a Certificate of Cancellation from the court. If you pay the debt in full after one month you can ask the court to mark the entry on the Register as satisfied and (for a fee) obtain a Certificate of Satistaction to prove that the debt has been paid.

How to Pay

- **PAYMENT(S) MUST BE MADE to the person named at the address for payment quoting their reference and the court case number**
- **DO NOT bring or send payment to the court. THEY WILL NOT BE ACCEPTED**
- You should allow at least 4 days for your payment to reach the claimant or his represenitive
- Make sure that you keep records and can account for all payments made. Proof may be required if there is any disagreement. It is not safe to send cash unless you are registered post
- A leaflet giving further advice about payment can be obtained from the court. If you need more information you should contact the claimant or his representative

The court office at

is open between 10 am and 4 pm Monday to Friday. When corresponding the court, please address forms or letters to the Court Manager and quote the claim number.

N32 (3)HP/CCA

Variation Order (Return of Goods)

In the	
Claim No.	
Claimant's Ref.	
Defendant's Ref.	

Claimant

Defendant

seal

District Judge **ordered** that, instead of the conditions mentioned in the judgment of this action dated the day of [19][20], the operation of the order shall be suspended on the following conditions, namely:(1)

(1) state the varied conditions

And that the terms of the regulated agreement referred to in the judgment be further modified in the following respect:(2)

(2) state the respects in which the agreement is to be modified

Or that the suspension of the operation of the order in the judgment in this action dated the day of [19][20], be revoked and that the defendant(3)

(3) insert name of hirer

do return the goods specified in the judgment to the claimant by

And that the defendant(3) do pay the sum of £ for costs (or costs of those proceedings when assessed) to the claimant by
(or within 14 days of assessment) (or by instalments of £ for every calendar month, the first instalment to reach the claimant by)

Dated

Important Notice

To the defendant

If you do not pay in accordance with this order your goods may be removed and sold or other enforcement proceedings may be taken against you. If your circumstances change and you cannot pay, ask at the court office about what you can do

This judgment has been registered in the Register of County Court Judgments. **This may make it difficult for you to get credit. If you pay in full within one month** you can ask the court to cancel the entry on the Register. You will need to give proof of payment. You can (for a fee) also obtain a Certificate of Cancellation from the court. If you pay the debt in full after one month you can ask the court to mark the entry on the Register as satisfied and (for a fee) obtain a Certificate of Satisfaction to prove the debt has been paid

Address for Payment

How to Pay

- **PAYMENT(S) MUST BE MADE to the person named at the address for payment quoting their reference and the court case number.**
- **DO NOT bring or send payments to the court. THEY WILL NOT BE ACCEPTED.**
- You should allow at least 4 days for your payment to reach the claimant or his representative.
- Make sure that you keep records and can account for all payments made.
- Proof may be required if there is any disagreement. It is not safe to send cash unless you use registered post.
- A leaflet giving further advice about payment can be obtained from the court. If you need more information you should contact the claimant or his representative.

The court office at

is open between 10 am and 4 pm Monday to Friday. Address all communications to the Court Manager quoting the claim number

N32(4) Variation order (return of goods)

Order for Balance of Purchase Price
(return of goods)

In the	
Claim No.	
Claimant's Ref	
Defendant's Ref	

Claimant

Defendant

seal

District Judge **has ordered** that the order in this action dated the day of [19][20]
for the return of the specified goods be revoked and that the defendant do pay the sum of £ in respect of the

balance of the total price of the goods and £ for the costs to the claimant
by
(or by instalments of £ for every calender month, the first instalment to reach the claimant
by)

Dated

To the defendant

If you do not pay in accordance with this order your goods may be removed and sold or other enforcement proceedings may be taken against you. If your circumstances change and you cannot pay, ask at the court office about what you can do.

Address for payment

Important Notice

This judgment has been registered in the Register of County Court Judgments This may make it difficult for you to get credit. **If you pay in full within one month** you can ask the court to cancel the entry on the Register. You will need to give proof of payment. You can (for a fee) also obtain a Certificate of Cancellation from the court. If you pay the debt in full after one month you can ask the court to mark the entry on the Register as satisfied and (for a fee) obtain a Certificate of Satisfaction to prove that the debt has been paid.

How to Pay

- **PAYMENT(S) MUST BE MADE to the person named at the address for payment quoting their reference and the court case number** DO NOT bring or send payment to the court. THEY WILL NOT BE ACCEPTED
- You should allow at least 4 days for your payment to reach the claimant or his representative
- Make sure that you keep records and can account for all payments made. Proof may be required if there is any disagreement. It is not safe to send cash unless you use registered post
- A leaflet giving further advice about payment can be obtained from the court.
- If you need more information you should contact the claimant or his representative

The court office at

is open between 10 am and 4 pm Monday to Friday. When corresponding the court, please address forms or letters to the Court Manager and quote the claim number.

N32 (5) HP/CCA

Judgment for Delivery of Goods

In the	
Claim No.	
Claimant's Ref.	
Defendant's Ref.	

Claimant

Defendant

seal

(1) specify the goods to which the court decides have been detained

District Judge **has ordered** that the claimant do recover against the defendant the following goods of the claimant wrongly detained by the defendant, namely:(1)

of the vale of £ and also the sum of £ for arrears of hire rent
and the sum of £ for costs

District Judge **has ordered** that the defendant do return the goods to the claimant, or do pay the sum of £ , their value, to reach the claimant by

And also that the defendant do pay the sum of £ arrears and £ for costs, amounting together to the sum of £ , to the claimant by instalments of £ for every calendar month, the first instalment to reach the claimant by

Dated

Take Notice

To the defendant

If you do not pay in accordance with this order your goods may be removed and sold or other enforcement proceedings may be taken against you. If your circumstances change and you cannot pay, ask at the court office about what you can do

Address for Payment

This judgment has been registered in the Register of County Court Judgments. **This may make it difficult for you to get credit. If you pay in full within one month** you can ask the court to cancel the entry on the Register. You will need to give proof of payment. You can (for a fee) also obtain a Certificate of Cancellation from the court. If you pay the debt in full after one month you can ask the court to mark the entry on the Register as satisfied and (for a fee) obtain a Certificate of Satisfaction to prove that the debt has been paid.

How to Pay

- **PAYMENT(S) MUST BE MADE to the person named at the address for payment quoting their reference and the court case number.**
- **DO NOT bring or send payments to the court. THEY WILL NOT BE ACCEPTED.**
- You should allow at least 4 days for your payment to reach the claimant or his representative.
- Make sure that you keep records and can account for all payments made Proof may be required if there is any disagreement. It is not safe to send cash unless you use registered post.
- A leaflet giving further advice about payment can be obtained from the court.
- If you need more information you should contact the claimant or his representative.

The court office at

is open between 10 am and 4 pm Monday to Friday. Address all communications to the Court Manager quoting the claim number

N33 Judgment for delivery of goods (simple hire agreement)

Judgment for Claimant
(after court decided amount)

In the High Court of Justice	Division District Registry
Claim No.	
Claimant (including Ref)	
Defendant (including Ref)	
Date	

To [Claimant][Defendant]['s Solicitor]

Seal

To the Defendant

The claimant obtained judgment against you on for an amount to be decided by the court.

[Master][District Judge] has decided the amount and ordered that you should pay £ [including interest to date of judgment] and £ for costs [with costs to be assessed]

You must pay to the claimant a total of £

[by instalments of £ per [week][month]

[the first payment to reach the claimant] by [and on or before this date each [week][month] until the debt has been paid]

If costs are to be assessed, you will be told when those costs have to be paid after the assessment has taken place.

Warning

If you ignore this order your goods may be removed and sold, or other enforcement proceedings may be taken against you. If this happens further costs will be added. If your circumstances change and you cannot pay, ask at the court office what you can do.

Address for payment

How to pay

- **Payment(s) must be made to the person named at the address for payment, giving the claimant's reference and claim number**
- **DO NOT bring or send payments to the court - they will not be accepted**
- You should allow at least 4 days for your payment to reach the claimant or his representative
- Make sure that you keep records and can account for all payments made. Proof may be required if there is any disagreement. It is not safe to send cash unless you use registered post
- Leaflets on how to pay and what to do if you cannot pay are available from the court

The court office at

is open between 10 am and 4.30 pm Monday to Friday. When corresponding with the court, please address forms or letters to the Court Manager and quote the claim number.

N34HC

Judgment for Claimant
(after court decided amount)

In the **County Court**	
Claim No.	
Claimant (including ref.) **Defendant** (including ref)	
Date	

Seal

To [Claimant][Defendant]['s Solicitor]

To the Defendant

The claimant obtained judgment against you on for an amount to be decided by the court.

District Judge has decided the amount and ordered that you should pay £ [including interest to date of judgment] and £ for costs [with costs to be assessed]

You must pay to the claimant a total of £

[by instalments of £ per [week][month]

[the first payment to reach the claimant] by [and on or before this date each [week][month] until the debt has been paid]

If costs are to be assessed, you will be told when those costs have to be paid after the assessment has taken place.

Warning

If you ignore this order your goods may be removed and sold, or other enforcement proceedings may be taken against you. If this happens further costs will be added. If your circumstances change and you cannot pay, ask at the court office what you can do.

If judgment is for £5,000 or more, or is in respect of a debt which attracts contractual or statutory interest for late payment, the claimant may be entitled to further interest.

Address for payment

Note to the defendant

This judgment has been registered on the Register of County Court Judgments. This may make it difficult for you to get credit. **If you pay in full within one month** you can ask the court to cancel the entry on the Register. You will need to give proof of payment. You can (for a fee) also obtain a Certificate of Cancellation from the court. If you pay the debt in full after one month you can ask the court to mark the entry on the Register as satisfied and (for a fee) obtain a Certificate of Satisfaction to prove that the debt has been paid.

How to pay

- **Payment(s) must be made to the person named at the address for payment, giving the claimant's reference and claim number**
- **DO NOT bring or send payments to the court - they will not be accepted**
- You should allow at least 4 days for your payment to reach the claimant or his representative
- Make sure that you keep records and can account for all payments made. Proof may be required if there is any disagreement. It is not safe to send cash unless you use registered post
- Leaflets on registered judgments, how to pay and what to do if you cannot pay are available from the court

The court office at

is open between 10 am and 4 pm Monday to Friday. When corresponding with the court, please address forms or letters to the Court Manager and quote the claim number.

N34 Judgment for claimant

Hardship payment order

In the

Claim No.

Claimant

Defendant

Third Party

SEAL

On 20 , [Master] [District Judge]
sitting at [county court] [district registry] [the Royal Courts of Justice] at

considered the application of the [defendant] [claimant] ('the judgment debtor') and
heard .

An interim third party debt order made on 20 forbids the third party from paying to the judgment debtor or any other person £ or (if less) the amount due from it to the judgment debtor until the application of the [claimant] [defendant] ('the judgment creditor') is heard, unless the court orders otherwise; it appears that the amount which is due from the third party to the judgment debtor (after deducting the expenses allowed on receiving the interim third party debt order) is £ ;

and the court orders that the third party may pay [to the judgment debtor] [to] out of the amount due from it to the judgment debtor £ [on 20] [on the day of each [week] [month]].

The question whether one party should bear the other party's costs of this application and, if so, how will be considered on the hearing of the judgment creditor's application.

To

N37 Hardship payment order (03.02)

Order to attend court for questioning

In the

Claim No.

Claimant

Defendant

On 20 , [the court] [[Master][District Judge]
sitting at]
considered the application of the [claimant] [defendant] ('the judgment creditor'), which shows that:

a judgment or order given on 20 [by the
in claim no.] ordered the [defendant] [claimant] ('the judgment debtor') [to pay money to the judgment creditor, and that the amount now owing under the judgment or order is £]
[and] [to
]

and the court orders that

1. [who is an officer of] the judgment debtor [company] [corporation] attend [the court] [county court]
at on 20
before a [judge][court officer] at [a.m] [p.m.]
to provide information about the judgment debtor's means and any other information needed to enforce the judgment or order.
[The questioning will take place before a judge.]

2. The [judgment debtor] [officer] at that time and place produce at court all documents in the judgment debtor's control [which relate to the judgment debtor's means of paying the amount due under the judgment or order and] which relate to those matters mentioned in paragraph 1. [The documents produced must include those shown in the attached list.]

3. The [judgment debtor] [officer] at that time and place answer on oath, all the questions which the court asks and which the court allows the judgment creditor to ask.

[**4.** The court where the questioning is to take place may make an order for payment of the costs of the application and of the hearing.]

To

You must obey this order. If you do not, you may be sent to prison for contempt of court.

Amount owing

The application shows that the amount owing under the judgment or order
(including any costs and interest) is £
The judgment creditor has paid a court fee of £__________
Total £__________

If the total amount owing is paid (together with any further interest falling due), the judgment creditor may agree that the questioning need not take place (but may ask for an order for costs).

N39 Order to attend court for questioning (03.02)

To the person ordered to attend

How to pay

Do not send payments to the court office. They will not be accepted.

Payment must be made to the judgment creditor at the address below, quoting the reference and the claim number. Allow at least 4 days for payments sent by post to arrive. It is not safe to send cash unless you use registered post.

Keep records and make sure you can account for all payments made. Proof may be needed if there is a disagreement.

If you need more information about paying, contact the judgment creditor or representative.

Correspondence for the court relating to the hearing should be addressed to 'The Court Manager' of the court where the hearing is to take place.

Travelling expenses

You may ask the judgment creditor to pay you a sum reasonably sufficient to cover your travelling expenses to and from court. You should ensure your request reaches the judgment creditor within 7 days of receiving this order.
If the court orders you to pay the judgment creditor's costs, the order may include any amount which has been paid to you for travelling expenses.

The information required

You will be required to disclose full details of your income and outgoings and your assets (what you own) and liabilities (what you owe) and the matters referred to in paragraph 1 of the order.
(If you have been ordered to attend as an officer of a company or corporation, you will be required to disclose the same details about the company or corporation.)

Documents in your control

You must produce all documents which confirm the information required. If you do not have them in your possession, you must get them if you can.
These will include

- pay slips
- bank statements
- building society books
- share certificates
- rent book
- mortgage statement
- hire-purchase and similar agreements
- court orders on which you still owe money
- other outstanding bills
- electricity, gas, water and council tax bills for the last year.

If you have a business or you are a partner in a business, or the judgment debtor is a company or corporation, they will include the above documents so far as they relate to the business and

- bills or invoices owed to the judgment debtor
- two years' balance sheets and profit and loss accounts
- current management accounts.

If a list of additional documents is attached to this order, these too must be produced.

Judgment Creditor's address

ref. Tel.

To the judgment creditor

If the hearing is to be before a judge, you or your representative **must attend** and conduct the questioning.
If the questioning is to be carried out by a court officer, you need not attend, but you or your representative may attend if you wish to ask questions.

Warrant of arrest for disobedience
(order to attend court for questioning)

In the

County Court

Claim No.

Warrant No.

Claimant

Defendant

SEAL

To the bailiffs of the court and every constable within the district of the court:

On 20 , [His] [Her] Honour Judge
sitting at
found that of
('the judgment debtor') had
committed a breach of the order to attend court for questioning dated 20 and is accordingly in contempt of court and

ordered that [he] [she] be committed for contempt to Her Majesty's Prison
for a period of days
and that the order for committal be suspended so long as [he] [she] attend court at the time and place specified in that order and otherwise comply with the order to attend court for questioning dated 20 [and
].

The court is satisfied that the suspended commital order dated 20 was served on the judgment debtor on 20 [but [he] [she] failed to attend court at that time and place.] [and that [he] [she] attended court but failed to comply with the order in that [he] [she]
]

You the bailiffs and constables are therefore required to arrest the judgment debtor and to bring [him] [her] before a judge to consider whether the committal order should be discharged.

Dated

N40A Warrant of arrest for disobedience (order to attend court for questioning) (03.02)

Bailiff's Certificate

I arrested ____
the judgment debtor, on __________________________ and brought [him][her]
before the judge on __________________________

Signed ________________________
Bailiff of the County Court

Warrant of committal for disobedience
(order to attend court for questioning)

In the

County Court

Claim No.

Warrant No.

Claimant

Defendant

To the bailiffs of the court and every constable within the district of the court and to the Governor of Her Majesty's Prison

SEAL

On 20 , [His] [Her] Honour Judge
sitting at
found that of
('the judgment debtor') had committed
a breach of the order to attend court for questioning dated 20 and is accordingly in contempt of court and

ordered that [he] [she] be committed for contempt to Her Majesty's Prison
for a period of days
and that the order for committal be suspended so long as [he] [she] attend court at the time and place specified in that order and otherwise comply with the order to attend court for questioning dated 20 [and
]

On 20 , the judgment debtor was arrested and brought before [[His] [Her] Honour] [District] Judge sitting at
on 20 .

The judge was satisfied that

- the judgment debtor [did not attend court] [refused to take the oath] [refused to answer the questions asked] as required by the order to attend court for questioning dated 20
- at the time and place mentioned in the order for committal dated 20 the judgment debtor did not [attend court] [take the oath] [answer the questions] [
]
- the conditions for suspension of that order of committal were therefore not met
- the judgment debtor persists in the contempt of court

and that the order for committal dated the 20 should not be discharged.

You the bailiffs and constables are therefore required to deliver to the Governor of Her Majesty's Prison

and you the Governor to receive [him] [her] and safely keep [him] [her] in prison for days from the date of [his] [her]arrest or until lawfully discharged if sooner.

Dated

N40B Warrant of committal for disobedience (order to attend court for questioning) (03.02)

Bailiff's Certificate

I arrested ______________________________

the judgment debtor, on ______________________ and brought [him][her]

[before the judge on ______________________]

[into the custody of the Governor of Her Majesty's Prison at ______________________

on ______________________]

Signed ______________________

Bailiff of the County Court

FORM N40A(HC)

Warrant of arrest for disobedience
(order to attend court for questioning)

In the High Court of Justice
[Queen's Bench] [Chancery] Division
[District Registry]

Claim No.

Warrant No.

Claimant

Defendant

To the Tipstaff attending on Her Majesty's Supreme Court, his deputy or assistants, and all police constables and other peace officers whom it may concern:

SEAL

On 20 , The Honourable [Mr] [Mrs] Justice
sitting at
found that of
('the judgment debtor') had committed a breach of the order to attend court for questioning dated 20 and is accordingly in contempt of court and

ordered that [he] [she] be committed for contempt to Her Majesty's Prison
for a period of days
and that the order be suspended so long as [he] [she] attend court at the time and place specified in that order and otherwise comply with the order to attend court for questioning dated 20 [and]

The court is satisfied that the suspended committal order dated 20 was served on the judgment debtor on 20 [but [he] [she] [failed to attend court at that time and place.] [and that [he] [she] attended court but failed to comply with the order in that [he] [she]]

THIS WARRANT COMMANDS you and every one of you in Her Majesty's name to arrest and to bring [him] [her] before a judge to consider whether the committal order should be discharged.

Dated

N40A(HC) Warrant of arrest for disobedience (order to attend court for questioning) (03.02)

Warrant of committal for disobedience
(order to attend court for questioning)

In the High Court of Justice
[Queen's Bench] [Chancery] Division
[District Registry]

Claim No.

Warrant No.

Claimant

Defendant

To the Tipstaff attending on Her Majesty's Supreme Court, his deputy or assistants, and all police constables and other peace officers whom it may concern:

SEAL

On 20 , The Honourable [Mr] [Mrs] Justice
sitting at
found that of
('the judgment debtor') had committed a breach of the order to attend court for questioning dated 20 and is accordingly in contempt of court and

ordered that [he] [she] be committed for contempt to Her Majesty's Prison
for a period of days
and that the order for committal be suspended so long as [he] [she] attend court at the time and place specified in that order and otherwise comply with the order to attend court for questioning dated 20 [and
]

On 20 , the judgment debtor was arrested and [on 20]brought before [The Honourable [Mr] [Mrs] Justice] [[His] [Her] Honour Judge] [Master] [District Judge] sitting at

The judge was satisfied that

- the judgment debtor [did not attend court] [refused to take the oath] [refused to answer the questions asked] as required by the order to attend court for questioning dated 20
- at the time and place mentioned in the order for committal dated 20 the judgment debtor did not [attend court] [take the oath] [answer the questions] [
]
- the conditions for suspension of that order of committal were therefore not met
- the judgment debtor persists in the contempt of court

and that the order for committal dated the 20 should not be discharged.

THIS WARRANT COMMANDS you and every one of you in Her Majesty's name to convey to the Governor of Her Majesty's Prison to be detained there and kept in safe custody for a period of days from the date of [his] [her] arrest or until lawfully discharged if sooner.

Dated

N40B(HC) Warrant of committal for disobedience (order to attend court for questioning) (03.02)

Notice of eviction

In the

County Court

Claim No.

Warrant no.

To

The court has issued a warrant for the possession of the above property (land) at the request of the claimant. The warrant gives a county court bailiff the authority to evict you and hand over possession to the claimant. This notice tells you the time and date when the eviction will take place, what will happen on that date, and what you can do.

The eviction will take place on 20 at am/pm.

You should arrange to leave the property (land) with your belongings before this date and time.

What will happen
A possession warrant gives the bailiff authority to remove **anyone** still in the property (on the land) at the time the eviction is due to take place. A representative of the claimant will attend with the bailiff. That representative will change any locks, or take any other steps necessary to prevent re-entry. If you have not removed all of your belongings when the eviction takes place, you will only be allowed time to do so if the claimant's representative agrees.

Important notes

- Get help and advice about the eviction, or about re-housing. **Act immediately.** You can get advice from an advice agency, a solicitor or your local Housing Department.
- **In some circumstances, the court can decide to suspend the warrant and postpone the date for eviction.** You should get advice now about whether the court may do so in your case. If it can, you must tell the court your grounds (reasons) for asking that it should. It is not sufficient just to say that you have not been able to find somewhere else to live. If you wish to apply, you should ask the court for a Form N244 (Application Notice). Once you have filled in the form with your request and the grounds on which you are making it, you will be given an appointment to see a judge. The claimant will be sent a copy of your application. You will have to pay a fee unless you qualify for fee exemption or remission. A member of the court's staff will be able to give you more details about this.
- You must attend at the time and date given on the notice. The claimant, or the claimant's representative, may also attend. If you do not go to the hearing, the judge may simply dismiss your application and you could incur additional court costs.
- **If you can pay off any arrears,** contact the claimant, or the claimant's solicitor, immediately you get this notice. Any payments must be made to the claimant and not to the court. Make sure that you get a receipt for any payments you make. It will be for the claimant to decide whether your payment is sufficient to stop the eviction. If it is, the claimant must let the court know before the eviction is due to take place.

You can contact the bailiff who will be responsible for the eviction, by telephoning Monday to Friday between the hours of and

The claimant (claimant's solicitor) is of

whose telephone number *(if available)* is

Quote reference

N54 Notice of eviction (06.01) *The Court Service Publications Branch*

Suspended committal order for disobedience
(order to attend court for questioning)

In the	Claim No.
	Claimant
	Defendant

On 20 , [[Mr] [Mrs] Justice] [[His] [Her] Honour Judge]
sitting at

[heard and]
read the order made on 20 , [the certificate dated 20 of the bailiff,] the affidavit[s] of sworn on 20 [and sworn on 20 respectively as to service of the order and] as to the provision of travelling expenses and the certificate dated 20 of the [Master][District Judge][Court Officer]

and the court is satisfied that

1. was ordered to attend court on 20 to be questioned
2. the order to attend was served on *name* on 20

[3. did not within seven days of the service of the order request from the judgment creditor payment of a sufficient sum for travelling expenses.]

[3. on 20 the judgment creditor paid *name* a sufficient sum for travelling expenses.]

[4. did not attend court on 20 to be questioned]

[3. , having attended court, refused to be sworn]

[3. , having attended court, refused to answer [any question][the question

]

And that has been guilty of contempt of court by disobeying the order of 20

and the court orders that

be committed to Her Majesty's Prison

for a period of days

N79A Suspended committal for disobedience (order to attend for questioning) (03.02)

and the court orders that

1. this order shall be suspended so long as attends court at a.m / p.m. on 20 at

and complies with the order made on 20 .

[and]

2. if does not comply with these terms, a warrant of arrest shall be issued and shall, when arrested, be brought before a judge to consider whether the committal order should be discharged.

[**3.** and that pay the judgment creditor's costs of attending of £ , on or before 20 .]

Certificate of Service

I certify that a copy of this order was served by me on ______________________________ the judgment debtor, on ____________________

Signed ____________________

Bailiff of the County Court

Interim third party debt order

In the

Claim No.

Claimant

Defendant

Third Party

SEAL

On 20 , [Master] [District Judge]
considered the application of the [claimant] [defendant] ('the judgment creditor'),
from which it appears:

a) there is an amount owing by the [claimant] [defendant] ('the judgment debtor') under the judgment or order given on 20 [by the in claim no.] and

b) there is a debt due or accruing due by the third party to the judgment debtor

and the court orders that

1. The application will be heard at [a.m.][p.m.] on 20 at when a judge will decide whether a final third party debt order should be made.

2. Until that hearing the third party must not, unless the court orders otherwise, pay to the judgment debtor, or to any other person, any sum of money due or accruing due by the third party to the judgment debtor, except for any part of that sum which exceeds the total shown below.

Amount now owing under the judgment or order including any costs and interest		£
Court fee		£
Costs of this application which may be allowed to the judgment creditor		£
	Total	**£**

This interim order does not authorise the third party to pay any money to the judgment creditor at this stage.

To

Hardship
If the third party is a bank or building society, and the judgment debtor or their family suffers hardship through not being able to meet ordinary living expenses as a result of not being able to withdraw money from the account, a court may make a hardship payment order allowing some money to be paid out. An application form (N244) can be obtained from any court office *(see overleaf for further details).*

N84 Interim Third Party Debt order (03.02)

Hardship payment orders

An application for a hardship payment order may be made to:

- **any county court** where the interim third party debt order was made to a county court; or
- **the Royal Courts of Justice in London or to any district registry,** where the interim third party debt order was made by the High Court.

A fee may be payable for the application, but in certain circumstances, the applicant can apply for exemption or remission of the fee. Court staff can provide further details about remission and exemption and provide the necessary forms.

The application should be made using Form N244. It must include details of the judgment creditor, the court where the interim third party debt order was made, if different, and the claim number. The form must include evidence of the hardship caused by not being able to meet ordinary living expenses and must be accompanied by documentary evidence such as mortgage statements or rent book, wage or salary slips and bank statements proving the applicant's financial position. There will usually be a hearing.

In cases of exceptional urgency, the court may agree to deal with the application without notice being given to the judgment creditor. Details of why the application is exceptionally urgent and why it should be dealt with without notice to the creditor, should be set out in the application.

If the judge makes a hardship payment order, the court will draw up an order which will be faxed to the appropriate bank or building society who will then be authorised to pay out the amount, or amounts, specified in the order.

What the third party will do

If the third party **is a bank or building society**, it must search for all accounts held solely by the judgment debtor and, within 7 days of receiving this order, give details of them to the court and the judgment creditor, stating whether it holds sufficient to cover the total shown and, if not, the amounts in them.

A bank or building society may deduct an amount from any money held for the judgment debtor, for its expenses in complying with this order. This would be in addition to the total amount shown above.

If the third party **is not a bank or building society** and claims to owe the judgment debtor no money or less money than the total shown above, the third party must tell the court and the judgment creditor within 7 days of receiving this order.

The final order

If a final third party debt order is made at the hearing, it will require the third party to pay direct to the judgment creditor some or all of the money which the third party owes to the judgment debtor.

Party details

The judgment creditor
Name:
Address for service:

Postcode
reference:
Telephone:

The judgment debtor
Name:
Address:

Postcode
reference:
Telephone:

The third party
Name:
Address for service:

Postcode
reference:
Telephone:

Banks and Building Societies
The name and address of the branch:

Postcode

Sort code
Account no(s):

Final third party debt order

In the

Claim No.

Claimant

Defendant

Third Party

SEAL

On 20 , [Master] [District Judge]

sitting at

heard

and the court orders that

1. The third party pay to the [claimant] [defendant] ('the judgment creditor') £ on or before the 20 .

2. The judgment creditor's costs of this application £ are to be retained out of the money recovered by the judgment creditor under this order in priority to the judgment debt.

The effect of this order

The amount owed **to** the judgment debtor by the third party will be reduced by what the third party pays under this order **and** any costs and expenses to which the third party is entitled.

The amount owed **by** the judgment debtor to the judgment creditor will be reduced by what the third party pays under this order **less** the judgment creditor's costs of the application, including the court fee.

To

N85 Final Third Party Debt Order (03.02)

Interim charging order

In the

Claim No.

Claimant

Defendant

SEAL

On 20 ,[Master] [District Judge] considered the application of the [claimant] [defendant] ('the judgment creditor'), from which it appears:

(a) a judgment or order given on 20 , [by the in claim no.] ordered the [defendant] [claimant] ('the judgment debtor') to pay money to the judgment creditor;

(b) the amount now owing under the judgment or order is £ (including any interest and costs); and

(c) the judgment debtor is the owner of or has a beneficial interest in the asset described in the schedule below;

and the court orders that

1. The interest of the judgment debtor in the asset described in the schedule below stand charged with payment of £ together with any further interest becoming due and the costs of the application.

2. The application will be heard at [a.m.] [p.m.] on 20 at
when a judge will decide whether the charge created by this order should continue (with or without modification) or should be discharged.

The Schedule

[The address of the land or property charged is

[the title to which is registered at H. M. Land Registry under Title No.]]

[*particulars of securities, funds etc. charged*

].

N86 Interim Charging Order (03.02)

Final charging order

In the

Claim No.

Claimant

Defendant

SEAL

On 20 , [Master] [District Judge]

sitting at

heard

and the court orders that

1. The charge created by the order made on the 20 shall continue [as modified by this order].

2. The interest of the [defendant] [claimant] in the asset described in the schedule below stand charged with payment of the sum of £ the amount now owing under a judgment or order given on 20 [by the in claim no.] together with any further interest becoming due and £ the costs of the application.

3. Those costs are to be added to the judgment debt.

The Schedule

[The address of the land or property charged is

[the title to which is registered at H. M. Land Registry under Title No.]]

[*(particulars of securities, funds etc. charged)*

].

[**STOP NOTICE**

To [the Bank of England] [ ]

Take notice that, in relation to the securities specified in the schedule to this order, you may not, without notice to at register any transfer, or make any redemption payment, or, in the case of a unit trust, deal with the units, or, where dividends or interest are included in the order, pay any dividend or interest.]

N87 Final Charging Order (03.02)

Anti-social Behaviour Injunction Power of Arrest

Name of court	Claim No.
Name of Claimant	
Claimant's Ref.	
Defendant's name	

Seal

Claimant

Phone number:

(here set out the provisions of the injunction to which the power of arrest relates)

Power of arrest

And the judge finding:

Delete as required

(a) that the condition(s) in section 153A of the Housing Act 1996 [is] [are] satisfied; or
(b) that the condition in section 153B(1) of the Housing Act 1996 is satisfied; or
(c) that the conditions in section 153D(1) of the Housing Act 1996 are satisfied; or
(d) that the conditions in section 91(2) of the Anti-social Behaviour Act 2003 are satisfied; or
(e) that the conditions in section 27(2) of the Police and Justice Act 2006 are satisfied.

[And, in proceedings under Section 222 of the Local Government Act 1972, the local authority having applied to the court]

And the court being satisfied that:

(a) the conduct consists of or includes the use or threatened use of violence; [and] [or]
(b) there is a significant risk of harm to a person mentioned in [section 153A(3) of the Housing Act 1996] [section 153A(4) Housing Act 1996] [section 153D(2) of the Housing Act 1996] [section 91(2) of the Anti-social Behaviour Act 2003] [section 27 of the Police and Justice Act 2006]*

* delete as appropriate

Note: The reference to section 153A(3) Housing Act 1996 applies to applications made that are subject to section 153A Housing Act 1996 introduced by section 26 of the Police and Justice Act 2006. The reference to section 153A(4) Housing Act 1996 applies to applications made that are subject to section 153A Housing Act 1996 as unamended by section 26 of the Police and Justice Act 2006.

A power of arrest is attached to this injunction whereby any constable may [under the power given in section 155 of the Housing Act 1996] [under the power given in section 27 of the Police and Justice Act 2006]*, arrest the [respondent] [defendant] if the constable has reasonable cause for suspecting the [respondent] [defendant] is in breach of this injunction.

This power of arrest was ordered on 20 and expires on the day of 20

Defendant

Note to Arresting Office

Where the defendant is arrested under the power given by section 155 of the Housing Act 1996, or section 27 of the Police and Justice Act 2006:-

- the defendant shall be brought before the judge within the period of 24 hours beginning at the time of his arrest;
- a constable shall inform the person on whose application the injunction was granted, forthwith where the defendant is arrested under the power given by section 155 of the Housing Act 1996 or as soon as reasonably practicable where the defendant is arrested under the power given by section 27 of the Police and Justice Act 2006.

Nothing in section 155 of the Housing Act 1996 or section 27 of the Police and Justice Act 2006 shall authorise the detention of the respondent after the expiry of the period of 24 hours beginning at the time of his arrest.

In calculating any period of 24 hours, no account shall be taken of Christmas Day, Good Friday or any Sunday.

The court office at

is open between 10am and 4pm. When corresponding with the court, please address forms or letters to the Court Manager and quote the claim number.

N110A Power of arrest attached to injunction (04.07)

Click here to reset form | Click here to print form

Particulars of claim for possession
(rented residential premises)

Name of court	Claim No.
Name of Claimant	
Name of Defendant	

1. The claimant has a right to possession of:

2. To the best of the claimant's knowledge the following persons are in possession of the property:

About the tenancy

3. (a) The premises are let to the defendant(s) under a(n) tenancy which began on .

(b) The current rent is £ and is payable each (week) (fortnight) (month).
(*other*)

(c) Any unpaid rent or charge for use and occupation should be calculated at £ per day.

4. The reason the claimant is asking for possession is:

(a) because the defendant has not paid the rent due under the terms of the tenancy agreement.
(Details are set out below)(Details are shown on the attached rent statement)

(b) because the defendant has failed to comply with other terms of the tenancy.
Details are set out below.

(c) because: (including any (other) statutory grounds)

N119 Particulars of claim for possession (rented residential premises) (04.10)

5. The following steps have already been taken to recover any arrears:

6. The appropriate (notice to quit) (notice of breach of lease) (notice seeking possession) (notice seeking a demotion order) (*other*) was served on the defendant on 20 .

About the defendant

7. The following information is known about the defendant's circumstances:

About the claimant

8. The claimant is asking the court to take the following financial or other information into account when making its decision whether or not to grant an order for possession:

Forfeiture

9. (a) There is no underlessee or mortgagee entitled to claim relief against forfeiture.

or (b) of

is entitled to claim relief against forfeiture as underlessee or mortgagee.

What the court is being asked to do:

10. The claimant asks the court to order that the defendant(s):

(a) give the claimant possession of the premises;

(b) pay the unpaid rent and any charge for use and occupation up to the date an order is made;

(c) pay rent and any charge for use and occupation from the date of the order until the claimant recovers possession of the property;

(d) pay the claimant's costs of making this claim.

11. In the alternative to possession, is the claimant asking the court to make a demotion order or an order suspending the right to buy?

☐ Yes ☐ No

Demotion/Suspension claim

This section must be completed if the claim includes a claim for demotion of tenancy or suspension order in the alternative to possession

12. The (demotion) (suspension) claim is made under:

☐ section 82A(2) of the Housing Act 1985

☐ section 6A(2) of the Housing Act 1988

☐ section 121A of the Housing Act 1985

13. The claimant is a:

☐ local authority

☐ housing action trust

☐ registered social landlord or a private registered provider of social housing

☐ other please specify (suspension claims only)

(Demotion claims only)

14. Has the claimant served on the tenant a statement of express terms of the tenancy which are to apply to the demoted tenancy?

☐ Yes ☐ No

If Yes, please give details:

15. The claimant is claiming delete as appropriate (demotion of tenancy) (and) (an order suspending the right to buy) because: *State details of the conduct alleged and **any** other matters relied upon.*

Statement of Truth

*(I believe)(The claimant believes) that the facts stated in these particulars of claim are true.
* I am duly authorised by the claimant to sign this statement.

signed ______________________ date ______________________

(Claimant)(Litigation friend(where claimant is a child or a patient)*)(Claimant's solicitor)
**delete as appropriate*

Full name ______________________

Name of claimant's solicitor's firm ______________________

position or office held ______________________
(if signing on behalf of firm or company)

Click here to print form

Notes for guidance on completing particulars of claim form (rented residential premises)

The following notes are a step by step guide to completing form N119. They tell you what information is needed for each of the numbered paragraphs in the form.

1. Give the full address of the premises of which you are seeking possession.
2. Name each person, to the best of your knowledge, in possession of the premises.

About the tenancy

3. (a) State the type of the tenancy (e.g. assured, assured shorthold) and when it began.

   (b) Give details of how much the agreed rent is and when it is payable.

   (c) Give the daily rate at which rent is charged.

4. (a) If you are claiming possession because the rent has not been paid, set out details of how much rent is outstanding up to the time the claim is issued, including a rent statement showing how the arrears arose. You must give sufficient detail to support your claim for possession. Set out the details in accordance with Paragraph 2.3 of Practice Direction accompanying Part 55 of the Civil Procedure Rules i.e. rent arrears history of 2 years preceeding date of issue or first date of default if less than 2 years. If a longer history is relied on, this should be stated in particulars of claim and the history exhibited to a witness statement.

   (b) If you are claiming possession on the grounds of rent arrears only, delete this paragraph. Give details if the defendant has failed to comply with any other terms of the tenancy agreement.

   (c) Complete this paragraph if you are claiming possession on a ground other than rent arrears or breach of tenancy. Otherwise delete it.

5. Give full details of steps taken to recover any arrears. If there have been previous court proceedings, give the date they were started and concluded and the terms of any order(s) made.
6. Give the date the notice to quit, notice of breach of lease, or notice seeking possession was given to the defendant. Delete the words in brackets to show which type of notice was served.

If you are a local authority on housing action trust and are claiming possession of premises let on a demoted tenancy, you must attach to the particulars of claim a copy of the notice of proceedings under Section 143E of the Housing Act 1996.

N119A Notes for guidance on completing particulars of claim form (rented residential premises) (04.10)

About the defendant

7. Give what details you know of the defendant's financial and other circumstances. Say in particular whether:
   - housing benefit is being paid to you or to the defendant;
   - deductions are being made from the defendant's benefits, towards the arrears. If so, say how much.

About the claimant

8. Delete this paragraph if you do not wish to give details of your financial and other circumstances to support the claim for possession.

Forfeiture

9. (a) Delete this paragraph if there is no underlessee or mortgagee.

   (b) If there is, give that person's name and address and file, in court, an additional copy of the particulars of claim for service on that person.

What the court is being asked to do

10. Delete paragraphs (a) to (d) as appropriate.

11. Tick as appropriate.

Demotion/Suspension claim

If you are claiming demotion of tenancy or an order suspending the right to buy in the alternative to possession, you must complete paragraphs 12-15

12. Specify under which section the claim is made.

13. Indicate whether you are a local authority, housing action trust, registered social landlord or a private provider of social housing, or if appropriate (in the case of suspension claims only) other category of landlord.

14. If you served on the tenant a statement of express terms of the tenancy which are to apply to a demoted tenancy, you must set out the details

15. State details of the conduct alleged and any other matters relied upon.

Statement of truth

- This must be signed by you, by your solicitor or your litigation friend, as appropriate. Where the claimant is a registered company or a corporation the claim form must be signed by either a director, treasurer, secretary, chief executive, manager or other officer of the company or (in the case of a corporation) the mayor, chairman, president or town clerk.
- Proceedings for contempt of court may be brought against any person who signs a statement of truth without an honest belief in its truth.

Particulars of claim for possession
(mortgaged residential premises)

In the

Claim No.

Claimant

Defendant

1. The claimant has a right to possession of:

About the mortgage

2. On the claimant(s) and the defendant(s) entered into a mortgage of the above premises.

3. To the best of the claimant's knowledge the following persons are in possession of the property:

[Delete (a) or (b) as appropriate]

4 (a) The agreement for the loan secured by the mortgage (or at least one of them) is a regulated consumer credit agreement. Notice of default was given to the defendant(s) on 20 .

(b) The agreement for the loan secured by the mortgage is not (or none of them is) a regulated consumer credit agreement.

5. The claimant is asking for possession on the following ground(s):

(a) the defendant(s) (has)(have) not paid the agreed repayments of the loan and interest.
Give details (as required under paragraph 2.5 of Practice Direction accompanying Part 55 of the Civil Procedure Rules):

N120 Particulars of claim for possession (mortgaged residential premises)(10.05) HMCS

(b) because:

6. (a) The amount loaned was £

(b) The current terms of repayment are: *(include any current periodic repayment and any current payment of interest)*

(c) The total amount required to pay the mortgage in full as at 20 (not more than 14 days after the claim was issued) would be £ taking into account any adjustment for early settlement. This includes £ payable for solicitor's costs and administration charges.

(d) The following additional payments are also required under the terms of the mortgage:

£ for [not] included in 6(c)

£ for [not] included in 6(c)

£ for [not] included in 6(c)

(e) Of the payments in paragraph 6(d), the following are in arrears:

arrears of £

arrears of £

arrears of £

[(f) The total amount outstanding under the regulated loan agreement secured by the mortgage is £]

(g) Interest rates which have been applied to the mortgage:

(i) at the start of the mortgage % p.a.

(ii) immediately before any arrears were accrued % p.a.

(iii) at the start of the claim % p.a.

7. The following steps have already been taken to recover the money secured by the mortgage:

About the defendant(s)

8. The following information is known about the defendant's circumstances:
(in particular say whether the defendant(s) (is)(are) in receipt of social security benefits and whether any payments are made directly to the claimant)

[Delete either (a) or (b) as appropriate]

9. (a) There is no one who should be given notice of these proceedings because of a registered interest in the property under section 31(10) of the Family Law Act 1996 or section 2(8) or 8(3) of the Matrimonial Homes Act 1983 or section 2(7) of the Matrimonial Homes Act 1967.

(b) Notice of these proceedings will be given to who has a registered interest in the property.

Tenancy

[Delete if inappropriate]

10. A tenancy was entered into between the mortgagor and the mortgagee on .
A notice was served on .

What the court is being asked to do

11. The claimant asks the court to order that the defendant(s):
(a) give the claimant possession of the premises;
(b) pay to the claimant the total amount outstanding under the mortgage.

Statement of Truth

*(I believe)(The claimant believes) that the facts stated in these particulars of claim are true.
* I am duly authorised by the claimant to sign this statement.

signed .... date ______________________

*(Claimant)(Litigation friend *(where claimant is a child or a patient)*)(Claimant's solicitor)
**delete as appropriate*

Full name ....

Name of claimant's solicitor's firm ....

position or office held
(if signing on behalf of firm or company)

Particulars of claim for possession
(trespassers)

In the

Claim No.

Claimant

Defendant(s)

1. The claimant has a right to possession of:

which is occupied by the defendant(s) who entered or (has)(have) remained on the land without the claimant's consent or licence.

2. The defendant(s) (has)(have) never been a tenant or sub-tenant of the land.

3. The land mentioned at paragraph 1 does (not) include residential property.

4. The claimant's interest in the land (or the basis of the claimant's right to claim possession) is
Give details:

5. The circumstances in which the land has been occupied are
Give details:

N121 Particulars of claim for possession (trespassers)(10.01) *Printed on behalf of The Court Service*

6. The claimant does not know the name(s) of (all) the defendant(s).

7. The claimant asks the court to order that the defendant(s):

(a) give the claimant possession of the land;

(b) pay the claimant's costs of making this claim.

Statement of Truth

*(I believe)(The claimant believes) that the facts stated in these particulars of claim are true.
* I am duly authorised by the claimant to sign this statement.

signed______________________________ date ______________________________

*(Claimant)(Litigation friend *(where claimant is a child or a patient)*)(Claimant's solicitor)
**delete as appropriate*

Full name ______________________________

Name of claimant's solicitor's firm ______________________________

position or office held ______________________________
(if signing on behalf of firm or company)

Click here to reset form | Click here to print form

Particulars of claim for demotion order/suspension of right to buy

Name of court	Claim No.
Name of Claimant	
Name of Defendant	

The claimant

1. The claimant is making this claim under:

☐ section 82A(2) of the Housing Act 1985
☐ section 121A of the Housing Act 1985
☐ section 6A(2) of the Housing Act 1988

In relation to the tenancy of:

2. The claimant is a:

☐ local housing authority
☐ registered social landlord or a private registered provider of social housing
☐ housing action trust
☐ other please specify (suspension claims only)

The tenancy

3. The premises are let under:

☐ a secure tenancy
☐ an assured tenancy

4. The tenancy began on: / / DD/MM/YY

5. The rent is: £

6. The rent is paid:

☐ weekly
☐ monthly
☐ fortnightly
☐ other (please specify)

N122 Particulars of claim for demotion order/suspension of right to buy (04.10)

7. The claimant is seeking the order because (State details of the conduct alleged and any other matters relied upon.)

Demotion Orders

8. Have you served on the defendant any statement of express terms of the tenancy which are to apply to the demoted tenancy? ☐ Yes ☐ No

If Yes, please give details of the terms

9. (a) Have you served the appropriate notice on the defendant giving particulars of the conduct alleged and of these proceedings? ☐ Yes ☐ No

(b) If Yes, when did you serve this notice? / / DD/MM/YY

Statement of Truth
*(I believe)(The claimant believes) that the facts stated in these particulars of claim are true.
* I am duly authorised by the claimant to sign this statement.

signed ______________________ date ______________________
*(Claimant)(Claimant's solicitor)
**delete as appropriate*

Full name ______________________

Name of claimant's solicitor's firm ______________________

Position or office held ______________________
(if an authorised signatory not acting as a solicitor)

Click here to print form

Mortgage pre-action protocol checklist

Name of court		Claim no.
Name of claimant		
Name of defendant		
Mortgage account number		

You must produce two copies of the Checklist on the day of the hearing.

Checklist

1. Is the possession claim within the scope of the Protocol? ☐ Yes ☐ No

2. Have you provided the defendant with the information/notice in the Protocol —
   (a) paragraph 5.1(1) ☐ Yes ☐ No If Yes, date provided: ☐☐/☐☐/☐☐☐☐
   (b) paragraph 5.1(2) ☐ Yes ☐ No If Yes, date provided: ☐☐/☐☐/☐☐☐☐
   (c) paragraph 5.7 ☐ Yes ☐ No If Yes, date of notice: ☐☐/☐☐/☐☐☐☐

3. Do you have evidence that the defendant has made a claim for —
   - Support for Mortgage Interest (SMI) ☐ Yes ☐ No
   - Mortgage Rescue Scheme (MRS), or ☐ Yes ☐ No
   - mortgage payment protection. ☐ Yes ☐ No

   If Yes, please explain why possession proceedings are continuing.

4. Is there an unresolved complaint by the defendant to the Financial Ombudsman Service that could justify postponing the possession claim? ☐ Yes ☐ No
   If Yes, please explain why possession proceedings are continuing.

5. Summarise the number and dates, in the three months prior to the date of this checklist, you attempted to discuss with the defendant ways of repaying the arrears.

N123 Pre-action protocol for possession claims based on mortgage or home purchase plan arrears in respect of residential property (04.10)

6. In the three months prior to the date of this checklist have you rejected any proposals by the defendant to change the date or method of regular payments? ☐ Yes ☐ No

If Yes, did you respond in accordance with paragraph 5.4 of the Protocol? ☐ Yes ☐ No

If No, please explain why.

[ ]

7. Have you rejected a proposal for repayment by the defendant in the three months prior to the date of this checklist? ☐ Yes ☐ No

If Yes, have you responded in accordance with paragraph 5.5 of the Protocol? ☐ Yes ☐ No

If No, please explain why.

[ ]

8. Has the defendant indicated that the property will be or is being sold? ☐ Yes ☐ No

If Yes, explain why possession proceedings are proceeding.

[ ]

Statement of Truth

*I believe that the facts stated in this Checklist are true.

*I am duly authorised by the claimant to sign this statement.

Signed ______________________ Date ______________

Full name [ ]

Name of claimant's solicitor's firm [ ]

Position or office held [ ]

Delete as appropriate

Guidance for the mortgage pre-action protocol checklist

The Checklist

This guidance is provided for those using the new Mortgage Pre-Action Protocol Checklist. Use of the Checklist came into effect on 1 October 2009 for all claims issued on or after that date in order to provide a uniform format for the provision of information to demonstrate compliance with the Protocol.

This guide must be read with the Mortgage Pre-Action Protocol, the Civil Procedure Rules and Practice Direction 55.

The Checklist (form N123), must be completed by all claimants (lenders) or their representatives making a possession claim. The claimant or their representative should be able to explain to the court the actions taken or not by the claimant, and the reason for issuing a possession claim.

Once the claimant and defendant (borrower) have been notified by the court of the date of the hearing, a Checklist must be completed indicating the action taken by the claimant within the previous three months to reach an agreement with the defendant, and comply with the Protocol.

The claimant must present two copies of the Checklist on the day of the hearing. No additional documents are necessary unless an issue arises.

Claimants can copy this form onto their systems but the form must not go beyond two sides.

Scope

The following mortgages fall within the scope of the Protocol and Checklist –

(i) first charge residential mortgages and home purchase plans regulated by the Financial Services Authority under the Financial Services and Markets Act 2000;

(ii) second charge mortgages over residential property and other secured loans regulated under the Consumer Credit Act 1974 on residential property; and

(iii) unregulated residential mortgages.

Where a potential claim includes a money claim and a claim for possession, these are also within scope.

Q1 – requires confirmation of the type of mortgage and whether it is within scope of the Protocol as indicated above. If the answer is No, there is no need to compete the rest of the form. However, you must be prepared to explain to the court why you consider that the mortgage does not fall within the scope of the Protocol.

If the answer to Q1 is Yes, all the remaining questions must be answered in full.

Q2 – answer the questions Yes or No, as appropriate, and insert the dates where relevant. Where you have not complied with one or more of these requirements, you must be prepared to explain to the court in full why that is the case.

Q3 – answer the questions Yes or No, as appropriate. Where a claim, either for Support for Mortgage Interest (SMI), Mortgage Rescue Scheme (MRS) or under a mortgage payment protection policy, has been made, you must set out clearly and succinctly why you are proceeding with a claim for possession.

Q4 – answer the question Yes or No, as appropriate. If the defendant has an unresolved complaint you must set out clearly and succinctly why you are proceeding with a claim for possession.

Q5 – you should provide here a list of dates and details of the associated media (for example, letter, telephone, etc). Where use has been made of automated diallers, which do not necessarily keep an individual record of each attempted call, you should confirm the number of attempts and frequency that your system is programmed to make.

Q6 – answer the question Yes or No, as appropriate. Where you have answered:

- No, then no further information is required.
- Yes, you must also confirm whether or not you have complied with the requirements of paragraph 5.4 of the Protocol when notifying the defendant of your decision. If the answer to that question is:
    - Yes – then no further information is required on the Checklist but you must be prepared to explain to the court what action you took if requested to do so.
    - No – you should set out your reasons for non-compliance clearly and succinctly.

Q7 – answer the question Yes or No, as appropriate. Where you have answered:

- No, then no further information is required.
- Yes, you must also confirm whether or not you have complied with the requirements of paragraph 5.5 of the protocol when notifying the defendant of your decision. If the answer to that question is:
    - o Yes – then no further information is required on the Checklist but you must be prepared to explain to the court what action you took if requested to do so.
    - o No – you should set out your reasons for non-compliance clearly and succinctly.

Q8 – answer the question Yes or No, as appropriate. Where the defendant is trying to sell their property you need to explain clearly and succinctly why you are bringing proceedings including, specifically, whether or not the defendant has complied with the requirements of paragraphs 6.2 and 6.3 of the Protocol.

The statement of truth
The statement of truth must be signed and completed by the claimant or representative. This section must be completed in order to validate the information provided.

Service of the Checklist
Two copies of the Checklist must be brought to the hearing.

Application for an interim possession order

In the	
Claim No.	

Claimant's full name and address

Address for service (if different from above) Ref / Tel No.

Defendant's name (if known including title e.g. Mr, Mrs or Miss) and address

Seal

The claimant is claiming possession of

on the grounds that the claimant has an immediate right to possession and that the person(s) in occupation of the premises is (are) in occupation without consent.

Application issued on

The court will consider whether an interim possesion order should be made on

at am/pm

at

Service

nsert time, lay and late 24 ɩours after ime of ssue

For this notice to be valid it **must** be served before am/pm on the day of 20 . It must be **affixed** to the main door or another conspicuous part of the premises and, if practicable, inserted through the letterbox in a sealed transparent envelope addressed to 'the occupiers'. In addition it may be attached to stakes in the ground in conspicuous parts of the adjoining land if this is appropriate.

N130 Application for possession including application for interim possession order (12.02) *Printed on behalf of The Court Service*

What you should do

- if you have no right to occupy the premises you must leave.
- if you think you have a right to occupy the premises or you believe that the applicant is not entitled to an interim possession order you may file a witness statement at the court before the date and time shown on this notice. The form you must use is attached to this notice.
- if you need advice you should go to a Solicitor, Legal Advice Centre or Citizens Advice Bureau. Court staff are unable to give legal advice.

If you give a false or misleading information in your witness statement you will be guilty of a criminal offence and on conviction you may be sent to prison and/or fined.

What can happen next

- if the court makes an interim possession order you will have 24 hours from the time it is served on you to leave the premises. It will be served on you in the same way that this notice was – it does not have to be served on you personally. The interim possession order must be served within 48 hours of its being approved by the court.
- after you have left the premises you may apply to the court for the interim possession order to be set aside. If you wish to do so, you should go to a Solicitor, Legal Advice Centre or Citizens Advice Bureau.
- if you do not obey an interim possession order (by leaving the premises within 24 hours) you may be arrested and on conviction sent to prison and/or fined.
- a date for hearing (when the claim for possession will be considered) will be shown on the interim possession order. You have a right to attend that hearing.
- if the court does not make an interim possession order you will be told in writing.

Further Information

- a leaflet is available free of charge from any county court office.

Statement to support an application for possession and for an interim possession order

Paragraph 1
Insert your full name, address and occupation of person making this statement.

1 I

make this statement in support of the claim for possession and for an interim possession order

Paragraph 2
Give the address of the premises

2 I

have an immediate right to possession of

Give a description of the premises (house, flat, shop etc)

which is a

and have had this right since

Paragraph 3
Give details of proof of interest (deeds, lease etc)

3 Proof of my interest in the premises is in the form of

Paragraph 4
Give the date when you found out that the premises were being occupied illegally. Explain how you found out and why you could not have been expected to find out sooner

4 I

first knew of the occupation of the premises on the day of 20 by

and could not reasonably have been aware of this earlier because

5 The defendant(s) entered the premises without my consent and without the consent of anyone who on the date of entry had an immediate right to possession of the premises. Since that date I have not granted the defendant(s) any such consent.

Paragraph 6
Delete if you do not know the names of any of the occupier(s)

6 As well as the defendant(s) named in this application there are (no) other occupiers whose names I do not know.

Paragraph 7
Give the names of those people and which part of the building they occupy. Delete the words in brackets as appropriate.

7 There are (no) other people who are entitled to possession of other parts of the building in which the premises are situated (and they are:)

Paragraph 8
The court must take into account whether or not you have given undertakings when deciding whether to make an interim possession order.
Delete any undertakings you are not prepared to give.

8 I hereby give the following undertakings:

(a) to re-instate the defendant, if so ordered by the court

(b) to pay such damages as the court may order

AND

(c) before the claim for possession is finally decided, not to damage the premises

(d) not to grant a right of occupation to any other person

(e) not to damage or dispose of any of the defendant's property

9 **I ask the court to grant me an interim possession order in relation to the premises described at paragraph 2.**
I also ask the court to grant me possession of the premises.

10 **I understand the undertaking(s) I have given, and that if I break any of my promises to the court I may be sent to prison for contempt of court and/or fined.**

11 **I understand that if I make a false or misleading statement without an honest belief in its truth proceedings for contempt of court may be brought against me.**

Statement of truth

I believe that the facts stated in this statement are true.

Signed Date

Witness statement of the defendant to oppose the making of an interim possession order

Witness statement of
(defendant)

made on ______________________

completed by defendant

Between ______________________ Claimant

and ______________________ Defendant

the occupier(s) of

Claim No.	
In the **County Court**	

For completion by the court

Appointment on **20**

at **am/pm**

(1) Insert full name, address and occupation of witness

I, (1)

make oath and say as follows:

(2) Insert address of premises

1. I consider that I have a right to occupy the premises at (2)

2. I have been in occupation since

Give date

3. The claimant (name)

was aware of my occupation of the premises. I know this because

N133 Witness statement of the defendant to oppose the making of an interim possession order (12.02)

Printed on behalf of The Court Service

(3) Give name, address and date

4. I was told by [(3)]

of

on that I could occupy the premises named in paragraph 1.

(4) Say who this person is and describe any documents they showed you

I believe that he/she had the right to allow me to occupy the premises because [(4)]

5. I have written evidence to show my right of occupation. It is in the form of (eg rent book, tenancy agreement) and a copy is attached and marked 'A' [(5)]

(5) Delete if you have no written evidence

6. The claimant is **not** entitled to an interim possession order because

7. **I understand that if I have made a false or misleading statement in this witness statement I will be guilty of a criminal offence and on conviction may be sent to prison or fined or both.**

Statement of Truth

*(I believe)(The defendant(s) believe(s)) that the facts stated in this witness statement (and any continuation sheets) are true.

* I am duly authorised by the defendant(s) to sign this form.

signed ______________________ date ______________________

(Defendant(s))(Litigation friend(where the defendant is a child or a patient)*)(Defendant's solicitor)

**delete as appropriate*

Full name ______________________

Name of defendant's solicitor's firm ______________________

position or office held ______________________
(if signing on behalf of firm or company)

Defendant's or defendant's solicitor's address to which documents should be sent.

Postcode

if applicable	
Ref. no.	
Tel. no.	
fax no.	
e-mail	
DX no.	

Interim possession order

In the	
County Court	
Claim No.	
Claimant's Ref.	
Defendant's Ref.	

Between . . . . Claimant

and . . . . Defendant

For completion by the claimant
Served on 20
at am/pm

To the Defendant

of

Seal

If you do not obey this order within 24 hours of the time of service you may be arrested and on conviction sent to prison and/or fined

As a result of this order any person entering the premises as a trespasser while this order is in force may also be arrested and on conviction sent to prison and/or fined. In addition, if those in occupation at the time of service of this order, return as trespassers within a year of service of this order they may be arrested and on conviction sent to prison and/or fined

On the of 20 the court considered an application for an interim possession order

The court ordered that all person(s) in occupation of

must vacate the premises within 24 hours of service of this order.

The court further ordered

Insert the terms of any other orders eg costs

Notice of return date

The court will consider making a final possession order

at

on the day of 20 at o'clock

If you do not attend at the time shown the Court may make a final possession order in your absence.

You are entitled to apply to the Court to set aside this interim possession order before the date given above provided that you have left the premises.

To the Claimant-What you must do

Insert time and date 48 hours after approval by the court

- You **must** serve this order before am/pm on the day of 20 .
- It **must** be affixed to the main door or another conspicuous part of the premises and, if practicable, inserted through the letter box in a sealed transparent envelope addressed to 'the occupiers'. In addition it may be attached to stakes in the ground in conspicuous parts of the adjoining land if that is appropriate.
- Immediately before you serve this order you **must** write in the date and time in the box in the top right-hand corner of this form.

To the Defendant-What you must do

- You **must** leave the premises within 24 hours of the time this interim possession order is served
- **If you do not leave the police may arrest you and on conviction you may be sent to prison and/or fined**
- If you think you have a right to occupy the premises or any of the information given is incorrect you should go to a Solicitor, Legal Advice Centre or Citizens Advice Bureau after you have left the premises. Take any evidence with you (e.g. rent book, tenancy agreement)

The court office at

is open between 10am and 4pm. Monday to Friday. When writing to the court, please address forms or letters to the Court Manager and quote the claim number.

N134 Interim posession order (12.02)

Interim possession order record of appointment

Claim no. . . . .

On . . . . the . . . . day of 20

Before (H Honour) (District) Judge. . . . .

The court was sitting at . . . .

The Claimant

- ☐ was represented by Counsel
- ☐ was represented by a Solicitor
- ☐ attended in person
- ☐ did not attend

The Defendant

- ☐ was represented by Counsel
- ☐ was represented by a Solicitor
- ☐ attended in person
- ☐ did not attend

The court read the witness statement of

- ☐ the Claimant dated . . . .
- ☐ the Defendant dated . . . .

And of . . . . dated . . . .

Delete as appropriate

The Claimant gave undertaking(s) (through his counsel or solicitor) (in his witness statement):

(a) to re-instate the defendant if, so ordered by the court

(b) to pay such damages as the court may order

(c) not to damage the premises

(d) not to grant a right of occupation to any other person

(e) not to damage or dispose of any of the defendant's property

---

The court made this interim possession order on the grounds that

Signed
(H Honour) (District) Judge

Dated

Order for Possession

In the

County Court

Claim No.

Applicant's Ref.

Applicant

Respondent

Seal

(enter name of Judge) **ordered** that the applicant do recover possession of the premises mentioned in the originating application and interim possession order in this matter, namely: *(description of the premises)*

And that the applicant do recover against the respondent the sum of £ for costs (or his costs of this action to be assessed)

And further that the respondent do pay the applicant the sum mentioned above by (or do pay the amount of costs when assessed by that day or, if the costs have not been assessed, within 14 days of assessment)

Dated

Take Notice

To the respondent

If you were occupying these premises when an interim possession order was served and you return as a trespasser within **one year** of that date you may be arrested and on conviction sent to prison and/or fined. (Criminal Justice and Public Order Act 1994 section 76)

If you do not pay the costs when they are due and the applicant takes steps to enforce payment, the order will be registered in the Register of County Court Judgments. **This may make it difficult for you to get credit.** Further information about registration is available in a leaflet which you can get from any county court office.

Address for Payment

How to Pay

- **PAYMENT(S) MUST BE MADE** to the person named at the address for payment quoting their reference and the court case number.
- **DO NOT** bring or send payments to the court. **THEY WILL NOT BE ACCEPTED.**
- You should allow at least 4 days for your payment to reach the applicant or his representative.
- Make sure that you keep records and can account for all payments made. Proof may be required if there is any disagreement. It is not safe to send cash unless you use registered post.
- A leaflet giving further advice about payment can be obtained from the court.
- If you need more information you should contact the applicant or his representative.

The court office at

is open between 10 am and 4 pm Monday to Friday. When corresponding with the court, please address forms or letters to the Court Manager and quote the claim number.

N136 Order for possession (4.99)

Allocation questionnaire
(Small claims track)

Name of court	
Claim No.	
Last date for filing with court office	

Completed by, or on behalf of, (print name)

[ ]

who is the [Claimant][Defendant] in this claim.

Please read the notes on pages 4 before completing the questionnaire.

You must complete **all** sections of this questionnaire. It will be used to assist the court in the management of the claim.

You should note the date by which it must be returned and the name of the court it should be returned to since this may be different from the court where proceedings were issued. This information is shown on the Form N152 which came with this questionnaire.

If you have settled this claim (or if you settle it on a future date) and therefore do not need a hearing, you must let the court know immediately.

A Settlement

Would you like to use the free small claims mediation service provided by Her Majesty's Courts Service, to help you settle your claim with the other party? ☐ Yes ☐ No

B Location of hearing

The claim will be heard in the court to which this form must be returned. Is there any reason why it should be transferred to another court to be heard? ☐ Yes ☐ No

If Yes, say which court and why

[ ]

C Track

Do you agree that the small claims track is the most suitable track for this claim? ☐ Yes ☐ No

If No, please say why

[ ]

N149 Allocation questionnaire (Small claims tracks) (04.08)

D Witnesses

So far as you know at this stage, how many witnesses (other than yourself) do you intend to call to give evidence at the hearing? ☐

E Experts

Do you want permission to use an expert's report at the hearing? ***(see notes)*** ☐ Yes ☐ No

If Yes, what will the expert's evidence deal with?

☐

Have you already obtained an expert's report? ☐ Yes ☐ No

If Yes, have you given a copy of that report to the other party? ☐ Yes ☐ No

In addition to using an expert's report do you want your expert to attend the hearing and give evidence? ☐ Yes ☐ No

If Yes, give the reasons why you think their attendance is necessary:

☐

The court may order the appointment of a single expert who can be instructed by both parties. If you think this would not be appropriate, please say why.

☐

F Hearing

Are there any days within the next four months when you, an expert or a witness will not be able to attend court for the hearing? ☐ Yes ☐ No

If Yes, please give details

	Dates not available
Yourself	
Expert	
Other essential witness	

Will you be using an interpreter at the hearing either for yourself or for a witness? ***(see notes)*** ☐ Yes ☐ No

If Yes, please specify the type of interpreter

☐

2

G Other information

In the space below, set out any other information you consider will help the judge to manage or clarify the claim, including any other information you consider should be supplied by the other party.

H Fee

Have you attached the fee for filing this allocation questionnaire? ☐ Yes ☐ No

An allocation fee is payable if your claim or counterclaim exceeds £1,500.

Additional fees will be payable at further stages of the court process.

I Signature *(see notes)*

Signed   Date

Print full name

If a solicitor is acting for you please enter the firm's name, reference number and full postal address including (if appropriate) details of fax number, e-mail address, Document Exchange (DX) number. Otherwise, please enter your details as appropriate. This will assist the court in contacting you, if necessary at short notice.

	Ref. no.	
	Telephone no.	
	Mobile no.	
	Fax no.	
	e-mail address	
	DX no.	

3

Notes for completing a small claims track allocation questionnaire

- If the claim is not settled, a judge must allocate it to an appropriate case management track and if necessary give directions for the conduct of the case. The most just and cost-effective track for this claim appears to be the small claims track and you must now complete the attached questionnaire to help the judge decide.
- If you fail to return the allocation questionnaire by the date given, the judge may make an order that leads to your claim or defence being 'struck out' (Rule 3.4): this means you could not proceed with it. Alternatively the judge may order an allocation hearing at which the judge can order any party who has not filed their questionnaire to pay, immediately, the costs of that hearing.
- The letters below refer to the corresponding sections of the questionnaire and tell you what information is needed, including where appropriate other guidance and references to court rules (Civil Procedure Rules).

A Settlement

Even at this stage, you should still think about whether you and the other party can settle your dispute without going to court. You may seek to settle the claim either by direct discussion or negotiation with the other party or by mediation. Mediation is a way of resolving disputes without needing to go to a court hearing, where parties are assisted in achieving mutually beneficial resolutions with the help of an impartial mediator. You may use any mediation provider, but if you would like to try the free Her Majesty's Courts Service small claims mediation service, or find out more about how mediation could help, you should tick 'Yes' to this question. The court will then refer your case to the small claims mediator and provide you with a contact telephone number. Experience has shown that it is often possible for the mediator to help resolve disputes over the telephone without either party having to attend court. However, since mediation is a voluntary process, it will only take place if the parties agree.

You can find out more about the various settlement options in the Legal Services Commission leaflet 'Alternatives to Court' which is free from any county court or the LSC leaflet line on 0845 3000 343.

B Location

Automatic transfer to a defendant's local court applies to certain claims (Rule 26.2). This claim will be heard at the court to which you have been asked to return this questionnaire but the court will consider an application for it to be transferred to another court **if there is a good reason to do so**.

C Track

The basic guide by which claims are normally allocated to a track is the amount in dispute, although other factors such as the complexity of the case will also be considered (Rules 26.6 - 26.8). Leaflet EX307 - The Small claims track, explains this in greater detail.

D Witnesses

Enter the number of witnesses you intend to call to give evidence **not** including yourself or any expert witness.

E Experts

You should **not** obtain an expert's report until you receive the court's direction. If you have already obtained a report, please attach it to your completed questionnaire.

F Hearing

Dates to avoid: You should only enter those dates where you, your expert or an essential witness will not be able to attend court because of a holiday or other commitments.

Interpreters: In some circumstances the court will arrange for, and meet the cost of, an interpreter. If you require an interpreter, you should contact the court immediately. For further details visit our website www.hmcourts-service.gov.uk under 'Information about'

G Other information

Give details of any other information that you consider will help the judge to manage the claim, referring as necessary to any documents you have attached. Bear in mind however that at this stage you need not attach all other documents which you wish the court to consider at the hearing. This is something you will later be asked to provide.

H Fee

For more information about court fees please go our website www.hmcourts-service.gov.uk or pick up a fees leaflet EX50 from any county court. If you cannot afford the fee, you may be eligible for remission of the fee. More details can be found in the leaflet EX160A, which can be downloaded from our website or you can pick up a copy from any county court.

I Signature

This questionnaire must be signed by only the party to the claim or litigation friend or legal representative.

Click here to reset form | Click here to print form

Allocation questionnaire

To be completed by, or on behalf of,

Name of court	
Claim No.	
Last date for filing with court office	

who is [1st][2nd][3rd][ ][Claimant][Defendant] [Part 20 claimant] in this claim

Please read the notes on page six before completing the questionnaire.

You should note the date by which it must be returned and the name of the court it should be returned to since this may be different from the court where the proceedings were issued.

If you have settled this claim (or if you settle it on a future date) and do not need to have it heard or tried, you must let the court know immediately.

Have you sent a copy of this completed form to the other party(ies)? ☐ Yes ☐ No

A Settlement

Under the Civil Procedure Rules parties should make every effort to settle their case before the hearing. This could be by discussion or negotiation (such as a roundtable meeting or settlement conference) or by a more formal process such as mediation. The court will want to know what steps have been taken. Settling the case early can save costs, including court hearing fees.

For legal representatives only

I confirm that I have explained to my client the need to try to settle; the options available; and the possibility of costs sanctions if they refuse to try to settle. ☐

For all

Your answers to these questions may be considered by the court when it deals with the questions of costs: see Civil Procedure Rules Part 44.3 (4).

1. Given that the rules require you to try to settle the claim before the hearing, do you want to attempt to settle at this stage? ☐ Yes ☐ No
2. If Yes, do you want a one month stay? ☐ Yes ☐ No
3. Would you like the court to arrange a mediation appointment? ☐ Yes ☐ No
   (A fee will be payable to the mediation provider appointed by the National Mediation Helpline.)
4. If you answered 'No' to question 1, please state below the reasons why you consider it inappropriate to try to settle the claim at this stage.

Reasons:

B Location of trial

Is there any reason why your claim needs to be heard at a particular court? ☐ Yes ☐ No

If Yes, say which court and why?

C Pre-action protocols

You are expected to comply with the relevant pre-action protocol.

Have you done so? ☐ Yes ☐ No

If No, explain why?

D Case management information

What amount of the claim is in dispute? £

Applications

Have you made any application(s) in this claim? ☐ Yes ☐ No

If Yes, what for?
(e.g. summary judgment, add another party)

For hearing on

Witnesses

So far as you know at this stage, what witnesses of fact do you intend to call at the trial or final hearing including, if appropriate, yourself?

Witness name	Witness to which facts

2

Experts

Do you wish to use expert evidence at the trial or final hearing? ☐ Yes ☐ No

Have you already copied any experts' report(s) to the other party(ies)? ☐ None yet obtained ☐ Yes ☐ No

Do you consider the case suitable for a single joint expert in any field? ☐ Yes ☐ No

Please list any single joint experts you propose to use and any other experts you wish to rely on. Identify single joint experts with the initials 'SJ' after their name(s).

Expert's name	Field of expertise (eg. orthopaedic surgeon, surveyor, engineer)

Do you want your expert(s) to give evidence orally at the trial or final hearing? ☐ Yes ☐ No

If Yes, give the reasons why you think oral evidence is necessary:

Track

Which track do you consider is most suitable for your claim? Tick one box

☐ small claims track
☐ fast track
☐ multi-track

If you have indicated a track which would not be the normal track for the claim, please give brief reasons for your choice

3

Disclosure of electronic documents

If you are proposing that the claim be allocated to the multi-track:

1. Have you reached agreement, either using the Electronic Documents Questionnaire in PD31B or otherwise, about the scope and extent of disclosure of electronic documents on each side? ☐ Yes ☐ No

2. If No, is such an agreement likely? ☐ Yes ☐ No

3. If there is no agreement and no agreement is likely, what are the issues about disclosure of electronic documents which the court needs to address, and should they be dealt with at the Case Managment Conference or at a separate hearing?

E Trial or final hearing

How long do you estimate the trial or final hearing will take? days hours minutes

Are there any days when you, an expert or an essential witness will not be able to attend court for the trial or final hearing? ☐ Yes ☐ No

If Yes, please give details

Name	Dates not available

F Proposed directions *(Parties should agree directions wherever possible)*

Have you attached a list of the directions you think appropriate for the management of the claim? ☐ Yes ☐ No

If Yes, have they been agreed with the other party(ies)? ☐ Yes ☐ No

G Costs

Do ***not*** *complete this section if you have suggested your case is suitable for the small claims track* ***or*** *you have suggested one of the other tracks and you do not have a solicitor acting for you.*

What is your estimate of your costs incurred to date? £

What do you estimate your overall costs are likely to be? £

In multi-track cases these questions should be answered in compliance with CPR Part 43.

4

H Fee

Have you attached the fee for filing this allocation questionnaire? ☐ Yes ☐ No

An allocation fee is payable if your claim or counterclaim exceeds £1,500.

Additional fees will be payable at further stages of the court process.

I Other information

Have you attached documents to this questionnaire? ☐ Yes ☐ No

Have you sent these documents to the other party(ies)? ☐ Yes ☐ No

If Yes, when did they receive them?

Do you intend to make any applications in the immediate future? ☐ Yes ☐ No

If Yes, what for?

In the space below, set out any other information you consider will help the judge to manage the claim.

Signed

[Counsel] [Solicitor] [for the][1st][2nd][3rd][ ]
[Claimant] [Defendant] [Part 20 claimant]

Date

Please enter your name, reference number and full postal address including (if appropriate) details of telephone, DX, fax or e-mail

Postcode

If applicable	
Telephone no.	
Fax no.	
DX no.	
Your ref.	

E-mail

5

Click here to reset form | Click here to print form

Notes for completing an allocation questionnaire

- If the claim is not settled, a judge must allocate it to an appropriate case management track. To help the judge choose the most just and cost-effective track, you must now complete the attached questionnaire.
- If you fail to return the allocation questionnaire by the date given, the judge may make an order which leads to your claim or defence being struck out, or hold an allocation hearing. If there is an allocation hearing the judge may order any party who has not filed their questionnaire to pay, immediately, the costs of that hearing.
- Use a separate sheet if you need more space for your answers marking clearly which section the information refers to. You should write the claim number on it, and on any other documents you send with your allocation questionnaire. Please ensure they are firmly attached to it.
- The letters below refer to the sections of the questionnaire and tell you what information is needed.

A Settlement

Under the Civil Procedure Rules parties should make every effort to settle their case before the hearing. This could be by discussion or negotiation (such as a roundtable meeting or settlement conference) or by a more formal process such as mediation. The court will want to know what steps have been taken. If you think that it would be worthwhile you and the other party trying to negotiate a settlement at this stage you should tick the 'Yes' box. The court may order a stay, whether or not all the other parties to the claim agree. Even if you are requesting a stay, you should still complete the rest of the questionnaire.

More information about settlement options is available in the Legal Services Commission leaflet 'Alternatives to Court' free from any county court or the LSC leaflet line on 0845 3000 343. If you would like to find out more about mediation, and the fees charged, contact the National Mediation Helpline on 0845 60 30 809 or go to www.nationalmediationhelpline.com. Although you may appoint a mediator of your choice, if you would like the court to arrange a mediation for you please tick 'Yes'. By ticking this box you are consenting to your contact details being passed via the Helpline to an accredited external registered provider.

B Location of trial

High Court cases are usually heard at the Royal Courts of Justice or certain Civil Trial Centres. Fast or multi-track trials may be dealt with at a Civil Trial Centre or at the court where the claim is proceeding.

C Pre-action protocols

Before any claim is started, the court expects you to have complied with the relevant pre-action protocol, and to have exchanged information and documents relevant to the claim to assist in settling it. To find out which protocol is relevant to your claim see: http://www.justice.gov.uk/civil/procrules_fin/menus/protocol.htm

D Case management information

Applications

It is important for the court to know if you have already made any applications in the claim, what they are for and when they will be heard. The outcome of the applications may affect the case management directions the court gives.

Witnesses

Remember to include yourself as a witness of fact, if you will be giving evidence.

Experts

Oral or written expert evidence will only be allowed at the trial or final hearing with the court's permission. The judge will decide what permission it seems appropriate to give when the claim is allocated to track. Permission in small claims track cases will only be given exceptionally.

Track

The basic guide by which claims are normally allocated to a track is the amount in dispute, although other factors such as the complexity of the case will also be considered. Leaflet EX305 - The Fast Track and the Multi-track, explains this in greater detail.

E Trial or final hearing

You should enter only those dates when you, your expert(s) or essential witness(es) will not be able to attend court because of holiday or other commitments.

F Proposed directions

Attach the list of directions, if any, you believe will be appropriate to be given for the management of the claim. Agreed directions on fast and multi-track cases should be based on the forms of standard directions set out in the practice direction to CPR Part 28 and form PF52.

G Costs

Only complete this section if you are a solicitor and have suggested the claim is suitable for allocation to the fast or multi-track.

H Fee

For more information about court fees please go our website www.hmcourts-service.gov.uk or pick up a fees leaflet EX50 from any county court. If you cannot afford the fee, you may be eligible for remission of the fee. More details can be found in the leaflet EX160A, which can be downloaded from our website or you can pick up a copy from any county court.

I Other Information

Answer the questions in this section. Decide if there is any other information you consider will help the judge to manage the claim. Give details in the space provided referring to any documents you have attached to support what you are saying.

6

Claim no.	
Claimant	
Defendant	

Master/District judge

Allocation to track

Master's/District judge's directions

N150A Allocation to track - Master's/District judge's directions (4.99)

No AQs filed
No allocation questionnaite(s) filed, issue standard 'unless' order

to all parties ☐

to [ ] ☐

Stay for settlement
Claim to be stayed for 1 month for settlement

issue standard order ☐

Transfer
Transfer claim to

[ ] county court ☐
district registry ☐
Division at the RCJ ☐

for

allocation and ase management directions ☐
reference to judge in charge of [ ] list ☐

Allocation hearing
List claim for allocation hearing with time estimate of

[ ] mins

Request for further information
Request further information from

(party) [ ]
by (date) [ ]

as to: [ ]

Allocation
Allocate claim to:

(with parties consent) ☐

small claims track ☐
fast track ☐
multi-track ☐

(a) note details of directions opposite ☐ ➔

(b) confirm parties' agreed directions as attached ☐
as amended ☐

(c) estimated length of trial [ ] ☐

(d) timetable to trial or trial window to be [ ] weeks/months ☐

(e) fixed date for trial to be given within [ ] weeks/months ☐

(f) see details of directions opposite - transfer to civil trial centre at [ ] ☐ ➔

Reasons for allocation decision

Reasons for decision if allocated to other than 'presumed' track including any comments on costs:

Trial Judge

Refer to Presiding/Designated Civil Judge for consideration of trial by High Court Judge ☐

Other directions or order

Master/District Judge ______ Date ______

Details of directions (where (a) or (f) applies)

Allocation questionnaire
(amount to be decided by the court)

In the	
Claim No.	
Last date for filing with court office	

To

SEAL

Please read the notes on page six before completing the questionnaire.

Please note the date by which it must be returned and the name of the court it should be returned to since this may be different from the court where proceedings were issued.

If you have settled this case (or if you settle it on a future date) and do not need to have it heard or tried, you must let the court know immediately.

A Settlement

Under the Civil Procedure Rules parties should make every effort to settle their case before the hearing. This could be by discussion or negotiation (such as a roundtable meeting or settlement conference) or by a more formal process such as mediation. The court will want to know what steps have been taken. Settling the case early can save costs, including court hearing fees.

For legal representatives only

I confirm that I have explained to my client the need to try to settle; the options available; and the possibility of costs sanctions if they refuse to try to settle. ☐

For all

Your answers to these questions may be considered by the court when it deals with the questions of costs: see Civil Procedure Rules Part 44.3 (4).

1. Given that the rules require you to try to settle the claim before the hearing, do you want to attempt to settle at this stage? ☐ Yes ☐ No
2. If Yes, do you want a one month stay? ☐ Yes ☐ No
3. Would you like the court to arrange a mediation appointment? ☐ Yes ☐ No
   (A fee will be payable to the mediation provider appointed by the National Mediation Helpline.)
4. If you answered 'No' to question 1, please state below the reasons why you consider it inappropriate to try to settle the claim at this stage.

Reasons:

N151 Allocation questionnaire (amount to be decided by the court) (04.08) 1

B Track

Which track do you consider is most suitable for your case? *(Tick one box)*

☐ small claims ☐ fast track ☐ multi-track

If you think your case is suitable for a specialist list, say which:

If you have indicated a track which would not be the normal track for the case, please give brief reasons for your choice:

C Pre-action protocols

You are expected to comply with the relevant pre-action protocol.

Have you done so? ☐ Yes ☐ No

If No, explain why?

D Applications

If you have not already issued a claim in the case against someone not yet a party, do you intend to apply for the court's permission to do so? ☐ Yes ☐ No

Do you intend to make any other applications eg. for special directions? ☐ Yes ☐ No

In either case, if Yes, please give details:

2

E Witnesses of fact

So far as you know at this stage, what witnesses of fact do you intend to call at the hearing?

Witness name	Witness to which facts

F Experts' evidence

Do you wish to use expert evidence at the hearing? ☐ Yes ☐ No

Have you already copied any experts' report(s) to the other party(ies)? ☐ None obtained as yet ☐ Yes ☐ No

Please list the experts whose evidence you think you will use:

Expert's name	Field of expertise (eg. orthopaedic surgeon, mechanical engineer)

Will you and the other party use the same expert(s)? ☐ Yes ☐ No

If No, please explain why not:

Do you want your expert(s) to give evidence orally at the hearing or trial? ☐ Yes ☐ No

If Yes, give the reasons why you think oral evidence is necessary:

3

G Location of trial

Is there any reason why your case needs to be heard at a particular court? ☐ Yes ☐ No

If Yes, give reasons
(eg. particular facilities required, convenience of witnesses, etc.)

and specify the court:

H Representation and estimate of trial time

Do you expect to be represented by a solicitor or counsel at the trial? ☐ No ☐ Solicitor ☐ Counsel

How long do you estimate it will take to put your case to the court at the trial?

days	hours	minutes

If there are days when you, your representative, expert or an essential witness will not be able to attend court, give details:

Name	Dates not available

I Costs (only relates to costs incurred by legal representatives)

What is your estimate of costs incurred to date? £

What do you estimate the overall costs are likely to be? £

J Fee

Have you attached the fee for filing this allocation questionnaire? ☐ Yes ☐ No

An allocation fee is payable if your claim or counterclaim exceeds £1,500.

Additional fees will be payable at further stages of the court process.

4

K Other information

Have you attached documents you wish the judge to take into account when allocating the case? ☐ Yes ☐ No

Have they been served on the other parties? ☐ Yes ☐ No

If Yes, say when

Have the other parties agreed their content? ☐ Yes ☐ No

Have you attached a list of the directions you think appropriate for the management of your case? ☐ Yes ☐ No

Are they agreed with the other parties? ☐ Yes ☐ No

Are there any other facts which might affect the timetable the court will set?
If so, please state

Signed Date

[Counsel][Solicitor][for the][Claimant][Defendant]

Please enter your name, reference number and full postal address including (if appropriate) details of telephone, DX, fax or e-mail

	If applicable	
	Telephone no.	
	Fax no.	
	DX no.	
Postcode	Your ref.	

E-mail

5

Notes for completing an allocation questionnaire

- If the case is not settled, a judge must allocate it to an appropriate case management track. To help the judge choose the most just and cost-effective track, you must now complete the attached questionnaire.
- If you fail to return the allocation questionnaire by the date given, the judge may make an order which leads to your claim being struck out, or hold an allocation hearing. If there is an allocation hearing the judge may order any party who has not filed their questionnaire to pay, immediately, the costs of that hearing.
- If you wish to make an application, for example, for special directions, or for permission to add another party to the claim, you should send it and any required fee with the completed allocation questionnaire. If a hearing is fixed for your application, it may also be used as an allocation hearing.
- Any other documents you wish the judge to take into account should be filed with the questionnaire. But you must confirm that the documents have been sent to the other party, or parties, saying when they would have received them and whether they agreed their contents.
- Use a separate sheet if you need more space for your answers marking clearly which section the information refers to. Write the case number on it, sign and date it and attach it securely to the questionnaire.
- The letters below refer to the sections of the questionnaire and tell you what information is needed.

A Settlement

Under the Civil Procedure Rules parties should make every effort to settle their case before the hearing. This could be by discussion or negotiation (such as a roundtable meeting or settlement conference) or by a more formal process such as mediation. The court will want to know what steps have been taken. If you think that it would be worthwhile you and the other party trying to negotiate a settlement at this stage you should tick the 'Yes' box. The court may order a stay, whether or not all the other parties to the claim agree. Even if you are requesting a stay, you should still complete the rest of the questionnaire.

More information about settlement options is available in the Legal Services Commission leaflet 'Alternatives to Court' free from any county court or the LSC leaflet line on 0845 3000 343. If you would like to find out more about mediation, and the fees charged, contact the National Mediation Helpline on 0845 60 30 809 or go to www.nationalmediationhelpline.com. Although you may appoint a mediator of your choice, if you would like the court to arrange a mediation for you please tick 'Yes'. By ticking this box you are consenting to your contact details being passed via the Helpline to an accredited external mediation provider.

B Track

The basic guide by which cases are normally allocated to a track depends on the money value of the claim, although other factors such as the complexity of the case will also be considered. Leaflet EX305 - The Fast Track and the Multi-track explains this in greater detail.

C Pre-action protocols

Before any claim is started, the court expects you to have complied with the relevant pre-action protocol, and to have exchanged information and documents relevant to the claim to assist in settling it. To find out which protocol is relevant to your claim see: http://www.justice.gov.uk/civil/procrules_fin/menus/protocol.htm

D Applications

If you intend to make an application, for example for special directions, you should, if you have not already filed an application, file it with your completed allocation questionnaire.

E Witnesses of fact

Remember to include yourself, if you will be giving evidence; but not experts, who should be included in section F.

F Experts' evidence

Oral or written expert evidence will only be allowed at the trial with the court's permission.The judge will decide what permission it seems appropriate to give when the case is allocated to track.

G Location of trial

Only complete this section if you are a solicitor and have suggested the claim is suitable for allocation to the fast or multi-track.

H Representation and estimate of trial time

If the case is allocated to the fast track, no more than one day will be allowed for the trial of the whole case.

I Costs

Estimates should be given using Form 1 which can be found in the Schedule of Costs Forms set out in the Civil Procedure Rules. The form should be attached to and returned with your completed questionnaire.

J Fee

For more information about court fees please go our website www.hmcourts-service.gov.uk or pick up a fees leaflet EX50 from any county court. If you cannot afford the fee, you may be eligible for remission of the fee. More details can be found in the leaflet EX160A, which can be download from our website or you can pick up a copy from any county court.

Click here to reset form | Click here to print form

Claim no.	
Claimant	
Defendant	

Master/District judge

Allocation to track

Master's/District judge's directions

N151A Allocation to track - Master's/District judge's directions (4.99) 1

TO BE COMPLETED BY THE COURT

No AQs filed
No allocation questionnaite(s) filed, issue standard 'unless' order

to all parties ☐

to [ ] ☐

Stay for settlement
Claim to be stayed for 1 month for settlement

issue standard order ☐

Transfer
Transfer claim to

[ ] county court ☐
district registry ☐
Division at the RCJ ☐

for

allocation and ase management directions ☐

reference to judge in charge of [ ] list ☐

Allocation hearing
List claim for allocation hearing with time estimate of

[ ] mins

Request for further information
Request further information from

(party) [ ]
by (date) [ ]

as to: [ ]

Allocation
Allocate claim to:

(with parties consent) ☐

small claims track ☐

fast track ☐

multi-track ☐

(a) note details of directions on page opposite ☐ ➔

(b) confirm parties' agreed directions as attached ☐

as amended ☐

(c) estimate length of trial [ ] ☐

(d) timetable to trial or trial window to be [ ] weeks/months ☐

(e) fis date for trial to be given within [ ] weeks/months ☐

(f) see details of directions opposite - transfer to civil trial

centre at [ ] ☐ ➔

2

Reasons for allocation decision
Reasons for decision if allocated to other than 'presumed' track including any comments on costs:

Trial Judge
Refer to Presiding/Designated Civil Judge for consideration of trial by High Court Judge ☐

Other directions or order

Master/District Judge | Date

Details of directions (where (a) or (f) applies)

3

4

Notice that a [Defence] [Counterclaim] has been filed

In the	
Claim No.	
Claimant including ref.	
Defendant including ref.	
Date	

To [Claimant][Defendant] ['s Solicitor]

[The defendant has filed a [defence][counterclaim], [a copy][copies] of which [is][are] enclosed with this notice. An allocation questionnaire is also enclosed which contains notes for guidance on how to complete it.]

[You have already been sent [a copy of a defence][copies of defences] received from [one][ ]of the defendants in this claim. The time for all the defendants to file their defences has now elapsed and I am enclosing an allocation questionnaire for you to complete.[No further defences have been received.][A copy][Copies] of the final [defence][counterclaim] received [is][are] also enclosed.]]

You must complete the allocation questionnaire on or before [ ] and return it to

the court office at [ ]

[If you intend to defend the counterclaim, you must file a copy of your defence with your completed allocation questionnaire. Your defence must contain a statement of truth.]

The court office at

is open between 10 am and 4 pm Monday to Friday. When corresponding with the court, please address forms or letters to the Court Manager and quote the claim number.

N152 Notice that a [Defence] [Counterclaim] has been filed

Notice of Allocation or Listing Hearing

In the	
Claim No.	
Claimant (including ref.)	
Defendant (including ref.)	
Date	

To [Claimant][Defendant][s' Solicitor]

Seal

[Master][District Judge] has considered the statements of case and allocation [listing] questionnaires filed in this claim [counterclaim] and decided that a hearing is necessary before a final decision about [allocation][listing] can be made.

[Reasons for the hearing are as follows:-

]

The [Master][District Judge] orders you to attend at [am][pm] on the of

at

[The [Master][District Judge] directs the [claimant][defendant] to provide the following [further] information and send copies to the court and the other parties by .... :-]

Note: If you fail to attend the hearing, the court may order you to pay the costs of the other party, or parties, that do attend. Failure to pay those costs within the time stated may lead to your statement of case being struck out.

The court office at

is open between 10 am and 4 pm Monday to Friday. Address all communications to the Court Manager quoting the claim number.

N153 Notice of Allocation or Listing Hearing

Notice of Allocation to the Fast Track

In the	
Claim No.	
Claimant (including ref)	
Defendant (including ref)	
Date	

To [Claimant][Defendant]['s Solicitor]

Seal

[Master][District Judge] has considered the statements of case and allocation questionnaires filed, and allocated the [claim] [counterclaim] to **the fast track.**

The trial of this [claim] [counterclaim] will take place during the period commencing of and ending on of at a venue to be notified.

The [Master][District Judge] orders that you and the other parties prepare for the trial as follows:-

[The reason[s] the judge has given for allocation to this track [is][are] that .]

Notes:

- You and the other party, or parties, may agree to extend the time periods given in the directions above provided this **does not** affect the date given for returning the listing questionnaire or the date of the trial or trial period.
- If you do not comply with these directions, any other party to the claim will be entitled to apply to the court for an order that your statement of case (claim or defence) be struck out.
- Leaflets explaining more about what happens when your case is allocated to the fast track are available from the court office.

The court office at

is open between 10 am and 4 pm Monday to Friday. Address all communications to the Court Manager quoting the claim number.

N154 Notice of Allocation to the Fast Track

Notice of Allocation to the Multi-track

In the	
Claim No.	
Claimant (including ref)	
Defendant (including ref)	
Date	

To [Claimant][Defendant]['s Solicitor]

Seal

[Master][District Judge] has considered the statements of case and allocation questionnaires filed and allocated the claim [counterclaim] to **the multi-track.**

The [Master][District Judge] has ordered that:-

[The claim is being transferred to the [Civil Trial Centre at County Court] [Division of the Royal Courts of Justice] where all future applications, correspondence and so on will be dealt with]

[The reason[s] the judge has given for allocation to this track [is][are] that .]

Notes:

- You and the other party, or parties, may agree to extend the time periods given in the directions above provided this **does not** affect the date given for any case management conference, for returning the listing questionnaire, for any pre trial review or the date of the trial or trial period.
- If you do not comply with these directions, any other party to the claim will be entitled to apply to the court for an order that your statement of case (claim or defence) be struck out.
- Leaflets explaining more about what happens when your case is allocated to the Multi-track are available from the court office.

The court office at

is open between 10 am and 4 pm Monday to Friday. Address all communications to the Court Manager quoting the claim number.

N155 Notice of Allocation to Multi-track

Order for Further Information (allocation)

In the	
Claim No.	
Claimant (including ref.)	
Defendant (including ref.)	
Date	

To [Claimant][Defendant]['s Solicitor]

Seal

[Master][District Judge] has considered the statements of case and allocation questionnaires filed and requires further information before making a final decision about allocation.

The [Master][District Judge] orders the [claimant][defendant] to provide information about:-

This information and any accompanying documents should be delivered to the court and copied to the other parties on or before[ ]

Note: Where an allocation hearing is necessary because a party does not provide the information ordered above, the court may order that party to pay the costs of any other party attending the hearing.

The court office at

is open between 10 am and 4 pm Monday to Friday. Address all communications to the Court Manager quoting the claim number.

N156 Request for Further Information (allocation)

Notice of Allocation to the Small Claims Track

In the	
County Court	
Claim No.	
Claimant (including ref)	
Defendant (including ref)	
Date	

To Claimant][Defendant]['s Solicitor]

Seal

District Judge has considered the statements of case and allocation questionnaires filed and allocated the claim [counterclaim] to **the small claims track**.

The hearing of this claim [counterclaim] will take place at [am][pm]on the of at

The judge has estimated that the hearing of this claim [counterclaim] should take no longer than [mins][hours]. This is the total time for you, the other party [parties] and any witnesses to put your evidence and for the judge to reach a decision. To help prepare the claim [counterclaim] for hearing, the judge has ordered that you comply with the following directions:-

[The reason[s] the judge has given for allocation to this track [is][are] that .]

Notes

- If you cannot, or choose not to, attend the hearing, you must write and tell the court **at least 7 days before the date of the hearing**. The district judge will hear the case in your absence, but will take account of your statement of case and any other documents you have filed.
- If you do not attend the hearing and do not give notice that you will not attend, the district judge may strike out your claim, defence or counter claim. If the claimant attends but the defendant does not, the district judge may make a decision based on the evidence of the claimant only.
- Leaflets explaining more about what you should do and what happens when your case is allocated to the small claims track are available from the court office.

The court office at

is open between 10 am and 4 pm Monday to Friday. Address all communications to the Court Manager quoting the claim number.

N157 Notice of Allocation to the Small Claims Track

Notice of Allocation to the Small Claims Track (preliminary hearing)

In the	
Claim No.	
Claimant (including ref.)	
Defendant (including ref.)	
Date	

To [Claimant][Defendant]['s Solicitor]

Seal

District Judge .... has considered the statements of case and allocation questionnaires filed and allocated the claim [counterclaim] to the **small claims track**.

Before the claim [counterclaim] is listed for hearing, the judge has ordered that a preliminary hearing should take place [because] :-

[special directions are needed in this claim [counterclaim] to prepare for the final hearing which the judge would prefer to explain to you in person.]

[to consider whether the [claim][counterclaim] can be disposed of because the [claimant][defendant] has no real prospect of success at a final hearing.]

The preliminary hearing will take place at [am][pm] on the of

at

[The reason[s] the judge has given for allocation to this track [is][are] that .]

Notes

- If you do not attend the hearing the court may make an order in your absence.
- If it is practical to do so and you and the other parties agree, the judge may decide to treat the preliminary hearing as a final hearing.
- Leaflets explaining more about what you should do and what happens when your case is allocated to the small claims track are available from the court office.

The court office at

is open between 10 am and 4 pm Monday to Friday. Address all communications to the Court Manager quoting the claim number.

N158 Notice of Allocation to the Small Claims Track (preliminary hearing)

Notice of Allocation to the Small Claims Track
(no hearing)

In the	
County Court	
Claim No.	
Claimant (including ref)	
Defendant (including ref)	
Date	

To [Claimant][Defendant]['s Solicitor]

Seal

District Judge has considered the statements of case and allocation questionnaires filed and allocated the claim [counterclaim] to the **small claims track.**

The judge proposes to deal with the claim [counterclaim] without a hearing, that is, on the papers alone but can only do this if all parties agree.

Please tell the court whether or not you agree to your case being dealt with in this way by completing the lower half of this form and returning a copy to the court on or before ______. You must at the same time send a copy of it to all other parties.

Leaflets explaining more about what you should do and what happens when your case is allocated to the Small Claims Track are available from the court office.

Reply to the court

Tick A or B and C

A ☐ I agree that the claim [counterclaim] should be dealt with on the papers alone.

or

B ☐ I do not agree that the claim [counterclaim] should be dealt with on the papers alone.

and

C ☐ I have sent a copy of this completed form to the other party.

In the	
County Court	
Claim No.	
Claimant (including ref)	
Defendant (including ref)	

Signed ______ (Claimant)(Defendant)('s Solicitor)('s litigation friend)

Position or office held ______ (if signing on behalf of firm or company)

Date ______

The court office at

is open between 10 am and 4 pm Monday to Friday. Address all communications to the Court Manager quoting the claim number.

N159 Notice of Allocation to the Small Claims Track (no hearing)

FORM N160 NOTICE OF ALLOCATION TO SMALL CLAIMS TRACK (PARTIES' CONSENT)

Notice of Allocation to the Small Claims Track
(with parties' consent)

To [Claimant][Defendant]['s Solicitors]

In the County Court	
Claim No.	
Claimant (including ref)	
Defendant (including ref)	
Date	

Seal

District Judge has considered the statements of case and allocation questionnaires filed and, with the consent of the parties, allocated the claim [counterclaim] to **the small claims track**.

The hearing of the claim [counterclaim] will take place at [am][pm] on the of at

The judge has estimated that the hearing of this claim [counterclaim] should take no longer than mins/hours and has ordered that you must comply with the following directions which will tell you what to do to prepare for the trial:

Notes

- If you cannot, or choose not to, attend the hearing, you must write and tell the court at **least 7 days before the date of the hearing** The district judge will hear the case in your absence, but will take account of your statement of case and any other documents you have filed.
- As you have consented to your claim [counterclaim] being heard in the small claims track, any costs allowed to the successful party will be limited to the maximum sum which can be awarded in the fast track.
- If you do not attend the hearing and do not give notice that you will not attend, the district judge may strike out your claim, defence or counterclaim. If the claimant attends but the defendant does not, the district judge may make a decision based on the evidence of the claimant only.
- Leaflets telling you more about the small claims track are available from the court office.

The court office at

is open between 10 am and 4 pm Monday to Friday. When corresponding with the court, please address forms or letters to the Court Manager and quote the claim number

N160 Notice of Allocation to the Small Claims Track (with parties' consent)

FORM N161

Appellant's notice
(All appeals except small claims track appeals)

For Court use only	
Appeal Court Ref. No.	
Date filed	

Notes for guidance are available which will help you complete this form. Please read them carefully before you complete each section.

SEAL

Section 1 Details of the claim or case you are appealing against

Claim or Case no.

Name(s) of the ☐ Claimant(s) ☐ Applicant(s) ☐ Petitioner(s)

Name(s) of the ☐ Defendant(s) ☐ Respondent(s)

Details of the party appealing ('The Appellant')

Name

Address (including postcode)

Tel No.	
Fax	
E-mail	

Details of the Respondent to the appeal

Name

Address (including postcode)

Tel No.	
Fax	
E-mail	

Details of additional parties (if any) are attached ☐Yes ☐No

N161 Appellant's notice (07.06)

Section 2 Details of the appeal

From which court is the appeal being brought?

☐ The County Court at

☐ High Court District Registry at

☐ The Royal Courts of Justice

☐ Other (please specify)

What is the name of the Judge whose decision you want to appeal?

What is the status of the Judge whose decision you want to appeal?

☐ District Judge or Deputy ☐ Circuit Judge or Recorder

☐ Master or Deputy ☐ High Court Judge or Deputy

What is the date of the decision you wish to appeal?

To which track, if any, was the claim or case allocated?

☐ Fast track

☐ Multi track

☐ Not allocated to a track

Nature of the decision you wish to appeal

☐ Case management decision ☐ Grant or refusal of interim relief

☐ Final decision ☐ A previous appeal decision

Section 3 Legal representation

Are you legally represented? ☐ Yes ☐ No
If 'Yes', please give details of your solicitor below

Your solicitor's name

Your solicitor's address (including postcode)

Tel No.	
Fax	
E-mail	
DX	
Ref.	

Are you, the Appellant, in receipt of a Legal Aid Certificate or a Community Legal Service Fund (CLSF) certificate? ☐ Yes ☐ No

Is the respondent legally represented? ☐ Yes ☐ No
If 'Yes', please give details of the respondent's solicitor below

The respondent's solicitor's address (including postcode)

Tel No.	
Fax	
E-mail	
DX	
Ref.	

Section 4 Permission to appeal

Do you need permission to appeal? ☐ Yes ☐ No

Has permission to appeal been granted ?

☐ **Yes**

Date of order granting permission

Name of Judge granting permission

☐ **No**

I

the Appellant('s solicitor) seek permission to appeal.

Section 5 Other information required for the appeal

Please set out the order (or part of the order) you wish to appeal

Does your appeal include any issues arising from the Human Rights Act 1998? ☐ Yes ☐ No

Are you asking for a stay of execution of any judgment against you? ☐ Yes ☐ No
If **'Yes'** you must complete **Part A of Section 8**

Have you lodged this notice with the court within 21 days of the date on which the Judge made the decision you wish to appeal? ☐ Yes ☐ No
If **'No'** you must complete **Part B of Section 8**

Are you making any other applications? ☐ Yes ☐ No
If **'Yes'** you must complete **Part C of Section 8**

Section 6 Grounds for appeal and arguments in support

Please state, in numbered paragraphs, **on a separate sheet** attached to this notice and entitled 'Grounds of Appeal' (also in the top right hand corner add your claim or case number and full name), why you are saying that the Judge who made the order you are appealing was wrong.

☐ The arguments (known as a 'Skeleton Argument') in support of the 'Grounds of Appeal will follow within 14 days of filing this Appellant's Notice

OR

☐ The arguments (known as a 'Skeleton Argument') in support of the 'Grounds of Appeal' are set out **on a separate sheet** and attached to this notice.

Section 7 What are you asking the Appeal Court to do?

I am asking the appeal court to:-
(please tick the appropriate box)

☐ set aside the order which I am appealing

☐ vary the order which I am appealing and substitute the following order. Set out in the following space the order you are asking for:-

☐ order a new trial

Section 8 Other applications

Complete this section **only** if you are asking for orders **in addition** to the order asked for in Section 7.

Part A
I apply for a stay of execution because:

Part B

☐ I do not need an extension of time for filing my appeal notice because it has been filed within the extended time granted by the Judge whose decision I am appealing.

OR

☐ I apply for an extension of time for filing my appeal notice because (set out the reasons for the delay. You must also set out in Section 9 what steps you have taken since the decision you are appealing).

Part C
I apply for an order that:

because

Section 9 Evidence in support

In support of my application(s) in Section 8, I wish to rely upon the following evidence:

Statement of Truth

I believe (The appellant believes) that the facts stated in this section are true.

Full name

Name of appellant's solicitor's firm

signed
Appellant ('s solicitor)

position or office held
(if signing on behalf of firm or company)

Section 10 Supporting documents

To support your appeal you should file with this notice all relevant documents listed below. To show which documents you are filing, please tick the appropriate boxes.

If you do not have a document that you intend to use to support your appeal complete the box over the page.

- ☐ two additional copies of your appellant's notice for the appeal court;
- ☐ one copy of your appellant's notice for each of the respondents;
- ☐ one copy of your skeleton argument for each copy of the appellant's notice that is filed;
- ☐ a sealed *(stamped by the court)* copy of the order being appealed;
- ☐ a copy of any order giving or refusing permission to appeal, together with a copy of the judge's reasons for allowing or refusing permission to appeal;
- ☐ any witness statements or affidavits in support of any application included in the appellant's notice;
- ☐ a copy of the order allocating the case to a track *(if any)*; and
- ☐ a copy of the legal aid or CLSF certificate (if legally represented).

A bundle of documents for the appeal hearing containing copies of all the papers listed below:-

- ☐ a sealed copy *(stamped by the court)* of your appellant's notice;
- ☐ a sealed copy *(stamped by the court)* of the order being appealed;
- ☐ a copy of any order giving or refusing permission to appeal, together with a copy of the judge's reasons for allowing or refusing permission to appeal;
- ☐ any affidavit or witness statement filed in support of any application included in the appellant's notice;
- ☐ a copy of the skeleton argument;
- ☐ a transcript or note of judgment, and in cases where permission to appeal was given by the lower court or is not required those parts of any transcript of evidence which are directly relevant to any question at issue on the appeal;
- ☐ the claim form and statements of case (where relevant to the subject of the appeal);
- ☐ any application notice (or case management documentation) relevant to the subject of the appeal;
- ☐ in cases where the decision appealed was itself made on appeal (eg from district judge to circuit judge), the first order, the reasons given and the appellant's notice used to appeal from that order;
- ☐ in the case of judicial review or a statutory appeal, the original decision which was the subject of the application to the lower court;
- ☐ in cases where the appeal is from a Tribunal, a copy of the Tribunal's reasons for the decision, a copy of the decision reviewed by the Tribunal and the reasons for the original decision and any document filed with the Tribunal setting out the grounds of appeal from that decision;
- ☐ any other documents which are necessary to enable the appeal court to reach a decision; and
- ☐ such other documents as the court may direct.

FORM N161

Reasons why you have not supplied a document and date when you expect it to be available:-

Title of document and reason not supplied	Date when it will be supplied

Signed [ ] Appellant('s Solicitor)

Guidance notes on completing form N161 - Appellant's notice (all appeals except small claims track appeals)

Please note form N161 is to be used for fast track and multi-track cases and statutory appeals from tribunals and other outside bodies only. Appeals in small claims track cases should use form **N164 - Appellant's notice (small claims track only)**.

A free leaflet **'EX340 - I want to appeal'** giving information about making an appeal in or to the High Court or a county court is available from:

- any county court,
- our website, www.hmcourts-service.gov.uk; or
- the Clerk of the lists General Office/ Appeals Office at the Royal Courts of Justice, Strand, London WC2A 2LL.

The leaflet will also explain the meaning of some of the terms and expressions used in this guidance.

Information is available about making an appeal to the Court of Appeal, from the Civil Appeals Office Registry, Room E307, Royal Courts of Justice, Strand, London WC2A 2LL.

- Court staff can help you complete the appellant's notice and tell you about procedure, they cannot give legal advice - for example, whether you should appeal or whether your appeal will be successful.
- If you need legal advice about bringing your appeal, you should contact a solicitor or a Citizens Advice Bureau immediately.
- If you are legally represented, your solicitor should complete this form on your behalf.

N161A - Guidance notes on completing the appellant's notice (07.06)

Important - time limits for issuing (filing) your appeal.

You have only a limited time in which to file your appellant's notice at the appeal court, so you must act quickly.

The leaflet **'EX340 - I want to appeal'** will tell you which is the appropriate appeal court in your case.

You must file your appellant's notice:-

- within the time limit set by the judge whose order you are appealing against; or
- where that judge set no time limit, within **21 days** after the date of the decision you wish to appeal against was made.

General notes on completing the notice

Set out below are notes to help you fill in the form. You should read the notes to each section carefully before you begin to complete that particular section.

Use a separate sheet if you need more space for your answers, marking clearly which section the information refers to. Write the claim or case number on it and attach it securely to the notice.

If you do not have all the documents or information you need for your appeal, you must **not** allow this to delay sending or taking the form to the appeal court within the correct time. Complete the form as fully as possible and provide what documents you have. The notes to Section 10 will explain more about what you have to do in these circumstances.

Section 1: Details of the claim or case you are appealing against

Give the claim or case number you wish to appeal against. You are required to provide the full name of all parties and to indicate whether they were the claimant, applicant or petitioner, defendant or respondent by ticking the appropriate box. You can find this and other information in the order or decision you are appealing against.

Give your (appellant's) full name, and the address to which you would like all documents relating to the appeal to be sent. Include contact information e.g telephone and any other contact information.

You will also need to include the above details for the respondent to enable the court to send correspondence and other details to the respondent. If there is more than one respondent, list their names, addresses and contact details on a separate sheet of paper and tick the 'details of additional parties' box to indicate that you have done so. Write the claim number on it and attach it securely to your notice.

Section 2: Details of the appeal

Most of the information you will need to complete this section will be found on the order or decision you are appealing against.

Give the name of the court or tribunal whose order you are appealing against.

Give the name of the Judge, whose decision you wish to appeal and indicate, by ticking the relevant box, the status of the judge.

If the order being appealed was made in the High Court or a county court, and did not relate to a family matter, it will usually have been allocated to the fast track or multi-track for the purpose of preparation of evidence and trial. If it was allocated to a track, you should tick the appropriate box to show which. (The notice of allocation or other order should give this information.)

You should also tick the appropriate box if the order you are appealing against was a case management decision to indicate the nature of the decision you wish to appeal. Case management decisions include orders relating to:

- the timetable for trial;
- the filing and exchange of information (of witnesses and experts);
- disclosure of documents (papers the court said you must make available to the other parties); or
- adding a party to a claim.

A grant or refusal of interim relief might include an injunction, freezing order, an order for the detention or custody or preservation of relevant property, or a financial order. You should tick the previous appeal decision box if this is a second appeal and you wish to appeal against the outcome of the first appeal hearing.

Section 3: Legal representation

Confirm whether you are legally represented and if so, give your solicitor's name and contact details.

Indicate whether or not your case is being funded.

Confirm whether the respondent is legally represented and, if so, provide the name and contact details of their solicitor.

4

Section 4: Permission to appeal

You will usually need permission to appeal the decision of a judge of the High Court or a county court. If you are appealing the decision of a tribunal, you should check with that tribunal whether you need permission to appeal and, if so, whether you need to ask for that permission from the tribunal, or from the appeal court.

> If you wish to make a **second appeal** against the same order, you can only do so if the Court of Appeal in London gives you permission. You must make your application for permission to that court permission for a second appeal will only be given exceptionally.

You should note that permission will only be given where the court considers that your appeal has a real prospect of success. Where your appeal is against a case management decision, the court will also consider:-

- whether the issue is significant enough to justify the costs of an appeal;
- the overall effect on the case management timetable, e.g. whether the loss of the trial date is more significant than the procedural point you wish to appeal; and
- whether it would be more convenient to deal with your point at the trial.

You **do not** need permission if the order you are appealing against is one of the following:

- a committal order;
- an order refusing the grant of habeas corpus;
- a secure accommodation order under Section 25 of the Children Act 1989.

5

You need only request permission in this notice if:-

- you did not ask for permission to appeal at the hearing at which the decision you are appealing against was made; or
- you asked for permission, but it was refused, and you wish the appeal court to reconsider your request.

The court when giving permission to appeal may, **exceptionally,** direct that your appeal be referred to the Court of Appeal if it considers that it raises an important point of principle or practice or there is some other important reason for the Court of Appeal to hear it. Where the court gives this direction, it will be shown on form **N460 Reasons for allowing or refusing permission to appeal (including referral to the Court of Appeal)** which the court will send you.

If you need more time than is allowed for filing your appellant's notice, you must make an application in the notice itself. (See the notes to Section 8).

Section 5: Other information required for the appeal

You are required to state the order you wish to appeal. If you are appealing only part of an order or tribunal decision, you must write out that part (or parts) of the order in the box provided.

You should also indicate whether your appeal includes any Human Rights Act issues and whether you are asking the appeal court to issue a stay on enforcing the order which you are appealing. (You do not need to do this if you have already obtained a stay from the lower court or your appeal is from the Immigration Appeal Tribunal). If you are asking for a stay, extension of time or other order you will also need to complete the relevant part of Section 8.

6

Section 6: Grounds for appeal and arguments in support

An appeal must be based on relevant grounds (reasons for appealing). An appeal court will only allow an appeal against a decision that was either:-

- wrong; or
- unjust because of a serious procedural or other irregularity in the lower court proceedings.

The appeal court will be unlikely to overturn a decision where no real difference would be made to the outcome of the case; or the appeal would involve re-examining the factual investigation undertaken by the lower court.

Set out briefly and **on a separate sheet** your reasons why you think the judge's decision was wrong or unjust. If possible, list your reasons in short separately numbered paragraphs.

Remember that you **must not** include any grounds for appealing which rely on new evidence, that is evidence that has become available since the order was made. You may not produce new evidence in your appeal without first obtaining the permission of the appeal court. (See the notes to Section 4)

Please indicate by ticking the relevant box whether you are attaching your arguments (referred to as a skeleton argument) to this notice or whether you intend to send them separately within 14 days of filing this appellant's notice with the court.

The separate skeleton argument should be filed and served on the respondent either with your completed notice or, if you are unable to complete your skeleton argument in time, no later then 14 days after filing your notice.

7

Skeleton arguments should contain a numbered list of points that you intend to argue at the hearing. Each point should be stated in no more than a few sentences. Refer at each point to any documents you are filing with your appellant's notice which supports that argument (see Section 10 on documents).

Other useful information
Try to consider what other information the appeal court might find useful. For example, the court may find it helpful to have a list of people who feature in the case, an explanation of technical terms used in the papers, or a list of events in date order (a chronology). If you are providing any of these, they should be on a separate piece of paper attached to your notice marked with the case or claim number and names of the parties.

Section 7: What you are asking the appeal court to do?

Indicate by ticking the relevant box whether you are asking the appeal court to set aside or vary the order you are appealing or whether you would like it to order a new trial.

Section 8: Other applications

You only need to complete this section if you are asking for orders in addition to those requested in Section 7.

Any application for an extension of time for appealing must be made in the appeal notice itself. You should state the reason for the delay and the steps taken up to the time of filing the notice.

You may wish to make additional applications to the appeal court in connection with your appeal. Any other applications may be made either in the notice, or in a separate application notice (Form N244 - Application notice). This form can be obtained from

8

the court or our website. You may have to pay additional fees if it is filed at a later date than your appellant's notice.

Section 9: Evidence in support

Include here any information you have to support your application under Section 8.

State whether you are producing new evidence in your appeal or asking for permission to produce oral evidence at the appeal hearing. You will need to give reasons why the new evidence was not before the original court and, where oral evidence is requested, the reasons why you think it is necessary. You should sign the statement of truth at the bottom of this section to support any evidence you provide.

Section 10: Supporting documents

Do not delay filing your appellant's notice at the appeal court. If you have not been able to obtain any of the documents listed below within the time allowed, complete the notice as best you can and ensure the notice is filed on time. Tick the appropriate boxes to show the documents you are filing with the appeal notice. List any documents that you intend to use but which you do not have available in the box over the page. Set out the reasons why you have been unable to obtain any of the information or documents and give the date when you expect them to be available.

Whenever possible, the following documents should be filed with your appellant's notice:-

- two additional copies of your appellant's notice for the appeal court;
- one copy of your appellant's notice for each of the respondents;

9

- one copy of your skeleton argument for each copy of the appellant's notice that is filed;
- a sealed (stamped by the court) copy of the order being appealed;
- a copy of any order giving or refusing permission to appeal, together with a copy of the judge's reasons for allowing or refusing permission to appeal;
- any witness statements or affidavits in support of any application included in the appellant's notice;
- a copy of the order allocating the case to a track (if any); and
- a copy of the legal aid or CLSF certificate (if legally represented).

Your bundle of documents in support which should include copies of:

- a sealed copy (stamped by the court) of your appellant's notice;
- a sealed copy (stamped by the court) of the order being appealed;
- a copy of any order giving or refusing permission to appeal, together with a copy of the judge's reasons for allowing or refusing permission to appeal;
- any affidavit or witness statement filed in support of any application included in the appellant's notice;
- a copy of the skeleton argument;

10

- a transcript or note of judgment, and in cases where permission to appeal was given by the lower court or is not required those parts of any transcript of evidence which are directly relevant to any question at issue on the appeal;
- the claim form and statements of case (where relevant to the subject of the appeal);
- any application notice (or case management documentation) relevant to the subject of the appeal;
- in cases where the decision appealed was itself made on appeal (eg. from district judge to circuit judge), the first order, the reasons given and the appellant's notice used to appeal from that order;
- in the case of judicial review or a statutory appeal, the original decision which was the subject of the application to the lower court;
- in cases where the appeal is from a Tribunal, a copy of the Tribunal's reasons for the decision, a copy of the decision reviewed by the Tribunal and the reasons for the original decision and any document filed with the Tribunal setting out the grounds of appeal from that decision;
- any other documents which are necessary to enable the appeal court to reach a decision; and
- such other documents as the court may direct.

A transcript or note of judgment may be either an approved transcript of the judgment where the hearing was recorded or a copy of the written judgment (endorsed with the judge's signature) or a note of the judgment. If you were not legally represented in the lower court but the respondent was, the respondent's advocate should make their note of the judgment available to you free of charge.

11

You should remember that if you file any of the documents at a later date, you must check whether or not the information contained in the later documents alters any of the details already given in your appellant's notice. If it does, you will need to apply to the court for permission to amend the notice. The court can tell you how to do this.

What happens next?

Filing your completed notice and documents

Send or take the notice and copies of all the other documents to the appeal court office with the appropriate fee. The court can tell you how much this is. The court will seal the notice (stamp the notice with the court seal).

The court will serve your appellant's notice, your skeleton argument and any other documents on the respondent, unless you tell the court that you wish to serve them yourself.

Please note that the above paragraph does not apply to the Court of Appeal and the Civil Appeals Office will not serve documents where service is required by the Civil Procedure Rules (See CPR 52 PD para 15.1(2)). For further guidance see the Civil Appeals website www.hmcourts-service.gov.uk/cms/civilappeals.htm forms and guidance.

The respondent must be served with -

- **a sealed copy of your appellant's notice** as soon as practicable but no later than 7 days after it is filed at the court;

12

- **any separate skeleton argument** at the same time as the notice. If you have been unable to complete your skeleton argument in time, it must be served no later than 14 days after filing your notice at the court;
- **your bundle of documents**
- if you have already obtained permission to appeal or do not need permission, the bundle must be served at the same time as your notice; **or**
- if you have asked for permission to appeal in your notice and permission has been granted without a hearing, the bundle must be served within 7 days of receiving notice that permission has been given; **or**
- if you have asked for permission to appeal in your notice which is to be considered at a hearing, the bundle must be served within 7 days of receiving notice of that hearing.

Important

notes for respondents

You have been served with a copy of an appellant's notice (an appeal).

If the notice includes an application for permission to appeal, you need do nothing unless and until you receive notice from the court that permission has been given.

If permission is given, you will only have a limited time in which to reply to the appeal. You must decide what to do quickly.

You can:

- also appeal against the same order; or
- ask for the order to be varied; or
- ask that the order be upheld by the appeal court for different or additional reasons than those given by the lower court (the court who made the order being appealed); or
- ask that the order be upheld for the same reasons relied on by the lower court; or
- do nothing

If you wish to appeal, vary or uphold the order being appealed for different or additional reasons, **you will need to complete a Respondent's Notice** (Form N162) and send it to the court. **You have a very limited time to do this.** This form, the notes for guidance for completing it and a leaflet *I want to appeal* can be obtained free from any court office or Judges' Interim Applications Office at the Royal Courts of Justice, Strand, London, WC2A 2LL. They will explain about time limits and tell you the documents you will need to support your appeal.

You may also complete a respondent's notice if you simply wish to ask the appeal court to uphold the order for the reasons given in the lower court but have additional arguments to make to the appeal court. Alternatively you may set these additional arguments out in a 'skeleton argument', i.e. a document which just sets out the points you wish to make to the appeal court. Form N163 can be used to set out your skeleton argument. This form can also be obtained from any court office or the Royal Courts of Justice at the above address.

Information about making an appeal to the Court of Appeal can be obtained from the Civil Appeals Office Registry, Room E307, Royal Courts of Justice, Strand, WC2A 2LL.

If you do not complete a respondent's notice or file a skeleton argument, you will not be able to rely on any additional arguments at the hearing of the appeal which were not raised in the lower court unless the court gives you permission.

N161B Important Notes for Respondent (4.00) *Printed on behalf of The Court Service*

Respondent's Notice

In the	
Appeal Court Reference No.	

Notes for guidance are available which will help you complete this form. Please read them carefully before you complete each section.

For Court use only	
Date filed	

Seal

Section 1 Details of the claim or case

Name of court ______ Case or claim number ______

Name or title of case or claim ______

In the case or claim, were you the
(tick appropriate box)

☐ claimant ☐ applicant ☐ petitioner

☐ defendant ☐ respondent ☐ other *(please specify)* ______

Section 2 Your (respondent's) name and address

Your (respondent's) name ______

Your solicitor's name ______ *(if you are legally represented)*

Your (your solicitor's) address

Your reference or contact name ______

Your contact telephone number ______

DX number ______

Details of other respondents are attached ☐ Yes ☐ No

Section 3 Time estimate for appeal hearing

Do not complete if appealing to the Court of Appeal

How long do you estimate it will take to put your case to the appeal court at the hearing?

Days	Hours	Minutes

Who will represent you at the appeal hearing? ☐ Yourself ☐ Solicitor ☐ Counsel

N162 Respondent's Notice (04.07)

Section 4 Details of the order(s) or part(s) of order(s) you want to appeal

Name of Judge

Date of order(s)

If only part of an order is appealed, write out that part (or those parts)

Section 5 Permission to file a respondent's notice

Has permission to appeal been granted?

☐ Yes complete box **A**

☐ No complete box **B**
if you are asking for permission or it is not required

A

Date of order granting permission ____________

Name of judge ____________

Name of court ____________

B

☐ I do not need permission

☐ I ____________
respondent('s solicitor) seek permission to appeal the order(s) at **section 4** above.

Are you making any other applications? If Yes, complete section 9	☐ Yes	☐ No
Is the respondent in receipt of legal aid certificate or a community legal service fund (CLSF) certificate?	☐ Yes	☐ No
Does your appeal include any issues arising from the Human Rights Act 1998?	☐ Yes	☐ No

2

Section 6 Grounds for appeal or for upholding the order

I (the respondent)

☐ appeal(s) the order

☐ wish(es) the appeal court to uphold the order on different or additional grounds

because:-

3

Section 7	Arguments in support of grounds

My skeleton argument is:-

☐ set out below ☐ attached ☐ will follow within 14 days of receiving the appellant's skeleton arguments

I (the respondent) will rely on the following arguments at the hearing of the appeal:-

4

Section 8 What decision are you asking the appeal court to make?

I (the respondent) am (is) asking that:-

(tick appropriate box)

- ☐ the order(s) at **section 4** be set aside
- ☐ the order(s) at **section 4** be varied and the following order(s) substituted :-
- ☐ a new trial be ordered
- ☐ the appeal court makes the following additional orders :-
- ☐ the appeal court upholds the order but for the following different or additional reasons

Section 9 Other applications

I wish to make an application for additional orders

☐ in this section

☐ in the Part 23 application form (N244) attached

Part A

I apply (the respondent applies) for an order (a draft of which is attached) that :-

because :-

Part B

I (the respondent) wish(es) to rely on :

☐ evidence in Part C

☐ witness statement (affidavit)

6

Part C

I (the respondent) wish(es) to rely on the following evidence in support of this application:-

Statement of Truth

I believe (the respondent believes) that the facts stated in Section 9 are true.

Full name ______________________

Name of respondent's solicitor's firm ______________________

Signed ______________________ position or office held ______________________

Respondent ('s solicitor) (if signing on behalf of firm or company)

7

Section 10 Supporting documents

Please tick the papers you are filing in your bundle:-

- ☐ your respondent's notice and any skeleton arguments (if separate);
- ☐ any witness statements or affidavits in support of any application included in section 5 or 9 of your notice or in a separate Part 23 application notice;
- ☐ any other affidavit or witness statement filed in support of your arguments;
- ☐ a copy of the legal aid or CLSF certificate (if legally represented); and
- ☐ any other documents directed by the court to be filed in your appeal *(give details).*

Reasons why you have not supplied a document and date when you expect it to be available:-

Signed____________________________ Respondent/'s Solicitor

Click here to print form

8

Guidance notes for completing the respondent's notice

A free leaflet *I want to appeal* giving information about making an appeal in or to the High Court or county court is available from any county court or the Clerk of the Lists General Office/ Appeals Office at the Royal Courts of Justice, Strand, London WC2A 2LL. The leaflet will also explain some of the terms and expressions used in these notes of guidance.

Information is available about making an appeal to the Court of Appeal, from the Civil Appeals Office Registry, Room E307, Royal Courts of Justice, Strand, WC2A 2LL

- Court staff can help you complete the respondent's notice and tell you about the procedure. But they cannot give legal advice, for example, about the likely success of the appellant's appeal, whether you should reply to it or whether you should yourself appeal.
- If you need legal advice about this appeal, you should contact a solicitor or a law or advice centre.
- If you are legally represented, your solicitor should complete this form on your behalf.

When to file a respondent's notice

You need to file a notice if you wish:

- to appeal against the order (appealing includes asking for the order to be varied); or
- to ask the appeal court to uphold the order for different or additional reasons. (This is not treated as an appeal by the appeal court.)

1

If you wish the appeal court to uphold the lower court's order and reasons, and have arguments to support this you wish to make, you have two options.

You can:

- either complete a respondent's notice (you will not need to complete sections 4,5,6 or 8);
- or, set out your arguments in a skeleton argument. The notes to section 7 of the Respondent's Notice will explain more about this.

Important - time limits for filing your notice

You have only a limited time in which file a respondent's notice.

You must file your respondent's notice with the appeal court:-

- within the time limit set by the judge whose order or decision is being appealed; **or**
- where that judge set no time limit, within **14 days** after the date of service of:

  the appellant's notice where permission to appeal was given by the lower court or permission to appeal is not required; **or**

  the notification that the appeal court has given the appellant permission to appeal; **or**

  the notification that the application for permission to appeal and the appeal itself are to be heard together

You must file your notice with the court at which the appellant's appeal is proceeding.

2

General notes on completing the notice

Set out below are notes to help you fill in the form. You should read the notes to each section carefully before you begin to complete that particular section.

Use a separate sheet if you need more space for your answers marking clearly which section the information refers to. Write the claim or case number on it, sign and date it and attach it securely to the notice.

If you do not have all the information to complete your respondent's notice (or any documents that you need to file with it), you must **not** allow this to delay sending or taking it to the appeal court within the correct time. Complete the form as fully as possible and provide what documents you have. The notes to Section 9 will explain more about what you have to do in these circumstances.

Enter the appeal court's reference number in the top right hand corner of the respondent's notice. This number will appear on the top left hand side of the appellant's notice.

Section 1

Details of claim or case

Give the name of the court or tribunal whose order is being appealed, the number of the case or claim, and the title of the claim or case, eg. 'John Smith v Eric James'. You can take these details from the order being appealed.

Indicate, by ticking the appropriate box, which party you were in those proceedings.

3

Section 2

Respondent's details

Give your full name and an address to which all documents relating to the appeal can be sent. Include contact information, e.g. telephone and any other reference numbers.

If there is more than one respondent, list their names, addresses and contact details on a separate sheet of paper. Write the claim or case number on it and attach it securely to your notice.

Tick the box to let the court know if separate details are attached.

Section 3

Time estimate for appeal hearing

> You do not need to complete this section if your appeal is being made to the Court of Appeal in London.

Please give an estimate of how long you believe it will take you to present your case to the court at the appeal hearing. The court needs this information to assess how much of a judge's time to allow.

Section 4

Details of the order you are seeking to appeal

If you are appealing only part of an order or tribunal decision, you must write out that part (or those parts) of the order in the box provided.

You should give the full title and name of the judge, e.g. 'His Honour Judge Jones' or 'District Judge Smith', and the date of the order or decision being appealed.

Section 5

Permission to file a respondent's notice

You will usually need permission to file a respondent's notice to appeal the decision of a judge of the High Court or a county court (appealing includes asking for the judge's order to be varied).

Permission will only be given where the court considers that your appeal (or application to vary) has a real prospect of success. Where your appeal is against a case management decision, the court will also consider:-

- whether the issue is significant enough to justify the costs of an appeal;
- the overall effect on the case management timetable, e.g. whether the loss of the trial date is more significant than the procedural point you wish to appeal; and
- whether it would be more convenient to deal with your point at the trial.

If you are appealing the decision of a tribunal, you should check with that tribunal whether you need to ask for permission to appeal and, if so, whether you need to ask for that permission from the tribunal or from the appeal court.

5

You need only request permission to appeal in this notice if

- you did not ask for permission to appeal at the hearing at which the decision you are appealing against was made; or
- you asked for permission, but it was refused, and you wish the appeal court to reconsider your request.

You do **not** need permission if the order you are appealing against is one of the following:

- a committal order;
- an order refusing the grant of habeus corpus;
- a secure accommodation order under Section 25 of the Children Act 1989;
- to ask the appeal court to uphold the decision of the lower court, even though it is for different or additional reasons

If you need more time than that allowed for filing your respondent's notice, you must make an application in the notice itself. *(See the notes to Section 9).*

Section 6

Grounds for appealing, or for upholding the order

If you are appealing against the lower court's order, your appeal (appealing includes asking for the order to varied) must be based on relevant 'grounds' (reasons). An appeal court will only allow an appeal against a decision that was either:

- wrong; or
- unjust because of a serious procedural or other irregularity in the lower court proceedings.

The appeal court will be unlikely to overturn a decision where no real difference would be made to the outcome of the case; or the appeal would involve re-examining the factual investigation undertaken by the lower court.

Asking the court to uphold a decision is not an appeal but you must give reasons if asking for it to be upheld on different or additional grounds.

Set your reasons out briefly. If possible, list your reasons in short separately numbered paragraphs.

Remember that you must not include any grounds which rely on new evidence, that is, evidence that has become available since the order was made. You may not produce new evidence without first obtaining the permission of the appeal court. *(See the notes to Section 9).*

Section 7

Arguments in support of grounds

Your arguments (together referred to as a 'skeleton argument') may be set out in this section or in a separate document attached to this notice. They should, where appropriate, answer the arguments set out in the appellant's skeleton argument.

Any separate skeleton argument has to be filed and served on the appellant with your completed notice no later than 14 days after you receive the appellant's skeleton argument.

Skeleton arguments should contain a numbered list of points that you intend to argue at the hearing. Each point should be stated in no more than a few sentences. Refer at each point to any document you are filing with your respondent's notice which supports that argument. *(See Section 10 on documents)*

7

Form N163 can be used to set out your skeleton argument. This form can be obtained from any court office or from the Clerk of the Lists General Office/ Appeals Office, The Royal Courts of Justice, Strand, London WC2A 2LL.

Other useful information
Try to consider what other information the appeal court might find useful. For example, the court would find it helpful to have a list of people who feature in the case, an explanation of technical terms use in the papers or a list of events in date order (a chronology). If you are providing any of these, they should be on a separate piece of paper attached to your notice marked with the case or claim number and the names of the parties. You do not need to duplicate any of the documents which the appellant has already provided.

Section 8

What decision are you asking the court to make

Set out details of the order(s) (or the variation to the original order(s)) that you want the appeal court to make.

Section 9

Other applications

If you wish to apply for an extension of time to file a fully completed respondent's notice with any supporting documents, this must be made in the notice itself. You should state the reason for the delay and the steps taken up to the time of filing the notice.

You may wish to make additional applications to the appeal court in connection with your appeal or application to vary or uphold the order. Any other applications may be made either in the notice, or in a separate application notice (Form N244). This form can be obtained from the

8

court. You may have to pay additional fees if it is filed at a later date than your respondent's notice.

The types of application you might want to make will include:

- amending (make changes to) your respondent's notice after it has been filed at court. But note that you can amend your skeleton argument (even if it is set out in part 7 of your notice) without making an application;
- asking the appeal court to issue a stay on executing the order or suspend any action in the case pending the outcome of the appeal. (You do not need to do this if you have already obtained a stay from the lower court or the appeal is from the Immigration Appeal Tribunal.);
- producing new evidence in the appeal or asking for permission to produce oral evidence at the appeal hearing. You will need to give reasons why the new evidence was not before the original court and, where oral evidence is requested, the reasons why you think it is necessary;
- asking for security for costs, ie that the appellant be ordered to pay a sum of money into court sufficient to cover any costs the appellant may be ordered to pay in the appeal.

Section 10

Supporting documents

You may have additional documents to those filed by the appellant to support your appeal or your request to vary or uphold the order. These should be in a bundle and filed with your respondent's notice.

Do not delay filing your respondent's notice at the appeal court. If you have not been able to obtain any of the documents that you wish to file with your notice, complete the notice as best you can and ensure that it is filed on time.

Your bundle should include any of the following (unless they are already included in the bundle filed by the appellant):-

- your respondent's notice and any skeleton argument (if separate);
- any witness statements or affidavits in support of any application included in Sections 5 or 9 of your notice or in a separate Part 23 application notice;
- any other affidavit or witness statement filed in support of your arguments; and
- any other documents directed by the court to be filed in the appeal.

You should remember that if you file any of the documents at a later date, you must check whether or not the information you are providing alters any of the details already given in your respondent's notice. If it does, you will need to apply to the court for permission to amend the notice. The court can tell you how to do this.

10

What happens next?

Filing your completed notice

Copy the completed notice (and any separate skeleton argument or bundles of documents) so that you have one copy for yourself, two copies for the court and one copy for each respondent. Send or take the notice and any supporting documents or bundles to the court office with the appropriate fee. The court can tell you how much this is.

Serving your respondent's notice

The appellant must be served with a sealed copy of this notice any separate skeleton arguments or bundle of documents as soon as practicable but no later than 7 days after it is filed at court. The court will serve all the documents filed on the appellant and any other respondents unless you tell the court that you wish to serve it yourself. Any separate skeleton argument (see the notes to Section 7 above) must be served with the respondent's notice where possible or within 21 days of receiving the appellant's skeleton argument.

If you have made an application for additional time to provide all information you need for appeal, the respondent will have the right to attend the hearing of your application.

N162A Notes for completing appellant's notice (04.07)

FORM N163

Skeleton argument

The contents of the skeleton arguments must comply with the practice direction to Part 52 of the Civil Procedure Rules

In the
Appeal Court Reference No. *(if known)*

For Court use only	
Date filed	

Details of the claim or case

Name of court ________ Case or claim number ________

Name or title of case or claim ________

In the case or claim, were you the
(tick appropriate box)

☐ claimant ☐ applicant ☐ petitioner

☐ defendant ☐ respondent ☐ other *(please specify)* ________

Your name and address

Your name ________

Your Solicitor's name ________ *(if you are legally represented)*

Your Advocate's name ________

Your (your solicitor's /advocate's) address

Your reference or contact name ________

Your contact telephone number ________

DX number ________

In the appeal, are you the ☐ appellant ☐ respondent

complete your skeleton argument overleaf ➡

N163 Skeleton argument (4.00) *The Court Service Publications Unit*

Skeleton argument

I (the appellant)(the respondent) will rely on the following arguments at the hearing of the appeal:-

Signed ____________________________________ Appellant/ Respondent ('s solicitor)('s advocate)

Appellant's notice
(Small Claims Track only)

For Court use only	
Appeal Reference no.	
Date filed	

I wish to appeal against an order made in the ______ County Court

I was the ☐ Claimant ☐ Defendant

Seal

Note: In the appeal you will be known as the 'appellant'

Section 1 Details of the claim

Claim number

Name(s) of claimant(s)	Name(s) of defendant(s)

Section 2 Details for the appeal

What is the name of the Judge who made the order(s) you are appealing?

On what date was the order(s) you are appealing made?

If only part of an order is appealed please say which numbered paragraphs of the order you wish to appeal against **or** if they are not numbered, set out the words of that part of the order.

N164 Appellant's notice (04.07) 1

Section 3 Permission to appeal

Has permission to appeal been granted? ☐ Yes ☐ No

If permission to appeal has **NOT** been granted please tick the box opposite. ☐ I ask for permission to appeal

Section 4 Other information required

Does your appeal include any issues arising from the Human Rights Act 1998? ☐ Yes ☐ No

Are you asking for a stay of execution of any judgment against you? (If granted this means that no further action will be taken on the judgment until your appeal has been dealt with) ☐ Yes ☐ No

If you answer 'Yes' you ***must*** *complete Section 7 Part A*

Will you be lodging this appellant's notice with the court within 21 days of the date on which the Judge made his decision? ☐ Yes ☐ No

If you answer 'No' you ***must*** *complete Section 7 Part B*

Are you making any other applications? ☐ Yes ☐ No

If you answer 'Yes' you ***must*** *complete Section 7 Part C*

Section 5 Grounds for appeal

Please state in numbered paragraphs, why you say that the Judge who made the order you are appealing against was wrong.

2

Section 6 What are you asking the Appeal Court to do?

I am asking the Appeal Court to:-
(tick the appropriate box)

☐ set aside the order which I am appealing

☐ vary the order which I am appealing and substitute the following order. Set out in the following space the order you are asking for:-

☐ order a new hearing

Section 7 Other applications

Complete this section **only** if you are asking for orders **in addition** to the order asked for in Section 6

PART A

I apply for a stay of execution because:

PART B *(tick only **one** box)*

☐ I do not need an extension of time for filing my appellant's notice because it has been filed within the extended time granted by the District Judge

☐ I apply for an extension of time for filing my appeal notice because (*Set out the reasons for the delay. You must also set out in Section 8 what steps you have taken since the District Judge's decision)*

PART C

I apply for an order that:

Because

3

Section 8 Evidence in support

In support of my applications in Section 7, I wish to rely upon the following evidence:

Statement of Truth

I believe (The appellant believes) that the facts stated in Section 8 are true.

Signed ______________________ Position or office held ______________________
Appellant ('s solicitor) (if signing on behalf of firm or company)

Full name ______________________

Name of appellant's solicitor's firm ______________________

4

Section 9 Documents in support of your appeal

Note: You **must** send to the court with this appellant's notice a copy of the order being appealed and where permission to appeal has already been considered by the court, a copy of Form N460 containing the reasons for the decision allowing or refusing permission to appeal.

Please note that your appeal cannot be processed until the court has received the document(s)

I attach *(please tick)*

☐ a copy of the Order being appealed

and

☐ a copy of Form N460 *(see note above)*

Signed ______________________________ Dated ______________________________
(Appellant/Appellant's Solicitor)

Listing questionnaire (Pre-trial checklist)

To be completed by, or on behalf of,

who is [1st][2nd][3rd][ ][Claimant][Defendant] [Part 20 claimant][Part 20 defendant] in this claim

In the	
Claim No.	
Last date for filing with court office	
Date(s) fixed for trial or trial period	

This form must be **completed** and **returned** to the court no later than the date given above. If not, your statement of case may be struck out or some other sanction imposed.

If the claim has settled, or settles before the trial date, you must let the court know immediately.

Legal representatives only: You must **attach** estimates of costs incurred to date, and of your likely overall costs. In substantial cases, these should be provided in compliance with CPR Part 43.

For multi-track claims only, you must also **attach** a proposed timetable for the trial itself.

A Confirmation of compliance with directions

1. I confirm that I have complied with those directions already given which require action by me. ☐Yes ☐No

If you are unable to give confirmation, state which directions you have still to comply with and the date by which this will be done.

Directions	Date

2. I believe that additional directions are necessary before the trial takes place. ☐Yes ☐No

If Yes, you should attach an application and a draft order.

Include in your application all directions needed to enable the claim ***to be tried on the date, or within the trial period, already fixed.*** *These should include any issues relating to experts and their evidence, and any orders needed in respect of directions still requiring action by any other party.*

3. Have you agreed the additional directions you are seeking with the other party(ies)? ☐Yes ☐No

B Witnesses

1. How many witnesses (including yourself) will be giving evidence on your behalf at the trial? *(Do not include experts - see Section C)* ☐

Continued over

Witnesses continued

2. If the trial date is not yet fixed, are there any days within the trial period you or your witnesses would wish to avoid if possible? *(Do not include experts - see Section C)*

Please give details

Name of witness	Dates to be avoided, if possible	Reason

Please specify any special facilities or arrangements needed at court for the party or any witness (e.g. witness with a disability).

3. Will you be providing an interpreter for any of your witnesses? ☐ Yes ☐ No

C Experts

You are reminded that you may not use an expert's report or have your expert give oral evidence unless the court has given permission. If you do not have permission, you must make an application (see section A2 above)

1. Please give the information requested for your expert(s)

Name	Field of expertise	Joint expert?	Is report agreed?	Has permission been given for oral evidence?
		☐Yes ☐No	☐Yes ☐No	☐Yes ☐No
		☐Yes ☐No	☐Yes ☐No	☐Yes ☐No
		☐Yes ☐No	☐Yes ☐No	☐Yes ☐No

2. Has there been discussion between experts? ☐ Yes ☐ No

3. Have the experts signed a joint statement? ☐ Yes ☐ No

4. If your expert is giving oral evidence and the trial date is not yet fixed, is there any day within the trial period which the expert would wish to avoid, if possible? ☐ Yes ☐ No

If Yes, please give details

Name	Dates to be avoided, if possible	Reason

2 of 3

D Legal representation

1. Who will be presenting your case at the trial? ☐ You ☐ Solicitor ☐ Counsel

2. If the trial date is not yet fixed, is there any day within the trial period that the person presenting your case would wish to avoid, if possible? ☐ Yes ☐ No

If Yes, please give details

Name	Dates to be avoided, if possible	Reason

E The trial

1. Has the estimate of the time needed for trial changed? ☐ Yes ☐ No

If Yes, say how long you estimate the whole trial will take, including both parties' cross-examination and closing arguments ☐ days ☐ hours ☐ minutes

2. If different from original estimate have you agreed with the other party(ies) that this is now the **total** time needed? ☐ Yes ☐ No

3. Is the timetable for trial you have attached agreed with the other party(ies)? ☐ Yes ☐ No

Fast track cases only

The court will normally give you 3 weeks notice of the date fixed for a fast track trial unless, in exceptional circumstances, the court directs that shorter notice will be given.

Would you be prepared to accept shorter notice of the date fixed for trial? ☐ Yes ☐ No

F Document and fee checklist

Tick as appropriate

I attach to this questionnaire -

☐ An application and fee for additional directions

☐ A proposed timetable for trial

☐ A draft order

☐ An estimate of costs

☐ Listing fee

Signed

[Counsel][Solicitor][for the][1st][2nd][3rd][ ]
[Claimant][Defendant]
[Part 20 claimant][Part 20 defendant]

Date

Please enter your [firm's] name, reference number and full postal address including (if appropriate) details of DX, fax or e-mail

Postcode

Tel. no.		DX no.		E-mail	
Fax no.		Ref. no.			

3 of 3

Notice of Date for Returning Listing Questionnaire

To the

In the County Court	
Claim Number	
Claimant (including ref.)	
Defendant (including ref.)	
Date	

Enclosed with this notice is a listing questionnaire which you must complete and return on or before

to the court office at

Note: You should read the notes for guidance on the first page of the listing questionnaire and note particularly the possible sanctions for failure to complete and return it.

The court office at EDMONTON County Court, is open between 10am and 4pm Monday to Friday. When corresponding with the court, please address forms or letters to the Court Manager and quote the claim number. Tel: 0181 807 1666/7 Fax:

Produced by: TRAIN8
CJR0176

N171 Notice for date for return of listing questionnaire

Notice of Trial Date

In the	
Claim No.	
Claimant (including ref)	
Defendant (including ref)	
Date	

To [Claimant][Defendant]['s Solicitor]

The trial of the above claim [counterclaim] will take place at [am][pm]

on the of

at

[Any application in the case must be made to the court where the case is to be tried.]

[Master][District Judge] .... has ordered that:

Note for fast track cases: At the end of the trial, in addition to deciding which party will pay the costs of the case, the judge will also normally assess the amount to be paid. All parties should ensure that they bring all relevant information in respect of their costs to the trial to enable the judge to carry out that assessment.

The court office at

is open between 10 am and 4 pm Monday to Friday. When corresponding with the court, please address forms or letters to the Court Manager and quote the claim number.

N172 Notice of Trial Date

Notice to Pay Fee

In the	
Claim No.	
Claimant including ref.	
Defendant including ref.	
Date	

To the [Claimant][Defendant] ['s Solicitor]

[On the [ ] the court received your [allocation] [listing] questionnaire.

Either a fee of £ or an application for a fee exemption or remission should have accompanied the questionnaire. Neither was enclosed.]

[Your [claim] [counterclaim] was [allocated to the] [fast track] [multi-track] [listed for trial] on [ ]. A fee of £ was payable unless you had made an application for a fee exemption on remission. Neither have been received.]

If by [ ] you have not paid the fee or applied for a fee exemption or remission, your [claim] [counterclaim] will be struck

out and you will be liable for the costs which the [claimant][defendant] has incurred.

Note:

If your [claim][counterclaim] is struck out, you may apply to the court for it to be reinstated. An order reinstating your [claim][counterclaim] will only have effect if within two days of the order you:-

- pay the fee; or
- send the court evidence of your exemption from payment or remission of the fee

The court office at

is open between 10 am and 4 pm Monday to Friday. When corresponding with the court, please address forms or letters to the Court Manager and quote the claim number.

N173 Notice to Pay Fee

Notice of Issue (specified amount)

To the Claimant ['s Solicitor]

In the	
The court office at is open between 10 am & 4 pm Monday to Friday Tel:	
Claim No.	
Claimant (including ref.)	
Defendant(s)	
Issue fee	£

Your claim was issued on [ ].
The court sent it to the defendant by first class post on [ ]
and it will be deemed to be served on [ ].
The defendant has until [ ] to reply.

The defendant may

- **Pay** you your total claim.
- **File an acknowledgment of service.** This will allow the defendant 28 days from the date of service of your particulars of claim to file a defence or contest the court's jurisdiction.
- **Dispute the whole claim.** The court will send you a copy of the defence.
- **Admit that all the money is owed.** The defendant will send you a completed admission form and you may ask the court to enter judgment using the request below.
- **Admit that only part of your claim is owed.** The court will send you a copy of the reply form and you will have to decide what to do next.
- **Not reply at all.** You may ask the court to enter judgment using the request below.

Note: If the claim is disputed and the defendant is an individual, the claim may be transferred to either the defendant's local court or, if he or she is represented, the one nearest the business address of the solicitor.

For further information please turn over

Request for Judgment

In the	
Claim No.	
Claimant (including ref.)	
Defendant(s) (including ref.)	

- *Tick and complete either A or B. Remember to sign and date the form. Your signature certifies that the information you have given is correct.*
- *If the defendant has given an address on the form of admission to which correspondence should be sent. which is different from the address shown on the claim form, you must tell the court.*
- *Complete all the judgment details at C.*

A ☐ **The defendant has not filed an admission or defence to my claim or an application to contest the court's jurisdiction.**

Decide how and when you want the defendant to pay. You can ask for the judgment to be paid by instalments or in one payment.

B ☐ **The defendant admits that all the money is owed**

Tick only **one** box below and return the completed slip to the court.

☐ **I accept the defendant's proposal for payment**
Say how the defendant intends to pay. The court will send the defendant an order to pay. You will also be sent a copy.

☐ **The defendant has not made any proposal for payment**
Say how you want the defendant to pay. You can ask for the judgment to be paid by instalments or in one payment. The court will send the defendant an order to pay. You will also be sent a copy.

☐ **I do NOT accept the defendant's proposal for payment**
Say how you want the defendant to pay. Give your reasons for objecting to the defendant's offer of payment in Part D overleaf. Return this slip to the court **with the defendant's admission** (or a copy). The court will fix a rate of payment and send the defendant an order to pay. You will also be sent a copy.

C Judgment details

I would like the defendant to be ordered to pay

☐ (immediately)
☐ (by instalments of £ per month)
☐ (in full **by**)

Amount of claim as stated in claim form (including interest at date of issue)		
Interest since date of claim (if any) .... Period from .... to .... Rate ....%		
Court fees shown on claim		
Solicitor's costs (if any) on issuing claim		
Sub Total		
Solicitor's costs (if any) on entering judgment		
Sub Total		
Deduct amount (if any) paid since issue		
Amount payable by defendant		

I certify that the information given is correct

Signed .... **Date** ....
(Claimant)(Claimant's Solicitor)(Litigation friend)

N205A Notice of Issue (specified amount) and request for judgment

JANUARY 1999

Notes for Guidance

- The claim form must be served on the defendant within 4 months of the date of issue (6 months if you are serving outside England or Wales). You may be able to apply to extend the time for serving the claim form but the application must generally be made before the 4-month or 6-month period expires.
- It the defendant does not file an admission, defence or counterclaim, or if the defendant admits the whole claim with or without an offer of payment, you may ask for judgment. If you do not request judgment within 6 months of the end of the period for filing a defence, your claim mill be stayed. This means that the only action you can take is to apply to a judge for an order lifting of the stay.
- You should keep a record of any payments you receive from the defendant. If there is a hearing, or you wish to take steps to enforce the judgment, you will need to satisfy the court about the balance outstanding. You should give the defendant a receipt and payment in cash should always be acknowledged. You should tell the defendant how much he owes if he asks.
- **You must inform the court IMMEDIATELY if You receive any payment before a hearing date or after you have sent a request for enforcement to the court.**
- Further information in leaflet form can be obtained free of charge from the court.

Part D

Objections to the defendant's proposal for payment **Claim Number** ____________

Notice of Issue (unspecified amount)

In the	
The court office at is open between 10 am & 4 pm Monday to Friday Tel:	
Claim No.	
Claimant (including ref.)	
Defendant(s)	
Issue fee	£

To the Claimant['s Solicitor]

Your claim was issued on [ ].

The court sent it to the defendant by first class post on [ ] and it will be deemed to be served on [ ].

The defendant has until [ ] to reply.

The defendant may either

- **Pay an amount into court to satisfy your claim.** This is called a 'payment in satisfaction'. The court will notify you of the payment and you will have to decide whether to accept the amount offered.
- **Offer to pay you an amount to satisfy your claim and/or ask for time to pay.** The court will send you a copy of the defendant's reply and you will have to decide what you want to do.
- **Admit liability for your claim but not offer an amount in satisfaction.** The court will send you a copy of the defendants's reply and you will be able to request judgment for amount to be decided by the court and costs.
- **File an acknowledgment of service.** This will allow the defendant 28 days from the date of service of your particulars of claim to file a defence or contest the court's jurisdiction. The court will send you a notice that an acknowledgment has been filed.
- **Dispute your claim.** The court will send you a copy of the defence and tell you what to do next.
- **Not reply at all.** You may ask the court to enter judgment for an amount to be decided by the court by completing the tear off portion on this form. A hearing will be arranged to determine the amount the defendant should pay you. **If you do not request judgment within 6 months of the date for filing a defence, your claim will be stayed. This means that the only action open to you would be to apply to a judge for an order lifting the stay.**

✂ ---

Request for Judgment

In the	
Claim No.	
Claimant (including ref)	
Defendant(s)	

Notes:

- The court will notify both you and the defendant of any steps you should take to prepare for the hearing at which the court will decide what amount you are entitled to.
- You should notify the court immediately if your claim is settled or you decide that you do not wish to proceed.

To the court

The defendant has not filed an admission or defence to my claim, or an application to contest the court's jurisdiction and the time for doing so has expired.

I request that judgment be entered for an amount including costs, to be decided by the court.

Signed [ ] **Date** [ ]

(Claimant)(Claimant's solicitor)(Litigation friend)

N205B Notice of Issue (unspecified amount) and request for judgment

Notice of Issue
(non-money claim)

In the	
Claim No.	
Claimant (including ref.)	
Defendant(s)	
Issue fee	£

To the Claimant ['s Solicitor]

Your claim was issued on [ ].

[The court sent it to the defendant by the first class post on [ ] and it will be deemed served on [ ]. The defendant has until [ ] to reply.]

[The claim form [which includes particulars of claim] is returned to you, with the relevant response forms for you to serve them on the defendant[s].]

Notes for guidance

- The claim form and the particulars of claim, if served separately, must be served on the defendant within 4 months of the date of issue (6 months if you are serving outside England and Wales). You may be able to apply to extend the time for serving the claim form but the application must generally be made before the 4-month or 6-month period expires.
- You must inform the court immediately if your claim is settled or discontinued.

The defendant may

- **admit the truth of the whole or any part of your claim.** The court will send you a copy of the defendant's admission and tell you what to do next.
- **file an acknowledge of service.** This will allow the defendant 28 days from the date of service of your particulars of claim to file a defence or contest the court's jurisdiction.
- **dispute the whole claim.** The court will send you a copy of the defence.
- **not reply at all.** You may make an application to the court for judgment. A fee may be payable.

The court office at

is open between 10 am and 4 pm Monday to Friday. When corresponding with the court, please address forms or letters to the Court Manager and quote the claim number.

N205C Notice of Issue (non-money claim)

Notice of issue
(probate claim)

In the	Claim No.
Claimant(s)	
Defendant(s)	
	Issue fee

In the estate of deceased (Probate)

Your claim was issued on [ ]

[The court sent it to the defendants(s) by first class post on [ ]

and it will be deemed served on [ ]].

[The claim form (which includes particulars of claim) is returned to you, with the relevant response forms, for you to serve them on the defendant(s)]

Notes for guidance
The claim form and particulars of claim, if served separately, must be served on the defendant within 4 months of the date of issue (6 months if you are serving outside England and Wales). You may be able to apply to extend the time for serving the claim form but the application must generally be made before the 4 month or 6 month period expires.

You must inform the court immediately if your claim is settled.

The defendant must file an acknowledgment of service and defence within 28 days of service of the Particulars of Claim (whether they are served with the claim form or separately). A longer period applies if the defendant is served outside England and Wales.

Default judgment **cannot** be obtained in a probate claim.

If no defendant acknowledges service or files a defence, and the time for doing so has expired, you may apply to the court for an order, that the claim proceed to trial.

To

Ref.

N205D Notice of issue (probate) (10.01)

Notice of issue
(accelerated possession procedure)
(assured shorthold tenancy)

In the County Court

Claim No.

Claimant

Defendant

Issue fee

To the claimant ('s solicitor)

Ref.

Seal

Your claim was issued on

The court has sent it to the defendant and it will be deemed served on 20 .
(The court will send you a separate notice of service if no date is given here.)

The defendant has 14 days from service to file a defence. If a defence is filed, the court will send you a copy.

If the defendant does not file a defence, you may ask the court to make a possession order and (if applied for) an order for costs. Complete the tear-off portion of this form and return it to the court office.

On receiving either the defence or your request for an order, the court staff will refer the claim to a judge to decide whether or not to make an order without a hearing.

You have three months from the date by which the defendant should file a defence to file your request for an order. If by then the court has not received either a defence or your request, the claim will be stayed.

Request for possession order and costs
(accelerated possession procedure)
(assured shorthold tenancy)

In the County Court

Claim No.

Claimant

Defendant

To the court

The defendant has not filed a defence to my claim and the time for doing so has expired.

I ask the court to order the defendant to give me possession of the premises [and to pay my costs].

[The defendant has given me possession of the premises. I ask the court to order the defendant to pay my costs.]

Signed ______________________ Date ______________________
Claimant('s solicitor)(Litigation friend*(where the claimant is a child or a patient)*)

N206A Notice of issue (accelerated possession procedure)(assured shorthold tenancy)

Notice of issue
(possession claim)

In the

Claim No.

Claimant

Defendant

Issue fee

Your claim was issued on .

Seal

Date of hearing:

The claim will be heard on 20 at am/pm

at

Evidence

- If you intend to rely on any witness statements, you must file them in the court office and serve copies on all the other parties **no later than 2 clear working days before the hearing.**
- In a claim for possession against trespassers, any witness statements must be served with the claim form.

Hearing

At the hearing the court may:

- decide the claim;
- adjourn the claim to be heard on another day, or
- give case management directions and, in some cases, allocate the claim to a track.

Claimant's (solicitor's) address

Ref.

N206B Notice of issue (possession claim)

Notice of issue
(demotion/suspension claim)

Name of court	Claim No.
Name of Claimant	
Name of Defendant	
Date of hearing	

Your claim was issued on

SPECIMEN

Seal

Date of hearing:

The claim will be herd on 20 at am/pm
at

Evidence

- If you intend to rely on any witness statements, you must file them in the court office and serve copies on all the other parties **no later than 2 clear working days before the hearing.**

Hearing

At the hearing the court may:

- decide the demotion/suspension claim; or
- adjourn the claim to be heard on another day; and
- give case management directions.

Claimant's (solicitor's) address

Ref.

N206D Notice of issue (demotion/suspension claim) (08.05) HMCS

Claim Form
(CPR Part 8)

In the	
Claim No.	

Claimant

SEAL

Defendant(s)

Does your claim include any issues under the Human Rights Act 1998? ☐ Yes ☐ No

Details of claim *(see also overleaf)*

Defendant's name and address

	£
Court fee	
Solicitor's costs	
Issue date	

The court office at

is open between 10 am and 4 pm Monday to Friday. When corresponding with the court, please address forms or letters to the Court Manager and quote the case number.

N208 Claim form (CPR Part 8) (10.00) *Printed on behalf of The Court Service*

Claim No.	

Details of claim *(continued)*

Statement of Truth
*(I believe)(The Claimant believes) that the facts stated in these particulars of claim are true.
* I am duly authorised by the claimant to sign this statement

Full name ______________________________

Name of claimant's solicitor's firm ______________________________

signed ______________________ position or office held ______________________
*(Claimant)(Litigation friend)(Claimant's solicitor) (if signing on behalf of firm or company)

**delete as appropriate*

Claimant's or claimant's solicitor's address to which documents should be sent if different from overleaf. If you are prepared to accept service by DX, fax or e-mail, please add details.

Notes for claimant on completing a Part 8 claim form

- Please read all of these guidance notes before you begin completing the claim form. The notes follow the order in which information is required on the form.
- Court staff can help you fill in the claim form and give information about procedure once it has been issued. But they cannot give legal advice. If you need legal advice, for example, about the likely success of your claim or the evidence you need to prove it, you should contact a solicitor or a Citizens Advice Bureau.
- If you are filling in the claim form by hand, please use black ink and write in block capitals.
- You must file any written evidence to support your claim either in or with the claim form. Your written evidence must be verified by a statement of truth.
- Copy the completed claim form, the defendant's notes for guidance and your written evidence so that you have one copy for yourself, one copy for the court and one copy for each defendant. Send or take the forms and evidence to the court office with the appropriate fee. The court will tell you how much this is.

Notes on completing the claim form

Heading

You must fill in the heading of the form to indicate whether you want the claim to be issued in a county court or in the High Court (The High Court means either a District Registry (attached to a county court) or the Royal Courts of Justice in London).

Use whichever of the following is appropriate:

'In the ....County Court'
(inserting the name of the court)

or

'In the High Court of Justice.........................Division'
(inserting eg. 'Queen's Bench' or 'Chancery' as appropriate)
'............................District Registry'
(inserting the name of the District Registry)

or

'In the High Court of Justice.........................Division,
(inserting eg. 'Queen's Bench' or 'Chancery' as appropriate)
Royal Courts of Justice'

Claimant and defendant details

As the person issuing the claim, you are called the 'claimant'; the person you are suing is called the 'defendant'. Claimants who are under 18 years old (unless otherwise permitted by the court) and patients within the meaning of the Mental Health Act 1983 must have a litigation friend to issue and conduct court proceedings on their behalf. Court staff will tell you more about what you need to do if this applies to you.

You must provide the following information about yourself **and** the defendant according to the capacity in which you are suing and in which the defendant is being sued. When suing or being sued as:-

an individual:

All known forenames and surname, whether Mr, Mrs, Miss, Ms or Other (e.g. Dr) and residential address (**including** postcode and telephone and any fax or e-mail number) in England and Wales. Where the defendant is a proprietor of a business, a partner in a firm or an individual sued in the name of a club or other unincorporated association, the address for service should be the usual or last known place of residence **or** principal place of business of the company, firm or club or other unincorporated association.

Where the individual is:

under 18 write '(a child by Mr Joe Bloggs his litigation friend)' after the child's name.

a patient within the meaning of the Mental Health Act 1983 write '(by Mr Joe Bloggs his litigation friend)' after the patient's name.

trading under another name

you must add the words 'trading as' and the trading name e.g. 'Mr John Smith trading as Smith's Groceries'.

suing or being sued in a representative capacity

you must say what that capacity is e.g. 'Mr Joe Bloggs as the representative of Mrs Sharon Bloggs (deceased)'.

suing or being sued in the name of a club or other unincorporated association

add the words 'suing/sued on behalf of' followed by the name of the club or other unincorporated association.

a firm

enter the name of the firm followed by the words 'a firm' e.g. 'Bandbox - a firm' and an address for service which is either a partner's residential address or the principal or last known place of business.

a corporation (other than a company)

enter the full name of the corporation and the address which is either its principal office **or** any other place where the corporation carries on activities and which has a real connection with the claim.

a company registered in England and Wales

enter the name of the company and an address which is either the company's registered office **or** any place of business that has a real, or the most, connection with the claim e.g. the shop where the goods were bought.

an overseas company (defined by s744 of the Companies Act 1985)

enter the name of the company and either the address registered under s691 of the Act **or** the address of the place of business having a real, or the most, connection with the claim.

N208A - w3 Notes for claimant (CPR Part 8) (4.99) *Printed on behalf of The Court Service*

Details of claim

Under this heading you must set out either

- the question(s) you wish the court to decide; **or**
- the remedy you are seeking and the legal basis for your claim; **and**
- if your claim is being made under a specific CPR Part or practice direction, you must state which.

Defendant's name and address

Enter in this box the full name and address of the defendant to be served with the claim form (i.e. one claim form for each defendant). If the defendant is to be served outside England and Wales, you may need to obtain the court's permission.

Address for documents

Insert in this box the address at which you wish to receive documents, if different from the address you have already given under the heading 'Claimant'. The address you give must be either that of your solicitors or your residential or business address and must be in England or Wales. If you live or carry on business outside of England and Wales, you can give some other address within England and Wales.

Statement of truth

This must be signed by you, by your solicitor or your litigation friend, as appropriate.

Where the claimant is a registered company or a corporation the claim must be signed by either the director, treasurer, secretary, chief executive, manager or other officer of the company or (in the case of a corporation) the mayor, chairman, president or town clerk.

Notes for defendant (Part 8 claim form)

Please read these notes carefully - they will help you to decide what to do about this claim.

- You have 14 days* from the date on which you were served with the claim form to respond to the claim
- If you **do not return** the acknowledgment of service, you will be allowed to attend any hearing of this claim but you will **not** be allowed to take part in the hearing unless the court gives you permission to do so
- Court staff can tell you about procedures but they cannot give legal advice. If you need legal advice, you should contact a solicitor or Citizens Advice Bureau immediately

Time for responding

The completed acknowledgment of service must be returned to the court office within *(14 days) ( ) of the date on which the claim form was served on you. If the claim form was:

- sent by post, the *(14 days) ( ) begins 2 business days from the date of the postmark on the envelope.
- delivered or left at your address, the *(14 days) ( ) begins the second business day after it was delivered.
- handed to you personally, the *(14 days) ( ) begins on the second business day it was given to you.

Completing the acknowledgment of service

You should complete sections A - E as appropriate. In **all** cases you must complete sections F and G.

Section A - not contesting the claim

If you do **not** wish to contest the remedy sought by the claimant in the claim form, you should complete section A. In some cases the claimant may only be seeking the court's directions as to how to act, rather than seeking a specific order. In these circumstances, if you wish the court to direct the claimant to act in a certain way, give brief details.

Section B - contesting the claim

If you do wish to contest the remedy sought by the claimant in the claim form, you should complete section B. If you seek a remedy different from that sought by the claimant, you should give brief details in the space provided.

Section C - disputing the court's jurisdiction

You should indicate your intention by completing section C and filing an application disputing the court's jurisdiction within 14 days of filing your acknowledgment of service at the court. The court will arrange a hearing date for the application and tell you and the claimant when and where to attend.

Section D - objecting to use of procedure

If you believe that the claimant should not have issued the claim under Part 8 because:

- there **is** a substantial dispute of fact involved; and
- you do not agree that the rule or practice direction stated does provide for the claimant to use this procedure

you should complete section D setting out your reasons in the space provided.

Section E - written evidence

Complete this section if you wish to rely on written evidence. You must send your written evidence to the court with your acknowledgment of service. It must be verified by a statement of truth or the court may disallow it. If you have agreed with the other party(ies) an extension of time for filing your written evidence, a copy of your written agreement must be filed with your acknowledgment of service. Please note that the agreement can only extend time by 14 days from the date you file your acknowledgment of service.

Claims under section 1 of the Inheritance (Provision for Family and Dependants) Act 1975

A defendant who is a personal representative of the deceased must file and serve written evidence which must state to the best of that person's ability:

- full details of the value of the deceased's net estate, as defined in section 25 of the Act;
- the person or classes of person beneficially interested in the estate, and
  - the names and (unless they are parties to the claim) addresses of all living beneficiaries; and
  - the value of their interests in the estate so far as they are known;
- whether any living beneficiary (and if so, naming him) is a child or protected party within the meaning of Rule 21.1(2); and
- any facts which might affect the exercise of the court's powers under the Act.

Section F - name of defendant

Print your full name, or the full name of the defendant on whose behalf you are completing this form.

Serving other parties

You must send to any other party named on the claim form, copies of both the acknowledgment of service and any written evidence, at the same time as you file them with the court.

What happens next

The claimant may, within 14 days of receiving any written evidence from you, file further evidence in reply. On receipt of your acknowledgment of service, the court file will be referred to the judge for directions for the disposal of the claim. The court will contact you and tell you what to do next.

Statement of truth

This must be signed by you, by your solicitor or your litigation friend, as appropriate.

Where the defendant is a registered company or a corporation the statement must be signed by either the director, treasurer, secretary, chief executive, manager or other officer of the company or (in the case of a corporation) the mayor, chairman, president or town clerk.

**For claims under the Inheritance (Provision for Family and Dependants) Act 1975 the period is 21 days.*

N208C Notes for defendant (CPR Part 8) (07.09)

Notice of Issue
(Part 8 claim)

In the	
Claim No.	
Claimant (including ref.)	
Defendant(s)	
Issue fee	£

To the Claimant ['s Solicitor]

Your claim was issued under Part 8 of the CPR on [ ].

The court sent it with a copy of your witness statement(s) to the defendant by the first class post on [ ] and it will be deemed served on [ ]. The defendant has until [ ] to reply.

[As you requested the claim form is returned to you, with copy[ies] of your witness statement(s) for you to serve on the defendant[s]].

Notes for guidance

Service of the claim form

- The claim form must be served on the defendant within 4 months of the date of issue (6 months if you are serving outside England & Wales). You may apply for an order extending the time for serving the claim form but the application must generally be made before the 4-month or 6-month period expires.

Replying to the claim form

- the defendant must file an acknowledgment of service with the court together with any written evidence to be relied on within 14 days of service of the claim form. At the same time, the defendant must send copies to you and all other parties.
- if the defendant files written evidence, you will have 14 days from receiving it in which to file any further evidence in reply. You must at the same time send copies to all other parties to the claim.

The defendant may

- contest your claim and seek a remedy different from that sought by yourself
- object to your using this procedure and set out his reasons for doing so
- dispute the court's jurisdiction

What happens next

- the court file will be referred to a judge for directions for the disposal of the claim 14 days after the expiry of the time for filing the acknowledgment of service
- the file will not be referred if the court has already arranged a hearing date or given directions

Failure to reply

- if an acknowledgment of service is not filed, the defendant may attend any hearing in the claim but may not take part at the hearing unless the court gives permission.

You must inform the court immediately if your claim is settled or discontinued.

The court office at

is open between 10 am and 4 pm Monday to Friday. When corresponding with the court, please address forms or letters to the Court Manager and quote the claim number.

N209 Notice of Issue (CPR Part 8) (4.99) *Printed on behalf of The Court Service*

Acknowledgment of Service
(Part 8 claim)

You should read the 'notes for defendant' attached to the claim form which will tell you how to complete this form, and when and where to send it.

In the	
Claim No.	
Claimant (including ref)	
Defendant	

Tick and complete sections A - E as appropriate.
In all casesyou must complete sections F and G

Section A

☐ I do notintend to contest this claim

Give details of any order, direction, etc. you are seeking from the court.

Section B

☐ I intend to contest this claim

Give brief details of any different remedy you are seeking.

Section C

☐ I intend to dispute the court's jurisdiction
(Please note, any application must be filed within 14 days of the date on which you file this acknowledgment of servic

The court office at

is open between 10 am and 4 pm Monday to Friday. When corresponding with the court, please address forms or letters to the Court Manager and quote the claim number.

N210 Acknowledgment of Service (CPR Part 8) (3.01) *Printed on behalf of The Court Service*

Claim No.	

Section D

☐ I object to the claimant issuing under this procedure

My reasons for objecting are:

Section E

☐ I intend to rely on written evidence

My written evidence:

☐ is filed with this form

☐ will be filed within 14 days as agreed with the other party(ies). A copy of the written agreement is attached to this form

Section F

Full name of defendant filing this acknowledgment ______________________

Section G

Signed (To be signed by you or by your solicitor or litigation friend)

*(I believe)(The defendant believes) that the facts stated in this form are true. *I am duly authorised by the defendant to sign this statement

**delete as appropriate*

Position or office held (if signing on behalf of firm or company)

Date

Give an address to which notices about this case can be sent to you

Postcode

Tel. no.

if applicable	
Ref. no.	
fax no.	
DX no.	
e-mail	

Acknowledgment of Service
(Part 8 costs-only claim)

In the	
Claim No.	
Claimant (including ref)	
Defendant	

Tick and complete sections A - C as appropriate.

In all cases you must complete sections D and E.

Section A

☐ I do not intend to contest this claim

Section B

☐ I intend to contest the amount of costs claimed but not the making of an order for costs

Section C

I intend to

☐ contest the making of an order for costs

or

☐ seek a different remedy

or

☐ dispute the court's jurisdiction
(Please note, any application must be filed within 14 days of the date on which you file this acknowledgment of service)

Section D

Full name of defendant filing this acknowledgment

Section E

Signed (To be signed by you or by your solicitor or litigation friend)	*(I believe)(The defendant believes) that the facts stated in this form are true. *I am duly authorised by the defendant to sign this statement **delete as appropriate*
Position or office held (if signing on behalf of firm or company)	
Date	
Give an address to which notices about this case can be sent to you	Postcode
	Tel. no.

if applicable	
Ref. no.	
fax no.	
DX no.	
e-mail	

The court office at

is open between 10 am and 4 pm Monday to Friday. When corresponding with the court, please address forms or letters to the Court Manager and quote the claim number.

N210A Acknowledgment of Service (Part 8 costs-only claim) (12.02) *The Court Service Publications Branch*

Acknowledgment of Service

(Practice Direction 8B – Pre-Action Protocol for Low Value Personal Injury Claims in Road Traffic Accidents)

Name of court	
Claim no.	
Claimant *(including ref.)*	
Defendant *(including ref.)*	

Section A

Tick only **one** box

- ☐ I do not intend to contest the claim
- ☐ I intend to contest the amount of damages claimed but not the making of an order for damages
- ☐ I intend to contest the making of an order for damages
- ☐ I intend to dispute the court's jurisdiction
  (Please note, any application must be filed within 14 days of the date on which you file this acknowledgment of service)
- ☐ I object to the use of the procedure in Practice Direction 8B. My reasons for objecting are:

Section B

I want the claim to be determined by the court:

Tick only **one** box

- ☐ on the papers only
  (not applicable where the claimant is a child)
- ☐ at a hearing

Section C

Full name of defendant filing this acknowledgment

Section D

*[I believe] [The defendant believes] [The defendant's insurer believes] that the facts stated in this form are true.
*[I am duly authorised by the [defendant] [defendant's insurer] to sign this statement].

**delete as appropriate*

Signed

(To be signed by you, your insurer or by a solicitor on behalf of you or your insurer)

Position or office held

(If signing on behalf of firm or company)

Dated ☐☐/☐☐/☐☐☐☐

Phone no.

Give an address to which notices about this case can be sent to you

	If applicable	
	Fax no.	
	DX no.	
	Your ref.	
Postcode	E-mail	

N210B Acknowledgment of Service (Practice Direction 8B – Pre-Action Protocol for Low Value Personal Injury Claims in Road Traffic Accidents) (04.10)

Notes for defendant - Acknowledgment of Service

(Practice Direction 8B – Pre-Action Protocol for Low Value Personal Injury Claims in Road Traffic Accidents)

Please read these notes carefully – they will help you to decide what to do about this claim.

- You have 14 days from the date on which you were served with the claim form to respond to the claim.
- If you do not return the acknowledgment of service, you will be allowed to attend any hearing of this claim but you will not be allowed to take part in the hearing unless the court gives you permission to do so.
- Court staff can tell you about procedures but they cannot give legal advice. If you need legal advice, you should contact a solicitor or Citizens Advice Bureau immediately.

Time for responding

This completed acknowledgment of service must be returned to the court office within 14 days of the date on which the claim form was served on you. If the claim form was:

- sent by post, the 14 days begins 2 business days from the date of the postmark on the envelope.
- delivered or left at your address, the 14 days begins the second business day after it was delivered.
- handed to you personally, the 14 days begins on the second business day after it was given to you.

Completing the acknowledgment of service

Section A

You can only choose **one** of the following options in this section.

- **not contesting the claim**
  If you do not wish to contest the claim.
- **contesting the amount of damages**
  If you do wish to contest the amount of damages sought by the claimant in the claim form.
- **contesting an order for damages**
- **disputing the courts jurisdiction**
  Where you intend to dispute the court's jurisdiction you should file an application disputing the court's jurisdiction within 14 days of filing your acknowledgment of service at the court.
- **objecting to use of the procedure**
  If you believe that the claimant should not have started proceedings under Practice Direction 8B you should set out your reasons in the space provided.

Section B

You should state whether you want the claim to be determined by the court on the papers or at a hearing. A paper hearing is not available for a child claim.

Section C

Print your full name, or the full name of the defendant on whose behalf you are completing this form.

Section D

This must be signed by you, your solicitor, your insurer, your insurer's solicitor or your litigation friend, as appropriate.

Evidence - general

You may only file further evidence as set out in Practice Direction 8B (paragraphs 8.2 and 11.3).

Serving other parties

You must serve on any other party named on the claim form, copies of the acknowledgment of service at the same time as you file it with the court.

What happens next

On receipt of your acknowledgment of service, the court file will be referred to the judge for directions for the determination of the claim. The court will contact you and tell you what to do next.

Claim Form
(Additional claims- CPR Part 20)

In the	
Claim No.	

Claimant(s)

SEAL

Defendant(s)

Part 20 Claimant(s)

Part 20 Defendant(s)

Brief details of claim

Value

Defendant's name and address

	£
Amount claimed	
Court fee	
Solicitors costs	
Total amount	
Issue date	

The court office at

is open between 10 am and 4 pm Monday to Friday. When corresponding with the court, please address forms or letters to the Court Manager and quote the claim number.

N211 - w3 Claim Form (CPR Part 20 - additional claims)(4.99) *Printed on behalf of The Court Service*

Claim No.	

Particulars of Claim (attached)

Statement of Truth
*(I believe)(The Part 20 Claimant believes) that the facts stated in these particulars of claim are true.
* I am duly authorised by the Part 20 claimant to sign this statement

Full name ....

Name of Part 20 claimant's solicitor's firm ....

signed.. position or office held..
*(Part 20 Claimant)('s solicitor)(Litigation friend) (if signing on behalf of firm or company)
*delete as appropriate

Part 20 Claimant ('s solicitor's) address to which documents or payments should be sent if different from overleaf. If you are prepared to accept service by DX, fax or e-mail, please add details.

Nodiadau i hawlydd Rhan 20 ar lenwi ffurflen hawlio Rhan 20

- Os gwelwch yn dda, darllenwch yr holl nodiadau arweiniol hyn cyn dechrau llenwi'r ffurflen hawlio. Mae'r nodiadau yn dilyn yr un drefn â'r cwestiynau ar y ffurflen. Oni fyddwch yn codi eich hawliad Rhan 20 cyn neu ar yr un pryd ag y byddwch yn ffeilio eich amddiffyniad i'r prif hawliad (hynny yw, yr hawliad a wneir yn eich erbyn chi fel diffynnydd) bydd rhaid yn gyntaf i chi gael caniatâd y llys i wneud hynny.
- Gall staff y llys eich helpu i lenwi'r ffurflen hawlio a rhoi gwybod i chi am y drefniadaeth ar ôl codi'r hawliad. Ond ni allant roi cyngor cyfreithiol. Os oes arnoch angen cyngor cyfreithiol, er enghraifft ynghylch y tebygrwydd o lwyddo gyda'ch hawliad, neu'r dystiolaeth y bydd arnoch ei hangen i'w brofi, dylech gysylltu â thwrnai neu Ganolfan Cyngor ar Bopeth.
- Os ydych yn llenwi'r ffurflen hawlio mewn llawysgrifen, defnyddiwch inc du os gwelwch yn dda, ac ysgrifennwch mewn priflythrennau.
- Pan fyddwch wedi llenwi'r ffurflen hawlio, gwnewch gopïau o'r ffurflen hawlio a'r nodiadau arweiniol i'r diffynnydd, fel bod gennych un copi i chi eich hunan, un copi i'r llys, un copi i'r diffynnydd Rhan 20 a chopi i bob un o'r partïon eraill i'r prif hawliad. Anfonwch neu ewch a'r ffurflenni i swyddfa'r llys ynghyd â'r ffi briodol. Bydd y llys yn dweud wrthych faint yw'r swm.
- Oni bai fod y llys wedi gorchymyn fel arall, dylid cyflwyno'r ffurflen hawlio i'r diffynnydd Rhan 20 o fewn 14 diwrnod ar ôl ffeilio eich amddiffyniad, ynghyd â chopïau o'r holl ddatganiadau achos a ffeiliwyd yn y prif hawliad. Rhaid cyflwyno copïau o'r ffurflen hawlio Rhan 20 a manylion yr hawliad i'r partïon i'r prif hawliad hefyd, os ydynt ar wahân i'r prif hawliad.
- Ychwanegir y diffynnydd fel parti i'r prif hawliad, unwaith y cyflwynir y ffurflen hawlio Rhan 20 iddo.

Notes for Part 20 claimant on completing a Part 20 claim

- Please read all of these guidance notes before you begin completing the claim form. The notes follow the order in which information is required on the form. Unless you issue your Part 20 claim before or at the same time as filing your defence to the main claim, (in other words the claim being brought against you as defendant) you will first need to obtain the court's permission to do so.
- Court staff can help you fill in the claim form and give information about procedure once it has been issued. But they cannot give legal advice. If you need legal advice, for example about the likely success of your claim or the evidence you need to prove it, you should contact a solicitor or a Citizens Advice Bureau.
- If you are filling in the claim form by hand, please use black ink and write in block capitals.
- When you have completed the claim form, copy the claim form and the defendant's note for guidance so that you have one copy for yourself, one copy for the court, one copy for the Part 20 defendant and a copy for each of the other parties to the main claim. Send or take the forms to the court office with the appropriate fee, the court will tell you how much this is.
- Unless the court has ordered otherwise, the Part 20 defendant should be served with the claim form within 14 days of your defence being filed, together with copies of all the statements of case filed in the main claim. The parties to the main claim must also at the same time be served with copies of the Part 20 claim form and particulars of claim, if these are separate from the claim.
- The defendant is added as a party to the main claim once served with the Part 20 claim form.

Nodiadau ar lenwi'r ffurflen hawlio

Pennawd

Yr un fydd enw'r llys a rhif yr hawliad â'r hyn sydd ar y ffurflen hawlio yn y prif hawliad. Dylech gopïo'r manylion hynny ar eich ffurflen hawlio Rhan 20.

Notes on completing the claim form

Heading

The name of the court and the claim number will be the same on the claim form in the main claim. You should copy those details on to your Part 20 claim form.

N211A Nodiadau i'r hawlydd (RTS Rhan 20) (4.99)
Argraffwyd ar ran Y Gwasanaeth Llys

N211A Notes for claimant (CPR Part 20) (4.99)
Printed on behalf of The Court Service

Manylion yr hawlydd a'r diffynnydd

Dylech gopïo manylion yr hawlydd a'r diffynnydd o'r prif hawliad i'r blychau hawlydd a diffynnydd. Dylech ysgrifennu eich enw chi yn y blwch hawlydd Rhan 20, ac enw'r person yr ydych yn hawlio yn ei erbyn yn y blwch diffynnydd Rhan 20. Rhaid i hawlwyr sydd dan 18 oed (oni chaniateir yn wahanol gan y llys), a chleifion o fewn ystyr Deddf Iechyd Meddwl 1983, gael cyfaill cyfreitha i godi a chynnal achos llys ar eu rhan. Gall staff y llys ddweud rhagor am yr hyn fydd yn rhaid i chi ei wneud, os yw hyn yn berthnasol i chi.

Rhaid i chi roi'r wybodaeth ganlynol amdanoch eich hunan **ac** am y diffynnydd Rhan 20, ar sail y statws yr ydych chi yn siwio ac y mae y diffynnydd yn cael ei siwio.

Wrth siwio neu gael eich siwio fel:-

unigolyn

Pob enw blaen sydd yn wybyddus a'r cyfenw, un ai Mr, Mrs, Miss, Ms neu Arall (er enghraifft Dr) a'r cyfeiriad preswyl (**gan gynnwys** y côd post a'r rhif teleffon ac unrhyw rif ffacs neu gyfeiriad e-bost) yng Nghymru a Lloegr. Pan fo'r diffynnydd yn berchennog busnes, yn bartner mewn ffyrm neu'n unigolyn yn cael ei siwio yn enw clwb neu gymdeithas anghorfforedig arall, dylid defnyddio, fel cyfeiriad cyflwyno, y breswylfan arferol neu'r olaf y gwyddys amdani neu brif safle busnes y cwmni, ffyrm neu glwb neu gymdeithas anghorfforedig arall.

Pan fo'r unigolyn:

dan 18 oed ysgrifennwch '(plentyn trwy Mr Huw Puw ei gyfaill cyfreitha)' ar ôl enw'r plentyn

yn glaf o fewn ystyr Deddf Iechyd Meddwl 1983 ysgrifennwch '(trwy Mr Huw Puw ei gyfaill cyfreitha)' ar ôl enw'r claf

yn masnachu dan enw arall rhaid i chi ychwanegu'r geiriau 'yn masnachu fel' a'r enw masnachol, er enghraifft 'Mr John Jones yn masnachu fel Siop Siôn'

yn siwio neu'n cael ei siwio mewn swyddogaeth gynrychiadol rhaid i chi ddweud beth yw'r swyddogaeth honno, er enghraifft 'Mr Huw Puw fel cynrychiolydd Mrs Henrietta Puw (ymadawedig)'.

yn siwio neu'n cael ei siwio yn enw clwb neu gymdeithas anghorfforedig arall ychwanegwch y geiriau 'yn siwio/yn siwio ar ran' gydag enw'r clwb neu gymdeithas anghorfforedig arall yn dilyn.

ffyrm nodwch enw'r ffyrm gyda'r gair 'ffyrm' yn dilyn, er enghraifft 'Crempog - ffyrm' a chyfeiriad cyflwyno sydd un ai'n gyfeiriad preswyl partner, neu'r prif safle busnes, neu'r safle busnes olaf sy'n wybyddus.

corfforaeth (ac eithrio cwmnïau) rhowch enw llawn y gorfforaeth a chyfeiriad un ai ei phrif swyddfa **neu** unrhyw fan arall lle bydd y gorfforaeth yn cynnal gweithgareddau ac sydd â chysylltiad real â'r hawliad.

Claimant and defendant details

You should copy the claimant and defendant details from the main claim into the claimant and defendant boxes. You should enter your name into the Part 20 claimant box and the name of the person you are claiming against into the Part 20 defendant box. Claimants who are under 18 years old (unless otherwise permitted by the court), and patients within the meaning of the Mental Health Act 1983 must have a litigation friend to issue and conduct court proceedings on their behalf. Court staff will tell you more about what you need to do if this applies to you.

You must provide the following information about yourself and the Part 20 defendant according to the capacity in which you are suing and in which the defendant is being sued.

When suing or being sued as:-

an individual

All known forenames and surname, whether Mr, Mrs, Miss, Ms or Other (e.g. Dr) and residential address (**including** postcode, telephone and any fax or e-mail number) in England and Wales. Where the defendant is a proprietor of a business, a partner in a firm or an individual sued in the name of a club or other unincorporated association, the address for service should be the usual or last known place of residence or principal place of business of the company, firm or club or other unincorporated association.

Where the individual is:

under 18 write '(a child by Mr Joe Bloggs his litigation friend)' after the child's name.

a patient with the meaning of the Mental Health Act 1983 write '(by Mr Joe Bloggs his litigation friend)' after the patients name.

trading under another name you must add the words 'trading as' and the trading name e.g. 'Mr John Smith trading as Smith's Groceries'.

suing or being sued in a representative capacity you must say what capacity is e.g. 'Mr Joe Bloggs as the representative of Mrs Sharon Bloggs (deceased)'.

suing or being sued in the name of a club or other unincorporated association add the words 'suing/sued on behalf of' followed by the name of the club or other unincorporated association.

a firm enter the name of the firm followed by the words 'a firm' e.g. 'Bandbox - a firm' and an address for service which is either a partner's residential address or the principal or last known place of business.

a corporation (other than a company) enter the full name of the corporation and the address which is either its principal office or any other place where the corporation carries on activities and which has a real connection with the claim.

cwmni a gofrestrwyd yng Nghymru a Lloegr rhowch enw'r cwmni a chyfeiriad un ai'r swyddfa gofrestredig **neu** unrhyw safle busnes sydd â chysylltiad real, neu'r cysylltiad mwyaf â'r hawliad, er enghraifft y siop lle y prynwyd y nwyddau.

cwmni tramor (a ddiffinnir yn Adran 744 Deddf Cwmnïau 1985) rhowch enw'r cwmni ac un ai'r cyfeiriad a gofrestrwyd yn rhinwedd adran 691 y Ddeddf **neu** gyfeiriad safle busnes sydd â chysylltiad real, neu'r cysylltiad mwyaf â'r hawliad.

Manylion byr o'r hawliad

Noder: Dylech roi'r ffeithiau a'r manylion llawn am eich hawliad, gan nodi a ydych yn hawlio llog ai peidio, yn yr adran 'manylion yr hawliad' ***(gweler y nodyn dan 'Manylion yr Hawliad')***

O dan y pennawd **hwn** rhaid cynnwys:
- datganiad cryno o natur eich hawliad
- y feddyginiaeth a geisiwch

Gwerth

Noder:-
Os ydych yn codi eich hawliad Rhan 20 yn yr Uchel Lys, nid oes raid i chi roi datganiad gwerth

Os ydych yn codi'r hawliad yn y llys sirol ac yn hawlio swm pendant o arian ('swm penodol'), ysgrifennwch y swm gyferbyn â 'swm a hawlir' yn y blwch yng nghornel isaf y ffurflen hawlio ar y dde.

Os <u>nad</u> ydych yn hawlio swm pendant o arian ('swm amhenodol'), ysgrifennwch "Rwy'n disgwyl adennill swm sydd" o dan y pennawd 'Gwerth' ac i ddilyn hynny, pa un bynnag o'r canlynol sydd yn briodol i'ch hawliad:
- "ddim yn rhagor na £5,000" **neu**
- "yn rhagor na £5,000 ond ddim yn rhagor na £15,000" **neu**
- "yn rhagor na £15,000"

Os yw eich hawliad am 'ddim rhagor na £5,000' ac yn cynnwys hawliad am **anafiadau personol**, rhaid i chi hefyd ysgrifennu "Mae fy hawliad yn cynnwys hawliad am anafiadau personol. Rwy'n disgwyl ennill, fel iawndal am boen, dioddefaint a cholled mwynderau, swm sydd" ac i ddilyn, un ai:
- "ddim yn rhagor na £1,000" **neu**
- "yn rhagor na £1,000"

Os yw eich hawliad am 'ddim rhagor na £5,000' ac yn cynnwys hawliad ar sail **diffyg atgyweirio cyflwr tŷ** mewn perthynas ag adeiladau preswyl, rhaid i chi hefyd ysgrifennu "Mae fy hawliad yn cynnwys hawliad yn erbyn fy landlord am ddirywiad yng nghyflwr tŷ mewn perthynas ag adeiladau preswyl. Amcangyfrifir bod cost yr atgyweiriadau neu waith arall yn swm sydd" ac i ddilyn, un ai:
- "ddim yn rhagor na £1,000" **neu**
- "yn rhagor na £1,000"

a company registered in England and Wales enter the name of the company and an address which is either the company's registered office **or** any place of business that has a real, or the most, connection with the claim e.g the shop where the goods were bought

an overseas company (defined by s744 of the Companies Act 1985) enter the name of the company and either the address registered under s691 of the Act **or** the address of the place of business having a real, or the most, connection with the claim.

Brief details of claim

Note: The facts and full details about your claim and whether or not you are claiming interest, should be set out in the 'particulars of claim' ***(see note under 'Particulars of Claim')***

You must set out under **this** heading:
- a concise statement of the nature of your claim
- the remedy you are seeking

Value

Note:-
If you are issuing your Part 20 claim in the High Court, you do not have to give a statement of value.

If you are issuing in the county court and claiming a fixed amount of money (a 'specified amount') write the amount in the box at the bottom right-hand corner of the claim form against 'amount claimed'.

If you are <u>not</u> claiming a fixed amount of money (an 'unspecified amount') under 'Value' write "I expect to recover" followed by whichever of the following applies to your claim:
- "not more than £5,000" **or**
- "more than £5,000 but not more than £15,000" **or**
- "more than £15,000"

If your claim is for 'not more than £5,000' and includes a claim for **personal injuries,** you must also write "My claim includes a claim for personal injuries and the amount I expect to recover as damages for pain, suffering and loss of amenity is" followed by either:
- "not more than £1,000" **or**
- "more than £1,000"

If your claim is for 'not more than £5,000' and includes a claim for **housing disrepair** relating to residential premises, you must also write "My claim includes a claim against my landlord for housing disrepair relating to residential premises. The costs of the repairs and other work is estimated to be" followed by either:
- "not more than £1,000" **or**
- "more than £1,000"

"Rwy'n disgwyl adfer, fel iawndal am atgyweirio a gwaith arall, swm sydd" ac i ddilyn un ai:

- "ddim yn rhagor na £1,000" **neu**
- "yn rhagor na £1,000"

Os na ellwch bennu gwerth i'ch hawliad, ysgrifennwch "Ni allaf ddweud faint yr wyf yn disgwyl ei adennill".

"I expect to recover as damages in respect of repairs and other work" followed by either:

- "not more than £1,000" **or**
- "more than £1,000"

If you are not able to put a value on your claim, write "I cannot say how much I expect to recover".

Enw a chyfeiriad y diffynnydd

Yn y blwch hwn ysgrifennwch enw llawn a chyfeiriad y diffynnydd Rhan 20 sydd yn cael y ffurflen hawlio (hynny yw, un ffurflen hawlio i bob diffynnydd Rhan 20). Os bwriedir cyflwyno'r ffurflen y tu allan i Gymru a Lloegr, mae'n bosib y bydd yn rhaid i chi gael caniatâd y llys.

Defendant's name and address

Enter in this box the full names and address of the Part 20 defendant receiving the claim form (ie. one claim form for each Part 20 defendant). If the defendant is to be served outside of England and Wales, you may need to obtain the court's permission.

Manylion yr hawliad

Gellwch gynnwys manylion eich hawliad yn y blwch a ddarperir ar y ffurflen hawlio, neu mewn dogfen ar wahân, a ddylai fod â'r pennawd 'Manylion yr Hawliad'. Dylai gynnwys enwau'r partïon, y llys, rhif yr hawliad a'ch cyfeiriad chi ar gyfer cyflwyno, yn ogystal â datganiad gwirionedd. Dylech gadw copi i chi eich hunan, darparu un i'r llys ac un i bob un o'r partïon eraill yn y prif hawliad. Os yw manylion yr hawliad ar wahân, mae'n **rhaid** eu cyflwyno gyda'r ffurflen hawlio. Dylech hefyd atodi copïau o'r holl ddatganiadau achos sydd eisoes wedi eu cyflwyno yn y prif hawliad i'w cyflwyno i'r diffynnydd.

Rhaid i fanylion eich hawliad gynnwys

- datganiad cryno o'r ffeithiau yr ydych yn dibynnu arnynt
- datganiad (os yn briodol) i'r perwyl eich bod yn ceisio iawndal gwaethygedig neu iawndal cosbedigaethol
- manylion am unrhyw log a hawlir
- unrhyw faterion eraill sydd yn ofynnol i'ch math chi o hawliad fel a bennir yn y cyfarwyddyd ymarfer perthnasol

Particulars of claim

You may include your particulars of claim on the claim form in the space provided or in a separate document which you should head 'Particulars of Claim'. It should include the names of the parties, the court, the claim number and your address for service and also contain a statement of truth. You should keep a copy for yourself, provide one for the court, one for each defendant and one for all other parties in the main claim. Separate particulars of claim **must** be served with the claim form. You should also attach copies of all statements of case already served in the main claim for service on the defendant.

Your particulars of claim must include

- a concise statement of the facts on which you rely
- a statement (if applicable) to the effect that you are seeking aggravated damages or exemplary damages
- details of any interest which you are claiming
- any other matters required for your type of claim as set out in the relevant practice direction

Cyfeiriad ar gyfer dogfennau

Nodwch yn y blwch hwn y cyfeiriad lle y dymunwch dderbyn dogfennau os yw'n wahanol i'r cyfeiriad a roesoch eisoes o dan y pennawd 'Hawlydd'. Mae'n rhaid i'r cyfeiriad a roddwch fod un ai'n gyfeiriad eich twrnai neu eich cyfeiriad preswyl neu fusnes, ac y mae'n rhaid iddo fod yng Nghymru neu Loegr. Os ydych yn byw neu'n cynnal busnes y tu allan i Gymru a Lloegr, gellwch roi rhyw gyfeiriad arall o fewn Cymru a Lloegr.

Address for documents

Insert in this box the address at which you wish to receive documents and/or payments, if different from the address you have already given under the heading 'Claimant'. The address you give must be either that of your solicitors or your residential or business address and must be in England or Wales. If you live or carry on business outside England and Wales, you can give some other address within England and Wales.

Datganiad gwirionedd

Rhaid i hwn gael ei lofnodi gennych chi, gan eich twrnai neu gan eich cyfaill cyfreitha, fel sydd yn briodol.
Pan fo'r hawlydd yn gwmni cofrestredig neu'n gorfforaeth, rhaid i'r hawliad gael ei lofnodi un ai gan gyfarwyddwr, trysorydd, ysgrifennydd, prif weithredwr, rheolwr neu swyddog arall gyda'r cwmni, neu (yn achos corfforaeth) gan y maer, y cadeirydd, y llywydd neu glerc y dref.

Statement of truth

This must be signed by you, by your solicitor or your litigation friend, as appropriate.
Where the claimant is a registered company or a corporation the claim must be signed by either the director, treasurer, secretary, chief executive, manager or other officer of the company or (in the case of a corporation) the mayor, chairman, president or town clerk.

Notes for defendant on replying to the Part 20 claim form

Please read these notes carefully - they will help you decide what to do about this claim.

- You must reply to this claim form within 14 days of the date it was served on you. If the claim was
  - sent by post, the date of service is taken as the second day after posting (see post mark).
  - delivered or left at your address, the date of service will be the day after it was delivered.
  - handed to you personally, the 14 days begins on the day it was given to you.
- You may either
  - pay the amount claimed
  - admit the truth of all or part of the claim or
  - dispute the claim
- If you do not reply, the court will consider that you have admitted the claim and judgment may be entered against you.
- The notes below tell you what to do and which forms to use for your reply.
- Court staff can help you complete the forms of reply and tell you about court procedures. But they cannot give legal advice. If you need legal advice, for example about the likely success of disputing the claim, you should contact a solicitor or a Citizens Advice Bureau immediately.

Registration of Judgments: If the claim results in a judgment being made against you in a **county court**, your name and address may be entered in the Register of County Court Judgments. This may make it difficult for you to obtain credit.
Costs and Interest: Additional costs and interest may be added to the amount claimed on the front of the claim form if judgment is entered against you. In a county court, if judgment is for £5,000 or more, or is in respect of a debt which attracts contractual or statutory interest for late payment, the claimant may be entitled to further interest.

Your response and what happens next

How to pay

Do not bring any payments to the court - they will not be accepted.

When making payments to the claimant, quote the claimant's reference (if any) and the claim number.

Make sure that you keep records and can account for any payments made. Proof may be required if there is any disagreement. It is not safe to send cash unless you use registered post.

Admitting the Claim

Claim for a specified amount
Complete Form N9A and send it to the claimant at the address given for payment on the claim form within 14 days. You should at the same time send a copy to all the other parties to the main claim (in other words the claim where the Part 20 claimant is the defendant).

Claim for an unspecified amount
Complete Form N9C and send it to the court within 14 days. A copy will be sent to the claimant.

What happens next
The claimant may apply to the court for judgment to be entered on your admission. The court will arrange a hearing and tell you and the claimant where and when to attend.

Disputing the claim

Complete the form of defence (either N9B if the claim is for a specified amount or N9D if the claim is for an unspecified amount) and return it to the court within 14 days. On receipt of your defence, the court will arrange a hearing and tell you and the claimant when and where to attend. At the hearing the judge will usually give directions as to the future case management of the claim but may make any other order, e.g. striking out all or part of a statement of case.

If you need longer than 14 days to prepare your defence, complete the acknowledgment of service Form N213 and return it to the court. This will allow you 28 days from the date of service of the claim form to file your defence.

Contesting the court's jurisdiction

Complete the acknowledgment of service Form N213 and return it to the court within 14 days. You should make an application to the court within 28 days of service of the claim. An application form (N244) can be obtained from the court and a fee may be payable.

If you do nothing

If you do nothing or you send an acknowledgment of service to the court but fail to send your defence, you will be considered to have admitted the claim and be bound by any judgment or decision made in the main claim where it relates to this claim against you.

Statement of truth

This must be signed by you, by your solicitor or your litigation friend, as appropriate.

Where the defendant is **a registered company or a corporation** the response must be signed by either the director, treasurer, secretary, chief executive, manager or other officer of the company **or** (in the case of a corporation) the mayor, chairman, president or town clerk.

N211C Notes for defendant (CPR Part 20) (10.02)

The Court Service Publications Branch

Notice of Issue
(Part 20 claim)

In the	
Claim No.	
Claimant (including ref.)	
Defendant(s) (including ref.)	
Part 20 Claimant (including ref.)	
Part 20 Defendant(s)	
Issue fee	£

To the Claimant ['s Solicitor]

Your Part 20 claim was issued on [ ].

The court sent it and accompanying papers to the defendant by the first class post on [ ] and it will be deemed served on [ ]. The defendant has until [ ] to reply.

[As you requested the claim form [which includes particulars of claim] is returned to you, [with the relevant response forms] for you to serve them on the defendants[s]. You must also serve copies of any statements of case already filed in the main claim.]

Notes for guidance

Service
- The claim form must be served on the Part 20 defendant within 14 days of filing your defence to the main claim unless the court has directed otherwise.

Entering default judgment
- you will need the court's permission to enter judgment in default if you have **not** satisfied any default judgment against you in the main claim **or** you wish to obtain judgment for any remedy other than a contribution or an indemnity

The defendant may
- **admit the truth of the whole or any part of your claim.** You may apply to the court for judgment to be entered on the admission.
- **dispute all or part of your claim.** The court will arrange a hearing and tell you and the other parties to the claim when and where to attend. At the hearing the judge will usually give directions about the future case management of the claim but may make any other order considered appropriate, e.g. striking out all or part of a statement of case.
- **not reply at all.** The defendant will be considered to have admitted your claim and be bound by any judgment or decision made in the main claim where it relates to this claim.

You must inform the court immediately if your claim is settled or discontinued.

The court office at

is open between 10 am and 4 pm Monday to Friday. When corresponding with the court, please address forms or letters to the Court Manager and quote the claim number.

N212 Notice of Issue (CPR Part 20 claim)

Printed on behalf of The Court Service

Click here to reset form | Click here to print form

Acknowledgment of Service
(Part 20 claim)

Defendant's full name if different from the name given on the claim form

Name of court	
Claim No.	
Claimant (including ref.)	
Defendant(s) (including ref.)	
Part 20 Claimant (including ref.)	
Part 20 Defendant(s)	

Address to which documents about this claim should be sent (including reference if appropriate)

Postcode

	if applicable
Tel. no.	
Fax no.	
DX no.	
e-mail	

Tick the appropriate box

1. I intend to defend all of this claim ☐
2. I intend to defend part of this claim ☐
3. I intend to contest jurisdiction ☐
4. My date of birth is D D M M Y Y Y Y

If you file an acknowledgment of service but do not file a defence within 28 days of the date of service of the claim form, you will be considered to have admitted the claim and will be bound by any judgment entered against the Part 20 claimant in the main claim.

If you do not file an application within 28 days of the date of service of the claim form, it will be assumed that you accept the court's jurisdiction and judgment may be entered against you.

Part 20 claimant should alter where appropriate (if the claim form is to be served out of the jurisdiction see CPR rules 6.35 and 6.37(5).

Signed

(Defendant) (Defendant's solicitor) (Litigation friend)

Date

Position or office held
(if signing on behalf of firm, company or corporation)

The court office at

is open between 10 am and 4 pm Monday to Friday. When corresponding with the court, please address forms or letters to the Court Manager and quote the claim number.

N213 Acknowledgment of Service (CPR Part 20) (10.08)

Certificate of service

Name of court	Claim No.
Name of Claimant	
Name of Defendant	

On what day did you serve? ☐☐/☐☐/☐☐☐☐

What documents did you serve?
Please attach copies of the documents you have not already filed with the court.

On whom did you serve?
(If appropriate include their position e.g. partner, director).

How did you serve the documents? - *please tick the appropriate box*

☐ by first class post or other service which provides for delivery on the next business day

☐ by delivering to or leaving at a permitted place *(see notes overleaf)*

☐ by personally handing it to or leaving it with (.................time left, where document is other than a claim form) *(please specify)*

☐ by Document Exchange

☐ by fax machine (.................time sent, where document is other than a claim form) *(you may want to enclose a copy of the transmission sheet)*

☐ by other electronic means (.................time sent, where document is other than a claim form) *(please specify)*

☐ by other means permitted by the court *(please specify)*

Give the address where service effected, include fax or DX number, e-mail address or other electronic identification

Being the ☐ claimant's ☐ defendant's ☐ solicitor's ☐ litigation friend

☐ usual residence
☐ last known residence
☐ place of business
☐ principal place of business
☐ last known place of business

☐ principal office of the partnership
☐ principal office of the corporation
☐ principal office of the company
☐ other *(please specify)*

The date of service is *(see overleaf for guidance)* ☐☐/☐☐/☐☐☐☐

I believe that the facts stated in this certificate are true.

Full name

Signed

(Claimant) (Defendant) ('s solicitor) ('s friend)

Position or office held

(If signing on behalf of firm or company)

Date ☐☐/☐☐/☐☐☐☐

N215 Certificate of service (10.08)

Notes for guidance

Please note that these notes are only a guide and are not exhaustive. If you are in doubt you should r
Part 6 of the rules

Where to serve	
Nature of party to be served	**Permitted place of service**
Individual	Usual or last known residence
Individual being sued in the name of a business	Usual or last known residence; **or** place of business or last known place of business
Individual being sued in the name of a partnership	Usual or last known residence; **or** place of business or last known place of business of the partnership
Limited liability partnership	Principal office of the partnership; **or** any place of business of the partnership within the jurisdiction which has a real connection with the claim
Corporation (incorporated in England and Wales) other than a company	Principal office of the corporation; **or** any place of within the jurisdiction where the corporation carries on its activities and which has a real connection with the claim
Company registered in England and Wales	Principal office of the company or corporation; **or** any place of business of the company within the jurisdiction which has a real connection with the claim
Any other company or corporation	Any place within the jurisdiction where the corporation carries on its activities; **or** any place of business of the company within the jurisdiction

Personal Service - A document is served personally on an individual by leaving it with that individual. A document is served personally on a company or other corporation by leaving it with a person holdin senior position within the company or corporation. In the case of a partnership, you must leave it with partner or a person who at the time of service has the control or management of the partnership busin its principal place of business.

Service on a solicitor - Where a solicitor is authorised to accept service, see CPR rule 6.7.

Deemed Service - Rule 6.14. A document which is served in accordance with these rules or any relevant practice direction shall be deemed to be served on the day shown in the following table.

Method of service	**Deemed day of service**
First class post or other service which provides for delivery on the next business day.	The second day after it was posted, left with, delivered to or collected by the relevant service provider provided that day is a business day; or if not, the next business day after that day
Document exchange	The second day after it was left with, delivered to or collected by the relevant service provider provided that day is a business day; or if not, the next business day after that day
Delivering the document to or leaving it at a permitted address	If it is delivered to or left at the permitted address on a business day before 4.30pm, on that day; or in any other case, on the next business day after that day
Fax	If the transmission of the fax is completed on a business day before 4.30pm, on that day; or in any other case, on the next business day after the day on which it was transmitted
Other electronic method	If the email or other electronic transmission is sent on a business day before 4.30pm, on that day; or in any other case, on the next business day after the day on which it was sent
Personal service	If the document is served personally before 4.30pm on a business day, it is served on that day; or in any other case, on the next business day after that day

In this context 'business day' means any day except Saturday, Sunday or a bank holiday; and 'bank holi includes Christmas Day and Good Friday.

Service of documents on children and protected parties - The rules relating to service on children and protected parties are contained in rule 6.13.

Claim Forms - The general rules about service are subject to the special rules about service of claim forms contained in rules 6.3 to 6.19.

Notice of non-service

In the	
Claim No.	
Local No.	
Claimant (including ref)	
Defendant	
Date	

Take Notice that the court has attempted to serve the

[claim form]

[particulars of claim]

[application for
please specify]

[[order][judgment] of *date*]

[*other to be specified*]

by first class post and the envelope has been returned by the Post Office marked:

["Not known at the address given"]

["Gone away"]

["No such address"]

["Insufficient address"]

[The document has been returned to the Home Court and any further correspondence should be sent there.]

You must now attempt service of the document yourself

The court office at

is open between 10 am and 4 pm Monday to Friday. Address all communications to the Court Manager quoting the claim number.

N216 Notice of non-service

Order for Substituted Service

In the	
Claim No.	
Claimant (including ref)	
Defendant	

Seal

Upon reading the evidence of

dated

[Master] [District Judge] **ORDERED**

[that the delivery of a sealed copy of the issued in this claim, together with a sealed copy of this order, to an adult at

being the usual or last known address [or place of business] of the defendant]

[that the posting of a sealed copy of the issued in this action, together with a sealed copy of this order, by [special delivery][recorded delivery] post addressed to the defendant at

being the usual or last known address [or place of business] of the defendant]

[that notice of the issued in this action be published in the newspaper and that publication of such notice]

shall be deemed to be good and sufficient service of the on the defendant [on the day after it was delivered][on the day it was published]

Dated

The court office at

is open between 10 am and 4 pm Monday to Friday. Address all communications to the Court Manager quoting the claim number.

N217 Order of Substituted Service

Notice of service on partner

In the	
Claim No.	
Claimant (including ref.)	
Defendant	

The (claim form) (particulars of claim) served with this notice (is) (are) served on you

(tick only one box)

☐ as a partner of the business

☐ as a person having control or management of the partnership business

☐ as both a partner and as a person having control or management of the partnership business

named in the claim form (particulars of claim).

Signed ______ **Date** ______

Claimant ('s solicitor)

N218 -w3- Notice of service on partner (4.99) *Produced on behalf of The Court Service*

Request for judgment and reply to admission (specified amount)

In the	
Claim No.	
Claimant (including ref)	
Defendant (including ref)	

Complete section A or B.
If you complete section A you must also confirm, where applicable, that particulars of claim have been served in accordance with the rules.

In all cases you must complete sections C and D.
If the defendant has given an address on the form of admission to which correspondence should be sent, which is different from the address shown on the claim form, you must tell the court.

Remember to sign and date the form. Your signature certifies that the information you have given is correct.

A ☐ **The defendant has not filed an admission or defence to my claim**

☐ I confirm that particulars of claim have been served on the defendant in accordance with the rules.

Now complete section C and all the judgment details at section D. Decide how and when you want the defendant to pay. You can ask for the judgment to be paid by instalments or in one payment.

B ☐ **The defendant admits that all the money is owed**

Tick only **one** box below and complete section C and all the judgment details at section D.

☐ **I accept the defendant's proposal for payment**
Say how the defendant intends to pay. The court will send the defendant an order to pay. You will also be sent a copy.

☐ **The defendant has not made any proposal for payment**
Say how you want the defendant to pay. You can ask for the judgment to be paid by instalments or in one payment. The court will send the defendant an order to pay. You will also be sent a copy.

☐ **I do NOT accept the defendant's proposal for payment**
Say how you want the defendant to pay. Give your reasons for objecting to the defendant's offer of payment on the back of this form. Send this form to the court **with defendant's admission N9A.** The court will fix a rate of payment and send the defendant an order to pay. You will also be sent a copy.

C Defendant's date of birth

☐ Defendant's date of birth is not stated in the form of reply but is known to the claimant as: ☐☐/☐☐/☐☐☐☐

☐ Defendant's date of birth is not stated in the form of reply and is not known to the claimant.

D Judgment details

I would like the defendant to be ordered to pay:

☐ immediately

☐ by instalments of £ ______ per month

☐ in full by ☐☐/☐☐/☐☐☐☐

Amount of claim as admitted (including interest at date of issue)	
Interest since date of claim (if any) Period from .... to ______ Rate ___ %	
Court fees shown on claim	
Solicitor's costs (if any) on issuing claim	
Sub Total	
Solicitor's costs (if any) on entering judgment	
Sub Total	
Deduct amount (if any) paid since issue	
Amount payable by defendant	

I certify that the information given is correct.

Signed ______________________
(Claimant) (Claimant's solicitor) (Litigation friend)

Position or office held ______________________
(if signing on behalf of firm or company)

Date ☐☐/☐☐/☐☐☐☐

Please return the completed form to the court.

The court office at

is open between 10 am and 4 pm Monday to Friday. When corresponding with the court, please address forms and letters to the Court Manager and quote the claim number.

N225 Request for judgment and reply to admission (specified amount) (04.09)

Notice of Part Admission (specified amount)

To the Claimant['s Solicitor]

In the	
Claim No.	
Claimant (including ref)	
Defendant (including ref)	
Date	

The defendant has partly admitted your claim (see the attached forms N9A and N9B)

Please tell the court what you wish to do by completing the lower half of this form and returning it to the court on or before [ ]
At the same time you must send a copy to the defendant. If you do not return this form to the court by the date shown, your claim will be stayed. No further action will be taken by the court until the form is received.

You must tick box A or B. If you tick box B you must also complete the details in that part and part C.

Remember to sign and date the notice.

A ☐ I DO NOT accept the defendant's part admission

If you tick this box the claim will proceed as a defended claim. If the defendant is an individual and lives in, or carries on business in, another court's area, the claim may be transferred to that court. You and the defendant will be sent an allocation questionnaire and the date by which it must be returned to the court. The information you give will help a judge decide whether your case should be dealt with in the small claims, fast or multi-track. Leaflets telling you more about the tracks are available from the court office. You will be sent a notice of allocation setting out the judge's decision.

B ☐ I ACCEPT the amount admitted by the defendant in satisfaction of my claim

Tick only **one** box and follow the instructions given.

☐ **I accept the defendant's proposal for payment**

Complete all the judgment details at C. The court will enter judgment in accordance with the offer and will send the defendant an order to pay. You will also be sent a copy.

☐ **The defendant has not made any proposal for payment**

Complete all the judgment details at C. Say how you want the defendant to pay. You can ask for the judgment to be paid by instalments or in one payment. The court will send the defendant an order to pay. You will also be sent a copy.

☐ **I do NOT accept the defendant's proposal for payment**

Complete all the judgment details at C and say how you want the defendant to pay. Give your reasons for objecting to the defendant's offer of payment in the space opposite. (Continue on the back of this form if necessary.) The court will fix a rate of payment and send the defendant an order to pay. You will also be sent a copy.

C Judgment details

If you are not accepting the defendant's proposal for payment, say how you would like the judgment to be paid.

I would like the judgment to be paid

☐ (immediately)

☐ (by instalments of £ per month)

☐ (in full by)

Amount of claim as admitted	
Court fees entered on claim	
Solicitor's costs (if any) on issuing claim	
Sub Total	
Solicitor's costs (if any) on entering judgment	
Sub Total	
Deduct amount (if any) paid since issue	
Amount payable by defendant	

I certify that the information given is correct

Signed . . . . **Dated** . . . .

N225A Notice of part admission (specified amount)

Notice of Admission (unspecified amount)

To the Claimant['s Solicitor]

In the	
Claim No.	
Claimant (including ref)	
Defendant (including ref)	
Date	

Important notes for claimant

- Enclosed with this notice is a copy of the defendant's admission of your claim (Form N9C).
- You must tick either A or C **or** complete B and D and return the form to the court **on or before [ ]**. At the same time you must send a copy to the defendant. If you do not return the form by this date, your claim will be stayed.No further action will be taken by the court until the form is received.
- Remember to sign and date the notice.

A ☐ I DO NOT accept the amount offered by the defendant in satisfaction of my claim. I wish judgment to be entered for an amount to be decided by the court.

The court will enter judgment and refer the court file to a judge for directions for management of the case. You and the defendant will be sent a copy of the court's order.

B ☐ I ACCEPT the amount admitted by the defendant in satisfaction of my claim

Tick only **one** box and follow the instructions given.

☐ **I accept the defendant's proposal for payment**

Complete all the judgment details at D. The court will enter judgment in accordance with the offer and will send the defendant an order to pay. You will also be sent a copy.

☐ **I do NOT accept the defendant's proposal for payment**

Complete all the judgment details at D and say how you want the defendant to pay. Give your reasons for objecting to the defendant's offer of payment in the space opposite. (Continue on the back of this form if necessary.) The court will fix a rate of payment and send the defendant an order to pay. You will also be sent a copy.

C ☐ The defendant has admitted liability but has not made any proposal for payment

The court will enter judgment and refer the court file to a judge for directions for management of the case. You and the defendant will be sent a copy of the court's order.

D Judgment details

If you are not accepting the defendant's proposal for payment, say how you would like judgment to be paid.

I would like the judgment to be paid

☐ (immediately)

☐ (by instalments of £ per month)

☐ (in full by)

Enter amounts as shown	£	
Amount of offer		
Court fees entered on claim		
Solicitor's costs (if any) on issuing claim		
Solicitor's costs (if any) on entering judgment		
Sub Total		
Deduct amount (if any) paid since issue		
Balance payable by defendant		

I certify that the information given is correct

Signed .... **Date** ....

N226 Notice of Admission (unspecified amount)

Request for judgment by default
(amount to be decided by the court)

Click here to reset form | Click here to print form

In the	
Claim No.	
Claimant (including ref)	
Defendant	

To the court

The defendant has not filed (an acknowledgment of service)(a defence) to my claim and the time for doing so has expired.

I request judgment to be entered against the defendant for an amount to be decided by the court and costs.

Defendant's date of birth (if known) D D M M Y Y Y Y

Signed (Claimant)(Claimant's solicitor)(Litigation friend)

Position or office held (if signing on behalf of firm or company)

Date

Note: The court will enter judgment and refer the court file to a judge who will give directions for the management of the case including its allocation to track.

The Court Manager

The court office at

is open between 10 am and 4 pm Monday to Friday. When corresponding with the court, please address forms or letters to the Court Manager and quote the claim number.

N227 Request for judgment by default (amount to be decided by the court) (04.06) HMCS

Notice of Admission – Return of Goods

(hire-purchase or conditional sale)

To the Claimant['s solicitor]

In the	
Claim No.	
Claimant (including ref)	
Defendant (including ref)	
Date	

Enclosed with this notice is a copy of the defendant's admission of your claim

- *Tick and complete either A or B and make sure that the judgment details at C are completed.*
- *Remember to sign and date the form. Your signature certifies that the information you have given is correct.*
- *Return the form to the court within 14 days.*

A ☐ I DO NOT accept the amount admitted by the defendant in satisfaction of my claim

You should attend court on the day fixed for the hearing. If you do not attend, an order may be made in your absence.

B ☐ I ACCEPT the amount admitted by the defendant in satisfaction of my claim

Tick only **one** box below and follow the instructions given.

☐ **I accept the defendant's proposal for payment**

Complete all the judgment details at C. The court will make an order under sections 133 and 135 of the Consumer Credit Act 1974 for the return of the goods, suspended in accordance with the offer.

You will not have to attend court on the day fixed for the hearing.

☐ **The defendant has not made any proposal for payment**

Complete all the judgment details at C. Say how you want the defendant to pay. You can ask for the judgment to be paid by instalments or in one payment. The court will send the defendant an order to pay. You will also be sent a copy.

☐ **I do NOT accept the defendant's proposal for payment**

Complete all the judgment details at C and say how you want the defendant to pay. Give your reasons for objecting to the defendant's offer of payment in the space opposite. (Continue on the back of this form if necessary.) The court will fix a rate of payment and send the defendant an order to pay. You will also be sent a copy.

C Judgement details

If you are not accepting the defendant's offer, say how you would like the judgement to be paid.

I would like the judgment to be paid

☐ (immediately)

☐ (by instalments of £ per month)

☐ (in full by)

....

List goods to be returned...

Enter amounts as shown	£	
Amount of the unpaid balance of total price as stated in the claim		
Deduct amount (if any) paid since issue		
Balance of total price		
Court fees entered on claim		
Solicitor's costs (if any) on issuing claim		
Solicitors's costs (if any) on entering judgment		
Total of fees and solicitor's costs		

I certify that the information given is correct

Signed .... **Date** ....

N228 Notice of Admission – Return of Goods (hire-purchase or conditional sale agreement)

Click here to reset form | Click here to print form

Certificate of suitability of litigation friend

If you are acting

- **for a child**, you must serve a copy of the completed form on a parent or guardian of the child, or if there is no parent or guardian, the carer or the person with whom the child lives
- **for a protected party**, you must serve a copy of the completed form on one of the following persons with authority in relation to the protected party as: (1) the attorney under a registered enduring power of attorney (2) the donee of the lasting power of attorney; (3) the deputy appointed by the Court of Protection; or if there is no such person, an adult with whom the protected party resides or in whose care the protected party is. You must also complete a certificate of service (obtainable from the court office)

You should send the completed form to the court with the claim form (if acting for the claimant) or when you take the first step on the defendant's behalf in the claim together with the certificate of service (if applicable).

Name of court	
Claim No.	
Claimant (including ref.)	
Defendant (including ref.)	

You do not need to complete this form if you are a deputy appointed by the Court of Protection with power to conduct proceedings on behalf of the protected party.

I consent to act as litigation friend for ______________________
(claimant)(defendant)

I believe that the above named person is a

☐ child ☐ protected party *(give your reasons overleaf and attach a copy of any medical evidence in support)*

I am able to conduct proceedings on behalf of the above named person competently and fairly and I have no interests adverse to those of the above named person.

*I undertake to pay any costs which the above named claimant may be ordered to pay in these proceedings subject to any right I may have to be repaid from the assets of the claimant.

* delete if you are acting for the defendant

Please write your name in capital letters

☐Mr ☐Mrs ☐Miss Surname ______________________

☐Ms ☐Other ________ Forenames ______________________

Address to which documents in this case are to be sent.

I certify that the information given in this form is correct

Signed ______________________

Date ______________________

The court office at

is open between 10 am and 4 pm Monday to Friday. When corresponding with the court, please address forms or letters to the Court Manager and quote the claim number.

N235 Certificate of suitability of litigation friend (10.07)

Claim No.	

My reasons for believing that the (claimant)(defendant) is a protected party are:-

Notice of Defence that Amount claimed has been paid

In the	
Claim No.	
Claimant (including ref.)	
Defendant (including ref.)	

To the Claimant ['s Solicitor]

The defendant says that the amount you are claiming has been paid (see attached Form N9B).

Please tell the court what you wish to do by completing the lower half of this form and returning it to the court on or before [ ]. You must send a copy of the completed form to the defendant as well as to the court.

- If you disagree with the defendant and wish to proceed with your claim, the court will contact you and tell you what to do next. If the defendant is an individual and lives in, or the defendant's solicitor's business is in, another court's area, the claim may be transferred to that court.
- If you do not return this form to the court by the date shown, your claim will be stayed. The only action which you will be able to take will be to apply to a judge for an order lifting the stay. A fee is payable on the application.

Claimant's reply

In the	
Claim No.	
Claimant (including ref.)	
Defendant (including ref.)	

To the court

I have read Form N9B and

please tick 1 or 2 and 3

1. ☐ I wish to proceed with the claim

or

2. ☐ I do not wish to proceed with the claim.

and

3. ☐ I have sent a copy of this completed form to the defendant.

Signed

(Claimant)(Claimant's Solicitor)(Litigation friend)

Position or office held (if signing on behalf of firm or company)

Date

The court office at

is open between 10 am and 4 pm Monday to Friday. Address all communication to the Court Manager quoting the claim number

N236 Notice of Defence that Amount Claimed has been Paid - Claimant's Reply

Notice of payment into court
(under order - Part 37)

In the	
Claim No.	
Claimant (including Ref.)	
Defendant (including Ref.)	
Date	

To the [Claimant(s)][Defendant (s)][Solicitor] and to the court

TAKE NOTICE the [claimant][defendant] has paid £ into court pursuant to the order dated

And the [claimant][defendant] does not wish the payment to be treated as a payment in satisfaction.

Signed ______________________
[Claimant][Defendant] ('s solicitor)

Position held ______________________
(if signing on behalf of a firm or company)

Date ____________

Note:

Payment must be made to the Court Funds Office, 22 Kingsway, London, WC2B 6LE and accompanied by a completed Form100 and a sealed copy of the order/judgment.

Do not take or send payments to the court which made the order - they will not be accepted. Cheques must be made payable to 'The Accountant General of the Supreme Court'.

Copies of Form100 are available from every county court office, the Court Funds Office or from the Court Service website: www.courtservice.gov.uk

A copy of this notice must be sent to the other side and to the court when payment into court is made. If the payment is to be treated as a payment in satisfaction, Form N242A Notice of payment into court (in satisfaction - Part 36) should be used instead.

N242 Notice of payment into court (under order Part 37)

Notice of offer to settle - Part 36

Name of court *(If proceedings have started)*	
Claim No. (or other ref)	
Claimant (including ref)	
Defendant (including ref)	

To the Offeree ('s Solicitor) *(Insert name and address)*

Take notice the (defendant)(claimant) offers to settle the claim. This offer is intended to have the consequences of Part 36. If the offer is accepted within ________ days (must be at least 21 days) of service of this notice the defendant will be liable for the claimant's costs in accordance with Rule 36.10 of the Civil Procedure Rules.

The offer is to settle:

(tick as appropriate)

☐ the whole of the claim

☐ part of the claim *(give details below)*

☐ a certain issue or issues in the claim *(give details below)*

The offer is:

(Insert details - expand box as necessary)

Note: Rule 36.5 specifies details that must be included in an ofer including periodical payments of damages for future pecuniary loss.

Rule 36.11 requires that an offer by a defendant to pay a sum of money (other than periodical payments) must be paid within 14 days of acceptance.

☐ It (does)(does not) take into account all(part) of the following counterclaim:

(give details of the counterclaim)

:**42A** Notice of offer to settle - Part 36 (in settlement) (04.07)

Include only if claim for provisional damages

☐ The offer is made in satisfaction of the claim on the assumption that the claimant will not [develop (state the disease)] **OR** [suffer (state type of deterioration)].

But if that does occur, the claimant will be entitled to claim further damages at any time before (insert date).

OR

☐ This offer does not include an offer in respect of the claim for provisional damages.

To be completed by defendants only

☐ This offer is made without regard to any liability for recoverable benefits under the Social Security (Recovery of Benefits Act) 1997.

OR

☐ This offer is intended to include any relevant deductible benefits for which I am liable under the Social Security (Recovery of Benefits Act) 1997.

The amount of [£] is offered by way of gross compensation.

[I have not yet received a certificate of recoverable benefits]

OR

[The following amounts in respect of the following benefits are to be deducted (insert details)

Type of benefit **Amount**

The net amount offered is therefore [£0.00]]

Signed

Offeror('s solicitor)

Position held (If signing on behalf of a firm or company)

Date

Application notice

For help in completing this form please read the notes for guidance form N244Notes.

Name of court	
Claim no.	
Warrant no. (if applicable)	
Claimant's name (including ref.)	
Defendant's name (including ref.)	
Date	

1. What is your name or, if you are a solicitor, the name of your firm?

2. Are you a ☐ Claimant ☐ Defendant ☐ Solicitor

   ☐ Other *(please specify)*

   If you are a solicitor whom do you represent?

3. What order are you asking the court to make and why?

4. Have you attached a draft of the order you are applying for? ☐ Yes ☐ No

5. How do you want to have this application dealt with? ☐ at a hearing ☐ without a hearing

   ☐ at a telephone hearing

6. How long do you think the hearing will last? ☐ Hours ☐ Minutes

   Is this time estimate agreed by all parties? ☐ Yes ☐ No

7. Give details of any fixed trial date or period

8. What level of Judge does your hearing need?

9. Who should be served with this application?

10. What information will you be relying on, in support of your application?

- ☐ the attached witness statement
- ☐ the statement of case
- ☐ the evidence set out in the box below

If necessary, please continue on a separate sheet.

Statement of Truth

(I believe) (The applicant believes) that the facts stated in this section (and any continuation sheets) are true

Signed ______________________ Dated ______________________
Applicant('s Solicitor)('s litigation friend)

Full name

Name of applicant's solicitor's firm ______________________

Position or office held ______________________
(if signing on behalf of firm or company)

11. Signature and address details

Signed Dated
Applicant('s Solicitor)('s litigation friend)

Position or office held
(if signing on behalf of firm or company)

Applicant's address to which documents about this application should be sent

	If applicable	
	Phone no.	
	Fax no.	
Postcode	DX no.	
	Ref no.	

E-mail address	

2

Application Notice (Form N244) – Notes for Guidance

Court Staff cannot give legal advice. If you need information or advice on a legal problem you can contact Community Legal Service Direct on 0845 345 4 345 or www.clsdirect.org.uk, or a Citizens Advice Bureau. Details of your local offices and contact numbers are available via their website www.citizensadvice.org.uk

Paying the court fee
A court fee is payable depending on the type of application you are making. For example:

- To apply for judgment to be set aside
- To apply to vary a judgment or suspend enforcement
- To apply for a summons or order for a witness to attend
- To apply by consent, or without service of the application notice, for a judgment or order.

No fee is payable for an application by consent for an adjournment of a hearing if it is received by the court at least 14 days before the date of the hearing.

What if I cannot afford the fee?
If you show that a payment of a court fee would involve undue hardship to you, you may be eligible for a fee concession.

For further information, or to apply for a fee concession, ask court staff for a copy of the combined booklet and form EX160A - Court fees - Do I have to pay them? This is also available from any county court office, or a copy of the leaflet can be downloaded from our website www.hmcourts-service.gov.uk

Completing the form

Question 3
Set out what order you are applying for and why; e.g. to adjourn the hearing because..., to set aside a judgment against me because... etc.

Question 5
Most applications will require a hearing and you will be expected to attend. The court will allocate a hearing date and time for the application. Please indicate in a covering letter any dates that you are unavailable within the next six weeks.

The court will only deal with the application 'without a hearing' in the following circumstances.

- Where all the parties agree to the terms of the order being asked for;
- Where all the parties agree that the court should deal with the application without a hearing, or
- Where the court does not consider that a hearing would be appropriate.

Telephone hearings are only available in applications where at least one of the parties involved in the case is legally represented. Not all applications will be suitable for a telephone hearing and the court may refuse your request.

Question 6
If you do not know how long the hearing will take do not guess but leave these boxes blank.

Question 7
If your case has already been allocated a hearing date or trial period please insert details of those dates in the box.

Question 8
If your case is being heard in the High Court or a District Registry please indicate whether it is to be dealt with by a Master, District Judge or Judge.

Question 9
Please indicate in the box provided who you want the court to send a copy of the application to.

Question 10
In this section please set out the information you want the court to take account of in support of the application you are making.
If you wish to rely on:

- **a witness statement,** tick the first box and attach the statement to the application notice. A witness statement form is available on request from the court office.
- **a statement of case,** tick the second box if you intend to rely on your particulars of claim or defence in support of your application.
- **written evidence** on this form, tick the third box and enter details in the space provided. You must also complete the statement of truth. Proceedings for contempt of court may be brought against a person who signs a statement of truth without an honest belief in its truth.

Question 11
The application must be signed and include your current address and contact details. If you agree that the court and the other parties may communicate with you by Document Exchange, telephone, facsimile or email, complete the details

Before returning your form to the court

Have you:

- signed the form on page 2,
- enclosed the correct fee or an application for fee concession,
- made sufficient copies of your application and supporting documentation. You will need to submit one copy for each party to be served and one copy for the court.

N244 Notes Application Notice (Form N244) – Notes for Guidance (07.08)

Notice of Hearing of Application

In the	
Claim No.	
Claimant (including ref)	
Defendant (including ref)	
Date	

To [Claimant][Defendant]['s solicitor]

The hearing of the [claimant's][defendant's] application for

(see copy attached) will take place at [am][pm] on the of

at

The court office at

is open between 10 am and 4 pm Monday to Friday. When corresponding with the court, please address forms or letters to the Court Manager and quote the claim number.

N244A Notice of Hearing of Application

Notice of funding of case or claim

Notice of funding by means of a conditional fee agreement, insurance policy or undertaking given by a prescribed body should be given to the court and all other parties to the case:

- on commencement of proceedings
- on filing an acknowledgment of service, defence or other first document; and
- at any later time that such an arrangement is entered into, changed or terminated.

In the	
The court office is open between 10 am and 4 pm Monday to Friday. When writing to the court, please address forms or letters to the Court Manager and quote the claim number.	
Claim No.	
Claimant (include Ref.)	
Defendant (include Ref.)	

Take notice that in respect of

☐ all claims herein

☐ the following claims

☐ the case of *(specify name of party)*

[is now][was] being funded by:

(Please tick those boxes which apply)

☐ a conditional fee agreement
Dated
which provides for a success fee

☐ an insurance policy issued on
Date **Policy no.**
Name and address of insurer

Level of cover

Are the insurance premiums staged?

☐ Yes ☐ No

If Yes, at which point is an increased premium payable

☐ an undertaking given on
Date
by
Name of prescribed body
in the following terms

The funding of the case has now changed:

☐ the above funding has now ceased

☐ the conditional fee agreement has been terminated

☐ a conditional fee agreement
Dated
which provides for a success fee has been entered into;

☐ an insurance policy
Date
has been cancelled

☐ an insurance policy has been issued on
Date **Policy no.**
Name and address of insurer

continued over the page ➪

Level of cover

Are the insurance premiums staged?

☐ Yes ☐ No

If Yes, at which point is an increased premium payable

☐ an undertaking given on

Date

has been terminated

☐ an undertaking has been given on

Date

Name of prescribed body

in the following terms

Signed

Solicitor for the (claimant) (defendant)
(Part 20 defendant) (respondent) (appellant)

Dated

Notice of commencement of assessment of bill of costs

In the	
Claim No.	
Claimant (include Ref.)	
Defendant (include Ref.)	

To the claimant(defendant)

Following an . . . . *(insert name of document eg. order, judgment)* dated . . . . (copy attached) I have prepared my Bill of Costs for assessment. The Bill totals *£ . . . . If you choose to dispute this bill and your objections are not upheld at the assessment hearing, the full amount payable (including the assessment fee) will be £ . . . . (together with interest *(see note below)*). I shall also seek the costs of the assessment hearing

Your points of dispute must include

- details of the items in the bill of costs which are disputed
- concise details of the nature and grounds of the dispute for each item and, if you seek a reduction in those items, suggest, where practicable, a reduced figure

You must serve your points of dispute by . . . . *(insert date 21 days from the date of service of this notice)* on me at:- *(give full name and address for service including any DX number or reference)*

You must also serve copies of your points of dispute on all other parties to the assessment identified below *(you do not need to serve your points of dispute on the court).*

I certify that I have also served the following person(s) with a copy of this notice and my Bill of Costs:- *(give details of persons served)*

If I have not received your points of dispute by the above date, I will ask the court to issue a default costs certificate for the full amount of my bill *(see above*)* plus fixed costs and court fee in the total amount of £ . . . .

Signed . . . . **Date** . . . .
(Claimant)(Defendant)('s solicitor)

Note: Interest may be added to all High Court judgments and certain county court judgments of £5,000 or more under the Judgments Act 1838 and the County Courts Act 1984.

The court office at

is open between 10 am and 4 pm Monday to Friday. When corresponding with the court, please address forms or letters to the Court Manager and quote the claim number.

N252 Notice of commencement of assessment of bill of costs (12.99) *The Court Service Publications Unit*

Notice of Amount Allowed on Provisional Assessment

In the	
Claim No.	
Claimant (including Ref.)	
Defendant (including Ref.)	
Date	

To [Claimant][Defendant]['s Solicitor]

Take notice that the [claimant's][defendant's][receiver's] bill of costs has been provisionally assessed and is returned with this notice

If you wish to be heard on the assessment, you must, within 14 days of the receipt of this notice inform the court in writing and return the bill of costs to the court. A date for assessment will then be fixed.

If you accept the provisional assessment as final, please complete and return the bill together with the balance of the assessment fee.

Note: In Legal aid only/LSC only cases

1) Within 7 days of receipt of the notice the solicitor must notify counsel in writing where the fees claimed on counsel's behalf have been provisonally reduced or disallowed.
2) The solicitor should not accept the provisonal assessment as final without first enquiring whether any counsel whose fees have been provisionally reduced or disallowed has also accepted it.
3) Attention is drawn to the need to endorse on the bill a certificate in the form of precedent F(4) before returning the bill to the court.

The court office at

is open between 10 am and 4 pm Monday to Friday. Address all communications to the Court Manager quoting the claim number

N253 Notice of amount allowed on provisional assessment (7.00)

Request for a Default Costs Certificate

In the	
Claim No.	
Claimant (include Ref.)	
Defendant (include Ref.)	

I certify that (1) notice of commencement (2) the bill of costs and (3) a copy of the document giving the right to detailed assessment, were served on the paying party
(*and give details of any other party served with the notice*)

on (*insert date*)

Copies of (1) and (3) are attached.

I also certify that I have not received any points of dispute and that the time for receiving them has now elapsed.

I now request the court to issue a certificate for the amount of the bill of costs plus such fixed costs and court fees as are appropriate in this case.

Signed **Date**
(Claimant)(Defendant)('s Solicitor)

The court office at

is open between 10 am and 4 pm Monday to Friday. When corresponding with the court, please address forms or letters to the Court Manager and quote the claim number.

N254 Request for a Default Costs Certificate (07.02) *The Court Service Publications Branch*

 FORM N255(HC)

Default costs certificate

Name of court	Claim No.
Name of Claimant (including ref.)	
Name of Defendant (including ref.)	
[Defendant's][Claimant's] date of birth	
Date	

To [Claimant][Defendant]['s Solicitor]

As you have not raised any points of dispute on the [defendant's][claimant's] bill of costs, the costs of the claim have been allowed and the total sum of £ is now payable.

You must pay this amount to the [defendant][claimant] [within 14 days from the date of this order] [on or before [ ]]

The date from which any entitlement to interest under this certificate is to run is:-

1. as to the amount of the bill as assessed excluding the costs of assessment, [the date of the order]
2. and as to [£] being the fixed costs of assessment, the date of this certificate.

Take Notice

To the defendant (claimant)

If you do not pay in accordance with this order your goods may be removed and sold or other enforcement proceedings may be taken against you. If your circumstances change and you cannot pay, ask at the court office about what you can do

If you do not pay as ordered, this judgment may be registered on the Register of Judgments, Orders and Fines. This may make it difficult for you to get credit. **If you then pay in full within one month** you can ask the court to cancel the entry on the Register. You will need to give proof of payment. You can (for a fee) also obtain a Certificate of Cancellation from the court. If you pay the debt in full after one month you can ask the court to mark the entry on the Register as satisfied and (for a fee) obtain a Certificate of Satisfaction to prove that the debt has been paid.

Address for Payment

How to Pay

- **PAYMENT(S) MUST BE MADE to the person named at the address for payment quoting their reference and the court case number. DO NOT bring or send payments to the court. THEY WILL NOT BE ACCEPTED.**
- You should allow at least 4 days for your payment to reach the claimant (defendant) or his representative.
- Make sure that you keep records and can account for all payments made.
- Proof may be required if there is any disagreement. It is not safe to send cash unless you use registered post.
- A leaflet giving further advice about payment can be obtained from the court.
- If you need more information you should contact the claimant (defendant) or his representative.

The court office at

is open between 10 am and 4 pm Monday to Friday. Address all communications to the Court Manager quoting the claim number

N255HC Default costs certificate (04.06)

Default costs certificate

Name of court	Claim No.
Name of Claimant (including ref.)	
Name of Defendant (including ref.)	
[Defendant's][Claimant's] date of birth	
Date	

To [Claimant][Defendant]['s Solicitor]

As you have not raised any points of dispute on the [defendant's][claimant's] bill of costs, the costs of the claim have been allowed and the total sum of £ is now payable.

You must pay this amount to the [defendant][claimant] [within 14 days from the date of this order] [on or before [ ]]

The date from which any entitlement to interest under this certificate is to run is:-

1. as to the amount of the bill as assessed excluding the costs of assessment, [the date of the order]
2. and as to [£] being the fixed costs of assessment, the date of this certificate.

Take Notice

To the defendant (claimant)

If you do not pay in accordance with this order your goods may be removed and sold or other enforcement proceedings may be taken against you. If your circumstances change and you cannot pay, ask at the court office about what you can do

Further interest may be added if judgment has been given for £5,000 or more or is in respect of a debt which attracts contractual or statutory interest for late payment.

If you do not pay as ordered, this judgment may be registered on the Register of Judgments, Orders and Fines. This may make it difficult for you to get credit. **If you then pay in full within one month** you can ask the court to cancel the entry on the Register. You will need to give proof of payment. You can (for a fee) also obtain a Certificate of Cancellation from the court. If you pay the debt in full after one month you can ask the court to mark the entry on the Register as satisfied and (for a fee) obtain a Certificate of Satisfaction to prove that the debt has been paid.

Address for Payment

How to Pay

- **PAYMENT(S) MUST BE MADE to the person named at the address for payment quoting their reference and the court case number.**
- **DO NOT bring or send payments to the court. THEY WILL NOT BE ACCEPTED.**
- You should allow at least 4 days for your payment to reach the claimant (defendant) or his representative.
- Make sure that you keep records and can account for all payments made. Proof may be required if there is any disagreement. It is not safe to send cash unless you use registered post.
- A leaflet giving further advice about payment can be obtained from the court.
- If you need more information you should contact the claimant (defendant) or his representative.

The court office at

is open between 10 am and 4 pm Monday to Friday. Address all communications to the Court Manager quoting the claim number

N255 Default costs certificate

FORM N256(HC)

Final costs certificate

Name of court	Claim No.
Name of Claimant (including ref.)	
Name of Defendant (including ref.)	
[Defendant's][Claimant's] date of birth	
Date	

To [Claimant][Defendant]['s Solicitor]

In accordance with [identify the document giving the right to detailed assessment]

Master/District Judge [ ] has assessed the total costs as £ [including £ for the costs of the detailed assessment]

[And £ already having been paid under the interim costs certificate issued on [ ]]

You must pay [the balance of]£ to the [claimant][defendant] [within 14 days from the date of this order] [on or before[ ]]

The date from which any entitlement to interest under this certificate is to run is:-

1. as to the amount of the bill as assessed excluding the costs of assessment, [the date of the order]
2. and as to [£] being the costs of assessment, the date of this certificate.

Take Notice

To the defendant (claimant)

If you do not pay in accordance with this order your goods may be removed and sold or other enforcement proceedings may be taken against you. If your circumstances change and you cannot pay, ask at the court office about what you can do.

Further interest may be added if judgment has been given for £5,000 or more or is in respect of debt which attracts contractual or statutory interest for late payment.

If you do not pay as ordered, this judgment may be registered on the Register of Judgments, Orders and Fines. This may make it difficult for you to get credit. **If you then pay in full within one month** you can ask the court to cancel the entry on the Register. You will need to give proof of payment. You can (for a fee) also obtain a Certificate of Cancellation from the court. If you pay the debt in full after one month you can ask the court to mark the entry on the Register as satisfied and (for a fee) obtain a Certificate of Satisfaction to prove that the debt has been paid.

Address for Payment

How to Pay

- **PAYMENT(S) MUST BE MADE to the person named at the address for payment quoting their reference and the court case number. DO NOT bring or send payments to the court. THEY WILL NOT BE ACCEPTED.**
- You should allow at least 4 days for your payment to reach the claimant (defendant) or his representative.
- Make sure that you keep records and can account for all payments made.
- Proof may be required if there is any disagreement. It is not safe to send cash unless you use registered post.
- A leaflet giving further advice about payment can be obtained from the court.
- If you need more information you should contact the claimant (defendant) or his representative.

The court office at

is open between 10 am and 4 pm Monday to Friday. Address all communications to the Court Manager quoting the claim number

N256 (HC) Final cost certificate (04.06)

Final costs certificate

Name of court	Claim No.
Name of Claimant (including ref.)	
Name of Defendant (including ref.)	
[Defendant's][Claimant's] date of birth	
Date	

To [Claimant][Defendant]['s Solicitor]

In accordance with [identify the document giving the right to detailed assessment]

District Judge [ ] has assessed the total costs as £ [including £ for the costs of the detailed assessment]

[And £ already having been paid under the interim costs certificate issued on [ ]]

You must pay [the balance of]£ to the [claimant][defendant] [within 14 days from the date of this order] [on or before[ ]]

The date from which any entitlement to interest under this certificate is to run is:-

1. as to the amount of the bill as assessed excluding the costs of assessment, [the date of the order]
2. and as to [£] being the costs of assessment, the date of this certificate.

Take Notice

To the defendant (claimant)

If you do not pay in accordance with this order your goods may be removed and sold or other enforcement proceedings may be taken against you. If your circumstances change and you cannot pay, ask at the court office about what you can do.

Further interest may be added if judgment has been given for £5,000 or more or is in respect of debt which attracts contractual or statutory interest for late payment.

Address for Payment

If you do not pay as ordered, this judgment may be registered on the Register of Judgments, Orders and Fines. This may make it difficult for you to get credit. **If you then pay in full within one month** you can ask the court to cancel the entry on the Register. You will need to give proof of payment. You can (for a fee) also obtain a Certificate of Cancellation from the court. If you pay the debt in full after one month you can ask the court to mark the entry on the Register as satisfied and (for a fee) obtain a Certificate of Satisfaction to prove that the debt has been paid.

How to Pay

- **PAYMENT(S) MUST BE MADE to the person named at the address for payment quoting their reference and the court case number.**
- **DO NOT bring or send payments to the court. THEY WILL NOT BE ACCEPTED.**
- You should allow at least 4 days for your payment to reach the claimant (defendant) or his representative.
- Make sure that you keep records and can account for all payments made. Proof may be required if there is any disagreement. It is not safe to send cash unless you use registered post.
- A leaflet giving further advice about payment can be obtained from the court.
- If you need more information you should contact the claimant (defendant) or his representative.

The court office at

is open between 10 am and 4 pm Monday to Friday. Address all communications to the Court Manager quoting the claim number.

N256 Final cost certificate (04.06)

Interim costs certificate

In the	
Claim No.	
Claimant (including ref)	
Defendant (including ref)	
Date	

To [Claimant][Defendant]['s Solicitor]

Upon application by the [claimant][defendant] for [a detailed assessment hearing] [the issue of an interim costs certificate by agreement].

[Master][District Judge][ ] has ordered that you must pay £ to the [claimant][defendant] [within 14 days from the date of this order][on or before [ ]] [into court to await the issue of a final costs certificate].

Take Notice

To the defendant (claimant)

If you do not pay in accordance with this order your goods may be removed and sold or other enforcement proceedings may be taken against you. If your circumstances change and you cannot pay, ask at the court office about what you can do

Address for Payment

How to Pay

- **PAYMENT(S) MUST BE MADE to the person named at the address for payment quoting their reference and the court case number.**
- **DO NOT bring or send payments to the court. THEY WILL NOT BE ACCEPTED.**
- You should allow at least 4 days for your payment to reach the claimant (defendant) or his representative.
- Make sure that you keep records and can account for all payments made. Proof may be required if there is any disagreement. It is not safe to send cash unless you use registered post.
- A leaflet giving further advice about payment can be obtained from the court.
- If you need more information you should contact the claimant (defendant) or his representative.

The court office at

is open between 10 am and 4 pm Monday to Friday. Address all communications to the Court Manager quoting the claim number

N257 Interim Costs Certificate

Request for detailed assessment hearing (general form)

In the	
Claim No.	
Claimant (include Ref.)	
Defendant (include Ref.)	

I certify that the Notice of Commencement was served on the paying party ....

(*and give details of any other party served with the notice*)

on .... (*insert date*)

I now ask the court to arrange an assessment hearing.

I enclose copies of (*tick as appropriate*)

- ☐ the document giving the right to detailed assessment;
- ☐ a copy of the Notice of Commencement;
- ☐ the bill of costs;
- ☐ the paying party's points of dispute, annotated as necessary in order to show (1) which items have been agreed and their value and (2) which items remain in dispute and their value;
- ☐ points in reply (if any);
- ☐ a statement giving the names, addresses for service and references of all persons to whom the court should give notice of the hearing;
- ☐ the relevant details of any additional liability claimed;
- ☐ a copy of all the orders made by the court relating to the costs of the proceedings which are to be assessed;
- ☐ any fee notes of counsel and receipts or accounts for other disbursements relating to items in dispute;
- ☐ [where solicitors' costs are disputed] the client care letter delivered to the receiving party or the solicitor's retainer.

I believe the hearing will take .... (*give estimate of time court should allow*).

I enclose my fee of £ ....

Signed .... **Date** ....

(Claimant)(Defendant)('s solicitor)

The court office at

is open between 10 am and 4 pm Monday to Friday. When corresponding with the court, please address forms or letters to the Court Manager and quote the claim number

N258 Request for detailed assessment hearing (general form) (7.00) *The Court Service Publications Unit*

Request for detailed assessment
(Legal aid/ Legal Services Commission only)

In the	
Claim No.	
Claimant (include Ref.)	
Defendant (include Ref.)	

I now ask the court to provisionally assess the bill (arrange an assessment hearing as the assisted person/LSC funded client wishes to be heard)

I enclose copies of (*tick as appropriate*)

- ☐ The document giving the right to detailed assessment;
- ☐ the bill of costs;
- ☐ a statement giving the names, addresses for service and references of all persons to whom the court should give notice of the hearing;
- ☐ a copy of all the orders made by the court relating to the costs of the proceedings which are to be assessed;
- ☐ any fee notes of counsel and receipts or accounts for other disbursements relating to items claimed;
- ☐ all civil legal aid certificates and LSC certificates and amendments to them; notice of discharge or revocation and specific legal aid authorities;
- ☐ the relevant papers in support of the bill (Supreme Court Costs Office/ PRFD assessments only)

I certify that the assisted person/LSC funded client wishes to attend the assessment hearing and I believe the hearing will take* .... (*give estimate of time court should allow*).

I enclose my fee of £ ....

*(*delete if not applicable*)

Signed .... **Date** ....

(Claimant)(Defendant)('s solicitor)

The court office at

is open between 10 am and 4 pm Monday to Friday. When corresponding with the court, please address forms or letters to the Court Manager and quote the claim number.

N258A Request for detailed assessment (legal aid/LSC only) (7.00) *The Court Service Publications Unit*

Request for detailed assessment
(Costs payable out of a fund other than the Community Legal Service Fund)

In the	
Claim No.	
Claimant (include Ref.)	
Defendant (include Ref.)	

I now ask the court to provisionally assess the bill or arrange an assessment hearing.

I enclose copies of (*tick as appropriate*)

- ☐ The document giving the right to detailed assessement;
- ☐ the bill of costs;
- ☐ a statement giving the name and address for service of any person having a financial interest in the outcome of the assessment;
- ☐ a copy of all the orders made by the court relating to the costs of the proceedings which are to be assessed;
- ☐ any fee notes of counsel and receipts or accounts for other disbursements relating to items claimed;
- ☐ the relevant details of any additional liability claimed;
- ☐ the relevant papers in support of the bill (Supreme Court Costs Office/ PRFD assessments only)

I enclose my fee of £ . . . .

Signed .... **Date** ....

(Claimant)(Defendant)(Receiver)('s solicitor)

The court office at

is open between 10 am and 4 pm Monday to Friday. When corresponding with the court, please address forms or letters to the Court Manager and quote the claim number.

N258B Request for detailed assessment (cost payable out of a fund other than the Community Legal Service Fund) (7.00) *The Court Service Publications Unit*

Request for detailed assessment hearing pursuant to an order under Part III of the Solicitors Act 1974

In the	
Claim No.	
Claimant (include Ref.)	
Defendant (include Ref.)	

I certify that the [party] . . . . has served a breakdown of costs in this case and the [party] . . . . has served points of dispute thereon.

I now ask the court to arrange an assessment hearing.

I enclose copies of (*tick as appropriate*)

- ☐ the order made under Part III of the Solicitors Act 1974 in this case;
- ☐ the bill(s) of costs to be assessed;
- ☐ the breakdown(s);
- ☐ any fee notes of counsel and receipts or accounts for other disbursements served with the breakdown of costs;
- ☐ a statement giving names, addresses and references of the persons to whom the court should give notice of the hearing;
- ☐ the [party's] points of dispute plus copies to be sent to the other parties to these proceedings details of whom are given above;
- ☐ the points in reply (if any)

I believe the hearing will take . . . . (*give estimate of time court should allow*).

I enclose my fee of £ . . . .

Signed .... **Date** ....

(Claimant)(Defendant)('s solicitor)

The court office at

is open between 10 am and 4 pm Monday to Friday. When corresponding with the court, please address forms or letters to the Court Manager and quote the claim number

N258C Request for detailed assessment hearing pursuant to an order under Part III of the Solicitors Act 1974 (7.00) *The Court Service Publications Unit*

Notice of Appeal against a detailed assessment

Each ground must be numbered. Grounds which relate to decisions on items in the bill of costs must also state the number of the item, a short description of the item, the amount claimed and the amount allowed.
Some examples are given below.

Ground 1
Decision to refuse permission to amend the Points of Dispute. [*Then state the grounds upon which you intend to rely*]

Ground 2
Bill item 6, counsel's fee, £250 plus VAT claimed, £250 plus VAT allowed. [*Then state the grounds upon which you intend to rely*]

Ground 3
Bill item 28, attendances on expert witnesses, £480 plus VAT claimed, £420 plus VAT allowed. [*Then state the grounds upon which you intend to rely*]

In the	
Claim Number	
Claimant *(including reference)*	
Defendant *(including reference)*	
Date	

[The party wishes] [I wish] to appeal against [some of] the decision(s) made by the costs officer at the hearing on [date] concerning the detailed assessment of [the party's] bill of costs. The grounds of appeal are:

[*State the grounds upon which you intend to rely (see above left for examples). Continue on further sheet if needed.*]

I now enclose copies of *(tick as appropriate)*

- ☐ The Costs Certificate or other order being appealed
- ☐ Cost's Officer's written reasons (or order dispensing with written reasons)
- ☐ Bill of Costs
- ☐ Points of Dispute lodged with request for detailed assessment hearing
- ☐ Points in Reply (in any)
- ☐ The authority for the detailed assessment

To [*Costs Officer whose decision is being appealed*] and to [*the intended respondents to the appeal*]

Signed ______________________ Date ____________

[Party] [Party's Solicitor]

N259 - **w3** Notice of appeal against a detailed assessment (4.99)

Printed on behalf of The Court Service

Click here to reset form | Click here to print form

Statement of Costs (summary assessment)

In the Court	
Case Reference	

Judge/Master

Case Title

[Party]'s Statement of Costs for the hearing on *(date)* **(interim application/fast track trial)**

Description of fee earners*	
(a) *(name) (grade) (hourly rate claimed)*	
(b) *(name) (grade) (hourly rate claimed)*	
(c) *(name) (grade) (hourly rate claimed)*	
(d) *(name) (grade) (hourly rate claimed)*	

Attendances on *(party)*				
(a) *(number)*		hours at £		£
(b) *(number)*		hours at £		£
(c) *(number)*		hours at £		£
(d) *(number)*		hours at £		£
Attendances on opponents				
(a) *(number)*		hours at £		£
(b) *(number)*		hours at £		£
(c) *(number)*		hours at £		£
(d) *(number)*		hours at £		£
Attendance on others				
(a) *(number)*		hours at £		£
(b) *(number)*		hours at £		£
(c) *(number)*		hours at £		£
(d) *(number)*		hours at £		£
Site inspections etc				
(a) *(number)*		hours at £		£
(b) *(number)*		hours at £		£
(c) *(number)*		hours at £		£
(d) *(number)*		hours at £		£

N260 Statement of Costs (summary assessment) (06.09)

Brought forward £

Counsel's fees *(name) (year of call)*

Fee for [advice/conference/documents] £

Fee for hearing £

Other expenses

[court fees] £

Others *(give brief description)* £

Total £

Amount of VAT claimed

on solicitors and counsel's fees £

on other expenses £

Grand Total £

The costs stated above do not exceed the costs which the (*party*) is liable to pay in respect of the work which this statement covers. Counsel's fees and other expenses have been incurred in the amounts stated above and will be paid to the persons stated.

(party)

Dated

Signed

Name of firm of solicitors [partner] for the *(party)*

* 4 grades of fee earner are suggested:

(A) Solicitors with over eight years post qualification experience including at least eight years litigation experience.

(B) Solicitors and legal executives with over four years post qualification experience including at least four years litigation experience.

(C) Other solicitors and legal executives and fee earners of equivalent experience.

(D) Trainee solicitors, para legals and other fee earners.

"Legal Executive" means a Fellow of the Institute of Legal Executives. Those who are not Fellows of the Institute are not entitled to call themselves legal executives and in principle are therefore not entitled to the same hourly rate as a legal executive.

In respect of each fee earner communications should be treated as attendances and routine communications should be claimed at one tenth of the hourly rate.

Click here to print form

List of documents: standard disclosure

Notes

- The rules relating to standard disclosure are contained in Part 31 of the Civil Procedure Rules.
- Documents to be included under standard disclosure are contained in Rule 31.6
- A document has or will have been in your control if you have or have had possession, or a right of possession, of it **or** a right to inspect or take copies of it.

In the	
Claim No.	
Claimant (including ref)	
Defendant (including ref)	
Date	

Disclosure Statement

I, the above named

☐ Claimant ☐ Defendant

☐ Party (if party making disclosure is a company, firm or other organisation identify here who the person making the disclosure statement is and why he is the appropriate person to make it)

state that I have carried out a reasonable and proportionate search to locate all the documents which I am required to disclose under the order made by the court on (date of order)

☐ I did not search for documents:-

☐ pre-dating

☐ located elsewhere than

☐ in categories other than

☐ for electronic documents

☐ I carried out a search for electronic documents contained on or created by the following: (list what was searched and extent of search)

N265 Standard disclosure (10.05) HMCS

☐ I did not search for the following:-

☐ documents created before ☐

documents contained on or created by the ☐ Claimant ☐ Defendant

☐ PCs ☐ portable data storage media
☐ databases ☐ servers
☐ back-up tapes ☐ off-site storage
☐ mobile phones ☐ laptops
☐ notebooks ☐ handheld devices
☐ PDA devices

documents contained on or created by the ☐ Claimant ☐ Defendant

☐ mail files ☐ document files
☐ calendar files ☐ web-based applications
☐ spreadsheet files ☐ graphic and presentation files

documents other than by reference to the following keyword(s)/concepts
(delete if your search was not confined to specific keywords or concepts)

I certify that I understand the duty of disclosure and to the best of my knowledge I have carried out that duty. I further certify that the list of documents set out in or attached to this form, is a complete list of all documents which are or have been in my control and which I am obliged under the order to disclose.

I understand that I must inform the court and the other parties immediately if any further document required to be disclosed by Rule 31.6 comes into my control at any time before the conclusion of the case.

☐ I have not permitted inspection of documents within the category or class of documents (as set out below) required to be disclosed under Rule 31(6)(b)or (c) on the grounds that to do so would be disproportionate to the issues in the case.

Signed ☐ **Date** ☐

(Claimant)(Defendant)('s litigation friend)

List and number here, in a convenient order, the documents (or bundles of documents if of the same nature, e.g. invoices) in your control, which you do not object to being inspected. Give a short description of each document or bundle so that it can be identified, and say if it is kept elsewhere i.e. with a bank or solicitor

I have control of the documents numbered and listed here. I do not object to you inspecting them/producing copies.

List and number here, as above, the documents in your control which you object to being inspected. (Rule 31.19)

I have control of the documents numbered and listed here, but I object to you inspecting them:

Say what your objections are

I object to you inspecting these documents because:

List and number here, the documents you once had in your control, but which you no longer have. For each document listed, say when it was last in your control and where it is now.

I have had the documents numbered and listed below, but they are no longer in my control.

Notice to admit facts

In the	
Claim No.	
Claimant (include Ref.)	
Defendant (include Ref.)	

I (We) give notice that you are requested to admit the following facts or part of case in this claim:

I (We) confirm that any admission of fact(s) or part of case will only be used in this claim.

Signed (Claimant)(Defendant)('s Solicitor)

Position or office held (If signing on behalf of firm or company)

Date

Admission of facts

I (We) admit the facts or part of case (set out above)(in the attached schedule) for the purposes of this claim only and on the basis that the admission will not be used on any other occasion or by any other person.

Signed (Claimant)(Defendant)('s Solicitor)

Position or office held (If signing on behalf of firm or company)

Date

The court office at

is open between 10 am and 4 pm Monday to Friday. Address all communication to the Court Manager quoting the claim number

N266 - w3 Notice to admit facts (4.99)

Notice to prove documents at trial

In the	
Claim No.	
Claimant (include Ref.)	
Defendant (include Ref.)	

I (We) give notice that you are requested to prove the following documents disclosed under CPR Part 31 in this claim at the trial:

Signed
(Claimant)(Defendant)('s Solicitor)

Position or office held
(If signing on behalf of firm or company)

Date

The court office at

is open between 10 am and 4 pm Monday to Friday. Address all communication to the Court Manager quoting the claim number

N268 - W3 Notice to prove documents at trial (4.99) Printed on behalf of The Court Service

Notice of Transfer of Proceedings

In the	
Claim No.	
Claimant (including ref.)	
Defendant (including ref.)	
Date	

To the [Claimant][Defendant]['s Solicitor]

To all parties

ıe court office at

open between 10 am and 4 pm Monday to Friday. When corresponding with the court, please address forms or letters to the Court Manager and quote the claim number.

?71 Notice of transfer of proceedings

A defence to this claim has been filed. As the defendant is an individual the claim has been transferred to the court [covering the area where the defendant lives][nearest the business address of defendantÕs solicitor]. Please read the accompanying documents carefully and note that the allocation questionnaire should be returned to the [..................................][County Court][District Registry][Royal Courts of Justice].

This claim has been transferred to [..................................... County Court][.....................................District Registry][the Royal Courts of Justice] for that court to [deal with][hear] the[claimant's] [defendant's] **application** for ....

....

That [court][district registry] will refer the application to a judge, or, if there is to be a hearing, will send you and the other parties notice of the time, date and place of the hearing. You will be sent a copy of the judge's decision. [After the hearing the court file will be returned to this court.]

This [claim][counterclaim] is to be treated as a **defended** case. The procedural judge has identified it as a [claim][counterclaim] which may be suitable for handling in a specialist list. It has therefore been transferred to the [Civil Trial Centre at .... County Court][the .... list at the .... Division of the Royal Courts of Justice] where it will be referred to [a procedural judge for case management directions][the judge in charge of the specialist list for the judge to decide if it is a suitable case for that list and, if so, for case management directions to be given.] You will be sent [a notice of allocation] [an order] setting out the judge's directions.

As a result of an order made on the [....................................] of [...................] this [claim][counterclaim] has been transferred to the .... County Court for **trial**. [You will be sent a notice of the date and time of the trial shortly.] If you wish to make any further applications in this claim, they should be made to the court to which the claim has been transferred. [After the trial, the claim will be transferred back to this court. You will be told when this happens.]

This claim has been transferred to the .... County Court for **enforcement**. [The [claimant][defendant] wishes to issue an application for [................................][a copy of which is attached]]

This claim has been transferred to the .... County Court following an application made by the[claimant][defendant]. On receipt, the file will be referred to a procedural judge who will allocate the claim[counterclaim] to track and give case management directions. Details of the judgeÕs decision will be sent to you in a notice of allocation.

As a result of an order made on the [....................................] of [...................], this claim has been transferred to [................................][County Court][District Registry][the Royal Courts of Justice].

Notice of discontinuance

In the	
Claim No.	
Claimant (including ref.)	
Defendant (including ref.)	

Note: Where another party must consent to the proceedings being discontinued, a copy of their consent must be attached to, and served with, this form.

To the court

The claimant (defendant)

(tick only one box)

☐ discontinues all of this (claim) (counterclaim)

☐ discontinues that part of this claim (counterclaim) relating to: *(specify which part)*

against the (defendant) (following defendants) (claimant) (following claimants)

(... *(enter name of Judge)* granted permission for the claimant to discontinue (all) (part) of this (claim)(counterclaim) by order dated ....)

I certify that I have served a copy of this notice on every other party to the proceedings

Signed ☐ (Claimant)(Defendant)('s solicitor)(Litigation friend)

Position or office held ☐ (if signing on behalf of firm or company)

Date ☐

The court office at

is open between 10 am and 4 pm Monday to Friday. When corresponding with the court, please address forms or letters to the Court Manager and quote the claim number.

N279 - w3 Notice of discontinuance(6.99) *Printed on behalf of The Court Service*

Order on settlement on behalf of child or patient

In the	
Claim No.	
Claimant (including ref)	
Defendant (including ref)	

To [Claimant] [Defendant] ['s Solicitor]

Seal

If the defendant fails to pay the said sum into court by the date ordered, the defendant shall also pay into court such further sum as the Court Funds Office shall certify as being the amount lost by the claimant by the late payment, forthwith upon service of such certificate.

An application was made on [date] by [counsel] [solicitors] for the claimant [and was attended by [counsel] [solicitors] for the defendant].

[Master] [District Judge] approved the following terms of settlement and made them an Order of the Court.

BY CONSENT IT IS ORDERED that:-

The claimant may accept the sum of [£............] in satisfaction of the claim[s].

(where the claim is in respect of a Fatal Accident)

[The said sum of [£..............] is apportioned as follows:-

a) under the Law Reform (Miscellaneous Provisions) Act 1934 the sum of [£............]

b) under the Fatal Accidents Act 1976;

(i) [£.............] to the personal claim of the claimant,

(ii) [£.............] to the personal claim of the child dependant[s]

[.............................] [............................]]

[The defendant pay the sum of [£.............] to the claimant's [solicitors] [litigation friend] on or before [.................].]

The defendant pay the [further] sum of [£................] into the [Court Funds Office] on or before [............] [subject to a first charge under section 16(6) of the Legal Aid Act 1988] to be invested and accumulated in the Special Investment Account pending further order.

The claimant's solicitor attend a hearing for further investment directions on [date] at [time] at [address of court].

[The fund to be paid to the child on majority as [he] [she] may request]

[The claimant's solicitor to apply to the Court of Protection for the appointment of a receiver on or before [...............] and upon such appointment being made the sum of [£...........] [subject to a first charge under section 16(6) of the Legal Aid Act 1988] together with any interest accrued on that sum from the date of this order to be carried over to the Court of Protection to the credit of the claimant there to be dealt with as the Court of Protection thinks fit.]

[Any interest accrued up to the date of this order on any money in court paid in by or on behalf of the defendant be paid out to the defendant's solicitors.]

The defendant pay the claimant's costs be assessed with permission to request assessment to be dispensed with [and the claimant's solicitor waiving any claim to further costs].

The court office at

is open between 10 am and 4 pm Monday to Friday. When corresponding with the court, please address forms or letters to the Court Manager and quote the claim number

N292 Order on settlement on behalf of child or patient (04.09)

[The claimant's costs be [assessed] in accordance with Regulation 107 of the Civil Legal Aid (General) Regulations 1989.]

Upon payment of the sum(s) and costs referred to above, the defendant be discharged from further liability in respect of all claims made by the claimant against him in these proceedings.

All further proceedings be stayed except that either party has permission to apply to the court for the purpose of carrying this order into effect.

Claimant's application for a variation order (without hearing)

In the	
Claim No.	
Claimant (including ref.)	
Defendant (including ref.)	

Defendant's address

seal

I apply to the court for an order that the amount due and unpaid under the judgment or order

in this claim be paid by instalments of £ for every month/week because

(give your reason for making this application in the box below)

Signed .... **Date** ....
Claimant('s solicitor)('s litigation friend)

Judgment details

Date of judgment or order

How payment was ordered

Outstanding debt
**including any interest where judgment was entered for £5,000 or more, or is in respect of a debt which attracts contractual or statutory interest for late payment*

AMOUNT REMAINING DUE* £

The court office at

is open between 10 am and 4 pm Monday to Friday. Address all communications to the Court Manager quoting the claim number

N294 - w3 Claimant's application for a variation order (4.99) *Printed on behalf of The Court Service*

Application for order that debtor attend court for questioning

In the

Claim No.

Appn. No.

Claimant

Defendant

The [claimant] [defendant] ('the judgment creditor') applies for an order that the [defendant] [claimant] ('the judgment debtor') attend court to provide information about the judgment debtor's means and any other information needed to enforce the judgment or order given on 20 [by the in claim no.].

1. Judgment debtor

The judgment debtor is

whose address is

Postcode

2. Judgment debt or order

[The judgment or order required the judgment debtor to pay £ (including any costs and interest). The amount now owing is £ [which includes further interest payable on the judgment debt]].

[The judgment or order required the judgment debtor to]

Note:

Questioning and documents

Questioning will be by a court officer unless a judge agrees there are compelling reasons for questioning to take place before a judge. Normally the court officer will ask the questions set out in Form EX140 and the judgment debtor will be told to produce all relevant documents including:

- pay slips
- bank statements
- building society books
- share certificates
- rent book
- mortgage statement
- hire purchase and similar agreements
- court orders
- any other outstanding bills
- electricity, gas, water and council tax bills for the past year.

and in the case of a business

- bills owed to it
- 2 years' accounts
- current management accounts.

Complete sections 3,4 and 5 only if applicable.
The statement of truth overleaf must be completed.

N316 Application for order that debtor attend court for questioning (03.02) *Printed on behalf of The Court Service*

3. [Attached is a list of questions which the judgment creditor wishes the court officer to ask the judgment debtor in addition to those in Form EX140.]

4. [Attached is a list of documents which the judgment creditor wishes the judgment debtor to be ordered to produce in addition to those listed in the note above.]

5. [The judgment creditor requests that the judgment debtor be questioned by the judgment creditor before a judge. The reason for this request is

]

Statement of Truth

*(I believe)(The judgment creditor believes) that the facts stated in this application form are true.
* I am duly authorised by the judgment creditor to sign this statement.

signed ______________________ date ______________________

*(Judgment creditor)(Litigation friend *(where judgment creditor is a child or a patient)*)(Judgment creditor's solicitor)
**delete as appropriate*

Full name ______________________

Name of judgment creditor's solicitor's firm ______________________

position or office held ______________________
(if signing on behalf of firm or company)

Judgment creditor's or judgment creditor's solicitor's address to which documents should be sent.

Address		if applicable
Postcode	Ref. no.	
	fax no.	
	DX no.	
Tel. no.	e-mail	

Application for order that officer of debtor company attend court for questioning

In the

Claim No.

Appn. No.

Claimant

Defendant

The [claimant] [defendant] ('the judgment creditor') applies for an order that an officer of the [defendant] [claimant] company or corporation ('the judgment debtor') attend court to provide information about the judgment debtor's means and any other information needed to enforce the judgment or order given on 20
[by the in claim no.].

1. Judgment debtor

The judgment debtor is
whose address is

Postcode

2. The officer

The officer is the judgment debtor's
whose name is
and whose address is

Postcode

3. Judgment debt or order

[The judgment or order required the judgment debtor to pay £ (including any costs and interest). The amount now owing is £ [which includes further interest payable on the judgment debt]].

[The judgment or order required the judgment debtor to
]

Note:

Questioning and documents

Questioning will be by a court officer unless a judge agrees there are compelling reasons for questioning to take place before a judge. Normally the court officer will ask the questions set out in Form EX141 and the officer of the company will be told to produce all relevant documents including:

- bank statements
- share certificates
- hire purchase and similar agreements
- court orders on which money is still owed
- any outstanding bills
- bills owed to the company
- 2 years' accounts
- current management accounts.

Complete sections 4,5 and 6 only if applicable.
The statement of truth overleaf must be completed.

N316A Application for order that officer of the debtor company attend court for questioning (03.02) *Printed on behalf of The Court Service*

4. [Attached is a list of questions which the judgment creditor wishes the court officer to ask the officer of the company in addition to those in Form EX141.]

5. [Attached is a list of documents which the judgment creditor wishes the officer of the company to be ordered to produce in addition to those listed in the note above.]

6. [The judgment creditor requests that the officer of the company be questioned by the judgment creditor before a judge. The reason for this request is

]

Statement of Truth

*(I believe)(The judgment creditor believes) that the facts stated in this application form are true.
* I am duly authorised by the judgment creditor to sign this statement.

signed ______________________ date ______________________

(Judgment creditor)(Litigation friend(where judgment creditor is a child or a patient)*)(Judgment creditor's solicitor)
**delete as appropriate*

Full name ______________________

Name of judgment creditor's solicitor's firm ______________________

position or office held ______________________
(if signing on behalf of firm or company)

Judgment creditor's or judgment creditor's solicitor's address to which documents should be sent.		if applicable	
		Ref. no.	
		fax no.	
	Postcode	DX no.	
	Tel. no.	e-mail	

Order for recovery of award

In the

Claim No.

Applicant

Respondent

SEAL

On 20 , [the court] [[Master] [District Judge]
sitting at]
considered the application and the award made to the applicant on 20
by the under reference

and the court orders that

1. The applicant may enforce the award in this court.

2. The respondent pay the applicant's costs of the application, which are to be added to the amount unpaid under the award.

3. The amount enforceable is:

Unpaid under the award *(including interest)*	£
Court fee	£
Solicitor's costs	£
Total	**£**

together with any further interest becoming due.

Notes to the respondent

- This order means that your goods may be removed and sold or that some other enforcement proceedings may be taken against you. Further costs may then be payable.
- The applicant may be entitled to further interest on the award until the amount due is paid.

The court office is at:

To

N322 Order for recovery of award (03.02)

Application for an order to allow enforcement of a decision or ACAS conditional settlement (Form COT3) that requires permission to proceed

Name of court
Claim number *(To be completed by the court)*
Applicant
Respondent

The applicant applies to enforce a ☐ decision *Dated* __/__/____

☐ settlement *Dated* __/__/____

(If settlement, go to section 1 - Applicants details)

and for an order that the respondent pay the costs of this application.

What is the name of the Tribunal/ court that granted your award.

Give the reference number of your decision

Please give details of the legislation that allows you to enforce this decision

A copy of the decision or ACAS conditional settlement (Form COT3) is attached.

1. Applicant's details

Name of applicant

Applicant's address

Postcode

Telephone no.

Ref.

Email address

Address for service *(if different from opposite)*

Postcode

2. Respondent's details

Name of respondent

Respondent's address

Postcode

continued over the page

N322A Application for an order to allow enforcement of a decision or ACAS conditional settlement (Form COT3) that requires permission to proceed (06.09)

3. The amount now owing and the costs claimed

The amount of the decision/settlement *(including costs)* £

If your legislation allows you to claim interest on the amount award please complete this section.
You must show details of your calculations.

[Interest on £

from ☐☐/☐☐/☐☐☐☐ to ☐☐/☐☐/☐☐☐☐

at %]

or

[As shown in the attached calculation]	£34234234234234234
sub-total	£23423423423423423
Less amount paid	£23423423423423423
Balance remaining unpaid	£23423423422342342
Court fee	£234234234234234
Solicitor's costs	£234234234234
Total now owing	£23423423423423422

2

4. ACAS conditional settlement (Form COT3)

I certify that

☐ I have ☐ the applicant has

complied with the terms contained in the notice of settlement.

By *(please give details - continue on a separate sheet if necessary)*

Condition 1

What was the condition attached to your settlement?

Please give details of how the condition has or has not been fulfilled?

Condition 2

What was the condition attached to your settlement?

Please give details of how the condition has or has not been fulfilled?

3

5. Declaration in ACAS matters

☐ I certify that a declaration that this sum would not be recoverable against the respondent under general law of contract has not been made and that no application for such a declaration is pending.

6. Statement of truth

☐ I believe ☐ The applicant believes

that the facts stated in this application are true.

Signed ______________________ Dated ☐☐/☐☐/☐☐☐☐

(Applicant) (Litigation friend(where applicant is a child or a Protected Party)*) (Applicant's solicitor)

**delete as appropriate*

Full name

Name of applicant's solicitor's firm

Position or office held
(if signing on behalf of firm or company)

Request to register a High Court Judgment or Order for enforcement

In the

County Court

For court use only

Claim no:

Issue date:

Checklist

Answer the following questions, ticking the appropriate boxes **Yes No**

- if an order for transfer is required under s 40(2) CCA, is a copy attached?
- is an office copy of the High Court judgment or order (or evidence of the order under 025, r11(1) attached?
- does the date of judgment or order agree with the first date on the certificate?
- is the certificate signed and dated?
- is the amount of the judgment or order at **4A** the same amount?
- is the balance outstanding at **4B** the same as or less than the amount of the judgment or order at **4A**?
- do **4B** and **4C** add up to the amount given in box **4D**?
- if execution was issued in the High Court is a copy of the Enforcement Officers return attached?

If you ticked the first box for every question, you can allocate a claim number. The (proper) officer must sign this form before you can process any request for enforcement

Signed

If you ticked the second box for any question, return the papers and fee to the sender (with an explanation if necessary)

1 Claimant's name and address

2 Name and address for service and payment (if different from above)

Ref/Tel No.

3 Defendant's name and address

4 Payment details

A Amount of award

B Balance outstanding

C Interest since date of award (if any)*
period rate %

D **Amount now due**

5 Certificate

I wish to enforce a judgment or order of the High Court against the defendant

dated , an (office) copy of which is attached to this application.

I certify that the whole or part of the judgment or order has not been paid and that the balance now due is as shown.

*delete as appropriate ***(Execution was issued in the High Court and I attach a copy of the Enforcement Officer return)**

Signed Claimant(Claimant's solicitor)

Dated

N322H Request to register a High Court Judgment or Order for enforcement (04.04) *The Court Service Publications Branch*

Application for third party debt order

In the

Claim No.

Appn. No.

Claimant

Defendant

Third Party

The [claimant] [defendant] ('the judgment creditor') applies for an order that the third party pay to the judgment creditor the debt which the third party owes to the [defendant] [claimant] ('the judgment debtor') (or so much of it as is necessary to discharge the amount owing under the judgment or order given on 20 [by the in claim no.] and the costs of this application).

1. **Judgment debtor**
The judgment debtor is
whose address is

Postcode

2. **Judgment debt**
The judgment or order required the judgment debtor to pay £ (including any costs and interest). The amount now due is £ [which includes further interest].

☐ £ of the instalments due under the judgment or order has fallen due and remains unpaid.

☐ The judgment or order did not provide for payment by instalments.

3. **Third party**
The third party is within England and Wales and owes money to (or holds money to the credit of) the judgment debtor.

The third party is a bank or building society.
Its name is
Its head office address in England and Wales is:

The branch at which the account is held is
☐ not known

☐ the
whose address is

The account number is
☐ not known
☐

The sort code is
☐ not known
☐

N349 Application for third party debt order (03.02) *Printed on behalf of The Court Service*

[The third party is not a bank or building society.

☐ the third party is

whose address in England and Wales is

4. Other persons' interests

The persons (in addition to the judgment debtor) who have a claim to the money owed by the third party are

☐ None

☐ The following: *(names and address(es))*

Information known about each person's claim:

5. Sources and grounds of information

The judgment creditor knowns or believes that the information in section 3 and 4 is correct because:

6. Other applications

In respect of the judgment debt,

☐ the judgment creditor has made no other applications for third party debt orders.

☐ the judgment creditor has already made the following application(s) for third party debt order:

Details of application(s)

Third party's name

Address

Postcode

Statement of Truth

*I believe (the judgment creditor believes) that the facts stated in this application form are true.

*I am duly authorised by the judgment creditor to sign this statement

signed ______________________________ date ________________

*(Judgment creditor)(Litigation friend *(where judgment creditor is a child or a patient)*)(Judgment creditor's solicitor)

**delete as appropriate*

Full name ____

Name of judgment creditor's solicitor's firm ______________________________

position or office held ___________________________ *(if signing on behalf of a firm or company)*

Judgment creditor's or judgment creditor's solicitor's address to which documents should be sent.

Postcode

if applicable

Ref. no.	
fax no.	
DX no.	
e-mail	
Tel. no.	

Notice of Hearing to consider why Fine should not be imposed

In the	
Claim No.	
Claimant	
Defendant	

To

seal

If there is any reason why you think a fine should not be imposed upon you for [your failure to attend as a witness summoned to attend this court][your refusal to be sworn or give evidence][your failure to produce documents] you should either attend the hearing

at [am][pm] on

at

to give your reasons orally to the court **or**

set out your reasons in a witness statement

DATED

e court office at

ɔpen between 10 am and 4 pm Monday to Friday. When corresponding with the court, please address forms or letters to the Court Manager and quote the claim number.

ɩ67 Notice to show cause why Fine should not be imposed.

Application for charging order on land or property

In the

Claim No.

Appn. No.

Claimant

Defendant

The [claimant] [defendant] ('the judgment creditor') applies for an order imposing a charge on the interest of the [defendant] [claimant] ('the judgment debtor') in the land or property mentioned below to secure payment of the amount owing under the judgment or order given on 20 [by the in claim no.].

1. Judgment debtor
The judgment debtor is
whose address is

Postcode

2. Judgment debt
The judgment or order required the judgment debtor to pay £ (including any costs and interest). The amount now owing is £ [which includes further interest payable on the judgment debt].

☐ £ of the instalments due under the judgment or order has fallen due and remains unpaid.

☐ The judgment or order did not provide for payment by instalments.

3. The land or property
The address of the land or property upon which it is sought to impose a to charge is

[the title to which is registered at H. M. Land Registry under Title No.
An Office Copy of the Land Register entries for this title is attached.]

4. Judgment debtor's interest in the land or property
The judgment debtor is:
☐ the sole owner ☐ a joint owner ☐ a beneficiary under a trust

☐ This is shown by the Office Copy Land Register entries attached.

☐ The judgment creditor believes this to be so because

N379 Application for charging order on land or property (03.02) *Printed on behalf of The Court Service*

5. **Other creditors**

☐ The judgment creditor does not know of any other creditors of the judgment debtor.

☐ The judgment creditor knows of the following other creditors of the judgment debtor:
(names and addresses and, if known, nature of debt and amount)

6. **Other persons to be served**

☐ No other person has an interest in the property (including any co-owners, trustees and persons with rights of occupation).

☐ The following persons have or may have an interest in the property:
(name and address and, if known, nature of interest)

7. **Further information**

The judgment creditor asks the court to take account of the following:

8. **Sources of information** *(Complete only where the judgment creditor is a firm or a company or other corporation)*

[The information in this application is given [by me] [by of who is the of the judgment creditor] after making proper enquiry of all persons within the judgment creditor's organisation who might have knowledge of the facts.]

Statement of Truth

*I believe (the judgment creditor believes) that the facts stated in this application form are true.
*I am duly authorised by the judgment creditor to sign this statement

signed ______________________ date ______________

*(Judgment creditor)(Litigation friend *(where judgment creditor is a child or a patient)*)(Judgment creditor's solicitor)

**delete as appropriate*

Full name ______________________________

Name of judgment creditor's solicitor's firm ______________________

position or office held ______________________ *(if signing on behalf of a firm or company)*

Judgment creditor's or judgment creditor's solicitor's address to which documents should be sent.

Postcode

if applicable

Ref. no.	
fax no.	
DX no.	
e-mail	
Tel. no.	

Application for charging order on securities

In the

Claim No.

Appn. No.

Claimant

Defendant

The [claimant] [defendant] ('the judgment creditor') applies for an order imposing a charge on the interest of the [defendant] [claimant] ('the judgment debtor') in the securities mentioned below to secure payment of the amount owing under the judgment or order given on ________________ 20 ___ [by the____ in claim no. ______________________].

1. Judgment debtor

The judgment debtor is____

whose address is____

____

____ Postcode ________________

2. Judgment debt

The judgment or order required the judgment debtor to pay £________________(including any costs and interest). The amount now owing is £________________ [which includes further interest payable on the judgment debt].

☐ £________________ of the instalments due under the judgment or order has fallen due and remains unpaid.

☐ The judgment or order did not provide for payment by instalments.

3. The securities

The securities on which it is sought to impose a change are:____

____

____

____

4. Judgment debtor's interest

The interest of the judgment debtor in the securities is: ____

____

____

____

The judgment creditor believes this to be so because: ____

____

____

____

N380 Application for charging order on securities (03.02) *Printed on behalf of The Court Service*

5. **Other creditors**

☐ The judgment creditor does not know of any other creditors of the judgment debtor.

☐ The judgment creditor knows of the existence of the following other creditors of the judgment debtor:
(names and addresses and, if known, nature of debt and amount)

____
____
____
____

6. **Other persons to be served**

☐ No other persons have or may have an interest in the securities (including any co-owners and trustees).

☐ The following persons have or may have an interest in the securities:
(names and addresses and, if known, nature of interest)

____
____
____
____

7. **Further information**

The judgment creditor asks the court to take account of the following: ______________________________
____
____

8. **Sources of information** *(Complete only where the judgment creditor is a firm, a company or corporation)*

[The information in this application is given [by me] [by______________ of ______________ ______________ who is the ______________ of the judgment creditor] after making proper enquiry of all persons within the judgment creditor's organisation who might have knowledge of the facts.]

Statement of Truth

*I believe (the judgment creditor believes) that the facts stated in this application form are true.
*I am duly authorised by the judgment creditor to sign this statement

signed ______________ date ______________
*(Judgment creditor)(Litigation friend *(where judgment creditor is a child or a patient)*)(Judgment creditor's solicitor)
**delete as appropriate*
Full name ______________
Name of judgment creditor's solicitor's firm ______________
position or office held ______________ *(if signing on behalf of a firm or company)*

Judgment creditor's or judgment creditor's solicitor's address to which documents should be sent.

Postcode

if applicable

Ref. no.	
fax no.	
DX no.	
e-mail	
Tel. no.	

Notice of change of solicitor

Name of court	Claim No.
Name of Claimant *(including ref.)*	
Name of Defendant	

Note:
You should tick either box A **or** B as appropriate **and** box C. Complete details as necessary.

I (We) give notice that

A ☐ my solicitor *(insert name and address)*

has ceased to act for me and I shall now be acting in person.

B ☐ we *(insert name of solicitor)*

have been instructed to act on behalf of the claimant (defendant) in this claim

in place of *(insert name and address of previous solicitors)*.

C ☐ I (we) have served notice of this change on every party to the claim (and on the former solicitor).

Address to which documents about this claim should be sent (including any reference)

	If applicable	
	Telephone no.	
	Fax no.	
	DX no.	
Postcode	Your ref.	

E-mail	

Signed
(Claimant)(Defendant)('s solicitor)(Litigation friend)

Position or office held
If signing on behalf of firm or company

Date __/__/____

The court office at

is open between 10 am and 4 pm Monday to Friday. When corresponding with the court, please address forms or letters to the Court Manager and quote the claim number.

N434 Notice of change of solicitor (09.09)

REQUEST FOR RE-ISSUE OF ENFORCEMENT OF AN ORDER TO OBTAIN INFORMATION FROM JUDGMENT DEBTOR (NOT WARRANT) **FORM N446**

Request for Reissue of Enforcement or Oral Examination (not warrant)

In the

County Court

Claim No.

Type of process

Tick appropriate box and enter claim number and number of process

☐	**Attachment of earnings**	**A/E No.**
☐	**Oral examination**	**O/E No.**
☐	**Judgment summons**	**J/S No.**
☐	**Other** *please specify, charging order, garnishee etc.*	**No.**

1 Claimant's name

2 Name and address for service and payment

Ref/Tel No.

3 Defendant's name and address

For court use only

Hearing Date:

on

at o'clock

at (address)

Reissue date:

4 Outstanding debt

(A) Balance due* at date of this request (including costs of issue of post - judgment process, and unsatisfied warrant costs†

*this may include interest to the date of request where judgment is for £5,000 or more, or is in respect of a debt which attracts contractual or statutory interest for late payment
†except where reissuing oral examination

Unsatisfied warrant costs (oral examinations only)

(B) **Judgment summonses only**
Amount due under the judgment summons (do not include amounts for which defendant imprisoned)

IMPORTANT
You must inform the court immediately of any payments you receive after you have sent this request to the court

I certify that (*the whole or part of any instalments due under the judgment or order have not been paid and that) the balance now due under this judgment is as shown (†and that the amount due under the judgment summons is as shown at (B))

Signed

Claimant (Claimant's solicitor)

Date

**delete if you are applying to reissue an oral examination*
†delete if not applying to reissue judgment summons

Reasons for requesting reissue *(information you are relying on to support your application for reissue eg defendant's address (or employment) has changed, he has failed to make payments under a suspended order etc.)*

Reissue No.

N446-w3 Request for reissue of post-judgment process (other than warrant) (4.99)

Printed on behalf of The Court Service

Reasons for allowing or refusing permission to appeal (including referral to the Court of Appeal (Civil Division))

The judge must complete this form on allowing or refusing an application for permission to appeal at a hearing or trial

Title of case/claim

Case/claim no

Heard/tried before *(insert name of Judge)*

Date of hearing/trial

Nature of hearing/ trial

Result of hearing/trial

Claimant's/defendant's application for permission to appeal

☐ allowed ☐ refused

Brief reasons for decision to allow or refuse appeal
(to be completed by the Judge):

Judge's signature

If permission is given the judge must also complete the reverse of this form

Note: The appellant must file a copy of this completed form at the appeal court with the appellant's notice when issuing the appeal.

N460 Reasons for allowing or refusing permission to appeal and referral to the Court of Appeal (7.00)

Do you consider the appeal should be referred to the Court of Appeal (Civil Division)?

☐ Yes ☐ No

If Yes, please indicate which of the following criteria apply:

☐ There appear to be conflicting authorities.

☐ There is a point of practice and procedure of significant importance.

☐ There is a point of general principle and importance in the development of the substantive law.

☐ A number of appeals on similar points suggest that a theme, or trend, is developing which the Court of Appeal needs to consider.

Additional reasons *(please set out below)*

Judicial Review
Claim Form

In the High Court of Justice
Administrative Court

Notes for guidance are available which explain how to complete the judicial review claim form. Please read them carefully before you complete the form.

For Court use only	
Administrative Court Reference No.	
Date filed	

Seal

SECTION 1 Details of the claimant(s) and defendant(s)

Claimant(s) name and address(es)

name

address

Telephone no. Fax no.

E-mail address

Claimant's or claimant's solicitors' address to which documents should be sent.

name

address

Telephone no. Fax no.

E-mail address

Claimant's Counsel's details

name

address

Telephone no. Fax no.

E-mail address

1st Defendant

name

Defendant's or (where known) Defendant's solicitors' address to which documents should be sent.

name

address

Telephone no. Fax no.

E-mail address

2nd Defendant

name

Defendant's or (where known) Defendant's solicitors' address to which documents should be sent.

name

address

Telephone no. Fax no.

E-mail address

SECTION 2 Details of other interested parties

Include name and address and, if appropriate, details of DX, telephone or fax numbers and e-mail

name

address

Telephone no. Fax no.

E-mail address

name

address

Telephone no. Fax no.

E-mail address

SECTION 3 Details of the decision to be judicially reviewed

Decision:

Date of decision:

Name and address of the court, tribunal, person or body who made the decision to be reviewed.

name

address

SECTION 4 Permission to proceed with a claim for judicial review

I am seeking permission to proceed with my claim for Judicial Review.

Is this application being made under the terms of Section 18 Practice Direction 54 (Challenging removal)? ☐ Yes ☐ No

Are you making any other applications? If Yes, complete Section 7. ☐ Yes ☐ No

Is the claimant in receipt of a Community Legal Service Fund (CLSF) certificate? ☐ Yes ☐ No

Are you claiming exceptional urgency, or do you need this application determined within a certain time scale? If Yes, complete Form N463 and file this with your application. ☐ Yes ☐ No

Have you complied with the pre-action protocol? If No, give reasons for non-compliance in the box below. ☐ Yes ☐ No

Have you issued this claim in the region with which you have the closest connection? (Give any additional reasons for wanting it to be dealt with in this region in the box below). If No, give reasons in the box below. ☐ Yes ☐ No

Does the claim include any issues arising from the Human Rights Act 1998?
If Yes, state the articles which you contend have been breached in the box below. ☐ Yes ☐ No

SECTION 5 Detailed statement of grounds

☐ set out below ☐ attached

SECTION 6 Details of remedy (including any interim remedy) being sought

SECTION 7 Other applications

I wish to make an application for:-

3 of 6

SECTION 8 Statement of facts relied on

Statement of Truth

I believe (The claimant believes) that the facts stated in this claim form are true.

Full name ______________________________

Name of claimant's solicitor's firm ______________________________

Signed ______________________________ Position or office held ______________________________

Claimant ('s solicitor) (if signing on behalf of firm or company)

4 of 6

SECTION 9 Supporting documents

If you do not have a document that you intend to use to support your claim, identify it, give the date when you expect it to be available and give reasons why it is not currently available in the box below.

Please tick the papers you are filing with this claim form and any you will be filing later.

- ☐ Statement of grounds ☐ included ☐ attached
- ☐ Statement of the facts relied on ☐ included ☐ attached
- ☐ Application to extend the time limit for filing the claim form ☐ included ☐ attached
- ☐ Application for directions ☐ included ☐ attached
- ☐ Any written evidence in support of the claim or application to extend time
- ☐ Where the claim for judicial review relates to a decision of a court or tribunal, an approved copy of the reasons for reaching that decision
- ☐ Copies of any documents on which the claimant proposes to rely
- ☐ A copy of the legal aid or CSLF certificate *(if legally represented)*
- ☐ Copies of any relevant statutory material
- ☐ A list of essential documents for advance reading by the court *(with page references to the passages relied upon)*

If Section 18 Practice Direction 54 applies, please tick the relevant box(es) below to indicate which papers you are filing with this claim form:

- ☐ a copy of the removal directions and the decision to which the application relates ☐ included ☐ attached
- ☐ a copy of the documents served with the removal directions including any documents which contains the Immigration and Nationality Directorate's factual summary of the case ☐ included ☐ attached
- ☐ a detailed statement of the grounds ☐ included ☐ attached

5 of 6

Reasons why you have not supplied a document and date when you expect it to be available:-

Signed ______________________________ Claimant ('s Solicitor)______________________________

Click here to print form

Guidance notes on completing the Judicial Review claim form

Set out overleaf are notes to help you complete the form. You should read the notes to each section carefully before you begin to complete that particular section.

Use a separate sheet if you need more space for your answers, marking clearly which section the information refers to.

If you do not have all the documents or information you need for your claim, you must not allow this to delay sending or taking the form to the Administrative Court Office within the correct time. Complete the form as fully as possible and provide what documents you have. The notes to section 9 will explain more about what you have to do in these circumstances.

The Court and venue

- CPR part 54 – claims for Judicial Review are dealt with by the Administrative Court.
- Subject to the considerations in Practice Direction 54D 5.2, the general expectation is that proceedings will be administered and determined in the region in which the claimant has closest connection.
- Where the claim is proceeding in the Administrative Court in **London**, documents must be filed in the Administrative Court Office, Room C315, Royal Courts of Justice, Strand, London, WC2A 2LL.
- Where the claim is proceeding in the Administrative Court in **Birmingham**, documents must be filed in the Administrative Court Office, Birmingham Civil Justice Centre, Priory Courts, 33 Bull Street, Birmingham B4 6DS.
- Where the claim is proceeding in the Administrative Court in **Wales**, documents must be filed in the Administrative Court Office, Cardiff Civil Justice Centre, 2 Park Street, Cardiff, CF10 1ET.
- Where the claim is proceeding in the Administrative Court in **Leeds**, documents must be filed in the Administrative Court Office, Leeds Combined Court Centre, 1 Oxford Row, Leeds, LS1 3BG.
- Where the claim is proceeding in the Administrative Court in **Manchester**, documents must be filed in the Administrative Court Office, Manchester Civil Justice Centre, 1 Bridge Street West, Manchester, M3 3FX.

Time limit for filing a claim

- Unless Section 18 Practice Direction 54 applies in relation to the deferral of removal, the claim must be filed promptly and in any event **no later than three months** after the grounds to make the claim first arose.

Note: Section 18 Practice Direction 54 and Practice Direction 54D are set out on our website (www.hmcourts-service.gov.uk). Should you need a hard copies of these Practice Directions, please contact the Administrative Court office or your local Citizen's Advice Bureau.

If you need help to complete the form you should consult a solicitor or your local Citizen's Advice Bureau.

Section 1

Details of the claimants and defendants
Give full name(s) and address(es) to which all documents relating to the judicial review are to be sent. Include contact information e.g. telephone numbers and any other reference numbers.

Section 2

Details of other interested parties
Where the claim for judicial review relates to proceedings in a court or tribunal, any other parties to those proceedings must be named in the claim form as interested parties. Full details of interested parties must be included in the claim form.

For example, if you were a defendant in a criminal case in the Magistrates or Crown Court and are making a claim for judicial review of a decision in that case, the prosecution must be named as an interested party.

In a claim which does not relate to a decision of a court or tribunal, you should give details of any persons directly affected by the decision you wish to challenge.

Section 3

Details of the decision to be judicially reviewed
Give details of the decision you seek to have judicially reviewed. Give the name of the court, tribunal, person or body whose decision you are seeking to judicially review, and the date on which the decision was made.

Section 4

Permission to proceed with a claim for judicial review
This section must be completed. You must answer all the questions and give further details where required.

Section 5

Detailed statement of grounds
Set out, in detail, the grounds on which you contend the decision should be set aside or varied.

Section 6

Details of remedy
Complete this section stating what remedy you are seeking:
(a) a mandatory order;
(b) a prohibiting order;
(c) a quashing order; or
(d) an injunction restraining a person from acting in any office in which he is not entitled to act.

A claim for damages may be included but only if you are seeking one of the orders set out above.

Section 7

Other applications
You may wish to make additional applications to the Administrative Court in connection with your claim for Judicial Review. Any other applications may be made either in the claim form or in a separate application (Form PF244). This form can be obtained from any of the Administrative Court Offices listed overleaf or from our website at www.hmcourts-service.gov.uk.

Section 8

Statement of facts relied on
The facts on which you are basing your claim should be set out in this section of the form, or in a separate document attached to the form. It should contain a numbered list of the points that you intend to rely on at the hearing. Refer at each point to any documents you are filing in support of your claim

Section 9

Supporting documents
Do not delay filing your claim for judicial review. If you have not been able to obtain any of the documents listed in this section within the time limits referred to on the previous page, complete the notice as best you can and ensure the claim is filed on time. Set out the reasons why you have not been able to obtain any of the information or documents and give the date when you expect them to be available.

Judicial Review
Acknowledgment of Service

In the High Court of Justice Administrative Court	
Claim No.	
Claimant(s) (including ref.)	
Defendant(s)	
Interested Parties	

Name and address of person to be served

name

address

SECTION A

Tick the appropriate box

1. I intend to contest all of the claim ☐ } complete sections B, C, D and E
2. I intend to contest part of the claim ☐ }
3. I do not intend to contest the claim ☐ complete section E
4. The defendant (interested party) is a court or tribunal and **intends** to make a submission. ☐ complete sections B, C and E
5. The defendant (interested party) is a court or tribunal and **does not intend** to make a submission. ☐ complete sections B and E

Note: If the application seeks to judicially review the decision of a court or tribunal, the court or tribunal need only provide the Administrative Court with as much evidence as it can about the decision to help the Administrative Court perform its judicial function.

SECTION B

Insert the name and address of any person you consider should be added as an interested party.

name

address

Telephone no. Fax no.

E-mail address

name

address

Telephone no. Fax no.

E-mail address

SECTION C

Summary of grounds for contesting the claim. If you are contesting only part of the claim, set out which part before you give your grounds for contesting it. If you are a court or tribunal filing a submission, please indicate that this is the case.

SECTION D

Give details of any directions you will be asking the court to make, or tick the box to indicate that a separate application notice is attached.

If you are seeking a direction that this matter be heard at an Administrative Court venue other than that at which this claim was issued, you should complete, lodge and serve on all other parties Form N464 with this acknowledgment of service.

SECTION E

**delete as appropriate*

*(I believe)(The defendant believes) that the facts stated in this form are true.

*I am duly authorised by the defendant to sign this statement.

(if signing on behalf of firm or company, court or tribunal)

Position or office held

(To be signed by you or by your solicitor or litigation friend)

Signed

Date

Give an address to which notices about this case can be sent to you

name

address

Telephone no.

Fax no.

E-mail address

If you have instructed counsel, please give their name address and contact details below.

name

address

Telephone no.

Fax no.

E-mail address

Completed forms, together with a copy, should be lodged with the Administrative Court Office (court address, over the page), at which this claim was issued within 21 days of service of the claim upon you, and further copies should be served on the Claimant(s), any other Defendant(s) and any interested parties within 7 days of lodgement with the Court.

3 of 4

Administrative Court addresses

- Administrative Court in **London**

  Administrative Court Office, Room C315, Royal Courts of Justice, Strand, London, WC2A 2LL.

- Administrative Court in **Birmingham**

  Administrative Court Office, Birmingham Civil Justice Centre, Priory Courts, 33 Bull Street, Birmingham B4 6DS.

- Administrative Court in **Wales**

  Administrative Court Office, Cardiff Civil Justice Centre, 2 Park Street, Cardiff, CF10 1ET.

- Administrative Court in **Leeds**

  Administrative Court Office, Leeds Combined Court Centre, 1 Oxford Row, Leeds, LS1 3BG.

- Administrative Court in **Manchester**

  Administrative Court Office, Manchester Civil Justice Centre, 1 Bridge Street West, Manchester, M3 3FX.

Judicial Review
Application for urgent consideration

This form must be completed by the Claimant or the Claimant's advocate if exceptional urgency is being claimed and the application needs to be determined within a certain time scale.

The claimant, or the claimant's solicitors must serve this form on the defendant(s) and any interested parties with the N461 Judicial review claim form.

To the Defendant(s) and Interested Party(ies) Representations as to the urgency of the claim may be made by defendants or interested parties to the relevant Administrative Court Office by fax:-

For cases proceeding in

London – 020 7947 6802 **Birmingham** – 0121 250 6730

Cardiff – 02920 376461 **Leeds** – 0113 306 2581

Manchester – 0161 240 5315

In the High Court of Justice Administrative Court	
Claim No.	
Claimant(s) *(including ref.)*	
Defendant(s)	
Interested Parties	

SECTION 1 Reasons for urgency

SECTION 2 Proposed timetable *(tick the boxes and complete the following statements that apply)*

☐ a) The application for interim relief should be considered within .... hours/days

☐ b) The N461 application for permission should be considered within .... hours/days

☐ c) Abridgement of time is sought for the lodging of acknowledgments of service

☐ d) If permission for judicial review is granted, a substantive hearing is sought by ....(date)

SECTION 3 Interim relief *(state what interim relief is sought and why in the box below)*

A draft order must be attached.

SECTION 4 Service

A copy of this form of application was served on the defendant(s) and interested parties as follows:

Defendant

☐ by fax machine to — Fax no.
time sent — time

☐ by handing it to or leaving it with — name

☐ by e-mail to — e-mail address

Date served — Date

Interested party

☐ by fax machine to — Fax no.
time sent — time

☐ by handing it to or leaving it with — name

☐ by e-mail to — e-mail address

Date served — Date

Name of claimant's advocate — name

Claimant (claimant's advocate) — Signed

2 of 2

No. 32
Order for examination within jurisdiction of witness before trial (Rule 34.8)

IN THE HIGH COURT OF JUSTICE
[ ] DIVISION
[ ] District Registry
Claim No.

Before *(Judge/Master/District Judge)* [sitting in Private]

Claimant

Defendant

AN APPLICATION was made by [application notice/letter] dated (*date*) *or* by [Counsel][solicitor] for (*party*) and was attended by ( )

The Master [District Judge] read the written evidence filed

IT IS ORDERED that:

1. (*name*) a witness on behalf of the (*party*) be examined orally on oath or affirmation before [a Judge][a Master][a District Judge][an examiner of the court][(*name*) whom the court hereby appoints].
2. the (*party's*) solicitor is to give to the (*party's*) solicitor ( ) days notice in writing of the time and place where the examination is to take place (*or as ordered*)
3. the depositions taken at the examination be filed in the Central Office of the Supreme Court (*or as appropriate - see note below*) and that official copies of them may be read and given in evidence at the trial of these proceedings, saving all just exceptions.
4. the costs of this application are [summarily assessed in the sum of £] [to be the subject of a detailed assessment] and to be paid by (*party*).

Dated

Note- the depositions should be filed in the court office where the claim is proceeding.

No. 33
Application for issue of letter of request to judicial authority out of jurisdiction (Rule 34.13)

Parties should use form PF 244/N244 and add the following text:

"......for an order that:

1. a letter of request be issued to the proper judicial authority of (*country*) for the examination of (*names of witnesses*) on the (*party*)'s behalf at (*address*) in (*country*).
2. the claim be stayed until the return of the letter of request and examination.
3. the costs of this application, letter of request and examination be assessed and paid to (*party*)."

No. 34
Order for issue of letter of request to judicial authority out of jurisdiction (rule 34.13)

IN THE HIGH COURT OF JUSTICE
QUEEN'S BENCH DIVISION
[ ] District Registry
Claim No.

Before (*Master/District Judge*)

Claimant

Defendant

An Application was made by [application notice/letter] dated (*date*) *or* by [Counsel][solicitor] for (*party*) and was attended by ( )

The Master [District Judge] read the written evidence filed

IT IS ORDERED that:

1. a letter of request be issued directed to the proper judicial authority of (*country*) for the examination of the following witnesses, namely:

   (*give names and addresses of witnesses*)

2. the depositions of those witnesses when received be filed in the Central Office of the Supreme Court (*or as appropriate- see note below*) and that official copies of them may be read and given in evidence at the trial of these proceedings, saving all just exceptions.

[3. the trial of these proceedings be stayed until the depositions are filed.]

4. the costs of and caused by this application and the letter of request and examination are [summarily assessed in the sum of £][to be the subject of a detailed assessment] and to be paid by (*party*).

   Dated

Note- the depositions should be filed in the court office where the claim is proceeding.

No. 35
Letter of request for examination of witness out of jurisdiction (Rule 34.13)

To the Competent Judicial Authority of (*name of court*) in (*country*)

I (*name*) Senior Master of the Queen's Bench Division of the Supreme Court of England and Wales respectfully request the assistance of your court with regard to the following matters.

1. A claim is now pending in the [ ] Division of the High Court of Justice in England and Wales [County Court] entitled as follows:

   (*set out full title and claim number*)

   in which (*name*) of (*address*) is the claimant and (*name*) of (*address*) is the defendant.

2. The names and addresses of the representatives or agents of the parties are:

   (*set out names and addresses of representatives of the parties*).

3. The claim by the claimant is for:-

   (a) (*set out the nature of the claim*)
   (b) (*the relief sought*) and
   (c) (*a summary of the facts*).

4. It is necessary for the purposes of justice and for the due determination of the matters in dispute between the parties that you cause the following witnesses, who are resident within your jurisdiction, to be examined. The names and addresses of the witnesses are as follows:-

5. The witnesses should be examined on oath or if that is not possible within your laws or is impossible of performance by reason of the internal practice and procedure of your court or by reason of practical difficulties, they should be examined in accordance with whatever procedure your laws provide for in these matters.

6. *Either:*
   The witnesses should be examined in accordance with the list of questions annexed hereto.

   Or:
   The witnesses should be examined regarding (*set out full details of evidence sought*)

   (N.B. Where the witness is required to produce documents, these should be clearly identified.)

7. I would ask that you cause me, or the agents of the parties (if appointed), to be informed of the date and place where the examination is to take place.

8. Finally, I request that you will cause the evidence of the said witnesses to be reduced into writing and all documents produced on such examinations to be duly marked for identification and that you will further be pleased to authenticate such examinations by the seal of your court or in such other way as is in accordance with your procedure and return the written evidence and documents produced to me addressed as follows:-

   Senior Master of the Queen's Bench Division
   Royal Courts of Justice
   Strand
   London WC2A 2LL
   England

Dated

Signed:

Senior Master of the Queen's Bench Division

No. 37
Order for appointment of special examiner to take evidence of witness out of jurisdiction (Rule 34.13(4) PD para 5)

IN THE HIGH COURT OF JUSTICE
QUEEN'S BENCH DIVISION
[ ] District Registry
Claim No.

Before (*Master/District Judge*) [sitting in Private]

Claimant

Defendant

An Application was made by [application notice/letter] dated (*date*) *or* by [Counsel][solicitor] for (*party*) and was attended by ( )

The Master [District Judge] read the written evidence filed

IT IS ORDERED that:

1. the British Consul or his deputy at (*place*) is appointed as special examiner for the purpose of taking the examination, cross-examination and re-examination orally, on oath or affirmation, of (*names of witnesses*) on the part of (*party*) at (*place*) in (*country*). The examiner shall not exercise any compulsory powers but may invite the attendance of witnesses and the production of documents. Otherwise the examination shall be taken in accordance with the English procedure.
2. the solicitors for the (*party*) give to the solicitors for the (*party*) [ ] days notice in writing of the date on which they propose to send out this order to (*country*) for execution, and that [ ] days after service of that notice the solicitors for the parties respectively exchange the names of their agents at (*place*) to whom notice relating to the examination of the witnesses may be sent.
3. the agent of the party on whose behalf the witness is to be examined must give to the agent of the other party [ ] days notice (exclusive of Sundays) of the examination, before the examination of any witness under this order.
4. the depositions when taken together with any documents referred to in them, or certified copies of those documents or of extracts from them be sent by the examiner under seal to the Senior Master of the Supreme Court of England and Wales, Royal Courts of Justice, Strand, London WC2A 2LL (*or as appropriate- see note below*) to be filed in the Central Office (*or as appropriate- see note below*).
5. either party has permission to read and give the depositions in evidence at the trial of these proceedings, saving all just exceptions.

[6. the trial of these proceedings be stayed until the depositions are filed.]

7. the costs of and caused by this application and the examination are [summarily assessed in the sum of £][to be the subject of a detailed assessment] and to be paid by (*party*).

Dated

Note- Where appropriate the depositions should be sent to the Admiralty Registrar at the Royal Courts of Justice, the District Judge of a District Registry of the High Court or the Senior District Judge of the Family Division, First Avenue House, Holborn, London and should be filed in the appropriate court office.

No. 41
Default judgment in claim relating to detention of goods (Rule 12.4(1)(c))

IN THE HIGH COURT OF JUSTICE
[ ] DIVISION
[ ] District Registry
Claim No.

Claimant

Defendant

A Request for judgment was received from the claimant stating that no acknowledgment of service or defence to the claim had been filed and that the time for doing so had expired.

IT IS ORDERED that the defendant:

1. either deliver to the claimant the goods described in the [claim form] [particulars of claim] as (*description of goods*), or pay the claimant the value of the goods to be decided by the court, and

[2. pay damages for their detention to be decided by the court.]

3. pay the claimant costs [summarily assessed in the sum of £] [to be the subject of a detailed assessment].

Dated

No. 44
Part 24 judgment for claimant

IN THE HIGH COURT OF JUSTICE
[ ] DIVISION
[ ] District Registry
Claim No.

Before (*Master/District Judge*) [sitting in Private]

Claimant

Defendant

An Application was made on (*date*) by [Counsel][solicitor] for the claimant under Part 24 for judgment and was attended by

The Master [District Judge] read the written evidence filed

And the Court having found that the defendant has no real prospect of successfully defending the claim *or* [issue of (*define the issue*)] and that there is no other reason why the claim *or* [issue of (*define the issue*)] should be disposed of at a trial

IT IS ORDERED that the defendant:

1. pay the claimant the sum of £ .

or

2. pay the claimant an amount of money to be decided by the court.

or

3. (a) deliver to the claimant the goods described in the [claim form] [particulars of claim] as (*description of goods*), or

   (b) pay the claimant the value of the goods to be decided by the court, [and

   (c) pay damages for their detention to be decided by the court.]

or

4. give the claimant possession of the land described in the [claim form][particulars of claim] as (*description of land*).
5. pay the claimant costs [summarily assessed in the sum of £] [to be the subject of a detailed assessment].

   Dated

No. 44A
Part 24 Judgment for Defendant

IN THE HIGH COURT OF JUSTICE
[ ] DIVISION
[ ] District Registry
Claim No.

Before (*Master/District Judge*)[Sitting in Private]

Claimant

Defendant

An Application was made on (*date*) by [Counsel][solicitor] for the defendant under Part 24 for judgment and was attended by

The Master [District Judge] read the written evidence filed

And the Court having found that the claimant has no real prospect of succeeding on the claim *or* [issue of (*define the issue*)] and that there is no other reason why the claim *or* [issue of (*define the issue*)] should be disposed of at a trial

IT IS ORDERED that:

1. there be judgment for the defendant on the claim *or* [issue of (*define the issue*)].
2. the claimant pay the defendant costs [summarily assessed in the sum of £] [to be the subject of a detailed assessment].

Dated

No. 45
Judgment after trial before judge without jury (Part 40 PD(B) para. 14)

IN THE HIGH COURT OF JUSTICE
[ ] DIVISION
[ ] District Registry
Claim No.

Before (*Judge's name and title*)

Claimant

Defendant

This claim having [been tried][come] before (*Judge's name and title*) without a jury at [the Royal Courts of Justice]

[And terms of settlement having been agreed between the parties],

(*Set out here any matters required by paragraphs 5, 6 and 14.2(3),(4) and (5) of the Part 40 Practice Direction (B)*).

And the Judge having ordered on (*date*) that judgment be entered for the claimant against the defendant (*or as may be*) as set out below [and that execution be stayed for the period and on the terms set out below]:

IT IS ORDERED that:

1. the defendant pay the claimant the sum of £ (being £ principal sum and £ [agreed interest] [interest at the rate of ( )% from (*date*) to the date of this order])

   or in a personal injury claim-

   the defendant pay the claimant the sum of £ (being (1) £ special damages and £ [agreed interest] [interest at the rate of ( )% from (*date*) to the date of this order] (2) £ general damages and £ [agreed interest] [interest at the rate of ( )% from (*date*) to the date of this order] and (3) £ in respect of loss of future earnings and/or earning capacity) (*or as ordered*).

[2. execution be stayed for (*period*) and if within that time the (*party*) gives notice of appeal and sets down the appeal, execution be further stayed until the conclusion of the appeal.]

[3. that the sum of £ now in court standing to the credit of this claim be paid out to the claimant's solicitors in part satisfaction of the judgment debt and costs together with any interest accrued from the date of this order and that the interest accrued up to the date of this order be paid out to the defendant's solicitors as specified in the payment schedule to this order.]

4. the defendant pay the claimant's costs [summarily assessed in the sum of £] [to be the subject of a detailed assessment]

   Dated

No. 46
Judgment after trial before judge with jury (Part 40 PD(B) para. 14)

IN THE HIGH COURT OF JUSTICE
[ ] DIVISION
[ ] District Registry
Claim No.

Before (*Judge's name and title*)

Claimant

Defendant

This claim having been tried before (*Judge's name and title*) and a jury,

(*Set out here any matters required by paragraph 14.2(3) and (4) of the Part 40 Practice Direction (B)*)

And the jury having found the answers as set out below to the following questions:- (*set out questions and answers*),

And the jury [unanimously][by a majority of] having found for the (*party*),

And the Judge having ordered on (*date*) that judgment be entered for the (*party*) against the (*party*) as set out below:

IT IS ORDERED that:

1. the defendant pay the claimant the sum of £ (*or as ordered*).

[2. that the sum of £ now in court standing to the credit of this claim be paid out to the claimant's solicitors in part satisfaction of the judgment debt and costs together with any interest accrued from the date of this order and that the interest accrued up to the date of this order be paid out to the defendant's solicitors as specified in the payment schedule to this order.]

3. the defendant pay the claimant's costs [summarily assessed in the sum of £] [to be the subject of a detailed assessment].

Dated

No. 47
Judgment after trial before a judge of the Technology and Construction Court, or a Master or district judge (Part 40B PD para. 14)

IN THE HIGH COURT OF JUSTICE
[ ] DIVISION
[ ] District Registry
Claim No.

Before (*Judge/Master/District Judge's name and title*) [sitting in Private]

Claimant

Defendant

This claim which was directed by the Order dated (*date*) to be tried before [Judge/Master/District Judge] (*name and title*) and the [Judge][Master][District Judge] having tried the claim,

(*Set out any matters required by paragraphs 5, 6 and 14.2 of the Part 40B Practice Direction*).

And the [Judge][Master][District Judge] having ordered on (*date*) that judgment be entered for the (*party*) against the (*party*) as set out below:

IT IS ORDERED that:

1. the defendant pay the claimant the sum of £ (*or as ordered*).
2. the defendant pay the claimant's costs [summarily assessed in the sum of £] [to be the subject of a detailed assessment].

Dated

No. 48
Order after trial of issue directed to be tried under rule 3.1(2)(i)

IN THE HIGH COURT OF JUSTICE
[ ] DIVISION
[ ] District Registry
Claim No.

Before (*Judge's name and title*) [sitting in Private]

Claimant

Defendant

The Issue (*or as may be*) namely (*set out issue or question to be tried*) which was directed to be tried by the Order of (*Judge's name and title*) dated (*date*) having [been tried][come] before (*Judge's name and title*) without a jury at [the Royal Courts of Justice].

IT IS ORDERED that:

1. the above issue is determined as follows:
2. *such order as may follow the determination - or as may be*
3. the (*party*) pay the (*party's*) costs of the issue [summarily assessed in the sum of £] [to be the subject of a detailed assessment].

Dated

No. 49
Judgment against personal representatives (Part 40B PD para. 14.3)

IN THE HIGH COURT OF JUSTICE
[ ] DIVISION
[ ] District Registry
Claim No.

Before (*Judge's name and title*) [sitting in Private]

Claimant

Defendant

This claim having [been tried][come] before (*Judge's name and title*) without a jury at [the Royal Courts of Justice].

And the Judge having ordered on (*date*) that judgment be entered for the claimant against the defendant as set out below:

IT IS ORDERED that:

1. the defendant as executor [*or* administrator] of the above-named (*name*) deceased pay the claimant the sum of £ and costs [summarily assessed in the sum of £] [to be the subject of a detailed assessment] such sum and costs to be levied of the real and personal estate within the meaning of the Administration of Estates Act 1925 of the deceased at the time of his death in the hands of the defendant as executor [*or* administrator] to be administered, if he has now or shall later have that much in his hands to be administered, and
2. if he has not that much in his hands to be administered, then as to those costs, to be levied of the goods, chattels and other property of the defendant authorised by law to be seized in execution (*or as may be according to the order made*).

   Dated

No. 52
Notice of Claim to non-parties (CPR 19.8A)

IN THE HIGH COURT OF JUSTICE
CHANCERY DIVISION
Claim No.

[ ] District Registry

Master

.... 20 ...

Between **Claimant**

Defendant

TO:............................[*person[s] affected by the claim*]

TAKE NOTICE THAT:

(1) Proceedings have begun in the Chancery Division of the High Court of Justice in accordance with the attached claim form.

(2) You are or may be one of the persons who are interested in the [estate] [trust property] to which the proceedings relate.

(3) You may within 14 days after service of this notice acknowledge service of the claim form by completing the attached acknowledgement of service and handing it in at, or sending it by post to, Chancery Chambers, Room 5.04, Thomas More Building, Royal Courts of Justice, Strand, London WC2A 2LL and you will then become a party to the claim.

(3) If you do not acknowledge service of the claim form within 14 days after service of this notice you will be bound by any judgment given in the proceedings as if you were a party to them.

Dated .... [*enter date of sealing*]

No. 52A (CPR 19.8A)
Notice of judgment or order to non-parties

IN THE HIGH COURT OF JUSTICE
CHANCERY DIVISION
Claim No.

Claimant

Defendant

TO..*(enter names of non-parties)*

TAKE NOTICE THAT:

(1) A judgment [An order] of this Court was given [made] on (*date*) by which it was (*state substance of judgment or order)* A copy of the judgment [order] is attached to this notice.

(2) From the time of service of this notice you will be bound by the judgment [order] as if you had been a party to the claim.

(3) If you file an acknowledgment of service of this notice within 14 days after service of it in [Room 5.04 Chancery Chambers, Thomas More Building, Royal Courts of justice, Strand, London WC2A 2LL] [District Registry] you may

(a) within 28 days of service apply to the Court to set aside or vary the judgment [order], and

(b) take part in any proceedings relating to the judgment [order]

(4) If you do not acknowledge service of this notice within 14 days after service of it you will be bound by the judgment [order] as if you had been a party.

(5) A copy of the claim form and a form of acknowledgment of service is attached to this notice

Dated *(enter date of sealing)*

No.82

Application for appointment of receiver

(Schedule 1 RSC O.51, r.3)

Parties should use form PF 244/N244 and include in Part A the following:

".... for an order that [a receiver be appointed] [*(name and address)* be appointed receiver] in this claim to receive the rents, profits and moneys receivable in respect of the interest of the *(party)* in the following property, namely *(describe the property)* in or towards satisfaction of the moneys and interest due to the *(party)* under the judgment [or order] in this claim dated *(date)* and for an order that the costs of this application be paid by the *(party)* to the *(party)*"

No.83
Order directing application for appointment of receiver and granting injunction meanwhile (Schedule 1 RSC O.51, r 3)

IN THE HIGH COURT OF JUSTICE
[ ] DIVISION
[ ] District Registry
Claim No.

Before (*Master/District Judge*) [Sitting in Private]

Claimant

Defendant

An Application was made by [application notice/letter] dated (*date*) *or* by [Counsel][solicitor] for (*party*) and was attended by ( )

The Master [District Judge] read the written evidence filed

The *(party)* [by his counsel/solicitor] undertook that, if the Court later finds that this Order has caused loss to the *(party)* and decides that the *(party)* should be compensated for that loss, the *(party)* will comply with any Order the Court may make,

IT IS ORDERED that:

(1) there be a hearing on *(date)* at *(time)* before Master/District Judge at *(address of Court)* of the application by the *(party)* for the appointment of *(name and address)* as receiver in this claim, on the usual terms, to receive the rents, profits and moneys receivable in respect of the *(party's)* interest in the following property, namely (*describe the property*) in or towards satisfaction of the sum of £ debt and £ costs, and interest at the rate of (*insert the appropriate rate of interest at date of entry of judgment*) per annum from *(date)* due under the judgment] [or order] in this claim of *(date)*

(2) the *(party)* by himself, his servants or agents, or otherwise, be restrained, and an injunction is hereby granted restraining him, until after the hearing of the above application, from assigning charging or otherwise dealing with the said property.

Dated

No.84
Order appointing receiver by way of equitable execution (Section 37 of the Senior Courts Act 1981, Part 69 of the CPR)

IN THE HIGH COURT OF JUSTICE
[ ] DIVISION
[ ] District Registry
Claim No.

Before (*Master/District Judge*) [Sitting in Private]

Claimant

Defendant

An Application was made by [application notice/letter] dated (*date*) *or* by [Counsel] [solicitor] for (*party*) and was attended by ( )

The Master [District Judge] read the written evidence filed

IT IS ORDERED that:

1

(a) *(Name and address)*, after giving security to the satisfaction of a Master [or a District Judge], be and is hereby appointed to receive the rents, profits and moneys receivable in respect of the *(party's)* interest in the following property, namely*[describe the property]*

[(b) *(If no security ordered and receiver is not the claimant)* the *(party)* being answerable for the acts and defaults of the receiver, *(name and address)* be and is hereby appointed to receive the rents, profits and moneys receivable in respect of the *(party's)* interest in the following property, namely (*describe the property)* but he shall not receive more than the amount of the judgment debt and allowed costs of obtaining this order without permission of the Court or first giving [at the *(party's)* cost] the usual security to the satisfaction of a Master/District Judge.]

[(c) (*If no security ordered and receiver is the claimant) (name and address)* be and is hereby appointed to receive the rents, profits and moneys receivable in respect of the *(party's)* interest in the following property, namely (*describe the property)* but he shall not receive more than the amount of the judgment debt and allowed costs of obtaining this order without permission of the Court]

(2) this appointment shall be without prejudice to the rights of any prior incumbrancers upon the said property who may think proper to take possession of or receive the same by virtue of their respective securities or, if any prior incumbrancer is in possession, then without prejudice to such possession.

(3) the tenants of premises comprised in the said property to attorn and pay their rents in arrears and growing rents to the receiver.

(4) the receiver has permission, if he shall think proper (but not otherwise), out of the rents, profits and moneys to be received by him to keep down the interest upon the prior incumbrances, according to their priorities, and be allowed such payments, if any, in passing his accounts.

(5) the receiver shall on (*date - 3 months after the date of order),* and at such other times as may be ordered by the Master/District Judge pass his accounts, and shall on *(date - 4 months after the date of order),* and at such further and other times as may be ordered by the Master/District Judge pay the balance or balances appearing due on the accounts, or such part as shall be certified as proper to be paid, such sums to be paid in or towards satisfaction of what shall for the time being be due in respect of the judgment signed (*date)* for the sum of £ debt and £ costs, totalling £ .

(6) the costs of the receiver (including his remuneration), the costs of obtaining his appointment, of completing his security (if any), of passing his accounts and of obtaining his discharge shall not exceed 10 per cent of the amount due under the said judgment or the amount recovered by the receiver, whichever is the less, provided that not less than £5 be allowed unless otherwise ordered.

(7) costs be [summarily assessed by the Master/District Judge in the sum of £] [the subject of a detailed assessment] and shall be primarily payable out of the sums received by the receiver, but if no sums are received or the amount is insufficient, then upon the certificate of the Master/District Judge being given stating the amount of the deficiency, the certificate to be given after passing the final account, the amount of the deficiency so certified shall be paid by the *(party)* to the *(party)*.

(8) the balance (if any) remaining in the hands of the receiver, after making the above payments, shall unless otherwise directed by the Master/District Judge forthwith be paid by the receiver into court to the credit of this claim, subject to further order.

(9) any party has permission to apply to the Master/District Judge for further orders or directions.

Dated

No. 93
Order under the Evidence (Proceedings in Other Jurisdictions) Act 1975 (Schedule 1 - RSC O.70 r.1)

IN THE HIGH COURT OF JUSTICE
QUEEN'S BENCH DIVISION
Claim No.

Before Master [sitting in Private]

In the matter of the Evidence (Proceedings in Other Jurisdictions) Act 1975

and

In the matter of a civil [*or* commercial] proceeding now pending [*or* contemplated] before (*give description of foreign court or tribunal*) entitled as follows:-

(*(1) give title of proceedings in foreign court or tribunal or (2) state "In proceedings contemplated between (party) and (party)"*)

AN APPLICATION was made by [application notice/letter] dated (*date*) *or* by [Counsel][solicitor] for (*party*) and was attended by (   )

The Master read the written evidence filed and the Letter of Request dated (*date*) from (*description of foreign court or tribunal and name of country*) from which it appears that proceedings are pending [or contemplated] in that court and that that court seeks to obtain the testimony of (*name and address of witness*)

IT IS ORDERED that:

1. the witness (*name*) attend before [(*name and address*)] [an examiner of the court][a District Judge of the (*name*) county court] who is hereby appointed examiner at (*place*) on (*date*) at (*time*), or on such other day and time as the examiner may appoint, to be examined [on oath or affirmation] in respect of the required testimony [and produce (*specify particular documents required to be produced*)].
2. the examiner record in writing or cause to be recorded in writing the evidence of the witness (*name*), according to the rules and practice of Her Majesty's High Court of Justice relating to the examination and cross-examination of witnesses [*or as otherwise ordered*].
3. the examiner (a) request the witness to sign his deposition in the examiner's presence, (b) sign the deposition and (c) when completed, send it together with this Order and the Letter of Request to the Senior Master, Foreign Process Section, Room E02, Royal Courts of Justice, Strand, London WC2A 2LL for transmission to the Court requesting the evidence of the witness.

Dated

No. 94
Order for production of documents in marine insurance claim (Part 49D PD para. 7)

IN THE HIGH COURT OF JUSTICE
QUEEN'S BENCH DIVISION
[ ] District Registry
COMMERCIAL COURT
Claim No

Before The Hon. Mr Justice (*name*) [sitting in Private]

Claimant

Defendant

An Application was made by [application notice/letter] dated (*date*) *or* by [Counsel][solicitor] for (*party*) and was attended by ( )

The Judge read the written evidence filed

IT IS ORDERED that:

(1) the claimant and all other persons interested in this claim, and in the insurance the subject of this claim, give specific disclosure to the defendant, his solicitors or agents, of the classes of documents set out in the schedule to this order by (*date*) by list verified by witness statement/affidavit specifying which documents or classes of documents;

(a) are in his control,

(b) have never been in his control,

(c) have been but are no longer in his control, and in that case, when they last were and what has become of them.

(2) the persons giving disclosure under paragraph (1) above give inspection to the defendant by (*date*),

(3) the costs of this application are [summarily assessed in the sum of £][to be the subject of a detailed assessment] and to be paid by (*party*).

[(4) in the meantime all further proceedings be stayed.]

Schedule of Documents

1. all insurance slips, policies, letters of instruction or other orders for effecting the slips or policies, or relating to the insurance or the subject matter of the insurance on the ship (*name of ship*) or the cargo on board or the freight,
2. all documents relating to the sailing or alleged loss of the ship, cargo or freight and all correspondence with any person relating in any manner to (a) effecting insurance of the ship, cargo or freight or (b) any other insurance effected on the ship, cargo or freight on the voyage insured by the policy in this claim, or (c) any other policy effected on the ship, cargo or freight on the same voyage,
3. all correspondence between the captain or agent of the ship and any other person with the owner or any person before commencement of or during the voyage on which the alleged loss happened,
4. all books and documents, whatever their nature and whether originals, duplicates or copies, which in any way relate or refer to any matter in question in this claim.

No. 109
Order for reference to the European Court
(Schedule 1 – RSC O.114 r.2)

IN THE HIGH COURT OF JUSTICE
[ ] DIVISION
[ ] District Registry
(ENGLAND & WALES)
Claim No.

Before (*Judge's name and title*)

Claimant

Defendant

An Application was made by [application notice/letter] dated (*date*) *or* by [Counsel][solicitor] for (*party*) and was attended by ( )

The Judge [Master] [District Judge] read the written evidence filed

IT IS ORDERED that:

1. the question[s] set out in the Schedule to this Order concerning the interpretation [or validity] of (*specify Treaty provision or Community instrument or act concerned*) be referred to the Court of Justice of the European Communities for a preliminary ruling in accordance with Article 234 (formerly Article 177) of the Treaty establishing the European Economic Community *[or Article 150 of the Treaty establishing the European Atomic Energy Community or Article 41 of the Treaty establishing the European Coal and Steel Community or for a ruling under Schedule 2 to the Civil Jurisdiction and Judgments Act 1982, or as the case may be].*
2. all further proceedings in this claim be stayed until the Court of Justice has given its ruling on the said question[s] or until further order.

Schedule

REQUEST FOR PRELIMINARY RULING OF THE COURT OF JUSTICE OF THE EUROPEAN COMMUNITIES

(Here set out a clear and succinct statement of the case giving rise to the request for the ruling of the European Court of Justice in order to enable the European Court of Justice to consider and understand the issues of Community Law raised and to enable Governments of member States and other interested parties to submit observations.

The statement of the case should:

(a) identify the parties and summarise the nature and history of the proceedings;
(b) summarise the salient facts, indicating whether these are proved or admitted or assumed;
(c) make reference to the rules of national law (substantive and procedural) relevant to the dispute;
(d) summarise the contentions of the parties;
(e) explain why a ruling of the Court of Justice is sought, identifying the European Community provisions whose effect is in issue;

(f) formulate, without avoidable complexity, the question(s) to which an answer is requested.)

The preliminary ruling of the Court of Justice of the European Communities is accordingly requested on the following question(s):

(here set out the questions, without avoidable complexity, on which the ruling is sought, identifying the Treaty provisions or other Acts, Instruments or Rules of Community Law concerned).

Dated

Note

Reference should be made to
the Practice Direction (ECJ References: Procedure)
[1999] 1 WLR 260 where the
"Guidance of the Court of Justice of the European Communities
on References by National Courts for Preliminary Rulings"
is set out.

Form 111
Certificate of money provisions contained in a Judgment for Registration in another part of the United Kingdom (Schedule 6 to the Civil Jurisdiction and Judgments Act 1982 and Schedule 1 – RSC O.71 r.37(3))

IN THE HIGH COURT OF JUSTICE
[ ] DIVISION
[ ] District Registry

Claim No.

Claimant

Defendant

I, a Master of the Supreme Court [a District Judge of the High Court] of England and Wales, hereby certify:—

1. That *(name and address)*, the *(party)*, obtained judgment against *(name and address)*, the *(party)*, on *(date)* in the [ ] Division of the High Court of England and Wales for payment of the sum of £ in respect of *(state briefly the nature of the claim)* together with £ for costs.
2. That the judgment carries interest at the rate of per cent per annum calculated on the judgment debt and costs from the date of judgment until payment.
3. That the conditions specified in paragraph 3(a) and (b) of Schedule 6 to the Civil Jurisdiction and Judgments Act 1982 are satisfied in relation to the judgment.
4. This certificate is issued under Schedule 6 to the Civil Jurisdiction and Judgments Act 1982.

Dated

(Signed)

a Master of the Supreme Court [a District Judge of the High Court] of England and Wales

Produced for registration under Schedule 6 to the Civil Jurisdiction and Judgments Act 1982 by *(party)*.

Form 112
Certificate issued under Schedule 7 to the Civil Jurisdiction and Judgments Act 1982 in respect of Non-Money Provisions for Registration in another part of the United Kingdom (Schedule 1 – RSC O.71 r.38(7)

IN THE HIGH COURT OF JUSTICE
[ ] DIVISION
[ ] District Registry

Claim No.

Claimant

Defendant

I, a Master of the Supreme Court [a District Judge of the High Court] of England and Wales, hereby certify:—

(1) That the annexed copy judgment is a true copy of a judgment obtained in the High Court and that it is issued in accordance with section 18 of the Civil Jurisdiction and Judgments Act 1982.

(2) That the conditions specified in paragraph 3(a) and (b) of Schedule 7 to that Act are satisfied in relation to the judgment.

(3) This certificate is issued under paragraph 4(1)(b) of Schedule 7 to the Civil Jurisdiction and Judgments Act 1982.

Dated

(Signed)

a Master of the Supreme Court [a District Judge of the High Court] of England and Wales

PF 1
Application for time

Parties should use form PF 244/N244 and include in Part A the following:

"......for an order that:

1. the time for (*step in proceedings for which extension requested*) is extended to (*date to which extension requested*)"
2. *State when time would otherwise expire*
3. *Give brief grounds relied on.*

PF 2
Order for time (rule 3.1(2)(a))

IN THE HIGH COURT OF JUSTICE
[ ] DIVISION
[ ] District Registry
Claim No.

Before (*Master or District Judge*) [sitting in Private]

Claimant

Defendant

An Application was made by [application notice/letter] dated (*date*) *or* by [Counsel][solicitor] for (*party*) and was attended by ( )

The Master [District Judge] read the written evidence filed

IT IS ORDERED that:

1. the time for (*step in proceedings for which extension given*) is extended to (*date*).
2. the costs of this application are [summarily assessed in the sum of £][to be the subject of a detailed assessment] and to be paid by (*party*).

 Dated

PF 3
Application for an extension of time for serving a claim form (Rule 7.6)

Parties should use form PF 244/N244 and include in Part A the following:

"......for an order that:

1. the period within which the claim form may be served is extended to (*date to which extension requested*)"

Parties should set out in Part C when time would otherwise expire and the matters required to be stated in evidence under paragraph 8.2(1)-(4) of the Part 7 Practice Direction.

PF 4
Order for extension of time for serving a claim form (Rule 7.6)

IN THE HIGH COURT OF JUSTICE
[ ] DIVISION
[ ] District Registry
Claim No.

Before (*Master/District Judge*) [sitting in Private]

Claimant

Defendant

An Application was made by [application notice/letter] dated (*date*) *or* by [Counsel][solicitor] for (*party*) and was attended by ( )

The Master [District Judge] read the written evidence filed

IT IS ORDERED that the period within which the claim form may be served is extended to (*date*).

Dated

PF 6(A)
Application for permission to serve claim form out of jurisdiction (rule 6.21)

Parties should use form PF 244/N244 and include in Part A the following:

"......for an order that:

1. the claimant has permission under rule 6.20 to serve (*party*) at (*address at which party is to be served*) "

2. *The following written evidence must either be set out in Part C or referred to in Part B and filed with the application notice:*

   (a) the grounds and the paragraph(s) of rule 6.20 relied on,
   (b) that the claimant believes his claim has a reasonable prospect of success, and
   (c) the defendant's address or, if not known, in what place or country the defendant is, or is likely to be found, and
   (d) where the application is made in respect of a claim referred to in rule 6.20(3), the grounds on which it is believed that there is between the claimant and the person served, or to be served, a real issue which it is reasonable for the court to try.

PF 6(B)
Order for service out of the jurisdiction (Rule 6.21(4))

IN THE HIGH COURT OF JUSTICE
[ ] DIVISION
[ ] District Registry
Claim No.

Before (*Master/District Judge*) [sitting in Private]

Claimant

Defendant

An Application was made by [application notice/letter] dated (*date*) *or* by [Counsel][solicitor] for (*party*) and was attended by ( )

The Master [District Judge] read the written evidence filed

IT IS ORDERED that:

1. the claimant has permission to serve the claim form on (*party*) at (*address at which party is to be served*) or elsewhere in (*Country in which service is to be effected*).
2. the (*party*) has [ ] days after service on him of the claim form in which to respond by either;
   (a) filing or serving an admission,
   (b) filing and serving a defence, or
   (c) filing and serving an acknowledgment of service,

and, where an acknowledgment of service is filed and served, the (*party*) has a further 14 days in which to file and serve his defence.

Dated

Note:- For the times for making an admission or filing an acknowledgment of service or defence see rules 6.22 and 6.23 and the Table in the Part 6 Practice Direction.

PF 7
Request for Service of Document Abroad
(Rules 6.26(2)(a) and 6.27(2)(a))

IN THE HIGH COURT OF JUSTICE
QUEEN'S BENCH DIVISION
Claim No.

Claimant

Defendant

I hereby request that the claim form (*or describe the document*) be sent through the proper channel to (*name of country*) for service on the (*party*) at (*address*) or elsewhere in (*name of country*) and that it may be served as follows:-

(i) through the government of (*name of country*) (*where the government is willing to effect service*)
(ii) through the judicial authority of (*name of country*)
(iii) through the authority designated under the Hague Convention
(iv) through a British Consular authority at (*name of country*)
(v) through the receiving agency designated under regulation (EC) 1348/2000
(vi) *where service is to be effected on a State only;* through the Foreign and Commonwealth Office

(*delete methods not required*)

I hereby undertake personally to pay all expenses incurred by the [Foreign and Commonwealth Office] [foreign judicial authority] [receiving agency] in respect of the service requested, on receiving due notification of the amount of those expenses, to the [Finance Officer of the Foreign and Commonwealth Office] [foreign judicial authority] [receiving agency] and to produce a receipt for the payment to the court officer in the Central Office of the High Court.

Dated the
SOLICITOR
ADDRESS/DX
TELEPHONE NO
REF

(signature of party or solicitor)

PF 8

Standard "Unless" Order (rule 26.5(5), Part 26 PD para. 2.5 and N150A)

Notice of Allocation to the Multi-track

In the High Court of Justice
[ ] Division
[ ] District Registry

To all parties or their solicitors

Claim No.

Claimant

Defendant

Master (*name*) has considered the statements of case and no allocation questionnaire having been filed by the [claimant(s)] [defendant(s)]

The Master has ordered that:

1. unless the parties file their allocation questionnaires within [3] days after service of this order the claim [and counterclaim] be struck out.

or

2. unless the claimant files his allocation questionnaire within [3] days after service of this order the claim be struck out.

or

3. unless the defendant files his allocation questionnaire within [3] days after service of this order his defence [and counterclaim] be struck out.

or

4. (*as otherwise ordered*)

Dated

The court office at Queen's Bench Division, Royal Courts of Justice, Strand, WC2A 2LL is open between 10am and 4.30pm Monday to Friday. When corresponding with the court, please address forms or letters to room no E.14 and quote the claim number.

PF 11
Application for Part 24 Judgment (whole claim) (rule 24.2)

Parties should use form PF 244/N244 and include in Part A the following:

" I/We (*name of party or his solicitor*) [on behalf of] [the defendant] [the claimant] intend to apply for summary judgment under Part 24 against (*name or names of parties*) [for the amount set out in the particulars of claim [and interest]] *or* [on the whole claim] *or as may be* and costs, because *either*;

1. the claimant has no real prospect of succeeding on the claim *or*
2. the defendant has no real prospect of successfully defending the claim, and

there is no other reason why the claim should be disposed of at a trial.

Attention is drawn to rule 24.5(1) which provides that if a respondent to an application for summary judgment wishes to rely on written evidence at the hearing, he must, at least 7 days before the hearing, (a) file the written evidence and (b) serve copies on every other party to the application."

Where a party wishes to rely on evidence it should either be referred to in Part B and served with the application notice, or be set out in Part C. The application notice or evidence should include the matters referred to in the Part 24 practice direction paragraph 2(3).

PF 12
Application for Part 24 Judgment (one or some of several claims) (rule 24.2)

Parties should use form PF 244/N244 and include in Part A the following:

" I/We (*name of party or his solicitor*) [on behalf of] [the defendant][the claimant] intend to apply for summary judgment under Part 24 against (*name or names of parties*) for (*set out the particular claim(s) or parts of the claim referred to*) and costs, because *either*;

1. the claimant has no real prospect of succeeding on such particular claim(s) or parts of the claim *or*
2. the defendant has no real prospect of successfully defending such particular claim(s) or parts of the claim, and

there is no other reason why the claim(s) should be disposed of at a trial.

Attention is drawn to rule 24.5(1) which provides that if a respondent to an application for summary judgment wishes to rely on written evidence at the hearing, he must, at least 7 days before the hearing, (a) file the written evidence and (b) serve copies on every other party to the application."

Where a party wishes to rely on evidence it should either be referred to in Part B and served with the application notice, or be set out in Part C. The application notice or evidence should include the matters referred to in the Part 24 practice direction paragraph 2(3).

PF 13
Order under Part 24 (No. 1)

(for judgments under Part 24 see forms No 44 and No 44A)

IN THE HIGH COURT OF JUSTICE
[ ] DIVISION
[ ] District Registry
Claim No.

Before (*Master or District Judge*) [sitting in Private]

Claimant

Defendant

An Application was made by [application notice/letter] dated (*date*) *or* by [Counsel][solicitor] for (*party*) and was attended by ( )

The Master [District Judge] read the written evidence filed

IT IS ORDERED that:

1. if the defendant pays into the Court Funds Office the sum of £ by the (date) to remain there until further order he may defend the whole of the claimant's claim but if that sum is not paid into the Court Funds Office within the specified time, the claimant may enter judgment for that sum and the defendant may defend the remainder of the claimant's claim.

or, if judgment is for the whole sum claimed

2. unless the defendant pays into the Court Funds Office the sum of £ by the (*date*), to remain there until further order, the claimant may enter final judgment for the sum set out in the particulars of claim [and interest] and costs but if the defendant pays that sum into the Court Funds Office within the specified time, he may defend the claim.

under paragraph 1 or 2 above where payment is made

3. the defendant is to file his defence by the (*date*)
4. *further directions for management of the claim as in PF 52*
5. the costs of this application are [summarily assessed in the sum of £][to be the subject of a detailed assessment] and to be paid by (*party*).

Dated

PF 14
Order under Part 24 (No. 2)

IN THE HIGH COURT OF JUSTICE
[ ] DIVISION
[ ] District Registry
Claim No.

Before (*title and name of judge*) [sitting in Private]

Claimant

Defendant

An Application was made by [application notice/letter] dated (*date*) *or* by [Counsel][solicitor] for (*party*) and was attended by ( )

The Master [District Judge] read the written evidence filed

IT IS ORDERED that:

1. the application be refused
2. the defendant is to file his defence by the (*date*)

or

3. the defendant's written evidence stand as his [defence] [statement of case] and he may file any further particulars of his [defence] [statement of case] [in a witness statement] by the (*date*)
4. the parties give standard disclosure [relating to the issue of] under rule 31.6 and serve their lists of documents by the (*date*)
5. inspection of documents take place within ( ) days of service of the lists of documents

[and by consent

6. the claim be tried before a [Master][District Judge]].
7. *further directions for management of the claim as in PF 52*
8. the costs of this application are [summarily assessed in the sum of £][to be the subject of a detailed assessment] and to be paid by (*party*).

Dated

PF 15
Judgment under Part 24 for amount found due upon detailed assessment of solicitor's bill of costs

IN THE HIGH COURT OF JUSTICE
[ ] DIVISION
[ ] Registry
Claim No.

Before (*Master/District Judge*) [sitting in Private]

Claimant

Defendant

An Application was made by [application notice/letter] dated (*date*) *or* by [Counsel][solicitor] for (*party*) and was attended by ( )

The Master [District Judge] read the written evidence filed

IT IS ORDERED that:

1. in accordance with the Solicitors Act 1974, a detailed assessment of the bill of costs on which this claim is brought do take place before a Costs Officer under Parts 47 and 48,
2. the claimant;
   (1) give credit at the time of the assessment for all sums of money received by him for or on account of the defendant, and
   (2) may without further order enter judgment against the defendant for the amount (if any) found due together with the costs of this claim to be assessed at the same time.
3. in accordance with rule 48.10 (modified as follows);
   (1) the claimant serve a breakdown of costs by (*date*),
   (2) the defendant serve points of dispute by (*date*),
   (3) the claimant has permission to serve a reply (if any) by (*date*), and
   (4) the defendant file a request for a hearing date after the points of dispute have been served and in any event not later than [3 months after the date of this order].
4. if the defendant fails to comply with the provisions of paragraph 2 above, the claimant may without further order enter final judgment for the amount set out in the particulars of claim [and interest as claimed] together with costs of the claim [to be assessed] and of this application summarily assessed at £..............
5. if the claimant fails to comply with paragraph 2(1) above, the defendant has permission to apply to the court in which the detailed assessment hearing should take place for an order requiring compliance with rule 48.10.

   Dated

PF 16

NOTICE of court's intention to make an order of its own initiative
(rule 3.3(2) and (3))

In the High Court of Justice
[ ] Division
[ ] District Registry
[ ] County Court

Claim No.

Claimant

Defendant

To all the parties

TAKE NOTICE that:

1. The court intends to make an order that (*set out the order*). You may make representations in respect of this order by [filing a witness statement] setting out any objections to the making of this order and your reasons for your objections by (*date*).

or

2. The court intends, at a hearing to take place before [Master (*name*)] [District Judge (*name*)] at (*address of court*) on (*date to be given not less than 3 days after service of this notice*) at (*time*), to make an order that (*set out the order*). You may attend and make representations as to the proposed order and its terms.

Dated

To the Solicitors for:-
(*names, addresses and references*)

The court office is open between 10 am and 4.30pm Monday to Friday. Please address all communications to the Court Manager quoting the claim number.

PF 17
Order made on court's own initiative without a hearing
(rule 3.3(4) and (5))

IN THE HIGH COURT OF JUSTICE
[ ] DIVISION
[ ] District Registry

Claim No.

Before (*Master or District Judge*) [sitting in Private]

Claimant

Defendant

The Master [**District Judge**] read the [statements of case] [written evidence] filed [and the documents on the court file].

OF THE COURT'S OWN INITIATIVE

IT IS ORDERED that:

1. (*set out the order made*).

2. the (*party/parties*) [has][have] permission to apply not more than [7] days after the date of service of this order on [him][them] to set aside, vary or stay this order.

Dated

PF 19
Group Litigation Order (rule 19.11)

IN THE HIGH COURT OF JUSTICE
[ ] DIVISION
[ ] District Registry
[ ] County Court
Claim No.

Before (*Title and name of Judge or Master*)* [sitting in Private]

The Claimants are as set out in Schedule 1 to this Order

Defendant

An Application was made by [application notice/letter] dated (*date*) *or* by [Counsel][solicitor] for (*party*) and was attended by ( )

The [Judge] [Master] [District Judge] read the written evidence filed

And [The Lord Chief Justice of England and Wales] [The Head of Civil Justice] [The Vice-Chancellor] having consented to an Order being made in the following terms

....

....

IT IS ORDERED that:

1. This Order applies to claims in respect of the following common or related issues of fact or law:- (*specify the issues which will identify the claims to be managed as a group under this order*), and those claims will constitute the ( ) Group Litigation.
2. The Claimants are those individuals whose names are set out in Schedule 1 to this Order, and the Solicitors representing the Claimants are also set out in Schedule 1 to this Order, opposite the name of the Claimant they represent.
3. Further individuals whose claims fall within the group may hereafter apply to be entered in the group register referred to below and joined as Claimants under the terms of this Order.
4. the Solicitors (*name*) are the lead Solicitors for the purposes of service, receipt of documents (*or as ordered or agreed between the parties*).
5. a group register be set up on which details of the claims which are the subject of this order are to be entered and which will be maintained by [the management court specified in paragraph 9 below] [the lead Solicitors *or as Ordered*].

* Claims in a specialist list should be made to the senior judge of that list, and outside London, claims should be made to the Presiding Judge or to the Supervising Chancery Judge in the issuing district registry. In the Royal Courts of Justice application should be made in the Queen's Bench Division to the Senior Master and in the Chancery Division to the Chief Chancery Master.

6. the register shall include:
   (i) the full name, address and postcode of each Claimant and the litigation friend (*if appropriate*),
   (ii) the date of birth of the Claimant,
   (iii) the claim number of the Claimant's case and the date of commencement,
   (iv) the Solicitors on record,
   (v) all Notices of Funding including the number and date of issue,
   (vi) the National Insurance number of each Claimant, and
   (vii) the date of entry on the register.
7. the register shall be updated on (*date*) and thereafter (*as Ordered*), and after each update a copy of the register shall be served on [each] [the] defendant within [14] days of each update.
8. the defendant may give written notice to the [management court specified in paragraph 9 below] [lead Solicitors] of any issue it takes on the accuracy of the updated register within [28] days of receipt.
9. the [Royal Courts of Justice] [Division] [District Registry] [County Court] will be the court which will manage the claims on the group register, ("the management court") and any future claims to which this order applies are to be issued in that court and entered in the register.
10. any claims to which this order applies which are proceeding other than in the management court be transferred forthwith to that court and entered in the register in accordance with Rule 19.11(3)(a)(i) and (iii).
11. the claim(s) of (*claimant's name and claim number*) proceed as a test claim [and the following claims be stayed until further Order (*set out [in a schedule] the claimants' names and claim numbers*)].
12. (*Title and name of judge*) shall be the Judge responsible for the management of all claims to which this order applies.
13. the lead Solicitors file and serve on the Defendant(s) Group Particulars of Claim by (*date*). The Group Particulars of Claim;
    (a) shall contain
        (i) general allegations relating to all claims
        (ii) a schedule containing entries relating to each individual claim specifying which of the general allegations are relied on and any specific facts relevant to the Claimant
        (iii) (*as directed*)
    (b) [need not be verified by a statement of truth] [shall be verified by a statement of truth to be signed by [the lead Solicitor *or as directed*].
14. any documents or bundles in respect of claims to which this order applies should have endorsed on the top left hand corner the short title of the claim and ["Group Litigation" *or as directed*].
15. a copy of this order shall be lodged (i) with the Senior Master of the Queen's Bench Division in Room E115 at the Royal Courts of Justice, Strand, London WC2A 2LL and (ii) with the Law Society at 113 Chancery Lane, London WC2A 1PL.

16. the (i) individual costs relating to (*party*) are to be (*as ordered*), and (ii) common costs of this application are [to be costs in the case] [[summarily assessed in the sum of £] [to be the subject of a detailed assessment] and to be paid by (*party*)].

Dated

PF 20
Application for Part 20 directions

Parties should use form PF 244/N244 and

(a) adapt the form to show the Part 20 claimant(s) and Part 20 defendant(s) in the title in addition to the claimant(s) and defendant(s) to the claim, as set out in paragraph 7 of the Part 20 Practice Direction,

(b) attach the whole of Form PF 21(and such paragraphs of PF 52, suitably adapted, as may be appropriate) as a draft Order (with double spacing between the lines);

(i) completing those paragraphs or parts of paragraphs, for which an Order is sought, as appropriate, and

(ii) marking those paragraphs or parts of paragraphs for which an order is not sought, by striking through the paragraph or sub-paragraph ***number*** *only, and*

(c) in addition, include in Part A a request for the following orders and directions as appropriate:

"1. summary judgment under Part 24

2. an order to strike out the Part 20 [claimant's][defendant's] statement of case

3. case management directions of the Part 20 claim

4. what part the Part 20 defendant will take at the trial of the claim

5. to what extent the Part 20 defendant is to be bound by any judgment or decision made in the claim."

PF 21
Order for Part 20 directions

IN THE HIGH COURT OF JUSTICE
[ ] DIVISION
[ ] District Registry
Claim No.

Before (*title and name of judge*) [sitting in Private]

Claimant

Defendant

Part 20 Claimant

Part 20 Defendant

An Application was made by [application notice/letter] dated (*date*) *or* by [Counsel][solicitor] for (*party*) and was attended by ( )

The Master [District Judge] read the written evidence filed

IT IS ORDERED that:

1. the defendant (*name*) has permission to make a Part 20 claim against (*name*).
2. the Part 20 claim form as initialled by the Master [District Judge], together with the documents listed in rule 20.12(1) for responding to the Part 20 claim, be served on the Part 20 defendant by (*date*).
3. If the Part 20 defendant files and serves a defence to the Part 20 claim a case management conference will be held to include the Part 20 claim.
4. Where a case management conference is to be held, the Part 20 claimant, after consultation with the claimant;
   (a) not less than 14 days after the Part 20 defence is filed provide the court with convenient dates for holding the case management conference, and
   (b) not less than 7 days before the date fixed for the case management conference,
      (i) serve a list of proposed directions for management of the Part 20 claim (adapted from PF 52) including directions as to
      (ii) the right of the Part 20 defendant to appear at the trial of the claim,
      (iii) the extent to which the Part 20 defendant be bound by the result of the trial, and
      (iv) the manner in which the liability of the Part 20 defendant to the Part 20 claimant is to be determined.

Dated

PF 21A
Order to add person as defendant to counterclaim (Rule 20.5)

IN THE HIGH COURT OF JUSTICE
[ ] DIVISION
[ ] District Registry
Claim No.

Before (*Master/district judge*) [sitting in Private]

Claimant

Defendant

An Application was made by [application notice/letter] dated (*date*) *or* by [Counsel][solicitor] for the defendant [and was attended by ( )]

The Master [District Judge] read the written evidence filed

IT IS ORDERED that:

1. (*name of person*) be added as defendant to the counterclaim ("the Part 20 defendant").
2. the defendant/Part 20 claimant has permission to serve his defence and counterclaim on the Part 20 defendant together with:
   (a) a copy of this order,
   (b) a copy of the claim form and particulars of claim, and
   (c) form N211C (*suitably adapted*) and the forms for responding to the counterclaim as referred to in form N211C (*also suitably adapted*),

by (*date*).

3. the Part 20 defendant has 14 days in which to respond to the counterclaim by either;
   (a) filing or serving an admission,
   (b) filing and serving a defence, or
   (c) filing and serving an acknowledgment of service,

and, where an acknowledgment of service is filed and served, the Part 20 defendant has a further 14 days in which to file and serve his defence.

4. a copy of the counterclaim and of this order be served on all other defendants to the counterclaim.

   Dated

PF 22
Notice claiming contribution or indemnity against another defendant (Rule 20.6)

IN THE HIGH COURT OF JUSTICE
[ ] DIVISION
[ ] District Registry
Claim No.

Claimant

Defendant/Part 20 Claimant

Defendant/Part 20 Defendant

To (*name of Part 20 defendant*) of (*address*)

Take notice that the Part 20 claimant (*name*) claims against you [to be indemnified against the claimant's claim and costs of the claim][*or* contribution to the extent of (*proportion of claimant's claim*) of the claimant's claim][*or* the following remedy, namely (*set out remedy sought*)] on the following grounds (*set out grounds*):

Statement of Truth

*(I believe)(The Part 20 claimant believes) that the facts stated in this Part 20 notice are true.

*I am duly authorised by the Part 20 claimant to sign this statement

Full name____

Name of Part 20 claimant's solicitor's firm______________________

signed________________________position or office held________________

*(Part 20 claimant)('s solicitor)(Litigation friend) (if signing on behalf of firm or company)

* delete as appropriate

Note:- You may seek directions from the court in relation to this Part 20 claim by filing an application notice for hearing at a case management conference or otherwise as may be appropriate.

TO:- Part 20 defendant ('s solicitor) of (*address*) *Ref:* *Tel no:* *Fax no:*	*Part 20 claimant('s solicitor's) address, or DX or e-mail.* *Ref:* *Tel no:* *Fax no*

The court office at

is open between 10 am and (4 pm) (4.30 pm) on Monday to Friday. Address all communication to the Court manager quoting the claim number

PF 43
Application for security for costs
(rule 25.12, also Companies Act 1985 s.726)

Parties should use form PF 244/N244 and include in Part A the following:

"......for an order that:

1. the claimant give security for the defendant's costs in this claim to the satisfaction of the defendant or the [Master][District Judge] and in the manner ordered by the [Master][District Judge].

2. [all further proceedings be stayed until security is given].

3. [if security is not so given, there be judgment for the defendant]."

Written evidence in support of the application in respect of the conditions to be satisfied as set out in rules 25.13 and 25.14 must either be set out in Part C or referred to in Part B and served with the application notice.
A draft statement of costs based on costs form 1 should be filed with the application notice.

Note; precedent form under Section II of Part 25 with effect from 2/5/2000.

PF 44
Order for security for costs
(rule 25.12, also Companies Act 1985 s.726)

IN THE HIGH COURT OF JUSTICE
[ ] DIVISION
[ ] District Registry
Claim No.

Before (*Master/District Judge*) [sitting in Private]

Claimant

Defendant

An Application was made by [application notice/letter] dated (*date*) *or* by [Counsel][solicitor] for (*party*) and was attended by ( )

The Master [District Judge] read the written evidence filed

IT IS ORDERED that:

1. the claimant give security for the defendant's costs [of the claim][until (*specify stage in the claim*)] in the sum of £ [by paying the sum of £ into the Court Funds Office by (*date*)][by lodging with the defendant's solicitors a bankers draft (*describe form of bankers draft*)] [in the following manner (*describe*)].
2. [all further proceedings be stayed until security is given.]
3. [unless security is given as ordered,
   (a) the claim is struck out without further order, and
   (b) on production by the defendant of evidence of default, there be judgment for the defendant without further order with costs of the claim to be the subject of a detailed assessment.]
4. the costs of this application are [summarily assessed in the sum of £][to be the subject of a detailed assessment] and to be paid by (*party*).

   Dated

PF 48
COURT RECORD FORM

This form must be completed before an appointment with a Queen's Bench Master and handed to the Master at the beginning of the appointment

No ....

..v..

Date.. Time...

Claimant's Solicitors	**Defendant's Solicitors**

Counsel/ Solicitor	**Counsel/Solicitor**

APPLICATION

MASTER'S NOTES

	Tape recording details

ORDER	

signed...

dated.................................

—

To be drawn up by the [Solicitor for the Claimant/Defendant] [Court] and filed by

ONCE COMPLETED THE ORIGINAL OF THIS FORM MUST BE RETAINED BY THE COURT.

PF 49

FORM TO BE RETURNED WITH ALLOCATION QUESTIONNAIRE

AGREED DIRECTIONS

1.If the parties can agree proposals for the management of the case, the Court may agree such proposals and a case management conference may not be necessary.
Such directions should;
a) set out a timetable, by calendar dates, for taking steps for the preparation of the case:
b) include a date for the start of the trial window and specify the period in which the trial should take place
c) include provision about the disclosure of documents and
d) include provision about both factual and expert evidence.

DATES FOR CASE MANAGEMENT CONFERENCE

2. If a case management conference is necessary the Court will make efforts to fix it on a date convenient to the parties. However this cannot be guaranteed. On the basis the Court may fix a hearing date for the conference you should complete the questionnaire below. Where possible you should liaise with the other party/ies before completing this form.

This form, together with any agreed directions, should be returned to the Court with the completed allocation questionnaire. If it is not returned the Court will, in the event of deciding that a case management conference should take place, fix a date without reference to the parties.

PLEASE SUPPLY THE FOLLOWING INFORMATION;

1. Case name..v..

2. Case number...

3. Estimated length of conference

a) Claimant's estimate..

b) Defendant's estimate..

4. Earliest date when the Claimant/Defendants will be available and other convenient dates within the next three months

..

5. Dates that you wish to avoid during the next three months

..

6. Name of Counsel (if attending and if known)

a) For the Claimant..

b) For the Defendant..

Signed..Dated..

..Solicitors for the Claimant/ Defendant

Address..

Reference..Telephone No..............................

Fax no.. e-mail address..............................

PF 50
Application for case management directions in the multi-track (Part 29)

Use Form PF244/N244 attaching the whole of Form PF52 as a draft Order (with double spacing between the lines),

1 completing those paragraphs or parts of paragraphs, for which an Order is sought, as appropriate, and

2 marking those paragraphs or parts of paragraphs for which an order is not sought, by striking through the paragraph or sub-paragraph ***number*** *only.*

PF 52
Order for case management directions in the multi-track (Part 29)

IN THE HIGH COURT OF JUSTICE
QUEEN'S BENCH DIVISION

Claim No.

Before [sitting in Private]

Claimant

Defendant

An Application was made by application letter dated *or* by Solicitor for and was attended by

The Master [**District Judge**] read the written evidence filed

[The parties having agreed the directions set out in paragraph(s) below which are made by consent],

IT IS ORDERED that:

1. ALLOCATION
the case be allocated to the multi-track.

2. TRANSFER
(1) the claim be transferred to;
(a) the Division of the High Court,
(b) the District Registry [Mercantile List], or
(c) the County Court [Chancery List][Business List],
(2) the issue(s) be transferred to the County Court [Chancery List][Business List] for determination.
(3) the apply by to a Judge of the Technology and Construction Court [or other Specialist List] for an order to transfer the claim to that court.

(4) the claim commenced in the County Court be transferred from that court to the Queen's Bench Division of the High Court.

3. ALTERNATIVE DISPUTE RESOLUTION
the claim be stayed until while the parties try to settle it by mediation or other means. [The parties shall notify the Court in writing at the end of that period whether settlement has or has not been reached, and shall submit a draft consent order of any settlement]. The claim will be listed on for the court to make further directions unless;

(a) the claim has been settled and the claimant advises the court of the settlement in writing and files a draft consent order, or
(b) the parties apply not later than 3 days before the hearing for further directions without a hearing, or
(c) the parties apply for an extension of the stay and the extension is granted, upon which the hearing will be relisted on the date to which the extension is granted.

4. PROBATE CASES ONLY
the Defendant file his witness statement or affidavit of testamentary scripts and lodge any testamentary script at Room TM7.09 Thomas More Building, Royal Courts of Justice, Strand WC2A 2LL [District Registry/ County Court, at] by

5. CASE SUMMARY
the by prepare and serve a Case Summary [not exceeding words] on all other parties, to be agreed by and filed by and if it is not agreed the parties by that date file their own Case Summaries.

6. CASE MANAGEMENT CONFERENCE etc.

[*(a)* there be a [further] Case Management Conference/Listing Hearing before the Master/District Judge in [Court/Room No] [[Thomas More Building] Royal Courts of Justice][Court (trial centre)] on at of hours/minutes duration.] *or*

[*(b)* there be a Case Management Conference/Listing Hearing of hours/minutes duration. In order for the Court to fix a date the parties are to complete the accompanying questionnaire and file it by .] *or*

[*(c)* the apply for an appointment for a [further] Case Management Conference/Listing Hearing by .]

At the Case Management Conference, except for urgent matters in the meantime, the Court will hear any further applications for Directions or Orders and any party must file an Application Notice for any such Directions or Orders and serve it and supporting evidence (if any) by .

7. AMENDMENTS TO STATEMENTS OF CASE
(1) the has permission to amend his statement of case in accordance with the attached draft initialled by the District Judge
(2) the amended statement of case be verified by a statement of truth.
(3) the amended statement of case be filed by
(4) the amended statement of case be served by *or* service of the amended statement of case be dispensed with.
(5) any consequential amendments to other statements of case be filed and served by
(6) the costs of and caused by the amendment to the statement of case be in any event *or* are assessed in the sum of £ and are to be paid by

8. ADDITION OF PARTIES
(1) the has permission;
(a) to substitute as a ,and
(b) to amend his statement of case in accordance with the attached draft initialled by the District Judge
(2) the amended statement of case be verified by a statement of truth.
(3) the amended statement of case be;
(a) filed by and
(b) served on by
(4) a copy of this order be served on by
(5) any consequential amendments to other statements of case be filed and served by
(6) the costs of and caused by the amendment to the statement of case be in any event *or* are assessed in the sum of £ and are to be paid by

9. CONSOLIDATION
this claim be consolidated with claim number ,the lead claim to be claim number . [The title to the consolidated case shall be as set out in the Schedule to this order.]

10. TRIAL OF ISSUE
the issue of be tried as follows;
(1) with the consent of the parties, before a Master
(a) on in Room at the Royal Courts of Justice,
(b) with an estimated length of hearing hours,
(c) with the filing of listing questionnaires dispensed with,

or

(2) before a Judge
(a) with the trial of the issue to take place within after ("the trial window")
(b) with the to apply to the Clerk of the Lists at Room W15 by for a trial date within the trial window
(c) with the issue
(i) to be entered in the General List category "A" "B" or "C", with a time estimate of ,and
(ii) to take place in London
[(d) the filing of listing questionnaires be dispensed with [unless directed by the Clerk of the Lists] *or* each party file his completed listing questionnaire by], *or*
(3) before a [District Judge, with the consent of the parties] [Circuit Judge] [High Court Judge] [listing category [A][B][C]], at a hearing details of which [accompany this order][will be sent shortly] with an estimated length of hearing hours.

11. FURTHER INFORMATION
(1) the provide by the clarification sought in the Request dated attached and initialled by the District Judge
(2) any request for clarification ɔe served by

12. DISCLOSURE OF DOCUMENTS
(1) no disclosure is required.
(2) each party give by standard disclosure to every other party by list [by categories].
(3) the give specific disclosure of documents [limited to the issues of] described in the Schedule to this order [initialled by the Master/District Judge] by list [by categories] by
(4) the give by standard disclosure by list [by categories] to of documents limited to the issue(s) of by list.

13. INSPECTION OF DOCUMENTS
Any requests for inspection or copies of disclosed documents shall be made within days after service of the list.

14. PRESERVATION OF PROPERTY
the preserve until trial of the claim or further order *or other remedy under rule 25.1(1).*

15. WITNESS STATEMENTS

(1) each party serve on every other party the witness statement of the oral evidence which the party serving the statement intends to rely on in relation to [any issues of fact][the following issues of fact] to be decided at the trial, those statements and any Notices of intention to rely on hearsay evidence to be

(a) exchanged by *or*

(b) served by by and by by

(2) the has permission to serve a witness summary relating to the evidence of of on every other party by

16. NO EXPERT EVIDENCE

(1) no expert evidence being necessary, [no party has permission to call or rely on expert evidence][permission to call or rely on expert evidence is refused].

17. SINGLE EXPERT

(1) evidence be given by the report of a single expert in the field of ,instructed jointly by the parties, on the issue of [and his fees shall be limited to £].

(2) the claimant advise the court in writing by whether or not the single expert has been instructed.

(3) if the parties are unable to agree [by that date] who that expert is to be and about the payment of his fees any party may apply for further directions.

(4) unless the parties agree in writing or the court orders otherwise, the fees and expenses of the single expert shall be paid to him [by the parties equally](*or as ordered*).

(5) each party give his instructions to the single expert by

(6) the report of the single expert be filed by

(7) the evidence of the expert be given at the trial by written report/oral evidence of the expert.

18. SEPARATE EXPERTS

[(1) each party has permission to adduce [oral] expert evidence in the field of [limited to expert(s) [per party] [on each side]].

(2) the experts reports shall be exchanged by

(3) the experts shall hold a discussion for the purpose of:

(a) identifying the issues, if any, between them; and

(b) where possible, reaching agreement on those issues.

(4) the experts shall by prepare and file a statement for the Court showing:

(a) those issues on which they did agree; and

(b) those issues on which they disagree and a summary of their reasons for disagreeing.

(5) no party shall be entitled to recover by way of costs from any other party more than £ for the fees or expenses of an expert.]

or

[(1) the parties have permission to rely on expert evidence as follows:

Party	Identity of Expert	Field of Expertise	Issue to be addressed
Claimant			
Defendant			
(*other parties*)			

(2) the number of expert witnesses in each field be limited to for the and to for the .

[(3) the amount of the fees and expenses of the experts in the field[s] of that the may recover from the be limited to £ .

(4) the experts in the field(s) of prepare reports which are to be served as follows:

(a) by simultaneous exchange by

(b) by by and by by

(5) the reports be agreed if possible by .

(6) (a) if the reports are not agreed by that date, then the experts in the same field(s) shall, by , seek to identify, by "without prejudice" discussion, the issues between them and, where possible, to reach agreement on all/any issue(s),

(b) the experts shall by prepare and file a statement showing those issues on which they are agreed, those issues on which they disagree and a summary of their reasons for disagreeing.

(7) the expert evidence relied on by the in the field of be given at the trial by written report(s)/written summary of agreement/oral evidence of the expert(s).

(8) no party shall be entitled to recover by way of costs from any other party more than £ for the fees or expenses of an expert.]

19. TRIAL AND LISTING QUESTIONNAIRES

(1) (a) the trial of the claim/issue(s) take place [within after][between and ("the trial window").

(b) the make an appointment to attend on the Clerk of the Lists/Listing Officer at Room [W14][W15] in order to fix a trial date within the trial window, such appointment to be [within 14 days after][on] [not later than] and give notice of the appointment to all other parties.

1

(c) the claim
(i) be entered in the General List category "A" "B" or "C", with a time estimate of ,and
(ii) take place in London , *or*

(2) (a) Trial Date - the trial take place on a date to be fixed , a Notice of Hearing will be sent shortly at a venue to be notified
or
(b) Trial Window - the trial take place during the period beginning on and ending on at a venue to be notified,
(c) the present estimate of the time to be allowed for the trial is

(3) Listing Questionnaires -
[(a) the filing of listing questionnaires be dispensed with [unless directed by the Clerk of the Lists/Listing Officer]], *or*
[(b) each party file his completed listing questionnaire by 4.00pm on],

(4) the parties inform the Court forthwith of any change in the trial time estimate.

20. PRE TRIAL REVIEW
[[The trial being estimated to last more than 10 days], There be a Pre Trial Review on a date to be arranged by the Clerk of the Lists/Listing Officer in Room [W14][W15]] [there be a Pre-Trial Review on at] before the Judge at the Court at which, except for urgent matters in the meantime, the Court will hear any further applications for Directions or Orders.

21. DEFINITION AND REDUCTION OF ISSUES
by the parties list and discuss the issues in the claim [including the experts' reports and statements] and attempt to define and narrow the issues [including those issues the subject of discussion by the experts].

22. TRIAL BUNDLE
The parties agree and file a trial bundle and exchange and file skeleton arguments and chronologies not more than 7 and not less than 3 days before the start of the trial.

23. TRIAL TIMETABLE (*only for use at final CMC or PTR*)
(1) the parties agree a timetable for the trial, subject to the approval of the trial Judge, and file it with the trial bundle.
(2) subject to the approval of the trial Judge, the timetable for the trial will be:
(a) opening speeches to last no more than minutes,
(b) the statements served stand as the evidence in chief of the Claimants' witnesses of fact who are to give evidence on the [first] morning/afternoon/day of the trial,

(c) the statements served stand as the evidence in chief of the Defendants' witnesses of fact who are to give evidence on the morning/afternoon/day of the trial,
(d) the reports of the experts served stand as their evidence in chief and the experts in the field(s) of give oral evidence on the morning /afternoon/day of the trial,
(e) closing submissions be made on the morning /afternoon/day of the trial.

24. SETTLEMENT
If the claim or part of the claim is settled the parties must immediately inform the Court, whether or not it is then possible to file a draft Consent Order to give effect to the settlement.

25. OTHER DIRECTIONS

26 COSTS
the costs of this application be;
(a) in the case, or
(b) summarily assessed at £ and paid by , or
(c) the in any event to be the subject of a detailed assessment,
(d) the pay the the sum of £ on account of such costs on or before

Dated

PF 53
Order for separate trial of an issue (Rule 3.1(2)(i))

IN THE HIGH COURT OF JUSTICE
[ ] DIVISION
[ ] District Registry
[ ] County Court
Claim No.

Before (*Master/District Judge*) [sitting in Private]

Claimant

Defendant

An Application was made by [application notice/letter] dated (*date*) *or* by [Counsel][solicitor] for (*party*) and was attended by ( )

The Master [District Judge] read the written evidence [statements of case] filed

IT IS ORDERED that:

1. the issue(s) set out in the Schedule below be tried between (*name*) and (*name*).
2. in the trial of the issue(s) (*name*) will be the claimant and (*name*) will be the defendant.
3. the issue should be tried as follows;

   (a) with the consent of the parties, before a Master

      (i) on (*date*) in Room ( ) at the Royal Courts of Justice,
      (ii) with an estimated length of hearing ( ) hours,
      (iii) with the filing of listing questionnaires dispensed with, *or*

   (b) before a Judge

      (i) with the trial of the issue to take place within (*period*) after (*date*)("the trial window")
      (ii) with the (*party*) to apply to the Clerk of the Lists at Room [W14][W15] by (*date*) for a trial date within the trial window
      (iii) with the issue

         (i) to be entered in the [Jury List][Trial List][General List] category "A" "B" or "C", with a time estimate of (*specify number of days/weeks*), and
         (ii) to take place in London (*or identify venue*)

      [(iv) the filing of listing questionnaires be dispensed with [unless directed by the Clerk of the Lists] *or* each party file his completed listing questionnaire by (*date*)], *or*

   (c) before a [District Judge, with the consent of the parties] [Circuit Judge] [High Court Judge] [listing category [A][B][C]], at a hearing details of which [accompany this order][will be sent shortly] with an estimated length of hearing ( ) hours.

4. the costs of this application are [[summarily assessed in the sum of £] [to be the subject of a detailed assessment] and to be paid by (*party*)] [costs in the issue].

Schedule

(set out issue(s))

Dated

PF 56
Request for further information
(CPR Part 18 and Part 18 Practice Direction)

IN THE HIGH COURT OF JUSTICE
[ ] Division
[ ] District Registry
[ ] County Court
Claim No.

Claimant

Defendant

To [Claimant][Defendant]['s Solicitor]

You are requested to provide the following clarification or information under CPR Part 18 and the Part 18 Practice Direction by (*date*):-

Request:	Response:
1.*	1.*

* in numerical sequence

continued overleaf

Request:	Response:

Signed

(Claimant)(Defendant)('s Solicitor)

Position or office held

(If signing on behalf of firm or company)

Date

Applicant's/applicant's solicitor's address, or DX or e-mail.			TO:- Respondent/Respondent's solicitor of (address)		
Ref:	Tel no:	Fax no:	Ref:	Tel no:	Fax no:

The Statement of truth is to be completed by the Responding Party when responding on this form.

Statement of truth

*(I believe)(The [Claimant][Defendant] believes) that the facts contained in this Response are true.

* I am duly authorised by the [Claimant][Defendant] to sign this statement

Full name____________________________________

Name of [claimant][defendant]'s solicitor's firm________________________

signed__________________________position or office held______________

*(Claimant)(Defendant)(Litigation friend)(solicitor) (if signing on behalf of firm or company)

* delete as appropriate

PF 57
Application for clarification or further information (Part 18; PD 18 para.5)

Parties should use form PF 244/N244 and include in Part A the following:

"......for an order that the (*party*) give [clarification of][further information in relation to] the matter(s) set out [on the attached Request] [below]."

Parties should set out the matter(s) requiring clarification/further information using separate numbered paragraphs, and, where a request relates to a document, identify the document and (if relevant) the paragraph or words to which it relates.

Where a Request has been made, the Request together with any response to it, should be attached to the application notice.

If a Request for further information or clarification has not been made, the parties should state in Part B or C the reason why not.

If evidence is relied on in support of the application, it may be included in Part C.

PF 58
Order for clarification or further information (Rule 18.1)

IN THE HIGH COURT OF JUSTICE
[ ] DIVISION
[ ] District Registry
Claim No.

Before (*Master/District Judge*) [sitting in Private]

Claimant

Defendant

An Application was made by [application notice/letter] dated (*date*) *or* by [Counsel][solicitor] for (*party*) and was attended by ( )

The Master [District Judge] read the written evidence filed

IT IS ORDERED that:

1. the (*party*) provide by (*date*) the following [clarification] [further information] [as requested by (*party*) in the attached Request dated (*date*) initialled by the [Master][District Judge]] *or* [as set out below:]
2. the costs of this application are [summarily assessed in the sum of £] [to be the subject of a detailed assessment] and to be paid by

   Dated

PF 63
Interim Order for receiver in pending claim

IN THE HIGH COURT OF JUSTICE
[ ] DIVISION
[ ] District Registry
Claim No.

Before (*Master/District Judge*) [sitting in Private]

Claimant

Defendant

An Application was made by [application notice/letter] dated (*date*) *or* by [Counsel][solicitor] for (*party*) and was attended by ( )

The Master [District Judge] read the written evidence filed

IT IS ORDERED that:

(1) (*name and address*) be appointed [without security][on giving security in the following form (*describe by reference to directions under RSC O.30 r.2*)] until the (*date*) or further order to receive (*describe the property and income*) and that all questions as to passing his accounts and payments and all further questions be reserved until further order.

(2) (*parties*) have permission to apply in the meantime.

Dated

PF 67
Evidence in support of application to make an order of the Supreme Court an order of the High Court (paragraph 13.2 of practice direction 40B)

IN THE HIGH COURT OF JUSTICE
[ ] DIVISION
[ ] District Registry
Claim No.

Claimant

Defendant

I, (*name, address and description*), a solicitor of the Senior Courts and a partner in the firm of (*name*) Solicitors for the (*party*) state [on oath] that:

1. On (*date*) judgment was entered for the (*party*) for £ with costs.
2. On (*date*) upon the appeal of the (*party*) the Court of Appeal ordered that the said judgment in favour of the (*party*) be affirmed [*or* dismissed *or state the order of the Court of Appeal*] and that the said appeal be allowed [dismissed] with costs to be paid by (*party*) to the (*party*) [*or state the order of the Court of Appeal as regards costs*].
3. On (*date*) upon the appeal of the (*party*) to the Supreme Court, the Supreme Court made the order a copy of which [I refer to] [is now shown to me] marked ["A"].
4. The costs of the appeal to the Supreme Court have been assessed by the Registrar of the Supreme Court and allowed in the sum of £ as appears by his certificate dated (*date*) a copy of which [I refer to] [is now shown to me] marked ["B"].
5. In the circumstances, I respectfully ask for an order that the order of the Supreme Court be made an order [judgment] of the High Court and that the costs of this application be paid by (*party*).

I believe that the facts stated in this witness statement are true.

Signed: Name:

Dated

[SWORN, etc]

PF 68
Order making an order of the Supreme Court an order of the High Court (paragraph 13.3 of practice direction 40B)

IN THE HIGH COURT OF JUSTICE
[ ] DIVISION
[ ] District Registry
Claim No.

Before (*Master/District Judge*) [sitting in Private]

Claimant

Defendant

An Application was made by [application notice/letter] dated (*date*) *or* by [Counsel][solicitor] for (*party*) and was attended by ( )

The Master [District Judge] read the written evidence filed

IT IS ORDERED that:

1. the order made on (*date*) by the Supreme Court, in (*set out the case*) that (*set out the order*) be entered and made an order of the High Court.
2. The costs of this application are [summarily assessed in the sum of £] [to be the subject of a detailed assessment] and to be paid by

   Dated

PF 72
List of Exhibits handed in at Trial (Part 39 PD para. 7)

IN THE HIGH COURT OF JUSTICE
[QUEEN'S BENCH] DIVISION **Claim no.**

Claimant

Defendant

Tried on (*dates*) **before The Honourable Mr Justice** (*name*) **at**

Number of exhibit	Description of exhibit	Party who put in exhibit	Witness who proved exhibit	Notes

PF 74
Order for trial of whole claim or of an issue by Master or District Judge (PD Part 2B para. 4.1)

IN THE HIGH COURT OF JUSTICE
[ ] DIVISION
[ ] District Registry
Claim No.

Before (*Master/District Judge*) [sitting in Private]

Claimant

Defendant

An Application was made by [application notice/letter] dated (*date*) *or* by [Counsel][solicitor] for (*party*) and was attended by ( )

The Master [District Judge] read the written evidence filed

IT IS ORDERED BY CONSENT that:

1. [this claim] *or* [the question/issue arising in this claim] set out in the Schedule to this order be tried by a Master [District Judge].
2. the trial to take place
   (a) before a Master
      (i) on (*date*) in Room ( ) at the Royal Courts of Justice,
      (ii) with an estimated length of hearing ( ) hours,
      (iii) with the filing of listing questionnaires dispensed with, *or*

   completed listing questionnaire by (*date*)], *or*

   [(b) before a District Judge, at a hearing details of which [accompany this order][will be sent shortly] with an estimated length of hearing ( ) hours.]
3. (*directions as to the management and trial of the claim or issue.*)
4. the costs of this application be costs in the claim/issue (*or as ordered*).

Schedule
(state question or issue)

Dated

PF 78
Solicitor's undertaking as to Expenses (rule 34.13(6)(b))

IN THE HIGH COURT OF JUSTICE
QUEEN'S BENCH DIVISION
Claim No.

Claimant

Defendant

I [or We] (*name*) hereby undertake to be responsible for all expenses incurred by Her Majesty's Secretary of State for Foreign and Commonwealth Affairs in respect of the letter of request issued in these proceedings on (*date*) and on receiving due notification of the amount of such expenses undertake to pay them as directed by the Senior Master of the Supreme Court.

The following have been appointed as agents for the parties in connection with the execution of the above letter of request:

Claimant's Agent:— (*name and address*)

Defendant's Agent:— (*name and address*)

(*signed*)

Solicitors for (*party*)

Dated

PF 83
Judgment (non attendance of party) (Rule 39.3)

IN THE HIGH COURT OF JUSTICE
[ ] DIVISION
[ ] District Registry
Claim No.

Before (*Judge's name and title*) [sitting in Private]

Claimant

Defendant

This claim having been called on before (*Judge's name and title*) without a jury at [the Royal Courts of Justice].

And the defendant having failed to appear and on proof of the claimant's claim

or

And the claimant having failed to appear [and on proof of the defendant's counterclaim]

And the Judge having ordered on (*date*) that judgment be entered for the (*party*) against the (*party*) as set out below:

IT IS ORDERED that:

1. the defendant pay the claimant the sum of £ .

or

2. [the claimant pay the defendant the sum of £ in respect of the counterclaim and] the claim be dismissed.
3. the (*party*) pay the (*party's*) costs [summarily assessed in the sum of £] [to be the subject of a detailed assessment].

Dated

PF 84A
Order on application arising from a failure to comply with an order or condition (Rule 3.1(3))

IN THE HIGH COURT OF JUSTICE
[ ] DIVISION
[ ] District Registry
Claim No.

Before (*Master/District Judge*) [sitting in Private]

Claimant

Defendant

An Application was made on (*date*) by [Counsel][solicitor] for (*party*) and was attended by (*party*)

The Master [District Judge] read the written evidence filed and the Order dated (*date*) in which it was Ordered (*set out terms of order including the consequence ordered to follow the failure to comply*)

And the (*party*) having failed to comply with that [Order][condition],

IT IS ORDERED that:

1. (*set out the consequence ordered to follow the failure to comply or as may be otherwise ordered*)
2. the costs of this application are [summarily assessed in the sum of £] [to be the subject of a detailed assessment] and to be paid by (*party*).

   Dated

PF 84B
Judgment on application arising from a failure to comply with an order (Rules 3.5(1) and (4))

IN THE HIGH COURT OF JUSTICE
[ ] DIVISION
[ ] District Registry
Claim No.

Before (*Master/District Judge*) [sitting in Private]

Claimant

Defendant

An Application was made on (*date*) by [Counsel][solicitor] for (*party*) for judgment and was attended by (*party*)

The Master [District Judge] read the written evidence filed and the Order dated (*date*) in which it was Ordered (*set out terms of order*)

And the (*party*) having failed to comply with that Order,

IT IS ORDERED that:

1. the (*statement of case*) [the following part of the (*statement of case*) (*specify*)] of (*party*) be struck out.
2. there be judgment for;

   [the defendant dismissing the claim] *or*

   [(*party*) for a declaration that (*set out terms of declaration*)] *or*

   [(*party*) for specific delivery of the following goods (*describe goods*)] *or*

   (*such other remedy as may be ordered under rule 3.5(4)*)
3. the (*party*) pay the (*party*) costs [summarily assessed in the sum of £] [to be the subject of a detailed assessment].

   Dated

PF 85A
Request for judgmentJustice (under Rule 3.5(2))

IN THE HIGH COURT OF JUSTICE
[ ] Division
[ ] District Registry
[ ] County Court
Claim No.

Claimant

Defendant

To the Court

An order was made on (*date*) that unless (*party*) (*set out the order to be complied with*) his statement of case would be struck out.
The (*party*) has not complied with that order [within the specified time].
I request judgment to be entered against (*party*) for;

(1) the sum of £ and costs, *or*

(2) an amount to be decided by the court and costs, *or*

(3) delivery of (*specify goods*) or payment of their value to be decided by the court and costs

I Certify that the information given is correct

Signed____________________position or office held______________

*(Claimant)(Defendant)(Litigation friend)(solicitor) (if signing on behalf of firm or company)

* delete as appropriate

Dated

The court office is open between 10 am and [4.00pm] [4.30pm] Monday to Friday. Please address all communications to the Court Manager quoting the claim number.

PF 85B
Judgment on Request arising from a failure to comply with an order (Rule 3.5(2))

IN THE HIGH COURT OF JUSTICE
[ ] DIVISION
[ ] District Registry
Claim No.

Claimant

Defendant

A Request was received from (*party*) dated (*date*);

(a) which certified that (*party*) had failed to comply with the Order dated (*date*) that (*set out term(s) of order*) and that his statement of case be struck out (*or as may be*), and
(b) requesting judgment to be entered against (*party*).

IT IS ORDERED that there be judgment as follows:

1. [the (*party*) pay the (*party*) the sum of £]

or

[the (*party*) pay the (*party*) damages to be decided by the court]

or

[delivery of the goods described in the [claim form] [particulars of claim] as (*description of goods*) or (*party*) pay (*party*) the value of the goods to be decided by the court]

2. the (*party*) pay the (*party*) costs [summarily assessed in the sum of £] [to be the subject of a detailed assessment].

Dated

PF 113
Evidence on Application for Service by Alternative Method (Rule 6.8, Pt 6 PD para 9.1)

IN THE HIGH COURT OF JUSTICE
[ ] DIVISION
[ ] District Registry
Claim No.

Claimant

Defendant

I, (name, address and description) state [on oath] that:

(the following text may also be set out in Part C of form PF244/N244)

1. Having been directed by (*party/solicitor*) to serve the defendant with a copy of the Claim Form in these proceedings, which had been duly sealed with the seal of the Issuing Court and accompanied by the Response Pack, (*or specify other document(s) to be served*) on (*date*) I attended for the purpose of serving a copy of the/those document(s) on (*party*) at (*address*).
2. (*describe efforts to effect service*).
3. I believe that I have made all reasonable efforts and used all means in my power to serve the Claim Form and Response Pack (*or document(s) to be served*), but I have not been able to do so. I ask for an order for service by the following alternative method(s): (*set out proposed method(s)).*
4. I believe that a Claim Form (*or other document*) served by this/these method(s) will come to the attention of the defendant because (*set out grounds for belief*).

I believe that the facts stated in this witness statement are true.

Signed Name

Dated

[Sworn etc.]

PF 130
Form of advertisement (Rule 6.8)

IN THE HIGH COURT OF JUSTICE
[ ] DIVISION
[ ] District Registry
Claim No.

Claimant

Defendant

To: (*name*)

Take notice that:

(1) A Claim Form has been issued against you in the High Court of Justice, [ ] Division, [District Registry] Claim no. by (*claimant's name*) of (*address*). Details of the claim are set out in the Claim Form [and the particulars of claim attached to it].

(2) On (*date*) the Court ordered that the Claim Form is deemed to be served on you by this advertisement.

(3) You must within days from the date of publication of this advertisement respond to the Claim by;

(a) filing an Acknowledgement of Service form,
(b) admitting the claim, or
(c) filing and serving a defence,

otherwise judgment may be entered against you.

(4) The appropriate forms may be obtained from the Court Office, Room [ ], Royal Courts of Justice, Strand, London WC2A 2LL, (*or District Registry*), or from the solicitors whose name and address appear below.

Dated

Signed

[name of firm]

[claimant] ['s solicitor]

of (address)

PF 147
Application for Order declaring that Solicitor has ceased to act through death etc (Rule 42.4, PD para. 4)

Parties should use Form PF 244/N244 (noting the provisions of rule 42.4(2) as to notice) and include in Part A the following:

"........... for an order declaring that (*name of solicitor who has ceased to act*) has ceased to be the solicitor acting for (*party*) in this claim because he [has died] [has become bankrupt][has ceased to practice][cannot be found]."

PF 148
Order Declaring Solicitor has ceased to Act through Death etc (Rule 42.4)

IN THE HIGH COURT OF JUSTICE
[ ] DIVISION
[ ] District Registry
Claim No.

Before (*Master or District Judge*) [Sitting in private]

Claimant

Defendant

An Application was made by [application notice][letter] dated (*date*) *or* was made on (*date*) by [*counsel*][*solicitor*] for (*party)* and was attended by ( ).

The Master/District Judge read the written evidence filed.

And (*name*), the solicitor for (*party*) in these proceedings, having died [*or* become bankrupt*, or as appropriate*]

And (*party*) having failed to give notice of change of solicitor or intention to act in person, and notice of this application having been duly served on him.

It is Ordered and Declared that (*name*) has ceased to be the solicitor acting for (*name and address of party whose solicitor has ceased to act*) in this claim.

Dated

PF 149
Application by Solicitor for Declaration that He has Ceased to Act (rule 42.3, Pt. 42 PD para. 3)

The solicitor applying should use Form PF 244/N244 and include in Part A the following:

"...........for an order declaring that (*name of solicitor(s)*) has/have ceased to be the solicitor(s) acting for (*party*) in this claim because of the facts set out in [Part C][the written evidence served with this application notice]."

Note:- To be served only on the party for whom the solicitor applying has acted.

PF 150
Order Declaring that Solicitor has ceased to Act (rule 42.3 and Pt 42 PD para. 3.3)

IN THE HIGH COURT OF JUSTICE
[ ] DIVISION
[ ] District Registry
Claim No.

Before (*Master or District Judge*) [Sitting in Private]

Claimant

Defendant

An application was made by [application notice/letter] dated (*date*) *or* was made on (*date*) by [*counsel*][*solicitor*] for [*party*] and was attended by ( ).

The Master read the written evidence filed

It is Ordered and Declared that (*name*) has ceased to be the solicitor acting for (*party*) in these proceedings.

And it is Ordered that the written evidence be filed at Court separately from the other documents in this claim.

Dated

PF 152 QB
Evidence in support of application for Examination of a Witness under the Evidence (Proceedings in other Jurisdictions) Act 1975 (Schedule 1 – RSC O.70, r.2 and Pt. 34 PD para. 6.3)

IN THE HIGH COURT OF JUSTICE
QUEEN'S BENCH DIVISION
[ ] District Registry
Claim No

In the matter of the Evidence (Proceedings in Other Jurisdictions) Act 1975 and

In the matter of a civil [*or* commercial] proceeding now pending [*or* contemplated] before (*give description of foreign court or tribunal*) entitled as follows:-

((1) give title of proceedings in foreign court or tribunal or (2) state "In proceedings contemplated between (party) and (party)")

I, (*name, address and description*) state [on oath] that:

1. I am instructed by (*name and address of foreign lawyer and for whom he is acting or as the case may be*) to apply for an Order for the examination of the following witness[es], namely;

(*name*) of (*address*)

whose testimony the above-named foreign Court desires to obtain in connection with the above matter. [I refer to] [There is shown to me] a bundle marked ["A"] containing;

(a) the Letter of Request from the foreign court,
(b) a draft order,
(c) (*insofar as they are not contained in the Letter of Request*)
   (i) a statement of the issues relevant to the proceedings and
   (ii) a list of questions or the subject matter of questions to be put to the witness[es], and
(d) (*where appropriate*) a translation of the above documents.

2. It is proposed that the witness[es] be examined upon oath (*if the Letter of Request or other document requests that the examination be taken in a particular manner, such manner should be stated here*) in relation to the said proceedings [before one of the Examiners of the Court] *or* [before (*name*) a solicitor/barrister who, in my opinion, is a fit and proper person to take such examination].

I believe that the facts stated in this witness statement are true.

Signed: Name:

Dated:

[SWORN etc]

Note:

1) Should the Letter of Request not disclose the name of a witness, but describe him by an office e.g. "Secretary or other proper officer of Limited", a paragraph should be added to the effect that the deponent has ascertained that the proposed witness is the proper person to give the desired evidence.

PF 153
Certificate Under the Evidence (Proceedings in Other Jurisdictions) Act 1975 (Schedule 1 – RSC O.70, r.5)

I, , Senior Master of the Queen's Bench Division of the Supreme Court of England and Wales, hereby certify that the documents annexed to this Certificate are;

1. the original order of the Division of Her Majesty's High Court of Justice, dated the day of 20 , made in the matter of (*title of proceedings*) pending in the (*foreign court*) at in the of , directing the examination of certain witnesses to be taken before (*name*), and
2. the examination and deposition taken by the examiner pursuant to the said order and duly signed and completed by the examiner on the day of 20 , together with the original Letter of Request.

[Signed]

Senior Master

Dated the day of 20 .

PF 154
Order for registration of a foreign judgment under the Foreign Judgments (Reciprocal Enforcement) Act 1933

IN THE HIGH COURT OF JUSTICE
QUEEN'S BENCH DIVISION
[ ] District Registry

Before (*Master/District Judge*) [sitting in Private]

[In the matter of the Administration of Justice Act 1920]

or

[In the matter of the Foreign Judgments (Reciprocal Enforcement) Act 1933]

and

In the matter of a Judgment of the (*describe overseas court*) dated (*date*) entitled as follows:-

(*give title of proceedings in overseas court*)

An Application was made by [application notice/letter] dated (*date*) *or* by [Counsel][solicitor] for (*party*) and was attended by ( )

The Master [District Judge] read the written evidence filed

IT IS ORDERED that:

1. the judgment dated (*date*) of (*describe overseas court*) in which it was ordered that (*name, address and description*) the judgment creditor, recover against (*name, address and description*) the judgment debtor, the sum of (*state amount due under the judgment in the currency in which it is expressed*) for debt and costs (*or as may be*) be registered as a judgment in the Queen's Bench Division of the High Court of Justice under the Statute.
2. the judgment debtor has permission to apply to set aside the registration within [ ] days after service on him of notice of the registration under RSC O.71 r.7(3) (Schedule 1 to the Civil Procedure Rules 1998) if he has grounds for doing so and execution on the judgment will not issue until;
   (a) after the expiration of that period, or
   (b) after the expiration of any extension of that period granted by the court, or
   (c) where an application is made to set aside the registration, the application has been disposed of.
3. the costs of this application be the subject of a detailed assessment and be added to the judgment (*or as may be ordered*).

   Dated

PF 155
Certificates under section 10 of the Foreign Judgments (Reciprocal Enforcement) Act 1933

IN THE HIGH COURT OF JUSTICE
[ ] Division
[ ] District Registry
Claim No

In the matter of the Foreign Judgments (Reciprocal Enforcement) Act 1933

Claimant

Defendant

Certificate A

I, a [Master of the Supreme Court] [District Judge of the High Court] of England and Wales, hereby certify that:

1. The Claim Form (*or as the case may be*), a copy of which is annexed, was issued out of the Division of the High Court of Justice on (*date*) by (*name*) the above-named claimant against (*name*), the above-named defendant, for payment of the sum of £ in respect of (*state briefly the nature of the claim*).

2. [The claim form (*or as the case may be*) was duly served on the (*date*), on the defendant by (*state method of service*)] *or* [The defendant (*name*) [acknowledged service of the claim form] [filed a defence] on the (*date*)].

3. [The defendant objected to the jurisdiction of the court by application notice dated (*date*)] or [The defendant did not dispute the jurisdiction of the Court].

4. The following statements of case were served:

(*list statements of case*)

5. The (*party*) obtained judgment against the (*party*) in the Division of the High Court of Justice for the sum of £ as appears from the office copy of the judgment, sealed with the seal of the Supreme Court, annexed to this certificate. The grounds on which the judgment was based were:

(*set out grounds*)

6. [No application to set aside the judgment has been made] *or* [an application to set aside the judgment has been finally disposed of and dismissed].

7. [No appeal against the judgment has been brought within the time prescribed] *or* [An application for permission to appeal against the judgment has been finally disposed of and permission refused] *or* [An appeal against the judgment has been finally disposed of and dismissed].

(Signed)

A [Master of the Supreme Court] [District Judge of the High Court] of England and Wales.

Dated

Certificate B

I, a [Master of the Supreme Court] [District Judge of the High Court] of England and Wales, hereby certify that the judgment obtained by (*party*) against (*party*) in this claim on (*date*) for payment of the sum of £ and £ costs carries interest at the rate of £ per annum calculated on the sums of £ and £ from the date of the judgment until payment.

(signed)

A [Master of the Supreme Court] [District Judge of the High Court] of England and Wales.

Dated

PF 156 QB
Evidence in support of application for registration of a Community judgment

IN THE HIGH COURT OF JUSTICE
QUEEN'S BENCH DIVISION
[ ] District Registry

In the matter of the European Communities (Enforcement of Community Judgments) Order 1972

and

In the matter of RSC O. 71, Schedule 1 to the Civil Procedure Rules 1998

and

In the matter of a Judgment of the (*describe European institution*) dated (*date*) entitled as follows:

(*give title of proceedings*)

I, (*name, address and description*) state [on oath] as follows:-

1. I am instructed by the above-named (*party*) to apply for the registration of the above-mentioned Community judgment. A copy, duly authenticated by the seal of (*name of institution*) and to which the Secretary of State has appended an order for enforcement under Article 3 of the above-mentioned Order, [together with a translation [certified by a notary] [verified by the [witness statement] [affidavit] of (*name*)]], [I refer to] [is shown to me] marked ["A"].
2. (*Where the application is for registration of a Community judgment under which a sum of money is payable;*) The judgment is for (*state amount due under the judgment in the currency in which it is expressed*) and
   (a) so far as is known to me, the name, occupation and usual or last known abode or place of business of the judgment debtor is (*set out*), and
   (b) to the best of my information and belief, the European Court has not suspended enforcement of the judgment which remains [wholly unsatisfied] [unsatisfied to the extent of (*state amount in which the judgment remains unsatisfied*)].
3. The (*party*) accordingly seeks an order for registration of the Community judgment [in the sum of (*state amount*)].

I believe that the facts stated in this witness statement are true.

Signed: Name:

Dated

[SWORN etc]

PF 157 QB
Order for registration of a Community judgment

IN THE HIGH COURT OF JUSTICE
QUEEN'S BENCH DIVISION
[ ] District Registry

Before (*Master/District Judge*) [sitting in Private]

In the matter of the European Communities (Enforcement of Community Judgments) Order 1972

and

In the matter of RSC O. 71, Schedule 1 to the Civil Procedure Rules 1998

and

In the matter of a Judgment of the (*describe European institution*) dated (*date*) entitled as follows:

(*give title of proceedings*)

An Application was made by [application notice/letter] dated (*date*) *or* by [Counsel][solicitor] for (*party*) and was attended by ( )

The Master [District Judge] read the written evidence filed

IT IS ORDERED that:

1. the European Community judgment dated (*date*) in which it was ordered that the defendant pay the claimant the sum of (*state amount due under the judgment in the currency in which it is expressed*), be registered in the Queen's Bench Division of the High Court of Justice under the European Communities (Enforcement of Community Judgments) Order 1972.

   Dated

PF 158 QB
Notice of registration of a Community judgment

IN THE HIGH COURT OF JUSTICE
QUEEN'S BENCH DIVISION

In the Matter of the European Communities (Enforcement of Community Judgments) Order 1972

and

In the Matter of RSC O. 71, Schedule 1 to the Civil Procedure Rules 1998

and

In the Matter of a Judgment of the (*describe European institution*) dated (*date*) entitled as follows:

(*give title of proceedings*)

To the Defendant (*name and address*)

TAKE NOTICE that:

1. The above-mentioned judgment has been registered in the Queen's Bench Division of the High Court of Justice in England and Wales. A copy of the Judgment and of the Secretary of State's order for enforcement is annexed.
2. The application for the Judgment to be registered was made by *(name and address of party or his solicitor)* and any documents about the case may be served at that address.
3. Within 28 days of the date of this notice (or within such further period as the Court may permit) you may apply for the variation or cancellation of the registration on the ground that the Judgment had been partly or wholly satisfied at the date of the registration.

Dated

PF 159 QB
Evidence in support of application for registration of a judgment of another Contracting State or Regulation State

IN THE HIGH COURT OF JUSTICE
QUEEN'S BENCH DIVISION

In the Matter of section 4 of the Civil Jurisdiction and Judgments Act 1982

and

In the Matter of a Judgment of (*name Court and contracting State*) in a claim between:

Claimant

Defendant

I, (*name, address and description*) state [on oath] as follows:

1. By a Judgment of (*name Court and contracting State*) dated (*date*) in proceedings between the claimant and defendant it was ordered that (*summarise terms of Judgment*).
2. [I refer to] [there is shown to me] a bundle marked ["A"] containing the following documents;
   (a) the judgment [*or* a [verified] [certified] [*or otherwise* duly authenticated] copy of the judgment],
   (b) (*name the document[s] showing that the judgment is enforceable and has been served*),
   (c) (*in the case of a judgment given in default, name the [certified true copy of the] document establishing service of the document instituting the proceedings*),
   (d) (*where appropriate, name the document showing the claimant is in receipt of legal aid*).

[3. [I refer to] [there are shown to me] marked ["B"] translations of all the documents [certified by a notary public] [verified by the [witness statement] [affidavit] of (*name of person qualified for the purpose*)].]

4. The Judgment provides [does not provide] for payment of a sum [sums] of money.
5. In accordance with the laws of [*the contracting State*] interest is recoverable upon the Judgment at the rate of   per cent. per annum from the date of Judgment until payment (*or as the case may be*) [*or* Interest is not recoverable upon the Judgment or any part of it].
6. The claimant's address for service within the jurisdiction is (*address*). So far as is known to me the usual [last-known] address [place of business] of the defendant is (*address*).
7. To the best of my knowledge, information and belief the right to enforce the Judgment is vested in the claimant on the grounds that the Court pronounced Judgment in his favour in the terms summarised above and that in accordance with the laws of (*the contracting State*) such Judgment is immediately enforceable (*or as the case may be*).
8. At the date of this witness statement [affidavit] the Judgment remains wholly unsatisfied (*or as the case may be*).

9. The claimant accordingly applies for registration of the Judgment (*or describe part of judgment which is unsatisfied*) under section 4 of the Civil Jurisdiction and Judgments Act 1982.

I believe that the facts stated in this witness statement are true.

Signed: Name:

Dated:

[SWORN etc]

PF 160 QB
Order for registration of a judgment of another Contracting State or Registration State under section 4 of the Civil Jurisdiction and Judgments Act 1982

IN THE HIGH COURT OF JUSTICE
QUEEN'S BENCH DIVISION
[ ] District Registry

Before (*Master/District Judge*) [sitting in Private]

In the matter of the Civil Jurisdiction and Judgments Act 1982

and

In the matter of a Judgment of the (*name court and contracting state*) obtained in a claim between:

Claimant

Defendant

An Application was made by [application notice/letter] dated (*date*) or by [Counsel][solicitor] for (*party*) [and was attended by ( )]

The Master [District Judge] read the written evidence filed

IT IS ORDERED that:

1. the judgment dated (*date*) of (*name court and contracting state*) be registered in the Queen's Bench Division of the High Court of Justice under the Civil Jurisdiction and Judgments Act 1982.
2. the defendant has permission within one month or [two months if the defendant is domiciled in another contracting state] after service on him of notice of registration of the judgment to appeal against the registration and execution on the judgment will not issue until;
   (a) after the expiration of that period, or
   (b) in the event of an appeal, after the appeal has been determined.
3. the costs of and occasioned by this application and the registration of the judgment are [summarily assessed in the sum of £] [to be the subject of a detailed assessment] and to be added to the judgment as registered.

   Dated

PF 161 QB
Notice of Registration of a judgment of another Contracting State or Regulation State

IN THE HIGH COURT OF JUSTICE
QUEEN'S BENCH DIVISION

In the Matter of section 4 of the Civil Jurisdiction and Judgments Act 1982

and

In the Matter of a Judgment of *(name court and contracting state)* in a claim between:

Claimant

Defendant

To the Defendant (*name and address*)

TAKE NOTICE that:

1. By Order of Master *(name)* dated *(date)* a judgment of *(name court and contracting state)* dated *(date)* in which it was ordered *(state briefly terms of judgment)* has been registered in the Queen's Bench Division of the High Court of Justice in England and Wales under the Civil Jurisdiction and Judgments Act 1982 on the application of the claimant.
2. You may appeal against the order for registration within one month (*or* two months *if the defendant is domiciled in another contracting state*) after service on you of this notice.
3. The address for service of the claimant is (*address).*

Dated

PF 163 QB

Evidence in support of application for certified copy of a judgment for enforcement in another Contracting State or Regulation State

IN THE HIGH COURT OF JUSTICE
[QUEEN'S BENCH] DIVISION

In the matter of section 12 of the Civil Jurisdiction and Judgments Act 1982

and

In the matter of a claim between:

Claimant

Defendant

I, (*name, address and description*) state [on oath] as follows:-

1. On (*date*) the claim form was issued out of the Central Office by the claimant against the defendant for £ for (*give brief details of the claim*).
2. The claim form was served on the defendant on (*date*) by (*describe method*). (*briefly describe the course of proceedings leading up to judgment*)
3. [I refer to] [there are shown to me] marked ["A"] the following documents:

   (a) the claim form,
   (b) the [certificate of service] [notice of service by the court],
   (c) the statements of case,
   (d) the judgment of (*title and name of judge*),
   [(e) the Legal Aid Certificate issued to the claimant in respect of this claim.]

4. [The defendant did not dispute the jurisdiction of the court.] [The defendant disputed the jurisdiction of the court on the ground (*state ground*). An application by the defendant to set aside the claim on that ground was dismissed by Master (*name*) on (*date*).]
5. The judgment has been served on the defendant in accordance with the provisions of the Civil Procedure Rules 1998 and is not subject to any stay of execution.
6. That [no appeal against the judgment has been brought within the time prescribed] *or* [an application for permission to appeal against the judgment has been finally disposed of and permission refused] *or* [an appeal against the judgment has been finally disposed of and dismissed].
7. The judgment provides for payment of the sum of £ by the defendant to the claimant and interest is recoverable on the whole of the sum at the rate of per cent. per annum from the date of judgment until payment.

8. The claimant seeks an order to enforce the judgment in (*name of contracting state*) and applies for a certified copy of the judgment under section 12 of the Civil Jurisdiction and Judgments Act 1982.

I believe that the facts stated in this witness statement are true.

Signed: Name:

Dated

[SWORN etc]

PF 164

Evidence in support of application for certificate as to money provisions contained in a judgment of the High Court for registration elsewhere in the United Kingdom

IN THE HIGH COURT OF JUSTICE
[ ] DIVISION
[ ] District Registry
Claim No.

Claimant

Defendant

I, (*name, address and description*) state [on oath] as follows:-

1. On (*date*) the claimant obtained judgment against the defendant for £ in respect of (*state briefly the nature of the claim*) together with interest at the rate of per cent. per annum from (*date*) to the date of judgment amounting to £ and costs [summarily assessed] [the subject of a detailed assessment] in the sum of £ .
2. The aggregate of the sums payable under the judgment by the defendant to the claimant is £ . Interest is payable on the judgment sum at the rate of per cent. per annum from (*date*) the date of judgment until payment.
3. The judgment is wholly unsatisfied (*or as the case may be*) and the sum of £ remains payable under the judgment by the defendant to the claimant together with interest at the rate of per cent. per annum from (*date*).
4. That [no appeal against the judgment has been brought within the time prescribed] *or* [an application for permission to appeal against the judgment has been finally disposed of and permission refused] *or* [an appeal against the judgment has been finally disposed of and dismissed].
5. Enforcement of the judgment is not stayed or suspended.
6. To the best of my information and belief the following are correct:

   (*here set out the name and usual or last known address or place of business of the claimant and defendant*)
7. This witness statement [affidavit] is made [sworn] for the purpose of obtaining a certificate of judgment for registration in (*describe part of United Kingdom*) in accordance with schedule 6 to the Civil Jurisdiction and Judgments Act 1982 and I hereby apply for the same.

I believe that the facts stated in this witness statement are true.

Signed: Name:

Dated

[SWORN etc]

PF 165
Evidence in support of application for registration of a judgment of a court in another part of the United Kingdom containing non-money provisions

IN THE HIGH COURT OF JUSTICE
[ ] DIVISION
[ ] District Registry

In the matter of section 18 of the Civil Jurisdiction and Judgments Act 1982

and

In the matter of a Judgment of (*name of court of origin and other part of the United Kingdom*) in proceedings between:

Claimant

Defendant

I, (*name, address and description*) state [on oath] as follows:

1. By a Judgment of (*name court of origin and other part of the United Kingdom*) dated (*date*) it was ordered that (*summarise terms of Judgment and particularly non-money terms*).
2. [I refer to] [there is shown to me] a bundle marked ["A"] containing a copy of the judgment certified by (*name of court of origin*) to be a true copy together with a certificate of that court certifiying;
   (a) that the time for appealing against the judgment has expired and that no appeal was brought within that time (*or as the case may be*), and
   (b) that enforcement of the judgment is not stayed or suspended.
3. To the best of my information or belief the usual or last known address;
   (a) of the claimant is (*address*), and
   (b) of the defendant is (*address*).
4. The claimant accordingly applies for registration of the judgment in this Honourable Court under section 18 of and schedule 7 to the Civil Jurisdiction and Judgments Act 1982.

I believe that the facts stated in this witness statement are true.

Signed: Name:

Dated

[SWORN etc]

PF 166
Certificate as to finality, etc. of Arbitration Award for enforcement abroad (Arbitration Act 1996, s.58)

In the matter of the Arbitration Act 1996

and

In the matter of an Arbitration between:

Claimant

Respondent

I, a Master of the Supreme Court [a District Judge of the High Court] of England and Wales, hereby certify:—

1. That the award made by *(name of arbitrator)* and published on (*date*) is not subject to any appeal or to any application to remit or set it aside and that the time for any such appeal or application has expired [*or* an appeal against the award was dismissed by the order of The Honourable Mr Justice (*name*) (*dated*)] (*or as may be*),

2. That the award is by virtue of the provisions of sub-section (1) of section 58 of the Arbitration Act 1996 final and binding on the parties and any persons claiming through or under them.

Dated

(Signed)

a Master of the Supreme Court [a District Judge of the High Court] of England and Wales

PF 167
Order to stay proceedings under Section 9 of the Arbitration Act 1996

IN THE HIGH COURT OF JUSTICE
QUEEN'S BENCH DIVISION
Claim No.

Before (*Judge/Master/District Judge's name and title*) [sitting in Private]

Claimant

Defendant

An Application was made by [application notice/letter] dated (*date*) *or* by [Counsel][solicitor] for (*party*) and was attended by (   )

The [Judge][Master][District Judge] read the written evidence filed

IT IS ORDERED that:

1. all further proceedings in this claim be stayed under section 9 of the Arbitration Act 1996,
2. the costs of and caused by the claim [including the costs of this application] are [summarily assessed in the sum of £   ] [to be the subject of a detailed assessment] and to be paid by (*party*).

Dated

PF 168
Order to transfer claim from High Court to county court (County Courts Act 1984; High Court and County Courts Jurisdiction Order 1991; Rule 30.3)

IN THE HIGH COURT OF JUSTICE
[   ] DIVISION
[   ] District Registry
Claim No.

Before (*Master/District Judge*) [sitting in Private]

Claimant

Defendant

An Application was made by [application notice/letter] dated (*date*) *or* by [Counsel][solicitor] for (*party*) and was attended by (   )

The Master [District Judge] read the written evidence filed

IT IS ORDERED that:

1. this claim be transferred to the (*name of county court*) County Court under section 40 [(1)][(2)] of the County Courts Act 1984.
2. the costs of this application are [summarily assessed in the sum of £   ] [to be assessed in the County Court] [and to be paid by (*party*)].

Dated

PF 170(A)
Application for child or patient's settlement in personal injury or Fatal Accidents Act claims, before proceedings begun (Rule 21.10(2), Pt 21 PD paras. 6 and 7)

Parties should use the Part 8 Claim Form N208 and the information required by paragraphs 6.2 or 6.3 of the Practice Direction should either be included in the "Details of claim" section of the claim form or provided to the court.

In a Fatal Accidents Acts claim, the information set out in paragraph 7 of the practice direction should also be provided.

A draft order in form N292 containing the terms of settlement or compromise should be attached whenever possible; if that is not possible the terms should be set out in the claim form.

PF 170(B)
Application for child or patient's settlement in personal injury or Fatal Accidents Act claims, in existing proceedings (Rule 21.10(2), Pt. 21 PD paras. 6 and 7)

Parties should use form PF244/N244 and the information required by paragraphs 6.2 or 6.3 of the Practice Direction should either be included in Part A of the application notice or provided to the court.

In a Fatal Accidents Act claim, the information set out in paragraph 7 of the practice direction should also be provided.

A draft order in form N292 containing the terms of settlement or compromise should be attached whenever possible.

PF 172
Request for directions in respect of funds in court or to be brought into court (Rule 21.11 and Part 21 PD para 8)

IN THE HIGH COURT OF JUSTICE
QUEEN'S BENCH DIVISION
[ ] DISTRICT REGISTRY

Claimant

Defendant

The full name and date of birth of the child[1] is as follows:-

Name

Date of birth

Other income ❑ yes ❑ no

Liable for tax ❑ yes ❑ no

I will produce the birth certificate of the child at the appointment.

I apply for:-

1. A payment out of the fund of £ for *

*(*give name of child for whom payment is to be made*)

2. Investment of the fund as appropriate.

Specific liabilities and/or other factors which may affect investment policy are as follows:- (*give details*)

Names and addresses of persons to whom future correspondence and payments should be sent:-

(i) Correspondence to (*give name and address*)
(ii) Payments to (*give name and address*)

Name and address of claimant's solicitor:-

Signature of litigation friend:-

Address:-

Date:-

Note: *Notes for guidance for completion of this form may be obtained from the Masters' Support Unit, Room E.16 or from the Court Manager of the relevant District Registry.*

1 When directions are sought in respect of more than 1 child, a form for each child should be submitted.

To be completed by the court

1. Fund to be invested by the court £...............
2. Legal aid first charge ❑ yes ❑ no
3. Majority directions ❑ yes ❑ no
4. Investment requirements:-
   (i) capital growth ❑ yes ❑ no
   (ii) capital growth and income ❑ yes ❑ no
   (iii) maximum income ❑ yes ❑ no
5. Payment directions:-
   (i) pay income to (*give name*)
   ❑ during minority ❑ until (*insert date*)
   (ii) pay £...................monthly to (*give name*)
   commencing on (*insert date*) until (*insert date*)
   (iii) (*insert any other payment ordered*)
6. Income directions (subject to above payment directions):-
   (i) accumulate and reinvest ❑ yes ❑ no
   (ii) invest in a special account ❑ yes ❑ no
7. Tax directions- recovered tax to be:-
   (i) retained by litigation friend for benefit of child ❑ yes ❑ no
   (ii) paid by litigation friend into child's fund in court ❑ yes ❑ no
8. Date of birth confirmed ❑ yes ❑ no

(Signed)

Master/District Judge

Dated

PF 198

Order for transfer from the Royal Courts of Jusice to a district registry or vice-versa or from one district registry to another (rule 30.2(4)

IN THE HIGH COURT OF JUSTICE
[ ] DIVISION
[ ] District Registry
Claim No.

Before (*Master or District Judge*) [sitting in Private]

Claimant

Defendant

An Application was made by [application notice/letter] dated (*date*) *or* by [Counsel][solicitor] for (*party*) and was attended by ( )

The Master [District Judge] read the written evidence filed

IT IS ORDERED that:

1. the claim (*or as may be*) be transferred to [the Royal Courts of Justice] [the District Registry].
2. the costs of this application are [summarily assessed in the sum of £] [to be the subject of a detailed assessment] and to be paid by (*party*).

Dated

PF 205
Evidence in support of application for permission to execute for earlier costs of enforcement under s.15(3) and (4) of the Courts and Legal Services Act 1990

IN THE HIGH COURT OF JUSTICE
QUEEN'S BENCH DIVISION
Claim No.

Claimant

Defendant

I, (*name, address and description*) state [on oath] that:

1. I am [the judgment creditor in these proceedings] [(*give deponent's connection with the proceedings*) authorised by the judgment creditor to make this witness statement [affidavit] on his behalf].
2. [I am] [the claimant is] a judgment creditor of the [defendant] to the extent of £ inclusive of all interest which has accrued to date on the judgment debt.
3. [I am] [the claimant is] presently taking steps [*or* [I have] [the claimant has] taken steps] to enforce [the judgment] [the sum of £ being the balance of the judgment]. Details of the unsuccessful attempts and methods employed to enforce the judgment together with the costs of each attempt incurred by the claimant are set out in the following list:

(*list the attempts*)

4. The costs set out in the above list were all reasonably incurred. [I refer to] [there is shown to me] marked ["A"] a numbered bundle of documents containing the vouchers, receipts and other documents relied on in support of this application. The bundle is divided into sections which correspond with the costs claimed in respect of each previous attempt set out above.
5. I seek an order for permission to execute now for the costs set out above.

I believe that the facts stated in this witness statement are true.

Signed: Name:

Dated

[SWORN etc]

PF 244 R.C.J. (Application for Reconsideration) (Out of Country Application)
NOTICE under CPR 54.31(2)

Administrative Court Office ref CO/ /

s.103A Nationality, Immigration and Asylum Act 2002 and para 30(5)(b) of Schedule 2 to the Asylum and Immigration (Treatment of Claimants, etc.) Act 2004, (Civil Procedure Rule 54.31(2))

To: The Administrative Court Office Room C315, Royal Courts of Justice, Strand, London WC2A 2LL

I/We* apply for an order that the Asylum and Immigration Tribunal reconsider its decision on an appeal under s.82*/83* of the Nationality, Immigration and Asylum Act 2002, following the Tribunal's decision not to order reconsideration

Part A

Full Name of Applicant:
Address:
Date of birth:
Home Office Ref No:
Reporting Centre (if applicable): **AIT Ref No:**
Date of Tribunal decision on application for reconsideration:
Was your case dealt with under the fast track procedure in the AIT? Yes/No*
Deemed Date of receipt of AIT decision:** *(If you are seeking to file this application more than* **28** *days after the deemed date of receipt, you must apply for an extension of time in which to file this application and set out your grounds for seeking an extension of time in Part B below)*
Filed by - (Applicant) (Litigation friend) (Applicant's Solicitor) (Charity or Not for Profit Organisation) (Signing on behalf of firm or company)*
Solicitor's reference No (if applicable):
Solicitor's Name (if applicable):
Address:***
Tel:
Fax:

*delete as appropriate
**If you were the Respondent to the appeal and were required to serve the notice from the Tribunal on the appellant, please state the date on which, and the means by which, the notice from the Tribunal was served.
***If you are being assisted by a charity or not for profit organisation, you may give that organisation's address for the purpose of correspondence.

Part B – Grounds for extension of time

(If you are seeking to file this application out of time (see explanation under Deemed Date of receipt of AIT decision in Part A), you must apply for an extension of time and set out in this Part the grounds on which it is contended that the application notice could not reasonably practicably have been filed within the appropriate time limit. Those grounds must be supported by written evidence verified by a statement of truth.)

Statement of Truth (to be signed when part B is completed)

(I believe*)(The Applicant believes*) that the facts contained under part B in this application notice are true.

I am duly authorised by the Applicant to sign this statement*

Full name____

Name of Applicant's Solicitor's firm*______________________________

Signed____________________ position or office held ____________________

(Applicant) (Litigation Friend) (Applicant's Solicitor) (Charity or Not for Profit Organisation) (Signing on behalf of firm or company)*

*delete as appropriate

Part C – The grounds which the Court will consider are those you submitted to the AIT in your application for reconsideration (Form AIT/103A).

If you wish to respond to the reasons given by the Tribunal for its decision that it does not propose to make an order for reconsideration, you should set out in this Part the grounds upon which you dispute any of the reasons given by the Tribunal and give reasons in support of those grounds.

Part D – Is an order for the payment of costs from the Community Legal Service Fund sought under s.103D of the Nationality, Immigration and Asylum Act 2002?

Yes/No/Not Applicable*

Note: *If you are seeking an order for costs you must answer "yes" to ensure that consideration is given to whether or not an order should be made.*

Unrepresented parties, *if you do not have a legal representative acting for you, or you do not have a charity or not for profit organisation assisting you, you must answer "Not Applicable".*

If you were the Respondent to the original appeal, *you must also answer "Not Applicable".*

Signed: ** (name)
(Applicant) (Litigation friend) (Applicant's Solicitor) (Charity or Not for Profit Organisation) (Signing on behalf of firm or company)*
Address for Service:
Dated:

**** If you are acting in person you must sign this form personally and give an address for service in England or Wales. If you are being assisted by a charity or not for profit organisation, you may give their address as your address for service.**

You must file with this notice:

(a) A copy of the Tribunal's decision on your application for reconsideration;
(b) any other document which was served on you giving reasons for that decision;
(c) written evidence in support of part B, where applicable;
(d) A copy of your application for reconsideration (Form AIT/103A) as submitted to the AIT; and
(e) A cheque or postal orders for the issue fee of £400.00 or an Application for Fee Exemption or Remission in form EX160, if appropriate.

Note: Cheques or postal orders should be made out to Her Majesty's Courts Service.

*delete as appropriate

Please send your completed application, together with a copy, to The Administrative Court Office, Room C315, Royal Courts of Justice, Strand, London, WC2A 2LL.

PF 197
Application for order for transfer from the Royal Courts of Justice to a district registry or vice-versa or from one district registry to another (Rule 30.2(4))

Parties should use form PF 244/N244 and include in Part A the following:
"......for an order that:

1. this [claim] [Part 20 claim] [counterclaim] [application for (*state remedy sought*) *or as may be*] be transferred to [the Royal Courts of Justice] [the District Registry].

Parties should state their reasons for seeking a transfer in Part B.

PF 12CH
Advertisement for creditors (CPR 40PD10)

IN THE HIGH COURT OF JUSTICE
CHANCERY DIVISION

In the Estate of AB deceased **Claim No.**

By an Order of the Chancery Division of the High Court of Justice dated [ ] and made in these proceedings concerning the estate of AB deceased, the creditors of AB late of [ ] who died on [ ] are to send [forthwith]* by prepaid post to [ ] of [ ]:

(i) their full names, addresses and descriptions;
(ii) the full particulars of their claims; and
(iii) a statement of their accounts and the nature of the securities (if any) held by them.

Failure to do this will exclude them from the benefit of the Order unless the Court on application otherwise orders.

Dated

[Signature and address of solicitors of the party applying for the Order, stating on whose behalf they are acting]

* *CPR rule 40.PD 10(2) provides that the Court may fix the time within which the advertisement should require a reply.*

PF 13CH
Advertisement for claimants other than creditors Pursuant to Order (CPR 40 PD 10)

IN THE HIGH COURT OF JUSTICE
CHANCERY DIVISION

In the estate of AB deceased **Claim No.**

By an order of the Chancery Division of the High Court of Justice dated [ ] made in these proceedings concerning the estate of AB deceased, the following inquiry was [*or* inquiries were] ordered:

[Set out inquiry or inquiries]

Notice is given that all persons claiming to be entitled under the above inquiry [*or* inquiries] must send by prepaid post to [ ] of [ ], so as to reach that address on or before [ ]:

(i) their full names, addresses and descriptions; and
(ii) the full particulars of their claims.

And it is ordered that failure to do this will exclude them from the benefit of the Order unless the Court on application otherwise orders.

Dated

Signed *

* [Add name and address of solicitors of the inserting the advertisement, stating on whose behalf they are acting].

PF 14CH
[Witness statement][Affidavit] verifying list of creditors' claims (CPR 40 PD 10)

IN THE HIGH COURT OF JUSTICE
CHANCERY DIVISION

In the estate of AB deceased **Claim No.**

Before (Master)

Claimant*

Defendant*

We, CD of [ ] and EF of [ ] , the above-named claimants [*or* defendants] the executors [*or* administrators] of AB deceased, and GH of [*the person to whom claims are required by the advertisement to be sent*] severally state [on oath]:

1. In accordance with the directions given by the Master I, GH, caused an advertisement for claims to be inserted in the London Gazette on [ ] and in [*insert any further newspapers directed and the dates of the issues in which advertisements appeared*].
2. I have in the document shown to me marked A listed all the claims particulars of which have been sent to me by persons claiming to be creditors of AB deceased, following the advertisements.
3. We, CD and EF, have in the document shown to us marked B listed all the claims by persons claiming to be creditors of AB deceased which we have received, other than claims listed in Document A.
4. We have in the document shown to us marked C listed all the sums of money which were or may have been due and owing by AB at the time of his death and are or may be still due and owing, and which have come to the knowledge of one or both of us, but in respect of which no claim has been received by either or both of us or has been sent in following the advertisement.

We, CD, EF and GH state:

5. We have examined the particulars of the several claims and sums of money listed in documents A, B and C and we have compared them with the books, accounts and documents of AB [*or as may be, and state any other inquiries or investigations made*] in order to ascertain, as far as possible, to which of the claims and sums of money the estate of AB is liable.
6. From this examination [*and state any other reasons*] we are of the opinion and truly believe that the estate of AB is liable to the amounts listed in the sixth columns of the part I of documents A and B and in the fifth column of the part I of document C, and to the best of our knowledge such amounts are due from the estate of AB and may properly be allowed to the respective persons named in the documents.
7. We are of the opinion that the estate of AB is not liable to the amounts listed in the Part II of documents A, B and C and that these amounts

should not be allowed without proof by the respective claimants [*or*: we are not able to state whether the estate of AB is liable to the amounts listed in the Part II of documents A, B and C, or whether these amounts or any part of them should be allowed without further evidence.

8. Except as stated above, there are not, to the best of our knowledge, any claims of creditors against the estate of AB, or any sums of money due or owing by AB at the time of his death and still remaining due and owing.

*Where there is more than one claimant/defendant, the parties should be described as follows:

(1) AB

(2) CD

(3) EF Claimants

and

(1) GH

(2) IJ

(3) KL Defendants

PF 15CH
List of Claims by Persons Claiming to be Creditors Following Advertisement (Exhibit A Referred to in Affidavit/Witness Statement in Form 14)

A

IN THE HIGH COURT OF JUSTICE
CHANCERY DIVISION

In the estate of AB deceased

Claim No.

List of claims which have been sent to GH by persons claiming to be creditors of AB deceased following the advertisement issued for that purpose dated

This document was shown to me and marked A.

PART I – CLAIMS ALLOWABLE WITHOUT FURTHER EVIDENCE

Serial Number (*in continuation of numbers in list A*)	Names of claimants *(in alphabetical order)*	Addresses and descriptions	Particulars of claim	Amount claimed	Amount proper to be allowed
				£	£

PART II CLAIMS WHICH OUGHT TO BE PROVED BY CLAIMANTS

Serial Number (*in continuation of numbers in first part*)	Names of persons to whom sums may be due *(in alphabetical order)*	Addresses and descriptions	Particulars of claims	Amount claimed
				£

PF 16CH
List of claims by Persons Claiming to be Creditors other than those Sent in Following Advertisement (Exhibit B referred to in [Witness Statement][Affidavit] in Form 14)

B

IN THE HIGH COURT OF JUSTICE
CHANCERY DIVISION
In the estate of AB deceased **Claim No.**

List of claims by persons claiming to be creditors of AB deceased other than claims sent in following the advertisement dated .
This document was shown to me and marked B.

PART I – CLAIMS ALLOWABLE WITHOUT FURTHER EVIDENCE

Serial Number (*in continuation of numbers in list A*)	Names of claimants *(in alphabetical order)*	Addresses and descriptions	Particulars of claim	Amount claimed	Amount proper to be allowed
				£	£

PART II CLAIMS WHICH OUGHT TO BE PROVED

Serial Number (*in continuation of numbers in first part*)	Names of persons to whom sums may be due *(in alphabetical order)*	Addresses and descriptions	Particulars of claims	Amount claimed
				£

PF 17CH
List of Sums of Money which may be Due but in Respect of which no Claim has been Received(Exhibit C Referred to in [Witness Statement][Affidavit] in Form 14)

C

IN THE HIGH COURT OF JUSTICE
CHANCERY DIVISION
In the estate of AB deceased **Claim No.**

List of sums of money which may be due but in respect of which no claim has been received.
This document was shown to me and marked C.

PART I – SUMS ADMITTED TO BE DUE

Serial Number (*in continuation of numbers in list B*)	Names of creditors *(in alphabetical order)*	Addresses and descriptions	Particulars of debt	Amount of deby
				£

PART II SUMS WHICH MAY BE DUE BUT IN RESPECT OF WHICH LIABILITY OUGHT TO BE PROVED

Serial Number (*in continuation of numbers in first part*)	Names of persons to whom sums may be due *(in alphabetical order)*	Addresses and descriptions	Particulars of sums which may be due	Amount in respect of which proof is required
				£

PF 18CH
Notice to Creditor to prove claim (CPR Part 40 PD 12)

IN THE HIGH COURT OF JUSTICE
CHANCERY DIVISION

In the estate of AB deceased **Claim No.**

Before Master

Claimant*

Defendant*

You are required to prove the claim sent in by you against the estate of AB deceased; [*or, if no claim has been sent in*: If you claim to be allowed any sum against the estate of AB deceased, in respect of the mortgage dated etc *[or as may be*], and you must file such [witness statements][affidavits] as you may be advised in support of your claim, and give notice of them to me on or before [*date*] and attend in person or by your solicitor before Master , at Chancery Chambers, Room No. , Thomas More Building, Royal Courts of Justice, Strand, London WC2A 2LL at [*time*] on [*date*], when your claim will be adjudicated.

Dated

Signed GR of , solicitor for the claimant [*or* defendant]

To etc.

* Where there is more than one claimant/defendant, the parties should be described as follows:

(1) AB

(2) CD

(3) EF Claimants

and

(1) GH

(2) IJ

KL Defendants

PF 19CH
Notice to Creditor or other claimant to produce documents or particulars in support of claim (CPR Part 40 PD 12)

IN THE HIGH COURT OF JUSTICE
CHANCERY DIVISION
In the estate of AB deceased **Claim No.**

Before Master

Claimant*

Defendant*

You are required to produce in support of the claim sent in by you in the matter of the estate of AB deceased [*describe the document to be produced or particulars to be given*] before Master at Chancery Chambers, Room No. Thomas More Building, Royal Courts of Justice, Strand, London WC2A 2LL at [*time*] on [*date*]

Dated

Signed of , solicitor for the claimant [*or* defendant]

To etc.

* Where there is more than one claimant/defendant, the parties should be described as follows:

(1) AB

(2) CD

(3) EF Claimants

and

(1) GH

(2) IJ

(3) KL Defendants

PF 20CH
Notice to Creditor of Allowance of claim (CPR Part 40 PD 13)

IN THE HIGH COURT OF JUSTICE
CHANCERY DIVISION

In the estate of AB deceased

Claim No.

Before Master

Claimant*

Defendant*

The claim by you against the estate of AB deceased has been allowed as follows: [insert name, address and particulars of claim as proposed to be inserted in the Master's order certifying the account].

[If only part allowed, add: If you claim to have a larger sum allowed, you are required to prove this further claim, and you must file such affidavit as you may be advised in support of your claim, and give notice of them to me on or before [date] and attend in person or by your solicitor before Master , at Chancery Chambers, Room No. , Thomas More Building, Royal Courts of Justice, Strand, London WC2A 2LL at [time] on [date], when your claim will be adjudicated].

Dated

Signed of , solicitor for the claimant [*or* defendant]

To etc.

* Where there is more than one claimant/defendant, the parties should be described as follows:

(1) AB

(2) CD

(3) EF Claimants

and

(1) GH

(2) IJ

(3) KL Defendants

PF 21CH
Notice to Creditor of Disallowance of claim in whole or in part (CPR Part 40 PD 12)

IN THE HIGH COURT OF JUSTICE
CHANCERY DIVISION

In the estate of AB deceased **Claim No.**

Before Master

Claimant*

Defendant*

The claim by you against the estate of AB deceased has been wholly disallowed [*or* has been disallowed in part to the extent of].

Dated

Signed of , solicitor for the claimant [*or* defendant]

To etc.

* Where there is more than one claimant/defendant, the parties should be described as follows:

(1) AB

(2) CD

(3) EF Claimants

and

(1) GH

(2) IJ

(3) KL Defendants

PF 22CH
Order for Administration: Beneficiaries' Action Reconstituted as Creditors' Claim (Van Oppen Order)

IN THE HIGH COURT OF JUSTICE
CHANCERY DIVISION

In the estate of deceased Claim No.

Before Master

Claimant*

Defendant*

An Application by notice dated ( ) was made on *(date)* by the [claimant][defendant].

The Master heard [counsel] [solicitor] for [party]

[**The Master read** (*documents*)]

It appears from the above [affidavit][witness statement] that the applicant is a creditor in the estate of the above testator.

The claimants the executors of the will admit by their [counsel][solicitor] that the assets of the estate are insufficient for payment of all debts and liabilities in full.

IT IS ORDERED that all further proceedings be carried on by the applicant as claimant, against the claimants and defendants as defendants, [but the defendants CD and LM are not to attend such further proceedings until application is made for an order stating the result of the proceedings on the accounts and enquiries mentioned below or otherwise relating to payment of costs; notice of which application is to be given to them respectively by the applicant]

AND IT IS ORDERED that in lieu of the accounts and inquiries directed by the judgment dated , the following accounts and inquiries be taken and made, namely:1-6 (*include such of paragraph(2) 1 - 6 of Form PF 11CH as may be appropriate*).

AND in taking the accounts and making the inquiries hereby directed any proceedings had and taken under the judgment dated are to be adopted as far as may be applicable

AND IT IS ORDERED that the testator's property (continue as in Form PF 11CH)

AND IT IS ORDERED that the testator's real estate (continue as in Form PF 11CH)

AND IT IS ORDERED that the money (continue as in Form PF 11CH)

AND the costs of the original claimants and defendants of this action down to an including this order are reserved to be dealt with at the conclusion of the accounts and inquiries

AND the costs of this application are to be costs in the proceedings

Permission to apply for further consideration.

Note: the above is adapted from the order made in Re Van Oppen; Roberts v Gray

[1935] WN 51. It is envisaged that the defendants CD and LM are the beneficiaries who were parties to the action as originally constituted.

---

* Where there is more than one claimant/defendant, the parties should be described as follows:

(1) AB

(2) CD

(3) EF Claimants

and

(1) GH

(2) IJ

(3) KL Defendants

PF 23CH
[Witness Statement][Affidavit] verifying List of Claims other than Creditors' Claims (CPR 40 PD 11.2)

IN THE HIGH COURT OF JUSTICE
CHANCERY DIVISION
In the estate of AB deceased **Claim No.**

Before Master

Claimant*

Defendant*

We, CD of and EF of , the above-named claimants [*or* defendants], the executors [*or* administrators] of the above-named AB deceased [*or* trustees of the settlement etc] and GH, of *[the person to whom claims are required by the advertisement to be sent*] severally state [on oath]:

I, GH, for myself state:

1. I have in the document shown to me marked D set out a list of all the claims the particulars of which have been sent to me by the persons claiming under the inquiry [*or* inquiries, numbered and]directed by the judgment [*or* order] in this action dated .

We, CD and EF, for ourselves state:

2. We have in the document shown to us marked E set out a list of all the claims by persons claiming to be interested in the subject matter of the inquiry [*or* inquiries] which have come to our knowledge or to the knowledge of either of us other than claims contained in the document marked D.

We, CD, EF and GH, for ourselves state:

3. Except as mentioned above there are not to the best of our knowledge information and belief any claims under the inquiry [*or* inquiries].

* Where there is more than one claimant/defendant, the parties should be described as follows:

(1) AB
(2) CD
(3) EF Claimants
and
(1) GH
(2) IJ
(3) KL Defendants

PF 24CH
List of claims not being Creditors' Claims sent in Following Advertisement (being Exhibit D referred to in [Witness Statement] [Affidavit] No 23 (CPR Part 40 PD 11(2))

D

IN THE HIGH COURT OF JUSTICE
CHANCERY DIVISION

In the estate of AB deceased **Claim No.**

Before Master

Claimant*

Defendant*

List of claims the particulars of which have been sent in to GH by persons claiming under the inquiry [*or* inquiries and] directed by the Judgment [*or* Order] in these proceedings dated following the advertisement issued in that behalf, dated .

This document was shown to me and marked D.

* Where there is more than one claimant/defendant, the parties should be described as follows:

Serial number	Names of claimants (*in alphabetical order*)	Addresses and descriptions	Particulars of claim

(1) AB
(2) CD
(3) EF Claimants
and
(1) GH
(2) IJ
(3) KL Defendants

PF 25CH
List of Claims not being Creditors' Claims Other than those Sent in Following Advertisement (being Exhibit E referred to in [Witness Statement][Affidavit] No 23 (CPR Part 40 PD 11(2))

E

IN THE HIGH COURT OF JUSTICE
CHANCERY DIVISION
In the estate of AB deceased **Claim No.**

Before Master

Claimant*

Defendant*

List of claims by persons claiming to be interested in the subject of the inquiry [*or* inquiries and] directed by the Judgment [*or* Order] in these proceedings dated , other than claims sent in following the advertisement

Dated

This document was shown to me and marked E.

Serial number *(in continuation of numbers in List D)*	Names of claimants (*in alphabetical order*)	Addresses and descriptions	Particulars of claim

* Where there is more than one claimant/defendant, the parties should be described as follows:

(1) AB
(2) CD
(3) EF Claimants
and
(1) GH
(2) IJ
(3) KL Defendants

PF 26CH
Notice to Claimant other than Creditor to Prove a Claim

IN THE HIGH COURT OF JUSTICE
CHANCERY DIVISION
Claim No.

Before Master

Claimant*

Defendant*

You are hereby required to prove the claim sent in by you in answer to the inquiry directed by the order in this action dated . You are to *file [continue as in Form PF 18CH above to "adjudicating the claim"*].

Note that in default of giving such notice and attending as stated above you will be treated as having made no claim.

Dated [*etc as in Form PF 18CH*].

* Where there is more than one claimant/defendant, the parties should be described as follows:

(1) AB

(2) CD

(3) EF Claimants

and

(1) GH

(2) IJ

(3) KL Defendants

PF 27CH
[Witness Statement][Affidavit] Verifying Accounts and Answering Usual Inquiries in Administration Action

IN THE HIGH COURT OF JUSTICE
CHANCERY DIVISION

In the estate of GH deceased **Claim No.**

Before Master

Claimant*

Defendant*

We, AB of , CD of and EF of , the above defendants, state [on oath]:

1. We have according to the best of our knowledge, set out in Schedule 1 below a full account and inventory of the estate of or which the above testator GH, who died on possessed or was entitled to at the time of his death *[and not specifically devised or bequeathed by him*].
2. Apart from what is set out in the Schedule I [*and what is specifically devised or bequeathed by the above testator*] the testator was not, to the best of our knowledge, at the time of his death in possession of or entitled to any debt or sum of money due to him from us or any of us on any account whatsoever, nor to any property whatsoever.
3. The testator's funeral expenses have been paid. They consist of the items of disbursement numbered and in the account referred to below. *[Or if not paid, state accordingly, with the amount due and to whom due*].
4. We have in the account shown to us marked A, according to the best of our knowledge, set out a full account of the testator's property [*not specifically devised or bequeathed by him*] which has come into our hands or the hands of any of us, or the hands of a person by order of all or any of us, or for the use of all or any of us. The account shows the times when, the names of the persons from whom, and on what account the property has been received. There is also a similar account of the disbursements, allowances, and payments made by all or any of us on account of the testator's funeral expenses, debts and testamentary expenses, with the times when, names of persons to whom, and purposes for which they were disbursed, allowed or paid. [*if so ordered, add*: and in setting out the account we have distinguished in separate columns between capital and income].
5. We, each speaking positively for ourself and to the best of our knowledge for others persons, state that, except as appears in the account marked A, neither we (individually or severally) nor any persons by our order or for our use have possessed, received or got in any part of the testator's estate, or any money in respect of it, and that the account marked A does not contain any item of disbursement, allowance or payment other than those actually disbursed, allowed or paid on the account.
6. To the best of our knowledge, the estate of the testator now outstanding or undisposed of consists of the particulars set out in Schedule II.

7. Apart from what is set out in Schedule II, there is not to our knowledge any part of the testator's estate now outstanding or undisposed of.

8. We have, according to the best of our knowledge, set out in Schedule III the particulars of all the incumbrances affecting the testator's property and what part of it the incumbrances respectively affect.

"The account marked A". [If there are a large number of items of a particular class, e.g. rents, dividends or instalments of debts, they may for convenience be shown in separate sub-accounts, a total of which should be brought into the main account].

"*A full account of the testator's property*". [This account must include all rents, profits and other income received since the testator's death].

"A similar account of the disbursements" etc. [This account must include all outgoings in respect of the testator's estate since his death].

Schedule II. [This Schedule must include any arrears of rent, interest etc which may, if convenient, be given as total figures by reference to separate columns of arrears included in any of the sub-accounts mentioned in the note above relating to "The account marked A"].

Schedule I

1. £500 cash in house.
2. £1,000 cash in testator's bank (*specify*)
3. £10,000 Consolidated 3% annuities in the testator's name.
4. £3,000 debt due from Samuel Jones on a bond, with interest from , at %.
5. A leasehold house at held under a lease for a term of , which will expireon at a rent of £3,000 a year.
6. £1,500, half a year's rent due from Mary Evans to .
7. A freehold farm comprising acres, at , let to John James on annual tenancy at a rent of £5,000 a year.
8. £1,250, a quarter's rent due from the above John James.

Schedule II

[Set out the particulars in the same form as above].

Schedule III

[Give short particulars of the incumbrances and show what part of the estate is subject to each]

PF 28CH
Executors' (or Administrators') Account, being Account A referred to in Form PF 27CH

A

IN THE HIGH COURT OF JUSTICE
CHANCERY DIVISION
Claim No.

Before Master

Claimant*

Defendant*

This account marked A was produced and shown to AB, CD and EF, and is the account referred to in their [affidavit sworn on][witness statement dated]

[Before me (signature of Commissioner or officer before whom the affidavit is sworn)].

RECEIPTS

No. Of item	Date received	Names of persons from whom received	On what account received	Amount received £
1			Found in house	
2			Balance at Bank	
3		Evans & co.	Half years's dividend on	
4		John James	Debt of £3,000 and interest from to	
5		Samuel Jones	Debt of £3,000 and interest from to	
6		Mary Evans	Half year's rent of house No. due	
7		A Patel	Proceeds of sale of above house	

* Where there is more than one claimant/defendant, the parties should be described as follows:

(1) AB
(2) CD
(3) EF Claimants
and
(1) GH
(2) IJ
(3) KL Defendants

DISBURSEMENTS

No. of item	Date when paid or allowed	Names of persons to whom paid or allowed	For what purpose paid or allowed	Amount received £
1		James Price	Undertaker's bill for funeral	
2		A & B	Expenses of obtaining probate	
3		Jane George	for medical attendance	
4		James Price	Debt of £1,000 and interest from to	

PF 29CH
Master's Order stating the result of Proceedings before him on the Usual Accounts and Inquiries in an Administration Action

IN THE HIGH COURT OF JUSTICE
CHANCERY DIVISION
Claim No.

In the estate of

Before Master

Claimant*

Defendant*

On the accounts and inquiries directed by the judgment [*or* order] dated it is declared:

1. The defendants , the executors of the testator, have received property not specifically devised or bequeathed to the amount of £ and they have paid, or are entitled to be allowed on account, sums in the amount of £ , leaving a balance due from [*or* to] them of £ on that account.
2. The unpaid debts of the testator which have been allowed are set out in the attached Schedule and with the interest on them and costs mentioned in the Schedule are due to the persons named in the Schedule and amount altogether to £ .

The funeral expenses of the testator amounted to £ , which are allowed to the executors in the account.

3. The legacies given by the testator are set out in the attached Schedule and with the interest on them remain due to the persons named in the Schedule and amount altogether to £ .
4. The outstanding property of the testator consists of the particulars set out in the attached Schedule.
5. The incumbrances affecting the testator's property are specified in the attached Schedule.

[6. The parts of the testator's property directed to be sold have been sold and the purchase moneys, amounting altogether to £ , have been paid into Court].

[Note: *The above numbers are to correspond with the numbers in the order so far as appropriate*].

[*The order would then proceed to direct the distribution of the estate, having regard to the above findings, unless this was adjourned to be dealt with on further consideration*

PF 30CH
Security of Receiver or of Administrator Pending Determination of a Probate Claim

IN THE HIGH COURT OF JUSTICE
CHANCERY DIVISION

[Title]

I, of the receiver (and manager)(*or* administrator pending determination of the claim) appointed by order dated (*or* proposed to be appointed) hereby undertake to the Court duly to account for all money and property received by me as such receiver (and manager) (*or* administrator pending determination of the claim) at such times and in such manner in all respects as the Court directs.

And we hereby jointly and severally (in the case of a guarantee or other company delete "jointly and severally") undertake with the Court and guarantee to be answerable for any default by AB as such receiver (and manager) (or administrator pending determination of the claim) and upon such default to pay to any person(s) or otherwise as the Court directs any sum or sums not exceeding £ in total that may from time to time be certified by a Master of the Supreme Court (or a District Judge) to be due from AB as receiver (and manager) (or administrator pending determination of the claim) and we submit to the jurisdiction of the Court in this action to determine any claim made under this undertaking.

PF 31CH
Consent to Act as Trustee (CPR Part 33 r 8)

I, AB, (*name*) of (*address*) hereby consent to act as trustee of the [*describe the instrument]*

Dated

(*Signed*) AB

I, CD, (*name*) of (*address*) certify that the above signature is the signature of AB, the person mentioned in the above consent.

(*Signed*) CD

PF 32CH
[Witness Statement][Affidavit] in support of Application for Appointment by the Court of new Litigation Friend* of Child Claimant

[Title]

I of , the [solicitor] for the claimant CD , a child, state [on oath]:

1. (*Reasons why the appointment of a new litigation friend is sought*)
2. AB (*Name, address and description of proposed new litigation friend*) is *a (state relationship if any of AB to CD*) and has no interest in the matter in question in these proceedings adverse to that of CD. AB's consent to be appointed as litigation friend is annexed.
3. AB is a fit and proper person to act as the litigation friend of CD.

[Sworn etc][Signed]

*CPR Rule 21.7

PF 33CH
Order for Distribution of a Lloyd's Estate

IN THE HIGH COURT OF JUSTICE
CHANCERY DIVISION
Claim No.

In the Estate of **deceased (a Lloyd's Estate)**

And in the Matter of The Practice Direction dated 21st November 1997

Before Master

An Application by a Part 8 claim was made on *(date)* by .

The Master heard [counsel] [solicitor] for [*party*]

[**The Master** read the evidence filed]

IT IS ORDERED that:

(1) The Claimants as personal representatives of the estate ("the Estate") of the above named deceased "the Deceased" [and] [the trustees of the trusts of the Deceased's will dated [ ] ("the Will") have permission to distribute the Estate [and] [administer the trusts of the will and distribute capital and income in accordance with such trusts] without making any retention or further provision in respect of any contract of insurance or reinsurance underwritten by the Deceased in the course of his business as an underwriting member of Lloyd's of London.

(2) The costs of the Claimants of this Application [*either* in the agreed sum of [£]] [*or* summarily assessed in the sum of £[ ] (with permission to [the residuary beneficiaries] [*name beneficiaries*] to apply within 14 days after service of this order on them for the variation or discharge of this summary assessment) [*or* subject to a detailed assessment on the indemnity basis if not agreed by or on behalf of [the residuary beneficiaries] [*name beneficiaries*] be raised and paid or retained out of the Estate in due course of administration.

PF 34CH
Order in Inquiry as to Title in Proceedings to enforce Charging Order where the Defendant's Title is not disclosed

IN THE HIGH COURT OF JUSTICE
CHANCERY DIVISION
Claim No.

Before Master (*Sitting in Private*)

Claimant*

Defendant*

An Application by notice dated ( ) was made on *(date)* by the [claimant][defendant].

The Master heard [counsel] [solicitor] for [party]

[**The Master** read (*documents*)]

IT IS ORDERED

That the defendant (*name*) within days after service of this Order file [an affidavit][a witness statement] stating what (if any) deeds and other documents relating to the title of the property known as are in his possession or power and whether any deeds or other documents relating to the title to the property are known by the defendant to be in the possession or power of any other person(s) and, if so, stating the name and address of every such person

And it is ordered that the defendant within the same time lodge in Room TM 5.04, Thomas More Building, Royal Courts of Justice, Strand, London WC2A 2LL all (if any) such deeds and documents are stated by him to be in his own possession or power.

* Where there is more than one claimant/defendant, the parties should be described as follows:

(1) AB

(2) CD

(3) EF Claimants

and

(1) GH

(2) IJ

(3) KL Defendants

PF 36CH
Order appointing administrator pending determination of probate claim

IN THE HIGH COURT OF JUSTICE
CHANCERY DIVISION
Claim No.

In the estate of AB deceased

Before Master

Claimant

Defendant

An Application by notice dated ( ) was made on (*date*) by [counsel][solicitor] for [*party*] and was attended by ( ).

The Master heard [counsel][solicitor] for [*party*]

[**The Master** read the evidence filed]

The court appoints CD of administrator of the estate of the deceased pending the determination of this claim

CD has given security of £ to the satisfaction of the court

IT IS ORDERED that a grant of administration pending determination of this claim under section 117 of the Supreme Court Act 1981 be made to (*AB*)

AND IT IS ORDERED that (*AB*) pass his accounts as the court from time to time directs

* Where there is more than one claimant/defendant, the parties should be described as follows:

(1) AB

(2) CD

(3) EF Claimants

and

(1) GH

(2) IJ

(3) KL Defendants

PF 38CH
Order in Probate claim involving compromise

IN THE HIGH COURT OF JUSTICE
CHANCERY DIVISION

In the estate of AB (*deceased*) **Claim No.**

Before Master

Claimant*

Defendant*

An Application by notice dated was made on [*date*] by [*counsel*][*solicitor*] for [*party*] and was attended by .

The Master heard [*counsel*][*solicitor*] for [*party*]

[**The Master** read the evidence filed]

Probate of the alleged last will and testament of (*deceased*) dated was granted on [*date*] to .

The court is satisfied that :

(1) consents by or on behalf of every relevant beneficiary (as defined by s.49 of the Administration of Justice Act 1985) have been given to the making of this order; and

(2) the order is for the benefit of those relevant beneficiaries who are children

The Court pronounces for/against the force and validity of the last will and testament of the deceased a completed copy of which is the script dated and marked exhibit [ ] referred to in the [witness statement][affidavit] of scripts of [*name*] sworn on [*date*] and against the force and validity of the last will and testament of the deceased a completed copy of which is the script dated and marked exhibit [ ] referred to in the [witness statement][affidavit] of scripts of [*name*] sworn on [*date*]

IT IS ORDERED that

(1) this claim [and counterclaim] be discontinued

( ) the probate letters of administration be revoked

( ) the terms set out in the Schedule be carried into effect

( ) [probate of the will][and codicil][letters of administration of the estate] of AB deceased late of [*address*] be granted to [the claimant][the defendant] [ ] named as executor if entitled thereto

( ) on application for such a grant the caveat numbered [ ] and entered on [*date*] do if still subsisting cease to have effect

( ) there be assessed if not agreed

(a) the costs of this claim [and counterclaim] of the claimant/defendant [ ]the executor named in the will

(b) the costs of this claim [and counterclaim] of the claimant/defendant [ ] and [ ]

(c) the costs of the claimant/defendant under the Legal Aid Act 1988

( ) the costs specified in (a) and (b) above be paid out of the estate of the deceased in the due course of administration

SCHEDULE

[Set out the agreed terms]

* Where there is more than one claimant/defendant, the parties should be described as follows:

(1) AB

(2) CD

(3) EF Claimants

and

(1) GH

(2) IJ

(3) KL Defendants

Claim Form

In the High Court of Justice Queen's Bench Division Commercial Court Royal Courts of Justice	

	for court use only
Claim No.	
Issue date	

Claimant(s)

SEAL

Defendant(s)

Name and address of Defendant receiving this claim form

Amount claimed	
Court fee	
Solicitor's costs	
Total amount	

The court office at the Admiralty and Commercial Registry, Royal Courts of Justice, Strand, London WC2A 2LL is open between 10 am and 4.30 pm Monday to Friday. When corresponding with the court, please address forms or letters to the Court Manager and quote the claim number.

N1(CC) Claim form (CPR Part 7) (03.02)

Claim No.	

Brief details of claim

Particulars of claim (*attached)(*will follow if an acknowledgment of service is filed that indicates an intention to defend the claim)

Statement of Truth
*(I believe)(The Claimant believes) that the facts stated in this claim form *(and the particulars of the claim attached to this claim form) are true.
* I am duly authorised by the claimant to sign this statement

Full name ______________________________

Name of *(claimant)('s solicitor's firm) ______________________________

signed ______________________ position or office held ______________________
*(Claimant)('s solicitor) (if signing on behalf of firm, company or corporation)

delete as appropriate

Claimant's or solicitor's address to which documents or payments should be sent if different from overleaf including (if appropriate) details of DX, fax or e-mail.

Notes for defendant on replying to the Part 7 claim form
(Commercial Court)

Please read these notes carefully - they will help you decide what to do about this claim. Further information may be obtained from the **Admiralty and Commercial Court Guide**

Your response and what happens next

- In every case you should file the Acknowledgment of Service form N9(CC).
- Complete the acknowledgment of service within the time stated on it and send it to The Admiralty and Commercial Registry, Royal Courts of Justice, Strand, London WC2A 2LL.
- If you do not file an acknowledgment of service, judgment may be entered against you. Additional costs and interest may be added to the amount claimed on the front of the claim form if judgment is entered against you.

Address where notices can be sent

- In the acknowledgment of service you must give an address to which notices and document relating to this claim must be sent. This must be an address in the United Kingdom.
- The address must be either your solicitor's address, you own residential or business address, or (if you live elsewhere) some other address. Any address given must be in the United Kingdom.
- If you fail to provide an address for service within the United Kingdom, your acknowledgment of service may be struck out and judgment may be entered against you.

Admitting the claim

If you admit the claim, send a written admission to the court with the acknowledgment of service.

Disputing the jurisdiction

If you wish to dispute the court's jurisdiction to try the claim you must:

- complete the acknowledgment of service form and send it to the court within *(14 days) (   ); and
- make any application to contest the court's jurisdiction as soon as possible and in any event within 28 days after filing your acknowledgment of service

Disputing the claim

If you wish to dispute the claim you must:

- file an acknowledgment of service within *(14 days) (   ); and
- serve a defence within the period stated in the acknowledgment of service

**Claimant should alter as appropriate if the claim form is to be served out of the jurisdiction together with the particulars of claim - see CPR rule 6.30*

N1C(CC) Notes for defendant (10.08)

Acknowledgment of Service

Defendant's full name if different from the name given on the claim form

In the High Court of Justice Queen's Bench Division Commercial Court Royal Courts of Justice	
Claim No.	
Claimant(s) (including ref.)	
Defendant(s)	
Defendant returning this form	

Address in the United Kingdom to which documents about this claim should be sent (including reference if appropriate)

	if applicable	
	Tel. no.	
	Fax no.	
	DX no.	
Postcode	e-mail	

Tick the appropriate box

1. (I admit)(The Defendant admits) this claim ☐
2. (I intend)(The Defendant intends) to defend all of this claim ☐
3. (I intend)(The Defendant intends) to defend part of this claim ☐
4. (I intend)(The Defendant intends) to contest jurisdiction ☐
5. My date of birth is ☐☐/☐☐/☐☐☐☐

If you file an acknowledgment of service but do not file a defence within *(28 days) (days) of the date of service of the particulars of claim, and you have not indicated that you intend to contest jurisdiction, judgment may be entered against you.

If you do not file an application to contest the jurisdiction within 28 days of filing the acknowledgment of service, it will be assumed that you accept the court's jurisdiction.

**Claimant should alter as appropriate if the claim form is to be served out of the jurisdiction together with particulars of claim; see CPR rule 6.35 and 6.37(5).*

Signed

(Defendant)(Defendant's solicitor)

Date

Position or office held
(if signing on behalf of firm, company or corporation)

N9(CC) Acknowledgment of service (10.08)

Claim Form
(CPR Part 8)

In the High Court of Justice	
Queen's Bench Division	
Commercial Court	
Royal Courts of Justice	
	for court use only
Claim No.	
Issue date	

Claimant(s)

SEAL

Defendant(s)

Name and Address of Defendant receiving this claim form

Court fee	
Solicitor's costs	

The court office at the Admiralty and Commercial Registry, Royal Courts of Justice, Strand, London WC2A 2LL is open between 10 am and 4.30 pm Monday to Friday. When corresponding with the court, please address forms or letters to the Court Manager and quote the case number.

N208(CC) Claim form (CPR Part 8) (03.02)

Claim No.	

Details of claim

Statement of Truth
*(I believe)(The Claimant believes) that the facts stated in this claim form are true.
* I am duly authorised by the claimant to sign this statement

Full name ______________________________

Name of *(claimant)('s solicitor's firm) ______________________________

signed ______________________ position or office held ______________________
*(Claimant)('s solicitor) (if signing on behalf of firm, company or corporation)

delete as appropriate

Claimant's or solicitor's address to which documents or payments should be sent if different from overleaf. If you are prepared to accept service by DX, fax or e-mail, please add details.

Notes for defendant on replying to the Part 8 claim form

Please read these notes carefully - they will help you decide what to do about this claim. Further information may be obtained from the Commercial Court Guide

- You have *(14 days) (   ) from the date on which you were served with the claim form *(see below)* in which to respond to the claim by completing and returning the acknowledgment of service enclosed with this claim form.
- If you **do not return** the acknowledgment of service, you will be allowed to attend any hearing of the claim but you will **not** be allowed to take part in the hearing unless the court gives you permission to do so.

Responding to this claim

Time for responding

The completed acknowledgment of service must be returned to the court office within *(14 days) (   ) of the date on which the claim form was served on you. If the claim form was

- sent by post, the *(14 days) (   ) begins 2 business days from the date of the postmark on the envelope.
- delivered or left at your address, the *(14 days) (   ) begins the second business day after it was delivered.
- handed to you personally, the *(14 days) (   ) begins on the second business day it was given to you.

Completing the acknowledgment of service

You should complete section A, B, **or** C as appropriate **and all** of section D.

Section A - contesting the claim
If you wish to contest the remedy sought by the claimant in the claim form, you should complete section A. If you seek a remedy different from that sought by the claimant, you should give full details in the space provided.

Section B - disputing the court's jurisdiction
You should indicate your intention by completing section B and filing an application disputing the court's jurisdiction within 14 days of filing your acknowledgment of service at the court. The court will arrange a hearing date for the application and tell you and the claimant when and where to attend.

Section C - objecting to the use of procedure
If you believe that the claimant should not have issued the claim under Part 8 because:

- there **is** a substantial dispute of fact involved; and
- you do not agree that the rule or practice direction stated does provide for the claimant to use this procedure

you should complete section C setting out your reasons in the space provided.

Written evidence

- If you wish to serve and file evidence in answer to the claimant's written evidence, you must send it to the court and to any other party within 28 days after filing an acknowledgment of service.
- Where you intend to dispute jurisdiction, only evidence in support of your application under CPR Part 11 need be filed. Your application and evidence must be filed within 28 days after filing an acknowledgment of service.

Serving other parties

At the same time as you file your completed acknowledgment of service (and any written evidence) with the court, you must also send copies of both the form and any written evidence to any other party named on the claim form.

What happens next

The claimant may, within 14 days of receiving any written evidence from you, file further evidence in reply. The case management procedure set out in the Commercial Court Guide will apply.

Note: The court may already have given directions or arranged a hearing. If so, you will have received a copy with the claim form. You should comply with any directions and attend any hearing in addition to completing, filing and serving your acknowledgment of service.

Statement of truth

This must be signed by you or by your solicitor as appropriate.

Where the defendant is a registered company or a corporation the statement of truth must be signed by either the director, treasurer, secretary, chief executive, manager or other officer of the company or the company's solicitor or (in the case of a corporation which is not a registered company) any of the persons in the positions previously described or the mayor, chairman, president or town clerk or other similar officer of the corporation or the corporation's solicitor.

**claimant should alter where appropriate if the claim form is to be served out of the jurisdiction: see CPR Part 6.*

N208C(CC) Notes for defendant (CPR Part 8) (10.08)

Click here to reset form | Click here to print form

Acknowledgment of Service
(Part 8 claim)

You should read the 'notes for defendant' attached to the claim form which will tell you when and where to send this form.

If you wish to contest the claim	If you wish to dispute the court's jurisdiction	If you believe the claimant should not have used this procedure
complete section **A**	complete section **B**	complete section **C**

In the	**High Court of Justice Queen's Bench Division Commercial Court Royal Courts of Justice**
Claim No.	
Claimant(s) (including ref.)	
Defendant(s)	
Defendant returning this form	

**delete as appropriate*

A

☐ *(I intend)(The defendant intends) to contest this claim

And (if applicable) *(I)(the defendant) also seek(s) the following different remedy to that claimed by the claimant:

B

☐ *(I intend)(The defendant intends) to dispute jurisdiction
(you should file your application within 28 days of the date on which you file this acknowledgment of service with the court)

The court office at the Admiralty and Commercial Registry, Royal Courts of Justice, Strand, London WC2A 2LL is open between 10 am and 4.30 pm Monday to Friday. When corresponding with the court, please address forms or letters to the Court Manager and quote the claim number.

N210(CC) Acknowledgment of Service (CPR Part 8) (04.06) HMCS

Claim No.	

C

☐ *(I object)(The defendant objects) to the claimant issuing under this procedure

***And** *(my)(the defendant's) reasons for objecting are:

D

Signed (To be signed by you or by your solicitor)	*(I believe)(The defendant believes) that the facts stated in this form are true. *I am duly authorised by the defendant to sign this statement **delete as appropriate*	**Position or office held** (if signing on behalf of firm, company or corporation)	
Full name Name of *(defendant) ('s solicitor's firm)			
Defendant's date of birth	D D M M Y Y Y Y	**Date**	

Give an address to which notices about this case can be sent.

Postcode

if applicable	
fax no.	
DX no.	
e-mail	
Tel. no.	

Claim Form (Additional claims - CPR Part 20)

In the High Court of Justice
Queen's Bench Division
Commercial Court
Royal Courts of Justice

	for court use only
Claim No.	
Issue date	

Claimant(s)

SEAL

Defendant(s)

Part 20 Claimant(s)

Part 20 Defendant(s)

Name and address of Part 20 Defendant receiving this claim form

Amount claimed	
Court fee	
Solicitor's costs	
Total amount	

The court office at the Admiralty and Commercial Registry, Royal Courts of Justice, Strand, London WC2A 2LL is open between 10 am and 4.30 pm Monday to Friday. When corresponding with the court, please address forms or letters to the Court Manager and quote the claim number.

N211(CC) Claim Form (CPR Part 20) (03.02)

Brief details of claim

Claim No.	

Note: Particulars of Claim must be attached

Statement of Truth
*(I believe)(The Part 20 Claimant believes) that the facts stated in this claim form and the particulars of claim attached to this claim form are true.
* I am duly authorised by the Part 20 claimant to sign this statement

Full name ______________________________

Name of *(Part 20 claimant)('s solicitor's firm) ______________________________

signed ______________________________ position or office held ______________________________

*(Part 20 Claimant)('s solicitor) (if signing on behalf of firm, company or corporation)

delete as appropriate

Part 20 Claimant's or solicitor's address to which documents or payments should be sent if different from overleaf. If you are prepared to accept service by DX, fax or e-mail, please add details.

Notes for Part 20 defendant on replying to the Part 20 claim form
(Commercial Court)

Please read these notes carefully - they will help you decide what to do about this claim
Further information may be obtained from the **Admiralty and Commercial Court Guide**

You must reply to this claim form within *(14 days)( ) of the date it was served on you. If the claim was

- sent by post, the date of service is taken as the second day after posting (see post mark);
- delivered or left at your address, the date of service will be the day after it was delivered;
- handed to you personally, the *(14 days)( ) begins on the day it was given to you.

If you do not reply, the claimant may ask the court to enter judgment against you.

You may either

- admit all or part of the claim; or
- dispute the claim.

Address where notices can be sent

- In the acknowledgment of service you must give an address to which notices and document relating to this claim must be sent. This must be an address in the United Kingdom.
- The address must be either your solicitor's address, you own residential or business address, or (if you live elsewhere) some other address. Any address given must be in the United Kingdom.
- If you fail to provide an address for service within the United Kingdom, your acknowledgment of service may be struck out and judgment may be entered against you.

Admitting all or part of the claim

If you admit the claim, send a written admission to the court with the acknowledgment of service.

Disputing the jurisdiction

If you wish to dispute the court's jurisdiction to try the claim you must:

- complete the acknowledgment of service form and send it to the court within *(14 days) ( ); and
- make any application to contest the court's jurisdiction as soon as possible and in any event within 28 days after filing your acknowledgment of service.

Disputing the claim

If you wish to dispute the claim you must:

- file an acknowledgment of service within *(14 days) ( ); and
- serve a defence within the period stated in the acknowledgment of service.

**Claimant should alter as appropriate if the claim form is to be served out of the jurisdiction together with the particulars of claim - see CPR rule 6.30*

N211C(CC) Notes for defendant (10.08)

Acknowledgment of service (Part 20 claim)

In the	High Court of Justice Queen's Bench Division Commercial Court Royal Courts of Justice
Claim No.	
Claimant(s) (including ref.)	
Defendant(s)	
Defendant returning this form	

Defendant's full name if different from the name given on the claim form

Address in the United Kingdom to which documents about this claim should be sent (including reference if appropriate)

Postcode

	if applicable
Fax no.	
DX no.	
e-mail	
Tel. no.	

If you file an acknowledgment of service but do not file a defence within *(28 days) ( ) of the date of service of the particulars of claim (which will be contained in or served with Part 20 claim form) and you have not indicated that you intend to contest jurisdiction, judgment may be entered against you.

If you do not file an application under CPR Part 11 within 28 days of the date of filing your acknowledgment of service it will be assumed that you accept the court's jurisdiction and judgment may be entered against you.

**Part 20 claimant should alter where appropriate (if the claim form is to be served out of the jurisdiction): see CPR rules 6.35 and 6.37(5).*

Tick the appropriate box

1. (I admit) (The Part 20 defendant admits)
- ☐ this claim
- ☐ part of the claim (details attached)

2. (I intend) (The Part 20 defendant intends)
- ☐ to defend all of the claim
- ☐ to defend part of this claim
- ☐ to contest jurisdiction

3. My date of birth is D D M M Y Y Y Y

Signed (Part 20 defendant) (Part 20 defendant's Solicitor)

Position or office held (if signing on behalf of firm, company or corporation)

Date / /

The court office at the Admiralty and Commercial Registry, Royal Courts of Justice, Strand, London WC2A 2LL is open between 10am and 4.30pm Monday to Friday. When corresponding with the court, please address forms or letters to the Court Manager and quote the claim number.

N213(CC) Acknowledgment of Service (CPR Part 20) (10.08)

Application Notice

- You must complete Parts A **and** B, **and** Part C if applicable
- Send any relevant fee and the completed application notice to the court with any draft order, witness statement or other evidence
- It is for you (and not the court) to serve this application notice

In the	**High Court of Justice** **Queen's Bench Division** **Commercial Court** **Royal Courts of Justice**
Claim No.	
Warrant no. (if applicable)	
Claimant(s) (including ref.)	
Defendant(s) (including ref.)	
Date	

You should provide this information for listing the application

Time estimate (hours) (mins)

Is this agreed by all parties? Yes ☐ No ☐

Please always refer to the Commercial Court Guide for details of how applications should be prepared and will be heard, or in a small number of exceptional cases can be dealt with on paper.

Part A

1. Where there is more than one claimant or defendant, specify which claimant or defendant

(The claimant)(The defendant)(1)

2. State clearly what order you are seeking (if there is room) or otherwise refer to a draft order (which must be attached)

intend(s) to apply for an order (a draft of which is attached) that(2)

3. Briefly set out why you are seeking the order. Identify any rule or statutory provision

because(3)

The court office at the Admiralty & Commercial Registry, Royal Courts of Justice, Strand, London WC2A 211

is open from 10am to 4.30 pm Monday to Friday. When corresponding with the court please address forms or letters to the Clerk to the Commercial Court and quote the claim number.

N244 (CC) - w3 Application Notice (4.99) *Printed on behalf of The Court Service*

Part B

(The claimant)(The defendant)[1] wishes to rely on: *tick one:*

the attached (witness statement)(affidavit) ☐ (the claimant)(the defendant)'s[1] statement of case ☐

evidence in Part C overleaf in support of this application ☐

Signed		**Position or office held** (if signing on behalf of firm, company or corporation)	
	(Applicant)('s litigation friend) ('s solicitor)		

4. If you are not already a party to the proceedings, you must provide an address for service of documents

Address to which documents about this claim should be sent (including reference if appropriate)[4]

		if applicable	
		Tel. no.	
		fax no.	
		DX no.	
Postcode		e-mail	

Part C

Claim No.

(Note: Part C should only be used where it is convenient to enter here the evidence in support of the application, rather than to use witness statements or affidavits)

(The claimant)(The defendant)[1] wishes to rely on the following evidence in support of this application:

Statement of Truth

*(I believe)(The applicant believes) that the facts stated in this application notice are true

*I am duly authorised by the applicant to sign this statement

Full name...

Name of*(Applicant)('s litigation friend)('s solicitor)

....

Signed

*(Applicant)('s litigation friend)('s solicitor)

Position or office held
(if signing on behalf of firm, company or corporation)

**delete as appropriate*

Date

List of documents: standard disclosure

Notes:

- The rules relating to standard disclosure are contained in Part 31 of the Civil Procedure Rules and Section E of the Commercial Court Guide.
- Documents to be included under standard disclosure are contained in Rule 31.6
- A document has or will have been in your control if you have or have had possession, or a right of possession, of it **or** a right to inspect or take copies of it.

In the High Court of Justice **Queen's Bench Division** **Commercial Court** **Royal Courts of Justice**	
Claim No.	
Claimant(s) (including ref)	
Defendant(s) (including ref)	
Date	
Party returning this form	

Disclosure Statement of (Claimant)(Defendant)

1. (I/We), (name(s)) state that (I/we) have carried out a reasonable search to locate all the documents which (I am *or* ______ *here name the party* is) required to disclose under (the order made by the court *or* the agreement in writing made between the parties on) *(insert date)* ______

2. The extent of the search that (I/we) made to locate documents that (I am *or* ______ *here name the party* is) required to disclose was as follows:

N265(CC) - Standard disclosure (10.05) HMCS

3. (I/We) limited the search in the following respects:-

☐ I did not search for documents:-

- ☐ pre-dating
- ☐ located elsewhere than
- ☐ in categories other than
- ☐ for electronic documents

☐ I carried out a search for electronic documents contained on or created by the following:
(list what was searched and extent of search)

☐ I did not search for the following:-

- ☐ documents created before

documents contained on or created by the ☐ Claimant ☐ Defendant

- ☐ PCs
- ☐ portable data storage media
- ☐ databases
- ☐ servers
- ☐ back-up tapes
- ☐ off-site storage
- ☐ mobile phones
- ☐ laptops
- ☐ notebooks
- ☐ handheld devices
- ☐ PDA devices

documents contained on or created by the ☐ Claimant ☐ Defendant

- ☐ mail files
- ☐ document files
- ☐ calendar files
- ☐ web-based applications
- ☐ spreadsheet files
- ☐ graphic and presentation files

documents other than by reference to the following keyword(s)/concepts
(delete if your search was not confined to specific keywords or concepts)

4. The facts considered in arriving at the decision that it was reasonable to limit the search in the respects identified above were as follows
(the facts must be set out in detail: see paragraph E3.6 of the Commercial Court Guide):

5. (I/We) certify that (I/we) understand the duty of disclosure and to the best of (my/our) knowledge (I have *or* ____ *here name the party* has) carried out that duty. (I/We) further certify that the list above is a complete list of all documents which are or have been in (my *or* ____ *here name the party's*) control which (I am *or here name the party* is) obliged under (the said order *or* the said agreement in writing) to disclose.

6. (I *or* ____ *here name the party*) understand(s) that (I *or* ____ *here name the party*) must inform the court and the other parties immediately if any further documents required to be disclosed by Rule 31.6 comes into (my *or* ____ *here name the party's*) control at any time before the conclusion of the case.

7. ((I *or* ____ *here name the party*) (have/has) not permitted inspection of documents within the category or class of documents (as set out below) required to be disclosed under Rule 31(6)(b) or (c) on the grounds that to do so would be disproportionate to the issues in the case.

Signed ____ **Date** ____

Name(s) ____

Position or office held ____

Please state why you are the appropriate person(s) to make the disclosure statement.

List and number here, in a convenient order, the documents (or bundles of documents if of the same nature, e.g. invoices) in your/the claimant's/the defendant's control, which you/the claimant/ the defendant do/does not object to being inspected. Give a short description of each document or bundle so that it can be identified, and say if it is kept elsewhere i.e. with a bank or solicitor

A. (I)(The claimant)(The defendant) (have/has) control of the documents numbered and listed here. (I)(the claimant)(the defendant) (do not)(does not) object to you inspecting them/producing copies.

List and number here, as above, the documents in the claimant's/the defendant's control which the claimant/the defendant objects to being inspected. (Rule 31.19)

B. (I)(The claimant)(The defendant) (have)(has) control of the documents numbered and listed here, but (I)(the claimant)(the defendant) (object)(objects) to you inspecting them:

Say what the claimant's/the defendant's objections are

(I)(The claimant)(The defendant) (object)(objects) to you inspecting these documents because:

List and number here, the documents the claimant/the defendant once had in his/her/its control, but which the claimant/the defendant no longer has. For each document listed, say when it was last in the claimant's/the defendant's control and where it is now.

C. (I)(The claimant)(The defendant) (have)(had) the documents numbered and listed below, but they are no longer in (my)(the claimant's)(the defendant's) control.

Case management information sheet

To be completed by, or on behalf of,

who is [1st][2nd][3rd][ ][Claimant][Defendant]
[Part 20 claimant] in this claim

In the County Court High Court of Justice Queen's Bench Division Technology and Construction Court	
Claim No.	
Last date for filing with court office	
Assigned judge	

Please read the notes on page five before completing this form.

You should note the date by which it must be returned and the name of the court it should be returned to since this may be different from the court where the proceedings were issued.

If you have settled this claim (or if you settle it on a future date) and do not need to have it heard or tried, you must let the court know immediately.

A Settlement

Do you wish there to be a one month stay to attempt to settle the claim, either by informal discussion or by alternative dispute resolution? ☐ Yes ☐ No

B Location of trial

Is there any reason why your claim needs to be heard at a particular court? ☐ Yes ☐ No

If Yes, say which court and why?

C Pre-action protocols

The Construction and Engineering Disputes protocol applies to this claim.

Have you complied with it? ☐ Yes ☐ No

If No, please explain the reasons why on a separate sheet and attach it to this form.

D Case management information

What amount of the claim is in dispute? £

Is there a counterclaim to this claim? ☐ Yes ☐ No

If Yes, state value of counterclaim £

TCC/CM1 Case management information sheet (03.02) 1

Applications

Have you made any application(s) in this claim? ☐ Yes ☐ No

If Yes, what for? ☐ For hearing on ☐

(e.g. summary judgment, add another party)

Witnesses

So far as you know at this stage, what witnesses of fact do you intend to call at the trial or final hearing including, if appropriate, yourself?

Witness name	Witness to which facts

Experts

Do you wish to use expert evidence at the trial or final hearing? ☐ Yes ☐ No

Have you already copied any experts' report(s) to the other party(ies)? ☐ None yet obtained ☐ Yes ☐ No

Do you consider the case suitable for a single joint expert in any field? ☐ Yes ☐ No

Please list any single joint experts you propose to use and any other experts you wish to rely on. Identify single joint experts with the initials 'SJ' after their name(s).

Expert's name	Field of expertise (eg. orthopaedic surgeon, surveyor, engineer)

Do you want your expert(s) to give evidence orally at the trial or final hearing? ☐ Yes ☐ No

If Yes, give the reasons why you think oral evidence is necessary:

☐

Disclosure

Are there any special considerations concerning disclosure of any documents that should be brought to the attention of the judge? ☐ Yes ☐ No

If Yes, please give details on a separate sheet and attach it to this form.

2

continue over ➡

Transfer

If you think your case is suitable for a transfer to another court or track, say which:

Court: Chancery Division/Queen's Bench Division/another TCC court/Commercial Court/ County Court
Track: Small claims/Fast track

Please give brief reasons for your choice:

E Trial or final hearing

How long do you estimate the trial or final hearing will take? .... days .... hours .... minutes

Are there any days when you, an expert or an essential witness will not be able to attend court for the trial or final hearing? ☐ Yes ☐ No

If Yes, please give details

Name	Dates not available

F Proposed directions *(Parties should agree directions wherever possible)*

See CPR Part 60 Practice Direction paras 8.4 and 8.6 and The Technology and Construction Court Guide

Have you attached a list of the directions you think appropriate for the management of the claim? ☐ Yes ☐ No

If Yes, have they been agreed with the other party(ies)? ☐ Yes ☐ No

G Costs

*Do **not** complete this section if you have suggested your case is suitable for the small claims track **or** you have suggested one of the other tracks and you do not have a solicitor acting for you.*

What is your estimate of your costs incurred to date? £

What do you estimate your overall costs are likely to be? £

In substantial cases these questions should be answered in compliance with CPR Part 43

3

H Other information

Have you attached documents to this form? ☐ Yes ☐ No

Have you sent these documents to the other party(ies)? ☐ Yes ☐ No

If Yes, when did they receive them?

Do you intend to make any applications in the immediate future? ☐ Yes ☐ No

If Yes, what for?

Are video link facilities required? ☐ Yes ☐ No

In the space below, set out any other information you consider will help the judge to manage the claim, including any details about IT being used before or at trial

Signed

Date

[Counsel][Solicitor][for the][1st][2nd][3rd][ ]
[Claimant][Defendant][Part 20 claimant]

Please enter your firm's name, reference number and full postal address including (if appropriate) details of DX, fax or e-mail

	if applicable	
	fax no.	
	DX no.	
Tel. no. Postcode	e-mail	
Your reference no.		

4

Notes for completing a case management information sheet

- If you fail to return the form by the date given, the judge may give directions or make any order he thinks fit.
- Use a separate sheet if you need more space for your answers marking clearly which section the information refers to. You should write the claim number and the name of the assigned judge on it, and on any other documents you send with the form. Please ensure they are firmly attached to it.

A Settlement

If you think that you and the other party may be able to negotiate a settlement you should tick the 'Yes' box. The court may order a stay, whether or not all the other parties to the claim agree. You should still complete the rest of the form, even if you are requesting a stay. Where a stay is granted it will be for an initial period of one month. You may settle the claim either by informal discussion with the other party or by alternative dispute resolution (ADR). ADR covers a range of different processes which can help settle disputes. More information is available in the Legal Services Commission leaflet 'Alternatives to Court' free from the LSC leaflet line Phone: 0845 3000 343

B Location of trial

Whenever possible the trial of a claim will be heard by the assigned TCC judge. A TCC claim may be tried at any place where there is a TCC judge available to try the claim.

C Pre-action protocols

Before any claim is started, the court expects you to have exchanged information and documents relevant to the claim to assist in settling it, and to have complied with the construction and engineering disputes protocol

D Case management information

Applications

It is important for the court to know if you have already made any applications in the claim, what they are for and when they will be heard. The outcome of the applications may affect the case management directions the court gives.

Witnesses

Remember to include yourself as a witness of fact, if you will be giving evidence.

Experts

Oral or written expert evidence will only be allowed at the trial or final hearing with the court's permission. The judge will decide what permission it seems appropriate to give when the claim is allocated to track. Permission in small claims track cases will only be given exceptionally.

E Trial or final hearing

You should enter only those dates when you, your expert(s) or essential witness(es) will not be able to attend court because of holiday or other committments.

F Proposed directions

Attach the list of directions, if any, you believe will be appropriate to be given for the management of the claim. Agreed directions on fast and multi-track cases should be based on the forms of standard directions set out in the practice direction to CPR Part 28 and form PF52.

G Costs

Only complete this section if you are a solicitor and have suggested the claim is suitable for allocation to the fast or multi-track.

H Other Information

Answer the questions in this section. Decide if there is any other information you consider will help the judge to manage the claim. Give details in the space provided referring to any documents you have attached to support what you are saying.

5

Pre-trial review questionnaire

In the County Court High Court of Justice Queen's Bench Division Technology and Construction Court	
Claim No.	
Last date for filing with court office	
Assigned judge	

To be completed by, or on behalf of,

who is [1st][2nd][3rd][ ] [Claimant] [Defendant] [Part 20 claimant] in this claim

- The judge will use the information which you and the other party(ies) provide to conduct a pre-trial review
- If you do not complete and return the questionnaire the judge may
  - make an order which leads to your statement of case (claim or defence) being struck out.
  - conduct the pre-trial review without it. You may be ordered to pay (immediately) the other parties' costs of attending.

A Directions complied with

1. Have you complied with all the previous directions given by the court? ☐ Yes ☐ No

2. If no, please explain which directions are outstanding and why

Directions outstanding	Reasons directions outstanding

3. Are any further directions required to prepare the case for trial? ☐ Yes ☐ No *(If no go to section B)*

4. If yes, please explain directions required and give reasons

Directions required	Reasons required

TCC/PTR1 Pre-trial review questionnnaire (10.05)

B Experts

1. Has the court already given permission for you to use written expert evidence? ☐ Yes ☐ No *(If no go to section C)*

2. If yes, please give name and field of expertise.

Name of expert	Whether joint expert *(please tick, if appropriate)*	Field of expertise

3. Have the experts held discussions as directed? ☐ Yes ☐ No
4. Have they filed statements as directed following those discussions? ☐ Yes ☐ No
5. Have the expert(s') report(s) been served and filed as ordered? ☐ Yes ☐ No
6. Has the court already given permission for the expert(s) to give oral evidence at the trial? *(If yes go to Section C)* ☐ Yes ☐ No
7. If no, are you seeking that permission? ☐ Yes ☐ No *(If no go to section C)*
8. If yes, give your reasons for seeking permission.

9. If yes, what are the names, addresses and fields of expertise of your experts?

Expert 1	Expert 2	Expert 3	Expert 4

10. Please give details of any dates within the trial period when your expert(s) will not be available.

Name of expert	Dates not available

C Other witnesses

(If you are not calling other witnesses go to section D)

1. How many other witnesses (including yourself) will be giving evidence on your behalf at the trial? *(do not include experts - see section B above)* ☐ *(Give number)*

2. What are the names and addresses of your witnesses?

Witness 1	Witness 2	Witness 3	Witness 4

3. Please give details of any dates within the trial period when you or your witnesses will not be available?

Name of witness	Dates not available

4. Are any of the witness statements agreed? ☐ Yes ☐ No *(If no go to question C6)*

5. If yes, give the name of the witness and the date of his or her statement

Name of witness	Date of statement

6. Do you or any of your witnesses need any special facilities? ☐ Yes ☐ No *(If no go to question C8)*

7. If yes, what are they?

8. Will any of your witnesses be provided with an interpreter? ☐ Yes ☐ No *(If no go to section D)*

9. If yes, say what type of interpreter e.g. language (stating which), deaf/blind etc.

D Legal representation

1. Who will be presenting your case at the hearing or trial? ☐ You ☐ Solicitor ☐ Counsel

2. Please give details of any dates within the trial period when the person presenting your case will not be available.

Name	Dates not available

E Other matters

1. How long do you estimate the whole trial will take, excluding judgment?

Minutes	Hours	Days

2. What is the estimated number of pages of evidence to be included in the trial bundle?

(please give number)

3. Please provide a case summary and proposals (agreed if possible) for directions to be given.

Signed

Claimant/defendant or Counsel/Solicitor for the claimant/defendant

Dated

Claim Form
(Admiralty claim in rem)

In the	High Court of Justice Queen's Bench Division Admiralty Court
	for court use only
Claim No.	
Issue date	

Admiralty claim in rem against

SEAL

of the Port of

Claimant

Defendant

Brief details of claim

The Admiralty Registry within the Royal Courts of Justice, Strand, London WC2A 2LL is open between 10am and 4.30pm Monday to Friday. Please address all correspondence to the Admiralty Registry and quote the claim number.

ADM1 Claim form (Admiralty claim in rem) (03.02)

Claim No.	

Particulars of Claim (attached)(to follow)

Statement of Truth
*(I believe)(The Claimant believes) that the facts stated in these particulars of claim are true.
* I am duly authorised by the claimant to sign this statement

Full name ____________________

Name of claimant's solicitor's firm ____________________

signed____________________ position or office held____________________
*(Claimant)(Claimant's solicitor) (if signing on behalf of firm or company)

*delete as appropriate

Claimant's or claimant's solicitor's address to which documents or payments should be sent if different from overleaf including (if appropriate) details of DX, fax or e-mail.

Claim Form
(Admiralty claim)

In the High Court of Justice
Queen's Bench Division
Admiralty Court

	for court use only
Claim No.	
Issue date	

Claimant(s)

SEAL

Defendant(s)

Name and address of Defendant receiving this claim form

The court office at the Admiralty and Commercial Registry, Royal Courts of Justice, Strand, London WC2A 2LL is open between 10 am and 4.30 pm Monday to Friday. When corresponding with the court, please address forms or letters to the Court Manager and quote the claim number.

ADM1A Claim form (admiralty claim) (03.02)

Claim No.	

Brief details of claim

Particulars of claim (*attached)(*will follow if an acknowledgment of service is filed that indicates an intention to defend the claim)

Statement of Truth

*(I believe)(The Claimant believes) that the facts stated in this claim form *(and the particulars of the claim attached to this claim form) are true.

* I am duly authorised by the claimant to sign this statement

Full name ______________________________

Name of *(claimant)('s solicitor's firm) ______________________________

signed____________________ position or office held ____________________

*(Claimant)('s solicitor) (if signing on behalf of firm, company or corporation)

**delete as appropriate*

Claimant's or solicitor's address to which documents or payments should be sent if different from overleaf including (if appropriate) details of DX, fax or e-mail.

Notes for defendant on replying to an admiralty claim form

Please read these notes carefully - they will help you decide what to do about this claim.
Further information may be obtained from the **Admiralty and Commercial Court Guide.**

Your response and what happens next

- In every case you should file the acknowledgment of service form within 14 days of the date of service on your property (or a solicitor acting on your behalf).

- Complete the acknowledgment of service form ADM2 within the time stated and send it to The Admiralty and Commercial Registry, Royal Courts of Justice, Strand, London WC2A 2LL.

- If you do not file an acknowledgment of service, judgment may be entered against you and if the property described in the claim form is under arrest, it may be sold by order of the court. Additional costs and interest may be added.

Address where notices can be sent

- In the acknowledgment of service you must give your full name if it was not stated on the claim form and an address to which notices and document relating to this claim must be sent.

- **This must be an address in the United Kingdom.**

- The address must be either your solicitor's address, you own residential or business address, or (if you live elsewhere) some other address. Any address given must be in the United Kingdom.

Disputing the jurisdiction

If you wish to dispute the court's jurisdiction to try the claim you must:

- complete the acknowledgment of service form and send it to the court within *(14 days) ( ); and
- make any application to contest the court's jurisdiction as soon as possible and in any event within 28 days (2 months in the case of a collision claim) after filing your acknowledgment of service.

Disputing the claim

If you wish to dispute the claim you must:

- file an acknowledgment of service within *(14 days) ( ); and
- serve a defence within the period stated in the acknowledgment of service.

**Claimant should alter as appropriate if the claim form is to be served out of the jurisdiction together with the particulars of claim - see CPR rule 6.30.*

ADM1C Notes for defendant (10.08)

Acknowledgment of service (Admiralty claim)

In the High Court of Justice Queen's Bench Division Admiralty Court	
Claim No.	
Claimant(s) (including ref.)	
Defendant(s)	

Description of defendant(s):-

Full name of person described above:-

Nature of ownership of property

Address in the United Kingdom to which documents about this claim should be sent (including reference if appropriate).

Postcode

If applicable	
Telephone no.	
Fax no.	
DX no.	
Your ref.	

E-mail

If you do not file an acknowledgment of service within 14 days of the claim form being served on you, and whether or not particulars of claim are served with it, judgment may be given against you.

Tick the appropriate box

1. I intend to defend all of this claim ☐
2. I intend to defend part of this claim ☐
3. I intend to contest jurisdiction ☐
4. My date of birth is D D M M Y Y Y Y

If you file an acknowledgment of service but do not file:
- a defence within 28 days of the date of service of the particulars of claim; or
- a collision statement of case within 2 months (in the case of a collision claim),

judgment may be given against you.

If you do not file an application within 28 days of the date of service of the particulars of claim (2 months in the case of a collision claim) it will be assumed that you accept the court's jurisdiction and judgment may be given against you.

Signed

(Defendant) (Defendant's solicitor)

Date / /

Position or office held

(if signing on behalf of firm, company or corporation)

The court office at

is open between 10am and 4.30pm Monday to Friday. Please address forms or letters to the Court Manager and quote the claim number.

ADM2 Acknowledgment of service (10.08)

Collision statement of case

In the	**High Court of Justice Queen's Bench Division Admiralty Court**
Claim No.	

Claimant(s)

Defendant(s)

Collision statement of case on behalf of ....

PART 1

1.	The names of the ships which came into collision and their ports of registry	
2.	The length, breadth, gross tonnage, horsepower and draught at the material time of the ship and the nature and tonnage of any cargo carried by the ship	
3.	The date and time (including the time zone) of the collision	
4.	The place of the collision	
5 .	The direction and force of the wind	
6.	The state of the weather	
7.	The state, direction and force of the tidal or other current	
8.	The position, the course steered and speed through the water of the ship when the other ship was first seen or immediately before any measures were taken with reference to her presence, whichever was the earlier	

ADM3 Collision statement of case (03.02)

9. The lights or shapes (if any) carried by the ship

10. (a) The distance and bearing of the other ship if and when her echo was first observed by radar

(b) The distance, bearing and approximate heading of the other ship when first seen

11. What light or shape or combination of lights or shapes (if any) of the other ship was first seen

12. What other lights or shapes or combinations of lights or shapes (if any) of the other ship were subsequently seen before the collision, and when

13. What alterations (if any) were made to the course and speed of the ship after the earlier of the two times referred to in article 8 up to the time of collision, and when, and what measures (if any) other than alterations of course or speed, were taken to avoid the collision, and when

14. The heading of the ship, the parts of each ship which first came into contact and the approximate angle between the two ships at the moment of contact

15. What sound signals (if any) were given, and when

16. What sound signals (if any) were heard from the other ship, and when

PART 2

State:

(1) that the information in Part 1 is incorporated in Part 2;

(2) any other facts and matters upon which the party filing this collision statement of case relies;

(3) all allegations of negligence or other fault on which the party filing this collision statement of case relies;

(4) the relief or remedy which the party filing this collision statement of case claims.

Statement of Truth

*(I believes)(The Claimant believes)(The defendant believes) that the facts stated in this collision statement of case are true
*I am duly authorised by the (claimant) (defendant) to sign this statement

Full name..

Name of claimant's/defendant's solicitor's firm...

signed.. *(Claimant)(Defendant) (solicitor)

position or office held... (if signing on behalf of firm or company)

***delete as appropriate**

Application and undertaking for arrest and custody

In the	High Court of Justice Queen's Bench Division Admiralty Court
Claim No.	

Admiralty claim in rem against:

The Admiralty Marshal is requested to execute the Warrant in the above claim lodged herewith by the arrest of *(give details)*
lying/expected to arrive at *(give details)*

I (we) undertake personally to pay on demand the fees of the Marshal and all expenses incurred, or to be incurred, by him or on his behalf in respect of

1. the arrest, or endeavours to arrest, the property; and
2. the care and custody of it while under arrest; and
3. the release, or endeavours to release it.

I (we) request that a search be made in the Register before the warrant is issued to determine whether there is a caution against arrest in force in respect of the above property.

Date

Signed...

To be signed by the Solicitor

Office use only:

I confirm that at: on:
no cautions have been filed or entered against the arrest of the above property.

Signed...

ADM4 Application and undertaking for arrest and custody (03.02)

Declaration in support of application for warrant of arrest

'The claimant's claim is *(state nature of claim)*

I am informed by *(name and occupation of informant)*
that the claimant's claim has not been satisfied.

The property to be arrested is the ship *(name)*
of the port of *(port of registry)* .

The amount of security for the claim sought by the claimant is *(state amount if known)*

The relevant notice (if required)(exhibit no.) has been sent to the consular office
of *(name of country or State)* '.

If the claim falls under section 21(4) of the Supreme Court Act 1981 and it does ***not*** *carry a maritime lien or other charge the declaration should further include:-*

'The ship *(name of ship to be arrested)* is the ship (or is one of the ships) against which the claim is brought and is (is not) the ship in connection with which the claim arose.

The person who would be liable on the claim in an action in personam ("the relevant person")
is *(name)* .

When the right to bring the claim arose *(name of relevant person)* was (the owner or charterer)(in possession or in control) *(as the case may be)*
of the ship *(name of the ship in connection with which the claim arose)* .

(name of relevant person) was
on the *(date claim form was issued)* the beneficial owner of all the shares
in the ship *(name of ship in connection with which the claim arose and is the ship to be arrested)*
or was the charterer of it under a charter by demise.

*(**OR**, if the ship to be arrested is not the one in connection with which the claim arose)*

(name of relevant person) was
on the *(date claim form was issued)* the beneficial owner as respects all the
shares in the ship *(name of ship to be arrested)*.

In establishing that the court is not prevented from considering the claim by reason of section 166(2) of the Merchant Shipping Act 1995, the facts relied on are:

Statement of Truth

*(I believe)(The claimant believes) that the facts stated in this declaration form are true.

*I am duly authorised by the claimant to sign this statement.

Full Name

Name of claimant's solicitor's firm

signed
(Claimant)(Claimant's solicitor)

position or office held
(If signing on behalf of a firm or company)

*delete as appropriate

Notice to Consular Officer of intention to apply for warrant of arrest

To the Consular Officer of *(name of State)*
The ship *(give name)*
of the Port of *(give details)*

TAKE NOTICE that as solicitors for *(name or description of party seeking arrest)*

we did on the of [19][20]
(or we intend to) institute proceedings in the Queen's Bench Division, Admiralty Court,
of the High Court of Justice against the above-mentioned ship in respect of a claim (or counterclaim)
by *(name or description of party seeking arrest)*
for *(state nature of claim or counterclaim)*

and that we intend to apply to the Admiralty Court to arrest the ship.

Date

Signed ....
Solicitors for

ADM6 Notice to Consular Officer of intention to apply for warrant of arrest (03.02)

Request for caution against arrest

[Description of property giving name, if a ship]

I/We *(give name)*
of

[Solicitors for
of
]

request a caution against the arrest of *(description of property giving name, if a ship)*

[and undertake to acknowledge service of the claim form in any claim that may be begun in the High Court of Justice against the *(give name)*
and, within 3 days after receiving notice that a claim has been issued, to give security in the claim in the sum not exceeding *(enter amount)* or to pay that sum into court.]

[having constituted a Limitation Fund in Claim No. *(give number)*
in respect of damage arising from the relevant incident, namely *(describe briefly the incident)*

and undertake to acknowledge service of the claim form in any claim that may be begun against the property described in this request.]

I/We consent that the claim form and any other documents in the claim may be left for me/us at *(enter address)*

Date

Signed ....

ADM7 Request for caution against arrest(03.02)

Warrant of Arrest

In the High Court of Justice Queen's Bench Division Admiralty Court	
Claim No.	

Admiralty action in rem against:

Claimant(s)

Defendant(s)

ELIZABETH THE SECOND, by the Grace of God, of the United Kingdom of Great Britain and Northern Ireland and of Our other realms and territories Queen, Head of the Commonwealth, Defender of the Faith:

To the Admiralty Marshal of Our High Court of Justice, and to all singular his substitutes, Greeting.
We hereby command you to arrest the ship
of the port of and to keep same under arrest until you should receive further orders from Us.

WITNESS , Lord High Chancellor of Great Britain,
the day of

The Claimant's claim is for [copy from Claim Form]

Taken out by

Solicitors for the

ADM9 - w3 Warrant of arrest (4.99) *Printed on behalf of The Court Service*

Certificate as to Service

On the day of

the within-named ship

lying at

was arrested by virtue of

for a short time on*

of the said ship, and on taking off the process, by leaving a copy thereof fixed in its place.

Signed ______________________ Date ________________

*State on which part of the outside of the ship's superstructure

Standard Directions to the Admiralty Marshal

In the	High Court of Justice Queen's Bench Division Admiralty Court
Claim No.	

Admiralty claim in rem against:

Claimant(s)

Defendant(s)

IT IS ORDERED that the Admiralty Marshal may at any time:-

(a) take measures to preserve the ship *(give details)*

its machinery and equipment;

(b) move the ship up to 5 miles within the limits of the port where it is lying under arrest, either for its safety or to comply with the requirements of the Port Authority;

(c) supply the minimum victuals, domestic fuel and water necessary to avoid hardship to the crew.

Date

The Admiralty Registrar

ADM10 Standard Directions to the Admiralty Marshal (03.02)

Request for caution against Release

[Description of property giving name, if a ship)]

I/We
of

[Solicitors for   of

]
request the entry of a caution against the release of the above-named property or it's proceeds of sale paid into court by the Admiralty Marshal.

The applicant for a caution claims to have an in rem right against the above-mentioned property or proceeds of sale for *(state nature of claim in rem and the approximate amount claimed, if known)*

Date

Signed ....

Request and undertaking for release

In the	High Court of Justice Queen's Bench Division Admiralty Court
Claim No.	

Admiralty claim in rem against:

The Admiralty Marshal is requested to release from arrest in the above claim the *(give details)*

lying *(give details)*

I (We) personally undertake to pay the fees of the Marshal and all expenses incurred, or to be incurred, by him or on his behalf in respect of:

1. the arrest, or endeavours to arrest the property; and
2. the care and custody of it while under arrest; and
3. it's release, or endeavours to release it.

Date

Signed ....

To be signed by the Solicitor

Office use only:

I confirm that at: on: no cautions have been filed or entered against release of the above property.

Signed..

ADM12 Request and undertaking for release (03.02)

Request for withdrawal of caution against release

In the	High Court of Justice Queen's Bench Division Admiralty Court
Claim No.	

Admiralty claim in rem against:

I/We
of

[Solicitors for of

]

request that the caution entered on the day of 20 against the release of the above-named property or the proceeds of its sale into court by the Admiralty Marshal, be withdrawn

Dated the day of 20

Signed ....

ADM12A Request for withdrawal of caution against release (03.02)

Application for judgment in default of filing an acknowledgment of service and/or defence or collision statement of case

In the	High Court of Justice Queen's Bench Division Admiralty Court
Claim No.	

Admiralty claim in rem against:

Claimant(s)

Defendant(s)

To the Defendant(s) and/or all persons who have entered cautions against release.

TAKE NOTICE that the claimant(s) will make an application on the of
at am/pm, at by Counsel for an order that:

(1) Judgment in default of filing an acknowledgment of service (and/or defence) (or collision statement of case) be given for the claimant(s) in the sum of with interest (or in an amount to be assessed) and for the costs of this claim including the costs of this application to be (summarily) assessed if not agreed.

(2) *(if applicable)* The vessel *(give name)*
be appraised and sold by the Admiralty Marshal. (see Form ADM14 for the terms of the order for sale)

Date

ADM13 Application for judgment in default of filing an acknowledgment of service and/or defence or collision statement of case(03.02)

Order for sale of a ship

In the	High Court of Justice Queen's Bench Division Admiralty Court
Claim No.	

Admiralty claim in rem against:

Claimant(s)

Defendant(s)

BEFORE

UPON HEARING

and upon reading the written evidence of *(give details)*

(And no acknowledgment of service and/or defence or collision statement of case having been filed on behalf of the defendant(s)]

IT IS ORDERED that:

(1) the ship *(give details)*
be appraised and sold by the Admiralty Marshal (before judgment (if applicable))

(2) the Admiralty Marshal choose one or more experienced persons to appraise the vessel and certify its true value in writing.

(3) the Admiralty Marshal sell the vessel on his conditions of sale for the highest price that can be obtained for it, but not for less than the certified value without an order of court.

(4) the Admiralty Marshal pay the proceeds of sale of the vessel into court.

(5) on completion of the sale the Admiralty Marshal countersign and file the certificate of value together with an account of his fees and expenses.

(6) the Solicitors on behalf of the claimant (or as may be) within *(give details)*
give to the Admiralty Marshal a personal undertaking to pay on demand the fees and expenses of the Marshal incurred by him or on his behalf in respect of the appraisement and sale of the property, or of endeavours to appraise or to sell the property.

[OR BE SOLD IN SUCH OTHER WAY AS THE COURT MAY ORDER

]

Date

ADM14 Order for sale of a ship

Claim Form (Admiralty limitation claim)

Click here to reset form

In the	High Court of Justice Queen's Bench Division Admiralty Court
	for court use only
Claim No.	
Issue date	

Claimant(s)

SEAL

Defendant(s)

Details of limitation claim *(see also overleaf)*

Named defendant's name and address

The Admiralty Registry within the Royal Courts of Justice, Strand, London WC2A 2LC is open between 10am and 4.30pm Monday to Friday. Please address all correspondence to the admiralty registry and quote the claim number.

ADM15 Claim form Admiralty limitation claim (03.02)

Claim No.	

Details of limitation claim *(continued)*

Statement of Truth
*(I believe)(The Claimant believes) that the facts stated in these details of claim are true.
* I am duly authorised by the claimant to sign this statement

Full name ______________________________

Name of claimant's solicitor's firm ______________________________

signed______________________________ position or office held______________________________
*(Claimant)(Claimant's solicitor) (if signing on behalf of firm or company)

*delete as appropriate

Claimant's or claimant's solicitor's address to which documents or payments should be sent if different from overleaf including (if appropriate) details of DX, fax or e-mail.

Notes for defendant (admiralty limitation claim)

Please read these notes carefully - they will help you decide what to do about this claim.

Futher information may be obtained from the Admiralty and Commercial Registry, Room E200, Royal Courts of Justice, Strand, London WC2A 2LL. Tel: 020 7947 6112. Fax: 020 7947 6245.

You have only a limited time to reply to this claim - the notes below tell you what to do.

You may either:

dispute the court's jurisdiction or contend that the court should not exercise it

admit the claimant's right to limit liability

dispute the claim

The response pack, which should accompany the claim form, will tell you which forms to use for your reply

If you **do not** respond in any way the court may grant the claimant a General Limitation Decree in your absence

Court staff can tell you about procedures but they cannot give legal advice. If you need legal advice, you should contact a solicitor or Citizens Advice Bureau immediately.

Responding to this claim

Time for responding

You have from the date the claim form was served on you:

14 days to file an acknowledgment of service disputing the court's jurisdiction

or

28 days to file a completed defence or admission of the claimant's right to limit liability (or, if the claim form was served outside the United Kingdom, within the time specified by CPR Rule 6.35).

If the claim form was:

- sent by post, the date of service is taken as the second business day after posting (see date of postmark on the envelope)
- delivered or left at your address, the date of service will be the second business day after it was delivered
- handed to you personally, the date of service will be the second business day it was given to you.

Completing the acknowledgment of service

You should tick either

- Box A - if you dispute the court's jurisdiction **or**
- Box B - if you contend that the court should not exercise its jurisdiction

and complete all the other details on the form.

You should send the completed form to the court and at the same time send a copy to the claimant.

You should file also an application at the court within 14 days of filing of your acknowledgment of service.The court will arrange a hearing date for the application.

If you do not file the application you will be treated as having accepted that the court has jurisdiction to hear the claim.

Completing the admission

You should complete admission form ADM16 and send it to the court and at the same time send a copy to the claimant. The claimant may file an application for the court to issue a restricted limitation decree limiting liability against any of the named defendants in the claim form who have filed an admission.

Completing the defence

You should file defence form ADM16A at the court and at the same time send a copy to the claimant. Within 7 days of filing of your defence (or filing of defence of other named defendants or expiry of the time for doing so) the claimant must apply for an appointment before the Admiralty Registrar for a case management conference. The court will give directions at this appointment for the future conduct of the case.

Statement of truth

This must be signed by you or by your solicitor, as appropriate.

If you do nothing

The claimant may apply for a limitation decree against you.

ADM15B Notes for Defendant (admiralty limitation claim) (10.08)

Notice of admission of right of claimant to limit liability

In the	High Court of Justice Queen's Bench Division Admiralty Court
Claim No.	

Claimant(s)

Defendant(s)

TAKE NOTICE THAT, the following defendant(s) *(name them)*

admit the right of the claimant(s) in this claim to limit his/her/their liability in accordance with the provisions of *(give details of the relevant Act)*

Signed

Date

DM16 Notice of admission of right of claimant to limit liability (03.02)

Defence to admiralty limitation claim

In the	High Court of Justice Queen's Bench Division Admiralty Court
Claim No.	

Claimant(s)

Defendant(s)

You have a limited number of days to file and serve this form. See notes for guidance attached to the claim form.

Signed (To be signed by you or by your solicitor)	*(I believe)(The defendant believes) that the facts stated in this form are true. *I am duly authorised by the defendant to sign this statement **delete as appropriate*	**Position or office held** (if signing on behalf of firm or company)	
Date			

Give an address to which notices about this case can be sent to you	Postcode		if applicable
		fax no.	
		DX no.	
	Tel. no.	e-mail	

DM16A Defence to admiralty limitation claim

Acknowledgment of Service
(Admiralty limitation claim)

Defendant's full name if different from the name given on the claim form

In the	High Court of Justice Queen's Bench Division Admiralty Court
Claim No.	
Claimant(s) (including ref.)	
Defendant(s)	

Address in England or Wales to which documents about this claim should be sent (including reference if appropriate)

	if applicable	
	fax no.	
	DX no.	
Tel. no. Postcode	e-mail	

Tick the appropriate box

A I intend to dispute jurisdiction ☐

B I intend to argue that the court should not exercise its jurisdiction ☐

You should file an application at the court within 14 day of service of this acknowledgment of service or you wil be treated as having accepted the court's jurisdiction.

Signed (Defendant)(Defendant's solicitor)

Position or office held (if signing on behalf of firm or company)

Date

The Admiralty Registry within the Royal Courts of Justice, Strand, London WC2A 2LC is open between 10am and 4.30pm Monday to Friday. Please address all correspondence to the Admiralty Registry and quote the claim number.

ADM16B Acknowledgment of service (admiralty limitation claim) (03.02)

Application for restricted limitation decree

In the	High Court of Justice Queen's Bench Division Admiralty Court
Claim No.	

Claimant(s)

Defendant(s)

TAKE NOTICE that the claimant(s) will apply to the Admiralty Registrar
on the at am/pm at

for:

(1) permission (if necessary) to amend the claim form in this action so that the defendants are only those named defendants that have admitted the claimant's right to limit liability under the Merchant Shipping Act 19 .

(2) a restricted limitation decree pursuant to the Merchant Shipping Act 19 restricted to their liabilities against the above-named defendants described in paragraph (1) above.

(3) an Order that the fund in court be paid out and distributed as follows:
(give details)

(4) the costs of this application be

Date

To: The Defendant(s) as above

ADM17 Application for restricted limitation decree (03.02)

Application for general limitation decree

In the	High Court of Justice Queen's Bench Division Admiralty Court
Claim No.	

Claimant(s)

Defendant(s)

TAKE NOTICE that the claimant(s) will apply to the Admiralty Registrar
on the at am/pm at

for:

(1) a general limitation decree

(2) an Order that the fund in court be paid out and distributed as follows:
(give details)

(3) the costs of this application be

Date

To: The Defendant(s) as above

ADM17A Application for general limitation decree (03.02)

Restricted limitation decree

In the	High Court of Justice Queen's Bench Division Admiralty Court
Claim No.	

Claimant(s)

Defendant(s)
(restrict to those defendants who have admitted claimant's right to limit liability)

BEFORE

UPON CONSENT of the claimants and the above-named defendants

AND UPON reading the written evidence of

IT IS ORDERED BY DECREE that by reason of the Merchant Shipping Act 19

1. the claimants are not answerable in damages in respect of claims by the above-named defendants or persons claiming through or under them, beyond the amount *(give amount)* of Special Drawing Rights, in respect of the loss, damage and delay caused to any property or to the infringement of any rights through the claimants' act or omission or through the act or omission of any person on board
   the vessel *(give name)*
   in the navigation or management of the *(give name)*
   when the *(give name)*
   collided with the *(give name)*
   in the *(give details)*
   on the *(give date)* .

2. the limitation tonnage of the *(give name)* ascertained in accordance with the provisions of the Merchant Shipping Act 19 is *(enter figure)* tonnes, that the amount of the Limitation Fund calculated in accordance with the Act is Special Drawing Rights and that the liability of the claimants to the above named defendants is £ *(enter amount)* together with simple interest thereon from the *(enter date of collision)* to this day and no more *(or as may be agreed between the parties to the claim)*

3. the claimants having constituted a Limitation Fund by payment into court of the amount on the *(enter date of payment into court)* , all further proceedings against them by the above-named defendants arising out of this occurrence be stayed.

ADM18 Restricted limitation decree (03.02)

4. the fund in court including all accrued interest to the date of payment out be paid out and distributed as follows: *(give details)*

5. the costs of this application be

Date

General limitation decree

In the	High Court of Justice Queen's Bench Division Admiralty Court
Claim No.	

Claimant(s)

Defendant(s)

BEFORE

UPON HEARING Solicitors (Counsel) for the claimants and defendants

AND UPON reading the written evidence of

IT IS ORDERED BY DECREE that by reason of the Merchant Shipping Act 19

1. the claimants are not answerable in damages beyond the amount of *(give amount)* Special Drawing Rights, in respect of the loss, damage and delay caused to any property or to the infringement of any rights through their act or omission or through the act or omission of any person on board the vessel *(give name)* in the navigation or management of the *(give name)* when the *(give name)* collided with the *(give name)* on the *(give date)* .

2. the limitation tonnage of the *(give name)* ascertained in accordance with the provisions of the Merchant Shipping Act 19 is *(enter figure)* tonnes, that the amount of the Limitation Fund calculated in accordance with the Act is Special Drawing Rights and that the liability of the claimants is £ *(enter amount)* together with simple interest thereon from the *(enter date of collision)* to this day and no more.

3. the claimants having constituted a Limitation Fund by payment into court of the amount on the *(enter date of payment into court)* ,all further proceedings in any claim against them arising out of this occurrence be stayed.

ADM19 General limitation decree (03.02)

4. after deduction of the above amount together with the simple interest thereon, the remainder of amount paid into court by the claimants on the *(give date of payment into court)*, and any interest accrued thereon be paid out to the claimants.

5. the claimants place a single advertisement in each of three newspapers, namely *(give details of newspapers)*

identifying the claim and specifying the decree made in this claim and further specifying a period of *(state period)* for the filing of claims and the issue of applications to set the decree aside.

6. the sum of £ *(enter amount)* together with the simple interest thereon be rateably distributed among the several persons who make out their claims against the fund and that within 7 days of the time for filing claims or declarations, the Admiralty Registrar will fix a date for a case management conference at which directions will be given for the further conduct of the proceedings.

7. the costs of this application be

Date

Defendant's claim in a limitation claim

In the	High Court of Justice Queen's Bench Division Admiralty Court
Claim No.	

Claimant(s)

Defendant(s)

The defendant's claim is for damages arising out of the above-mentioned collision.

On *(give date)*, the claimants were granted a decree limiting their liability for the collision to Special Drawing Rights. Due to the collision the defendants suffered damage and loss as follows; *(give details)*

with interest pursuant to section 35A of the Supreme Court Act 1981 and costs.

To the Claimant(s) and Solicitors.

To all other Defendants and their Solicitors.

ADM20 Defendant's claim in a limitation claim (03.02)

Statement of Truth

*(I believe)(The defendant believes) that the facts stated in this defendant's claim are true
*I am duly authorised by the (defendant) to sign this statement

Full name......................................

Name of defendant's solicitor's firm...

signed.. position or office held..
(Defendant)(Defendant's solicitor) (if signing on behalf of firm or company)

*delete as appropriate

Declaration as to inability of a defendant to file and serve statement of case under a decree of limitation

"The defendant *(give name)*
is unable to file and serve a statement of case within the time fixed under the general limitation decree made in this claim on the *(give date)* as he requires further information to enable him to decide whether or not to dispute the claimant`s right to limit liability in the following respects: *(state them)*

OR

"The defendant *(give name)*
requires a further *(give period)* in which to file and serve an application to set aside the said general limitation decree *(state reasons for request]*"

OR

"The defendant *(give name)*
requires a further *(give period)* in which to file and serve his statement of case under the said general limitation decree *(state reasons for request]*"

Statement of Truth
*(I believe)(The defendant believes) that the facts stated in this declaration are true.
* I am duly authorised by the claimant to sign this statement

Full name ______________________________

Name of defendant's solicitor's firm ______________________________

signed ______________________ position or office held ______________________
*(Defendant)(Defendant's solicitor) (if signing on behalf of firm or company)

*delete as appropriate

ADM21 Declaration as to inability of a defendant to file and serve statement of case under a decree of limitation (03.02)

In the		
		for court use only
Claim Form (arbitration)	Claim No.	
	Issue date	

In an arbitration claim between

Claimant

SEAL

Defendant(s)

In the matter of an [intended] arbitration between

Claimant

Respondent(s) *Set out the names and addresses of persons to be served with the claim form stating their role in the arbitration and whether they are defendants.*

Defendant's name and address

☐ This claim will be heard on:

at am/pm

☐ This claim is made without notice.

The court office at

When corresponding with the court, please address forms or letters to the Court Manager and quote the case number.

N8 Claim form (arbitration)

Claim No.	

Remedy claimed and grounds on which claim is made

Claim No.	

The claimant seeks an order for costs against

Statement of Truth
*(I believe)(The Claimant believes) that the facts stated in these particulars of claim are true.
* I am duly authorised by the claimant to sign this statement

Full name ______________________________

Name of claimant's solicitor's firm ______________________________

signed ______________________________ position or office held ______________________________

*(Claimant)(Claimant's solicitor) (if signing on behalf of firm or company)

delete as appropriate

Claimant's or claimant's solicitor's address to which documents should be sent if different from overleaf. If you are prepared to accept service by DX, fax or e-mail, please add details.

Arbitration Claim - notes for the claimant

Please read these guidance notes before you begin completing the claim form

The arbitration claim form may be used to start proceedings and make an application in existing proceedings. Where an application is being made in existing proceedings, an acknowledgment of service form is not required and the references to an acknowledgment of service form in the Notes for the Defendant should be deleted.

With the exception of:

- applications under section 9 of the Arbitration Act 1996; and
- certain proceedings which may be started only in the High Court or only in a county court - see High Court and County Courts (Allocation of Arbitration Proceedings) Order 1996, arbitration proceedings may be started in the courts set out in the table opposite.

Court	List
Admiralty and Commercial Registry at the Royal Courts of Justice, London	Commercial
Technology and Construction Court Registry, St Dunstan's House, London	TCC
District Registry of the High Court *(where Mercantile court established)*	Mercantile
District Registry of the High Court *(where the Claim form marked 'Technology and Construction Court' in top right hand corner)*	TCC
Central London County Court	Mercantile

Heading

You must fill in the heading of the claim form with:

- the name of the court (High Court or county court); and
- if issued in a District Registry, the name of the District Registry

Claimant and defendant details

You must provide your full name and address, including postcode and the full names and addresses of the defendants to be served. If a defendant is to be served outside England and Wales, the court's permission may need to be sought *(see Rule 62.5)*.

Remedy claimed and grounds on which claim is made

You must:

- include a concise statement of
  - the remedy claimed; and
  - any questions on which you seek the decision of the court;
- give details of any arbitration award which you challenge, identifying which part or parts of the award are challenged and the grounds for the challenge;
- show that any statutory requirements have been met;
- specify under which section of the Act the claim is made;

Respondents

- if on notice, give the names and addresses of the persons on whom the arbitration claim form is to be served, stating their role in the arbitration and whether they are defendants; or
- state that the claim is made without notice under section 44(3) of the 1966 Act, and the grounds relied on.

Acknowledgment of service form

An acknowledgment of service form N15 must accompany the arbitration claim form. You should complete the heading on this form. Where the claim form is to be served out of the jurisdiction, you must amend the Notes for the Defendant to give the time within which the defendant must acknowledge service and file evidence. The claim form is valid for one month beginning with the date of its issue or, where required to be served out of the jurisdiction, for such period as the court may fix.

Address for documents

You must provide an address for service within England and Wales to which documents should be sent. That address must be either the business address of your solicitor, or your residential or business address.

Statement of Truth

The statement of truth must be signed by you or by your solicitor. Where the statement of truth is not signed by the solicitor and the claimant is a registered company or corporation, the statement of truth must be signed by either a director, the treasurer, secretary, chief executive, manager or other officer of the company and (in the case of a corporation) the mayor, chairman, president or town clerk.

You may rely on the matters set out in the claim form as evidence only if the claim form is verified by a statement of truth. You may also file an affidavit or witness statement in support of the arbitration claim, which must be served with the claim form.

N8A Arbitration claim - notes for claimant (04.06) HMCS

Arbitration Claim - notes for the defendant

Please read these guidance notes carefully before you respond to the arbitration claim form

Court staff can help you with procedures but they cannot give legal advice. If you need legal advice, you should contact a solicitor or a Citizens Advice Bureau immediately.

Responding to the claim

If you are:

- named as a defendant in the claim form; and
- served with a copy of it,

you should respond by completing and returning to the court office the acknowledgment of service form which was enclosed with the claim form, within *(14 days) (   ) of the date it was served on you. At the same time you must serve a copy on the claimant and any other party shown on the claim form.

If the claim form was:

- sent by post, the *(14 days) (   ) starts 2 business days from the date of the postmark on the envelope;
- delivered or left at your address, the *(14 days) (   ) starts on the second business day it was given to you;
- handed to you personally, the *(14 days) (   ) starts 2 business days from the day it was given to you.

The acknowledgment of service

If you:

- fail to complete and file the acknowledgment of service within the time specified; or
- if you indicate that you do not intend to contest the claim,

If you later change your mind, you will not be entitled to contest the claim without the court's permission.

Evidence

If you wish to rely on evidence before the court, you must file and serve your written evidence within *(21 days) (   ) of the date the claim form was served on you.

Statement of truth

The acknowledgment of service must be signed by you or by your solicitor. Where the acknowledgment of service is not signed by your solicitor and you are a registered company or corporation, it must be signed by either a director, the treasurer, secretary, chief executive, manager or other officer of the company and (in the case of a corporation) the mayor. Chairman, president or town clerk.

Notes for arbitrators

If you are:

- an arbitrator; or
- ACAS (in a claim under the 1996 Act as applied with modification by the ACAS (England and Wales) Order 2001),

who has been named as a defendant in the claim form, the above notes apply to you as they do to any other defendant.

If you were, or are:

- an arbitrator in the arbitration which led to this claim; and
- if you are not named as a defendant;

this claim form is sent to you for information.

You may either:

- make a request (with notice only to the claimant) to be made a defendant
- may make representations to the court *(see paragraph 4.3 of practice direction to Part 62)*

**Claimant should alter where appropriate if the claim form is to be served out of the jurisdiction (see CPR Part6)*

N8B Arbitration claim - notes for defendant (10.08)

Acknowledgment of Service
(arbitration claim)

In the	
Claim No.	
Claimant (including ref)	
Defendant	

You should read the 'notes for defendant' attached to the claim form which will tell you how to complete this form, and when and where to send it.

Tick and complete sections A - D as appropriate.
In all cases you must complete sections E and F

Section A

☐ I **do not** intend to contest this claim

Section B

☐ I intend to contest this claim

Give brief details of any different remedy you are seeking.

Section C

☐ I intend to dispute the court's jurisdiction
(Please note, any application must be filed within 14 days of the date on which you file this acknowledgment of service)

The court office at

When corresponding with the court, please address forms or letters to the Court Manager and quote the claim number.

N15 Acknowledgment of Service (arbitration) (03.02)

Claim No.	

Section D

☐ I intend to rely on written evidence

My written evidence:

☐ is filed with this form

☐ will be filed and served within 21 days after the date by which I am required to file this acknowledgment of service.

Section E

Full name of defendant filing this acknowledgment ______________________

Section F

Signed (To be signed by you or by your solicitor)

*(I believe)(The defendant believes) that the facts stated in this form are true. *I am duly authorised by the defendant to sign this statement

**delete as appropriate*

Position or office held (if signing on behalf of firm or company)

Date

Give an address in England or Wales to which notices about this case can be sent to you

Postcode

Tel. no.

if applicable	
Ref. no.	
fax no.	
DX no.	
e-mail	

No. 53 - Writ of fieri facias

In the High Court of Justice
[ ] Division
[ ] District Registry
High Court Claim No.
[County Court Claim No.]

[Sent from the [ ] County Court by Certificate dated]

Claimant

Defendant

ELIZABETH THE SECOND, by the Grace of God, of the United Kingdom of Great Britain and Northern Ireland and of Our other realms and territories Queen, Head of the Commonwealth, Defender of the Faith.

TO: *"........, an enforcement officer authorised to enforce writs of execution issued from the High Court."*
Or,
"The enforcement officers authorised to enforce writs of execution issued from the High Court who are assigned to the district of[1] .... in England & Wales.

[**Note** If you have chosen this option you must send this writ to the National Information Centre for Enforcement for allocation.]

IN THIS CLAIM a Judgment or Order was made as set out in the Schedule.

YOU ARE NOW COMMANDED to seize in execution the goods, chattels and other property of the defendant authorised by law and raise therefrom the sums detailed in the Schedule, [together with fees and charges to which you are entitled]. And immediately after execution to pay the [claimant][defendant](*name*) the said sums and interest.

YOU ARE ALSO COMMANDED to indorse on this writ immediately after execution a statement of the manner in which you have executed it and send a copy of the statement to the [claimant][defendant]

THIS WRIT WAS ISSUED by the Central Office [the District Registry] of the High Court on (*date*) on the application of (*name*) of (*address*) [agent for (*name*) of (*address*)] solicitor for [the claimant] [*or* the claimant (*name*) in person] who resides at (*address*).

WITNESS (name) Lord High Chancellor of Great Britain, the (date)

The address[es] for enforcement are (give address[es] including county and postcode).

SCHEDULE

1. Date of Judgment or Order: 20	
2. Amount of Judgment or Order (including interest awarded by Judgment or Order)	£
3. Fixed costs on Judgment or Order	£
4. Assessed costs (if any) [by costs certificate dated (date)]	£
5. (If sent from county court by certificate) Interest[2] post-Judgment or Order on county court judgment or order over £5,000) until date of certificate	£
6. LESS credits or payments received since Judgment or Order	£
Sub Total	£
7. Costs of execution	£
Total	£

Together with: -

A. Judgment interest[3] at [8]% from;________20__
date of Judgment on sub-total above, or
(if sent from county court by certificate) date of county court certificate on paragraphs 1,2 and 3 above until payment,

B. Fees and Charges to which you are entitled (where appropriate).

1 This should reflect the Districts as set out in the High Court Enforcement Officers Regulation 2004

2 Interest under s.74 of the County Courts Act 1984

3 S.17 Judgments Act 1838

No. 54
Writ of fieri facias on order for costs

IN THE HIGH COURT OF JUSTICE
[ ] DIVISION
[ ] District Registry
High Court Claim No.
[County Court Claim No.]

[Sent from the [ ] County Court by Certificate dated (*date*)]

Claimant

Defendant

ELIZABETH THE SECOND, by the Grace of God, of the United Kingdom of Great Britain and Northern Ireland and of Our other realms and territories Queen, Head of the Commonwealth, Defender of the Faith.

TO: *"......, an enforcement officer authorised to enforce writs of execution issued from the High Court."*
Or,
"The enforcement officers from the High Court who are assigned to the district of[1] ....in England & Wales."
[N.B. If you have chosen this option you must send this writ to "NICESheriffs" for allocation.]

IN THIS CLAIM it was on the (*date*) ordered in this Court [*or* in the [ ] County Court under claim number [ ]] that the defendant (*name*) do pay the claimant (*name*) costs [to be assessed, which costs have been assessed and allowed at] £ [as appears by the certificate of the costs officer dated (*date*)]:

YOU ARE NOW COMMANDED to seize in execution the goods, chattels and other property of the defendant authorised by law and raise therefrom the sums detailed in the Schedule, [together with fees and charges to which you are entitled.] and immediately after execution to pay the claimant[defendant](*name*) the said sums and interest.

YOU ARE ALSO COMMANDED to indorse on this writ immediately after execution a statement of the manner in which you have executed it and send a copy of the statement to the claimant [defendant].

THIS WRIT WAS ISSUED by the Central Office [the District Registry] of the High Court on (*date*) on the application of (*name*) of (*address*) [agent for (*name*) of (*address*)] solicitor for [the claimant] [*or* the claimant (*name*) in person] who resides at (*address*).

WITNESS (*name*) Lord High Chancellor of Great Britain, the (*date*)

The address[es] for enforcement are (give address[es] including county and postcode).

SCHEDULE

1. Date of Judgment or Order: ____________200__

2. Amount of Judgment or Order (including interest awarded by Judgment or Order) £

3. Fixed costs on Judgment or Order £

4. Assessed costs (if any) [by costs certificate dated (date)] £

5. (If sent from county court by certificate) Interest[2] post-Judgment or Order (on county court judgment or order over £5,000) until date of certificate £

6. LESS credits or payments received since Judgment or Order £

Sub Total £

7. Costs of execution £

Total £

Together with:-
A. Judgment interest[3] at [8]% from; ________200__
 i. date of Judgment on sub-total above, or
 ii. (if sent from county court by certificate) date of county court certificate on paragraphs 1,2 and 3 above until payment,
B. Fees and charges to which they are entitled (where appropriate).

[1] This should reflect the Districts as set out in the High Court Enforcement Officers Regulation 2004
[2] Interest under s. 74 of the County Court Act 1984
[3] S.17 Judgments Act 1838

No. 55
Notice of Seizure

IN THE HIGH COURT OF JUSTICE
QUEEN'S BENCH DIVISION
[ ] District Registry
High Court Claim No.
[County Court Claim No.]

[Sent from the [ ] County Court by Certificate dated ***(date)*****]**

Claimant

Defendant

Address of premises . ...

THIS NOTICE is left by *(name)*.................... of *(address)*.. an Enforcement Officer authorised to enforce writs of execution from the High Court.

High Court Enforcement Reference No. . ...

TAKE NOTICE THAT:

1. A formal seizure of the goods at the above address has been made under a Writ of Execution directed to an Enforcement Officer by the High Court. The Enforcement Officer accordingly has conduct of the execution.
2. The goods seized are now in the custody of the Enforcement Officer, authorised to enforce writs of execution from the High Court, and must not be removed, sold or otherwise disposed of. This will remain the position until the sum due under the execution has been paid in full. The only exceptions are goods of the type referred to in section 138(3A) of the Supreme Court Act 1981. (This section is set out overleaf). Enclosed with this NOTICE is a WALKING POSSESSION AGREEMENT in the form prescribed by law. You must read this agreement and sign it to acknowledge the seizure and hand it to the Enforcement Officer attending your premises or return it to this Office. Failure to sign the Walking Possession Agreement may result in the removal of the goods seized without further notice pending disposal by public auction.
3. The judgment debt of £ and £ costs of execution are due under the Writ [together with £ interest and fees and charges of the enforcement officer] *or* [You must be in touch IMMEDIATELY with this Office so that you can be told the exact amount due for interest and charges].

04/04

4. Payment must be made to this Office in CASH or by BANK DRAFT. Payment by cheque may be accepted if the Enforcement Officer agrees but may be subject to such charges (if any) as are made by his bankers for special clearance.
5. If payment is not made and the execution proceeds, the Enforcement Officer or their agents will attend and remove the goods seized for sale by public auction or as the Court may direct.
6. If any of the goods seized are not your property, you must tell the owner about the seizure and he must write to the Enforcement Officer claiming the goods.
7. If any of the goods seized are the subject of a hire purchase or any similar agreement, you must send full details in writing to the Enforcement Officer.
8. If any of the goods seized are not liable to seizure by virtue of section 138(3A) of the Supreme Court Act 1981 (set out overleaf) this Office must be sent full details in writing within 5 days of the seizure or within such greater period as the Court may, on your application, allow.
9. You must inform this Office if another bailiff seizes, levies on or distrains the goods to pay another debt and you must inform that bailiff of this seizure.
10. You must also inform this Office of any Petition in Bankruptcy or application to liquidate a limited company that may have been or is subsequently served on you.
11. The goods seized are all those referred to at 2 above but, in case there is any doubt, the following items *ARE INCLUDED IN THE SEIZURE*:
....
....
....

Dated

Signed:

Address:

[Reverse of form:]
Section 138(3A) of the Supreme Court Act 1981 provides as follows—
"(3A) Every enforcement officer executing any writ of execution issued from the High Court against the goods of any person may by virtue of it seize—

(a) any of that person's goods except—

(i) such tools, books, vehicles and other items of equipment as are necessary to that person for use personally by him in his employment, business or vocation;

(ii) such clothing, bedding, furniture, household equipment and provisions as are necessary for satisfying the basic domestic needs of that person and his family; and

(b) any money, bank notes, bills of exchange, promissory notes, bonds, specialities or securities for money belonging to that person."

04/04

No. 56 - Writ of fieri facias after levy of part

In the High Court of Justice
[ ] Division
[ ] District Registry
High Court Claim No.
[County Court Claim No.]

[Sent from the [ ] County Court by Certificate dated]

Claimant

Defendant

ELIZABETH THE SECOND, by the Grace of God, of the United Kingdom of Great Britain and Northern Ireland and of Our other realms and territories Queen, Head of the Commonwealth, Defender of the Faith.

TO: *"........, an enforcement officer authorised to enforce writs of execution issued from the High Court."*
Or,
"The enforcement officers authorised to enforce writs of execution issued from the High Court who are assigned to the district of[1] .... in England & Wales.

[**Note** If you have chosen this option you must send this writ to the National Information Centre for Enforcement for allocation.]

IN THIS CLAIM a Judgment or order was made on (*date*) under claim number [ ] for the defendant (*name*) to pay the claimant (*name*) £ [and £ costs *or* costs to be assessed, which costs have been assessed and allowed at £ as appears by the certificate of the costs officer dated (*date*)]:

AND BY THE WRIT issued the (*date*) you were commanded [*or* the Enforcement Officer of (*state District*) was commanded] to seize in execution the goods, chattels and other property of the defendant authorised by law and raise therefrom the sums detailed in the Schedule to the Writ issued the (*date*), [together with fees and charges to which you are entitled] and immediately after execution to pay the claimant [defendant] (*name*) the said sums and interest.

AND THE INDORSEMENT ON THE WRIT stated that by virtue thereof you [*or* he] caused to be made of the property aforesaid the sum of £

YOU ARE NOW COMMANDED to seize in execution th goods, chattels and other property of the defendant authorised by law and raise therefrom the sums detailec the Schedule, [together with fees and charges to which are entitled] and immediately after execution to pay the claimant [defendant] (*name*) the said sums and interest.

AND YOU ARE ALSO COMMANDED to indorse on this writ immediately after execution a statement of the man in which you have executed it and send a copy of the statement to the claimant [defendant].

THIS WRIT WAS ISSUED by the Central Office [the District Registry] of the High Court on (*date*) on the application of (*name*) of (*address*) [agent for (*name*) of (*address*)] solicitor for [the claimant] [*or* the claimant (*name*) in person] who resides at (*address*).

WITNESS (*name*) Lord High Chancellor of Great Britain the (*date*)

The address[es] for enforcement are (*give address[es] including county and postcode*).

SCHEDULE

1. Date of Judgment or Order: 20
2. Amount of Judgment or Order (including interest awarded by Judgment or Order) £
3. Fixed costs on Judgment or Order £
4. Assessed costs (if any) [by costs certificate dated (date)] £
5. (If sent from county court by certificate) Interest[2] post-Judgment or Order on county court judgment or order over £5,000) until date of certificate £
6. LESS credits or payments received since Judgment or Order £

Sub Total £

7. Costs of execution £

Total £

Together with:-

A. Judgment interest[3] at [8]% from;_________20__
date of Judgment on sub-total above, or
(if sent from county court by certificate) date of county court certificat paragraphs 1,2 and 3 above until payment,
B. Fees and Charges to which you are entitled (where appropriate).

[1] This should reflect the Districts as set out in the High Court Enforcement Officers Regulation 2004
[2] Interest under s.74 of the County Courts Act 1984
[3] S.17 Judgments Act 1838

No. 57
Writ of fieri facias against personal representatives

IN THE HIGH COURT OF JUSTICE
[ ] DIVISION
[ ] District Registry
High Court Claim No.
[County Court Claim No.]

[Sent from the [ ] County Court by Certificate dated (*date*)]

Claimant

Defendant

ELIZABETH THE SECOND, by the Grace of God, of the United Kingdom of Great Britain and Northern Ireland and of Our other realms and territories Queen, Head of the Commonwealth, Defender of the Faith.

TO: *"......, an enforcement officer authorised to enforce writs of execution issued from the High Court."*
Or,
"The enforcement officers from the High Court who are assigned to the district of[1] *...........in England & Wales."*
[N.B. If you have chosen this option you must send this writ to "NICESheriffs" for allocation.]

IN THIS CLAIM a Judgment or Order was made under claim number [ ] that the defendant (*name*) as executor [*or* administrator] of (*name*) deceased pay the claimant (*name*) the sums as set out in the Schedule below to be raised from the real and personal estate of (*name*) at the time of his death in the hands of the defendant (*name*) as his executor [*or* administrator] to be administered, if he had or should thereafter have so much thereof in his hands to be administered, [and if he had not, then the costs in the Schedule below to be raised from the goods, chattels and other property of the defendant (*name*) authorised by law to be seized in execution].

YOU ARE NOW COMMANDED to seize in execution sufficient of the real and personal estate within the meaning of the Administration of Estates Act 1925 of (*name*) deceased, at the time of his death, which is in your county and in the hands of the defendant (*name*) as his executor [*or* administrator] to be administered and raise therefrom the sums detailed in the Schedule [together with poundage, officers' fees, costs of levying and all other legal incidental expenses] [and, if the defendant (*name*) has not so much thereof in his hands to be administered, to seize in execution the goods, chattels and other property of the defendant (*name*) authorised by law and raise therefrom the costs in the Schedule below], and immediately after execution to pay the claimant[defendant] the said sums and interest.

YOU ARE ALSO COMMANDED to indorse on this writ immediately after execution a statement of the manner in which you have executed it and send a copy of the statement to the claimant[defendant].

THIS WRIT WAS ISSUED by the Central Office [the District Registry] of the High Court on (*date*) on the application of (*name*) of (*address*) [agent for (*name*) of (*address*)] solicitor for [the claimant] [*or* the claimant (*name*) in person] who resides at (*address*).

WITNESS (name) Lord Chancellor of Great Britain, the (date)

The address[es] for enforcement are (give address[es] including county and postcode).

SCHEDULE

1. Date of Judgment or Order: __________200 __

2. Amount of Judgment or Order (including interest awarded by Judgment or Order) £

3. Fixed costs on Judgment or Order £

4. Assessed costs (if any) [by costs certificate dated (date)] £

5. (If sent from county court by certificate) Interest[2] post-Judgment or Order (on county court judgment or order over £5,000) until date of certificate £

6. <u>LESS</u> credits or payments received since Judgment or Order £

Sub Total £

7. Costs of execution £

Total £

<u>Together with</u>:-
A Judgment interest[3] at [8]% from; ________200__
i. date of Judgment on sub-total above, or
ii. (if sent from county court by certificate) date of county court certificate on paragraphs 1,2 and 3 above until payment,
B. Fees and charges to which you are entitled (where appropriate).

---

[1] This should reflect the Districts as set out in the High Court Enforcement Officers Regulation 2004
[2] Interest under S.74 of the County Courts Act 1984
[3] S.17 Judgments Act 1838

No. 58
Writ of fieri facias de bonis ecclesiasticis (Schedule 1 – RSC O.45 r.12)

IN THE HIGH COURT OF JUSTICE
QUEEN'S BENCH DIVISION
Claim No.

Claimant

Defendant

ELIZABETH THE SECOND, by the Grace of God, of the United Kingdom of Great Britain and Northern Ireland and of Our other realms and territories Queen, Head of the Commonwealth, Defender of the Faith.

To the Right Reverend Father in God (*name*) by Divine permission Lord Bishop of (*place*) greeting:

IN THIS CLAIM it was on the (*date*) ordered that the defendant (*name*) do pay the claimant (*name*) £ [and £ costs [as appears from a [default][final] costs certificate dated (*date*)]]:

AND whereas our sheriff of (*county*) on a day now past informed the claimant (*name*) that the defendant (*name*) had not any property from which he could cause to be made the sums of £ and £ or any part thereof and that the defendant (*name*) was a beneficed clerk, namely, rector or priest in charge of the rectory [*or* vicar or priest in charge of the vicarage] and parish church of (*place*) in the sheriff's county and within your diocese:

YOU ARE NOW COMMANDED that of the ecclesiastical property of the defendant (*name*) in your diocese you cause to be made the sum(s) of £ and £ for costs of execution and also interest on £ at the rate of £ per cent per annum from the (*date*) until payment and that immediately after execution of the writ you pay the claimant (*name*) in pursuance of the said judgment [*or* order] the amount levied in respect of the said sums and interest.

YOU ARE ALSO COMMANDED to indorse on this writ immediately after execution thereof a statement of the manner in which you have executed it and send a copy of the statement to the claimant (*name*).

WITNESS (*name*) Lord High Chancellor of Great Britain, the (*date*)

This writ was issued by (*name*) of (*address*) [agent for (*name*) of (*address*)] solicitor for [the claimant] [or this writ was issued by the claimant (*name*) in person] who resides at (*address*).

The defendant resides (or as the case may be) at (address including county).

No. 59
Writ of sequestrari de bonis ecclesiasticis
(Schedule 1 – RSC O.45 r.12)

IN THE HIGH COURT OF JUSTICE
QUEEN'S BENCH DIVISION
Claim No.

Claimant

Defendant

ELIZABETH THE SECOND, by the Grace of God, of the United Kingdom of Great Britain and Northern Ireland and of Our other realms and territories Queen, Head of the Commonwealth, Defender of the Faith.

To the Right Reverend Father in God (*name*) by Divine permission Lord Bishop of (*place*) greeting:

IN THIS CLAIM it was on the (*date*) ordered that the defendant (*name*) do pay the claimant (*name*) £ [and £ costs [as appears from a [default][final] costs certificate dated (*date*)]:

AND whereas our sheriff of (*county*) on a day now past informed the claimant (*name*) that the defendant (*name*) had not any property from which he could cause to be made the sums of £ and £ or any part thereof and that the defendant (*name*) was a beneficed clerk, namely, rector or priest in charge of the rectory [*or* vicar or priest in charge of the vicarage] and parish church of (*place*) in the sheriff's county and within your diocese:

YOU ARE NOW COMMANDED to enter into the rectory [*or* vicarage] and parish church of (*place*) and take and sequester them into your possession and to hold them in your possession until from the rents, tithes, rentcharges in lieu of tithes, oblations, obventions, fruits, issues and profits thereof and other ecclesiastical property in your diocese of and belonging to the rectory [*or* vicarage] and parish church of (*place*) and to the defendant (*name*) as [rector][vicar][priest in charge] thereof you shall have made the sum(s) of £ and £ for costs of execution and also interest on £ at the rate of £ per cent per annum from the (*date*) until payment and that immediately after execution of the writ to pay the claimant (*name*) in pursuance of the said judgment [*or* order] the amount levied in respect of the said sums and interest.

YOU ARE ALSO COMMANDED to indorse on this writ immediately after execution thereof a statement of the manner in which you have executed it and send a copy of the statement to the claimant (*name*).

WITNESS (*name*) Lord High Chancellor of Great Britain, the (*date*)

This writ was issued by (*name*) of (*address*) [agent for (*name*) of (*address*)] solicitor for [the claimant] [or this writ was issued by the claimant (*name*) in person] who resides at (*address*).

The defendant resides (*or as the case may be*) at (*address including county*).

No. 62 - Writ of fieri facias to enforce Northern Irish or Scottish judgment

In the High Court of Justice
[ ] Division
[ ] District Registry
High Court Claim No.
[County Court Claim No.]

[Sent from the [ ] County Court by Certificate dated]

Claimant

Defendant

ELIZABETH THE SECOND, by the Grace of God, of the United Kingdom of Great Britain and Northern Ireland and of Our other realms and territories Queen, Head of the Commonwealth, Defender of the Faith.

TO: *"........, an enforcement officer authorised to enforce writs of execution issued from the High Court."*

Or,

"The enforcement officers authorised to enforce writs of execution issued from the High Court who are assigned to the district of[1] .... in England & Wales.

[**Note** If you have chosen this option you must send this writ to the National Information Centre for Enforcement for allocation.]

A JUDGMENT [*or* Decree] dated the (*date*) was given in our High Court of Justice in Northern Ireland [*or* our Court of Session in Scotland *or as may be*] as set out in the Schedule below, as appears from a certificate registered on (*date*) in the register for judgments in our High Court of Justice in England and Wales pursuant to Schedule 6 to the Civil Jurisdiction and Judgments Act 1982.

YOU ARE NOW COMMANDED to seize in execution the goods, chattels and other property of the defendant (*name*) authorised by law and raise therefrom the sums detailed in the Schedule, [together with fees and charges to which you are entitled] and immediately after execution to pay the claimant[defendant](*name*) the said sums and interest.

YOU ARE ALSO COMMANDED to indorse on this writ immediately after execution a statement of the manner in which you have executed it and send a copy of the statement to the claimant [defendant].

THIS WRIT WAS ISSUED by the Central Office [the District Registry] of the High Court on (*date*) on the application of (*name*) of (*address*) [agent for (*name*) of (*address*)] solicitor for [the claimant] [*or* the claimant (*name*) in person] who resides at (*address*).

WITNESS (*name*) Lord High Chancellor of Great Britain, the (*date*)

The address[es] for enforcement are (*give address[es] including county and postcode*).

SCHEDULE

1. Date of Judgment or Order:	20
2. Amount of Judgment or Order (including interest awarded by Judgment or Order)	£
3. Fixed costs on Judgment or Order	£
4. Assessed costs (if any) [by costs certificate dated (date)]	£
5. (If sent from county court by certificate) Interest[2] post-Judgment or Order on county court judgment or order over £5,000) until date of certificate	£
6. LESS credits or payments received since Judgment or Order	£
Sub Total	£
7. Costs of execution	£
Total	£

Together with:-

A. Judgment interest[3] at [8]% from;________20__
date of Judgment on sub-total above, or
(if sent from county court by certificate) date of county court certificate
paragraphs 1,2 and 3 above until payment,

B. Fees and Charges to which you are entitled.

1 This should reflect the Districts as set out in the High Court Enforcement Officers Regulation 2004.

2 Interest under s.74 of the County Courts Act 1984

3 S.17 Judgments Act 1838

No. 63
Writ of fieri facias to enforce foreign registered judgment

IN THE HIGH COURT OF JUSTICE
QUEEN'S BENCH DIVISION
[ ] District Registry

In the matter of the Administration of Justice Act 1920, Part II [*or* the Foreign Judgments (Reciprocal Enforcement) Act 1933, Part I] [*or* the Civil Jurisdiction and Judgments Act 1982]

and

In the matter of a judgment of (*describe the court*) **obtained in** (*describe the proceedings*) **and dated** (*date*)

ELIZABETH THE SECOND, by the Grace of God, of the United Kingdom of Great Britain and Northern Ireland and of Our other realms and territories Queen, Head of the Commonwealth, Defender of the Faith.

TO: "*......, an enforcement officer authorised to enforce writs of execution issued from the High Court.*"
Or,
"*The enforcement officers from the High Court who are assigned to the district of*[1] *...........in England & Wales.*"
[N.B. If you have chosen this option you must send this writ to "NICESheriffs" for allocation.]

A JUDGMENT dated the (*date*) of (*describe the court*) registered in our High Court of Justice in England and Wales pursuant to Part II of the Administration of Justice Act 1920 [*or* Part I of the Foreign Judgments (Reciprocal Enforcement) Act 1933] [*or* the Civil Jurisdiction and Judgments Act 1982] adjudged that the (*name of party liable*) pay (*name of party entitled*) (*amount in foreign currency*) and the amount now due and owing under the said judgment is now equivalent to the sum set out in the Schedule below.

YOU ARE NOW COMMANDED to seize in execution the goods, chattels and other property of (*name of party liable*) authorised by law and raise therefrom the sum(s) detailed in the Schedule, [together with fees and charges to which you are entitled] and immediately after execution to pay (*name of party entitled*) the said sums and interest.

YOU ARE ALSO COMMANDED to indorse on this writ immediately after execution a statement of the manner in which you have executed it and send a copy of the statement to (*name of party entitled*).

THIS WRIT WAS ISSUED by the Central Office [the District Registry] of the High Court on (*date*) on the application of (*name*) of (*address*) [agent for (*name*) of (*address*)] solicitor for [the claimant] [*or* the claimant (*name*) in person] who resides at (*address*).

[1] This should reflect the Districts as set out in the High Court Enforcement Officers Regulation 2004

04/04

WITNESS (*name*) Lord High Chancellor of Great Britain, the (*date*)

The address[es] for enforcement are (*give address[es] including county and postcode*).

SCHEDULE

1. Date of Judgment or Order:		______________200__
2. Amount of Judgment or Order, including costs awarded by Judgment or Order		£
3. Interest[2] on the sum in paragraph 1 above in accordance with the law of (*the State in which the Judgment was given*) at such rate and for such period as are included in the Judgment as registered (*or as may be*), namely at [ ]% from (*date*) to (*date of issue of writ of fieri facias*)		£
4. Costs of obtaining and registering the Judgment or Order		£
5. LESS credits or payments received since registration of the Judgment or Order		£
	Sub Total	£
6. Costs of execution		£
	Total	£

together with:-

A. Interest on the sum in paragraph 1 above in accordance with the law of (*the State in which the judgment was given*) at such rate and for such period as are included in the judgment as registered (*or as may be*), namely at [ ]% from the date of issue of the writ of fieri facias until payment,

B. Interest at [ ]% on the sum in paragraph 3 from the date of registration until payment,

C. Fees and charges to which you are entitled (where appropriate).

2 Interest under S. 7 of the Civil Jurisdiction and Judgments Act 1982

04/04

No. 64
Writ of delivery: delivery of goods, damages and costs

IN THE HIGH COURT OF JUSTICE
[ ] DIVISION
[ ] District Registry

Claim No.

Claimant

Defendant

ELIZABETH THE SECOND, by the Grace of God, of the United Kingdom of Great Britain and Northern Ireland and of Our other realms and territories Queen, Head of the Commonwealth, Defender of the Faith.

TO: *"......, an enforcement officer authorised to enforce writs of execution issued from the High Court."*
Or,
"The enforcement officers from the High Court who are assigned to the district of[1] ....in England & Wales."
[N.B. If you have chosen this option you must send this writ to "NICESheriffs" for allocation.]

IN THIS CLAIM a Judgment or Order was made for (1) specific delivery of the goods detailed in Schedule 1 below and (2) for interest, damages and costs as set out in Schedule 2 below.

YOU ARE NOW COMMANDED:
(1) to cause the goods detailed in Schedule 1 to be delivered to the claimant (*name*),
(2) to seize in execution the goods, chattels and other property of the defendant (*name*) authorised by law and raise therefrom the sums detailed in Schedule 2 [together with fees and charges to which you are entitled], and immediately after execution to pay the claimant[defendant] (*name*), the said sums and interest.

YOU ARE ALSO COMMANDED to indorse on this writ immediately after execution a statement of the manner in which you have executed it and send a copy of the statement to the claimant[defendant] (*name*).

THIS WRIT WAS ISSUED by the Central Office [the District Registry] of the High Court on (*date*) on the application of (*name*) of (*address*) [agent for (*name*) of (*address*)] solicitor for [the claimant] [*or* the claimant (*name*) in person] who resides at (*address*).

WITNESS (*name*) Lord High Chancellor of Great Britain, the (*date*)

[1] This should reflect the Districts as set out in the High Court Enforcement Officers Regulation 2004

04/04

The address[es] for enforcement are (*give address[es] including county and postcode*).

SCHEDULE 1

1. Date of Judgment or Order: ________________200__

2. Details of goods: ____
   (*describe the goods the subject of the Judgment or Order*)

SCHEDULE 2

1. Amount of damages (including interest awarded by Judgment or Order)		£
2. Fixed costs on Judgment or Order		£
3. Assessed costs (if any) [by costs certificate dated (*date*)]		£
4. LESS credits or payments received since Judgment or Order		£
	Sub Total	**£**
5. Costs of execution		£
	Total	**£**

together with:-

A. Judgment interest[2] at [8]% from date of Judgment on sub-total above until payment,

B. Fees and charges to which you are entitled (where appropriate).

[2] S. 17 Judgments Act 1838

04/04

No. 65
Writ of delivery: delivery of goods or value, damages and costs

IN THE HIGH COURT OF JUSTICE
[ ] DIVISION
[ ] District Registry

Claim No.

Claimant

Defendant

ELIZABETH THE SECOND, by the Grace of God, of the United Kingdom of Great Britain and Northern Ireland and of Our other realms and territories Queen, Head of the Commonwealth, Defender of the Faith.

TO: *"......, an enforcement officer authorised to enforce writs of execution issued from the High Court."*

Or,

"The enforcement officers from the High Court who are assigned to the district of[1] *...........in England & Wales."*

[N.B. If you have chosen this option you must send this writ to "NICESheriffs" for allocation.]

IN THIS CLAIM a Judgment or Order was made for (1) delivery of the goods detailed in Schedule 1 below or for payment of their assessed value as set out in Schedule 2 below and (2) for interest, damages and costs as set out in Schedule 2 below.

YOU ARE NOW COMMANDED:
(1) to cause the goods detailed in Schedule 1 to be delivered to the claimant (*name*), or
(2) if you are unable to obtain the goods detailed in Schedule 1, to seize in execution the goods, chattels and other property of the defendant (*name*) authorised by law and raise therefrom their assessed value as detailed in paragraph 1 of Schedule 2, and
(3) in any event, to seize in execution the goods, chattels and other property of the defendant (*name*) authorised by law and raise therefrom the remaining sums detailed in Schedule 2 [together with fees and charges to which you are entitled], and immediately after execution to pay the claimant[defendant] (*name*), the said sums and interest.
YOU ARE ALSO COMMANDED to indorse on this writ immediately after execution a statement of the manner in which you have executed it and send a copy of the statement to the claimant (*name*).

[1] This should reflect the Districts as set out in the High Court Enforcement Officers Regulation 2004

04/04

THIS WRIT WAS ISSUED by the Central Office [the District Registry] of the High Court on (*date*) on the application of (*name*) of (*address*) [agent for (*name*) of (*address*)] solicitor for [the claimant] [*or* the claimant (*name*) in person] who resides at (*address*).

WITNESS (*name*) Lord High Chancellor of Great Britain, the (*date*)

The address[es] for enforcement are (*give address[es] including county and postcode*).

SCHEDULE 1

1. Date of Judgment or Order: ______________________200__

2. Details of goods:-____
(*describe the goods the subject of the Judgment or Order*)

SCHEDULE 2

1. Assessed value of goods:- (*where delivery has not taken place*)		£
2. Amount of damages (including interest awarded by Judgment or Order)		£
3. Fixed costs on Judgment or Order		£
4. Assessed costs (if any) [by costs certificate dated (*date*)]		£
5. LESS credits or payments received since Judgment or Order		£
	Sub Total	**£**
6. Costs of execution		£
	Total	**£**

together with:-

A. Judgment interest[2] at [8]% from date of Judgment on sub-total above until payment,

B. Fees and charges to which you are entitled (where appropriate)

[2] S.17 Judgments Act 1838

04/04

No. 66 - Writ of possession

In the High Court of Justice
[ ] Division
[ ] District Registry
High Court Claim No.
[County Court Claim No.]

[Sent from the [ ] County Court by Certificate dated]

Claimant

Defendant

ELIZABETH THE SECOND, by the Grace of God, of the United Kingdom of Great Britain and Northern Ireland and of Our other realms and territories Queen, Head of the Commonwealth, Defender of the Faith.

TO: *"......., an enforcement officer authorised to enforce writs of execution issued from the High Court."*

Or,

"The enforcement officers authorised to enforce writs of execution issued from the High Court who are assigned to the district of[1] *......... in England & Wales.*

[**Note** If you have chosen this option you must send this writ to the National Information Centre for Enforcement for allocation.]

THIS WRIT WAS ISSUED by the Central Office [the District Registry] of the High Court on (*date*) on the application of (*name*) of (*address*) [agent for (*name*) of (*address*)] solicitor for [the claimant] [*or* the claimant (*name*) in person] who resides at (*address*).

WITNESS (*name*) Lord High Chancellor of Great Britain, the (*date*)

The address[es] for enforcement are (*give address[es] including county and postcode*).

IN THIS CLAIM a Judgment or Order was made that the defendant give the claimant (*name*) possession of the land detailed in Schedule 1 below and pay the sums set out in Schedule 2 below.

YOU ARE NOW COMMANDED:
(1) to enter the land detailed in Schedule 1 and cause the claimant (*name*) to have possession of it,
(2) to seize in execution the goods, chattels and other property of the defendant (*name*) authorised by law and raise therefrom the sums detailed in Schedule 2 [together with fees and charges to which you are entitled], and immediately after execution to pay the claimant[defendant] (*name*), the said sums and interest.

YOU ARE ALSO COMMANDED to indorse on this writ immediately after execution a statement of the manner in which you have executed it and send a copy of the statement to the claimant[defendant] (*name*).

SCHEDULE 1
1. Date of Judgment or Order: 20
2. Details of land: (describe the land the subject of the judgment order)

SCHEDULE 2

1. Amount of sums (including interest awarded by judgment or order)	£
2. Fixed costs on judgment or order	£
3. Assessed costs (if any) [by costs certificate dated (date)]	£
4. LESS credits or payments received since Judgment or Order	£
sub Total	£
5.Costs of execution	£
Total	**£**

Together with:-
A. Judgment interest[2] at [8]% from date of Judgment on sub-total above
B. Fees and charges to which you are entitled

[1] This should reflect the Districts as set out in the High Court Enforcement Officers Regulation 2004.
[2] S. 17 Judgments Act 1838

No. 66A - Writ of possession

In the High Court of Justice
[ ] Division
[ ] District Registry
High Court Claim No.
[County Court Claim No.]

[Sent from the [ ] County Court by Certificate dated]

Claimant

Defendant

ELIZABETH THE SECOND, by the Grace of God, of the United Kingdom of Great Britain and Northern Ireland and of Our other realms and territories Queen, Head of the Commonwealth, Defender of the Faith.

TO: *"......, an enforcement officer authorised to enforce writs of execution issued from the High Court."*
Or,
"The enforcement officers from the High Court who are assigned to the district of[1] ....in England & Wales."
[N.B. If you have chosen this option you must send this writ to "NICESheriffs" for allocation.]

IN THIS CLAIM a Judgment or Order was made that the claimant (*name*) recover possession of the land detailed in Schedule 1 below [and pay the sums set out in Schedule 2 below].

YOU ARE ALSO COMMANDED to indorse on this writ immediately after execution a statement of the manner in which you have executed it and send a copy of the statement to the claimant [defendant] (*name*).

THIS WRIT WAS ISSUED by the Central Office [the District Registry] of the High Court on (*date*) on the application of (*name*) of (*address*) [agent for (*name*) of (*address*)] solicitor for [the claimant] [*or* the claimant (*name*) in person] who resides at (*address*).

WITNESS (*name*) Lord High Chancellor of Great Britain, the (*date*)

The address[es] for enforcement are (*give address[es] including county and postcode*).

YOU ARE NOW COMMANDED:
(1) to enter the land detailed in Schedule 1 and cause the claimant (*name*) to have possession of it,
[(2) (*where there is an order for costs against a named defendant*) to seize in execution the goods, chattels and other property of the defendant (*name*) authorised by law and raise therefrom the sums detailed in Schedule 2 [together with fees and charges to which you are entitled], and immediately after execution to pay the claimant (*name*), the said sums and interest].

SCHEDULE 1

1. Date of Judgment or Order: 20
2. Details of land: (describe the land the subject of the judgment order)

SCHEDULE 2

1. Fixed costs on judgment or order	£
2. Assessed costs (if any) [by costs certificate dated (date)]	£
3. LESS credits or payments received since Judgment or Order	£
Sub Total	**£**
4. Costs of execution	£
Total	**£**

Together with:-
A. Judgment interest[1] at [8]% from date of Judgment on sub-total above
B. Fees and Charges to which they are entitled.

[1] This should reflect the Districts as set out in the High Court Enforcement Officers Regulation 2004

[1] S.17 Judgments Act 1838

No. 67
Writ of sequestration (Schedule 1 – RSC O.45 r.12(4), O.46 r.5)

IN THE HIGH COURT OF JUSTICE
[ ] DIVISION
[ ] District Registry
Claim No.

Claimant

Defendant

ELIZABETH THE SECOND, by the Grace of God, of the United Kingdom of Great Britain and Northern Ireland and of Our other realms and territories Queen, Head of the Commonwealth, Defender of the Faith.

To (*names of not less than four commissioners*) greeting:

Whereas in this claim:

(1) it was on the (*date*) ordered that the defendant (*name*) should (*state act defendant was ordered to do or abstain from doing*),
(2) on (*date*) the defendant was found guilty of contempt of court in failing to comply with that order, and
(3) on (*date*) the Court gave the claimant permission to issue this writ of sequestration.

Take notice therefore, that we, confident of your prudence, integrity and fidelity, do by this writ authorise and command you, or any two or three of you,

(1) to enter upon and take possession of all the real and personal estate of the defendant (*name*),
(2) to collect, receive and take into your hands the rents and profits of his real estate and all his personal estate, and
(3) keep the same under sequestration in your hands until the defendant (*name*) shall comply with the order dated (*date*) and clear his contempt and the court make other order to the contrary.

Witness (*name*) Lord High Chancellor of Great Britain, the (*date*)

This writ was issued by (*name*) of (*address*) [agent for (*name*) of (*address*)] solicitor for [the claimant] [or this writ was issued by the claimant (*name*) in person] who resides at (*address*).

The defendant resides (*or as the case may be*) at (*address including county*).

No. 68
Writ of restitution

IN THE HIGH COURT OF JUSTICE
[ ] DIVISION
[ ] District Registry

Claim No.

Claimant

Defendant

ELIZABETH THE SECOND, by the Grace of God, of the United Kingdom of Great Britain and Northern Ireland and of Our other realms and territories Queen, Head of the Commonwealth, Defender of the Faith.

TO: *"......, an enforcement officer authorised to enforce writs of execution issued from the High Court."*

Or,

"The enforcement officers from the High Court who are assigned to the district of[1] *...........in England & Wales."*

[N.B. If you have chosen this option you must send this writ to "NICESheriffs" for allocation.]

IN THIS CLAIM a Judgment or Order was made on (*date*) that the defendant (*name*) do give the claimant (*name*) possession of (*describe the land the subject of the judgment or order*):

AND A WRIT OF POSSESSION was issued on (*date*) pursuant to the Judgment or Order directing you to give possession of the land to the claimant (*name*), and you have given possession to the claimant, but it appears to the Court that certain persons other than the claimant have wrongfully taken possession of the land, and the Court has on (*date*) ordered that a writ of restitution should be issued in respect of the land:

YOU ARE NOW COMMANDED to enter the land and cause the claimant (*name*) to have restitution of the land.

YOU ARE ALSO COMMANDED to indorse on this writ immediately after execution a statement of the manner in which you have executed it and send a copy of the statement to the claimant (*name*).

THIS WRIT WAS ISSUED by the Central Office [the District Registry] of the High Court on (*date*) on the application of (*name*) of (*address*) [agent for (*name*) of (*address*)] solicitor for [the claimant] [*or* the claimant (*name*) in person] who resides at (*address*).

WITNESS (*name*) Lord High Chancellor of Great Britain, the (*date*)

[1] This should reflect the Districts as set out in the High Court Enforcement Officers Regulation 2004

04/04

The address[es] for enforcement are (*give address[es] including county and postcode*).

No. 69
Writ of assistance

IN THE HIGH COURT OF JUSTICE
[ ] DIVISION
[ ] District Registry

Claim No.

Claimant

Defendant

ELIZABETH THE SECOND, by the Grace of God, of the United Kingdom of Great Britain and Northern Ireland and of Our other realms and territories Queen, Head of the Commonwealth, Defender of the Faith.

TO: *"......, the present (and any future) enforcement officer authorised to enforce writs of execution issued from the High Court."*

Or,

"The enforcement officers from the High Court who are assigned to the district of[1] *...........in England & Wales."*

[N.B. If you have chosen this option you must send this writ to "NICESheriffs" for allocation.]

Whereas by an order dated (*date*) made in the above-named claim in the [ ] Division of our High Court between the claimant (*name*) and the defendant (*name*), the defendant (*name*) was ordered to give to the claimant (*name*) possession of the land [*or* goods] therein described (*describe the land or goods the subject of the order*) but the defendant (*name*), and other persons have refused to obey the order and keep the possession of the land [*or* goods] in contempt of us and our Court:

And whereas by an order made in this claim (*dated*) it was ordered that a writ of assistance should issue to give the claimant (*name*) possession of the said land [*or* goods]:

YOU ARE NOW COMMANDED to [enter the said land and eject the defendant (*name*), his tenants, servants and accomplices, each and every of them, from the said land and every part thereof and put the claimant (*name*) and his assigns into full, peaceable and quiet possession thereof] [*or* put the claimant (*name*) and his assigns into full peaceable and quiet possession of the said goods] and defend and keep him and his assigns in such peaceable and quiet possession, when and as often as any interruption thereof is at any time effected, according to the intent of the said orders. And herein you are not in any wise to fail.

THIS WRIT WAS ISSUED by the Central Office [the District Registry] of the High Court on (*date*) on the application of (*name*) of (*address*) [agent for (*name*) of (*address*)] solicitor for [the claimant] [*or* the claimant (*name*) in person] who resides at (*address*).

WITNESS (*name*) Lord High Chancellor of Great Britain, the (*date*)

The address[es] for enforcement are (*give address[es] including county and postcode*)

---

[1] This should reflect the Districts as set out in the High Court Enforcement Officers Regulation 2004

No. 71
Notice of renewal of writ of execution

I N THE HIGH COURT OF JUSTICE
[ ] DIVISION
[ ] District Registry

Claim No.

Claimant

Defendant

Take Notice that the writ (*describe type of writ of execution*) issued in this claim directed to (Name & Address) an enforcement officer authorised to enforce writs of execution issued from the High Court and dated (*date*) has by order dated (*date*) been renewed for one year beginning with the date of the order.

To: (*Name & Address)* an enforcement officer authorised to enforce writs of execution issued from the High Court.

(*Signed*)

([Claimant] or [claimant's solicitor])

04/04

No. 85
Order of committal or other penalty upon finding of contempt of court (Schedule 1 – RSC O.52)

IN THE HIGH COURT OF JUSTICE
[ ] DIVISION
[ ] District Registry
Claim No.

Before *(Judge's name and title)*

Claimant

Defendant

AN APPLICATION was made by Counsel for (*party*) and was attended by [Counsel for](*party*)

The Judge read the written evidence filed and the Order of (*title and name of Judge/Master/District Judge*) dated (*date of Order*) in which [it was ordered that (*set out details of Order(s) breached*)] [the following undertaking was given (*set out undertaking breached*)].

AND THE COURT being satisfied that the (*party*) (*name*) has been guilty of contempt of court in failing to comply with [the order dated (*date of Order*)] [paragraphs (*give paragraph numbers*) of the order dated (*date of Order*)] [the undertakings given to the court and contained in the order dated (*date of Order*)] by (*set out details of breach*).

IT IS ORDERED

(1) that for his contempt the (*party*) (*name*) stand committed to HM Prison (*name of prison*) for a period of (*number of days or as may be*) from the date of his apprehension.

[(2) that the warrant of committal remain in the court office at [the Royal Courts of Justice] and that execution of it be suspended so long as the (*party*) (*name*) (*set out terms of suspension*) until (*date or as may be*) after which the sentence and warrant of committal be discharged.]

or

(3) that for his contempt the (*party*) (*name*) pay to Her Majesty the Queen a fine of £ on or before (*date payment due*).

or

(4) that the (*party*) may issue a writ of sequestration directed to the commissioners named in it to sequester all the real and personal property of the (*party*) (*name*) for its[his] contempt of court and that the writ of sequestration shall remain in full force and operation until the (*party*) clears its[his] contempt or until further order.

(5) that the costs of the (*party*) [summarially assessed in the sum of £] [to be the subject of a detailed assessment] be paid by the (*party*) to the (*party*).

(6) that the contemnor has permission to apply to the Court to clear his contempt and ask for his release or discharge.

Dated

No. 95
Certificate of order against the Crown
(Schedule 1 – RSC O.77 r.15 and s.25 of the Crown Proceedings Act 1947)

IN THE HIGH COURT OF JUSTICE
[ ] DIVISION
[ ] District Registry
Claim No.

Claimant

Defendant

By a [judgment][order] of this court dated (*date*) it was ordered that (*set out details of judgment or order*).

I hereby certify that the amount payable by (*party*) to (*party*) under the [judgment] [order] is £ [together with interest at the rate of £ per cent per annum until payment]

[and together with costs which have been the subject of a detailed assessment in the sum of £ as appears from a final costs certificate dated (*date*) [and interest is payable on the costs at the rate of £ per cent per annum from (*date*) until payment]].

or

[This certificate does not include the amount payable under the [judgment][order] in respect of costs].

Dated

Signed (Court Officer)

No. 96
Certificate of order for costs against the Crown (Schedule 1 – RSC O.77 r.15 and s.25 of the Crown Proceedings Act 1947)

IN THE HIGH COURT OF JUSTICE
[ ] DIVISION
[ ] District Registry
Claim No.

Claimant

Defendant

By a [judgment][order] of this court dated (*date*) it was ordered that (*give details of judgment or order*).

I hereby certify that the costs payable by (*party*) to (*party*) under the [judgment] [order] have been the subject of a detailed assessment and allowed in the sum of £ as appears from a final costs certificate dated (*date*) [and interest is payable on the costs at the rate of £ per cent per annum from (*date*) until payment].

Dated

Signed (Proper Officer)

No. 97
Claim form to grant bail (criminal proceedings) (Schedule 1 - RSC O. 79 r.9(1))

Parties should use form N208 using the terms "Applicant" and "Respondent", and include in the Details of claim section the following:

"The claim is for an order that the applicant be granted bail as to his commitment on (*date*) by [a magistrates court sitting at (*place*)][the Crown Court at (*place*)][the High Court] and that the respondent at the hearing before the Judge show cause why the applicant should not be granted bail. The applicant relies on the evidence in the witness statement/affidavit of (*name*) signed/sworn on (*date*) served with this claim form"

No. 97A
Claim form to vary arrangements for bail (criminal proceedings) (Schedule 1 - RSC O. 79 r.9(1))

Parties should use form N208 using the terms "Applicant" and "Respondent", and include in the Details of claim section the following:

"The claim is for an order that the terms on which (*name*) was granted bail on (*date*) by (*court*) should be varied as follows:-

(*set out terms on which party was granted bail*)

(*set out proposed variation*)

and that the respondent at the hearing before the Judge show cause why the variation should not be made. The applicant relies on the evidence in the witness statement/affidavit of (*name*) signed/sworn on (*date*) served with this claim form"

No. 98
Order to release prisoner on bail
(Schedule 1 – RSC O.79 r.9(6), (6A) and (6B))

IN THE HIGH COURT OF JUSTICE
QUEEN'S BENCH DIVISION
Claim No.

Before (*title and name of Judge*) [sitting in Private]

Applicant

Respondent

A Claim form for grant of bail was issued by the applicant on (*date*)

The Applicant (*name*) having been [remanded in custody] [convicted by (*court*) [and having given notice of appeal] *or as may be*] on (*date*)

And the Applicant being in the custody of the Governor of Her Majesty's Prison (*name of prison*)

The Judge read the written evidence filed

The Hearing was attended by (   )

IT IS ORDERED that the applicant (*name*), after complying with the conditions set out in Schedule 1 to this order and subject to the conditions set out in Schedule 2 to this order, be released on bail with a duty to surrender to the [magistrates' court at (*place*) on (*date*) at   am/pm] [Crown Court at (*place*) on a date and time to be notified to the applicant by an officer of that court].

Dated

Schedule 1

Conditions to be complied with before release on bail

1. To provide [   ] surety/sureties in the sum of £   [each] before a justice of the peace (*or as may be*) to secure (*name*)'s surrender to custody at the time and place appointed.

[2. To surrender (*name*)'s passport to   ]

3. (*set out any further condition*)

Schedule 2

Conditions to be complied with after release on bail

1. (*set out condition(s)*)

Note:- This form may also be adapted for use in case of orders to release on bail made by the Court of Appeal under Schedule 1 RSC O.59 r.20(4).

No. 98A
Order varying arrangements for bail
(Schedule 1 – RSC O.79 r 9(10))

IN THE HIGH COURT OF JUSTICE
QUEEN'S BENCH DIVISION
Claim No.

Before (*title and name of Judge*) [sitting in Private]

Applicant

Respondent

A Claim form for a variation of the arrangements for bail granted to (*name*) was issued by (*name*) [*where applicant is prosecutor* as prosecutor/a constable of (*name*) Police Force] on (*date*)

And (*name*) having been granted bail with a duty to surrender to the [magistrates' court at (*place*) on (*date*) at am/pm] [Crown Court at (*place*) on a date and time to be notified to the applicant by an officer of that court] and subject to the following conditions:

(*set out conditions imposed on the grant of bail*)

The Judge read the written evidence filed

The Hearing was attended by ( )

IT IS ORDERED that the arrangements for bail be varied as follows:

Dated

No. 99
Order of Court of Appeal to admit prisoner to bail
(Schedule 1 – RSC O.59 r.20(5))

No.

In the Court of Appeal

on appeal from the ( ) court

Dated

Applicant

Respondent

On (*date*) the applicant (*name*) was ordered by (*description of court*) to be imprisoned for (*period*) for contempt of court and the applicant (*name*) having appealed to [this Honourable Court][the House of Lords] against that order,

And (*name*) having applied to this Honourable Court to be admitted to bail

The Court read the notice of appeal filed

The Hearing was attended by ( )

IT IS ORDERED that upon (*name*) giving security [by his own recognisance] in the sum of £ with [two] sufficient sureties in the sum of £ each before a justice of the peace [*or as may be*] for the personal appearance of (*name*) before the (*description of court*) within 10 days after the judgment of [this Honourable Court][the House of Lords] on his appeal has been given, unless the order of the (*description of court*) is reversed by that judgment, he (*name*) be discharged out of the custody of the Governor of Her Majesty's Prison at (*address of prison*) in respect of that commitment.

By the Court

No. 100
Notice of bail (Schedule 1 – RSC O.79 r.9(7))

IN THE HIGH COURT OF JUSTICE
QUEEN'S BENCH DIVISION
Claim No.

Applicant

Respondent

To: (*name of prosecutor*)

On (*date*) (*name*) was (*set out circumstances of commitment*)

And the Honourable Mr Justice (*name*) [*or* the Court of Appeal] having made an order dated (*date*) that (*set out order for bail*)

Take Notice that under the above order [ ][sufficient] surety/sureties will [enter into recognisance][give security] before (*specify person*) at (*address*) on (*date*) at am/pm.

SURETIES

(set out names and descriptions of sureties)

Dated

Signed

Solicitor for

No. 104
Attachment of earnings order under the Attachment of Earnings Act 1971

IN THE HIGH COURT OF JUSTICE (*Here put letter and number, if any*)
FAMILY DIVISION
[DISTRICT REGISTRY]

In the matter of the Attachment of Earnings Act 1971

Whereas (*name*) of (*address*), who works at (*state name and address of employer*) as a (*describe occupation*) (Work no.) (hereinafter called the defendant) is required under a maintenance order made on (*date*) by the High Court of Justice (*or as the case may be*) to make payments of £ a week (*or as the case may be*) to (*name*)

And whereas on the application of (*name*) it appears that earnings fall to be paid by (*name of employer*) to the defendant:

IT IS HEREBY ORDERED that:

1. (*name of employer*) do make payments out of those earnings in accordance with the Attachment of Earnings Act 1971 to the Accountant General of the Supreme Court [*or* to the District Judge of the High Court of Justice at][*or* to the District Judge of the County Court] for transmission to (*name*),
2. for the purpose of calculating the said payments the normal deduction rate shall be ( ) a week (*or as the case may be*) and that the protected earnings rate shall be ( ) a week (*or as the case may be*).

Dated

To (*name of defendant*) of (*address*)

And to (*name of employer*) of (*address*)

Note:- This order does not come into force until one week after its service on the said defendant.

No. 105
Notice under section 10(2) of the Attachment of Earnings Act 1971

IN THE HIGH COURT OF JUSTICE (*Here put letter and number, if any*)
FAMILY DIVISION
[DISTRICT REGISTRY]

In the matter of the Attachment of Earnings Act 1971

Whereas by an attachment of earnings order dated (*date*) (*name of employer*) was required, out of earnings falling to be paid by him to (*name*), to make payments to me in or towards satisfaction of the payments due to ( ) under a maintenance order made by the High Court of Justice (*or as the case may be*) on (*date*);

And whereas it appears that:

1. the aggregate of the payments made for the purposes of the maintenance order exceeds the aggregate of the payments required by that order, and
2. the normal deduction rate specified by the attachment of earnings order exceeds the rate of payments required by the maintenance order, and
3. no proceedings for the variation or discharge of the attachment of earnings order are pending,

TAKE NOTICE that unless (*name*) applies to the High Court of Justice, within 14 days after the date of this notice, for an order discharging the attachment of earnings order or varying it in some other manner, the court will make an order varying the attachment of earnings order by reducing the normal deduction rate to the rate of payments required by the maintenance order or to such lower rate as the court thinks fit having regard to the amount of the excess mentioned in paragraph 1 of this notice.

Dated

Signed

(*to be signed by the officer of the High Court or the District Judge to whom payments under the attachment of earnings order are directed to be made*).

To (*name of defendant*) of (*address*)

And to (*name of employer*) of (*address*)

No. 110
Certificate under section 12 of the Civil Jurisdiction and Judgments Act 1982

Applicant

Defendant

I, a [Master of the Supreme Court] [District Judge of the High Court] of England and Wales, hereby certify:-

1. That the claim form (*or as the case may be*), a copy of which is annexed, was issued out of the High Court of Justice on (*date*) by (*name*) the above-named claimant, against (*name*) the above-named defendant, for [payment of the sum of £] (*or state any other remedy claimed*)
2. That the claim form [or as the case may be] was duly served on the (date), upon the defendant by (*state method of service*).

[3. That the defendant (*name*) [acknowledged service of the claim form][filed a defence] on the (date).]

4. That the (*party*) obtained judgment against the (*party*) in the Division of the High Court of Justice for [payment of the sum of £] (*or state any other remedy ordered*), together with the sum of £ for costs.
5. That [no] objection has been made to the jurisdiction of the Court [on the grounds that (*state grounds of objection*)].
6. That the judgment carries interest at the rate of per cent per annum calculated on the judgment debt and costs from the date of judgment until payment.
7. That the judgment has been served on the (*party*) (*name*) in accordance with the provisions of the Civil Procedure Rules 1998.
8. That [no application to set the judgment aside has been made] *or* [an application to set the judgment aside has been finally disposed of and dismissed].
9. That [no appeal against the judgment has been brought within the time prescribed] *or* [an application for permission to appeal against the judgment has been finally disposed of and permission refused] *or* [an appeal against the judgment has been finally disposed of and dismissed].
10. That enforcement of the judgment is not for the time being stayed or suspended, that the time available for its enforcement has not expired and that the judgment is accordingly enforceable.
11. This certificate is issued under [section 12 of the Civil Jurisdiction and Judgments Act 1982]

Dated

(Signed)
A [Master of the Supreme Court] [District Judge of the High Court] of England and Wales.

PF 23
Notice by Enforcement Officer of claim to goods taken in execution

IN THE HIGH COURT OF JUSTICE
QUEEN'S BENCH DIVISION
High Court Claim No.
[County Court Claim No.]

[Sent from the [ ] County Court by Certificate dated (date)]

Claimant

Defendant

Take notice that (*name*) has claimed the goods specified in the attached schedule taken in execution by the Enforcement Officer of (*Name & Address*) authorised to enforce writs of execution from the High Court, under the warrant of execution issued in this claim.

You are hereby required to admit or dispute the title of (name) to those goods and give notice in writing to the Enforcement Officer within 7 days of receipt of this notice. If you do not do so the Enforcement Officer may make an interpleader application.

If you admit the title of (*name*) to the goods and give the required notice to the Enforcement Officer you will only be liable for any fees or expenses incurred prior to receipt of the notice admitting the claim.

Dated

(*Signed*)
To the execution creditor

((*Name & Address*) an Enforcement Officer authorised to enforce writs of execution issued from the High Court.)

PF 24
Notice by execution creditor of admission or dispute of title of Interpleader Claimant

IN THE HIGH COURT OF JUSTICE
QUEEN'S BENCH DIVISION
High Court Claim No.
[County Court Claim No.]

[Sent from the [ ] County Court by Certificate dated (dated)]

Claimant

Defendant

Take notice that I (*name*), the execution creditor, [admit][dispute] the title of (*name*), the interpleader claimant, to the goods (*set out goods*) seized by you under the execution issued under the judgment in this claim.

Dated

(*Signed*) (Execution Creditor or solicitor)

((Name & Address) an Enforcement Officer authorised to enforce writs of execution issued from the High Court.)

PF 25
Interpleader application

(A) Where there are no existing proceedings, the party seeking interpleader relief must use the Part 8 claim form N208, (i) naming as Defendants in the title the persons making adverse claims to the subject-matter of the claim, and (ii) setting out the relief sought in the Details of Claim section, e.g. as in 1 below.

1. that the defendants, being the persons making adverse claims to the subject-matter of the claim
   (a) state the nature and particulars of their respective claims to the debt, money, goods or chattels [the subject-matter of this claim][the subject-matter in dispute],
   (b) take such steps in the proceedings as the Court shall direct,
   (c) either pursue or give up their respective claims, and
   (d) abide by any order the court may make.

(B) Where there are existing proceedings, form PF 244/N244 should be used, including in Part A the names of the persons making adverse claims to the subject-matter of the claim, and seeking an order, e.g. as set out in 1, 2 and 3 below.

1. (*Where the person making adverse claims is not already a party*) that (*name*) be added as defendant to the claim.
2. that [the defendant][the claimant][(*name*)], being the person(s) making adverse claims to the subject-matter of the claim
   (a) state the nature and particulars of their respective claims to the debt, money, goods or chattels [the subject-matter of this claim][the subject-matter in dispute],
   (b) take such steps in the proceedings as the Court shall direct,
   (c) either pursue or give up their respective claims, and
   (d) abide by any order the court may make.
3. (*such further directions, including any order for a stay, as may be appropriate*).

PF 26
Interpleader application by an Enforcement Officer

Form PF 244/N244 should be used, adapting the form to show the Interpleader Claimant in the title after the Claimant and Defendant, and including in Part A the following:

".......for an order that:

1. the execution creditor and the interpleader claimant
   (a) state the nature and particulars of their respective cases and claims in relation to the debt, money, goods, or chattels seized or intended to be seized by the sheriff under the writ of fieri facias issued in the claim,
   (b) take such steps in the proceedings as the Court shall direct,
   (c) either pursue or give up their respective claims, and
   (d) abide by any order the court may make.
2. (*such further directions, including any order for a stay, as may be appropriate*)."

The PF 244/N244 should also contain the following notice:

"To the Interpleader Claimant:

Take notice that within 14 days of service of this application notice you are required to

(i) file a witness statement or affidavit specifying any money and describing any goods and chattels claimed and setting out the grounds on which your claim is based, and
(ii) serve copies of the witness statement or affidavit on the execution creditor and the sheriff."

PF 27
Evidence in support of Interpleader application (Schedule 1 – RSC O.17 r.3(4))

IN THE HIGH COURT OF JUSTICE
QUEEN'S BENCH DIVISION
Claim No.

Claimant

Defendant

I, (*name,address and description*) state [on oath] that:

(*the following text may also be set out in Part C of form PF 244/N244*)

1. The claim form was issued in the above proceedings on (*date*) and was served on me on (*date*).
2. The claim is brought to recover (*describe money/goods the subject of the claim*). The (*money/goods etc.*) is/are in my possession but I claim no interest in it/them [other than for charges or costs (*specify*)].
3. The right to the subject-matter of this claim has been and is claimed by (*party*).
4. I do not in any manner collude with (*party*) or with the claimant, but I am ready and willing to pay the money into court or to transfer or deal with the (*money/goods etc.*) or otherwise dispose of them as the court may direct.

I believe that the facts stated in this witness statement are true.

Signed: Name:

Dated

[SWORN etc]

Interpleader order (1) – Claim barred where an Enforcement Officer interpleads
Before (*Master or District Judge*)

In the High Court Of Justice
[ ] Division
[ ] District Registry
Claim No

Claimant

Defendant

Interpleader Claimant

Seal

An Application was made by [application notice/letter] dated (*date*) or by [Counsel] [solicitor] for (*party*) and was attended by ( )

The Master [District Judge] read the written evidence filed

IT IS ORDERED that:

1. the claim of the interpleader claimant be barred and that no claim be brought against the Enforcement Officer.
2. the interpleader claimant pay the execution creditor

   (i) his costs of the interpleader proceedings [summarily assessed in the sum of £] [to be the subject of a detailed assessment] and

   (ii) the costs the execution creditor is liable to pay the Enforcement Officer.
3. the execution creditor pay the Enforcement Officer his costs and charges of the interpleader proceedings including those of this application and his possession money caused by the claim of the interpleader claimant [summarily assessed in the sum of £] [to be the subject of a detailed assessment].

   Dated

Interpleader order (1a) – Enforcement Officer to withdraw

Before (*Master or District Judge*)

In the High Court Of Justice
[ ] Division
[ ] District Registry
Claim No

Claimant

Defendant

Interpleader Claimant

Seal

An Application was made by [application notice/letter] dated (*date*) or by [Counsel][solicitor] for (*party*) and was attended by ( )

The Master [District Judge] read the written evidence filed

IT IS ORDERED that:

1. the Enforcement Officer withdraw from possession of the goods seized by him under the writ of fieri facias issued in the claim and claimed by the interpleader claimant and that no claim be brought against him.

2. the execution creditor pay the Enforcement Officer his costs and charges of the interpleader proceedings and his possession money [summarily assessed in the sum of £][to be the subject of a detailed assessment].

Dated

PF 30
Interpleader order (2) – Interpleader claimant substituted as defendant (Schedule 1 – RSC O.17)

IN THE HIGH COURT OF JUSTICE
QUEEN'S BENCH DIVISION
Claim No.

Before (*Master/District Judge*) [sitting in Private]

Claimant

Defendant

Interpleader claimant

An Application was made by [application notice/letter] dated (*date*) *or* by [Counsel][solicitor] for (*party*) and was attended by (   )

The Master [District Judge] read the written evidence filed

IT IS ORDERED that:

1. the above-named interpleader claimant be substituted as defendant in this claim in place of the above-named defendant.
2. the costs this application are [summarily assessed in the sum of £   ] [to be the subject of a detailed assessment] and to be paid by (*party*).

   Dated

Interpleader order (3) – trial of issue

Before (*Master or District Judge*)

In the High Court Of Justice
[ ] Division
[ ] District Registry
Claim No

Claimant

Defendant

Interpleader Claimant

Seal

An Application was made by [application notice/letter] dated (*date*) or by [Counsel][solicitor] for (party) and was attended by ( )

The Master [District Judge] read the written evidence filed

IT IS ORDERED that:

1. [the Enforcement Officer proceed to sell the goods seized by him under the writ of fieri facias issued in the claim and claimed by the interpleader claimant and pay the net proceeds of the sale, after deducting the expenses of the sale, into the Court Funds Office, to remain there until further order.]

   or

   [the Enforcement Officer retain and preserve the goods seized by him under the writ of fieri facias issued in the claim and claimed by the interpleader claimant until the trial ordered in paragraph 2 below or further order on the following terms (*set out terms as to storage, maintenance and insurance etc. charges*).]
2. an issue be tried, namely, whether at the time of seizure by the Enforcement Officer the goods seized by him were the property of the interpleader claimant as against the execution creditor.
3. in the trial of the issue the interpleader claimant be the claimant and the execution creditor be the defendant.
4. (*directions as to the management and trial of the issue.*)
5. any questions as to costs, possession money or otherwise be dealt with at the trial of the issue and that no claim be brought against the Enforcement Officer in respect of the seizure of the goods.

   Dated

Interpleader order (4) – conditional order for the Enforcement Officer to withdraw and trial of issue

Before (*Master or District Judge*)

In the High Court Of Justice
[ ] Division
[ ] District Registry

Claim No

Claimant

Defendant

Interpleader Claimant

An Application was made by [application notice/letter] dated (*date*) *or* by [Counsel][solicitor] for (*party*) and was attended by ( )

The Master [District Judge] read the written evidence filed

Seal

IT IS ORDERED that:

1. [upon payment by the interpleader claimant of the sum of £ into the Court Funds Office by (*date*)]
   or
   [upon the interpleader claimant giving security to the satisfaction of the Master for payment of the sum of £ by (*date*)]
   and upon payment to the Enforcement Officer of the possession-money from the date of this order, the Enforcement Officer withdraw from possession of the goods seized by him under the writ of fieri facias issued in the claim and claimed by the interpleader claimant.
2. unless the above payment is made or security given within the time ordered, the Enforcement Officer proceed to sell the goods seized by him and pay the net proceeds of the sale, after deducting the expenses of the sale, and the possession money from the date of this order into the Court Funds Office, to remain there until further order.
3. an issue be tried, namely, whether at the time of seizure by the Enforcement Officer the goods seized by him were the property of the interpleader claimant as against the execution creditor.
4. in the trial of the issue the interpleader claimant be the claimant and the execution creditor be the defendant.
5. (*directions as to the management and trial of the issue.*)
6. any questions as to costs, possession money or otherwise be dealt with at the trial of the issue and that no claim be brought against the Enforcement Officer in respect of the seizure of the goods.

Interpleader order (6) – summary disposal

Before (*Master or District Judge*)

In the High Court Of Justice
[ ] Division
[ ] District Registry
Claim No
Claimant

Defendant
Interpleader Claimant

An Application was made by [application notice/letter] dated (*date*) *or* by [Counsel][solicitor] for (*party*) and was attended by ( )

The Master [District Judge] read the written evidence filed

And [1. the applicant being a Enforcement Officer authorised to enforce writs of execution issued from the High Court, and requesting that the merits of the interpleader claimant's claim be disposed of and decided in a summary manner] *or*
[2. the interpleader claimants consenting to the merits of the interpleader claimant's claim being disposed of and decided in a summary manner] *or*
[3. the interpleader claimant (*name*) requesting that the merits of the interpleader claimant's claim be disposed of and decided in a summary manner] *or*
[4. the question at issue between the interpleader claimants being a question of law]

And the Master [District Judge] having found (*as appropriate*)

IT IS ORDERED that:

1. the Enforcement Officer proceed to sell the goods and pay the proceeds of sale (less his expenses) to the execution creditor.
2. the interpleader claimant pay the execution creditor
   (i) his costs of the interpleader proceedings [summarily assessed in the sum of £] [to be the subject of a detailed assessment] and
   (ii) the costs the execution creditor is liable to pay the Enforcement Officer.
3. the execution creditor pay the Enforcement Officer his costs and charges of the interpleader proceedings including those of this application and his possession money caused by the claim of the interpleader claimant [summarily assessed in the sum of £][to be the subject of a detailed assessment].

   or

   the Enforcement Officer withdraw from possession of the goods and that no claim be brought against him.
2. the execution creditor pay the Enforcement Officer his costs and charges of the interpleader proceedings and his possession money [summarily assessed in the sum of £][to be the subject of a detailed assessment].

or

1. (*the Enforcement Officer not being involved*) the claim of (*party*) be dismissed and that (*party*) pay the costs of (*party/parties*) [summarily assessed in the sum of £] [to be the subject of a detailed assessment].

Dated

PF 86
Praecipe for writ of fieri facias
(Schedule 1 – RSC O.45 r.12(1) and O.46 r.6)

IN THE HIGH COURT OF JUSTICE
[QUEEN'S BENCH] DIVISION
High Court Claim No.
[County Court Claim No.]

[Sent from the [ ] County Court by Certificate dated (*date*)]
Claimant
Defendant

Seal a writ of fieri facias directed to the sheriff of (*County*) against the (*party*) (*name and address*) on a judgment [*or* order] dated (*date*) for the sum of £ debt and £ costs and interest.

Endorsed to levy £ and interest at (*insert rate*) per annum from (*date*) and costs of execution.

Signed

Dated

PF 87
Praecipe for writ of sequestration
(Schedule 1 – RSC O.45 r.12(4) and O.46 r.6)

IN THE HIGH COURT OF JUSTICE
[QUEEN'S BENCH] DIVISION
Claim No.

Claimant

Defendant

Seal a writ of sequestration against (*name and address of party*) directed to (*names of Commissioners*).

Permission to issue writ of sequestration given by (*title and name of Judge*) on (*date*).

Signed

Dated

PF 88
Praecipe for writ of possession
(Schedule 1 – RSC O.45 r.12(3), O.46 r.6 and O.113 r.7)

IN THE HIGH COURT OF JUSTICE
[QUEEN'S BENCH] DIVISION
Claim No.

Claimant

Defendant

Seal a writ of possession directed to the sheriff of (*County*) to give possession to the (*party*) (*name*) of the land described as (*specify*) in the judgment or order dated (*date*).

Signed

Dated

PF 89
Praecipe for writ of possession and fieri facias combined
(Schedule 1 – RSC O.45 r.12 and O.46 r.6)

IN THE HIGH COURT OF JUSTICE
[QUEEN'S BENCH] DIVISION
High Court Claim No.
[County Court Claim No.]

[Sent from the [ ] County Court by Certificate dated (*date*)]

Claimant

Defendant

Seal a writ of possession and fieri facias directed to the sheriff of (*County*) to give possession to the (*party*) (*name*) of the land described as (*specify*) in the judgment referred to below and also to levy against the (*party*) (*name and address*) for the sum of £ debt and £ costs and interest at (*insert rate*) per annum from (*date*) [*if part paid* endorsed to levy £ and interest at (*insert rate*) per annum from (*date*)].

Judgment dated (*date*).

Costs Officer's Certificate dated (*date*).

Signed

Dated

PF 90
Praecipe for writ of delivery
(Schedule 1 – RSC O.45 r.12(2) and O.46 r.6)

IN THE HIGH COURT OF JUSTICE
[QUEEN'S BENCH] DIVISION
Claim No.

Claimant

Defendant

Seal a writ of delivery directed to the sheriff of (*County*) to make delivery to the (*party*) (*name*) of the goods specified in the judgment dated (*date*).

Signed

Dated

PF 97

Order for sale by an Enforcement Officer by private contract

Before (*Master or District Judge*)

In the High Court Of Justice
[ ] Division
[ ] District Registry

Claim No

Claimant

Defendant

Seal

An Application was made by [application notice/letter] dated (*date*) *or* by [Counsel][solicitor] for (*party*) and was attended by ( )

The Master [District Judge] read the written evidence filed

IT IS ORDERED that:

1. (*insert name & address*) an Enforcement Officer authorised to enforce writs of execution from the High Court, has permission to sell the goods and chattels seized by him under the writ of [fieri facias/poss/delivery] in these proceedings by private contract.
2. the Enforcement Officer's costs of this application [summarily assessed in the sum of £] [to be the subject of a detailed assessment] be added to his execution charges.

PF 102
Bench warrant (Schedule 1 – RSC O.52)

To: The Tipstaff attending on Her Majesty's Supreme Court, his deputy or assistants, and all police constables and other peace officers whom it may concern.

IN THE HIGH COURT OF JUSTICE
[ ] DIVISION
[ ]
Claim No.

Claimant

Defendant

IT APPEARING to the satisfaction of The Honourable Mr Justice (*name*) one of the Justices of the (*name of Division*) Division of Her Majesty's High Court of Justice that (*name of contemnor*) has committed a breach of the Order dated (*date*) and is accordingly in contempt of Court.

THIS WARRANT COMMANDS you and every one of you in Her Majesty's name to apprehend (*name of contemnor*) and bring [him] before me or another of the Justices of the (*name of Division*) Division of Her Majesty's High Court of Justice at (*time*) on (*date*) or as soon as possible thereafter at the High Court in [London] to be dealt with according to law [and if you apprehend the contemnor after 4.00pm [he] shall be held in custody until such time as the Court shall next sit].

Dated

A JUSTICE OF THE HIGH COURT

PF 103

Warrant of committal (general) (Schedule 1 - RSC O.52)

To: The Tipstaff attending on Her Majesty's Supreme Court, his deputy or assistants, and all police constables and other peace officers whom it may concern.

IN THE HIGH COURT OF JUSTICE
[ ] DIVISION
[ ] District Registry

Claim No.

Claimant

Defendant

BY THE ORDER OF THIS COURT given this day it was Ordered that (*name of contemnor*) stands committed to Her Majesty's Prison (*name of prison*) for [his] contempt as set out in the Order.

THIS WARRANT COMMANDS you and every one of you in Her Majesty's name to apprehend (*name of contemnor*) and convey [him] safely to Her Majesty's Prison (*name of prison*) to be detained there and kept in safe custody for a period of (*specify period*) from the date of his apprehension.

Dated

A JUSTICE OF THE HIGH COURT

PF 104
Warrant of committal (contempt in face of court)
(Schedule 1 – RSC O.52)

To: The Tipstaff attending on Her Majesty's Supreme Court, his deputy or assistants, and all police constables and other peace officers whom it may concern.

IN THE HIGH COURT OF JUSTICE
[ ] DIVISION
[ ] District Registry
Claim No.

Claimant

Defendant

A CONTEMPT IN THE FACE OF THE COURT having been committed by (*name*)

NOW BY THE ORDER OF THIS COURT given this day (*name of contemnor*) stands committed to Her Majesty's Prison (*name of prison*) for [his] contempt.

THIS WARRANT COMMANDS you and every one of you in Her Majesty's name to apprehend (*name of contemnor*) and convey [him] safely to Her Majesty's Prison (*name of prison*) to be detained there and kept in safe custody for a period of (*specify period*) from the date of his apprehension.

Dated

A JUSTICE OF THE HIGH COURT

PF 105
Warrant of committal (failure of witness to attend)
(Schedule 1 – RSC O.52)

***To:** The Tipstaff attending on Her Majesty's Supreme Court, his deputy or assistants, and all police constables and other peace officers whom it may concern.*

IN THE HIGH COURT OF JUSTICE
[ ] DIVISION
[ ] District Registry
Claim No.

Claimant

Defendant

A WITNESS SUMMONS having been issued in this Claim for the attendance of (*name and address*) as a Witness.

AND (*name of witness*) having failed personally to appear before me The Honourable Mr Justice (*name*) one of the Justices of the (*name of Division*) Division of Her Majesty's High Court of Justice on the trial of the Claim, under the Witness Summons served on [him].

THIS WARRANT COMMANDS you and every one of you in Her Majesty's name to apprehend (*name of witness*) and bring [him] before me or another of the Justices of the (*name of Division*) Division of Her Majesty's High Court of Justice at (*time*) on (*date*) or as soon as possible thereafter at the High Court in [London] to be dealt with according to law [and if you apprehend the contemnor after 4.00pm [he] shall be held in custody until such time as the Court shall next sit].

Dated

A JUSTICE OF THE HIGH COURT

PF 106
Warrant of committal (of prisoner) (Schedule 1 – RSC O.52)

To:** **The Governor of Her Majesty's Prison (name) or his deputy and to the Tipstaff attending on Her Majesty's Supreme Court, his deputy or assistants, and all police constables and other peace officers whom it may concern.

IN THE HIGH COURT OF JUSTICE
[ ] DIVISION
[ ] District Registry
Claim No.

Claimant

Defendant

BY THE ORDER OF THIS COURT given this day it was Ordered that (*name of contemnor*) stands committed to Her Majesty's Prison (*name of prison*) for [his] contempt as set out in the Order.

AND (*name of contemnor*) is at present a prisoner in the custody of the Governor of Her Majesty's Prison (*name of prison*).

THIS WARRANT COMMANDS you and every one of you in Her Majesty's name to detain (*name of contemnor*) and keep [him] in safe custody at Her Majesty's Prison (*name of prison*) for a period of (*specify period*) from the completion of the sentence [he] is at present detained for.

Dated

A JUSTICE OF THE HIGH COURT

PF 141
Witness Statement/Affidavit of Personal Service of Judgment or Order (Schedule 1 – RSC O.45, r.7)

IN THE HIGH COURT OF JUSTICE
[ ] DIVISION
[ ] District Registry
Claim No.

Claimant

Defendant

I, (*name, address and description*) state [on oath]:

1. That I did on (*date*) at (*address*) personally serve the above defendant (*or as appropriate*) with a sealed copy of the [order][judgment] dated (*date*) in these proceedings, [which I refer to] [shown to me] marked ["A"] (*recite operative part of order or judgment*).
2. The copy of the [order][judgment] I served had endorsed on it on the front page the following words; "If you, the within-named (*name*), do not comply with this order you may be held to be in contempt of court and imprisoned or fined, or [in the case of a company or corporation] your assets may be seized".

I believe that the facts stated in this witness statement are true.

Signed Name

Dated

[Sworn, etc.]

PF 177
Order for written statement as to partners in firm (Schedule 1 – RSC O.81 r.2(1))

IN THE HIGH COURT OF JUSTICE
[ ] DIVISION
[ ] District Registry
Claim No.

Before (*Master/District Judge*) [sitting in Private]

Claimant

Defendant

An Application was made by [application notice/letter] dated (*date*) *or* by [Counsel][solicitor] for (*party*) and was attended by ( )

The Master [District Judge] read the written evidence filed

IT IS ORDERED that:

1. the claimant[defendant] or his solicitor furnish the defendant[claimant] with a statement in writing, verified by [an affidavit] [a statement of truth], setting out the names and places of residence of all the persons who where partners in the claimant[defendant] firm on (*date*), being the date when the cause of action arose, in accordance with Schedule 1-RSC Order 81, rule 2.
2. the costs of this application are summarily assessed in the sum of £ to be paid by (*party*).

Dated

PF 179
Evidence on registration of a Bill of Sale
(Bills of Sale Act 1878, s.8; Schedule 1 – RSC O.95)

IN THE HIGH COURT OF JUSTICE
QUEEN'S BENCH DIVISION
No.

Applicant

Respondent

I (*name, address and description*) state [on oath] that:

1. The document(s) annexed hereto and marked "A" is a true copy of a bill of sale and of every schedule or inventory to it or referred to in it and of every attestation of its execution as made and given by (*name of grantor or assignor*) on (*date of execution*).
2. The bill of sale was made and given by (*name of grantor or assignor*) on (*date*).
3. I was present and saw (*name of grantor or assignor*) duly execute the bill of sale on (*date*).
4. (*Name of grantor or assignor*) resides at (*state address at time witness statement/affidavit signed or sworn*) and his occupation is (*describe*).
5. The name (*name of witness*) signed on the bill of sale as being the name of the witness attesting its due execution, is in my handwriting. (*Where there is more than one witness, adapt paragraph 5 accordingly, including the name, address and description of the other witness*).

I believe that the facts stated in this witness statement are true.

Signed: Name:

Dated

[SWORN etc]

Note:- If the grantor or assignor is a limited company substitute the following paragraphs for paragraphs 3 and 4 above:

3. I was present and saw the common seal of (*name of company*) affixed in the presence of (*name*) a director and (*name*) [a director][the secretary] of (*name of company*) to the bill of sale. The seal is the common seal of (*name of company*) and the bill of sale was sealed in accordance with the provisions of the memorandum and articles of association of (*name of company*).
4. (*name*) and (*name*) are director(s) [and secretary] of the company and the signatures are their signatures.
5. The registered office of the company is at (*address*).

Note:- Where an application to rectify the register or extend the time for registration is being made, the following paragraphs should be included:

[6]. I seek an order that:

the omission to register a [witness statement/affidavit of renewal of a] bill of sale be rectified by extending the date for registration to (*date*).

or

the [omission][mis-statement] of the [name][address][occupation] of (*name*) be rectified by the insertion in the register of the correct [name][address][occupation] of (*name*).

[7]. The reasons for the [omission][mis-statement] are (*describe*).

[8]. To the best of my knowledge, information and belief no prejudice will be caused to any person by reason of the extension of time for registration.

PF 180
Evidence on registration of an Absolute Bill of Sale, Settlement and Deed of Gift
(Schedule 1 – RSC O.95)

IN THE HIGH COURT OF JUSTICE
QUEEN'S BENCH DIVISION
No.

Applicant

Respondent

I (*name and address*), a Solicitor of the Supreme Court, state [on oath] that:

1. The document(s) annexed hereto and marked "A" is a true copy of (*state nature of document*) and of every schedule or inventory to it or referred to in it and of every attestation of its execution as made and given by (*name of witness*) on (*date*).
2. The (*document*) was made and given by (*name of grantor or assignor*) on (*date*).
3. (*Name of grantor or assignor*) duly executed the (*document*) in my presence on (*date*) and I duly attested its execution.
4. (*Name of grantor or assignor*) resides at (*state address at time witness statement/affidavit signed or sworn*) and his occupation is (*describe*).
5. The name (*name of witness*) signed on the (*document*) as being the name of the witness attesting its due execution, is in my handwriting.
6. Before the execution of the (*document*) by (*name of grantor or assignor*) I fully explained to him its nature and effect.

I believe that the facts stated in this witness statement are true.

Signed: Name:

Dated

[SWORN etc]

Note:- Where an application to rectify the register or extend the time for registration is being made, the following paragraphs should be included:

[7]. I seek an order that:

the omission to register a [witness statement [affidavit] of renewal of a] (*document*) be rectified by extending the date for registration to (*date*).

or

the [omission][mis-statement] of the [name][address][occupation] of (*name*) be rectified by the insertion in the register of the correct [name] [address][occupation] of (*name*).

[8]. The reasons for the [omission][mis-statement] are (*describe*).

[9]. To the best of my knowledge, information and belief no prejudice will be caused to any person by reason of the extension of time for registration.

PF 181
Evidence in support of an application for re-registration of a Bill of Sale
(Bills of Sale Act 1878, s.11; Schedule 1 – RSC O.95)

IN THE HIGH COURT OF JUSTICE
QUEEN'S BENCH DIVISION
No.

Applicant

Respondent

I (*name, address and description*) state [on oath] that:

1. A bill of sale dated (*date*) and made between (*names, addresses and descriptions of the parties to the original bill of sale*), the registration [*or* last renewed registration] of which was effected on (*date*), is still a subsisting security.

I believe that the facts stated in this witness statement are true.

Signed: Name:

Dated

[SWORN etc]

Note:- Where an application to extend the time for re-registration is being made, the following paragraphs should be included:

[2]. I seek an order that the omission to register a witness statement [affidavit] of renewal of the bill of sale be rectified by extending the date for registration to (*date*).

[3]. The reasons for the omission are (*describe*).

[4]. To the best of my knowledge, information and belief no prejudice will be caused to any person by reason of the extension of time for registration.

PF 182
Order for extension of time to register or re-register a Bill of Sale (Bills of Sale Act 1878, s.14; Schedule 1 – RSC O.95 r.1)

IN THE HIGH COURT OF JUSTICE
QUEEN'S BENCH DIVISION
No.

Before Master (*name*) [sitting in Private]

In the Matter of a Bill of Sale made between (*name the parties to the bill of sale*) on (*date*)

An Application dated (*date*) was made by [[Counsel][solicitor] for] the applicant

The Master read the written evidence filed

IT IS ORDERED that the time for registering [re-registering] the above bill of sale is extended to (*date*), but this order is without prejudice to the rights of parties acquired prior to the time when this bill of sale is actually registered [re-registered].

Dated

PF 183
Evidence for permission to enter Memorandum of Satisfaction on a Bill of Sale
(Bills of Sale Act 1878, s.15; Schedule 1 – RSC O.95 r.2 and Practice Direction - Bills of Sale para. 1)

IN THE HIGH COURT OF JUSTICE
QUEEN'S BENCH DIVISION
No.

Applicant

Respondent

I (*name, address and description*) state [on oath] that:

1. On (*date*) I was present and saw (*name*) of (*address*) sign the annexed consent, marked "A", to an order that a memorandum of satisfaction be written on the registered copy of a bill of sale dated (*date*) and made between (*names and addresses of parties*).
2. I am informed by (*name*) and believe that the debt, interest and costs due under the bill of sale have been satisfied or discharged.
3. The signature on the consent is in the handwriting of (*name*) who is the grantee or assignee of the bill of sale. (*Where the grantee or assignee is a company, see the Note following the Annexed Consent*).
4. The name (*name of witness*) signed on the consent as being the witness to the signature of (*name*) is in my handwriting.
5. I seek an order that a memorandum of satisfaction be written on the registered copy of the bill of sale.

I believe that the facts stated in this witness statement are true.

Signed: Name:

Dated

[SWORN etc]

Annex

CONSENT

"A"

I CONSENT to a memorandum of satisfaction being written on the registered copy of the bill of sale for securing the sum of £ dated (*date*) made between (*names and addresses of parties*) and registered on (*date*), the debt for which the bill of sale was given as security having been satisfied.

Dated

Signed

Grantee or Assignee Signed

Signed

A solicitor of the Supreme Court

Note:- *Where the party giving consent is a limited company, the following paragraphs 1-4 should be substituted for paragraphs 1-3 above, re-numbering paragraphs 4-5 above:*

1. On (*date*) I was present and saw the common seal of (*name of company*) affixed in the presence of (*name*) a director and (*name*) [a director] [the secretary] to the annexed consent, marked A, to an order that a memorandum of satisfaction be written on the registered copy of a bill of sale dated (*date*) and made between (*names and addresses of parties*).
2. I am informed by (*name and position in the grantee or assignee company*) and believe that the debt, interest and costs due under the bill of sale have been satisfied or discharged.
3. The seal is the common seal of (*name of company*) which is the [grantee] [assignee] of the bill of sale and the consent was sealed in accordance with the provisions of the memorandum and articles of association of (*name of company*).
4. (*Name*) and (*name*) are director(s) [and secretary] of the company and the signatures are their signatures.

Annex

CONSENT

"A"

WE CONSENT to a memorandum of satisfaction being written on the registered copy of the bill of sale for securing the sum of £ dated (*date*) made between (*names and addresses of parties*) and registered on (*date*), the debt for which the bill of sale was given as security having been satisfied.

The common seal of (*name of company*) was affixed to this consent in the presence of (*names*).

Dated

Signed

Director

Signed

[Director][Secretary]

Signed

Witness

A solicitor of the Supreme Court

PF 184
Claim form for entry of satisfaction on a registered Bill of Sale (Bills of Sale Act 1878, s.15; Schedule 1 – RSC O.95 r.2; Bills of Sale PD para. 3)

Parties should use the Part 8 Claim Form N208 and the following information should be included in the "Details of claim" section of the claim form:

"A Bill of Sale was made between (*names and addresses of parties*) on (*date*) to secure the sum of £ . The debt for which the bill of sale was given as security has been satisfied. [The [grantee] [assignee] has [failed] [refused] to consent to an order in these terms] *or* [I have been unable to obtain the consent of the [grantee] [assignee]] [*or as may be*] and I seek an order that a memorandum of satisfaction be entered on the bill of sale."

PF 185
Order for entry of Satisfaction on a registered Bill of Sale (Bills of Sale Act 1878, s.14; Schedule 1 – RSC O.95 r.2)

IN THE HIGH COURT OF JUSTICE
QUEEN'S BENCH DIVISION
Claim No.

Before Master (name) [sitting in Private]

Claimant

Defendant

In the Matter of a Bill of Sale made between (*names of parties*) and dated (*date*).

A Claim form was issued on (*date*) and the claim was dealt with by the Master [at] [without] a hearing.

The Master read the written evidence filed.

IT IS ORDERED that a memorandum of satisfaction be written on the registered copy of the bill of sale.

Dated

PF 186 QB
Evidence on registration of Assignment of Book Debts (s. 344 Insolvency Act 1986; Schedule 1 – RSC O.95 r.6(2))

IN THE HIGH COURT OF JUSTICE
QUEEN'S BENCH DIVISION
No.

Applicant

Respondent

I (*name and address*), a Solicitor of the Supreme Court, state [on oath] that:

1. The document annexed hereto and marked "A" is a true copy of an assignment (*give short description of nature and extent of book debts assigned*) and of every schedule to it or referred to in it and of every attestation of its execution.
2. The assignment was executed on (*date and time*) by (*name of assignor*) ("the Assignor") in my presence and I saw the Assignor execute the assignment.
3. The Assignor resides at (*address*) and his occupation is (*describe*).
4. The name (*name of witness*) and signature on the assignment as being the name of the witness attesting its due execution, is in my handwriting.
5. Before the Assignor executed the assignment I explained to him its full nature and effect.

I believe that the facts stated in this witness statement are true.

Signed: Name:

Dated

[SWORN etc]

PF 187
Application for Solicitor's Charging Order (s. 73 Solicitors Act 1974; Schedule 1 – RSC O.106 r.2)

Parties should use the Part 8 Claim Form N208 and include in the "Details of claim" section the following:

"......for an order declaring that:

1. the applicant is entitled to a charge upon (*specify the nature and amount of the recovered or preserved property sought to be charged*) in respect of his costs, charges and expenses of this claim."

PF 188
Charging order: solicitor's costs
(s. 73 Solicitors Act 1974; Schedule 1 – RSC O.106 r.2)

IN THE HIGH COURT OF JUSTICE
[ ] DIVISION
[ ] District Registry
Claim No.

Before (Master/District Judge) [sitting in Private]

Claimant

Defendant

A Claim Form was issued on (*date*).

The Claim was dealt with at a hearing and was attended by [Counsel] [solicitor] for (*parties*)

The Master [District Judge] read the written evidence filed

IT IS ORDERED AND DECLARED that:

1. the property (*specify property recovered or preserved*) be charged in favour of the claimant (*name*) in respect of his costs, charges and expenses of this claim.
2. the costs of the claim be the subject of a detailed assessment and that after assessment the property (*describe*) be sold or sufficient of its value realised to satisfy the claimant's bill as assessed (*or as the court thinks fit*).

Dated

PF 6CH

Certificate of Application for Permission to Issue Execution on Suspended Order for Possession where defendant is in Default of Acknowledgment of service

IN THE HIGH COURT OF JUSTICE
CHANCERY DIVISION
Claim No.

Before Master

Claimant*

Defendant*

An Application by notice dated ( ) was made on (date) by the [claimant] [defendant].

The Master heard [counsel] [solicitor] for [party]

[**The Master** read (documents)]

I certify that on the day of a copy of the application herein dated , together with a copy of the witness statement/affidavit was sent by first class prepaid letter post addressed to the defendant at the defendant's last known address being [insert address]

NOTE: This Certificate is to be endorsed on the affidavit or witness statement in support of the application for leave to issue execution.

---

* Where there is more than one claimant/defendant, the parties should be described as follows:

(1) AB

(2) CD

(3) EF Claimants

and

(1) GH

(2) IJ

(3) KL Defendants

PF 7CH
Form of Inquiry for Persons Entitled to the Property of an Intestate

IN THE HIGH COURT OF JUSTICE
CHANCERY DIVISION
Claim No.

Before (*Master*)

In the Estate of (*Please see new Practice Direction*)

Claimant*

Defendant*

An Application by notice dated ( ) was made on (date) by the [claimant] [defendant].

The Master heard [counsel] [solicitor] for [party]

[**The Master** read (documents)]

IT IS ORDERED

That an inquiry be made who on the death of [A.B.] on the day of became beneficially entitled, either absolutely or contingently, to any property of [A.B.] as to which [A.B.] died intestate, and for what estates and interests and in what shares and proportions, and, if any such persons are since dead, when they died, and, if any persons died having attained an absolute vested interest, who are their personal representatives.

---

* Where there is more than one claimant/defendant, the parties should be described as follows:

(1) AB

(2) CD

(3) EF Claimants

and

(1) GH

(2) IJ

(3) KL Defendants

PF 8CH
Application Notice after Master's Findings on Kin Inquiry (Benjamin order)[1] giving permission to distribute estate upon footing(s)

IN THE HIGH COURT OF JUSTICE
CHANCERY DIVISION
Claim No.

Before (**Master**)

IN THE ESTATE OF

Claimant*

Defendant

An Application by notice dated (   ) was made on (date) by the [claimant] [defendant].

The Master heard [counsel] [solicitor] for [party]

[**The Master** read (documents)]

IT IS ORDERED

(1) That the claimant may distribute the estate of X.Y. deceased upon the footing that Y.Y. (a child of X.Y) predeceased him without leaving issue (or upon the footings set out in the Master's order dated   ).

(2) That the costs of the claimant [trustees] be paid on the indemnity basis and on the standard basis of the defendants and of the parties attending be assessed [from the foot of the taxation directed by the order dated   ] and be [retained and] paid out of the estate of the intestate X.Y.

---

1 See Re Benjamin, Neville v. Benjamin [1902] 1 Ch.723 at 726.

* Where there is more than one claimant/defendant, the parties should be described as follows:

(1) AB

(2) CD

(3) EF Claimant

and

(1) GH

(2) IJ

(3) KL Defendants

PF 9CH
Order giving Permission to Distribute Estate upon Footing (Re Benjamin)[1]

IN THE HIGH COURT OF JUSTICE
CHANCERY DIVISION
Claim No.

Before (Master)

Claimant*

Defendant*

IN THE ESTATE OF

An Application by notice dated ( ) was made on (date) by the [claimant] [defendant].

The Master heard [counsel] [solicitor] for [party]

[**The Master** read (documents)]

It appearing by the Master's order that [A.B. named in the order dated was last heard of on and that he/she was not married at that date and in the absence of any evidence that A.B. survived and X.Y. (who died on) or was married].

IT IS ORDERED that the claimants have permission to distribute the estate of the said X.Y. deceased on the footing [of the said L.Y. having died in the said X.Y's lifetime without having been married].

---

1. See Benjamin, Neville v. Benjamin [1902] 1 Ch 723 at 726.

* Where there is more than one claimant/defendant, the parties should be described as follows:

(1) AB

(2) CD

(3) EF Claimants

and

(1) GH

(2) IJ

(3) KL Defendants

PF 10CH
Judgment in Beneficiaries' Administration Action

IN THE HIGH COURT OF JUSTICE
CHANCERY DIVISION
Claim No.

Before (*Master*)

Claimant*

Defendant*

IN THE ESTATE OF

An Application by notice dated ( ) was made on (date) by the [claimant] [defendant].

The Master heard [counsel] [solicitor] for [party]

[**The Master** read (documents)]

IT IS ORDERED

(1) That the trusts of the will of the [ ] the testator be performed and carried into execution.

[Insert such of the following directions as are appropriate in the particular case]

(2) That the following accounts and inquiries be taken and made:

1. An account of the property not specifically devised or bequeathed by the testator coming into the hand of the defendant, the executor of the will of the testator, or into the hands of any other person by the order or for the use of the defendant [*add if necessary*] distinguishing between capital and income.

2. An account of the testator's debts and funeral and testamentary expenses, (or *where the deceased died more than six years before judgment*, an inquiry whether there is any debt or funeral or testamentary expense of the testator remaining unpaid).

3. An account of legacies and annuities.

4. An inquiry into what parts if any of the testator's property are outstanding or undisposed of, and whether any part of such property is subject to any and what incumbrances.

(3) That the testator's property not specifically devised or bequeathed be applied in payment of the testator's debts and funeral and testamentary expenses, and afterwards in payment of the legacies and annuities given by his will in a due course of administration.

[Adjourn for further consideration by the Court]

[Permission to apply for further consideration by the Court]

Note: *Paragraph (3) may require alteration where the property specifically devised or bequeathed has to be resorted to for debts, though the estate is solvent.*

* Where there is more than one claimant/defendant, the parties should be described as follows:

(1) AB

(2) CD

(3) EF Claimants

and

(1) GH

(2) IJ

(3) KL Defendants

PF 11CH
Judgment in Creditors' Administration Action

IN THE HIGH COURT OF JUSTICE
CHANCERY DIVISION
Claim No.

Before (*Master*)

Claimant*

Defendant*

An Application by notice dated (   ) was made on (date) by the [claimant] [defendant].

The Master heard [counsel] [solicitor] for [party]

[**The Master** read (documents)]

IT IS ORDERED

(1) That the trusts of the will of [   ] the testator be performed and carried into execution.

(2) That following accounts and inquiries be taken and made:

1. an account of what is due to the claimant and all other creditors of the testator
2. an account of the testator's funeral expenses
3. an account of the property of the testator's coming into the hands of the defendant, [the executor of his/her will] [into the hands of any person or persons by the order] for the use of the defendant
4. an inquiry into what parts if any of the testator's property are outstanding or undisposed of, and as to any part of such property as is outstanding or undisposed of, whether the same is subject to any and what incumbrance

[5. An account of what is due to such of the incumbrancers, if any, as consent to the sale below directed in respect of their incumbrances.

6. An inquiry as to the priorities of such last mentioned incumbrancers].

And it is ordered that the testator's property be applied in payment of the testator's debts and funeral expenses in a due course of administration.

[**And it is also ordered that** the testator's estate be sold subject to the directions of the Court free from the incumbrances, if any, of such incumbrancers as consent to a sale and subject to the incumbrances of such of them as do not consent.

And it is ordered that the money from the sale of the testator's estate be paid into Court to the credit of this action subject to further order and if such money or any part thereof arises from real estate sold with the consent of incumbrancers, the money so arising is to be applied in the first place in payment of what appears due to such incumbrancers, according to their priorities].

[Adjourn further consideration by the Court]

[Liberty to apply for further consideration by the Court]

Note: *It may be desirable in some cases to add an inquiry as to preferential debts. The portions in square brackets are to be included where by reason of the estate being insolvent or otherwise a sale is necessary.*

---

* Where there is more than one claimant/defendant, the parties should be described as follows:

(1) AB

(2) CD

(3) EF Claimants

and

(1) GH

(2) IJ

(3) KL Defendants

Judgment for Claimant in action of Forfeiture for Non-payment of Rent

In the	
County Court	
Claim No.	
Claimant's Ref.	
Defendant's Ref.	

Claimant

Defendant(s)

seal

To the defendant(s)

1 The court has decided that you should give the claimant possession of

because you have not paid the rent due under the terms of your lease.

2 You must also pay to the claimant £ for unpaid rent, £ for use and occupation of the property and

(1) delete if not applicable

(a) (1) £ for the claimant's costs in making the application for possession.

(b) (1) the claimant's costs to be assessed* on scale

* *If the claimant's costs are to be assessed, that is looked at by a judge to decide if they are reasonable, you will have to pay those costs within 14 days of assessment. You will be sent a copy of the claimant's bill and will be able to object to any amounts in it. The judge will decide if your objections are valid.*

3 You must pay:
(a) the total sum of £ to the claimant on or before
(b) the total sum of £ to the claimant by instalments of £ , the first instalment to be paid to the claimant on or before

4 **If you pay** the unpaid rent and costs as set out in paragraph 3, **the existing lease will continue** and the claimant will no longer be entitled to possession of the property under this order. **If you do not pay** the amounts owing, the claimant **can take steps to evict you and your goods may be sold** or other enforcement proceedings taken to obtain payment. This is called enforcing the order and money judgment.

5 Payments should be made to the claimant at the place where you would normally pay your rent. If you need more information about making payments you should contact the claimant. The court cannot accept any payments.

Date

Claimant's/Defendants address

Note

If you do not pay the money owed when it is due and the claimant takes steps to enforce payment, the order will be registered in the Register of County Court Judgments. **This may make it difficult for you to get credit.** Further information about registration is available in a leaflet which you can get from any county court office.

The court office at

is open between 10 am and 4 pm Monday to Friday. Address all communications to the Court Manager quoting the claim number

N27 Judgment for claimant in action of forfeiture for non-payment of rent

Variation Order

Claimant

In the		Court
Claim No.		
Claimant's Ref.		

Seal

On the application of the defendant/claimant

The judgment (or order) made against the defendant in this court

(1) or as the case may be

( )[1]

on the

for payment of £ and £ for costs is hereby varied

(2) Where judgment was entered for £5,000 or more, or was in respect of a debt which attracts contractual or statutory interest for late payment, the claimant may be entitled to further interest.

(enter name of judge) has now ordered that the defendant pay the claimant the outstanding sum, including any interest,[2]

(of £ [3]) (by instalments of £ for every calendar month,

the first payment to reach the claimant) by

(3) delete where balance is not known to the court

Dated

—— Take Notice ——

To the defendant

If you do not pay in accordance with this order your goods may be removed and sold or other enforcement proceedings may be taken against you. If your circumstances change and you cannot pay, ask at the court office about what you can do.

—— Address for Payment ——

—— How to Pay ——

- **PAYMENT(S) MUST BE MADE to the person named at the address for payment quoting their reference and the claim number.**
- **DO NOT bring or send payments to the court. THEY WILL NOT BE ACCEPTED.**
- You should allow at least 4 days for your payment to reach the applicant or his representative.
- Make sure that you keep records and can account for all payments made. Proof may be required if there is any disagreement. It is not safe to send cash unless you use registered post.
- A leaflet giving further advice about payment can be obtained from the court.
- If you need more information you should contact the applicant or his representative.

The court office at

is open between 10 am and 4 pm Monday to Friday. When corresponding with the court, please address letters to the Court Manager and quote the claim number.

N35 Variation order

Variation Order (determination)

Claimant

Defendant

In the	
County Court	
Claim No.	
Claimant's Ref.	

Seal

On the application of the defendant / claimant and the court having considered the papers received from the parties, the judgment (or order) made against the defendant in this court ( )[1] on the for payment of £ and £ for costs is hereby varied

(1) or as the case may be

It is now ordered that
the defendant pay the claimant the outstanding sum, including any interest, [2] (of £ [3])(by instalments of £ for every calendar month, the first payment to reach the claimant by

(2) Where judgment was entered for £5,000 or more, or was in respect of a debt which attracts contractual or statutory interest for late payment, the claimant may be entitled to further interest.

(3) delete where balance is not known to the court

Dated

Take Notice

If you (either the claimant or the defendant) object to the payment rate fixed by the court, you must write to the court with your reasons. You have 16 days from the date of the postmark to do this. A hearing will be arranged and you will both be told when to come to court. If the order is not from the defendant's local court, it will be automatically transferred to that court for the hearing.

To the defendant

If you do not pay in accordance with this order your goods may be removed and sold or other enforcement proceedings may be taken against you. If your circumstances change and you cannot pay, ask at the court office about what you can do.

Address for Payment

How to Pay

- **PAYMENT(S) MUST BE MADE to the person named at the address for payment quoting their reference and the claim number.**
- **DO NOT bring or send payments to the court. THEY WILL NOT BE ACCEPTED.**
- You should allow at least 4 days for your payment to reach the applicant or his representative.
- Make sure that you keep records and can account for all payments made. Proof may be required if there is any disagreement. It is not safe to send cash unless you use registered post.
- A leaflet giving further advice about payment can be obtained from the court.
- If you need more information you should contact the applicant or his representative.

The court office at

is open between 10 am and 4 pm Monday to Friday. When corresponding with the court, please address forms or letters to the Court Manager and quote the claim number.

N35A Variation order (determination)

Order Suspending Warrant / Judgment

Claimant

Defendant

In the **County Court**	
Claim No.	
Warrant No.	
Local No.	
Claimant's Ref.	

Seal

On the application of

And the court being satisfied that the defendant is unable to pay and discharge the sum payable by him in this action (or the instalments due under the judgment or order in this action)

(enter name of Judge) **ordered that**

(1) delete as necessary
(2) state time
(3) delete where balance is not known to the court

The judgment or order be suspended (1)(2)
The warrant of execution issued in this action be suspended (1)
The warrant of committal issued in this action be suspended for (1)(2)
so long as the defendant do pay the claimant the outstanding sum (of £ (3))
(by instalments of £ for every calendar month, the first instalment) to reach the claimant by and further payments to reach the claimant by the day of each month

Or

(4) state terms including liability to re-arrest if so ordered

that the defendant be discharged from custody under the warrant of committal (4)

(The warrant has been returned to the County Court
and any further correspondence should be sent there, quoting the claim number (1))

Dated

Take Notice

To the defendant
If you do not pay in accordance with this order, the warrant may be reissued or other enforcement proceedings may be taken against you. If your circumstances change and you cannot pay, ask at the court office about what you can do.

Address for Payment

How to Pay

PAYMENT(S) MUST BE MADE to the person named at the address for payment quoting their reference and the claim number.
DO NOT bring or send payments to the court. THEY WILL NOT BE ACCEPTED.
You should allow at least 4 days for your payment to reach the applicant or his representative.
Make sure that you keep records and can account for all payments made. Proof may be required if there is any disagreement. It is not safe to send cash unless you use registered post.
A leaflet giving further advice about payment can be obtained from the court.
If you need more information you should contact the applicant or his representative.

The court office at

is open between 10 am and 4 pm Monday to Friday. When corresponding with the court, please address forms or letters to the Court Manager and quote the claim number.

N41 Order suspending judgment or order and/or warrant of execution/committal

Order Suspending Warrant (determination)

Claimant

Defendant

In the	
County Court	
Claim No.	
Warrant No.	
Local No.	
Claimant's Ref.	

seal

On the application of the defendant

And the court having considered the papers received from the parties and being satisfied that the defendant is unable to pay and discharge the sum payable by him in this action (or the instalments due under the judgment or order in this action)

It is ordered that

This warrant of execution and the judgment (or order) be suspended and not enforced so long as the defendant do pay the claimant the outstanding sum of £ (by instalments of £ for every calendar month, the first payment to reach the claimant) by and further payments to reach the claimant by the day of each month.

delete as necessary (The warrant will be returned to the County Court after 16 days. After that date any further correspondence should be sent there, quoting the claim number)

Dated

Take Notice

If you (either the claimant or defendant) object to the payment rate fixed by the court, you must write to the court with your reasons. You have 16 days from the date of the postmark to do this. A hearing will be arranged and both parties will be told when to come to court.

To the defendant
If you do not pay in accordance with this order the warrant may be reissued or other enforcement proceedings may be taken against you. If your circumstances change and you cannot pay, ask at the court office about what you can do.

Address for Payment

How to Pay

- **PAYMENT(S) MUST BE MADE to the person named at the address for payment quoting their reference and the claim number.**
- **DO NOT bring or send payments to the court. THEY WILL NOT BE ACCEPTED.**
- You should allow at least 4 days for your payment to reach the claimant or his representative.
- Make sure that you keep records and can account for all payments made. Proof may be required if there is any disagreement. It is not safe to send cash unless you use registered post.
- A leaflet giving further advice about payment can be obtained from the court.
- If you need more information you should contact the claimant or his representative.

The court office at

is open between 10 am and 4 pm Monday to Friday. Address all communications to the Court Manager quoting the claim number

N41A Order suspending warrant (determination)

Warrant of Execution

In the County Court
Case no
Warrant no
Code
Date applied for at o'clock Local no

To the defendant
A judgment was made against you and as you have not paid the plaintiff has asked the court to issue a warrant. The warrant gives the bailiff the right to **take** and **sell your goods.**

Plaintiff

Defendant(s)
and address(es) to levy at

Plaintiff (solicitor)'s address

Ref no
Code no

Court Office address

Bailiff area no

Balance due	
Amount of warrant	
Fee	
Solicitor's costs	
Land Registry Fee	
Total	
Balance of debt after warrant paid	

The court office is open from 10 am to 4 pm Mondays to Fridays

Warrant of Execution

In the County Court
Case no
Warrant no
Code
Date applied for at o'clock Local no

To the district judge and the bailiff at
This warrant is sent to you for execution
Date sent Date received

Plaintiff

Defendant(s)
and address(es) to levy at

Plaintiff (solicitor)'s address

Ref no
Code no

Amounts received or passed through	
Date	Amount

N42 Warrant of execution (order 26, rule 1) (6.95)

Bailiff area no

Balance due	
Amount of warrant	
Fee	
Solicitor's costs	
Land Registry Fee	
Total	
Balance of debt after warrant paid	

To the bailiff

A judgment was made and is enforceable in this court. You are now required to levy for the total shown.

Date of levy	
First visit Give date and time	return code ☐
Second visit Give date and time	return code ☐
Third visit Give date and time	return code ☐
Fourth visit Give date and time	return code ☐
Fifth visit Give date and time	return code ☐

Any other comments

Walking possession agreement

(request **not** to remove goods)

Please do not take my goods listed here:

I agree that until payment is made or the warrant withdrawn, I will:

- not remove or damage the goods or allow anyone to do so
- show this form to anyone who calls and tries to take these goods and I will tell you that they called; and
- **allow you to re-enter the premises at any time (and as often as you want) to see the goods or to complete the enforcement of this warrant**

Signed　　　　　　　　Date

To the defendant

Notice of levy
The bailiff has levied on your goods. This means you must not dispose of them as the court may have to take them and sell them at public auction.

If you do not want the bailiff to remove your goods
You can ask the bailiff **not** to remove your goods but you should sign the walking possession agreement below.

If you pay the total money due
Your goods will not be taken and you will not have to pay any more costs.
You **must** pay the money to the bailiff or your local court (the address is shown on the front of this notice). When you pay any money you will be given a receipt.

If your goods are removed

- you will be given a list of the goods removed
- the goods will not be sold for at least 6 days (unless they are perishable)
- you will be given at least 4 days' notice of the date and place of the sale
- further fees may then be charged and will be added to the debt
- these fees could include the cost of removing your goods and the fees charged by the auctioneer

When the goods are sold
You will be given a detailed written account of the sale and distribution of the money.

If the sale is stopped
You will normally have to pay a fee and any expenses incurred in removing the goods or advertising the sale.

Walking pos session agreement

(request **not** to remove goods)

Please do not take my goods listed here:

I agree that until payment is made or the warrant withdrawn, I will:

- not remove or damage the goods or allow anyone to do so
- show this form to anyone who calls and tries to take these goods and I will tell you that they called; and
- **allow you to re-enter the premises at any time (and as often as you want) to see the goods or to complete the enforcement of this warrant**

Signed　　　　　　　　Date

If you have any questions about this warrant you should contact the court office

Returns other than payments **Date of levy** [19] [20]

Date	Time		Date	Time	

To the district judge and bailiff

The claimant obtained a judgment for return of the goods listed in the schedule overleaf. The goods have not been returned (or payment has not been made) as ordered and at the claimant's request this warrant has been issued. You are now required to seize the listed goods wherever they may be found within the district of the court and to deliver them to the claimant and you are further required to levy for the total amount shown overleaf.

Walking possession agreement

(request not to remove goods)

To the district judge and bailiff of the court
Please do not remove the goods seized (listed here)

Until payment is made or the warrant is withdrawn:

- ☐ I will not remove the goods or any part of them or allow any other person to do so without your permission;
- ☐ I will not damage the goods or any part of them or allow any other person to do so;
- ☐ I will show this form to any other person who may call with the intention of levying on the goods and tell you of their visit at once,

and I authorise you to re-enter the premises at any time (and as often as you want) to complete the enforcement of the warrant, or to inspect the goods

Signed **Dated**

In the

County Court

Warrant of Delivery

The court office is open from 10am to 4pm Mondays to Fridays

seal

To the defendant

The claimant obtained a judgment against you for recovery of goods listed here *(suspended on payment of the unpaid balance).

Schedule of goods

You have not returned the goods to the claimant or made payment as you were ordered to do and at the claimant's request this warrant has been issued.

You should now make all payments under the warrant to the bailiff or at the court named above, which is your local county court.

You should send any correspondence concerning this warrant, including claims to the goods, to the court at the address above.

Applies to orders for return of goods suspended on payment under CCA 1974. Delete if not applicable.

Case No.

Warrant number

Date applied for

at **o'clock**

CLAIMANT

Claimant (solicitor)'s address

Ref.

DEFENDANT(S)

Address(es) to levy at

Debt/damages and costs	
Fee	
Solicitor's costs	
Land Registry fee	
Total amount to be levied	

The bailiff should give a printed and numbered receipt from his official receipt book for every payment made to him under this warrant. You should not accept any other form of receipt.

For more information see over

Levy Notice ***(this does not apply to the goods listed overleaf)***

The bailiff has levied on your goods. This means you must not dispose of them as the court may have to seize and sell them at public auction to raise money to pay your debt. Certain goods will not be seized by the bailiff; these are (i) tools, books, vehicles and other items of equipment necessary for your personal use in your employment, business or vocation (ii) clothing, bedding, furniture, household equipment and provisions necessary for satisfying basic domestic needs for you and your family.
If you pay the total due, which is shown overleaf, your goods will not be removed and you will not have to pay further costs.

Payment under this warrant must be made to the bailiff or to the county court

Walking possession agreement
You may request the bailiff not to remove the goods; this is called a walking possession agreement. If you wish to do so you should sign the walking possession agreement and the copy on the bailiff's warrant form.

If your goods are removed
- ☐ You will be given a list of the goods removed.
- ☐ The goods will not be sold before the 6th day after their removal unless you request an earlier sale or the goods are perishable.
- ☐ You will be given at least 4 days' notice of the day, time and place of the sale.
- ☐ Further fees may be charged which will be listed.

Stopping the sale
If the sale is stopped because the warrant is withdrawn, paid or suspended you will normally have to pay a fee of 10p for every £1 of the assessed value of the goods and any expenses reasonably incurred in removing the goods or advertising the sale.

Auction fees
When your goods have been removed, they may be valued and sold. If they are, you may have to pay the following additional fees:
- ☐ **for valuing the goods:** 5p for every £1 of the assessed value.
- ☐ **for the sale:** this is normally 15p for every £1 for which the goods were sold.

When the goods are sold
You will be given a detailed written account of the sale and distribution of the money.

Walking possession agreement
(request not to remove goods)

To the district judge and bailiff of the court
Please do not remove the goods seized (listed here)

Until payment is made or the warrant is withdrawn:
I will not remove the goods or any part of them or allow any other person to do so without your permission;
I will not damage the goods or any part of them or allow any other person to do so;
I will show this form to any other person who may call with the intention of levying on the goods and tell you of their visit at once,
and I authorise you to re-enter the premises at any time (and as often as you want) to complete the enforcement of the warrant, or to inspect the goods

Signed **Dated**

In the
County Court

Warrant of Delivery

To the district judge and bailiff at

Take notice this warrant has been issued out of this court for execution at an address within the jurisdiction of your court. You are therefore required to execute the said warrant.
Date sent
Date received
seal

As the defendant has failed to return the goods and pay as ordered, you are now required to seize the goods listed here and to deliver them to the claimant *(unless the unpaid balance of the total price now amounting to £ is paid).

Schedule of goods

I acknowledge having received delivery of the goods described (with the exception of)

(for the) claimant

** Applies to orders for return of goods suspended on payment under CCA 1974. Delete if not applicable.*

N46 Warrant of delivery (4.99)

Claim No.
Warrant Number

Date applied for
at **o'clock**

CLAIMANT

Claimant (solicitor)'s address

Ref.

DEFENDANT(S)

Address(es) to levy at

Debt/damages and costs	
Fee	
Solicitor's costs	
Land Registry fee	
Total amount to be levied	

Amounts recovered or passed through:

Date taken	Amount	Date taken	Amount

Returns other than payments **Date of levy** [19][20]

Date	Time		Date	Time	

To the district judge and bailiff

The claimant obtained a judgment for return of the goods listed in the schedule overleaf. The goods have not been returned as ordered and at the claimant's request this warrant has been issued. You are now required to seize the listed goods wherever they may be found within the district of the court and if the goods cannot be found you are forthwith to levy for their value together with the damages and costs as shown overleaf.

Walking possession agreement

(request not to remove goods)

To the district judge and bailiff of the court
Please do not remove the goods seized (listed here)

Until payment is made or the warrant is withdrawn:
- I will not remove the goods or any part of them or allow any other person to do so without your permission;
- I will not damage the goods or any part of them or allow any other person to do so;
- I will show this form to any other person who may call with the intention of levying on the goods and tell you of their visit at once,

and I authorise you to re-enter the premises at any time (and as often as you want) to complete the enforcement of the warrant, or to inspect the goods

Signed **Dated**

In the County Court

Warrant of Delivery

The court office is open from 10am to 4pm Mondays to Fridays

seal

To the defendant

The claimant obtained a judgment against you for recovery of goods listed here

Schedule of goods

You have not returned the goods to the claimant or made payment as you were ordered to do and at the claimant's request this warrant has been issued.

You should now make all payments under the warrant to the bailiff or to the court named above, which is your local county court.

You should send any correspondence concerning this warrant, including claims to the goods, to the court at the address above.

Claim No.

Warrant number

Date applied for

at **o'clock**

CLAIMANT

Claimant (solicitor)'s address

Ref.

DEFENDANT(S)

Address(es) to levy at

Balance of assessed value of goods	
Damages and costs	
Fee	
Solicitor's costs	
Land Registry fee	
Total amount to be levied (goods not returned)	
Total amount to be levied (goods returned)	

The bailiff should give a printed and numbered receipt from his official receipt book for every payment made to him under this warrant. You should not accept any other form of receipt.

For more information see over

Levy Notice *(this does not apply to the goods listed overleaf)*

The bailiff has levied on your goods. This means you must not dispose of them as the court may have to seize and sell them at public auction to raise money to pay your debt. Certain goods will not be seized by the bailiff; these are (i) tools, books, vehicles and other items of equipment necessary for your personal use in your employment, business or vocation (ii) clothing, bedding, furniture, household equipment and provisions necessary for satisfying basic domestic needs for you and your family.

If you pay the total due, which is shown overleaf, your goods will not be removed and you will not have to pay further costs.

Payment under this warrant must be made to the bailiff or to the county court

Walking possession agreement

You may request the bailiff not to remove the goods; this is called a walking possession agreement. If you wish to do so you should sign the walking possession agreement and the copy on the bailiff's warrant form.

If your goods are removed

- ☐ You will be given a list of the goods removed.
- ☐ The goods will not be sold before the 6th day after their removal unless you request an earlier sale or the goods are perishable.
- ☐ You will be given at least 4 days' notice of the day, time and place of the sale.
- ☐ Further fees may be charged which will be listed.

Stopping the sale

If the sale is stopped because the warrant is withdrawn, paid or suspended you will normally have to pay a fee of 10p for every £1 of the assessed value of the goods and any expenses reasonably incurred in removing the goods or advertising the sale.

Auction fees

When your goods have been removed, they may be valued and sold. If they are, you may have to pay the following additional fees:

- ☐ **for valuing the goods:** 5p for every £1 of the assessed value.
- ☐ **for the sale:** this is normally 15p for every £1 for which the goods are sold.

When the goods are sold

You will be given a detailed written account of the sale and distribution of the money.

Walking possession agreement

(request not to remove goods)

To the district judge and bailiff of the court

Please do not remove the goods seized (listed here)

Until payment is made or the warrant is withdrawn:

- ☐ I will not remove the goods or any part of them or allow any other person to do so without your permission;
- ☐ I will not damage the goods or any part of them or allow any other person to do so;
- ☐ I will show this form to any other person who may call with the intention of levying on the goods and tell you of their visit at once,

and I authorise you to re-enter the premises at any time (and as often as you want) to complete the enforcement of the warrant, or to inspect the goods

Signed **Dated**

In the

County Court

Warrant of Delivery

To the district judge and bailiff at

Take notice this warrant has been issued out of this court for execution at an address within the jurisdiction of your court. You are therefore required to execute the said warrant.

Date sent

Date received

seal

As the defendant has failed to return the goods and pay as ordered, you are now required to seize the goods listed here and to deliver them to the claimant. If the goods cannot be found you are forthwith to levy the sum of £

(balance of the assessed value of the goods) together with any damages and costs.

Schedule of goods

I acknowledge having received delivery of the goods described (with the exception of)

(for the) claimant

N48 Warrant of delivery ☐ return of goods or value (4.99)

Claim No.

Warrant number

Date applied for

at **o'clock**

CLAIMANT

Claimant (solicitor)'s address

Ref.

DEFENDANT(S)

Address(es) to levy at

Balance of assessed value of goods	
Damages and costs	
Fee	
Solicitor's costs	
Land Registry fee	
Total amount to be levied (goods not returned)	
Total amount to be levied (goods returned)	

Amounts recovered or passed through:

Date taken	Amount	Date taken	Amount

Levy Notice

The bailiff has levied on your goods. This means you must not dispose of them as the court may have to seize and sell them at public auction to raise money to pay your debt. Certain goods will not be seized by the bailiff; these are (i) tools, books, vehicles and other items of equipment necessary for your personal use in your employment, business or vocation (ii) clothing, bedding, furniture, household equipment and provisions necessary for satisfying basic domestic needs for you and your family.

If you pay the total due, which is shown overleaf, your goods will not be removed and you will not have to pay further costs.

If your goods are removed
- ☐ You will be given a list of the goods removed.
- ☐ The goods will not be sold before the 6th day after their removal unless you request an earlier sale or the goods are perishable.
- ☐ You will be given at least 4 days' notice of the day, time and place of the sale.
- ☐ Further fees may be charged which will be listed.

Stopping the sale
If the sale is stopped because the warrant is withdrawn, paid or suspended you will normally have to pay a fee of 10p for every £1 of the assessed value of the goods and any expenses reasonably incurred in removing the goods or advertising the sale.

Auction fees
When your goods have been removed, they may be valued and sold. If they are, you may have to pay the following additional fees:
- ☐ **for valuing the goods:** 5p for every £1 of the assessed value.
- ☐ **for the sale:** this is normally 15p for every £1 for which the goods were sold.

When the goods are sold
You will be given a detailed account in writing of the sale and distribution of the money.
You should now make all payments under the warrant to the bailiff or at the court named below, which is your local county court.
You should send any correspondence concerning this warrant, including claims to the goods, to the court at the address below.

seal

The court office is open
from 10am to 4 pm Mondays to Fridays

Possession obtained and given to the claimant on

Bailiff

I acknowledge having received possession of the land described in this warrant on the

(for the) claimant

(for use only when sale or other charges incurred)

	£	£
Gross amount levied or received		
Transport charges		
Appraisement fee on £		
Sale fee on £		
Advertising		
Rent to landlord		
Costs of interpleader ordered to be deducted from proceeds		
Net amount paid into court		£
on		

In the
County Court

Warrant for Possession of Land

Returns other than payments

Date	*Time*	

Claim No. ____

Warrant number ____ ____

CLAIMANT

Claimant (solicitor)'s address

Ref.

DEFENDANT(S)

Address(es) to levy at

Balance of debt	
Amount of warrant	
Fee	
Solicitor's costs	
Land Registry fee	
Total	

Amounts recovered or passed through:

Date taken	Amount	Date taken	Amount

Levy Notice

The bailiff has levied on your goods. This means you must not dispose of them as the court may have to seize and sell them at public auction to raise money to pay your debt. Certain goods will not be seized by the bailiff; these are (i) tools, books, vehicles and other items of equipment necessary for your personal use in your employment, business or vocation (ii) clothing, bedding, furniture, household equipment and provisions necessary for satisfying basic domestic needs for you and your family.

If you pay the total due, which is shown overleaf, your goods will not be removed and you will not have to pay further costs.

If your goods are removed

- ☐ You will be given a list of the goods removed.
- ☐ The goods will not be sold before the 6th day after their removal unless you request an earlier sale or the goods are perishable.
- ☐ You will be given at least 4 days' notice of the day, time and place of the sale.
- ☐ Further fees may be charged which will be listed.

Stopping the sale

If the sale is stopped because the warrant is withdrawn, paid or suspended you will normally have to pay a fee of 10p for every £1 of the assessed value of the goods and any expenses reasonably incurred in removing the goods or advertising the sale.

Auction fees

When your goods have been removed, they may be valued and sold. If they are, you may have to pay the following additional fees:

- ☐ **for valuing the goods:** 5p for every £1 of the assessed value.
- ☐ **for the sale:** this is normally 15p for every £1 for which the goods were sold.

When the goods are sold

You will be given a detailed account in writing of the sale and distribution of the money.

You should now make all payments under the warrant to the bailiff or at the court named below, which is your local county court.

You should send any correspondence concerning this warrant, including claims to the goods, to the court at the address below.

seal

The court office is open
from 10am to 4 pm Mondays to Fridays

Possession obtained and given to the claimant on

Bailiff

I acknowledge having received possession of the land described in this warrant on the

(for the) claimant

(for use only when sale or other charges incurred)

Gross amount levied or received		£
Transport charges	£	
Appraisement fee on £		
Sale fee on £		
Advertising		
Rent to landlord		
Costs of interpleader ordered to be deducted from proceeds		
Net amount paid into court		£

on

In the

County Court

Warrant for Possession of Land

Returns other than payments

Date	*Time*	

N49 Warrant for possession of land (4.99)

Claim No. ______

Warrant number ______ ______

CLAIMANT

Claimant (solicitor)'s address

Ref.

DEFENDANT(S)

Address(es) to levy at

Balance of debt	
Amount of warrant Fee Solicitor's costs Land Registry fee	
Total	

Amounts recovered or passed through:

Date taken	Amount	Date taken	Amount

Claim No ____________
Warrant Number ______ ______
Restitution Number ______ ______

CLAIMANT

Claimant (solicitor)'s address

Ref. ____________

DEFENDANT(S)

Address(es) to levy at

Balance of debt
Amount of warrant Fee Solicitor's costs Land Registry fee
Total

The bailiff should give a printed and numbered receipt from his official receipt book for every payment made to him under this warrant. You should not accept any other form of receipt.

For more information see over

Warrant of Restitution

To the district judge and bailiffs of the court

On the day of [19][20],

(1) describe the land as set out in the judgment

It was adjudged that the claimant was entitled to possession of[1]

And on the day of [19][20] a warrant of possession was issued, requiring you to give possession of the land to the claimant and possession of the land was given by you to the claimant under the warrant on the day of [19][20]

(**And** the claimant having satisfied the court that the land has been re-entered wrongfully and the court having ordered, on the day of [19][20], that a warrant of restitution should issue in respect of the land (and that the defendant should pay the claimant the sum of £ for costs)

YOU ARE THEREFORE REQUIRED FORTHWITH TO ENTER THE LAND AND RESTORE POSSESSION OF IT TO THE CLAIMANT

(**You are further required** to levy forthwith for the total amount shown overleaf in accordance)

Application was made to this court for this warrant at minutes past the hour of o'clock

on

N50 Warrant of restitution (4.99)

Levy Notice

The bailiff has levied on your goods. This means you must not dispose of them as the court may have to seize and sell them at public auction to raise money to pay your debt. Certain goods will not be seized by the bailiff; these are (i) tools, books, vehicles and other items of equipment necessary for your personal use in your employment, business or vocation (ii) clothing, bedding, furniture, household equipment and provisions necessary for satisfying basic domestic needs for you and your family.

If you pay the total due, which is shown overleaf, your goods will not be removed and you will not have to pay further costs.

If your goods are removed

- ☐ You will be given a list of the goods removed.
- ☐ The goods will not be sold before the 6th day after their removal unless you request an earlier sale or the goods are perishable.
- ☐ You will be given at least 4 days' notice of the day, time and place of the sale.
- ☐ Further fees may be charged which will be listed.

Stopping the sale

If the sale is stopped because the warrant is withdrawn, paid or suspended you will normally have to pay a fee of 10p for every £1 of the assessed value of the goods and any expenses reasonably incurred in removing the goods or advertising the sale.

Auction fees

When your goods have been removed, they may be valued and sold. If they are, you may have to pay the following additional fees:

- ☐ **for valuing the goods:** 5p for every £1 of the assessed value.
- ☐ **for the sale:** this is normally 15p for every £1 for which the goods were sold.

When the goods are sold

You will be given a detailed account in writing of the sale and distribution of the money.

You should now make all payments under the warrant to the bailiff or at the court named below, which is your local county court.

You should send any correspondence concerning this warrant, including claims to the goods, to the court at the address below.

seal

The court office is open
from 10am to 4 pm Mondays to Fridays

Possession obtained and given to the claimant on the

Bailiff

I acknowledge having received possession of the land described in this warrant on the

(for the) applicant

(for use only when sale or other charges incurred)

Gross amount levied or received		£
Transport charges	£	
Appraisement fee on £		
Sale fee on £		
Advertising		
Rent to landlord		
Costs of interpleader ordered to be deducted from proceeds		
Net amount paid into court on		£

In the
County Court

Warrant of Restitution

Returns other than payments

Date	*Time*	

N50 Warrant of restitution (4.99)

Claim No ____

Warrant Number ____ ____

Restitution Number ____ ____

CLAIMANT

Claimant (solicitor)'s address

Ref.

DEFENDANT(S)

Address(es) to levy at

Balance of debt	
Amount of warrant Fee Solicitor's costs Land Registry fee	
Total	

Amounts recovered or passed through:

Date taken	Amount	Date taken	Amount

Warrant of Restitution

To the district judge and bailiffs of the court

On the day of [19][20],

It was adjudged that the applicant was entitled to possession of [1]

[1] describe the land as set out in the order

And on the day of [19][20] a warrant of possession was issued, requiring you to give possession of the land to the applicant and possession of the land was given by you to the applicant under the warrant on the day of [19][20]

(**And** the applicant having satisfied the court that the land has been re- entered wrongfully and the court having ordered, on the day of [19][20], that a warrant of restitution should issue in respect of the land (and that the respondent should pay the applicant the sum of £ for costs)

YOU ARE THEREFORE REQUIRED FORTHWITH TO ENTER THE LAND AND RESTORE POSSESSION OF IT TO THE APPLICANT

(**You are further required** to levy forthwith for the total amount shown overleaf in accordance with the provisions of sections 85 and 89 of the County Courts Act 1984)

Application was made to this court for this warrant at minutes past the hour of o'clock

on

Claim No ______

Warrant Number ______ ______

Restitution Number ______ ______

APPLICANT

APPLICANT(solicitors)'s address

Ref. ______

RESPONDENTS(S)

Address(es) to levy at

Balance of debt
Amount of warrant Fee Solicitor's costs Land Registry fee
Total

The bailiff should give a printed and numbered receipt from his official receipt book for every payment made to him under this warrant. You should not accept any other form of receipt.

For more information see over

N51 Warrant of restitution (4.99)

Levy Notice

The bailiff has levied on your goods. This mean you must not dispose of them as the court may have to seize and sell them at public auction to raise money to pay your debt. Certain goods will not be seized by the bailiff; these are (i) tools, books, vehicles and other items of equipment necessary for your personal news in your employment, business or vocation (ii) clothing, bedding, furniture, household equipment and provisions necessary for satisfying basic domestic need for you and your family.

If you pay the total due, which is shown overleaf, your goods will not be removed and you will not have to pay further costs.

If your goods are removed

- ☐ You will be given a list of goods removed.
- ☐ The goods will not sold beforethe 6th day after their removal unless you request an earlier sale or the goods are perishable.
- ☐ You will be given at least 4 days' notice of the day, time and place of the sale
- ☐ Further fees may be charged which will be listed.

Stopping the sale

If the sale is stopped because the warrant is withdrawn, paid or suspended you will normally have to pay a fee of 10p for every £1 of the assessed value of the goods and any expenses reasonably incurred in removing the goods or advertising the sale.

Auction fees

When your goods have been removed, they may be valued and sold. If they are, you may have to pay the following additional fees:

- ☐ for valuing the goods: 5p for every £1 of the assessed value.
- ☐ for the sale: this is normally 15p for every £1 for which the goods were sold.

When the goods are sold

You will be given a detail account in writing of the sale and distribution of the money.

You should now make all payments under the warrant to the bailiff or at the court named below, which is your local county court.

You should sent any correspondence concerning this warrant, including claims to the goods, to the court at the address below.

seal

The court office is open
from 10 am to 4 pm Mondays to Fridays

Possession obtained and given to the applicant on the

Bailiff

I acknowledge having received possession of the land described in this warrant on the

(for the) applicant

(for use only when sale or other charges incurred)

Gross amount levied or received		£
Transport charges	£	
Appraisement fee on £		
Sale fee on £		
Advertising		
Rent to landlord		
Cost of interpleader ordered to be deducted from proceeds		
Net amount paid into court on		£

In the

County Court

Warrant of Restitution (Order 24)

Returns other than payments

Date	*Time*	

N51 Warrant of restitution (4.99)

Claim No __________

Warrant Number __________

Restitution Number __________

APPLICANT

APPLICANT(solicitors)'s address

Ref.

RESPONDENTS(S)

Address(es) to levy at

Balance of debt	
Amount of warrant Fee Solicitor's costs Land Registry fee	
Total	

Amount recovered or passed through:

Date Taken	Amount	Date Taken	Amount

Warrant for Possession of Land under Order 24

To the district judge and bailiffs of the court

Claim No __________
Warrant number ______ ______

APPLICANT

Applicant (solicitor)'s address

Ref.

RESPONDENT(S)

Address(es) to levy at

On the day of [19][20],

(1) describe the land as set out in the order

It was ordered that the applicant recover possession of(1)

(And it was ordered that the applicant do recover against the respondent the sum of £ for costs, making together the sum of £ , which the respondent was ordered to pay to the applicant by)

THE RESPONDENT HAS FAILED TO OBEY THE ORDER AND AT THE APPLICANT'S REQUEST THIS WARRANT HAS BEEN ISSUED. YOU ARE NOW REQUIRED TO GIVE POSSESSION OF THE LAND TO THE APPLICANT.

(You are further required to levy for the total shown overleaf, in accordance with the provisions of sections 85 and 89 of the County Courts Act 1984.)

Application was made to this court for this warrant at minute past the hour of o'clock on

Balance of debt	
Amount of warrant	
Fee	
Solicitor's costs	
Land Registry fee	
Total	

The bailiff should give a printed and numbered receipt from his official receipt book for every payment made to him under this warrant. You should not accept any other form of receipt.

For more information see over

N52 Warrant for possession of land under (Order 24, rule(6(1)) (4.99)

Levy Notice

The bailiff has levied on your goods. This means you must not dispose of them as the court may have to seize and sell them at public auction to raise money to pay your debt. Certain goods will not be seized by the bailiff; these are (i) tools, books, vehicles and other items of equipment necessary for your personal news in your employment, business or vocation (ii) clothing, bedding, furniture, household equipment and provisions necessary for satisfying basic domestic need for you and your family.

If you pay the total due, which is shown overleaf, your goods will not be removed and you will not have to pay further costs.

If your goods are removed

- You will be given a list of goods removed.
- The goods will not sold beforethe 6th day after their removal unless you request an earlier sale or the goods are perishable.
- You will be given at least 4 days' notice of the day, time and place of the sale
- Further fees may be charged which will be listed.

Stopping the sale
If the sale is stopped because the warrant is withdrawn, paid or suspended you will normally have to pay a fee of 10p for every £1 of the assessed value of the goods and any expenses reasonably incurred in removing the goods or advertising the sale.

Auction fees
When your goods have been removed, they may be valued and sold. If they are, you may have to pay the following additional fees:

- **for valuing the goods:** 5p for every £1 of the assessed value.
- **for the sale:** this is normally 15p for every £1 for which the goods were sold.

When the goods are sold
You will be given a detailed account in writing of the sale and distribution of the money.
You should now make all payments under the warrant to the bailiff or at the court named below, which is your local county court.
You should send any correspondence concerning this warrant, including claims to the goods, to the court at the address below.

seal

The court office is open
from 10am to 4 pm Mondays to Fridays

Possession obtained and given to the claimant on the

Bailiff

I acknowledge having received possession of the land described in this warrant on the

(for the) applicant

(for use only when sale or other charges incurred)

Gross amount levied or received		£
Transport charges	£	
Appraisement fee on £		
Sale fee on £		
Advertising		
Rent to landlord		
Costs of interpleader ordered to be deducted from proceeds		
Net amount paid into court on		£

In the

County Court

Warrant for Possessionm of Land (Order 24)

Returns other than payments

Date	*Time*	

N52 Warrant for possession of land (Order 24)

Claim No ________

Warrant Number ________

Restitution Number ________

APPLICANT

Applicant (solicitor)'s address

Ref.

RESPONDENT(S)

Address(es) to levy at

Balance of debt	
Amount of warrant	
Fee	
Solicitor's costs	
Land Registry fee	
Total	

Amounts recovered or passed through:

Date taken	Amount	Date taken	Amount

To the Governor of Her Majesty's Prison

at

Seal

IN THE

COUNTY COURT

CASE No.

WARRANT OF
COMMITTAL No.

DEFENDANT
(or otherwise)

TAKE NOTICE that, in accordance with the provisions of section 122 of the County Courts Act 1984, this warrant of committal has been sent to this court and the defendant, if arrested within the jurisdiction of this court, is to be conveyed to the prison of this court, and is to be kept there for the time mentioned in the warrant of committal or until lawfully discharged if sooner.

DATED

(1) Here insert name of prison of Foreign Court

N75 Indorsement on a warrant of committal sent to a foreign court Order 28 Rule 11(3)

I arrested the within-named on the

and delivered him into the custody of

the Governor of HM prison at

on the

To the District Judge of the **County Court**

TAKE NOTICE that this warrant has been issued out of this court for execution at an address within the jurisdiction of your court.

Seal

YOU ARE THEREFORE required to execute the said warrant.

DATED

BAILIFF OF THE
COUNTY COURT

N53 Warrant of execution or committal to District Judge of foreign court Section 122 County Courts Act 1984

Notice of Application for Attachment of Earnings Order

Claimant

Defendant

In the **County Court**	
Claim No.	
Application No.	
Claimant's Ref.	

Seal

To the defendant

The claimant obtained a judgment (or order) against you in this court

[1] or as the case may be ( )[1]

And as you have failed to pay as ordered, the claimant has applied for an attachment of earnings order requiring your employer to make deductions from your earnings to pay the judgment (or order)

Unless you pay the claimant the amount now due (shown below), you must complete the enclosed form of reply, including the statement of means, and send it to reach the court office **within 8 days** after you receive this notice

Failure to return the reply form and statement of means is a punishable offence. It will result in your employer being contacted and you may also be sent to prison for up to 14 days

[2] Where judgment was entered for £5,000 or more, or was in respect of a debt which attracts contractual or statutory interest for late payment, the claimant may be entitled to further interest.

Balance of debt due at date of this notice (and any interest [2])	£	
Attachment issue fee	£	
AMOUNT NOW DUE	£	

Dated

Instructions - please read these carefully

If the claimant's claim includes interest(2) and you pay the amount now due within 8 days after you receive this notice, the claimant will not be entitled to further interest. If you wish to pay the amount due, see **How to Pay** below.
If you complete and return the form of reply, including the statement of means, within 8 days and the court is satisfied with the information you give, the court will make an order and send you a copy. You will not have to attend court.
If you are unemployed or self employed, you should say so on the form of reply and answer as many questions as you can.

If you want an opportunity to pay voluntarily without your employer being ordered to make deductions from your pay, you should ask for a suspended order on the form of reply. You should also enclose a copy of your most recent pay slip.
Read the notes on the form of reply before giving the details asked for.
You can obtain help in completing the enclosed form of reply at any county court office or Citizens' Advice Bureau

Address for Payment

How to Pay

PAYMENT(S) MUST BE MADE to the person named at the address for payment quoting their reference and the court case number.
DO NOT bring or send payments to the court. THEY WILL NOT BE ACCEPTED.
You should allow at least 4 days for your payment to reach the claimant or his representative.
Make sure that you keep records and can account for all payments made. Proof may be required if there is any disagreement. It is not safe to send cash unless you use registered post.
A leaflet giving further advice about payment can be obtained from the court.
If you need more information you should contact the claimant or his representative.

The court office at

is open between 10 am and 4 pm Monday to Friday. When corresponding with the court, please address forms or letters to the Court Manager and quote the claim number.

N55 Notice of application for attachment of earnings order

Notice of Application for Attachment of Earnings Order (maintenance)

In the	
County Court	
Claim No.	
Application No.	
Claimant's Ref.	

Claimant

Defendant

seal

To the defendant

The claimant obtained an order against you in this court

(1) or as the case may be

(1)( )

And as you have failed to pay as ordered, the claimant has applied for an attachment of earnings order requiring your employer to make deductions from your earnings for payment of the arrears and for future maintenance

The application will be heard by this court

on the at o'clock

(2) insert the address of courthouse

at(2)

You must also complete the enclosed form of reply and statement of means and send it to reach the court office **within 8 days** after you receive this notice

FAILURE TO RETURN THE REPLY FORM AND STATEMENT OF MEANS IS A PUNISHABLE OFFENCE. IT WILL RESULT IN YOUR EMPLOYER BEING CONTACTED AND IT MAY RESULT IN YOU BEING ORDERED TO ATTEND COURT

ARREARS NOW DUE £	

Dated

Notes to help you complete the form of reply

- If you are unemployed or self employed, you should say so on the form of reply and answer as many questions as you can.
- Read the notes on the form of reply before giving the details asked for.
- If you want an opportunity to pay voluntarily without your employer being ordered to make deductions from your pay, you should ask for a suspended order on the form of reply. You should also enclose a copy of your most recent payslip.
- You can obtain help in completing the form of reply at any county court office or citizens' advice bureau.

The court office at

is open between 10 am and 4 pm Monday to Friday. Address all communications to the Court Manager quoting the claim number

N55A Notice of application for attachment of earnings order (maintenance)

For court use only

Certificate of Service - Attachment of Earnings | **Claim No.**

I certify that the notice of which this is a true copy, together with a form of reply was served by me on ....

Service was effected *(tick and complete whichever applies)*

☐ by posting it to the defendant on at the address stated in the notice

☐ by delivering it to the defendant personally (or to)

apparently not less than 16 years old, who promised to give it to the defendant on the same day) (or on)

at the address stated in the notice (or at)

☐ by inserting it, enclosed in an envelope addressed to the defendant, in the letter box at the address stated on the notice. I have reason to believe that the notice will reach the defendant in sufficient time, because:

Bailiff/Officer of the Court

OR
I certify that the notice has not been served for the following reasons:

Bailiff/Officer of the Court

FORM N56 FORM FOR REPLYING TO AN ATTACHMENT OF EARNINGS APPLICATION

Form for replying to an attachment of earnings application

- Read the notes on the notice of application before completing this form.
- Tick the correct boxes and give as much information as you can. The court will make an order based on the information you give on this form. You must give full details of your employment and your income and outgoings. Enclose a copy of your most recent pay slip if you can.
- *Make your offer of payment in box 10. You will get some idea of how much to offer by adding up your expenses in boxes 6, 7, 8 and 9 and taking them from your total income (box 5).*
- Send or take this completed and signed form immediately to the court office shown on the notice of application.
- You should keep your copy of the notice of application unless you are making full payment. (This does not apply to maintenance applications).
- For details of where and how to pay see notice of application.

In the County Court

Claim No.

Application No.

Claimant *(including ref.)*

Defendant

1 Personal details

Surname

Forename

☐ Mr ☐ Mrs ☐ Miss ☐ Ms

☐ Married ☐ Single ☐ Other *(specify)*

Age

Address

Postcode

2 Dependants *(people you look after financially)*

Children *(under 19)*		Others *(give details)*
Age	*Date of Birth*	

(If more continue on a separate sheet)

3 Employment

I am ☐ employed as a

☐ self employed as a

☐ unemployed

☐ a pensioner

a. employment

My employer is

Employer's address

Address of employer's head office *(if different from above)*

My works number and/or pay reference is

Jobs other than main job *(give details)*

b. self employment

Length of time self employed years months

c. unemployment

Length of time unemployed years months

Give details of any outstanding interviews

4 Bank account and savings

☐ **I have a bank account**

☐ The account is in credit by . . . £

☐ The account is overdrawn by . . . £

☐ **I have a savings account or building society account**

The amount in the account is . . . £

N56 Statement of means - attachment of earnings (04.03) *Printed on behalf of The Court Service*

5 Income

My usual take home pay *(including overtime, commission, bonuses etc. but excluding tax credits)*	£	per
Working tax credit	£	per
My husband's or wife's usual take home pay	£	per
Income support	£	per
Child benefit(s)	£	per
Child tax credit	£	per
Other state benefit(s)	£	per
My pension(s)	£	per
Others living in my home give me	£	per
Other income *(give details below)*		
	£	per
	£	per
Total income	£	per

7 Priority debts

(This section is for arrears only. Do not include regular expenses listed in box 6)

Rent arrears	£	per
Mortgage arrears	£	per
Council Tax arrears	£	per
Water charges arrears	£	per
Fuel debts: Gas	£	per
Electricity	£	per
Other	£	per
Maintenance arrears	£	per
Others *(give details below)*		
	£	per
	£	per
Total priority debts	£	per

6 Expenses

(Do not include any payments made by other members of the household out of their own income)

I have regular expenses as follows:

Mortgage *(including second mortgage)*	£	per
Rent	£	per
Council Tax	£	per
Gas	£	per
Electricity	£	per
Water charges	£	per
Telephone	£	per
TV rental and licence	£	per
HP repayments	£	per
Mail order	£	per
Housekeeping, food, school meals	£	per
Travelling expenses	£	per
Children's clothing	£	per
Maintenance payments	£	per
Others *(not court orders or credit debts listed in boxes 8 and 9)*		
	£	per
	£	per
	£	per
Total expenses	£	per

8 Court orders

Court	Claim No.	£	per
Total court order instalments		£	per

Of the payments above, I am behind with payments to *(please list)*

9 Credit debts

Loans and credit card debts *(please list)*

	£	per
	£	per
	£	per

Of the payments above, I am behind with payments to *(please list)*

10 Offer of Payment

I offer to have £ week/month deducted from my pay

- If you want an opportunity to pay voluntarily without your employer being ordered to make deductions from your pay you should ask for a suspended order. Tick the box below and give your reasons.

☐ I would like a suspended order because

11 Declaration

I declare that the details I have given above are true to the best of my knowledge

Signed   **Date**

Order for Attendance at an Adjourned Hearing of Attachment of Earnings Application (maintenance)

To the defendant

In the	
County Court	
Claim No.	
Application No.	
Claimant	
Defendant	
Claimant's Ref.	

Seal

You failed to attend the court on the day and time fixed for the hearing of an application for an attachment of earnings order, after being served with the notice of application

The application has been adjourned to

the **at** **o'clock**

at

You are ordered to attend at that time on that day

You must also complete the enclosed form of reply and statement of means and send it to reach the court office **within 8 days** after you receive this order

IF YOU DO NOT ATTEND YOU MAY BE SENT TO PRISON FOR UP TO 14 DAYS OR ARRESTED AND BROUGHT BEFORE THE COURT

Dated

Notes to help you complete the form of reply

- **If you are unemployed or self employed, you should say so on the form of reply and answer as many questions as you can.**
- **Read the notes on the form of reply before giving the details asked for.**
- **If you want an opportunity to pay voluntarily without your employer being ordered to make deductions from your pay, you should ask for a suspended order on the form of reply. You should also enclose a copy of your most recent pay slip.**
- **You can obtain help in completing the form of reply at any county court office or citizens' advice bureau**

The court office at

is open between 10 am and 4 pm Monday to Friday. When corresponding with the court, please address forms or letters to the Court Manager and quote the claim number.

N58 Order for defendant's attendance at an adjourned hearing of an attachment of earnings application (maintenance)

Certificate of Service (to be completed by the court)
I certify that the order of which this is a true copy was served by me on the defendant personally at the address stated in the order, or at

on the day of 20

Bailiff/Officer of the Court
Date

I certify that the order has **not been served** for the following reason:

Bailiff/Officer of the Court
Date

Warrant of Committal under section 23(1) of the Attachment of Earnings Act 1971

In the County Court	
Claim No.	
Claimant	
Defendant	
A/E No.	
Committal Warrant No.	

seal

To ☐the District Judge and Bailiffs of the court
☐and every constable within his jurisdiction
☐the Governor of Her Majesty's Prison at (1)

(1) Name of Prison

The defendant(2)

of(3)

(2) Name and (3) address of person to be committed and, if known, place of employment

* having failed to complete and return a statement of his earnings, resources and needs in accordance with section 14 of the Attachment of Earnings Act 1971, has failed to attend an appointment to show cause as to why he should not be committed to prison for up to 14 days [or, having attended such a hearing, has refused to be sworn (or to give evidence)]

* delete whichever does not apply

or

* having been ordered to attend at a specified day for the adjourned hearing of an application for an attachment of earnings order, has failed to do so [or, having attended such a hearing, has refused to be sworn (or to give evidence)]

(enter name of judge) **has ordered** that the defendant be committed to prison for(4) days

(4) state term of imprisonment

You the District Judge, Bailiffs and others are therefore required to arrest the defendant and to deliver him to the prison and you the Governor to receive the defendant and safely keep him in prison for (4) days from the arrest under this order or until he shall be sooner discharged by due course of law

Dated

The court office at

is open between 10 am and 4 pm Monday to Friday. Address all communications to the Court Manager and quote the above claim number

N59 Warrant of committal under section 23 of the Attachment of Earnings Act 1971

Order for Production of Statement of Means

To the defendant

In the	
	County Court
Claim No.	
Application No.	
Claimant	
Defendant	
Claimant's Ref.	

You have failed to return the statement of means sent to you

*see below **It is ordered** that unless you pay the amount now due to the court office (£ *) you must complete the enclosed form of reply, including the statement of means, and send it to reach the court office **within 8 days** after you receive this order

Unless you pay the amount not due to the court office, or return the completed reply form and statement of means, you may be ordered to attend court to show why you should not be sent to prison for up to 14 days or fined up to £250 under Section 23 of the Attachment of Earnings Act 1971

Dated

Instructions - please read these carefully

- ☐ If you wish to pay the amount now due see **How to Pay** box. Where judgment was entered for £5,000 or more, or was in respect of a debt which attracts contractual or statutory interest for late payment, this amount may include interest.
- ☐ If you complete and return the form of reply, including the statement of means, within 8 days and the cout is satisfied with the information you give, it will send you a copy of the order.
- ☐ If you are unemployed or self employed, you should say so on the form of reply and answer as many questions as you can.
- ☐ If you want an opportunity to pay voluntarily without your employer being ordered to make deductions from your pay, you should ask for a suspended order on the form of reply. You should also enclose a copy of your most recent pay slip.
- ☐ Read the notes on the form of reply before giving the details asked for.
- ☐ You can obtain help in completing the enclosed form of reply at any county court office or citizens' advice bureau.

—Address for Payment—

—How to Pay—

You can pay the court by calling at the court office which is open 10 am to 4 pm Monday to Friday

You may only pay by:
- ☐ cash
- ☐ banker's or giro draft
- ☐ cheque supported by a cheque card
- ☐ cheque (unsupported cheques may be accepted, subject to clearance, if the Court Manager agrees)

Please bring this form with you.

By post
You may only pay by:
- ☐ postal order
- ☐ banker's or giro draft
- ☐ cheque (cheques may be accepted, subject to clearance, if the Court Manager agrees). The payment must be made out to HM Paymaster General and crossed.

This method of payment is at your own risk.

And you must:
- ☐ pay the postage
- ☐ enclose this form
- ☐ enclose a self addressed envelope so that the court can return this form with a receipt

The court **cannot** *accept stamps or payments by bank and giro credit transfers*

Note:
You should carefully check any future forms from the court to see if payments should be made directly to the claimant.

The court office at

is open between 10 am and 4 pm Monday to Friday. When corresponding with the court, please address forms or letters to the Cour Manager and quote the claim number.

N61 Order for production of statement of means

Certificate of Service *(to be completed by the court)*

I certify that the summons of which this is a true copy was served by me on the defendant personally at the address stated in the order, or at

on the day of 20

Bailiff/Officer of the Court

Date

I certify that the summons **has not been served** for the following reason:

Bailiff/Officer of the Court

Date

Order to employer for production of statement of earnings

In the	
County Court	
Claim No.	
Application No.	
Claimant	
Defendant	

seal

To the defendant's employer

For the purposes of an application for an attachment of earnings order in respect of the above named defendant

You are ordered to complete the enclosed statement of earnings and send it to reach the court office **within 8 days** after service of this order upon you

Dated

——— Take Notice ———

Failure to return the completed statement of earnings form may result in a fine of up to £250 under section 23 of the Attachment of Earnings Act 1971

The court office at

is open between 10 am and 4 pm Monday to Friday. Address all communications to the Court Manager quoting the claim number

N61A Order to employer for production of statement of earnings

Certificate of Service (to be completed by the court)

I certify that the order of which this is a true copy was served by me on the defendant's employer personally at the address stated on the order, or at

on the day of [19][20].

Bailiff/Officer of the Court

Date

I certify that the order has **not been served** for the following reason:

Bailiff/Officer of the Court

Date

Summons for Offence under Attachment of Earnings Act 1971

In the County Court	
Claim No.	
A/E No.	
Claimant	
Defendant	

seal

To

of

YOU ARE SUMMONED to appear at this Court at

on the

at o'clock, to show cause why an order should not be made against you under Section 23(3) of the Attachment of Earnings Act 1971, for the payment of a fine not exceeding £250 [or your committal to prison for not more than 14 days(1)] for failing to comply with an attachment of earnings order made by this Court on the , in that you(2)

(1) Add where appropriate

(2) State particulars of failure or as the case may be, giving details of the alleged offence

DATED

The court office at

is open between 10 am and 4 pm Monday to Friday. Address all communications to the Court Manager quoting the claim number

N62 Summons for offence under Attachment of Earnings Act 1971

CASE No.

I certify that the summons of which this is a true copy,

was served by me on (date)

on the personally,

at the address stated in the summons, or

at

(1) Or in accordance with an order for substituted service. (1)

Bailiff/Officer of the Court

I certify that the summons has not been served for the

following reasons:-

Bailiff/Officer of the Court

Failure to provide Statement of Means

To the defendant

In the County Court	
Claim No.	
Application No.	
Claimant	
Defendant	
Claimant's Ref.	

Seal

You have failed to give the court within the time specified a statement of your earnings, resources and means in accordance with section 14 of the Attachment of Earnings Act 1971.

You are therefore ordered to attend court in person

at

on the at o'clock

to give good reasons why you should not be sent to prison for up to 14 days or fined up to £250 under Section 23 of the Attachment of Earnings Act 1971.

Dated

see below* **If you immediately return the completed and signed form of reply and statement of means to the court **or pay into the court office** (£*) the sum remaining due, you may not have to attend.

Instructions - please read these carefully

- If you wish to pay the amount see **Payments into Court**. Where judgment was entered on or after 1 July 1991, this amount may include interest. If so, the plaintiff may claim further interest until final payment.
- If you complete and return the form of reply, including the statement of means, within 8 days and the court is satisfied with the information you give, it will send you a copy of the order.
- If you are unemployed or self employed, you should say so on the form of reply and answer as many questions as you can.
- If you want an opportunity to pay voluntarily without your employer being ordered to make deductions from your pay, you should ask for a suspended order on the form of reply. You should also enclose a copy of your most recent pay slip.
- Read the notes on the form of reply before giving the details asked for.
- You can obtain help in completing the enclosed form of reply at any county court office or citizens' advice bureau.

Payments into Court

please bring or enclose this form

You can pay the court by calling at the court office which is open from 10 am to 4 pm Monday to Friday.

You may only pay by:
- cash
- banker's or giro draft
- cheque supported by a cheque card
- cheque (unsupported cheques may be accepted, subject to clearance, if the Court Manager agrees)

Cheques/drafts must be made out to HM Paymaster General and crossed

By post
You may only pay by:
- postal order
- banker's or giro draft
- cheque (cheques may be accepted, subject to clearance, if the Court Manager agrees).

The payment must be made out to HM Paymaster General and crossed. This method of payment is at your own risk.
And you must:
- pay the postage
- enclose a self addressed envelope so that the court can return the form and a receipt.

The court cannot accept stamps or payments by bank and giro credit transfers.

Note: You should carefully check any future forms from the courts to see if payments should be made directly to the claimant

The court office at

is open between 10 am and 4 pm Monday to Friday. When corresponding with the court, please address forms or letters to the Court manager and quote the case number.

N63 Notice to show cause under Section 23 of the Attachment of Earnings Act 1971

Certificate of Service *(to be completed by the court)*
I certify that the summons of which this is a true copy was served by me on the defendant personally at the address stated in the order, or at

on the day of [19][20]

Bailiff/Officer of the Court
Date

I certify that the summons **has not been served** for the following reason:

Bailiff/Officer of the Court
Date

Suspended Attachment of Earnings Order

Claimant

Defendant

In the County Court	
Claim No.	
A/E No.	
Claimant's Ref.	

Seal

District Judge **ordered** that the attachment of earnings order made in this claim be suspended and not enforced so long as the defendant punctually pays the claimant the sum of £ by instalments of £ for every calendar month (week), the first instalment to reach the claimant by until £ , the amount payable under the order, together with any interest,* has been paid

*Where judgment was entered for £5,000 or more, or was in respect of a debt which attracts contractual or statutory interest for late payment, the claimant may be entitled to further interest.

It is further ordered that service of the order on the employer be deferred accordingly

Dated

* **If you (either the claimant or the defendant) object** to the terms contained in this order, you must write to the court with your reasons. You have 16 days from the date of the postmark to do this. A hearing will be arranged and both parties will be told when to come to court.
* Delete where order made by district judge at hearing

Take Notice

To the defendant

At your request the court has made a suspended attachment of earnings order. This means that your employer will not be told that an order has been made against you so long as you keep your payments up to date. If you fall behind with your payments, the claimant may ask the court to send the order to your employer for payments to be deducted from your earnings without further notice.

If you change your employer, you must notify the court in writing **within 7 days** giving the following details

- the name and address of your new employer (and the pay
- office if different)
- your works number and / or pay reference
- your new rate of pay
  the court claim number

IF YOU DO NOT DO WHAT THIS NOTICE TELLS YOU, YOU MAY BE FINED OR IMPRISONED OR BOTH

Address for Payment

How to Pay

- **PAYMENT(S) MUST BE MADE to the person named at the address for payment quoting their reference and the court claim number.**
- **DO NOT bring or send payments to the court. THEY WILL NOT BE ACCEPTED.**
- You should allow at least 4 days for your payment to reach the claimant or his representative.
- Make sure that you keep records and can account for all payments made. Proof may be required if there is any disagreement. It is not safe to send cash unless you use registered post.
- A leaflet giving further advice about payment can be obtained from the court.
- If you need more information you should contact the claimant or his representative.

The court office at

is open between 10 am and 4 pm Monday to Friday. When corresponding with the court, please address forms or letters to the Court Manager and quote the claim number.

N64 Suspended attachment of earnings order

Suspended Attachment of Earnings Order (Maintenance)

Claimant

Defendant

In the County Court	
Claim No.	
A/E No.	
Claimant's Ref.	

seal

The court has made an attachment of earnings order to secure payment of maintenance in the sum of £ per month (week) (and arrears of £)* and costs of £ and has fixed the normal deduction rate at £ per month (week) and the protected earnings rate at £ per month (week)

*delete if no arrears

It is ordered that the attachments of earnings order be suspended and not put into force so long as the defendant punctually pays to the court until further notice the amount payable under the order, by instalments of £ for every calenday month (week) the first instalment to reach the court by

It is further ordered that service of the order on the employer be deferred accordingly

Dated

Take Notice

To the defendant

At your request the court has made a suspended attachment of earnings order. This means that your employer will not be told that an order has been made against you so long as you keep your payments up to date. If you fall behind with your payments, the claimant may ask the court to send the order to your employer for payments to be deducted from your earnings without further notice.

If you change your employer, you must notify the court in writing **within 7 days** giving the following details:

- ☐ the name and address of your new employer (and the pay office if different
- ☐ your works number and/or pay reference
- ☐ your new rate of pay
- ☐ the court claim number

Address for Payment

You can pay the court by calling at the court office which is open 10 am to 4 pm Monday to Friday

You may only pay by:

- ☐ cash
- ☐ banker's or giro draft
- ☐ cheque supported by a cheque card
- ☐ cheque (unsupported cheques may be accepted, subject to clearance, if the Court Manager agrees).

Cheques and drafts must be made payable to HM Paymaster General and crossed.

Please bring this form with you

By post

You may only pay by:

- ☐ postal order
- ☐ banker's or giro draft
- ☐ cheque (cheques may be accepted, subject to clearance, if the Court Manager agrees).

The payment must be made out to HM Paymaster General and crossed.
This method of payment is at your own risk.
And you must:

- ☐ pay the postage
- ☐ enclose this form
- ☐ enclose a self addressed envelope so that the court can return this form with a receipt.

The court **cannot** *accept stamps or payments by bank or giro credit transfer*

Note: You should carefully check any future forms from the court to see if payments should be made directly to the claimant

Payments by standing order

If you have been ordered to pay the claimant direct by standing order, payment(s) must be made to the person named at the address for payment opposite, quoting their reference and the court claim number, or into that person's bank account.

The court office at

is open between 10 am and 4 pm Monday to Friday. Address all communications to the Court Manager quoting the claim number

N64A Suspended attachment of earnings order (maintenance)

Centralised Attachment of Earnings Payment System (CAPS)

Attachment of Earnings Order Priority Maintenance

Details of the court which made the order	
In the **County Court**	
Case No. *Always quote this*	
Application No.	
Plaintiff	
Defendant	
Dated	

To the defendant's employer

Seal

To the defendant's employer

Your employee
who is employed by you at

as a works no./pay ref
is required to make payments under a court maintenance order.

The court orders that you must deduct £ per week/month (the normal deduction rate) from the defendant's earnings and send it to the address below until further order.
You must no deduct any money which would reduce your employee's net pay below £ per week/month (the protected earnings rate).

The normal deduction and protected earnings rates may vary from time to time. This is because the Attachment of Earnings Act allows any shortfall to be carried forward from pay day to pay day until it is cleared.

All payments must be sent to CAPS

Detach this payment slip and send it to CAPS.
See overleaf for further information

Case No.

Application No.

Plaintiff

Defendant

To the Manager

Amount of payment

Notes

Further information

- ***Do not send this order to CAPS. Detach the payment slip. See How to make a payment to CAPS below.***
- The case and application numbers remain the same and should be quoted on all correspondence with CAPS.
- You should start deducting money from your employee's wages from the next pay day after you receive the order.
- Each time you make a deduction you must give your employee a written statement of the total amount deducted including your administrative charge, if any.
- Each time you make a deduction from your employee's wages you are entitled to deduct £1 to cover your administrative overheads.
- Money is required to be paid to the address below at monthly or weekly intervals.
- If your employee leaves your employment you should write to CAPS at the address below. Please give as much information as you have.
- **Failure to comply with the terms of the order can be an offence.**

How CAPS will help you

- CAPS provides you with one place to make all payments under county court attachment of earnings orders.
- If you require more information on how to operate an attachment of earnings order an explanatory booklet is available. Please phone the CAPS help line.

CAPS help line

- If you require further information please phone the CAPS helpline on

How to make payment to CAPS

- Payments should be made by crossed cheque or postal order made payable to HM Paymaster General.
- You should send your payment with the attached payment slip.
- If you would rather use a schedule instead of the payment slip you must ensure that the following information is included:
  - Case number and attachment of earnings number
  - The plaintiff's name
  - Your employee's name
  - Any pay reference
  - The amount of the payment.
- You should clearly show how much money has been deducted for each case.
- **The schedule will not be returned to you.**
- **A receipt will be sent to you for each payment.**
- **A new payment slip will be sent with the receipt.**
- The address for CAPS is

Consolidated Attachment of Earnings Order

In the **County Court**	
Consolidated A/E No. Always quote this	
Employer's Ref.	

seal

To the defendant's employer

The defendant is in arrears under several judgments and earnings are payable by you to the defendant.
You are therefore ordered to make deductions out of the earnings of the defendant in accordance with the Attachment of Earnings Act 1971 until £ , the total amount payable under the judgments, together with any interest*, has been paid. *see over

For the purpose of calculating the deductions

The normal deduction rate is £ per week/month
The protected earnings rate is £ per week/month

And you are ordered to pay the sums deducted into the office of this court at monthly intervals.

Dated

Note: This order replaces the order(s) listed here. It does NOT replace any existing PRIORITY attachment of earnings orders

Claim Number	Claimant	Balance due when order made (actual date calculated)	
	Fees due to the court for carrying out this order		
	Total due		

To the defendant

This is a copy of an attachment of earnings order sent to your employer

If you change your employer, you must notify the court in writing **within 7 days,** giving the following details:

Address for Payment

- the name and address of your new employer (and the pay office if different)
- your works number and/or pay reference
- your new rate of pay
- the court claim number

If you do not do what this notice tells you, you may be fined or imprisoned or both

The court office at

is open between 10 am and 4 pm Monday to Friday. Address all communications to the Court Manager quoting the claim number

N66 Consolidated attachment of earnings order

Employer's Record of Payments - consolidated attachment of earnings

To the employer

Employer's reference (if required)

- Please enter in the above box your name and address (if different from that shown overleaf). The form and a receipt will be returned to this address after each payment.
- Details of how to operate an attachment of earnings order are contained in the explanatory booklet enclosed (*or* which may be obtained from the court office).
- You are required to pay money deducted under this order to the court office at the intervals specified overleaf.
- Any of the claimants scheduled to this order may be able to claim interest on the amount payable to them (where judgment was for £5,000 or more, or was in respect of a debt which attracts contractual or statutory interest for late payment). You will be notified of the additional amounts to be deducted before the order is satisfied.
- Payment by post may be made by crossed cheque or postal order made payable to HM Paymaster General.
- Please enter the date and amount of each payment in the column to the right. Send the form with the payment to the court office in the envelope provided.

To the Court Manager

Date sent	Amount	

Notice of Application for Consolidated Attachment of Earnings Order

In the County Court	
Claim No.	
Consolidated A/E No.	
Claimant	
Defendant	
Claimant's Ref.	

Defendant's address

Seal

Take notice that an application for a consolidated attachment of earnings order has been made by

☐ the claimant ☐ the defendant ☐ the defendant's employer

or

☐ An attachment of earnings order is already in force and the court considers that a consolidated order should be made

This will mean that

☐ all existing attachment of earnings orders will be brought together with (1) (2)

(1) insert details of any other debts to be included in the consolidated order

(2) PRIORITY maintenance orders cannot be included

☐ the employer will be required to make only one deduction from his employee's earnings
☐ the court will hold the money and pay regular dividends
☐ the court will deduct an administration fee of 5p per £ from the money paid into court

Dated

If you (either the claimant or the defendant) object to a consolidated order being made, you must give your reasons in the space provided below and return the form to the court. You have 16 days from the date of the postmark to do this. A consolidated order will not be made only in exceptional circumstances. The court will inform the parties of its decision.

I object to a consolidated order being made because

Signed ____________________ ☐ Claimant ☐ Defendant **Dated** __________

Claimant's (solicitor's) address

When corresponding with the court, please address forms or letters to the Court Manager and quote the claim number.
The court office at

is open between 10 am and 4 pm Monday to Friday

N66A Notice of application for consolidated attachment of earnings order

Judgment Summons

Claimant

Defendant

In the **County Court**	
Claim No.	
J/S No.	
Claimant's Ref.	

Seal

(1) if the claim is issued against some or one only of several defendants name them or him

To the defendant (1)

On the the claimant obtained a court judgment or order against you

And as you have failed to pay as ordered the claimant has requested this judgment summons to be issued against you.

You are therefore summoned to appear personally in this court at
on **at** **o'clock**

to be examined on oath as to the means you have had since the date of the judgment or order to comply with the terms of the judgment or order and also to give good reasons why you should not be committed to prison for such default

Dated

Amount for which judgment summons is to issue	£	
Fee on issue of summons	£	
(Travelling expenses to be paid or offered to the defendant)	£	
AMOUNT NOW DUE	**£**	

Amount, if any, which will remain outstanding when the above sum has been paid £

Where judgment was entered for more than £5000 on or after 1 July 1991, the claimant may be entitled to interest. If you pay the amount due, together with any further amount outstanding within 8 days of service of this summons on you, the claimant will not be entitled to further interest. (The date of postal service will be 7 days after the date of posting as shown by the postmark.)

If payment is made too late to prevent the claimant attendance on the day of hearing, you may be liable for further costs

Name and address of claimant('s solicitor)

Important □ for instructions on how to pay, turn over

When corresponding with the court, please address forms and letters to the Court Manager and quote the claim number
The court office at

is open between 10 am and 4 pm

N67 Judgment summons under the Debtors Act 1869

How to Pay and Address for Payment

- PAYMENT(S) MUST BE MADE to the person named at the address for payment, quoting their reference and the court claim number.
- DO NOT bring or send payments to the court. THEY WILL NOT BE ACCEPTED.
- You should allow at least 4 days for your payment to reach the claimant or his representative.
- Make sure that you keep records and can account for all payments made. Proof may be required if there is any disagreement. It is not safe to send cash unless you use registered post.
- A leaflet giving further advice about payment can be obtained from the court.
- If you need more information you should contact the claimant or his representative.

Defendant's place of employment and description (if known)

Certificate of Service *(to be completed by the court)*

I certify that the summons of which this is a true copy was served by me on the defendant personally at the address given, or at

on the day of [19][20]
when I at the same time paid (or offered) to the defendant the sum of £ for his expenses in travelling to and from the court

Bailiff/Officer of the Court

I certify that the summons of which this is a true copy was served by me by posting it to the defendant at the address stated on the summons in accordance with the certificate of the claimant or his solicitor
or on the defendant by *(in accordance with an order for substituted service)*

on the day of [19][20]

Bailiff/Officer of the Court
Date

I certify that the summons **has not been served** for the following reason:

Bailiff/Officer of the Court
Date

Order for Debtor's Attendance at an Adjourned Hearing of a Judgment

In the County Court	
Claim No.	
J/S No.	
Claimant	
Defendant	
Claimant's Ref.	

Defendant

You failed to attend the county court on the day and time fixed for the hearing of a judgment summons after being served with the summons

The hearing was adjourned to

day the day of [19][20] at o'clock

at

when you are ordered to attend

Dated

Take Notice

To the defendant

- **You are ordered to attend the above hearing**
- **If you do not attend you may be sent to prison for up to 14 days**

Balance now due* (including costs of the hearing which you failed to attend)

*where judgment was entered for more that £5000 on or after 1 July 1991, the amount shown here may include interest to the date of the application. If so, the claimant may claim further interest until full payment

Payments into Court

You can pay the court by calling at the court office which is open 10 am to 4 pm Monday to Friday

You may only pay by:

- cash
- banker's or giro draft
- cheque supported by a cheque card
- cheque (unsupported cheques may be accepted, subject to clearance, if the Court Manager agrees).

Cheques and drafts must be made payable to HM Paymaster General and crossed.

Please bring this form with you

By post

You may only pay by:

- postal order
- banker's or giro draft
- cheque (cheques may be accepted, subject to clearance, if the Court Manager agrees).

The payment must be made out to HM Paymaster General and crossed.

This method of payment is at your own risk.

And you must:

- pay the postage
- enclose this form
- enclose a self addressed envelope so that the court can return this form with a receipt.

The court ***cannot*** *accept stamps or payments by bank or giro credit transfer*

Note: You should carefully check any future forms from the court to see if payments should be made directly to the claimant

*complete only if not paid previously

*Travelling expenses to be paid or offered to the defendant £

The court office at

is open between 10 am and 4 pm Monday to Friday. Address all communications to the Court Manager quoting the claim number

N69 Order for debtor's attendance at an adjourned hearing for a judgment summons (4.99)

Certificate of Service (to be completed by the court)

I certify that the order of which this is a true copy was served by me on the within named personally

at the address stated in the order, or at

on the day of [19][20]

when I paid (or offered) the defendant the sum of £ for his travelling expenses.

Bailiff/Officer of the Court
Date

I certify that the order has **not been served** for the following reason:

Bailiff/Officer of the Court
Date

Order of Commitment

In the County Court	
Claimant	
Defendant [1]	
Claim No.	
Judgment Summons No.	
Order of Commitment No.	

[1] Shown below present address, description and, if known, place of employment

seal

To the District Judge and Bailiffs of the court, and every constable within his jurisdiction, and to the Governor of Her Majesty's Prison at

The debtor

of

having been ordered to attend on a specified day for the adjourned hearing of a judgment summons, has failed to do so [or, having attended for the hearing of a judgment summons, has refused to be sworn [or to give evidence]]:

(enter name of judge) **has ordered** that the debtor be committed to prison for days.

YOU the District Judge, Bailiffs and others are therefore required to arrest the debtor and deliver him to the Prison and you the Governor to receive the debtor and safely keep him in prison for days from the arrest under this order or until lawfully discharged if sooner.

DATED

The court office at

is open between 10 am and 4 pm Monday to Friday . Address all communications to the Court Manager and quote the above claim number

N70 Order of commitment (4.99)

Order Revoking an Order of Commitment under Section 110 of the County Courts Act 1984

(1) Shown below present address, description and, if known, place of employment

In the County Court	
Claimant	
Defendant (1)	
Claim No.	
Judgment Summons No.	
Order of Commitment No.	

seal

UPON APPLICATION made this day by the debtor, who was committed to prison by order dated for failing to attend the adjourned hearing of a judgment summons [or for refusing to be sworn [or to give evidence] at the hearing of a judgment summons] and upon reading the affidavit [or statement] of the debtor showing the reasons for his failure [or refusal] and upon the undertaking of the debtor to attend the court [or to be sworn] [or to give evidence] when next ordered or required to do so:

(enter name of judge)has ordered that the order of commitment be revoked [and that be discharged out of the custody of the Governor of Her Majesty's Prison at as to the said failure or refusal].

THE GOVERNOR
H M PRISON

DATED

The court office at

is open between 10 am and 4 pm Monday to Friday. Address all communications to the Court Manager and quote the above claim number

N71 Order revoking an order of commitment under Section 110 of the County Courts Act 1984

FORM N72 NOTICE TO DEFENDANT WHERE A COMMITTAL ORDER MADE

Suspended Committal Order (judgment summons)

In the	
County Court	
Claim No.	
J/S No.	
Claimant's Ref.	

Claimant

Defendant

seal

Take notice that today (enter name of judge) made a committal order for your imprisonment for days

(1) where judgment entered for more than £5000 on or after 1 July 1991

This order will not be put into force if (in addition to the sum of £ paid since issue of the judgment summons) you pay to the claimant the sum, including any interest[(1)], of £

by (or by instalments of £ for every calendar month, the first instalment to reach the claimant by)

(2) delete if not applicable

(When you have paid the sum of £ there will remain a further sum of £ payable under the original judgment or order)[(2)]

Dated

Take Notice

To the defendant

If you do not pay (any instalment) in accordance with this order, a warrant for your committal may be issued without further notice, and you may be imprisoned for the period shown above.

- If you cannot pay as directed by this order you should write or go to the court office immediately, stating the reasons why you cannot pay.
- The court will send you notice of a day and time to attend before the judge.
- If you satisfy the judge that you are unable to pay, he has the power to grant a further suspension on such terms as he thinks fit

Address for Payment

How to Pay

- **PAYMENT(S) MUST BE MADE to the person named at the address for payment quoting their reference and the claim number.**
- **DO NOT bring or send payments to the court. THEY WILL NOT BE ACCEPTED.**
- You should allow at least 4 days for your payment to reach the claimant or his representative.
- Make sure that you keep records and can account for all payments made. Proof may be required if there is any disagreement. It is not safe to send cash unless you use registered post.
- A leaflet giving further advice about payment can be obtained from the court.
- If you need more information you should contact the claimant or his representative.

The court office at

is open between 10 am and 4 pm Monday to Friday. Address all communications to the Court Manager quoting the claim number

N72 Notice to defendant where a committal order made, but directed to be suspended under Debtors Act Order 28 rule 7(1)

New Order on Judgment Summons

In the	
County Court	
Claim No.	
J/S No.	
Claimant's Ref.	

Claimant

Defendant

seal

[1] where judgment has been given against more than one defendant adapt accordingly

[2] or as the case may be

[3] where judgment entered for more than £5000 on or after 1 July 1991

The defendant[1]
having failed to pay the sum of £ due under a judgment of this court
( )[2]
made on the day of 20

(enter name of judge) **has ordered** that, on hearing the judgment summons issued in this case, the defendant do pay the claimant the amount remaining due, including any interest[3], of £
(together with £ for costs, amounting to £)
by
(or by instalments of £ for every calendar month, the first instalment to reach the claimant by)

Dated

Take Notice

To the defendant

If you do not pay in accordance with this order, your goods may be removed and sold or other enforcement proceedings may be taken against you. If your circumstances change and you cannot pay, ask at the court office about what you can do.

Address for Payment

How to Pay

- **PAYMENT(S) MUST BE MADE to the person named at the address for payment quoting their reference and the claim number.**
- **DO NOT bring or send payments to the court. THEY WILL NOT BE ACCEPTED.**
- You should allow at least 4 days for your payment to reach the claimant or his representative.
- Make sure that you keep records and can account for all payments made. Proof may be required if there is any disagreement. It is not safe to send cash unless you use registered post.
- A leaflet giving further advice about payment can be obtained from the court.
- If you need more information you should contact the claimant or his representative.

The court office at

is open between 10 am and 4 pm Monday to Friday. Address all communications to the Court Manager quoting the claim number

N73 New order on judgment summons

Warrant of Committal on a Judgment Summons under the Debtors Act 1869

In the County Court	
Claim No.	
J/S No.	
Warrant No.	

Claimant

Defendant

Seal

To the district judge and bailiffs of the court, and every constable within his jurisdiction, and to the Governor of Her Majesty's Prison at

(1) state names — The claimant obtained a judgment or an order against the defendant(s)(1)

(2) or case the case may be — in this court ( )(2)
on the day of [19][20] , for payment of £ for debt/ damages
(3) where judgment entered for more than £5000 — together with any interest(3) , and cost forthwith (or by the)
(or by instalments of £ for every calendar month) and subsequent costs have been incurred amounting to £

And the defendant having failed to pay the sum of £ due under the said judgment or order

And on the hearing this day of a judgment summons issued against the defendant, it has been proved to the satisfaction of the court that the defendant has (or has had since the date of the judgment or order) the means to pay the sum and refuses or neglect (or has refused or neglected) to pay the same and the defendant has given no good reasons why he should not be committed to prison

It is therefore ordered that the defendant be committed to prison for days, unless he pays the sum stated below, or files an affidavit stating that a receiving order of adjudication in bankruptcy has been made against him

You, the district judge, bailiffs and others, are therefore required to arrest the defendant and to deliver him to Prison and you, the Governor, to receive the defendant, and safely keep him in prison for days from the arrest under this order, or until lawfully discharged if sooner

(4) date on which order was made in court — **Dated**(4)

Warrant issued on the day of [19][20]

Note: a separate warrant must be issued against every defendant required to be arrested

Sum in payment of which defendant had made default at the time of issue of judgment summons (including interest to date of judgment summons)(3)		
Fee and costs on issue and hearing of judgment summons		
Sub total		
Deduct amount paid since issue of judgment summons		
Sub total		
Deduct amount paid since issue of this order		
Interest from date judgment summons to date of request for warrant of committal(3)(5)		
Sum on payment of which the defendant is to be discharged		

(5) delete unless judgment summons issued for balance of debt

N74 Warrant of committal on a judgment summons under the Debtors Act 1869 (4.99)

I certify that this duplicate warrant of commital is in substitution for the original warrant dated

and numbered

and has been issued by order of the Judge by reason of the failure of the Debtor to comply with the terms imposed when the Debtor was discharged in respect of the original warrant of committal.

DATED

District Judge

N76 Certificate to be indorsed on duplicate warrant of committal issued for re-arrest of debtor. (4.99)

SEAL

-v-

Penal Notice

To

of

You must obey the directions contained in this order. If you do not, you will be guilty of contempt of court, and you may be sent to prison.

Date

N.77 - w3Notice as to consequences of disobedience to order of court

Notice to Show Good Reason why an Order for Your Committal to Prison should not be made

In the	
County Court	
Claim No	

Between

________________________ **Applicant Claimant**

and

________________________ **Respondent Defendant**

Seal

(1) Insert name of person against whom the committal order is sought.
(2) Insert full address.
(3) Set out the precise parts of the injunction or undertaking relevant to this committal application.

To [(1)]

of[(2)]

On the day of [19][20] , the Court made an order [or you gave an undertaking] as follows:[(3)]

(4) Insert name of applicant.
(5) List the ways in which it is alleged that the respondent has disobeyed the order or broken the undertaking. If necessary continue on a separate sheet.

[(4)] has applied for an order that you should be committed to prison. It is alleged that you have disobeyed the order [*or* broken the undertaking] by[(5)]

You must attend Court

at

on the day of [19][20], at o'clock

to show good reason why you should not be sent to prison.

☐ If the Court is satisfied that any of the allegations are true, it may order that you be imprisoned for your contempt of this Court.

☐ **Important instructions about what you should do are set out overleaf.**

The applicant's solicitors are
Name
Address

Ref/tel no

The Court Office at
is open from 10 am to 4 pm Monday to Friday.

N78 Notice of an application to commit

Claim No.

Important notes

- ☐ The Court has the power to send you to prison if it finds that any of the allegations made against you are true. Full details of the allegations are contained in the applicant's sworn statement (the affidavit).
- ☐ You must attend court on the date shown on the front of this form. It is in your own interest to do so. You should bring any witnesses and documents with you which you think will help you put your side of the case.
- ☐ If you can show good reason why you should not be sent to prison you must tell the Court.
- ☐ If you need advice you should show this document at once to your Solicitor or go to a Citizens Advice Bureau.
- ☐ Even if you do not seek advice you can, if you wish, file a sworn statement at the Court setting out your side of the case. The Court Office can give you a form for this purpose and it can be sworn before a Court Officer. If you have disobeyed the order you can apologise for it on this form. You must still attend court on the date shown, however.

For Court use only

I certify that the notice, of which this is a true copy, was served by me on

(date) ....

or: the   personally,

at the address stated in the notice, or at

Or *in accordance with an order for substituted service.*

Bailiff/Officer of the Court

....

Notice of Non-Service

I certify that this notice has not been served for the following reasons:

Bailiff/Officer of the Court

Committal or Other Order upon Proof of Disobedience of a Court Order or Breach of an Undertaking

In the ______ **County Court**

Claim No. *Always quote this*

Between ______ **Applicant Claimant Petitioner**

and ______ **Respondent Defendant**

seal

Before His (Her) Honour Judge
Sitting at on *(date)*

1 **An application having been made by**(1) for committal of(2) to prison for disobeying the order [breach of the undertaking] dated The relevant terms of the order (undertaking) and the allegations made by the applicant are recited on the attached notice to show good reason

or

2 **Whereas**(2) has been suspected of a breach of the attached order dated and has been arrested by a constable and brought before the Judge under section 47(6) of the Family Law Act 1996.

or

3. **Whereas**(2) has been suspected of a breach of the attached order [undertaking] dated and has been arrested under a warrant of arrest and brought before the Judge under [section 47(8) of the Family Law Act 1996] [section 3(3) of the Protection from Harassment Act 1997].

IMMEDIATE CUSTODIAL ORDER

It is ordered that(2) be committed for contempt to Her Majesty's Prison (be detained under section 9(1) of the Criminal Justice Act 1982) at(3) for a (total) period of(4) or until lawfully discharged if sooner, and that a warrant of arrest and committal be issued forthwith.

And the contemnor can apply to the (court) (judge) to purge his contempt and ask for release.

[**And**, as the court by order dated dispensed with service of the notice of application for a committal order,
It is ordered that the contemnor be brought before a judge of this court as soon as practicable.]

ALTERNATIVE DISPOSAL

It is ordered that(2) be committed for contempt to prison for a (total) period of(4)

The order is suspended until [19][20] and will not be put in force if during that time the contemnor complies with the following terms:

And it is further ordered that in the event of non compliance any application for issue of the warrant shall be made to a judge (on notice to the contemnor)

It is ordered that(2) be fined the sum of £
Such sum to be paid into the office of the court within 14 days of the date of this order.

It is ordered that consideration of the penalty for the contempts found proved be adjourned until [19] [20] and may be restored for decision if during that time(2) does not comply with the following terms

PROVISION FOR COSTS

And it is ordered that

Date

For record of service, hearing and contempts found proved, see overleaf

N79 Committal or other order upon proof and disobedience of a court order or breach of an undertaking (Family Law Act 1996) (Protection from Harassment Act 1997)
(4.99)

RECORD OF SERVICE, HEARING AND CONTEMPTS FOUND PROVED

At the hearing

(1) [appeared personally] [was represented by solicitor / counsel] [did not attend]
(2) [appeared personally] [was represented by solicitor / counsel] [did not attend]

The court read the affidavits of (Names)	Date affidavit(s) sworn

And the court heard oral evidence given by
Name(s)

And the court is satisfied having considered the facts disclosed by the evidence and/or admitted in court by him/her that(2) has been guilty of contempt of this court by disobeying the order (breaking the undertaking) dated by (and as set out in the attached schedule)

	And for the particular contempt the court imposed the penalty of:
1.	1.
2.	2.

RECORD OF SERVICE

Service of Injunction Order with Penal Notice incorporated or indorsed	Service of Notice to show good reason in form N78	Arrest under warrant of arrest
(Order dated [19][20]	(Order dated [19][20]	respondent arrested on
(for substituted) (dispensing with) service)	(for substituted) (dispensing with) service)	by
Service proved by	Service proved by	
☐ certificate of service dated [19][20]	☐ certificate of service dated [19][20]	in accordance with a warrant of arrest issued on
☐ certificate of bailiff	☐ certificate of bailiff	
☐ oral evidence of	☐ oral evidence of	

Service of Immediate Custodial Order

I *(name of Officer)* certify that I served the contemnor with a copy of this order by:

☐ delivery by hand to the contemnor before he was taken from the court building or other place of arrest to the place of detention
☐ delivery by hand to the contemnor at *(time)* on *(date)* [19][20] at *(place)*

Where a suspended committal order is made, the applicant is responsible for service. (Rules of the Supreme Court Order 52 rule 7(2).) Where there is suspended committal order or penalty is adjourned on terms, personal service is advisable.

The court office is open from 10 am to 4 pm Monday to Friday.

When corresponding with the court, please address forms and letters to the Court Manager and quote the case number.

Notes on completion of page 2 ⬅
(Record of service, hearing and contempts found proved)

REPRESENTATION

The parties and their legal representative (advocate only)

AFFIDAVIT EVIDENCE

Only those affidavits which the judge has considered at the hearing. There is unlikely to be any affidavit evidence offered where the respondent has been brought to court under a power of arrest.

ORAL EVIDENCE

Only those witnesses sworn and examined

CONTEMPTS FOUND PROVED

List and give exact details of only those allegations of contempt which the judge has found proved.

If separate penalties are imposed for each contempt found proved these are to be recorded in the right-hand column showing whether or not periods of detention are to run consecutively or concurrently.

If necessary annex additional page and continue list on it. If an additional page is not used delete the words (and as set out in the attached schedule).

JUDGE'S APPROVAL

The Judge must be asked to initial the order here

RECORD OF SERVICE

Enter details of certificates of service.

Record of delivery of an undertaking need not be made on this document as it can be found on the form of undertaking.

A sealed copy of the approved order must be served on the contemnor, see Order 29 rule 1(5) recited opposite. ➡

Where the respondent is brought before the court under a power of arrest delete record of service of form N78.
Where the respondent is brought before the court under a warrant of arrest delete record of service of form N78 and complete record of service of warrant of arrest.

Disobedience of a Court Order or Breach of an Undertaking (Form N79)

Notes for Guidance on Completion

The Court Officer responsible for the forms completion should note the following:

- **Where the respondent is brought before the court after being arrested under a power of arrest** (Section 47(6) of the Family Law Act 1996) a sealed copy of the injunction order giving the power of arrest (not Power of Arrest form FL406) with penal notice indorsed becomes part of form N79 and must be attached to the approved order.

- **Where the respondent is brought before the court after being arrested under a warrant of arrest** (section 47(8) of the Family Law Act 1996) (section 3(3) of the Protection from Harassment Act 1997) a sealed copy of the injunction order becomes part of form N79 and must be attached to the approved order.

- **In all other cases** Form N78 (notice to show good reason why an order for committal should not be made) becomes part of form N79 and a sealed copy of N78 must be attached to the approved order.

- In all cases the warrant is in form N80.

- **When the form has been fully completed it must be passed to the judge for approval.** If the judge is available he/she should be asked to approve and initial or sign the final (typed) version. If this is not possible the judge must be asked to initial or sign the final hand-written draft. In either case the document endorsed by the judge **must be retained on the court file.**

- Before the order is served it must also be checked by an officer of no less than HEO grade.

- Before the order is served these notes should be detached, they are for the guidance of Court Staff only.

When an immediate custodial order is made:

- A copy of N79 (with attached N78 or injunction) must be sent to the Office of the Official Solicitor.

- A sealed copy of the approved order must be served on the contemnor. Order 29 rule 1(5) CCR states:

  If a committal order is made, the order shall be for the issue of a warrant of committal and unless the judge otherwise orders:-

  (a) a copy of the order shall be served on the person to be committed either before or at the time of the execution of the warrant;
  or
  (b) where the warrant has been signed by the Judge, the order for issue of the warrant may be served on the person to be committed at any time within 36 hours after execution of the warrant.

Notes for completion of page 1

Terms or names that may be used more than once in the order are numbered in brackets as follows:

(1) Person making application for committal
(2) Person against whom the committal order is made (contemnor)
(3) Name of prison or young offender institution
(4) Period of detention

If the respondent has been brought before the court under a power of arrest (Family Law Act 1996) delete 1 and 3.

If the respondent has been brought before the court under a warrant of arrest (Family Law Act 1996 or Protection from Harassment Act 1997) delete 1 and 2.

In all other cases delete 2 and 3.

Enter the date of order (with penal notice incorporated or indorsed) or undertaking.

Date of form N78 Notice to show good reason (applies to 1 only).

Date of the warrant of arrest (applies to 3 only).

Note: A warrant of arrest cannot be issued on an undertaking under the Protection from Harassment Act 1997.

IMMEDIATE CUSTODIAL ORDER

Complete this section if an immediate custodial order is made otherwise delete and complete section below

Section 9(1) of CJA is for persons aged less than 21 and at least 18.

The total period of detention must be specified by the Judge. The maximum period for contempt of court (including a county court) is 2 years.

If the offence is failure to do a specific act and the judge decides that the application may be made to a district judge upon proof that the act has been done delete (judge) otherwise delete (court).

Complete only if order dispensing with service of notice of application was granted otherwise delete.

ALTERNATIVE DISPOSAL

Delete this section if an immediate custodial order is made otherwise delete alternatives not selected by judge.

Enter the exact terms of any suspended committal order or adjournment of penalty.

There are further possible alternative disposals, eg under sections 35, 37 and 38 of the Mental Health Act and sequestration.

COSTS

Enter any order for costs here or show that no order for costs has been made if applicable

Date the order here

N329 Notes for guidance on completion (Form N79)

Warrant of Committal to prison

In the	
County Court	
Claim No.	
Warrant No.	

Between

Applicant
Petitioner

and

Respondent
Defendant

Seal

To
- **the District Judge and Bailiffs of the Court**
- **every constable within his jurisdiction**
- **the Governor(of Her Majesty's Prison at)**(1)

(1) Name of Prison

(2) Name and (3) address of person to be committed.

On the **day of** [19][20] ,
(enter name of judge) has ordered that (2)

of (3)

should be committed to Prison (4) (detained under Section 9(1) Criminal Justice Act 1982) for a period of (5)

(4) Where the person to be committed is aged less than 21 years and at least 18 delete all references to prison otherwise delete reference to Sec 9(1)CJA

You the District Judge and Bailiff are therefore required forthwith to arrest and deliver
(2)

to (Her Majesty's Prison at) (1)

(5) State term of imprisonment

And you, the Governor, are required to receive and keep (2)
safely (in prison) from the arrest under this warrant for a period of (5) or until lawfully discharged, if sooner.

(6) Add if so ordered otherwise delete

[(6) **And**, as the court by order dated dispensed with service of the notice of application for a committal order,
It is ordered that you, the Governor, bring (2)
before a judge of this court at such time and place as the court shall specify and afterwards, return him to the prison unless the court orders his discharge.]

Date

I arrested the person named in this warrant on (date)
and delivered him into the custody of the Governor (of Her Majesty's Prison) at (1)
on *(date)*

Bailiff of the County Court

The Court Office is open from 10am to 4pm Monday to Friday

Address all communications to the Court Manager and quote the above claim number.

N80 Warrant for committal to prison (4.99)

Notice to Solicitor to show cause why an undertaking should not be enforced by committal to prison

In the County Court	
Claim No.	
Claimant	
Defendant	

To

of

seal

TAKE NOTICE that you are required to attend at a court to be held at

on

at o'clock to show cause why an order should not be made committing you to prison

for failing to carry out the undertaking given by you on the day of [19][20],

to this court to[1]

(1) Here set out terms of undertaking

DATED

The court office at

is open between 10 am and 4 pm Monday to Friday. Address all communications to the Court Manager quoting the above Claim Number

N81 Notice to solicitor to show cause why an undertaking should not be enforced by committal to prison (4.99)

New Order on Judgment Summons

In the	
County Court	
Claim No.	
Claimant's Ref.	

Claimant

Defendant

seal

(1) enter name of person against whom order is made

(2) state terms of undertaking

By an undertaking given to this court on the day of [19][20],
(1) of
as solicitor for the claimant (or defendant) undertook to(2)

Now upon reading the affidavit of
dated the day of [19][20], and upon hearing

(3) add if solicitor giving the undertaking does not appear in person

((3)and being satisfied upon oath [or by the indorsement of a bailiff of this court (or the County Court)], that a copy of the notice to show cause why(1) should not be committed has been served personally upon him and being satisfied that(1) has failed to carry out the undertaking before referred to)

(enter name of judge) has ordered that (1)

(4) insert name of prison used by the court

be committed for contempt to Her Majesty's Prison at(4)
for a period of or until lawfully discharged if sooner and that a warrant for the arrest and committal of(1) be issued forthwith

And it is ordered that (1)
do pay the costs of this application and of the committal of, (to be assessed by the District Judge) and paid by(1)

(5) insert name of party to receive the costs and where payable

to(5)
on or before (within 14 days of assessment)

(6) delete if inapplicable

[And it is further ordered that any application for the release from custody of(1)
should be made to the Judge](6)

Dated

Address for Payment

How to Pay

- **PAYMENT(S) MUST BE MADE to the person named at the address for payment quoting their reference and the claim number**
- **DO NOT bring or send payments to the court. THEY WILL NOT BE ACCEPTED.**
- You should allow at least 4 days for your payment to reach the claimant or his representative.
- Make sure that you keep records and can account for all payments made. Proof may be required if there is any disagreement. It is not safe to send cash unless you use registered post.
- A leaflet giving further advice about payment can be obtained from the court.
- If you need more information you should contact the claimant or his representative.

The court office at

is open between 10 am and 4 pm Monday to Friday. Address all communications to the Court Manager quoting the claim number

N82 Order for committal for failure by solicitor to carry out undertaking (4.99)

Order for Discharge from Custody under Warrant of Committal

In the	
County Court	
Claim No.	
Claimant's Ref.	

seal

Claimant

Defendant

Upon application made this day of [19][20],
by
who was committed to prison for contempt by an order of this court dated the day of [19][20], and upon reading the application of
attested on the day of [19][20], showing that he is desirous of purging his contempt, and upon hearing

(1) or, if no one appears for him

(1)(and upon being satisfied that the notice of this application has been duly served upon the
)

It is ordered that

(2) insert name of prison

be discharged out of the custody of Her Majesty's Prison at(2)

(3) add if so ordered

(3)**And it is ordered** that
do pay the sum of £ , the costs of this application, such costs to be assessed and paid to(4)
by (or within 14 days of assessment)

(4) insert name of person to whom payment is to be made

Dated

Address for Payment

How to Pay

- **PAYMENT(S) MUST BE MADE to the person named at the address for payment quoting their reference and the claim number.**
- **DO NOT bring or send payments to the court. THEY WILL NOT BE ACCEPTED.**
- You should allow at least 4 days for your payment to reach the claimant or his representative.
- Make sure that you keep records and can account for all payments made. Proof may be required if there is any disagreement. It is not safe to send cash unless you use registered post.
- A leaflet giving further advice about payment can be obtained from the court.
- If you need more information you should contact the claimant or his representative.

The court office at

is open between 10 am and 4 pm Monday to Friday. Address all communications to the Court Manager quoting the claim number.

N83 Order for discharge from custody under warrant of committal

Interpleader Summons to Execution Creditor

In the	
County Court	
Claim No.	
Interpleader No.	
Warrant No.	

TO THE EXECUTION CREDIT OR

seal

BETWEEN... *Execution Creditor*

OF...

AND... *Execution Debtor*

OF...

AND... *Claimant*

OF...

The claimant having made a claim to certain goods [or the proceeds of sale (or value) of certain goods] [or to certain rent alleged to be due to him in respect of the premises upon which certain goods were] seized under a warrant of execution issued out of this court at your request,

You are summoned to appear at

on

at o'clock, when the claim will be decided, and such order made as the court thinks fit.

DATED

The court office at

is open between 10 am and 4 pm Monday to Friday. Address all communications to the Court Manager quoting the above Claim Number

N88 Interpleader Summons to Execution Creditor

"INTERPLEADER NO.

I certify that the summons of which this is a true copy was served by me on

(date)

Service was effected

(a) By posting it to the Execution Creditor on
at the address stated in the summons.

(b) At the address stated in the summons (or at

)

by delivering it to the Execution Creditor personally (or to

apparently not less than 16 years old, who promised to give it to the Execution Creditor on the same day or on).

(c) By inserting it, enclosed in an envelope addressed to the Execution Creditor in the letter box at the address stated on the summons for the reason at (1).

Bailiff/Officer of the Court

(1) I have reason to believe the summons will reach the Execution Creditor in sufficient time, because:

Bailiff

OR I certify that this summons has not been served for the following reasons:

Bailiff/Officer of the Court"

Interpleader Summons to Claimant claiming goods or rent under an execution

In the County Court	
Claim No.	
Interpleader No.	
Warrant No.	

seal

TO THE CLAIMANT

BETWEEN .... *Execution Creditor* AND .... *Execution Debtor*

OF.. OF ....

AND.. *Claimant*

OF..

You are summoned to appear at

on

at o'clock

To support a claim made by you to certain goods
[or to the proceeds of sale (or value) of certain goods]
[or to certain rent alleged to be due to you in respect of the premises upon which certain goods were]
seized under a warrant of execution issued out of this court at the request of the execution creditor.

If you are unable to prove your claim the goods will be sold and the proceeds paid over
[or the proceeds of sale (or value) will be paid over],
according to the requirements of the said warrant.

DATED

The court office at

is open between 10 am and 4 pm Monday to Friday Address all communications to the Court Manager quoting the above Claim Number

N88(1) Interpleader summons to claimant claiming goods or rent under an execution

"INTERPLEADER NO.

I certify that the summons of which this is a true copy was served by me on

(date)

Service was effected

(a) By posting it to the claimant on
at the address stated in the summons.

(b) At the address stated in the summons (or at
by delivering it to the claimant personally (or to

apparently not less than 16 years old, who promised to give it to the claimant on the same day or on).

(c) By inserting it, enclosed in an envelope addressed to the claimant in the letter box at the address stated on the summons for the reason at (1).

Bailiff/Officer of the Court

(1) I have reason to believe the summons will reach the Execution Creditor in suf ficient time, because:

Bailiff

OR I certify that this summons has not been served for the following reasons:

Bailiff/Officer of the Court"

Interpleader Summons to persons making Adverse Claims to Debt, or other Thing in Action, Money or Goods not the Subject Matter of an Action

In the County Court	
Claim No.	

seal

TO THE CLAIMANTS

BETWEEN..*Applicant*

OF..

....

AND...*Claimant* AND..*Claimant*

OF... OF ....

....

(1) Enter name & address

(1)

of

has filed an affidavit (a copy of which is attached) stating that he has received adverse claims from

of

and

of

(2) Here state the debt, thing in action, money or goods to which the adverse claims are made

to(2)

YOU ARE THEREFORE SUMMONED to appear at a court to be held at

on at o'clock

(3) Delete as necessary

when the District Judge will consider giving directions for the determination of this action [or when judgment will be given determining the rights and claims of the said claimants](3)

DATED

TAKE NOTICE you are each required within fourteen days after the service of this summons on you to file in the court office either three copies of a notice that you make no claim or three copies of particulars stating the grounds of your claim.

The court office at

is open between 10 am and 4 pm Monday to Friday. Address all communications to the Court Manager quoting the above Claim Number

N89 Interpleader Summons to persons making adverse claims to debt, or other thing in action, money or goods not the subject matter of an action

Summons for Assaulting an officer of the Court or rescuing goods

In the County Court	
Claim No.	
Claimant	
Defendant	
Claimant's Ref.	

To

seal

You are summoned to appear at a court to be held at

on the at o'clock

to answer a complaint made against you by

an Officer of this Court, and to show cause why an order should not be made against you

under the County Courts Act 1984, for payment of a fine or for your committal to prison or both,

for an assault committed by you on the day of [19][20],

upon the said Officer whilst in the execution of his duty [or for rescuing or attempting to rescue,

on the day of [19][20], certain goods seized under process of

this Court].

DATED

Note: to be served personally not less than eight days before the return date

The court office at

is open between 10 am and 4 pm Monday to Friday. Address all communications to the Court Manager quoting the above Claim Number

N90 Summons for assaulting an officer of the court or rescuing goods

Order of Commitment and/or imposing a fine for Assaulting an Officer of the Court or Rescuing Goods

In the

County Court

seal

To the District Judge and bailiffs of the court, and every constable within his jurisdiction, and to the Governor of Her Majesty's Prison at

(1) Enter name & address of offender

IT has been proved to the satisfaction of the court that
(1)

on the day of [19][20], [assaulted an officer of this court, whilst in the execution of his duty] or [(and) rescued or attempted to rescue certain goods seized under process of this court]

(2) Delete as necessary

1. (enter name of judge) **has ORDERED**(2) that

do pay a fine of £ for the offence(s) and the sum of £ for costs, amounting together to the sum of £ and do pay that sum into the office of this court forthwith [or by instalments of £ for every the first instalment to be paid on or before the

2. (enter name of judge) **has ORDERED**(2) that

shall be committed to prison for

AND YOU the District Judge, bailiffs and others are therefore required to arrest

and deliver him to Prison

AND YOU the Governor to receive

and keep him safely in prison for

from the arrest under this order or until he shall sooner be discharged by due course of law.

DATED

The court office at

is open between 10 am and 4 pm Monday to Friday. Address all communications to the Court Manager

N91 Order of commitment and/or imposing a fine for assaulting an officer of the court or rescuing goods.

Claim No.

Warrant No.

Defendant

Address

Occupation

I arrested the within named person on

the day of [19][20],

and delivered him into the custody of

the Governor of HM Prison at

on

the day of [19][20].

Bailiff of the
County Court

Application for an administration order

Please read the notes for guidance (form N270) before completing this form. Complete all details in black ink.

Name of court

Application no.
(For court use only)

Part A - Statement of means

Please complete the following statement of means as fully as possible. Continue on a separate sheet if necessary.

1. Personal details

Full name

Address (including postcode)

Mr ☐ Mrs ☐ Miss ☐ Ms ☐

Married ☐ Civil partner ☐ Single ☐ Other

Date of birth D D M M Y Y Y Y

2. Dependants *(people you look after financially)*

Number of children in each age group

under 11 ☐ 11-15 ☐ 16-17 ☐ 18 and over ☐

Other dependants *(give details)*

3. Bank/Building society accounts and savings

☐ I have a current account

☐ The account is in **credit** by £

☐ The account is **overdrawn** by £

☐ I have a savings or deposit account

☐ The amount in the account is £

I have other savings or investments *(give details)*

4. Employment

Complete all the boxes that apply. If you are not in paid employment and are not seeking work eg. a homemaker, you should say so in the unemployment section.

☐ **I am employed as a**

My employer (including full address)

My works number and/or pay reference

Jobs other than main job *(give details)*

☐ **I have been unemployed for** *(say how long)*

Do you have any reason to believe that you may be able to obtain employment within the next three months?

☐ **I am self employed as a**

Give details of:
a) contracts and other work in hand

b) any sums due for work done £

☐ I receive a pension

5. Property

I live in

jointly owned property ☐ my own property ☐ lodgings ☐

rented property ☐ other eg. with parents ☐

amount due under a mortgage/ charges against property £

value of property £

N92 Application for an Administration Order (Order 35, rule 2(1) (04.06) HMCS

Statement of means - income and expenditure

Important: It will help the court if you give all sums for income and expenditure as either monthly or weekly figures. Try not to mix the two.

6. Income - See page 2 of the notes for guidance before completing this section

	specify weekly/monthly		specify weekly/monthly
My usual take home pay	£	sub total brought forward	£
My partner contributes to the expenses listed in section 7	£	Income support (see notes for guidance)	£
Others living in my home give me	£	Child benefit(s)	£
My pension(s)	£	Other state benefits	
Other income (give details)			£
	£		£
Sub total	£	**Total**	£

7. Regular expenses and arrears

See page 3 of the notes for guidance before completing any part of this section	**(a) Regular payments** Enter the amount you usually spend or must pay for each item, weekly or monthly (please complete each entry: write n/a if not applicable) *weekly/monthly*	**(b) Total arrears** If you are in arrears with any of the items in the regular payments column(a), enter the total arrears owed in column (b). Full details should be given in the list of creditors (see notes for guidance).	**(c) Regular arrears payments** If you are paying off the arrears shown in column (b) show much you are paying weekly or monthly in column (c). Do not include these amounts as regular payments in column (a). *weekly/monthly*
Rent	£	£	£
Mortgage/home loan	£	£	£
Second mortgage/secured loan	£	£	£
Life insurance/endowment	£	£	£
House contents insurance	£	£	£
Council tax/community charge arrears	£	£	£
Maintenance/child support	£	£	£
Water/sewerage charges	£	£	£
Ground rent/service charge	£	£	£
Gas (or other fuel eg coal, oil)	£	£	£
Electricity	£	£	£
TV rental / licence	£	£	£
Magistrates' Court fine(s)	£	£	£
DSS Social Fund Loan/overpaid benefit	£	£	£
Telephone *(line, phone rental, essential calls only)*	£	£	£
Child care	£	£	£
Food and household essentials	£	£	£
Clothing	£	£	£
Laundry	£	£	£
Travelling expenses *(essential eg work, school)*	£	£	£
School meals/meals at work	£	£	£
Prescriptions/dentists/optician	£	£	£
Others *(eg hire purchase)* see guidance notes			
	£	£	£
	£	£	£
	£	£	£
	7a Total expenses	**7b Total arrears**	
	£ per w/m	£	£

Part B - List of creditors *(see page 4 of the notes for guidance)*

Applicant's name	Application no. *(For court use only)*	

Name of creditor, if known, and address to which payment should be sent. Give reference/account number. If judgment debt, also state court and case number *(see example 3 in notes for guidance).*	If someone else is jointly responsible for part of this debt give details (eg. guarantor, joint account etc.)	Amount outstanding £	p
	Sub total		

List of creditors - continued

Name of creditor, if known, and address to which payment should be sent. Give reference/account number. If judgment debt, also state court and case number	If someone else is jointly responsible for part of this debt give details (eg. guarantor, joint account etc.) **Sub total brought forward**	Amount outstanding £	p
	Total		

continue on a separate sheet if necessary

Part C - Offer of payment

You do not have to make an offer of payment as the court will fix a rate for you to pay based on the information you have given on this form. If you do make an offer, it should be one you can afford to pay.

I offer to pay by instalments of

£ ______ per week/month

☐ **Please tick if you object to the court making an attachment of earnings order and give your reasons in the space opposite** *(see notes for guidance).*

If you wish the court to take anything else into account when making an order, please give details *(see notes for guidance).*

Part D - Declaration *(to be signed and sworn or affirmed before an officer of the court)*

Before you sign this form take it to the court office with a copy of the judgment or order *(see notes for guidance)*

I ask the court to make an administration order.

I ______ (full name)

of ______ (address)

declare on oath/affirm that to the best of my knowledge, the names of all creditors, and the debts I owe them, are truly recorded in the list of creditors and that the information I have given in my application and the statement of means is true.

______ Signature

Sworn/affirmed at:

in the County of this day of 20

before me

Officer of the court, appointed by the Judge to take affidavits pursuant to s.58 of the County Courts Act 1984

 FORM N93

IN THE **COUNTY COURT**

BETWEEN .... CLAIMANT CLAIM No.

AND .... DEFENDANT ATTACHMENT APPLICATION No.

I, ...

of ....
the above named defendant, state that I owe the persons mentioned in the list below, including the claimant in this action, the sums given opposite their names, which do not total more than £5000. To the best of my knowledge I am not indebted to any other person whatsoever.

If an order is made for the administration of my estate, I request that it may provide for the payment of my debts in full [or to the extent of pence in the pound] by instalments of £ for every month

LIST OF CREDITORS

PLEASE COMPLETE USING BLACK INK

Name of creditor (and claim number in the claim of a judgment debt). If known, give creditor's reference number.	Address and description of creditor	Amount of debt £	p	Name and address of any other person liable for the debt.	Particulars and estimated value of any security in respect of the debt.
	CARRIED FORWARD £				

NOTE: The claimant's judgment debt must be inserted as well as all other debts.
If any of the above creditors, in addition to the claimant, has sued the defendant in any court, the claim or order in each case must be produced to the District Judge.

N93 - wList of Creditors (4.99) Printed on behalf of The Court Se

LIST OF CREDITORS *(Continued)*

Name of creditor (and claim number in the claim of a judgment debt). If known, give creditor's reference number.	Address and description of creditor	Amount of debt £	p	Name and address of any other person liable for the debt.	Particulars and estimated value of any security in respect of the debt.
	BROUGHT FORWARD £				
	TOTAL £				

I, ... aforesaid make oath and say that to the best of my knowledge, the names of all my creditors, and the debts due from me to them, are truly set forth in the above list of my creditors, and that the above particulars and statements are true.

Sworn at in the
of this
day of [19][20]

Before me *Officer of a court, appointed by the Judge to take affidavits*

Administration order

To the debtor and creditors *(address for service)*

In the County Court	
Administration Order Number	
Debtor	
Creditor	
Creditor's ref	

Seal

An order is made for the administration of the debtor's estate in the following terms:
(enter name of judge) **ordered** that the debtor pay into the office of the court the debts listed in the schedule below in full [or to the extent of pence in the pound] by monthly instalments of £ until this order is satisfied, the first instalment to be paid by
(**and it is directed** that this order by subject to review after (or at intervals of)).

Dated

Schedule of debts

Name of creditor	Amount £	p	Name of creditor	Amount £	p
			Brought forward		
Carried forward					
			Fee due to the court for carrying out this order		
			TOTAL	£	

To the debtor

- **If you do not keep up your payments this ordemay be revoked. This means that your creditors will be able to pursue the money owed to them separately.**
- **If you cannot pay as ordered oryou change your address, you should contact the court immediately.**

You must make payments into court

You can pay the court by calling at the court office which is open 10 am to 4 pm Monday to Friday
You may only pay by:
- cash
- banker's or giro draft
- cheque supported by a cheque card
- cheque (unsupported cheques may be accepted,
- subject to clearance, if the Court Manager agrees)

Cheques and drafts must be made payable to HM Paymaster General and crossed. *Please bring this form with you.*

This administration order has been registered in the Register of County Court Judgments. When the order is paid in full you can ask the court to mark the entry in the register as satisfied and for a certificate proving payment. You will need to pay a fee for this.

By post

You may only pay by:
- postal order
- banker's or giro draft
- cheque (cheques may be accepted, subject to
- clearance, if the Court Manager agrees).

The payment must be made out to HM Paymaster General and crossed. This method of payment is at your own risk.
And you must:
- pay the postage
- enclose this form
- enclose a self addressed envelope so that the court can return
- this form with a receipt

The court **cannot** *accept stamps or payments by bank and giro credit transfers.*

The court office is open from 10 am till 4 pm Monday to Friday

When corresponding with the court, please address forms and letters to the Court Manager and quote the above administration order number.

N94 Administration order

Order Revoking an Adminstration Order

In the County Court	
Administration Order No.	
Debtor	
Creditor	
Creditor's Ref.	

seal

To the debtor and creditors *(address for service)*

(enter name of judge) **has ordered that**

the administration order made on

in favour of the above named debtor be revoked

(because) (unless)

Dated

*delete where order made by District Judge at hearing

* If you (the debtor or any of his creditors) object to the making of this order, you must write to the court with your reasons. You have 16 days from the date of the postmark to do this. A hearing will be arranged and you will be told when to come to court.

To the debtor

The instructions below tell you how to pay your creditors after the administration order has been revoked

How to Pay

- **PAYMENT(S) MUST NOW BE MADE TO THE CREDITORS OR THEIR REPRESENTATIVES** quoting their reference (and the claim number if applicable)
- **DO NOT** bring or send payments to the court. **THEY WILL NOT BE ACCEPTED.**
- You should allow at least 4 days for your payment to reach the creditor or his representative.
- Make sure that you keep records and can account for all payments made. Proof may be required if there is any disagreement. It is not safe to send cash unless you use registered post.
- A leaflet giving further advice about payment of court judgments can be obtained from the court.
- If you need more information you should contact the creditor or his representative.

*** To the Creditor**

The court has declared a dividend on the amount paid by the debtor.

Enclosed is a payable order for £

* *delete if not applicable*

The court office at

is open between 10 am and 4 pm Monday to Friday. Address all communications to the Court Manager quoting the administration order number

N95 Order revoking an administration order

Order Suspending or Varying an Administration Order

In the County Court	
Administration Order No.	
Debtor	
Creditor	
Creditor's Ref.	

seal

To the debtor and creditors *(address for service)*

(enter name of judge) **has ordered that**

the administration order made on

in favour of the above named debtor be (suspended) (varied)

as follows

Dated

(1) delete where order made by District Judge at hearing

(1) If you (the debtor or any of his creditors) object to the making of this order, you must write to the court with your reasons. You have 16 days from the date of the postmark to do this. A hearing will be arranged and you will be told when to come to court.

(2) delete if not applicable

(2) **To the Creditor**

The court has declared a dividend on the amount paid by the debtor.

Enclosed is a payable order for £

The court office at

is open between 10 am and 4 pm Monday to Friday. Address all communications to the Court Manager quoting the administration number.

N95A Order suspending or varying an administration order

Power of Arrest attached to injunction
under section 2 Domestic Violence and Matrimonial Proceedings Act 1976 **F.P.R. 3.9**

In the	
County Court	
Claim No.	
Applicant's Ref.	

Applicant

Respondent

seal

(here set out the provisions of the injunction to which the power of arrest relates)

Power of Arrest

(1)Name each child

And the judge being satisfied that the respondent has caused actual bodily harm to the applicant (*or* and/the children)(1)

(2)Delete as required

and being of the opinion that he is likely to do so again, a power of arrest is attached to this injunction whereby any(2)) constable may under the power given by section 2(3) of the Domestic Violence and Matrimonial Proceding Act 1976 arrest without warrant the respondent if the constable has reasonable cause for suspecting the respondent of (using violence)(or)(entering any premises or area)(2) in breach of this injunction.

This power of arrest expires on the day of [19][20]

Note to Arresting Officer

Where the respondent is arrested under the power given by section 2 of the Domestic Violence and Matrimonial Proceedings Act 1976, that section requires that:

- the respondent shall be brought before the judge within the period of 24 hours beginning at the time of his arrest;
- the respondent shall not be released within that period except on the direction of the judge;
- the arresting constable shall forthwith seek the directions of the court as to the time and place at which the respondent is brought before a judge.

Nothing in section 2 authorises the detention of the respondent after the expiry of the period of 24 hours beginning at the time of his arest.

In calculating any period of 24 hours, no account shall be taken of Christmas Day, Good Friday or any Sunday.

The court office at

is open between 10 am and 4 pm Monday to Friday. Address all communications to the Court Manager quoting the claim number

N110 Power of arrest attached to injunction under section 2 Domestic Violence and Matrimonial Proceedings Act 1976 (F P R 3.9)

Order for Defendant to be Arrested and brought before the Court

Claimant

Defendant

In the County Court	
Claim No.	
A/E Number	
J/S Number	
Claimant's Ref.	

Seal

(1) delete as appropriate

To the (district judge and)[(1)] bailiffs of the court and every constable within the jurisdiction of the district judge

The defendant was ordered to attend on a specified day for the adjourned hearing of (an application for a maintenance attachment of earnings order) (a judgment summons)[(1)] and has failed to do so

(enter name of Judge) **has ordered** that the defendant be arrested and brought before this court (immediately)[(1)]

(or

at

on at o'clock)

You, the (district judge,)[(1)] bailiffs and others are therefore required to arrest the defendant and to bring him before this court

Dated

Description of defendant	*Defendant's place of employment*

The court office at

is open between 10 am and 4 pm Monday to Friday. When corresponding with the court, please address forms or letters to the Court Manager and quote the claim number

N112 Power of arrest (4.99)

Certificate of Service (to be completed by the court)

I certify that I arrested the person named in this order

on the day of [19][20]and brought him before the court.

Bailiff/Officer of the Court

Date

I certify that the order has **not been served** for the following reason

Bailiff/Officer of the Court

Date

N112A
POWER OF ARREST, SECTION 23
ATTACHMENT OF EARNINGS ACT 1971

Order for Defendant to be Arrested and brought before the Court

Claimant

Defendant

In the	
County Court	
Claim No.	
AE Number	
Claimant's Ref.	

Seal

To the bailiffs of the court and every constable within the jurisdiction of the district judge

The defendant was ordered to attend on a specified day to give good reasons why he should not be fined or imprisoned for failure to provide a statement of means in accordance with section 14 of the Attachment of Earnings Act 1971 and the defendant failed to attend the hearing

(1) delete as appropriate

(enter name of Judge) **therefore ordered** that the defendant be arrested and brought before this court (immediately)(1)

(or

at

on at o'clock)

You, the bailiffs and others are therefore required to arrest the defendant and to bring him before this court

Dated

Description of defendant	*Defendant's place of employment*

The court office at

is open between 10 am and 4 pm Monday to Friday. When corresponding with the court, please address forms or letters to the Court Manager and quote the claim number

N112A Power of arrest section 23 (Attachment of Earnings Act 1971)

Certificate of Service (to be completed by the court)

I certify that I arrested the person named in this order

on the day of 20 and brought him before the court.

Bailiff/Officer of the Court

Date

I certify that the order has **not been served** for the following reason:

Bailiff/Officer of the Court

Date

General Form of Undertaking

In the	
County Court	
Claim No.	
Claimant's Ref.	
Defendant's Ref.	

Between ______________________ **Claimant Applicant Petitioner**

and ______________________ **Defendant Respondent**

This form is to be used only for an undertaking not for an injunction

(1) Name of the person giving undertaking

(2) Set out terms of undertaking

(3) Give the date and time or event when the undertaking will expire

(4) The judge may direct that the party who gives the undertaking shall personally sign the statement overleaf

(5) Set out any other directions given by the court

(6) Address of the person giving undertaking

On the day of [19][20]

Seal

(1)

[appeared in person] [was represented by Solicitor / Counsel]

and gave an undertaking to the Court promising (2)

And to be bound by these promises until (3)

The Court explained to (1)

the meaning of his undertaking and the consequences of failing to keep his promises,

And the Court accepted his undertaking (4) [and *if so ordered* directed that

(1) should sign the statement overleaf].

And (enter name of Judge) **ordered** that (5)

Dated

To (1)

of (6)

Important Notice

- You may be sent to prison for contempt of court if you break the promises that you have given to the Court.
- If you do not understand anything in this document you should go to a Solicitor, Legal Advice Centre or a Citizens' Advice Bureau

The Court Office at

is open from 10 am to 4 pm. When corresponding with the court, address all forms and letters to the Court Manager and quote the claim number.

N117 General form of undertaking (4.99) *Printed on behalf of The Court Service*

The Court may direct that the party who gives the undertaking shall personally sign the statement below.

Statement

I understand the undertaking that I have given, and that if I break any of my promises to the Court I may be sent to prison for contempt of court.

Signed

To be completed by the Court

Delivered

☐ By posting on:

☐ By hand on:

☐ Through solicitor on:

Officer:

FORM N118 NOTICE TO DEFENDANT WHERE COMMITTAL ORDER MADE

Suspended Committal Order (Attachment of Earnings)

In the	
County Court	
Claim No.	
A/E Number	
Claimant's Ref.	

Claimant

Defendant

seal

Take notice that today (enter name of Judge) made a committal order for your imprisonment for days

This order will not be put into force so long as you attend this court

on

at

at **o'clock**

You must also complete the enclosed form of reply and statement of means and send it to reach the court office **within 8 days** after you receive this order

Dated

Take Notice

To the defendant

If you do not comply with this order, a warrant for your committal may be issued without further notice and you may be imprisoned for the period shown above.

If you cannot attend on the specified date, you should write or go to the court office immediately, stating the reason why you cannot attend. The court will send you notice of a day and time to attend before the judge.

Notes to help you complete the form of reply

- If you are unemployed or self employed, you should say so on the form of reply and answer as many questions as you can.
- Read the notes on the form of reply before giving the details asked for.
- If you want an opportunity to pay voluntarily without your employer being ordered to make deductions from your pay, you should ask for a suspended order on the form of reply. You should also enclose a copy of your most recent payslip.
- You can obtain help in completing the form of reply at any county court office or Citizens' Advice Bureau.

e court office at

ɔpen between 10 am and 4 pm Monday to Friday. Address all communications to the Court Manager quoting the claim number

18 Notice to defendant where committal order made but directed to be suspended under Attachment of Earnings Act 1971

Application for possession including application for interim possession order

Claim No.	
In the County Court	
The court office is open from 10am to 4pm Monday to Friday Telephone	

Applicant's full name address

Address for service (if different from above) Ref / Tel No.

Respondent's name (if known including title e.g. Mr, Mrs or Miss) and address

Seal

The applicant is claiming possession of

on the grounds that he has an immediate right to possession and that the person(s) in occupation of the premises is (are) in occupation without consent.

Application issued on

N130 - w3 Application for possession including application for interim possession order (4.99)

Printed on behalf of The Court Service

Affidavit to support an application for possession and for an interim possession order

Sworn by ____________ *(deponent)*	on ____________ *(date)*
This is the ____________ *(1st, 2nd etc)*	affidavit
filed on behalf of ____________ *(party)*	by this deponent
on ____________ *(date filed)*	
	completed by deponent

Paragraph 1 Insert full name, address and occupation of person making this affidavit.	**1**	I make this affidavit to support my application for possession and for an interim possession order
Paragraph 2 Give the address of the premises	**2**	(I) (has) (have) an immediate right to possession of
Give a description of the premises (house, flat, shop etc)		which is a and (has) (have) had this right since
Paragraph 3 Give details of proof of interest (deeds, lease etc)	**3**	Proof of (my) (the applicant's) interest in the premises is in the form of A copy of that is marked 'A' and is attached to this affidavit
Paragraph 4 Give the date when you found out that the premises were being occupied illegally. Explain how you found out and why you could not have been expected to find out sooner	**4**	(I) first knew of the occupation of the premises on the day of [19][20] by and could not reasonably have been aware of this earlier because

Paragraph 6
Delete if you do not know the names of any of the occupier(s)

Paragraph 7
Give the names of those people and which part of the building they occupy.
Delete the words in brackets as appropriate.

Paragraph 8
The court must take into account whether or not you have given undertakings when deciding whether to make an interim possession order.
Delete any undertakings you are not prepared to give.

5 The respondent(s) entered the premises without my consent and without the consent of anyone who on the date of entry had an immediate right to possession of the premises. Since that date I have not granted the respondent(s) any such consent.

6 As well as the respondent(s) named in this application there are (no) other occupiers whose names I do not know.

7 There are (no) other people who are entitled to possession of other parts of the building in which the premises are situated (and they are:)

8 I hereby give the following undertakings:

(a) **to re-instate the respondent if, after an interim possession order has been made, the court holds that I was not entitled to the order**

(b) **to pay damages if, after an interim possession order has been made, the court holds that I was not entitled to the order**

(c) **not to damage the premises pending final determination of the possession proceedings**

(d) **not to grant a right of occupation to any other person pending final determination of the possession proceedings**

(e) **not to damage or dispose of any of the respondent's possessions pending final determination of the procession proceedings**

9 **I ask the court to grant me an interim possession order in relation to the premises described at paragraph 2.**
I also ask the court to grant me possession of the premises.

10 **I understand the undertaking(s) I have given, and that if I break any of my promises to the court I may be sent to prison for contempt of court and/or fined.**

11 **I understand that if I make a false or misleading statement in this application or at the appointment to consider this application I will be guilty of a criminal offence and on conviction may be sent to prison and/or fined.**

Sworn at

in the of

this day of [19][20]

Before me ....

Solicitor / Commissioner for oaths / Officer of the court, appointed by the Circuit Judge to take affidavits

Notice of application for interim possession order

Claim No.	
In the County Court	
The court office is open from 10am to 4pm Monday to Friday	
Telephone	

Applicant's full name address

Address for service (if different from above) Ref / Tel No.

Respondent's name (if known including title e.g. Mr, Mrs or Miss) and address

Seal

This notice is only valid if sealed by the court
If it is not sealed it should be reported to the court

The applicant is claiming possession of

on the grounds that he has an immediate right to possession and that the person(s) in occupation of the premises is (are) in occupation without consent.

The court will consider whether an interim possession order should be made
on
at am/pm
at

Application issued on

- Service

Insert time, day and date 24 hours after time of issue

For this notice to be valid it **must** be served before am/pm on the day of [19][20]. It **must** be affixed to the main door or another conspicuous part of the premises and, if practicable, inserted through the letter box in a sealed transparent envelope addressed to 'the occupiers'. In addition it may be attached to stakes in the ground in conspicuous parts of the adjoining land if that is appropriate.

See the back of this form for important information

What you should do

- if you have no right to occupy the premises you **must** leave.
- if you think you have a right to occupy the premises or you believe that the applicant is not entitled to an interim possession order you may file an affidavit (sworn statement) at the court **before** the date and time shown on this notice. The form you must use is attached to this notice.
- if you need advice you should go to a Solicitor, Legal Advice Centre or Citizens Advice Bureau. Court staff are unable to give legal advice.
- you can attend the court at the date and time shown on this notice **only** if you have sworn and filed an affidavit. The judge may ask you about what you have written in your affidavit. You must state your case fully in this affidavit. You may not produce any new information at the appointment.

If you make a false or misleading statement in the affidavit you will be guilty of a criminal offence and on conviction you may be sent to prison and/or fined

What can happen next

- if the court makes an interim possession order you will have **24 hours** from the time it is served on you to leave the premises. It will be served on you in the same way that this notice was – it does not have to be served on you personally. The interim possession order must be served within 48 hours of its being approved by the court.
- after you have left the premises you may apply to the court for the interim possession order to be set aside. If you wish to do so, you should go to a Solicitor, Legal Advice Centre or Citizens Advice Bureau.
- **if you do not obey an interim possession order (by leaving the premises within 24 hours) you may be arrested and on conviction sent to prison and/or fined.**
- a date for hearing (when the claim for possession will be considered) will be shown on the interim possession order. You have a right to attend that hearing.
- if the court does **not** make an interim possession order you will be told in writing.

Further Information

- a leaflet is available free of charge from any county court office.

Affidavit of service of Notice of application for interim possession order

Sworn by (deponent)		on (date)	
This is the (1st, 2nd etc)		affidavit	
filed on behalf of (party)		by this deponent	
on (date filed)			
			completed by deponent

In the County Court	
Claim No.	
Applicant including reference	
Respondent	

(1) Insert full name, address and occupation of deponent

I, (1)

make oath and say as follows:

1. That I am over 16 years of age and
(a) acting as agent for the applicant, **or**
(b) employed by
of
(solicitor, acting as agent for
of) solicitor for the above named applicant

(2) Insert date and time of service

(3) Insert name(s) of person(s) served

(4) Give description and address of premises i.e. a room shop unit, flat, house

delete (a) or (b), or both as appropriate

Service

2. That on the(2) at am/pm
which was within 24 hours of its being issued
I served the notice of application and the form of occupier's affidavit, true copies of which are attached and marked "A" , on the occupier(s)(3)

of(4)

by affixing a copy of each of the documents to the main door or other conspicuous part of the premises and

(a) (by inserting through the letter box at the premises a copy of those documents enclosed in a sealed transparent envelope to "the occupiers")

(b) (by placing stakes in the ground at conspicuous parts of the adjoining land, to each of which is affixed a sealed transparent envelope addressed to "the occupiers" containing a copy of each of the documents)

Sworn at	in the	
of	this	Before me ....
day of	[19][20]	Solicitor / Commissioner for oaths / Officer of the court, appointed by the Circuit Judge to take affidavits

Indorse the documents as follows: These papers marked "A" are the copy notice of application and form of occupiers affidavit referred to in the attached affidavit. This affidavit is filed on behalf of the applicant.

Note: This affidavit must be completed and returned to the court office at or before the date when the application for an interim possession order will be considered

N132 Affidavit of service notice of application for interim possession order (4.99)

Affidavit of occupier to oppose the making of an interim possession order

Sworn by ______ on ______
(deponent) *(date)*
This is the ______ affidavit
(1st, 2nd etc)
filed on behalf of ______ by this deponent
(party)
on ______
(date filed)
completed by deponent

Claim No.	
In the County Court	

Between Applicant

and Respondent

the occupier(s) of

For completion by the court

Appointment on **[19][20]**

at **am/pm**

Please note: You must state your case fully in this affidavit. You may not produce any new information at the appointment.

(1) Insert full name, address and occupation of deponent

I, (1)

make oath and say as follows:

(2) Insert address of premises

1. I consider that I have a right to occupy the premises at (2)

2. I have been in occupation since

Give date

N133 - w3 Affidavit of occupier to oppose the making of an interim possession order

3. The applicant (name)

was aware of my occupation of the premises. I know this because

(3) Give name, address and date

4. I was told by [3]

of

on that I could occupy the premises named in paragraph 1.

(4) Say who this person is and describe any documents they showed you

I believe that he/she had the right to allow me to occupy the premises because [4]

(5) Delete if you have no written evidence

5. I have written evidence to show my right of occupation. It is in the form of

(eg rent book, tenancy agreement) and a copy is

attached and marked 'A' [5]

6. The applicant is **not** entitled to an interim possession order because

7. I understand that if I have made a false or misleading statement in this affidavit I will be guilty of a criminal offence and on conviction may be sent to prison or fined or both.

Sworn/Affirmed at

in the of

this day of [19][20]

Before me . . . .

Solicitor / Commissioner for oaths / Officer of the court, appointed by the Circuit Judge to take affidavits

Interim possession order

Between .... Applicant

and .... Respondent

In the	
County Court	
Claim No.	
Applicant's Ref.	
Respondent's Ref.	

For completion by the applicant
Served on **[19][20]**
at **am/pm**

Seal

To the Respondent

of

If you do not obey this order within 24 hours of the time of service you may be arrested and on conviction sent to prison and/or fined

As a result of this order any person(s) entering the premises as trespassers while this order is in force may also be arrested and on conviction sent to prison and/or fined. In addition, if those in occupation at the time of service of this order, return as trespassers within a year of service of this order they may be arrested and on conviction sent to prison and/or fined

On the of [19][20] the court considered an application for an interim possession order
The court ordered that all person(s) in occupation of

must vacate the premises within 24 hours of service of this order.
The court further ordered

Insert the terms of any other orders eg costs

Notice of return date
The court will consider making a final possession order
at
on the day of [19][20] at o'clock

If you do not attend at the time shown the Court may make a final possession order in your absence.
You are entitled to apply to the Court to set aside this interim possession order before the date given above provided that you have left the premises.

To the Applicant What you must do

Insert time and date 48 hours after approval by the court

You **must** serve this order before am/pm on the day of [19][20].
It **must** be affixed to the main door or another conspicuous part of the premises and, if practicable, inserted through the letter box in a sealed transparent envelope addressed to the occupiers. In addition it may be attached to stakes in the ground in conspicuous parts of the adjoining land if that is appropriate.
Immediately before you serve this order you **must** write in the date and time in the box in the top right-hand corner of this form.

To the Respondent What you must do

You **must** leave the premises within 24 hours of the time this interim possession order is served
If you do not leave the police may arrest you and on conviction you may be sent to prison and/or fined
If you think you have a right to occupy the premises or any of the information given is incorrect you should go to a Solicitor, Legal Advice Centre or Citizens Advice Bureau after you have left the premises. Take any evidence with you (e.g. rent book, tenancy agreement)

The court office at

is open between 10am and 4pm. Monday to Friday. When writing to the court, please address forms or letters to the Court Manager and quote the claim number.

N134 Interim posession order (4.99)

Interim possession order record of appointment

Claim no. ____________________

On ____________________ the ____________ day of ______________________________ [19][20]

Before (H Honour) (District) Judge ______________________________

The court was sitting at ______________________________

The Applicant

- ☐ was represented by Counsel
- ☐ was represented by a Solicitor
- ☐ attended in person
- ☐ did not attend

The Respondent

- ☐ was represented by Counsel
- ☐ was represented by a Solicitor
- ☐ attended in person
- ☐ did not attend

The court read the affidavit(s) of

- ☐ the Applicant sworn on ______________________________
- ☐ the Respondent sworn on ______________________________

And of ____________________ sworn on ______________________________

Delete as appropriate

The Applicant gave undertaking(s) (through his counsel or solicitor) (in his affidavit) promising:

(a) to re-instate the respondent if, after an interim possession order has been made, the court holds that the applicant was not entitled to the order

(b) to pay damages if, after an interim possession order has been made, the court holds that the applicant was not entitled to the order

(c) not to damage the premises pending final determination of the possession proceedings

(d) not to grant a right of occupation to any other person pending final determination of the possession proceedings

(e) not to damage or dispose of any of the respondent's possessions pending final determination of the possession proceedings

---

The court made this interim possession order on the grounds that

Signed
(H Honour) (District) Judge

Dated

FORM N135 AFFIDAVIT OF SERVICE OF INTERIM POSSESSION ORDER

Affidavit of service of interim possession order

Sworn by (deponent)		on (date)
This is the (1st, 2nd etc)		affidavit
filed on behalf of (party)		by this deponent
on (date filed)		
		completed by deponent

In the **County Court**	
Claim No.	
Applicant *including reference*	
Respondent	

(1) Insert full name, address and occupation of deponent

I, [1]

make oath and say as follows:

1. That I am over 16 years of age and

(a) acting as agent for the applicant, **or**

(b) employed by

of

(solicitor, acting as agent for

of) solicitor for the above named applicant

(2) Insert date and time of service

Service

2. That on the [2] at am/pm

which was within 48 hours of its being approved by the court

(3) Insert name(s) of person(s) served

I served the interim possession order, originating application and supporting affidavit, true copies of which are attached and marked "A", on the occupier(s) [3]

(4) Give description and address of premises i.e. a room, shop unit, flat, house

of [4]

by affixing a copy of each of the documents to the main door or other conspicuous part of the premises and

delete (a) or (b), or both, as appropriate

(a) (by inserting through the letter box at the premises a copy of those documents enclosed in a sealed transparent envelope addressed to "the occupiers")

(b) (by placing stakes in the ground at conspicuous parts of the adjoining land, to each of which is affixed a sealed transparent envelope addressed to "the occupiers" containing a copy of each of the documents)

Sworn at	in the	
of	this	Before me ....
day of	[19][20]	Solicitor / Commissioner for oaths / Officer of the court, appointed by the Circuit Judge to take affidavits

Indorse the documents as follows: These papers marked "A" are the copy interim possession order, originating application and supporting affidavit referred to in the attached affidavit. This affidavit is filed on behalf of the applicant.

Note: **This affidavit must be completed and returned to the court office at or before the return date**

If you wish the police to enforce the interim possession order against an occupier who has not left the premises 24 hours after the time of service of the order, you must take a copy of this form together with a copy of the interim possession order to the local police station

N135 Affidavit of service interim possession order (4.99)

Order for Possession

In the County Court	
Claim No.	
Applicant's Ref.	

Applicant

Respondent

Seal

(enter name of Judge) **ordered** that the applicant do recover possession of the premises mentioned in the originating application and interim possession order in this matter, namely: *(description of the premises)*

And that the applicant do recover against the respondent the sum of £ for costs
(or his costs of this action to be assessed)

And further that the respondent do pay the applicant the sum mentioned above by
(or do pay the amount of costs when assessed by that day or, if the costs have not been assessed, within 14 days of assessment)

Dated

Take Notice

To the respondent
If you were occupying these premises when an interim possession order was served and you return as a trespasser within **one year** of that date you may be arrested and on conviction sent to prison and/or fined. (Criminal Justice and Public Order Act 1994 section 76).
If you do not pay the costs when they are due and the applicant takes steps to enforce payment, the order will be registered in the Register of County Court Judgments. **This may make it difficult for you to get credit.** Further information about registration is available in a leaflet which you can get from any county court office.

Address for Payment

How to Pay

- **PAYMENT(S) MUST BE MADE** to the person named at the address for payment quoting their reference and the court case number.
- **DO NOT** bring or send payments to the court. **THEY WILL NOT BE ACCEPTED.**
- You should allow at least 4 days for your payment to reach the applicant or his representative.
- Make sure that you keep records and can account for all payments made. Proof may be required if there is any disagreement. It is not safe to send cash unless you use registered post.
- A leaflet giving further advice about payment can be obtained from the court.
- If you need more information you should contact the applicant or his representative.

The court office at

is open between 10 am and 4 pm Monday to Friday. When corresponding with the court, please address forms or letters to the Court Manager and quote the claim number.

N136 Order for possession (4.99)

Injunction Order

(Protection from Harassment Act 1997)

Between .... Claimant

and .... Defendant

In the	
County Court	
Claim No. *Always quote this*	
Claimant's Ref.	
Defendant Ref.	
For completion by the court Issued on	[19] [20]

Seal

To [1]

Of [2]

<u>If you do not obey this order you will be guilty of contempt of court and you may be fined or sent to prison or you may be guilty of a criminal offence for which you may be fined or sent to prison or both.</u>

On the of [19][20] the court considered an application for an injunction

The Court ordered that[1]

is forbidden (whether by himself or by instructing or encouraging any other person)[3]

This order shall remain in force until (the of [19][20] at o'clock unless before then it is revoked by a) further order of the court

And it is ordered that[1]

shall[4]

on or before[5]

It is further ordered that[6]

Notice of further hearing[7]

The court will re-consider the application and whether the order should continue at a further hearing at

on the day of [19][20]at o'clock

If you do not attend at the time shown the court may make an injunction order in your absence

You are entitled to apply to the court to re-consider the order before the day[8]

(1) The name of the person the order is directed to

(2) The address of the person the order is directed to

(3) The terms of the restraining order. If the defendant is a limited company, delete the words in brackets and insert "whether by its servants, agents, officers or otherwise"

(4) The terms of any orders requiring acts to be done

(5) Enter time (and place) as ordered

(6) The terms of any other orders costs etc.

(7) Use when the order is temporary or ex parte otherwise delete

(8) Delete if order made on notice

If you do not understand anything in this order you should go to a Solicitor, Legal Advice Centre or a Citizens' Advice Bureau

The court office at

is open between 10 am and 4 pm Monday to Friday. When corresponding with the court, please address forms or letters to the Court Manager and quote the claim number.

N138 Form of injunction (Protection from Harassment Act 1997) (4.99)

Injunction Order - Record of Hearing

Claim No.

On . . . . the . . . . day of . . . . [19][20]

Before (H Honour)(District) judge . . . .

The court was sitting at . . . .

. . . .

The ☐ **Claimant** **(Name)** . . . .

was ☐ represented by Counsel

☐ represented by a Solicitor

☐ in person

The ☐ **Defendant** **(Name)** . . . .

was ☐ represented by Counsel

☐ represented by a Solicitor

☐ in person

☐ did not appear having been given notice of this hearing

☐ not given notice of this hearing

The court read the written evidence of

☐ the Claimant sworn (signed) on . . . .

☐ the Defendant sworn (signed) on . . . .

And of . . . . sworn (signed) on . . . .

. . . .

The court heard spoken evidence on oath from

. . . .

. . . .

The Claimant gave an undertaking (through his counsel or solicitor) promising to pay any damages ordered by the court if it later decides that the Defendant has suffered loss or damages as a result of this order*

*Delete this paragraph if the court does not require the undertaking

Signed ____ Dated ____________________________

(Judge's Clerk)

N139
APPLICATION FOR WARRANT OF ARREST

In the

Claim Number

Application for a Warrant of Arrest
Protection from Harassment Act 1997

Claimant
Ref.
Defendant
Ref.

(1) Set out the precise pairs of the injunction order relevant to this application

On the day of [19][20], the Court made an injunction order as follows:(1)

(2) Insert name of claimant

(3) Insert name of person against whom the warrant of arrest is sought

I, (2) apply for an order that a warrant should be issued for the arrest of the defendant(3)

of

(4) List the ways in which it is alleged that the defendant has disobeyed the injunction order. If necessary continue on a separate sheet

The defendant has disobeyed the injunction order by(3)

I [have] [have not] informed the police that I believe the defendant has disobeyed the injunction order.

To the best of my knowledge, criminal proceedings [have] [have not] been instituted against the defendant.

Signed Date

N139 Application for a Warrant of Arrest (Protection from Harassment Act 1997)(4.99) *The Court Service Publications Unit*

In the

Claim Number

Warrant of Arrest

Protection from Harassment Act 1997

Claimant
Ref.
Defendant
Ref

The Court directs all police constables, [the district judge and bailiffs] [and the Tipstaff of the High Court] to arrest the defendant whose address is [believed to be]:

and to bring the defendant before this court immediately.

The Court heard an application, supported by [sworn affidavits] [signed written statements][evidence on oath], that the defendant had disobeyed the injunction order made

on

at the [County] [High] Court

by

The Next Hearing is

[on at [am][pm]]
[on a day and at a time to be specified]]

Ordered by
[Mr] [Mrs] Justice
[His] [Her] Honour Judge
District Judge
[Assistant] Recorder

on

N140 Warrant of Arrest (Protection from Harassment Act 1997)(4.99)

Notice of Issue of Fixed Date Summons

In the	
Court	
Claimant's Ref.	
Date	

Claimant

To the Claimant('s solicitor)

The court office at

is open from 10 am to 4 pm Monday to Friday
Please bring this notice with you to court

Claim Number	Defendant(s)	Issue Fee

The above claim was / were issued today and you must attend the hearing

tick the appropriate box

☐ when the proceedings will be heard OR ☐ when the district judge will give directions for the determination of this action.
(If you intend to ask the district judge to give any particular direction, you must give notice of your intention to him and the defendant)

at

on at o'clock

Notes

- **Always quote the claim number.**
- **You must inform the court IMMEDIATELY**
  If you receive any payment before the hearing date.
- Always bring this notice with you when you come to the court office for any purpose connected with your claim. On the day of hearing bring all books and papers necessary to prove the claim.
- If judgment is entered, the defendant will be ordered to pay you or your representative.
- You should keep a record of any payments you receive from the defendant. At the hearing if you wish to take steps to enforce the judgment, you will need to satisfy the court about the balance outstanding. You should give the defendant a receipt. Payment in cash should always be acknowledged. You should tell the defendant how much he owes if he asks.

Proceedings after judgement
You must inform the court IMMEDIATELY if you receive any payment while a warrant or other enforcement is current and/or before any hearing date.

N206 Notice of issue (fixed date summons)

IN THE COUNTY COURT

APPLICANTS ....

APPLICATION No.	NAME OF INFANT	APPLICATION FEE	DATE OF ISSUE

To the Applicants:

(1) You should attend before the Judge in chambers at

(1) Delete as necessary

on at o'clock

when this application will be heard

(1) It appears that the directions of the Judge as to the further conduct of this application must be given before the matter can proceed. You will be given notice of any directions made by him and if he wishes to see you, you will be sent a notice of appointment.

All letters should be sent to the Court Manager quoting the above Application Number

THE COURT OFFICE AT

is open from 10 a.m. to 4 p.m. Monday to Friday.

N207 Plaint note (freeing for adoption/adoption) (4.99)

N200
Petition

[General Title]

To His Honour the Judge of the said Court

THE PETITION OF of

SHOWS:

That [*here state the grounds upon which the petitioner claims to be entitled to an Order*]

Your petitioner prays that an Order may be made in the following terms [*here state the terms of the Order for which the petitioner prays*]

The names and addresses of the persons upon whom it is intended to serve this petition are: [*here state name and address of persons intended to be served*]

or

It is not intended to serve any person with this petition.

Your petitioner's address for service is: [*here state the petitioner's address for service*]

Dated this day of , 20 .

(Signed)

[Solicitors for the] Appellant

N201
Request for Entry of Appeal

CPR 52 and PD 52

[General Title]

To the District Judge of the County Court.

I desire to appeal against the order, decision or award of made on of which a copy is annexed hereto.

The grounds of my appeal are:

[*or* A copy of a notice of appeal served upon the respondents, which contains a statement of the grounds of my appeal, is annexed hereto.]

I request you to enter my appeal for hearing in the County Court.

The name and address of the respondent is:

My address for service is:

Dated this day of ,20 .

(Signed)

[Solicitors for the] Appellant

N203
Notice to persons on whose behalf party has obtained leave to sue or defend

[General Title]

TAKE NOTICE that has obtained an order, appointing him to sue [or defend] this action [*or* matter] on your behalf, or for your benefit, as well as on his own behalf.

A copy of the order and of the summons [or originating process] in the action [or matter] is served herewith and the affidavit on which the order was made has been files at the court office and mat be inspected by you.

Any judgment or order in these proceedings will be binding on you but may not be enforced against you without leave of the court. You will be given notice of any application for such leave and you may dispute liability to have the judgment or order enforced against you on the ground that by reason of facts and matters particular to your case you are entitled to be exempted from such liability.

N204
Notice to person against whom party has obtained leave to sue or defend on behalf of others

[General Title]

TAKE NOTICE that has obtained an order appointing him to sue [or defend] this action [*or* matter] on behalf of or for the benefit of [*state names of persons as in order*] as well as on his own behalf.

DATED

To the [defendant][claimant]

FORM N224

REQUEST FOR SERVICE OUT OF ENGLAND AND WALES AND WALES THROUGH THE COURT

In the County Court	
Claim No.	
Applicant *including reference*	
Respondent	

I/We request that the above-mentioned process may be served through the Court.

I/We personally undertake to be responsible for all expenses incurred by Her Majesty's Principal Secretary of State for Foreign and Commonwealth Affairs or the Senior Master in respect of the service requested, and on receiving notice of the amount of such expenses to pay them.

(1) Delete if the answer to question 4 below is NO.

I am/We are willing for service to be effected by whatever method the Secretary of State may choose. (1)

(*Signed*)

Claimant or other party or his solicitor.

1. Date of order giving leave to serve out of England and Wales.	
2. Nature of process to be served.	
3. Name of country in which service is to be effected.	
4. Is the party to be served a State as defined in Section 14 of the State Immunity Act 1978?	YES ☐ NO ☐
5. Name of party to be served.	
6. Address of party to be served.	
7. Is party to be served a United Kingdom National?	YES ☐ NO ☐

(2) Delete as appropriate.

Service is desired - (2)

a. through the authority designated under the Hague Convention

b. through the judicial authority of

c. through a British consular authority at

d. through the Government of
[where the government is willing to effect service]

N224 Request for service out of England and Wales through the Court (4.99)

Application for suspension of a warrant and/or variation of an order

Read these notes carefully before completing the form.

- Tick the correct boxes and give as much information as you can. It will help the court make a fair decision about how much you can afford to pay if the claimant refuses your offer.
- If you do not complete all the details and sign the form, the court will not be able to deal with your application.
- The form will be sent to the claimant to consider your offer.
- The court will send you an order giving details of how and when to pay or will tell you when to come to court. You will be informed of the court's decision.
- You will have to pay a fee for your application. You can get details of the fee to pay and information about what to do if you cannot pay all or part of a fee from any county court office.

In the Court	
Claim No.	
Warrant No.	Local No.
Claimant *(including ref.)*	
Defendant	

For court use only **Date copy sent to claimant** ☐

I cannot pay the amount ordered and I wish to apply for

☐ **suspension of the warrant**

and/or

☐ **a reduction in the instalment order**

1 Personal details

Surname

Forename

☐ Mr ☐ Mrs ☐ Miss ☐ Ms

☐ Married ☐ Single ☐ Other *(specify)*

Age

Address

Postcode

Daytime telephone

2 Dependants *(people you look after financially)*

Children *(under 19)*		Others *(give details)*
Age	*Date of Birth*	

(If more continue on a separate sheet)

3 Employment

☐ **I am employed as a**

My employer is

Jobs other than main job *(give details)*

☐ **I am self employed as a**

Annual turnover is .... £

☐ **I am not** in arrears with my national insurance contributions, income tax and VAT

☐ **I am** in arrears and I owe .... £

Give details of:
(a) contracts and other work in hand
(b) any sums due for work done

☐ **I have been unemployed for** years months

☐ **I am a pensioner**

4 Bank account and savings

☐ **I have a bank account**

☐ The account is in credit by £

☐ The account is overdrawn by £

☐ **I have a savings account or building society account**

The amount in the account is £

5 Property

I live in ☐ my own property ☐ lodgings
☐ jointly owned property ☐ council property
☐ rented property

6 Income

My usual take home pay *(including overtime, commission, bonuses etc.)*	£ per
Income support	£ per
Child benefit(s)	£ per
Other state benefit(s)	£ per
My pension(s)	£ per
Others living in my home give me	£ per
Other income *(give details below)*	
	£ per
	£ per
	£ per
Total income	£ per

8 Priority debts

(This section is for arrears only. Do not include regular expenses listed in box 7)

Rent arrears		£ per
Mortgage arrears		£ per
Council tax arrears		£ per
Water charge arrears		£ per
Fuel debts:	Gas	£ per
	Electricity	£ per
	Other	£ per
Maintenance arrears		£ per
Others *(give details below)*		
		£ per
		£ per
Total priority debts		£ per

7 Expenses

(Do not include any payments made by other members of the household out of their own income)

I have regular expenses as follows:

Mortgage *(including second mortgage)*	£ per
Rent	£ per
Council tax	£ per
Gas	£ per
Electricity	£ per
Water charges	£ per
TV rental and licence	£ per
HP repayments	£ per
Mail order	£ per
Housekeeping, food, school meals	£ per
Travelling expenses	£ per
Children's clothing	£ per
Maintenance payments	£ per
Others *(not court orders or credit debts listed in boxes 9 and 10)*	
	£ per
	£ per
	£ per
Total expenses	£ per

9 Court orders

Court	Claim No.	£ per
Total court order instalments		£ per

Of the payments above, I am behind with payments to *(please list)*

10 Credit debts

Loans and credit card debts *(please list)*

	£ per
	£ per
	£ per

Of the payments above, I am behind with payments to *(please list)*

11 Offer of Payment

If you take away the totals of boxes 7, 8 and 9 and the payments you are making in box 10 from the total in box 6, you will get some idea of the sort of sum you should offer. The offer you make should be one you can afford.

I can pay £ **a month**

(and I enclose £ **)**

I also enclose the fee of £

12 Declaration

I declare that the details I have given above are true to the best of my knowledge

Signed **Date**

Claimant's Reply to Defendant's Application

In the	Court
Claim No.	
Claimant	
Defendant	
Claimant's Ref.	

To the claimant('s solicitor)

Enclosed is a copy of an application made by the defendant

- The court will make an order in the terms of the defendant's offer (or as it thinks fit) unless you write to the court with your objections. You have 7 days from the date of the postmark to do this.
- Only **one** box should be ticked.
- Please remember to sign and date the form.

If you AGREE the defendant's application

1. ☐ **I accept the defendant's request**
- Return the form to the court office within the 7 day time limit (explained above).
- The court will make an order for payment in the terms of the offer.

If you DO NOT ACCEPT the defendant's offer

2. ☐ I do not agree to the applicants request and ask the court to arrange a hearing.
I have set out my reasons below/I enclose a statement of my objections.
- Return the form to the court office within the 7 day time limit (explained above).

Record here your objections to the defendant's proposals *(continue on a separate sheet if necessary)*

Signed ....

Dated ....

The court office at

is open between 10 am and 4 pm Monday to Friday. Address all communications to the Court Manager quoting the claim number

N246 Claimant's reply to defendant's application to vary instalment order

FORM N246A CLAIMANT'S REPLY TO DEFENDANT'S APPLICATION TO SUSPEND WARRANT OF EXECUTION

Claimant's Reply to Defendant's Application to Suspend Warrant of Execution

In the	
Court	
Claim No.	
Warrant No.	**Local No.**
Claimant	
Defendant	
Claimant's Ref.	

To the claimant('s solicitor)

Enclosed is a copy of an application made by the defendant for suspension of the warrant issued in this case (and/or for a variation of the order made).

- The court will make an order in the terms of the defendant's offer unless you write to the court with your objections. You have 16 days from the date of the postmark to do this.
- Only **one** box should be ticked.
- Remember to sign and date the form.

If you ACCEPT the defendant's offer

1. **I accept the defendant's offer**

- Return the form to the court office within the 16 day time limit (explained above).
- The court will make an order suspending the warrant (and varying the order) so long as payment is made in accordance with the order.

Note If the defendant does not keep up the payments, you may ask the court to reissue the warrant. Ask at the court office for Form N445.

If you AGREE to the suspension but DO NOT ACCEPT the defendant's offer (eg because you think the defendant could pay more)

2. **I do not accept the defendant's offer of payment but I will accept payment (by instalments of £ per month) or (in full by 20)**

- Give your reasons in the space below.
- Return the form to the court office within the 16 day time limit (explained above).
- The court will fix the rate of payment and will send you and the defendant a copy of the order.

If you DO NOT AGREE to the suspension and you DO NOT ACCEPT the defendant's offer

3. **I do not accept the defendant's offer of payment because I wish the bailiff to proceed with the warrant**

- Give your reasons in the space below.
- Return the form to the court office within the 16 day time limit (explained above).
- The court will return a copy of this form to you showing the date when the application and your objections will be heard. (The defendant will also receive a copy.)
- If you do not attend the hearing, the court will make an order in your absence.

Record here your objections to the defendant's proposals *(continue on a separate sheet if necessary)*

Signed ....(Claimant('s solicitor)

Dated ....

This section to be completed by the court

Date hearing notice sent

To the claimant and defendant

Take notice that the defendant's application will be heard by the court at

on

at o'clock

If you do not attend the hearing the court will make an order in your absence

The court office at

is open between 10 am and 4 pm Monday to Friday. Address all communications to the Court Manager quoting the claim number

N246A Claimant's reply to defendant's application to suspend warrant of execution

Administration orders

Notes for guidance

Please read these notes carefully. The notes will help you decide if you qualify for an administration order. They will also help you to complete the application (form N92).

What is an administration order?

If you are in financial difficulties and you are unable to pay your creditors (the people you owe money to) an administration order may help you.

- An administration order allows you to pay a sum that you can afford into the court each month to cover all your debts.
- In some circumstances the court may make an order for you to pay less than the total you owe (a "composition order"). This may be appropriate if it is clear that you will not be able to pay your debts in full in a reasonable period (say three years). You may ask the court to consider this by using the box in part C on the application form - but the final decision is for the court.
- The court will divide your monthly payment among your creditors (in proportion to the size of each debt).
- The court will manage your debts and deal directly with your creditors.
- While the order is in force none of the creditors named in your application or in the schedule to the order may try to enforce the debt or try to make you bankrupt (insolvent) without first asking the court.
- You will not need to pay a fee when you make the application. But, if an order is made, the court will deduct a sum for its costs from each of the payments you make. This is currently 10 pence in every £1 paid. For example, if you pay £20 each month, £2 will be paid to the court. To put it another way, if your total payments amount to £2,000 you will pay an additional sum of £200 to the court during the life of the order.

Do I qualify for an administration order?

To qualify for an administration order

- You must have two or more outstanding debts. At least one debt must be a High Court or county court judgment.
- Your total debts as stated on the list of creditors must not be more than £5,000.

If you satisfy these requirements, you may qualify for an administration order. If you do not qualify or you think you may qualify but need further advice, you should contact your local citizens advice bureau, money advice centre or legal advice centre.

What happens to my application?

- The court will look at your income and expenditure and consider your offer before fixing a rate of payment. This will normally be done without the need for a hearing and you and your creditors will have 16 days in which to write to the court with any objections.
- If there are no objections, an order will be made in the terms proposed by the court. You will be told how and when to pay the court.
- If you or any of your creditors object, or the court has difficulty in setting a rate of payment, you will be told to come to court for a hearing before the district judge.
- A creditor may object to their debt being included in the administration order. If the court agrees, the creditor will not be able to take action against you separately to recover the debt without first asking the court.
- If you are employed, the court may order your employer to send deductions direct from your earnings to the court. This is called an attachment of earnings order. If you object to this, you **must** tick the box in part C. You must give good reasons for objecting. The court may make a suspended attachment of earnings order. This means that as long as you regularly pay the administration order, your employer will not be asked to make deductions from your earnings. But if you do not keep up payments, the court may send the order to your employer without telling you.
- If an administration order is made, it will be registered in the Register of County Court Judgments. This will make it difficult for you to get credit. When the order is paid in full, you can ask the court to mark the entry in the register as satisfied and for a certificate proving payment. You will need to pay a fee for this.
- County court judgments included in the list of creditors may be registered separately. Court staff will be able to tell you how to have these entries on the Register marked satisfied.

What happens if I am unable to keep up the payments?

- If you cannot keep up payments **you must contact the court immediately.** The court may be able to help you. It is important that you do not get deeper into debt. Further debts can only be added after the order has been made if the court agrees.
- If you do not pay once the order has been made, the court may send the bailiff to take and sell your possessions, or make an attachment of earnings order to enforce payment. Alternatively, it may revoke (cancel) the order and your creditors will be able to take action against you separately to recover their debts.

N270 - w3 Notes for guidance (completing an application for an administration order)(4.99)

How do I complete the application form?

Please read these guidance notes carefully before you complete the application form for an administration order (form N92).

- Complete the application form and details of your income (section 6) and expenditure (section 7) as fully as possible. See the examples and notes below to help you complete the form. The court will use this information to fix the amount you will be expected to pay.
- It will help the court if you give all sums for income and expenditure as either monthly or weekly - try not to mix the two.

Completing Section 6 – income

- Complete details of all your income (section 6) as fully as possible.
- If you receive income from a second job or you regularly earn overtime you should show this in the 'other income' box.
- If you receive Income Support you should enter the figure you actually receive after any deductions are made.
- If you receive any other benefits (eg disablement benefit) you should say so and show how much you receive in 'other benefits' box.
- If your partner contributes to or pays any of the expenses in box 7, you must include the amount they pay in box 6.
- If you are in arrears with national insurance or income tax you should not deduct these from your take home pay. Instead, you should list them in section 7.

Example 1

Statement of means - income and expenditure

◆ Important: It will help the court if you give all sums for income and expenditure as either monthly or weekly figures. Try not to mix the two.

6. Income

See page 2 of the notes for guidance before completing this section

	specify weekly/monthly		specify weekly/monthly
My usual take home pay	£905 per month	**Sub total brought forward**	£1105 per month
My partner contributes to the expenses listed in section 7	£100 per month	Income support (see notes for guidance)	£—
Others living in my home give me	£—	Child benefit(s)	£41
My pension(s)	£—	Other state benefits (specify): none	£
Other income (give details): overtime	£100 per month		£
Sub total	£1105 per month	**Total**	£1146 per month

Completing Section 7 – expenditure

- You should list all the money you regularly pay out each month in regular expenses and arrears (section 7). List all the regular payments you make in column (a).
  If you are in arrears with any of these items, eg unpaid rent, you should list the total amount of the arrears you owe in column (b). Full details must also be given in the list of creditors (part B).
- If you are paying the arrears off by instalments, for example at a rate agreed with the creditor or under a court order, you should say how much you pay each week or month in column (c).
  Do not include this amount in column (a).
- If any amounts are deducted directly from your income (eg an attachment of earnings order for council tax or maintenance) or your benefit (eg refund of social fund loan or overpaid benefit) you should not include these sums anywhere in section 7. You must include them in the schedule and say that they are deducted direct from your income.
- Council tax has now replaced community charge. You should enter the amount you pay regularly for council tax in column a, and any arrears or arrears of community charge under column b and c.
- If you include travelling expenses in the regular expenses column you should only include expenses for bus or train fares or petrol. You should not include expenses for car insurance or road fund licence.
- If you make regular payments for items that are not listed, say what they are in the boxes marked 'others'. Examples might be repayment of a loan, hire purchase instalments or regular credit card payments.

Example 2

7. Regular expenses and arrears

See page 3 of the notes for guidance before completing any part of this section

	(a) Regular payments Enter the amount you usually spend or must pay for each item, weekly or monthly, *(please complete each entry: write n/a if not applicable)* *weekly/monthly*	(b) Total arrears If you are in arrears with any of the items in the regular payments column (a), enter the total arrears owed in column (b). Full details should be given in the list of creditors *(see notes for guidance)*	(c) Regular arrears payments If you are paying off the arrears shown in column (b), show how much you are paying weekly or monthly in column (c). Do not include these amounts as regular payments in column (a) *weekly/monthly*
Rent	£ 500 per month	£	£
Mortgage /home loan	£ n/a	£	£
Second mortgage/secured loan	£ n/a	£	£
Life insurance/endowment	£ 20 per month	£	£
House contents insurance	£ 60 per month	£	£
Council tax/community charge arrears	£ 40 per month	£	£
Maintenance/child support	£ 200 per month	£ 600	£ 40 per month
Water/sewerage charge	£ 16 per month	£	£
Ground rent/service charge	£ n/a	£	£
Gas (or other fuel eg coal, oil)	£ 30 gas per month	£	£
Electricity	£ 15 per month	£ 150	£ 10 per month
TV rental/licence	£ 6 per month	£	£
Magistrates' Court fine(s)	£ n/a	£	£
DSS Social Fund Loan/overpaid benefit	£ n/a	£	£
Telephone *(line, phone rental, essential calls only)*	£ 10 per month	£	£
Child care	£ n/a	£	£
Food and household essentials	£ 150 per month	£	£
Clothing	£ 5 per month	£	£
Laundry	£ n/a	£	£
Travelling expenses *(essential eg work, school)*	£ 15 per month	£	£
School meals/meals at work	£ n/a	£	£
Prescriptions/dentists/optician	£ n/a	£	£
Bank overdraft	£ 5 per month	£ 200	£
H.P. (3 piece suite)	£ 10 per month	£ 50	£ 5 per month
Visa Card	£ 50 per month	£ 500	£
	7a Total expenses £ 1132 per w/m	7a Total expenses £ 1500	

Completing Part B - list of creditors

- **You must list all your debts in the list of creditors** (you may be required to provide proof of each debt) and say what each debt is for (see the examples below).
- **At least one debt must be a High Court or county court judgment debt.** Remember to give the name of the court and case numbers for any county court or High Court debts (see example below). You must also provide a copy of the judgment or order, summons or writ.

Example 3

Part B: list of creditors *(see page 4 of the notes for guidance)*

Applicant's name	Application Number
John Slope	

Name of creditor, if known, and address to which payment should be sent. Give reference/account number. If judgment debt also state court and case number *(see example 3 in notes for guidance)*	If someone else is jointly responsible for part of this debt give details (eg guarantor, joint account etc)	Amount outstanding £	p
1. Furniture for You Ltd (for 3 piece suite) ref: 736527161 PH Pliwood House Barchester, Barsetshire Case no. 9210144 Barchester County Court		*362.*	*97*
2. Grantley Bank PLC (overdraft) a/c: 217/1894/202 30 High Street Barchester Barsetshire	*Mrs O Slope (joint account)*	*200.*	*00*
3. Midlays visa card a/c: 3991/4320/6191/7723 29 Old View Barchester Barsetshire		*500.*	*00*
4. B Bonds Sportwear (bounced cheque) 2 High Street Barchester Barsetshire payable to E M Wentworth (solicitor) ref: EMW/DTM 15 High Street Barchester Barsetshire		*27.*	*34*

Should I make an offer of payment?

- You may wish to suggest a rate at which you could pay back your debts (see part C of the application form). You do not have to make an offer but, if you do, it should be one you can afford to pay (however small).
- If you are employed, the court may ask your employer to send deductions direct from your earnings to the court. This is called an attachment of earnings order. If you object to this, you must tick the box in part C and say why you object. If you do not give good reasons, the court will consider making an order.

What should I do with the completed application form?

- Take the unsigned completed application form to your local county court. You will be asked to sign the form in front of a court officer and you will have to swear on oath that the information given in your application is true. If you can, bring any bills, statements and invoices to support the details of your income and expenditure.
- If you need help to complete the application form (N92) you should ask at your local county court office, citizens advice bureau, money advice centre or legal advice centre.
- **Take a photocopy of the completed application you may need to refer to it.**

Notice of Hearing of Interpleader Proceedings transferred from High Court

In the **Court**	
Claim No.	
Claimant	
Defendant	

To all parties and the Enforcement Officer of

In the matter of an action in the High Court of Justice Division

[No.]

being interpleader proceedings directed by the High Court to be transferred to this court.

TAKE NOTICE that these proceedings will be heard at

on

at o'clock.

NOTE - The claimant is required, within eight days of the receipt by him of this notice, to file in the court office three copies of the particulars of the goods alleged to be his property and the grounds of his claim.

DATED

The court office at

is open between 10 am and 4 pm Monday to Friday. Address all communications to the Court Manager quoting the claim number

N276 Notice of hearing of interpleader proceedings transferred from High Court (04.04) *The Court Service Publications Branch*

Notice of Pre-trial Review of Interpleader Proceedings transferred from High Court

In the **County Court**	
Claim No.	
Claimant	
Defendant	

To all parties and the Enforcement Officer of

In the matter of an action in the High Court of Justice Division

[No.]

being interpleader proceedings directed by the High Court to be transferred to this court.

TAKE NOTICE that you are required to attend at

on

at o'clock, when the District Judge will give directions for the determination of these proceedings.

NOTE - The claimant is required, within eight days of the receipt by him of this notice, to file in the court office three copies of the particulars of the goods alleged to be his property and the grounds of his claim.

DATED

The court office at

is open between 10 am and 4 pm Monday to Friday. Address all communications to the Court Manager quoting the claim number

N277 Notice of pre-trial review of interpleader proceedings transferred from High Court (04.04) *The Court Service Publications Branch*

Order of Reference of Proceedings or Questions for Inquiry and Report

In the	
County Court	
Claim No.	
Claimant	
Defendant	

To all parties

(insert name of judge) **HAS ORDERED** that these proceedings and all

(1) State the question

questions arising therein [or the following question arising in these proceedings]:[1]

be referred to the District Judge of this court [or to

of

for inquiry and report, pursuant to Section 93 of the County Courts Act 1959

(2) Add directions, if any, as to how reference is to be conducted

(2)

AND IT IS ORDERED that these proceedings stand adjourned for the consideration of the report [until the at o'clock.]

DATED

The court office at

is open between 10 am and 4 pm Monday to Friday. Address all communications to the Court Manager quoting the claim number

N280 Order of reference of proceedings or questions for inquiry and report (4.99)

General form of affidavit

Sworn by *(deponent)*	on
This is the *(1st, 2nd, etc.)*	affidavit
filed on behalf of *(party)*	by this deponent
on *(date filed)*	

In the **Court**
Claim No.

Claimant

Defendant

(1) Full names and occupation of deponent.

I (1)

of (2)

(2) Address

(3) Set out in numbered paragraphs, the facts deposed to.

make oath and say as follows:- (3)

Sworn at in the
County of
this day of [19][20]

Before me *Officer of a Court, appointed by the Judge to take Affidavits.*

N285 - w3 General form of affidavit (4.99) *Printed on behalf of The Court Service*

Order to Produce Prisoner

In the	
Court	
Claim No.	
Claimant	
Defendant	

seal

(1) Officer who has custody of prisoner

To[1]

The claimant [defendant] has made application to me, on affidavit, for an order under Section 57 of the County Courts Act 1984, to bring before this court
who it is said is detained as a prisoner in your custody, to be examined as a witness on his behalf in the above action.

Upon payment [or offer] to you of a reasonable sum for expenses and cost of conveyance of a proper officer or officers, and of
in going to, remaining at, and returning from this court.

YOU ARE REQUIRED to bring
before this court at

on
at o'clock, to be examined as a witness on behalf of the claimant [defendant] and immediately after he has given his testimony to this court, you are required to return him to the place from which he will have been brought under this order.

DATED

Signed

Judge
insert name of Judge

The court office at
is open between 10 am and 4 pm Monday to Friday. Address all communications to the Court Manager quoting the Claim number

N288 Order to produce prisoner (4.99)

Judgment for Defendant

In the County Court	
Claim No.	
Claimant	
Claimant's Ref.	
Defendant	
Defendant's Ref.	

To

seal

(insert name of judge) **Has ordered** that judgment be entered for the defendant and that the claimant do pay the sum of

£ for the defendant's costs (or the defendant's costs of this action, to be assessed on scale)

(insert name of judge) **Has ordered** that the claimant pays to the defendant the said sum (or costs) (immediately) (or by)

(and pays the assessed costs by that day, or if the costs have not been assessed, within 14 days of assessment)

Dated

Take Notice

To the claimant

If you do not pay in accordance with this order your goods may be removed and sold or other enforcement proceedings may be taken against you. If your circumstances change and you cannot pay, ask at the court office about what you can do

Address for Payment

(1) delete if debt is not to be registered

(1) This judgment has been recorded on the Register of County Court Judgments. This may make it difficult for you to get credit. **If you pay in full within one month you can ask the court to cancel the entry on the Register.** You will need to give proof of payment. You can (for a fee) also obtain a Certificate of Cancellation from the court. If you pay the debt in full after one month you can ask the court to mark the entry on the Register as satisfied and (for a fee) obtain a Certificate of Satisfaction to prove that the debt has been paid.

When judgment is for £5,000 or more, or is in respect of a debt which attracts contractual or statutory interest for late payment, the defendant may be entitled to further interest.

How to Pay

- **PAYMENT(S) MUST BE MADE to the person named at the address for payment quoting their reference and the court case number**
- **DO NOT bring or send payments to the court. THEY WILL NOT BE ACCEPTED.**
- You should allow at least 4 days for your payment to reach the defendant or his representative.
- Make sure that you keep records and can account for all payments made. Proof may be required if there is any disagreement. It is not safe to send cash unless you use registered post.
- A leaflet giving further advice about payment can be obtained from the court.
- If you need more information you should contact the defendant or his representative.

The court office at

is open between 10 am and 4 pm Monday to Friday. Address all communications to the Court Manager quoting the claim number

N289 Judgment for defendant

Certificate of Judgment or Order
(for Evidence only)

In the County Court	
Claim No.	
Claimant	
Defendant	
Claimant's Ref.	

seal

This certificate is granted for the purpose of

Claim details

Date of issue of proceedings	
Cause of action	
Date of judgment	

Judgment details

Amount of judgment	£ :
Debt or claim	£ :
Costs	£ :
Interest to date *(if any)*	£ :
Subsequent costs *(if any, including unsatisfied warrant costs)*	£ :
Interest from date of judgment* *(if any)*	£ :
Total amount	£ :

*Where judgment was entered for £5,000 or more, or was in respect of a debt which attracts contractual or statutory interest for late payment, the claimant may be entitled to further interest.

For court use only
(This certificate is only valid if sealed by the court and if this section is completed)

I certify that this is a true extract of the court record in this case

(for) **Court Manager** ....

Dated ....

The court office at

is open between 10 am and 4 pm Monday to Friday. Address all communications to the Court Manager quoting the claim number

N293 Certificate of judgment or order (for evidence only)

N293A
COMBINED CERTIFICATE OF JUDGMENT
AND REQUEST FOR WRIT OF FI FA

Combined certificate of judgment and request for writ of fieri facias or writ of possession

Creditor/Claimant

Debtor/Defendant

In the County Court	
Claim No.	
Creditor's/ Claimant's Ref.	
Debtor's/ Defendant's Ref.	
Date	

Part 1

Date of judgment or order

Total amount of judgment *including any costs*

or

Details of order for possession *including any costs*

Total amount of interest accrued at the rate of _____ per day to date *(if any)*

I certify that the details I have given are correct and that to my knowledge there is no application or other procedure pending.

I request an order for enforcement in the High Court by

☐ Writ of Fieri Facias

☐ Writ of Possession

I intend to enforce the judgment or order by execution against goods, and/or against trespassers in the High Court and require this Certificate for this purpose.

....

signed - (Creditor/Creditor's solicitor)
(Claimant/Claimant's solicitor)

....date

Part 2 ***(for court use only)***

I certify that this is a true extract of the court record in this case.

Seal

Order for enforcement in the High Court by

☐ Writ of Fieri Facias

☐ Writ of Possession

made on (date)...

....An Officer of the Court

Please Note:

This judgment or order has been sent to the High Court for enforcement by (Writ of Fieri Facias) (Writ of Possession against trespassers) only.

The county court claim has not been transferred to the High Court. Applications for other methods of enforcement or ancillary applications must be made to the county court in which the judgment or order was made, unless the case has since been transferred to a different court, in which case it must be made to that court.

The court office at

is open between 10 am and 4 pm Monday to Friday. When corresponding with the court, please address forms or letters to the Court Manager and quote the claim number.

THE ACTION DEPARTMENT of the High Court is open between 10am and 4.30pm. All correspondence should be sent to the Court Manager, Action Department, Royal Courts of Justice, Strand, London WC2A 2LL

N293A Combined certificate of judgment and request for writ of fieri facias or writ of possession (04.04)

/ continued overleaf

Part 3

In the High Court of Justice

Queen's Bench Division

(Sent from the County Court by Certificate dated the day of)

High Court Enforcement Number

County Court Claim Number

Address of (Debtor)
(property of which possession is to be given)

Seal a Writ of (Fieri Facias)(Possession) directed to the:

To: "____________________________, an enforcement officer authorised to enforce writs of execution from the High Court'.

Or,

'The enforcement officers authorised to enforce writs of execution from the High Court who are assigned to the district of [1] __________________ in England and Wales'.

Note: If you have chosen this option you must send this writ to the National Information Centre for Enforcement for allocation.

against ____________________________

for: *(Complete A, B, C as approriate)*

A. the sum of:

(a) debt £

(b) costs and interest £

(c) Subsequent costs £
(if any)

B. and interest thereon at ....% per annum from the date of transfer and costs of execution

C. possession of

and £ for costs.

Signed
Address for service
Date

Guidance Notes

Enforcement in the High Court of county court judgments or orders.

The practice for the enforcement in the High Court of those county court judgments or orders to which Article 8(A) and (B) of the High Court and County Court Jurisdiction Order 1991 applies shall be as follows:

1. The applicant shall present to the judgment counter clerk a certificate of judgment of the county court sealed with the seal of that court, setting out details of the judgment or order to be enforced, together with a copy of the same. There is no fee payable on registration.

2. The judgment counter clerk will check that the certificate has been signed by an officer of the issuing court (a rubber stamp is not sufficient), dated and that the certificate complies with CCR 0.22, r8 (1A) (Sched. 2 to the CPR), and in particular with the requirement that on its face it states that it is granted for the purpose of enforcing the judgment or order by execution against goods or for possession against trespassers in the High Court.

3. Provided that paragraphs 1 and 2 have been complied with, the counter clerk will:-
   (a) Allocate a reference number, and year and endorse that on the top right hand corner of the certificate and copy.
   (b) Date and seal the certificate and copy. Return the original to the applicant who should send the writ to the appropriate enforcement officer or the National Information Centre for Enforcement for allocation and retain a copy for the court records.

4. The Certificate shall be treated for enforcement purposes as a High Court judgment or order and interest at the appropriate rate shall run from the date of the certificate. Such interest as claimed on the judgment in the county court should be incorporated in the judgment as above.

5. The title of all subsequent documents shall be as follows:-

   IN THE HIGH COURT OF JUSTICE High Court No.
   QUEEN'S BENCH DIVISION County Court Claim No
   (Sent from the County Court by Certificate dated the day of .)

   A.B.
   Claimant

   C.D.
   Defendant

6. When the appropriate fee is paid and a writ of *fieri facias* or possession is issued, the Certificate of Judgment retained by the applicant shall be date sealed by the counter clerk on the bottom left hand corner.

7. **Any application for a stay of execution should be made by application notice in the High Court returnable before a Queen's Bench Master. All other applications for enforcement or ancillary relief must be made to the county court in which the judgment or order was made, unless the case has since been transferred to a different court, in which case that court.**

R L Turner, Senior Master
Queen's Bench Division

[1] This should reflect the Districts as set out in the High Court Enforcement Officers Regulation 2004

N295
Order for Sale of Land

[General Title]

UPON hearing

AND upon reading

It IS ORDERED that the [freehold] [leasehold] property (*description*) be sold [by public auction] [in such manner as the parties may agree or the court may direct in default of agreement]

AND IT IS ORDERED that the conduct of the Sale be committed to the [claimant].

[*Add any specific directions as to the sale e.g. fixing reserve or minimum price, giving leave to bid at auction, obtaining valuation, fixing auctioneers' remunerations*]

AND IT IS ORDERED that the [claimant's] costs of this action down to the date of this order be assessed in detail [*or* the standard basis or as the case may be] and paid by the [defendant].

And the further consideration of this action is adjourned [to be dealt with by the district judge in chambers]. And the parties are to be at liberty to apply.

DATED

N296
Notice of Judgment or Order to Party Directed to be Served with Notice thereof

Seal

[General Title]

TAKE NOTICE that on the day of , 20 , the judgment [*or* order] of which a copy is hereto annexed was made in this action [*or* matter] and that from the time of the service of this notice on you, you will be bound by the said judgment [*or* order] to the same extent as if you had been originally made a party.

AND FURTHER TAKE NOTICE that you may attend the proceedings under the said judgment [*or* order], and that you may apply to the [judge] [district judge] within one month after service upon you of this notice to discharge, vary or add to the said judgment or order.

DATED

N297
Order for Accounts and Inquiries in Creditor's Administration Action

Seal

[General Title]

THIS COURT ORDERS that the trusts of the Will of the above named testator be performed and carried in execution.

IT IS ORDERED that the following accounts and inquiries be taken and made, that is to say:

1. An account of what is due to the claimant and all other the creditors of the above-named intestate [*or* testator].

2. An account of the intestate's [*or* testator's] funeral expenses.

3. An Account of the intestate's [*or* testator's] property come to the hands of the defendants the administrators of his estate [*or* executors of his Will] or of any [*or* either] of them or to the hands of any other person or persons by the order or for the use of the said defendants or any [*or* either] of them.

4. An inquiry what parts (if any) of the intestate's [*or* testator's] property are outstanding or undisposed of and as to any part of such property as is outstanding or undisposed of whether the same is subject to any and what incumbrance.

5. [An Account of what is due to such of the incumbrancers (if any) as shall consent to the sale hereinafter directed in respect of the incumbrances.

6. An Inquiry what are the priorities of such last-mentioned incumbrancers.]

[And none of the above accounts or inquiries [except the accounts numbered
and] is to be prosecuted in chambers except with the leave of the [judge] [court].

[AND IT IS ORDERED that the intestate's [*or* testator's] property be applied in payment of his debts and funeral expenses in a due course of administration.]

AND IT IS ORDERED that the intestate's [*or* testator's] real estate be sold with the approbation of the judge free from the incumbrances (if any) of such of the incumbrancers as shall consent to the sale and subject to the incumbrances of such of them as shall not consent.

AND IT IS ORDERED that the money to arise by the sale of the intestate's [*or* testator's] real estate be paid into the court to the credit of the action subject to further Order. And if such money or any part thereof shall arise from real estate sold with the consent of incumbrancers the money so arising is to be applied in the first place in payment of what shall appear to be due in such incumbrancers according to their priorities.

The further consideration of this action be adjourned and the parties are at liberty to apply.

N298
Order for Administration

Seal

[General Title]

THIS COURT ORDERS that the trusts of the Will of the above-named testator be performed and carried into execution.

IT IS ORDERED that the following accounts and inquiry be taken and made, that is to say:

1. An account of the property [not specifically devised or bequeathed] of the above-named testator] [*or* Intestate] come to the hands of the claimants [*or* defendants] the executors of his said Will [*or* the administrators of his estate] or any [*or* either] of them or to the hands of any other person or persons by the order or for the use of the said claimant's [*or* defendants] or any [*or* either] of them.

[*Add if necessary* distinguishing between capital and income.]

2. An account of the testator's [*or* intestate's] debts.

3. An Account of the testator's [*or* intestate's] funeral [*and* testamentary] expenses.

4. An account of the legacies and annuities given by the testator's Will.

5. An Inquiry what parts (if any) of the testator's [*or* intestate's] property are outstanding or undisposed of and whether any part of such property so outstanding or undisposed of is subject to any and what incumbrance.
[And none of the above accounts or inquiries [except the account numbered and] is to be prosecuted in chambers except with the leave of the [judge] [court]]

[AND IT IS ORDERED that the testator's [*or* intestate's] property [not specifically devised or bequeathed] be applied in payment of his debts and funeral [and testamentary] expenses [and afterwards in payment of the legacies and annuities given by his Will] in a due course of administration.]

The further consideration of this action be adjourned and the parties are at liberty to apply.

N299
Order for Foreclosure nisi of legal mortgage of Land

Seal

[General Title]

[IT IS ORDERED that an account be taken of what is due to the claimant for principal and interest under or by virtue of the mortgage dated the day of , 20 , mentioned in the particulars of claim and of his costs of this action, to be taxed or assessed on scale .

AND IT IS ORDERED that the amount due to the claimant on such account be certified.]

And upon the defendant paying into court what shall be certified to be due to the claimant for principal and interest as aforesaid, together with the said costs, within six months after the date of the registrar's certificate.

[And the [judge] [court] being satisfied by the evidence that on 20 , there will be due to the claimant under and by virtue of the mortgage dated 20 mentioned in the particulars of claim the sum of £ for principal and the sum of £ for interest at £ per cent per annum on the said sum of £ from 20 to 20 and £ for the summarily assessed costs of the claimant of this action making together the sum of £ . And upon the defendant paying into court the said sum of £ on or before 20] IT IS ORDERED that the claimant do give to the defendant, or as he shall direct, a receipt pursuant to Section 115 of the Law of Property Act 1925, with regard to the moneys due under the said mortgage and do deliver up to the defendant, on oath if required, all deeds and writings in his custody or power relating thereto; and that upon such receipt being given and such deeds and writings being delivered up, the [district judge] shall pay out to the claimant the said sum so paid into court as aforesaid for principal, interest, and costs; but in default of the defendant paying into court such principal, interest, and costs as aforesaid by the time aforesaid, then IT IS ORDERED that the defendant do henceforth stand absolutely debarred and foreclosed of and from all right, title, interest, and equity of redemption of, in and to the property the subject of the said mortgage, and thereupon it is ordered that the defendant do forthwith deliver to the claimant possession of the said property [*describe property as in mortgage deed*]

And the parties are to be at liberty to apply.

N300
Order for Sale in Action by Equitable Mortgagee

Seal

[General Title]

THIS COURT DECLARES that the claimant is entitled to an equitable charge on the property referred to in the particulars of the claim.

AND IT IS ORDERED that an account be taken of what is due to the claimant for principal and interest on the said equitable charge and that the claimant's costs of this action be summarily assessed at £....... .

AND IT IS ORDERED that what shall be certified to be due to the claimant on taking the said account be considered as a charge on the said property. And upon the defendant paying into court what shall be certified to be due to the claimant for principal and interest as aforesaid, together with the said costs, within six months after the date of the district judge's certificate, IT IS ORDERED that the claimant do give to the defendant or as he shall direct a receipt pursuant to Section 115 of the Law of Property Act 1925, with regard to the moneys due on the said equitable charge and do deliver up to the district judge, on oath if required, all deeds and writings in his custody or power relating to the said property, and that upon such receipt being given and such deeds and writings being delivered up, the district judge shall pay out to the claimant the said sum so paid into court as aforesaid, for principal, interest and costs; but in default of the defendant paying into court such principal, interest and costs as aforesaid by the time aforesaid then it is ordered that the said property be sold by the claimant without further reference to the court AND IT IS ORDERED pursuant to s. 90 of the Law of Property Act 1925 that a term of (3000 years) (years less one day, but otherwise subject to the same terms and conditions as are contained in the lease mentioned in the particulars of claim) be vested in the claimant to enable him to carry out the sale. AND IT IS ORDERED that the money to arise by such sale be paid into court to abide further order,

AND the further consideration of this action is adjourned and the parties are to be at liberty to apply.

N302
Judgment in Action for Specific Performance (Vendor's action, title accepted)

Seal

[General Title]

THIS COURT orders that the agreement dated mentioned in the particulars of the claim be specifically performed and carried into execution.

AND IT IS ORDERED that interest be computed at the rate of £ per cent per annum on the sum of £ (the residue of the purchase money for the property mentioned in the agreement) from 20 , when the purchase ought to have been completed according to the terms of the said agreement to the day to be fixed hereinafter directed.

AND IT IS ORDERED that the following accounts be taken that is to say

1. An Account of what is due to the claimant for the balance of the said purchase price and interest.

2. An Account of the rents and profits of the said property received by the claimant or by any other person or persons by the order or for the use of the claimant since (*i.e. date for completion*) 20 . And it is ordered that the claimant's costs are summarily assessed at £........ .

AND IT IS ORDERED that what shall be found due on the said account of rents and profits be deducted from the said purchase money and interest and costs as aforesaid, and the balance certified by the district judge. And it appearing that the defendant has accepted the claimant's title to the said property IT IS ORDERED that the claimant be at liberty to prepare and execute a conveyance to the defendant (as to be delivered to the defendant as hereinafter provided) such conveyance to be settled by the court in case the parties differ.

And upon the claimant at a time and place to be appointed by the court after the said conveyance shall have been so executed as aforesaid delivering to the defendant the said conveyance together with all deeds and writings in his possession or power relating solely to the property and giving an acknowledgment and undertaking for production of deeds relating to other properties as provided by s. 64 of the Law of Property Act 1925.

IT IS ORDERED that the defendant do at the same time and place pay to the claimant the amount of the said certified balance.

N303
Order for Dissolution of Partnership

[General Title]

IT IS DECLARED AND ADJUDGED that the partnership mentioned in the claimant's particulars between the claimant and [defendant] [was dissolved as from the date of this judgment *or* the day of , 20 ;] (*or as the case may be*).

AND IT IS ORDERED that the following account and inquiry be taken:

1. An account of all dealings and transactions between the claimant and the defendant partners from 20

2. An inquiry as to what the credits property and effects now belonging to the partnership consist of

AND IT IS ORDERED that [*a proper person*] be appointed upon giving security to collect, get in, and receive the debts now due and accruing and other assets property and effects belonging to the partnership.

AND IT IS ORDERED that the defendant do within [10] days after service of this order [and of the order appointing the receiver] deliver over to the Receiver all the stock in trade and effects of the partnership and also all securities in his hands for such outstanding partnership estate together with all books and papers relating thereto.

AND IT IS ORDERED that the Receiver do out of the first money to be received by him pay the debts due from the partnership.

AND IT IS ORDERED that the Receiver do pass his accounts and pay the balances which may be certified to be due from him as the court shall direct. The further consideration of this action is adjourned.

And the parties to be at liberty to apply.

Notice to Parties to Attend upon taking Accounts

In the Court	
Claim No.	
Claimant	
Defendant	

To all Parties

TAKE NOTICE that all parties concerned are required to attend at the court office at

on

at o'clock, to proceed with the accounts and inquiries directed by the judgment [or order]

given herein, on the day of [19][20] .

DATED

The court office at

is open between 10 am and 4 pm Monday to Friday. Address all communications to the Court Manager quoting the claim number

N304 Notice of parties to attend upon taking accounts (4.99)

Notice to Creditor to Prove his Claim

In the County Court	
Claim No.	
Claimant	
Defendant	

To

TAKE NOTICE that you are required on or before the

[to file an affidavit] [or produce[1]

[1] State any deeds or documents to be produced

]

in support of your claim

[or, to attend at the court office at

on

at o'clock, for adjudication on the claim.]

DATED

The court office at

is open between 10 am and 4 pm Monday to Friday. Address all communications to the Court Manager quoting the claim number

N305 Notice to creditor to prove his claim (4.99)

Notice to Creditor of Determination of Claim

In the	
County Court	
Claim No.	
Claimant	
Defendant	

To

TAKE NOTICE that the claim sent in by you against the estate of

deceased has been [disallowed]

[or allowed at £ with interest thereon at per cent. per annum, from the day of

[19][20], and £ for costs.]

DATED

The court office at

is open between 10 am and 4 pm Monday to Friday. Address all communications to the Court Manager quoting the claim number

N306 Notice to creditor of determination of claim (4.99)

N307
District Judge's Order (Accounts and Inquiries)

Seal

[General Title]

The result of the accounts and inquiries which have been taken and made in pursuance of the judgment [*or* order] in this cause dated the day of , is as follows:

1. The defendants , the executors of the testator, have received property not specifically devised or bequeathed to the amount of £ and they have paid, or are entitled to be allowed on account thereof, sums to the amount of £ , leaving a balance due from [*or* to] them of £ on that account.

The particulars of the above receipts and payments appear in the account marked , verified by the witness statement of , filed on the day of , and which account is to be filed with this order, except that, in addition to the sums appearing on such account to have been received, the said defendants are charged with the following [*state the same here or in a schedule*], and except that the items of disbursement in the said account numbered , and are disallowed.

2. The unpaid debts of the testator which have been allowed are set forth in the schedule hereto and with the interest thereon and costs mentioned in the schedule are due to the persons therein named and amount altogether to £ .

The funeral expenses of the testator amounted to the sum of £ , which are allowed the said executors in the said account.

3. The legacies given by the testator are set forth in the schedule hereto and with the interest therein mentioned remain due to the persons therein named and amount altogether to £ .

4. The outstanding property of the testator consists of the particulars set forth in the schedule hereto.

5. The incumbrances affecting the said testators property are specified in the schedule hereto.

[6. The parts of the testator's property directed to be sold have been sold and the purchase-moneys, amounting together to £ , have been paid into Court.]

[*N.B.: the above numbers are to correspond with the numbers in the order so far as appropriate.*]

The evidence produced on these accounts [and inquiries] consists of the probate of the testator's will and the witness statements of A.B. and of C.D. filed and respectively.

DATED

DISTRICT JUDGE

N309
Order for Foreclosure Absolute

Seal

[General Title]

WHEREAS it appears to the Court that the defendant has not paid into Court the sum of £ which was by the district judge's order dated found to be due to the claimant for principal and interest upon the mortgage dated the day of mentioned in the particulars of claim, and for costs, pursuant to the order made in this action on the day of last, and that the period of six months has elapsed since the day of

IT IS ORDERED that the defendant do stand absolutely debarred and foreclosed of and from all right, title, interest, and equity of redemption of, in and to the property comprised in the said mortgage, the particulars of which property are set forth in the schedule hereto, and that the defendant do forthwith deliver up possession to the claimant of the property comprised in the said schedule.

The Schedule

N310
Partnership—Order on further consideration

Seal

[General Title]

IT IS ORDERED that the money now in court to the credit of this action amounting to the sum of £ , with any interest thereon, be applied as follows:

1. In payment of the debts due by the partnership set forth in the district judge's order, amounting to £ .

2. In payment to the claimant [*or* defendant] of the sum of £ being the amount found by the district judge's order to be due to the claimant [*or* defendant] by the partnership for advances as distinguished from capital.

AND IT IS ORDERED that it be referred to the district judge to assess in detail the costs of the claimant and the defendant in this action on scale.

AND IT IS ORDERED that out of the balance of the said sum of £ and interest, after payment of the said debts and of the said sum of £ so found due to the claimant [*or* defendant], the said costs of the claimant and defendant, or any such apportionment in respect thereof as hereinafter mentioned, be paid to the claimant and defendant respectively.

AND IT IS ORDERED that the residue (if any) of the said sum of £ and interest, be applied in payment to the claimant and defendant respectively, and rateably inter se, of the respective sums of £ and £ found by the district judge's order to be due to the claimant and defendant respectively in respect of capital, and that the ultimate balance (if any) of the said sum and interest be apportioned between and paid to the claimant and defendant respectively in the following proportions, viz. [*according to the shares in which profits were divisible*].

But if the balance of the said sum of £ and interest shall be insufficient to pay the said costs in full, then it is ordered that such balance be apportioned rateably between the claimant and the defendant in proportion to the amounts of their said costs when assessed in detail, and that the amounts so apportioned be certified and paid to the claimant and defendant respectively.

And the parties are to be at liberty to apply.

[*If any sum be found due from either partner to the partnership in respect of capital withdrawn or otherwise, order payment of that sum by him into court. If the sum in court is insufficient to pay the balance found due to the claimant or defendant, as the case may be, order the other party to pay to the party to whom such balance is found due a proportionate part of the deficiency, and insert directions as to costs.*]

N311
Administration Action—Order on Further Consideration

Seal

[General Title]

THIS ACTION coming on this day for further consideration AND UPON HEARING AND UPON READING the order dated , 20 , [*original order for accounts and inquiries*], and the order of the district judge, dated , 20 .

IT IS ORDERED that the costs of all parties to this action be assessed in detail, including the costs of the defendant, any costs, charges, and expenses properly incurred by him as executor and trustee of the will of the testator, not being costs of this action.

AND IT IS ORDERED that the defendant be at liberty, out of the sum of £ by the said order found due from him on account of the personal estate of the testator, to retain the amount of his said costs when taxed.

AND IT IS ORDERED that the said defendant do pay the balance of the said sum of £ found due from him as aforesaid remaining after such retainer as aforesaid into Court to the credit of this action.

AND IT IS ORDERED that the costs of all other parties when assessed in detail be paid out of the moneys in Court to the credit of this action.

AND IT IS ORDERED that out of any moneys remaining in court to the credit of this action after providing for the said costs, the debts of the testator included in the schedule to the district judge's order, with interest at £ per cent from the date of the district judge's order, the amount to be verified by (*state mode of verification*), be paid to the creditors to whom such debts are certified to be due and that out of any moneys to the credit of the last-mentioned account, after providing for payment of the costs and the debts as aforesaid the legacies by his said certificate found due to be paid, together with interest at £ per cent from the date of the order to the legatees respectively.

(AND THE COURT DECLARES that according to the true construction of the testator's will the ultimate balance of the testator's personal estate, and the proceeds of the sale of the testator's real estate, are divisible as follows:

Order for distribution amongst parties entitled, and payment, the shares of infants being carried over to accounts instituted according to circumstances.)

AND the parties are to be at liberty to apply.

I certify that this is a true extract of the court record in this case.

. . . . Dated . . . . District Judge

This certificate is issued for the purpose of issuing
in the County Court.

The present address of the defendant is that shown on the record card OR is belived to be:-(1)

(1) *Delete as necessary.*
N.313 Indorsement on certificate of judgment (transfer) *(4.99)*

F.C. No.

Bailiff's Report

In the	County Court
Claim no	
Warrant no	
Local no	
Creditor	
Debtor	

To the Creditor('s Solicitor)

And to the Court Manager of County Court

The warrant of execution in this action has not been executed for the reasons ticked below

☐ The bailiff is unable to trace the address you gave within the district of the court.

☐ The debtor is not known at the address you gave.

☐ The debtor is stated to have left the address you gave, leaving no effects on which to levy. [Premises empty]. *The debtor's new address is believed to be:*

☐ The debtor has no effects upon which to levy [Ceased trading].

☐ The debtor's goods are of insufficient value to cover the cost of removing and selling them (the debtor lives with parent(s)).

☐ The bailiff has been unable to gain peaceful entry to the premises.

☐ The address you gave is a registered office only and there are no effects of the debtor company on the premises.

☐ [Debtor bankrupt, petition number in the County Court] [company in liquidation, winding up order number].

☐ Other reason (specify):

Further information

☐ [The debtor is unemployed] [the debtor is believed to be employed by:].

☐ The bailiff has been unable to enter the premises to enforce the warrant. Efforts continue.

☐ The bailiff holds warrants to a total of £ which remain unsatisfied.

☐ Sheriff's Officer/Inland Revenue/VAT in possession on prior warrants.

☐ All goods on the premises are subject to conditional sale or hire purchase agreements.

☐ The warrant has been returned to the Home Court and any further correspondence should be sent there.

Dated

Address all correspondence to the Court Manager

The court office is open from 10 a.m. to 4 p.m. Mondays to Fridays

N317 Bailif's report

Bailiff's Report to the Claimant('s Solicitor)

In the County Court	
Claim No.	
Warrant No.	
Local No.	
Claimant	
Defendant	

The Bailiff has made visits at the dates and times shown below in connection with the above warrant and has been unable to meet the defendant or gain entry to the premises to make a levy.

	Date	Time
1.		
2.		
3.		

☐ It has proved impossible to obtain any information about the defendant locally

☐ Local enquiries have failed to confirm that the defendant lives at the above address

☐ Local enquiries have produced the following information

☐ No payments have been made to the court

In the circumstances the warrant is being treated as unenforceable

No further action will be taken unless you can give additional instructions which will help the bailiff.

DATED

Copy to the Court Manager County Court

The court office at

is open between 10 am and 4 pm Monday to Friday. Address all communications to the Court Manager quoting the claim number

N317A Bailiff's report to the claimant('s solicitor) (4.99)

FORM N319 NOTICE OF EXECUTION OF WARRANT OF COMMITTAL

IN THE **COUNTY COURT**

CASE No.

BETWEEN . . . . **CLAIMANT**

WARRANT No.

AND . . . . **DEFENDANT**

LOCAL No.

To the **County Court**

TAKE NOTICE that the warrant of committal in this action was executed on the
by lodging the person named in the warrant in Her Majesty's Prison at

DATED

N319 Notice of execution of warrant of committal.

IN THE **COUNTY COURT**

CASE No.

BETWEEN . . . . **CLAIMANT**

WARRANT No.

AND . . . . **DEFENDANT**

LOCAL No.

To the **County Court**

TAKE NOTICE that the warrant of committal in this action was executed on the
by lodging the person named in the warrant in Her Majesty's Prison at

DATED

N319 Notice of execution of warrant of committal.

Request for Warrant of Execution

to be completed and signed by the claimant or his solicitor and sent to the court with the appropriate fee

1 Claimant's name and address

2 Name and address for service and payment (if different from above) **Ref/Tel No.**

3 Defendant's name and address

In the County Court

Claim Number

for court use only

Warrant no.

Issue date:

Warrant applied for at o'clock

Foreign court code/name:

4 Warrant details

(A) Balance due at date of this request	
(B) Amount for which warrant to issue	
Issue fee	
Solicitor's costs	
Land Registry fee	
TOTAL	

If the amount of the warrant at (B) is less than the balance at (A), the sum due after the warrant is paid will be

I certify that the whole or part of any instalments due under the judgment or order have not been paid and the balance now due is as shown

Signed

Claimant (Claimant's solicitor)

Dated

IMPORTANT
You must inform the court immediately of any payments you receive after you have sent this request to the court

You should provide a contact number so that the bailiff can speak to you if he/she needs to:

Daytime phone number: Evening phone number (if possible):

Contact name (where appropriate):

Defendant's phone number (if known):

If you have any other information which may help the bailiff or if you have reason to believe that the bailiff may encounter any difficulties you should write it below.

Produced on behalf of The Court Service

Request for Warrant of Delivery of Goods

to be completed and signed by the claimant or his solicitor and sent to the court with the appropriate fee

1 Claimant's name and address

2 Name and address for service and payment *(if different from above)* **Ref/Tel No.**

3 Defendant's name and address

In the

County Court

Claim Number

for court use only

Warrant No.

Issue date:

Warrant applied for at o'clock

Foreign court code/name:

4 Warrant details

*(Balance of) assessed value of specified goods due at date of this request/ unpaid balance of total price	
(Debt/damages)	
(Costs)	
Issue fee	
Solicitor's costs	
AMOUNT TO BE LEVIED	

**Delete where specific delivery is ordered*

I apply for the issue of a warrant of delivery of goods (and execution) against the defendant(s) in respect of a judgment (an order) in this court for the delivery of the goods specified in the schedule below

I certify that the whole or part of any instalments due under the judgment or order have not been paid (*and the balance now due is as shown)

Signed

Claimant (Claimant's solicitor)

Date

*delete if not applicable

IMPORTANT

You must inform the court immediately of any payments you receive after you have sent this request to the court

Schedule of Goods *(Include here any other information that might assist the bailiff. You should also tell the court if you have reason to believe that the bailiff might encounter serious difficulties in attempting to execute the warrant.*

Warrant No.

N324 -w3 – Request for warrant of delivery (4.99)

Printed on behalf of The Court Service

Request for Warrant of Possession of Land

To be completed and signed by the claimant or his solicitor and sent to the court with the appropriate fee

1. Claimant's name and address

2. Name and address for service and payment (if different from above)

Ref/Tel No.

3. Defendant's name and address

In the

County Court

Claim No.

For court use only

Warrant No.

Issue date:

Warrant applied for at o'clock

Foreign court code/name (execution only):

4. Warrant details

(A) Balance due at the date of this request	
(B) Amount for which warrant to issue	
Issue fee	
Solicitor's costs	
Land Registry fee	
TOTAL	
If the amount of the warrant at (B) is less than the balance at (A), the sum due after the warrant is paid will be	

5. Property/land details

Date of judgment/order	
Date of possession	

Describe the land (as set out in the particulars of claim)

I certify that

(1) the defendant has not vacated the land as ordered (*and that the whole or part of any instalments due under the judgment or order have not been paid) († and the balance now due is as shown)

(2) notice has been given in accordance with The Dwelling Houses (Execution of Possession Orders by Mortgagees) Regulations 2010.

Signed

Claimant (Claimant's solicitor)

Dated

* *delete unless defendant is in arrears with the suspended possession order or judgment*

† *delete unless warrant is to issue for execution also*

IMPORTANT

You must inform the court immediately of any payments you receive after you have sent this request to the court

If there is more than one defendant and you are not proceeding against all of them, enter here the name(s) of the defendant(s) you wish to proceed against

You should provide a contact number so that the bailiff can speak to you if he/she needs to:

Daytime phone number: Evening phone number *(if possible)*:

Contact name *(where appropriate)*:

Defendant's phone number *(if known)*:

If you have any other information which may help the bailiff or if you have reason to believe that the bailiff may encounter any difficulties you should write it below.

N325 - Request for warrant for possession of land (10.10)

Notice of Issue of Warrant of Execution

Claimant

Defendant

In the County Court	
Claim Number	
Warrant Number	
Local Number	
Claimant's Ref.	

Quote all the above numbers on correspondence

Urgent
To the defendant

You have not made payment under the judgment as you were ordered. The claimant has therefore asked for a warrant to be issued to the bailiff to seize and sell your goods. Unless you pay the amount due to the county court **before the** **the bailiff will call and may remove your goods for sale at public auction**. This may mean that you will have to pay further costs.

Total to pay £
(including fees) on this warrant

Balance outstanding £
(after payment of this warrant)

Send or take your payment and this form to the court office at

Amount enclosed £
Enter the amount you are sending to the court

Payments into Court

You can pay the court by calling at the court office which is open 10 am to 4 pm Monday to Friday
You may only pay by:

- cash
- banker's or giro draft
- cheque supported by a cheque card
- cheque (unsupported cheques may be accepted subject to clearance, if the Court Manager agrees)

Cheques and drafts must be made payable to HM Paymaster General and crossed.
Please bring this form with you.

By post
You may only pay by:

- postal order
- banker's or giro draft
- cheque (cheques may be accepted, subject to clearance, if the Court Manager agrees)

The payment must be made out to HM Paymaster General and crossed. This method of payment is at your own risk. And you must:

- pay the postage
- enclose this form
- enclose a self adddressed envelope so that the court can return this form with a receipt

The court cannot accept stamps or payments by bank and giro credit transfers

Note:
You should carefully check any future forms from the court to see if payments should be made directly to the claimant
Where judgment was entered for £5,000 or more, or was in respect of a debt which attracts contractual or statutory interest for late payment, the claimant may be entitled to further interest. If you pay the total due on the warrant, together with the balance outstanding by the date shown above, the claimant will not be entitled to further interest.

N326 Notice of issue of warrant of execution

Notice of Issue of Warrant of Execution to Enforce a Judgment or Order of the High Court

In the County Court	
Claim No.	
Claimant	
Defendant	

(1) The proper officer of the High Court

To(1)

In the matter of an action in the High Court of Justice, Division

[No.]

TAKE NOTICE that a warrant of execution to enforce the judgment or order in the above action has this day been issued in this court against the defendant.

DATED

The court office at

is open between 10 am and 4 pm Monday to Friday. Address all communications to the Court Manager quoting the claim number

N327 Notice of issue of warrant of execution to enforce a judgment or order of the High Court (4.99)

Transfer of Proceedings to High Court

In the **County Court**	
Claim No.	
Claimant	
Defendant	
Claimant's Ref.	

Take notice, the judgment or order in the above action has been transferred to the High Court of Justice

Division

All future communications should be directed to the Claimant('s solicitor) whose name and address is

Name ....

Address ....

....

....

N328 Notice of transfer of proceedings to the High Court (4.99)

Transfer of Proceedings to High Court

Take notice, the judgment o
to the High Court of Justice

All future communications sl
whose name and address is

Name ....

Address ....

....

....

N328 Notice of transfer of proceeding

 FORM N330

In the County Court

CLAIM No.

BETWEEN .... CLAIMANT

WARRANT No.

AND .... DEFENDANT

LOCAL No.

To the County Court and to the Claimant

TAKE NOTICE that under the warrant of execution issued in this case [the defendant (1)
has paid £ in order to avoid a sale]

OR

[the goods of the defendant (1)
have been sold and after deduction of the costs of execution a balance of £ remains]
which will be retained in court for fourteen days

(1) Add 'Company' if so, and if the warrant issued against one or more of several defendants name him or them.

DATED

Address all communications to the Court Manager AND QUOTE THE ABOVE CLAIM NUMBER

THE COURT OFFICE AT

is open from 10 a.m. to 4 p.m. Monday to Friday.

N330 Notice of sale or payment under execution in respect of a judgment for a sum exceeding £500 (4.99)

Notice of Withdrawal from Possession, or Payment over of Moneys, on Notice of Receiving or Winding-up Order

In the County Court	
Claim No.	
Warrant No.	
Claimant	
Defendant	

To the Claimant and the Court Manager of County Court

TAKE NOTICE that the court has received notice that a Receiving Order has been made under the Bankruptcy Act, 1914, against the defendant [*or* that a provisional liquidator of the defendant company has been appointed] [*or* that an order/resolution for the (voluntary) winding-up of the defendant company has been made or passed under the Companies Act, 1948] and has withdrawn from possession of the goods seized under the warrant of execution issued in this action against the goods of the defendant [company] and has delivered them to the Official Receiver [or Trustee] [*or* to the Liquidator appointed] [*or* has paid over to the Official Receiver/Trustee/Liquidator appointed the proceeds of sale [*or* the money paid in order to avoid a sale] of the goods of the defendant [company] [*or* the money received in part satisfaction of the warrant of execution against the goods of the defendant [company]].

DATED

The court office at

is open between 10 am and 4 pm Monday to Friday. Address all communications to the Court Manager quoting the claim number

N331 Notice of withdrawal from possession, or payment over of money, on notice of receiving or winding-up order (4.99)

Note The Bankruptcy Act 1914 has been repealed. Please insert the correct statutory provision.

IN THE COUNTY COURT

CLAIM No.

WARRANT No.

LOCAL No.

. . . . v. . . . .

To the Defendant

TAKE NOTICE that the following goods have been removed by me in respect of the above warrant. You will be notified of the time and place where they will be sold.

DATED

Signed Bailiff

N332 - Inventory of goods removed. (4.99)

IN THE COUNTY COURT

CLAIM No.

WARRANT No.

LOCAL No.

. . . . v. . . . .

To the Defendant

TAKE NOTICE that the following goods have been removed by me in respect of the above warrant. You will be notified of the time and place where they will be sold.

DATED

Signed Bailiff

N332 - Inventory of goods removed. (4.99)

Notice of Time when and where Goods will be Sold

In the County Court	
Claim No.	
Warrant No.	
Local No.	
Claimant	
Defendant	

TAKE NOTICE that the goods which were seized under this warrant will be sold

by

at

on the day [19][20] , at o'clock unless the amount due

under the warrant, together with the additional fees incurred to the time of payment, are paid into the office of this court before that time.

DATED

The court office at

is open between 10 am and 4 pm Monday to Friday. Address all communications to the Court Manager quoting the claim number

N333 Notice of time when and where goods will be sold

 FORM N336

IN THE **COUNTY COURT**

BETWEEN . . . . CLAIMANT

AND . . . . DEFENDANT

To the Court Manager of the County Court

Please search your attachment of earnings order index and notify me whether any, and if so what, information is recorded in the name of

whose address is

against whom I have obtained a judgment in the Court,
under claim number

DATE

Signed
Claimant('s Solicitor)

Solicitor's Address

Solicitor's Ref:-

To the Claimant('s Solicitor)
A search of the attachment of earnings order index has been made against the above named defendant and I certify that:-

(1) delete where inapplicable

(1) There are no subsisting entries.

(1) An attachment of earnings order in respect of a judgment debt is in force in the County Court. The normal deduction rate is £ per week/month (1) and the balance outstanding is £

(1) A priority attachment of earnings order in respect of a fine/maintenance order (1) is in force in the Court.

DATE

Court Manager

N336 - w3 Request for and result of search in the attachment of earnings index (4.99) *Printed on behalf of The Court Service*

Request for Attachment of Earnings Order

to be completed and signed by the claimant or their solicitor and sent to the court with the appropriate fee

Name of county court

Claim number

For court use only

A/E application no.

Issue date:

Hearing date:

on

at o'clock

at (address)

1 Claimant's details name, address, and phone number

Postcode

Phone no.

2 Name and address for service and payment *(if different from above)* Ref/Phone no.

Postcode

Phone no.

3 Debtor's details name, address and phone number

Postcode

Phone no.

4 Judgment details

Court where judgment/order made if not court of issue

5 Outstanding debt

Balance due at date of request*
(excluding issue fee but including unsatisfied warrant costs)

Issue fee

AMOUNT NOW DUE

* you may also be entitled to interest to the date of request where judgment is for £5,000 or more, or is in respect of a debt which attracts contractual or statutory interest for late payment

6 Employment details *(please give as much information as you can – it will help the court to make an order more quickly)*

Employer's name and address

Postcode

Phone no.

6 Employment details *(continued)*

Debtor's place of work
(if different from employer's address)

The debtor is employed as

Works No. / Pay Ref.

7 Other details

Give any other details about the debtor's circumstances which may be relevant to the application.

I apply for an attachment of earnings order

I certify that the whole or part of any instalments due under the judgment or order have not been paid and the balance now due is as shown.

Signed

Claimant (Claimants solicitor)

Date

IMPORTANT
You must tell the court immediately of any payments you receive after you have sent this request to the court

N337 Request for attachment of earnings order (06.09)

Request for Statement of Earnings

In the County Court	
Claim No.	
Application No.	
Claimant	
Defendant	
Dated	

To the defendant's employer

Dear Sir,

*insert full name of defendant

Re your employee* ....

I understand that the defendant named above is in your employment. To assist the court in considering an application for an order attaching his/her earnings, will you please supply **within 7 days** the information requested overleaf.

If the defendant has never been employed by you or has now left your employment, please tick the correct box(es) below and return the completed form to me as soon as possible.

A pre-paid addressed envelope is enclosed for your reply.

Yours faithfully

Court Manager

The person named above is not employed by this company

☐ He/she has never been employed by this company

☐ He/she left this employment on (date) ....

☐ He/she is believed to be employed at ....

....

....

Signed ....

Position in company ....

Date ....

The court office at

is open between 10 am and 4 pm Monday to Friday. Address all communications to the Court Manager quoting the claim number

N338 Request for statement of earnings

Employer's Certificate(statement of earnings)

Employee's details

Full name of employee:

Works no./pay ref. *(if known)*:

Full address of employee:

Capacity in which employed:

Payment details

Please enter below payments for each of the past ten weeks/months

Payment week or month ended	Basic wages or salary		Overtime, bonuses, commission etc.		Deductions*		Net Payments	

***Deductions** - this item should only include Income tax (PAYE), National Insurance, and superannuation scheme contributions. It must **NOT** include other sums ordinarily deducted, such as National Savings or rent.

If the employee has received remuneration in kind, such as rent free accommodation, company car etc. please state the nature and the equivalent weekly or monthly amount.

Employer's details

Name of employer

Address of employer to which further communications should be sent:

Employer's reference:

Telephone no:

Registered office address *(if limited company)*:

Employer's signature.. **Date** ....

Position in company ....

Notice as to Payment under Attachment of Earnings Order made by High Court

In the	
County Court	
Claim No.	
Application No.	
Claimant	
Defendant	

To

An attachment of earnings order was made by the High Court of Justice on
requiring you to make payments into the office of this court out of the earnings payable by you to

of

who works at
as a [Works No./Pay ref.].

TAKE NOTICE that the payments may be made in cash at the office of this court or may be sent by post, at the payer's risk, by crossed postal order or cheque. This notice must be sent with each payment and will be returned to you with a receipt.

DATED

To

The court office at

is open between 10 am and 4 pm Monday to Friday. Address all communications to the Court Manager quoting the claim number

N340 Notice as to payment under attachment of earnings order made by High Court (4.99)

Notice of Intention to Vary Attachment of Earnings Order under Section 10(2) of Attachment of Earnings Act 1971

In the	County Court
Claim No.	
Application No.	
Claimant	
Defendant	

To all parties and

On , an attachment of earnings order was made to secure the payments required by a maintenance order obtained by the claimant aganst the defendant and it appears that:-

(a) the aggregate of the payments made under the maintenance order exceeds the aggregate of the payments required by that order, and

(b) the normal deduction rate specified by the attachment of earnings order exceeds the rate of payments required by the maintenance order,

(c) no proceedings for the variation or discharge of the attachment of earnings order are pending.

TAKE NOTICE that unless application is made to this court within 14 days after the date of this notice for an order discharging the attachment of earnings order or varying it in some other manner, the court will make an order varying the attachment of earnings order by reducing the normal deduction rate to the rate of payments required by the maintenance order or such lower rate as the court thinks fit having regard to the amount of the excess mentioned in paragraph (a) above.

DATED

The court office at

is open between 10 am and 4 pm Monday to Friday. Address all communications to the Court Manager quoting the claim number

N341 Notice of intention to vary attachment of earnings order under section 10(2) of Attachment of Earnings Act 1971 (4.99)

Request for Judgment Summons

to be completed and signed by the claimant and sent to the court with the appropriate fee

In the

County Court

Claim Number

1 Claimant's name and address

2 Name and address for service and payment (if different from above) **Ref/Tel No.**

For court use only

J/S no.

Issue date:

Hearing date:

On

at o'clock

at (address)

3 Defendant's name and address[1]

[1] enter names and addresses of all defendants against whom a summons is requested

4 Judgment details

Date of judgment/order

Court where judgment/order made if not court of issue

5 Judgment summons details

Balance due[2] at the date of this request

Amount in arrears under judgment or order (including costs)

[3]Amount for which judgment summons to issue

Issue fee

Travelling expenses to be paid or offered to defendant

TOTAL

Amount if any which will remain outstanding when the above sum has been paid

(2) and any interest to date of request where judgment over £5,000 and entered on or after 1 July 1991

(3) this figure must not include any amounts on previous judgment summons(es) where debtor imprisoned

I certify that the whole or part of any instalments due under the judgment or order have not been paid and the balance now due is as shown

My evidence in support is attached

Signed

Claimant

Date

IMPORTANT

You must inform the court immediately of any payments you receive after you have sent this request to the court

6 If service by post is required tick here

I request that the defendant(s) named here be served with the judgment summons in this action by post. I certify that I have reason to believe that the summons, if sent to the defendant(s) at the address(es) given, will come to his/her (their) knowledge in time for him/her (them) to comply with it.

I understand that no order of commitment will be made against the defendant(s) served by post unless he/she (they) appear(s) at the hearing of the summons (or the judge is satisfied that the summons came to his/her (their) knowledge in sufficient time for him/her (them) to appear) and I prove that the defendant has, or has had, the means to pay, but is refusing or neglecting, or has refused or has neglected, to do so.

Signed **Dated**

Claimant

Printed on behalf of The Court Service

Notice of Result of Hearing of a Judgment Summons issued on a Judgment or Order of the High Court

In the **County Court**	
Claim No.	
J/S No.	
Claimant	
Defendant	

(1) the proper officer of the High Court

To(1)

In the matter of an action in the High Court of Justice, Division

(No.)

(2) delete as appropriate

Take notice that, on the hearing of a judgment summons issued in this court, (no order was made *or*) (the following order was made by Judge :)(2)

(3) enter name

(2)**(a)** the defendant(3) was committed for days in respect of his default of payment of £ due under the judgment (or order) in the above action (and the issue of the warrant of committal was suspended until the day of [19] [20], or so long as the defendant pays the said amount to the claimant by instalments of £ for every)

or

(2)**(b)** a new order was made for payment of £ due under the judgment (or order) in the above action and £ , the costs of the judgment summons and hearing, by instalments of £ for every

DATED

The court office at

is open between 10 am and 4 pm Monday to Friday. Address all communications to the Court Manager quoting the claim number

N343 Notice of result of hearing of a judgment summons issued on a judgment or order of the High Court (4.99)

Request for Warrant of Committal (judgment summons)

to be completed and signed by the claimant and sent to the court

Click here to clear all fields

In the

County Court

Claim Number

J/S Number

1 Claimant's name and address

2 Name and address for service and payment (if different from above) **Ref/Tel No.**

3 Defendant's name and address[1]

[1] a separate warrant must be issued against every defendant required to be arrested

For court use only

Warrant no.

Issue date:

Warrant applied for at o'clock

Committed on

for days

Order suspended for

on payment of

4 Judgment summons detail

Committal order made on (date)	
Balance due at date of J/S request	
Interest from date of J/S request to date of warrant request[2]	
Amount in arrears under judgment or order (including costs)	
Amount for which judgment summons issued[3]	
Fee and costs on issue and hearing of judgment summons	
Sub total	
Less any amount paid since issue of this order	
Sum on payment of which defendant be discharged	

(2) where judgment entered for more than £5000

(3) not including any amounts on previous judgment summons(es) where defendant imprisoned

I request you to issue a committal warrant against the defendant named at Box 3

I certify that the whole or part of any instalments due under the judgment or order have not been paid and the balance now due is as shown, amounts shown are correct

Signed

Claimant

Dated

IMPORTANT

You must inform the court immediately of any payments you receive after you have sent this request to the court

Other information that might assist the bailiff, (and other address(es) at which the defendant might be found). You should also tell the court if you have reason to believe that the bailiff might encounter serious difficulties in attempting to arrest the defendant.

Committal warrant no.

Click here to print form

N344 Request for warrant of committal on judgment summons (03.02)

Publications Branch

Certificate of Payment by Prisoner under the Debtors Act 1869

In the County Court	
Claim No.	
Warrant No.	
Claimant	
Defendant	

To the Governor of Her Majesty's Prison at
[or the Court Manager of the County Court]

I CERTIFY that the defendant, who was committed to my [or your] custody under a warrant of committal issued by this court [or by the County Court], on
has now paid the amount for non-payment of which he was committed together with all costs due
[and that the defendant may, in respect of that warrant, be forthwith discharged out of your custody][(1)].

(1) Add where the certificate is sent by the District Judge

DATED
Governor of HM Prison
at

[or District Judge]

The court office at

is open between 10 am and 4 pm Monday to Friday. Address all communications to the Court Manager quoting the claim number

N345 Certificate of payment by prisoner under the Debtors Act 1869 (4.99)

N353
Order appointing Receiver of Real and Personal Property

[General Title]

UPON THE APPLICATION of and upon reading the affidavit of sworn on the day of , 20 , and upon hearing

IT IS ORDERED that of be appointed [*if so ordered*, without giving security] to receive the rents and profits of the real and leasehold estates and to get in the outstanding personal estate of the [testator] [intestate] named in the particulars of claim and to manage the business of lately carried on by the [testator] [intestate] at (address) and the tenants of the real and leasehold estates are to attorn and pay their rents in arrear and growing rents to such receiver [and manager].

AND IT IS ORDERED that the defendants, the executors of the testator [*or* administrators of the intestate], do deliver over to such receiver [and manager] all [the stock in trade and effects of the said business and also all] securities in their hands for such outstanding personal estate, together with all books and papers relating thereto.

[*Add, if so ordered* AND IT IS ORDERED that the said do on or before the day of , 20 , give security in the sum of £ .]

[*Add, if so ordered,* And the claimant undertaking to be responsible for the acts and defaults of the said receiver until such security is given, IT IS FURTHER ORDERED that the said receiver be at liberty to act at once.]

[But in case the said receiver [and manager] shall not have given such security by the time aforesaid or such further time as the [court] shall allow his appointment as such receiver [and manager] shall on the expiration of such time forthwith determine.]

[AND IT IS ORDERED that the said receiver [and manager] do submit [*state here the period e.g. annual, quarterly*] accounts to for the period commencing , and pay the balances which may be ordered to be due from him as the court shall direct.]

N354
Order appointing Receiver of Partnership

Seal

[General Title]

UPON THE APPLICATION of and upon reading the affidavit of sworn on the day of , 20 , and upon hearing

IT IS ORDERED that of be appointed [*if so ordered,* without giving security] to collect, get in, and receive the debts now due and outstanding and other assets and property belonging to the partnership business of at and out of the first moneys received to pay the debts due from the said business.

AND IT IS ORDERED that the claimant and defendant respectively do deliver over to the said all the stock-in-trade and effects of the said partnership, and also all securities in their or either of their hands for such outstanding partnership estate, together with all books and papers relating thereto.

[AND IT IS ORDERED that the said do on or before the day of , 20 , give security in the sum of £ .]

[*Add, if so ordered,* And the claimant undertaking to be responsible for the acts and defaults of the said receiver until such security is given, IT IS FURTHER ORDERED that the said receiver be at liberty to act at once.]

[But in case the said receiver shall not have given such security by the time aforesaid or such further time as the [court] shall allow, his appointment as such Receiver shall on the expiration of such time forthwith determine.

AND IT IS ORDERED that the said receiver do submit [*state here the period e.g. annual, quarterly*] accounts to for the period commencing , and pay the balances which may be ordered to be due from him as the court shall direct.]

N355
Interim Order for Appointment of Receiver

Seal

[General Title]

Upon hearing and upon reading the affidavit of sworn on the day of , 20 , and the claimant by undertaking to be answerable for all sums to be received by the receiver hereinafter named.

IT IS ORDERED that of be appointed without security until [the day of , 20 , next inclusive] *or* [further order] to receive the rents and profits of [specify the property] but without prejudice to the rights of any prior incumbrancer or his possession (if any), and the tenants of the said premises are (without prejudice as aforesaid) to attorn and pay their rents in arrears and growing rents to the said receiver so long as he shall continue to be such receiver; and that all further questions be reserved until further order. And the defendant is to be at liberty to apply.

DATED , 20 .

N356
Order for Appointment of Receiver by way of Equitable Execution

[General Title]

UPON HEARING , and upon reading the affidavits of filed the day of

IT IS ORDERED as follows:

1. That of be appointed [*if so ordered,* without giving security] to receive rents, profits and moneys receivable in respect of the defendant's interest in: [*specify the property*]

But this appointment is to be without prejudice to the rights of any prior incumbrancers upon the said property who may think proper to take possession of or receive the same by virtue of their respective securities or, if any prior incumbrancer is in possession, then without prejudice to such possession.

2. That the tenants of the said property do (without prejudice as aforesaid) attorn and pay their rents in arrear and growing rents to such receiver.

3. That the receiver be at liberty, if he shall think proper (but not otherwise), out of the rents, profits, and moneys to be received by him, to keep down the interest upon the prior incumbrances, according to their priorities, and be allowed such payments (if any) in his accounts.

4. That the remuneration of the receiver be £ .

5. That the receiver shall not without leave of the judge receive more than the amount required to keep down the interest upon prior incumbrances, and to provide for the allowance to the receiver and the allowed fees and costs of obtaining this order, and to pay to the claimant what shall be due to him in respect of the debt and costs due to him, amounting to £ for debt and £ for costs, making together the sum of £ .

6. That the receiver shall submit his accounts to the district judge and pay over the balance in his hands within [3] calendar months from the date of this order, or so soon as the amount receivable by him under the last preceding clause of this order has been received, whichever shall first happen, or whenever he may be called upon by the court so to do.

7. That the sums paid into court by the receiver shall be applied in or towards satisfaction of the remuneration of the receiver, and the fees and costs of obtaining this order, and the amount due to the claimant in respect of debt and costs as aforesaid; but if there shall be no sums received or the amount shall be insufficient to satisfy such fees and costs as aforesaid, then upon the order of the district judge being given stating the amount of the deficiency the amount of the deficiency so ordered shall be paid by the defendant to the district judge for the use of the claimant.

8. That the balance (if any) remaining after making the several payments aforesaid shall be paid by the receiver into Court to the credit of this action, subject to further order.

[9. AND IT IS ORDERED that the receiver do on or before the day of , 20 , give security in the sum of £ .

(*Add, if so ordered*, and the claimant undertaking to be answerable for the acts and defaults of the said receiver until such security is given, it is further ordered that the receiver be at liberty to act at once.)]

10. AND IT IS ORDERED that either of the parties is to be at liberty to apply to the Court as he may be advised.

Dated , 20 .

Notice of Claim to Goods taken in Execution

In the County Court	
Claim No.	
Warrant No.	
Local No.	
Claimant	
Defendant	

To the Claimant

TAKE NOTICE - That

of

(1) here specify them

has claimed [the proceeds of sale or value of] the goods [or the following goods[1]

]

taken in execution under the warrant of execution issued in this action. If within four days after receiving this notice you notify the court in writing that you admit the claim of , or request the District Judge to withdraw from possession [for which purpose the form below may be used], you will not be liable for any costs incurred after the receipt by the court of your notice.

DATED

The court office at

Is open between 10 am and 4 pm Monday to Friday. Address all communications to the Court Manager quoting the claim number
Retain this portion for your information

This portion may be detached and used as a reply to the Court Manager

In the County Court	
Claim No.	
Warrant No.	
Local No.	
Claimant	
Defendant	

To the Court Manager

of the County Court

TAKE NOTICE - That I admit the claim of
in respect of the goods seized by the court [or that I request the court to withdraw from possession] under the execution issued in this action.

DATED

Signed
(Claimant)

N358 Notice of claim to goods taken in execution (4.99)

Notice to Claimant to Goods taken in Execution to make deposit or give Security

In the County Court	
Claim No.	
Warrant No.	
Local No.	
Claimant	
Defendant	

To the Claimant

You have claimed the goods

[or the following goods[1]

(1) here specify them

]

taken in execution under the warrant of execution issued in this action:

TAKE NOTICE, that you are required, in accordance with section 100 of the County Courts Act, 1983.

EITHER

1. to deposit in the court office the amount of the value of the goods so claimed by you [such value to be fixed by appraisement in case of dispute] to abide the decision of the Judge upon your claim:

OR

2. to give security of the value of the goods so claimed by you in the following manner:-

AND FURTHER TAKE NOTICE, that if you fail to make the deposit or give the security the goods may be sold as if no such claim had been made by you, and the proceeds paid into court to abide the decision of the Judge.

DATED

The court office at

is open between 10 am and 4 pm Monday to Friday. Address all communications to the Court Manager quoting the claim number

N359 Notice to claimant to goods taken in execution to make deposit or give security (4.99)

N360
Affidavit in Support of Interpleader Summons other than under an Execution

CCR Ord 33, r 6(3)

[General Title]

I, of

[*if in an action*, the above named defendant] make oath and say as follows:

1. [*If in an action,* This action is brought to recover [*state what*] claimed by the claimant but I have received a claim adverse to that of the claimant from of

[*or, if no action,* I have received adverse claims from of
and of

to [*state what*], and expect to be sued on the said claims by the said claimants].

2. I claim no interest in the subject matter in dispute other than the sum of £

for costs or charges and I do not collude with either [*or any*] of the said claimants.

3. I am willing to bring into court or to pay or dispose of the subject matter in dispute as the Court may direct.

Notice of Application for Relief in Pending Action

In the County Court	
Claim No.	
Claimant	
Defendant	

seal

To all parties

(1) delete from notice sent to defendant

The defendant has filed an affidavit (a copy of which is attached)(1) stating that he has received a claim

from

of

to [part of] the subject matter in this action:

TAKE NOTICE, that you should attend at

on

at o'clock, [and that the pre-trial re view/or hearing of this action has been adjourned to the same place, and time] when judgment will be given determining the rights and claims of all the parties.

DATED

[**NOTE** - The claimant is required within fourteen days after the service of this notice on him, to file in the court office either a notice that he makes no claim, or particulars of the grounds of his claim to the subject matter in the action together with sufficient copies for service on all other parties. When the notice or particulars are filed a copy will be sent to you.]

The court office at

is open between 10 am and 4 pm Monday to Friday. Address all communications to the Court Manager quoting the claim number

N361 Notice of application for relief in pending action (4.99)

N362
Order on Interpleader Summons under an Execution where the Claim is not Established

CCR Ord 33, r 11

Seal

[Title as in Form N88]

UPON HEARING

AND upon reading

[And the claimant not having appeared on the hearing of this application]

IT IS ORDERED that the claimant be barred and that no action be brought against the district judge

add where security other than deposit of value of goods has been given

AND IT IS ORDERED that the said claimant do on or before the day of , 20 , pay to the district judge the sum of £ , being the value of the said goods and that in default of such payment the district judge do proceed to enforce the security given by the said claimant for such value.]

[*When money in hands of sheriff in interpleader transferred from High Court*

AND IT IS ORDERED that the sheriff of

do forthwith after service of this order upon him pay into this Court, the moneys in his hands in this proceeding after deducting therefrom his charges in respect of the said execution such charges to be taxed by the district judge in case of dispute.]

AND IT IS ORDERED that the money in court, being the proceeds of sale [*or* value] of the goods [*or* the sum paid by the claimant in respect of [*or* recovered by the enforcement of] the said security] be applied first in payment to the district judge of £ for the possession fees and charges payable in respect of the execution including the fees for keeping possession of the goods until this decision of the court could be obtained and then in payment to the execution creditor, so far as the same will extend, of the sum in respect of which the execution issued.

AND IT IS ORDERED that the execution creditor do on or before the day of , 20 , pay to the district judge of this court [the sum of £ for the costs of the district judge in respect of the claim for damages [*add, if the proceeds of sale of the goods is less than the charges payable* and] the sum of £ being the balance of the charges of the district judge not deducted from the proceeds of sale of the goods] with remedy over against the claimant.

AND IT IS ORDERED that the claimant do on or before the day of , 20 , pay to the district judge of this court the sum of £ for the costs of the execution creditor.

[AND IT IS FURTHER ORDERED that the execution creditor do pay to the said sheriff his costs of these proceedings down to and including the order directing transfer to this court, such costs in case of dispute to be assessed in detail by the district judge, and paid by the execution creditor to the district judge on the day of , 20 , within days after assessment, with remedy over against the claimant.]

N363
Order on Interpleader Summons under an Execution where the Claim is Established

Seal

CCR Ord 33, r 11

[Title as in Form N88]

IT IS ADJUDGED, that the goods *or* proceeds of sale, *or* value *or* part of the goods *or* proceeds of sale *or* value, of the goods taken in execution under process issuing out of this court to wit, *specifying them or it* are the property of the claimant that rent to the amount of £ is due to the claimant and for damages arising out of the said execution which the claimant claims against the execution creditor and the district judge of this court that the claimant is entitled to recover the sum of £ for damages against but is not entitled to recover any damages against .

AND IT IS ORDERED, that the do pay the said sum of £ for damages, and the sum of £ for costs to for the use of the claimant by , and that the do pay the sum of £ for costs to for the use of the by .

Here insert directions as to payment of charges, or sheriff's costs, and as to the disposal of any money in court or in the hands of the sheriff—See Form N362.

N364
Order on Interpleader Summons (other than under Execution) where there is an Action

CCR Ord 33, r 11(2)(3)

In the County Court
Case No.

BETWEEN *A.B.* *Claimant,*

and

C.D. *Defendant,*

and

E.F. *Claimant to the goods.*

Seal

IT IS THIS DAY ADJUDGED touching the claims of the claimant and the claimant to the goods that the claim of the claimant [*or* claimant to the goods] is valid and that the claimant to the goods [*or* claimant] has no claim to the subject matter in this action.

AND IT IS FURTHER adjudged that the claimant [*or* claimant to the goods] do recover against the defendant the sum of £ for debt and £ for costs amounting together to the sum of £ .

AND IT IS FURTHER adjudged that the claimant [*or* claimant to the goods] do recover the sum of £ from the claimant to the goods [*or* claimant] for costs [*add if any costs awarded to the defendant against the claimant or claimant to the goods*] *and it is further adjudged that the defendant do recover the sum of £ for costs from the claimant* [*or* claimant to the goods].

AND IT IS ORDERED that the defendant do pay the said sum of £ [*debt and costs*] to by , 20 , [*or* by instalments of £ for every , the first instalment to be paid by].

[*If the claimant to the goods fails to appear and an order is made barring his claim proceed as follows:*

And the claimant to the goods not appearing, it is declared that the said claimant to the goods and all persons claiming under him be for ever barred as against the claimant and all persons claiming under him.]

AND IT IS FURTHER ORDERED that the claimant [*or* claimant to the goods] do pay the said sum of £ for the costs of the claimant [*or* claimant to the goods] [*add if so ordered*] and that the claimant [do pay the said sum of £ for the costs of the defendant to by .]

N365
Order on Interpleader Summons (other than under Execution) where there is no Action

CCR Ord 33, r 11(3)(4)

In the **County Court**
Case No.

Seal

BETWEEN

A.B. *Applicant,*

and

E.F.

and

G.H. *Claimants.*

WHEREAS the applicant has applied to this Court for relief in the matter of adverse claims made upon him by the claimants in respect of [*here state the debt or other thing in action, money or goods to which the adverse claims were made.*]

NOW UPON HEARING

IT IS ADJUDGED [*here set out the judgment determining the claim as between the applicant and any claimant who appears or, if all the claimants appear, the judgment determining the rights and claims of all parties and the order as to payment.*]

[*If any claimant fails to appear and an order is made barring his claim proceed as follows:*

and the claimant not appearing, it is declared that the said and all persons claiming under him be for ever barred as against the applicant and all persons claiming under him.]

N366
Summons for Neglect to levy Execution

CCR Ord 34, r 1(6)

In the County Court

Seal

To of bailiff of the said Court.

YOU ARE HEREBY SUMMONED to appear at this Court, at on the day of , 20 , at o'clock, to answer a complaint made against you by of that you being employed to levy an execution against the goods and chattels of did by neglect, or connivance, or omission, lose the opportunity of levying such execution, and to show cause why an order should not be made against you under section 124 of the County Courts Act 1984, for payment of such damages as it shall appear that the said has sustained by your neglect, or connivance, or omission.

DATED THIS DAY , 20 .

To be served personally not less than eight days before the return day.

Order fining a Witness for Non-attendance

In the Court	
Claim No.	
Claimant	
Defendant	

seal

(1) state full name and address of witness

(1)

(2) delete as appropriate

(3) describe what he was required by the summons to produce

(2) was summoned to appear as a witness in this action at a court held on the
and at the time of being summoned was paid [or offered] his travelling expenses and compensation for loss of time according to the scale of allowances prescribed by the County Court Rules and he refused or neglected without sufficient cause shown, to appear at the court [or to produce(3)

]

OR

(2) was present in court, and being required by the court to give evidence in this action refused to be sworn [or to give evidence]

(enter name of Judge) HAS ORDERED that

do pay a fine of £ for such refusal or neglect into the office of this court on or before

DATED

The court office at

is open between 10 am and 4 pm Monday to Friday. Address all communications to the Court Manager quoting the claim number

N368 Order fining a winess for non-attendance (4.99)

Order for Commitment and/or Imposing a Fine for Insult or Misbehaviour

In the

Court

seal

To the District Judge and bailiffs of the court, and every constable within his jurisdiction, and to the Governor of Her Majesty's Prison at

On the

(1) state name and address of offender (1)

wilfully insulted the Judge during his sitting at court

(2) state the insult or misbehaviour (2)

(3) delete as necessary 1.(3) (enter name of Judge) **HAS ORDERED** that

do pay a fine of £ for the offence and do pay that sum into the office of this court forthwith

[or by instalments of £ for every the first such instalment to be paid on or before the]

2.(3) **IT IS ORDERED** that

shall be committed to prison for

AND YOU the District Judge, bailiffs and others, are therefore required to arrest

and deliver him to Prison and you the Governor

to receive

and keep him safely in prison for from the arrest under

this order or until he shall be sooner discharged by due course of law.

DATED

The court office at

is open between 10 am and 4 pm Monday to Friday. Address all communications to the Court Manager quoting the claim number.

N370 Order of commitment and/or imposing a fine for insult or misbehaviour (4.99)

Warrant of Committal No.

NAME OF CONTEMINOR

I arrested the above named on

the

and delivered him into the custody

of the Governor of HM Prison

at

on the

Bailiff of the County Court

Order for Rehearing

In the Court	
Claim No.	
Claimant	
Defendant	

seal

UPON THE APPLICATION of the

(enter name of Judge) **HAS ORDERED** that upon[1]

[1] set out the terms and conditions upon which the order is made

the judgment in this action, and all subsequent proceedings, be set aside and a rehearing take place between the parties at

on

at o'clock.

DATED

The court office at

is open between 10 am and 4 pm Monday to Friday .Address all communications to the Court Manager quoting the claim number

N372 Order for rehearing (4.99) *The Court Service Publications Unit*

Notice of Application for an Administration Order

In the	
County Court	
Application No. *Always quote this*	
Applicant	
Creditor	
Creditor's Ref.	

seal

To the applicant and creditors *(address for service)*

The applicant has asked the court to make an order for the administration of his estate.

- The applicant states that he owes the sums shown to each of the creditors shown on the attached list.
- A copy of the applicant's request and statement of means is also attached.
- After having read the application and statement of means, the court proposes to order the applicant to pay the debts listed in the application in full (or to the extent of pence in the pound) by monthly instalments of £
- The court will make an administration order in respect of the applicant's estate in these terms unless you (the applicant or any of his creditors) write to the court giving reasons why such an order should not be made (in the above terms). You have 16 days from the date of the postmark to do this.
- Only **one** box should be ticked.
- Please remember to sign and date the form.

1. ☐ **I do not object to the order being made in the terms stated above.**
   - Return the form to the court office within the 16 day time limit (explained above)
   - If there are no objections, the court will make an order and you will receive a copy.
   - If there are any objections then a hearing will be arranged and you will be informed of the details and of the date fixed in case you wish to attend.

2. ☐ **I object to the order being made (in the terms stated above).**
   - Give your reasons in the space below. Please state whether you (a creditor) object to the making of an order, to the inclusion of a particular debt or if you (debtor or creditor) object to the rate of payment proposed.
   - Return the form to the court office within the 16 day time limit (explained above).
   - The court will fix a hearing and you will be told when to attend and what to bring with you.

Record your objections here *(continue on a separate sheet if necessary)*

Signed

*credit or debtor

Dated

*delete as necessary

The court office at

is open between 10 am and 4 pm Monday to Friday. Address all communications to the Court Manager quoting the application number

N373 Notice of application for an administration order

Notice of Intention to Review an Administration Order

In the	
County Court	
Administration Order No. *Always quote this*	
Applicant	
Creditor	
Creditor's ref.	

seal

To the debtor and creditors (*address for service*)

The administration order made on **is to be reviewed by the court**

Tick whichever box applies
*delete as appropriate

- ☐ On the direction of the court
- ☐ At the request of the debtor (*who objects to the court's intention to revoke the order)
- ☐ At the request of a listed creditor

Take notice that this matter will be heard at

on

at o'clock

when the court will review the administration order

DATED

To the debtor

- If the review is being held at your request (or because you object to the court's intention to revoke the order) you must attend the court on the above date. If you do not attend the order may be revoked.
- If the review is being held at the direction of the court or a creditor, it is in your best interest to attend the court on the above date. **If you do not attend, an order may be made in your absence.**

The court office at

is open between 10 am and 4 pm Monday to Friday. Address all communications to the Court Manager quoting the administration order number

N374 Notice of intention to review an administration order

Notice of Intention to Revoke an Adminstration Order

In the	
County Court	
Administration Order No. *Always quote this*	

To the debtor

seal

You have failed to pay the sums due in accordance with the administration order made on

(There are currently instalments outstanding, amounting in total to £)

The adminstration order will be revoked unless within 16 days of the date shown on the postmark you either:

- make the payments due under the order (total shown above)
- explain your reasons for failing to make payments and make a proposal to pay the outstanding sum (in addition to the instalments ordered) or
- make a request to the court to vary the rate of payment ordered

Give your reasons for failing to make payments below (together with any proposals you wish to make for future payment)

Signed (debtor)	**Dated**

If you pay the amount shown within the 16 day time limit, the adminstration order will remain in force.

If you are unable to pay the amount shown above but you complete and return the form within the 16 day time limit, the court will either:

- **revoke, vary or suspend the order** (you will be told what the court has decided and you will be given the opportunity to object)
- **fix a hearing date** (you will be told when to come to court)

The court office at

is open between 10 am and 4 pm Monday to Friday. Address all communications to the Court Manager quoting the administration order number

N374A Notice of intention to revoke an adminstration order

Notice of further Creditor's Claim

In the	
County Court	
Administration Order No. *Always quote this*	
Applicant	
Creditor	
Creditor's Ref.	

seal

To the debtor and creditors *(address for service)*

(1) state name and address of further creditor

Take notice that (1)

of

(2) delete if the debt does not attract interest (a County Court judgment only attracts interest if over £5000 and if the judgment was entered on or after 1 July 1991)

claims that the above named debtor owes the sum of £ (including any interest(2)) and wishes to be included on the schedule of debts in the administration order.

If you object to the claim of the above named creditor you must **within nine days** of the date shown on the postmark send your written objections to a court (a hearing will be arranged and you will be told when to come to court).

And take notice that if no objection is received the claim will be taken as proved unless the court requires further proof of the debt, if further proof is required a hearing will be arranged. You will be told when to come to court.

Dated

The court office at

is open between 10 am and 4 pm Monday to Friday. Address all communications to the Court Manager quoting the application order number

N375 Notice of further creditor's claim

Notice of Hearing – Administration Order (by direction of the Court)

Order 39 Rule 5

In the	
County Court	
Application No. (Always quote this)	
Applicant	
Creditor	
Creditor's Ref.	

To the debtor and creditors (*address for service*)

seal

The applicant has asked the court to make an order for the administration of his estate

The court has directed that the application be listed for hearing

*delete if not applicable ***[as a notice of objection has been received by the court (copy attached)]**

Take notice that this matter will be heard at

on

at o'clock

when the court will consider whether an administration order should be made

DATED

To the creditor

*delete if not applicable

- The applicant states that he owes the sums shown to each of the creditors shown on the list of creditors.
- [*A copy of the list of creditors and his statement of means are attached].
- If you object to the inclusion (in the order) of any of the debts listed in the applicant's list of creditors, you must **at least 7 days before the hearing** state the grounds of your objection in writing to:
  1. the court
  2. the applicant
  3. the creditor (whose debt you object to)
- If you claim more than the amount shown on the applicant's list of creditors, you must bring with you to court any witnesses, books and documents necessary to prove your claim.

To the applicant

- You must attend the hearing and bring with you documents necessary to support your appplication.

The court office at

is open between 10 am and 4 pm Monday to Friday. Address all communications to the Court Manager quoting the application number

N376 Notice of hearing - Administration order (by direction of the court) Order 39 Rule 5

IN THE **COUNTY COURT**

Administration Order No.

Consolidated Attachment Order No.

Creditor .... v .... Debtor

Creditor's Reference ....

Claim No...

Amount of claim ....

The court has declared a dividend on the amount of money paid to the debtor.

Please find enclosed a payable order for £

Dated

The court office at

is open between 10 am and 4 pm Monday to Friday. Address all communications to the Court Manager and quote the above administration/consolidated attachment order number.

N377 Notice of Dividend (4.99)

N388
Notice to Probate Registry to produce Documents

Seal

[General Title]

WHEREAS an application has been made to this court to revoke the grant of probate of the Will [*or* letters of administration of the estate] of [*here insert the name and address of the testator or intestate*] granted out of the Probate Registry on the day of , 20

AND WHEREAS such application will be heard by this court at on the day of , 20 , at o'clock,

I THEREFORE REQUEST that you will cause to be produced before the court on that day [*add unless administration without will annexed has been granted* the will and] all documents in that registry relating to the matter.

Notice that a Claim has been entered against Crown (Crown Proceedings Act 1947)

In the County Court	
Claim No.	
Claimant	
Defendant	

(1) who may be ascertained from the list published by the Treasury under s.17 of the Crown Proceedings Act, 1947

To the Solicitor for the Crown[1]

TAKE NOTICE that a claim has been entered in the above action. A copy of the particulars of claim filed by the claimant accompanies this notice.

AND TAKE NOTICE that, if further information is required by the Crown, you should within 21 days after the service of this notice upon you file in the court office two copies of a demand specifying what information you require. If you are satisfied that you already have sufficient information, you may file a statement that no demand for further information will be made, whereupon the stay of proceedings cease to have effect.

DATED

The court office at

is open between 10 am and 4 pm Monday to Friday. Address all communications to the Court Manager quoting the claim number

N390 Notice that a claim has been entered against Crown (Crown Proceedings Act 1947) (4.99)

N391

Crown Proceedings Act 1947 Affidavit in support of application directing payment by Crown to Judgment Creditor of money due by Crown to Judgment Debtor

CCR Ord 42, r 14(3)

[As amended 1989]

In the .... County Court
Case No.

BETWEEN *Judgment Creditor*

AND *Judgment Debtor*

AND [*state Government Department concerned or the Attorney General*]

I of in the county of [*or* I, of in the county of solicitor for] the above-named judgment creditor, make oath and say as follows:

1. That I [*or*] recovered judgment [*or* obtained an order] in the county court against the above-named judgment debtor for payment of the sum of £ for debt [*or* damages] and costs.

2. That the said judgment [*or* order] is still wholly unsatisfied [*or* is still unsatisfied as to the sum of £ :].

3. That the Crown is indebted to the judgment debtor in the sum of £ being in respect of [*set out details of debt*] [*add if so* for payment of which sum the judgment debtor recovered judgment [*or obtained an order*] *in the County Court against the* *Department* [*or the Attorney General*] on the day of 20 and by the said judgment [*or* order] it was ordered that the Department [*or the Attorney General*] should pay the said sum of £ : to the judgment debtor on the day of 20 and the sum of £ : remains due and unpaid under the said judgment [*or* order]].

N392

Crown Proceedings Act 1947 Notice of application for order directing payment by the Crown to Judgment Creditor of money due by Crown to Judgment Debtor

CCR Ord 42, r 14(4)

In the County Court
Case No.

BETWEEN *Judgment Creditor*

AND *Judgment Debtor*

AND [state Government Department concerned or the Attorney General]

TAKE NOTICE that the judgment creditor will apply to the judge of this court at on the day of , 20 at the hour of in the noon for an order restraining the judgment debtor from receiving the amount of the debt due or accruing from the Crown to the judgment debtor or so much thereof as will satisfy the debt due under the judgment for £ : for debt (*or* damages) and costs given (*or* made) in the county court on the day of , 20 in an action in which the judgment creditor was plaintiff and the judgment debtor was defendant and directing payment thereof by the Department (*or the Attorney General*) to the judgment creditor or a receiver.

N432
Affidavit on Payment into Court under section 63 of the Trustee Act 1925, or section 136 of the Law of Property Act 1925

In the County Court

IN THE MATTER OF THE [*Citing Act*].
IN THE MATTER OF THE [*add the title of the particular trust*].

I of [*residence*] make oath and say as follows:

1. The address where I am to be served with any notice or application relating to the trust fund hereinafter mentioned is [*state it*].

2. [*Set out a short description of the trust and the instrument creating it stating the amount of the money or stock proposed to be paid or transferred, or security deposited, in trust to attend to orders of the court*].

3. Under the provisions of the above-mentioned Act I desire to pay into court, in trust to attend the orders of the court, the above-mentioned sum of £....... after retaining out of the said sum the taxed costs incurred in paying the said sum into court.

4. To the best of my knowledge and belief the only persons interested in, or entitled to, the said sum are [*state the names and addresses of the persons interested in, or entitled to, the money [*or *securities] to the best of the trustee's knowledge and belief*].

5. I submit to answer to the best of my ability such inquiries relating to the application to the said money [*or* securities] as the court may think proper to make or direct.

Sworn *etc* (*Jurat as in Form N285*)

Order for Sale of Land under Charging Order

In the County Court	
Claim No.	
Claimant	
Defendant	

seal

UPON HEARING

AND UPON READING

(enter name of Judge) **HAS ORDERED** that the defendant do within 28 days from the date of this order pay into court the sum of £ together with £ the claimant's assessed costs to the date of this order making together the sum of £ [and in default it is ordered that] the freehold/leasehold property known as

(1) delete as applicable

be sold by the claimant [at a price not less than £](1) without further reference to the court [save that the sale price or reserve be fixed by the court](1).

AND HAS ORDERED pursuant to Section 90 of the Law of Property Act 1925 that a term of [3,000 years] [years] less one day, but otherwise subject to the same terms and conditions as are contained in a lease dated and made between

be vested in the claimant to enable him to carry out the sale.

AND HAS ORDERED that the net proceeds of sale after discharge of all prior incumbrances, outgoings, the estate agents' commission and the said sum of £ be paid into court subject to further order.

DATED

The court office at

is open between 10 am and 4 pm Monday to Friday. Address all communications to the Court Manager quoting the claim number

N436 Order for sale of land under charging order (4.99)

N437
District Judge's Report

[General Title]

WHEREAS, by the order in this action dated the day of , 20 , the matters in question in this action [*or* the question of] was referred to me for enquiry and report.

Now I hereby report that I have been attended by [Counsel] [Solicitor], and have taken the evidence on oath of

The documents set forth in the Schedule hereto have been put in and proved where necessary.

AND I further report [here set out the evidence given, the facts found proved, the inferences drawn from the facts, and the result arrived at after applying the law to those facts and inferences].

Dated this day of , 20

DISTRICT JUDGE

The Schedule

Notice to Charge-holder under Matrimonial Homes Act 1983

In the	
County Court	
Claim No.	
Claimant	
Defendant	

seal

To:

(1) here describe the land as set out in the particulars

TAKE NOTICE the claimant claims possession of(1)

The attached summons is directed to you as a person having an interest in the property.

You may apply to the court to be made a party to the action and be heard on the claim. If you wish to do so, you should first seek legal advice from a solicitor or a Legal Advice Centre. Remember to take these papers with you.

DATED

The court office at

is open between 10 am and 4 pm Monday to Friday. Address all communications to the Court Manager quoting the claim number

N438 Notice to charge-holder under Matrimonial Homes Act 1983 (4.99)

Note The Matrimonial Homes Act 1983 has been repealed. See now the Family Law Act 1996.

FORM N440 NOTICE OF APPLICATION FOR TIME ORDER BY DEBTOR OR HIRER

IN THE **COUNTY COURT**

Claim no.

IN THE MATTER OF AN APPLICATION FOR A TIME ORDER

Between ______________________________ **Applicant**
(Insert your full name in block capitals)

and ______________________________ **Respondent**
(insert the full name in block capitals of the company to whom you make your payments)

1. *I (Name)* ______________________________

of (Address)

apply to the court for a time order

2. The following are the details of the regulated agreement in respect of which I am asking for a time order.

a. The agreement is dated ______________________________

and the reference number is ______________________________

b. The names and addresses of the other parties to the agreement are:

____

c. The name and address of the person (if any) who acted as surety

is ______________________________

of

____

d. *(Delete if not applicable)* The rights and duties of the party named ______________________________

at b. above passed to the respondent on __________ when *(here give the reasons why you now regard the respondent as your creditor)*

His address is

e. I signed the agreement at *(here give the address of the shop or other place where you signed the agreement)*

____

f. I agreed to pay instalments of £ a week ☐ a month ☐

____

g. ☐ The unpaid balance due under the agreement is £ ______________

or ☐ I do not know the unpaid balance

____

h. ☐ I am £ ______________ in arrear with my payments.

or ☐ I do not know how much the arrears are.

____

N440 Notice of application for time order by debtor or hirer (4.99)

The Court Service Publications Unit

i. On the Respondent served on me:

- ☐ a default notice
- ☐ a notice given under section 76(1)
- ☐ a notice given under section 98(1)

or I attach a copy of the notice which the Respondent served on me on

j. *You should complete this section if you are applying for time to pay, if not cross it out.*

My proposals for payment are £

to clear the arrears (if any) and then by instalments of £

k. *You should complete this section if you have failed to comply with the agreement in any other respect.*

I am in breach of the following provisions of the agreement:

And my proposals for remedying the breach(es) are as follows:

3. I have answered the questions about my financial circumstances set out in the schedule to this application.

4. The names and addresses of the persons to be served with this application are: *(You must include any sureties)*

5. My address for service is:

6. Signed

(Solicitor for the) Applicant.

Dated

Notification of Request for Certificate of Satisfaction or Cancellation

In the	
	County Court
Claim No.	
Claimant's ref.	
Date	

Claimant

Defendant (name and address)

Seal

To the claimant

The defendant is applying to the court for a certificate of satisfaction or cancellation of the judgment debt and for the entry in the Register of County Court Judgments to be

- ☐ marked to show that the debt including any interest[1] is satisfied
- ☐ removed *(only if payment has been made in full within one month of judgment)*

This judgment was registered by the County Court
Claim No. and the case was transferred to this court[2]

[1] where judgment is entered for £5,000 or more, or is in respect of a debt which attracts contractual or statutory interest for late payment, the claimant may be entitled to further interest

[2] delete if not applicable

Unless you object in writing to the court **within one month** of the above date a certificate will be granted automatically and the Register will be marked accordingly.

Defendant's name

- Surname ______________________
- Forename(s) ______________________

Defendant's address at time of judgment *(if different from above)*

____

____

Date of judgment ______________________

Amount of judgment £ ______________________

Date of final payment* ______________________

** The date of the final payment is that given by the defendant. If you do not agree the date shown you need inform the court **only** if the defendant is applying to have the entry **removed** from the register.*

N441 - w3 Notification of Request for Certificate of Satisfaction or Cancellation. (4.99)

Certificate of Satisfaction or Cancellation of Judgment Debt

In the **County Court**	
Claim No.	
Date	

To the defendant

Seal

This certificate confirms, for the purpose of the Register of County Court Judgments Regulations, that:

this debt including any interest(1) is satisfied; or

the judgment giving rise to the registration has been set aside

A notification will be issued to the Keeper of the Register of County Court Judgments for the entry to be

☐ marked to show that the debt including any interest(1) is satisfied

☐ removed *(only if payment has been made in full within one month of judgment)*

☐ removed *(because judgment was set aside)*

This judgment was registered by the County Court Claim No. and the case was transferred to this court(2)

(1) where judgment entered for more than £5000 on or before 1 July 1991

(2) delete if not applicable

This certificate is only valid if sealed by the court

Defendant's name

☐ Surname ______

☐ Forename(s) ______

Defendant's address at time of judgment *(if different from above)*

______

______

Date of judgment ______

Amount of judgment £ ______

Date of final payment (1) ______

Date judgment was set aside (2) ______

(1) delete if not known

(2) delete if not appropriate

N441A Certificate of Satisfaction or Cancellation of Judgment Debt

In the ______ County Court

Creditor ______ Claim No. ______

Debtor ______ Warrant No. ______

Local No. ______

Details of Sale

Gross amount levied or received

Transport Charges

Appraisement Fee on £

Sale Fee on £

Advertising

Rent to Landlord

Cost of Interpleader ordered to be deducted from proceeds

Net amount paid into Court on

the day of [19][20]

N444 Details of Sale under a warrant of execution

In the ______ County Court

Creditor ______ Claim No. ______

Debtor ______ Warrant No. ______

Local No. ______

Details of Sale

Gross amount levied or received

Transport Charges

Appraisement Fee on £

Sale Fee on £

Advertising

Rent to Landlord

Cost of Interpleader ordered to be deducted from proceeds

Net amount paid into Court on

the day of [19][20]

N444 Details of Sale under a warrant of execution

Request for Reissue of Warrant

Tick appropriate box and enter case number and warrant number

In the

County Court

Claim Number

Warrant Number

Type of warrant

- [ ] Warrant of execution
- [ ] Warrant of possession
- [ ] Warrant of delivery
- [ ] Warrant of committal

For court use only

Wt reissue no.

Reissue date:

Foreign court code/name:

1 Claimant's name

2 Name and address for service and payment

Ref/Tel No.

3 Defendant's name and address

4 Warrant details

(A) Balance of judgment or order due at date of this request including fee and costs of warrant issue and reissue, where appropriate. The reissue fee applies only to warrants of execution. (There is no fee to reissue a suspended warrant)

(B) Parts warrants only
Balance due under the warrant including the fee and costs of warrant issue and reissue, where appropriate. The reissue fee applies only to warrants of execution. (There is no fee to reissue a suspended warrant)

If the amount of the warrant at (B) is less than the balance at (A), the sum due after the warrant is paid will be

I certify that the whole or part of any instalments due under the judgment or order have not been paid and the balance now due is as shown (*and that the amount due under the part warrant is as shown at (B) †and/or the land which is subject of the judgment or order has not be vacated)

Signed

Claimant (Claimant's solicitor)

Date

**delete if not a part warrant*
†delete if not a possession warrant

IMPORTANT

You must inform the court immediately of any payments you receive after you have sent this request to the court

Reasons for requesting reissue *(information you are relying on to support your application for reissue eg address for execution has changed, failure to make payments under a suspended order etc. You should also tell the court if you have reason to believe that the bailiff might encounter any serious difficulty in attempting to execute the warrant.)*

Reissue No.

N445 Request for reissue of warrant (04.09)

Notice to Claimant of Date Fixed for Adjourned Hearing

In the	
County Court	
Claim No.	
Process No.	
Claimant	
Claimant's Ref.	
Defendant	

To the claimant('s solicitor)

TAKE NOTICE that the date shown below has been fixed for the defendant's attendance at an adjourned hearing of the

Tick the appropriate box

- ☐ oral examination (N39)
- ☐ attachment of earnings (N58)
- ☐ judgment summons (N69)

on [19][20], at o'clock

at

DATE

Travelling expenses

- Where the adjourned hearing is for an oral examination or judgment summons the defendant is entitled to request from you a reasonable sum to cover his travelling expenses to and from the court.
- In the case of an oral examination you should certify to the court not more than 4 days before the date fixed for the adjourned examination whether or not the defendant has made this request and if so how much has been paid to him.

You must inform the court immediately of any payments you receive before the hearing

The court office at

is open between 10 am and 4 pm Monday to Friday. Address all communications to the Court Manager quoting the claim number

N447 Notice to claimant of date fixed for adjourned hearing (4.99)

Attachment of Earnings – Request to Defendant for Employment Details

In the
County Court
The Court Office at is open from 10 am - 4 pm Monday to Friday
Dated:

To the defendant

Attachment of earnings proceedings have been issued (and are in force) against you at the above court.

☐ The court has been informed that you are no longer employed by ....

☐ The court believes that you have obtained employment.

- If you are currently employed or you are starting new employment you must complete the slip below (and the enclosed form N56) and return it (them) to the court without delay.
- While you remain unemployed the (application for) Attachment of Earnings Order will be adjourned. You should still complete and return the slip below. If you become employed at any time in the future, you must inform the court immediately.
- **If you fail to tell the court as soon as you become employed; action may be taken against you. You can be fined or imprisoned or both.**

- - *Please detach and return to the court* – – – – – – – – –

Defendant's Employment Details (Attachment of Earnings)

In the
County Court
Case Number
A/E Application No.
Plaintiff:
Defendant:

Please tick boxes and ensure that all details are completed as far as possible (including the case details on the right) before signing and returning this slip to the court.

☐ I am unemployed

☐ I am self employed as ....

☐ I will start/started new employment on *(date)* .... ☐ (and I enclose completed form N56)

My employer's name ....

My employer's address ....

....

My Works number/Pay reference is ....

My earnings/expected earnings are £ .... ☐ per week ☐ per month

Signed .... **Dated** ....

N448 Request to defendant for employment details/defendants reply

Click here to reset form | Click here to print form

Statement of Costs (summary assessment)

In the	
	Court
Case Reference	

Judge/Master

Case Title

[Party]'s Statement of Costs for the hearing on *(date)* **(interim application/fast track trial)**

Description of fee earners*

(a) *(name) (grade) (hourly rate claimed)*

(b) *(name) (grade) (hourly rate claimed)*

(c) *(name) (grade) (hourly rate claimed)*

(d) *(name) (grade) (hourly rate claimed)*

Attendances on *(party)*

(a) *(number)*		hours at £		£	
(b) *(number)*		hours at £		£	
(c) *(number)*		hours at £		£	
(d) *(number)*		hours at £		£	

Attendances on opponents

(a) *(number)*		hours at £		£	
(b) *(number)*		hours at £		£	
(c) *(number)*		hours at £		£	
(d) *(number)*		hours at £		£	

Attendance on others

(a) *(number)*		hours at £		£	
(b) *(number)*		hours at £		£	
(c) *(number)*		hours at £		£	
(d) *(number)*		hours at £		£	

Site inspections etc

(a) *(number)*		hours at £		£	
(b) *(number)*		hours at £		£	
(c) *(number)*		hours at £		£	
(d) *(number)*		hours at £		£	

N260 Statement of Costs (summary assessment) (06.09)

Work done on negotiations

(a) *(number)*		hours at £		£
(b) *(number)*		hours at £		£
(c) *(number)*		hours at £		£
(d) *(number)*		hours at £		£

Other work, not covered above

(a) *(number)*		hours at £		£
(b) *(number)*		hours at £		£
(c) *(number)*		hours at £		£
(d) *(number)*		hours at £		£

Work done on documents

(a) *(number)*		hours at £		£
(b) *(number)*		hours at £		£
(c) *(number)*		hours at £		£
(d) *(number)*		hours at £		£

Attendance at hearing

(a) *(number)*		hours at £		£
(b) *(number)*		hours at £		£
(c) *(number)*		hours at £		£
(d) *(number)*		hours at £		£

(a) *(number)*		hours travel and waiting time £		£
(b) *(number)*		hours travel and waiting time £		£
(c) *(number)*		hours travel and waiting time £		£
(d) *(number)*		hours travel and waiting time £		£

Sub Total £

Brought forward £

Counsel's fees *(name) (year of call)*

Fee for [advice/conference/documents] £

Fee for hearing £

Other expenses

[court fees] £

Others *(give brief description)* £

Total £

Amount of VAT claimed

on solicitors and counsel's fees £

on other expenses £

Grand Total £

The costs stated above do not exceed the costs which the (*party*) is liable to pay in respect of the work which this statement covers. Counsel's fees and other expenses have been incurred in the amounts stated above and will be paid to the persons stated.

(party)

Dated

Signed

Name of firm of solicitors [partner] for the *(party)*

* 4 grades of fee earner are suggested:

(A) Solicitors with over eight years post qualification experience including at least eight years litigation experience.

(B) Solicitors and legal executives with over four years post qualification experience including at least four years litigation experience.

(C) Other solicitors and legal executives and fee earners of equivalent experience.

(D) Trainee solicitors, para legals and other fee earners.

"Legal Executive" means a Fellow of the Institute of Legal Executives. Those who are not Fellows of the Institute are not entitled to call themselves legal executives and in principle are therefore not entitled to the same hourly rate as a legal executive.

In respect of each fee earner communications should be treated as attendances and routine communications should be claimed at one tenth of the hourly rate.

Click here to print form

FORM N500

Claim form
Directors disqualification application

In the	
Claim No.	

In the matter of

SEAL

And in the matter of The Company Directors Disqualification Act 1986.

Name of Claimant

Name(s) of Defendant(s)

The hearing

(This section will be completed by the court)

The defendant(s) must attend before the (Registrar/District Judge) on

Date ______ Time ______

Place ______

on the hearing of an application by ______, the claimant, for a disqualification order under section ______ of the Company Directors Disqualification Act 1986 that:

The grounds upon which the claimant seeks a disqualification order are set out (in the details of claim overleaf and) in the (affidavit/report) of ______ (sworn/dated______) a true copy of which is served herewith.

Note: If you do not attend, the court may make such order as it thinks fit

The court office at

is open between 10 am and 4 pm Monday to Friday. When corresponding with the court, please address forms or letters to the Court Manager and quote the claim number.

N500 Claim form - Directors disqualification proceedings (06.05) HMCS

Claim No.	

Does your claim include any issues under the Human Rights Act 1998? ☐ Yes ☐ No

Details of your claim

Defendant's name and address

	£
Court fee	
Solicitor's costs	
Issue date	

Endorsement

1. CPR Part 8 as modified by the Directors Disqualification Proceedings Pratice Direction applies to this claim.
2. Any evidence which the defendant wishes to be taken into consideration by the court must be filed in court within 28 days from the date of service of the claim form and copies must then be served forthwith on the claimant. The evidence must be in the form of one or more affidavits.

[3. This claim is made in accordance with the Insolvent Companies (Disqualification of Unfit Directors) Proceedings Rules 1987 (S.I. 1987/2023, as amended).]

4. The court has the power to impose a disqualification period as follows:

   where the application is under section 2 or section 4 of the Company Directors Disqualification Act, for a period of up to 15 years;

   where the application is under section 3 of the Company Directors Disqualification Act, for a period of up to 5 years;

   where the application is under section 7 of the Company Directors Disqualification Act, for a period of not less than 2 years and up to 15 years;

   where the application is under section 8 or section 9A of the Company Directors Disqualification Act, for a period of up to 15 years.

[5. On the first hearing of the claim, the court may hear and determine the claim summarily, without further or other notice to you and if it is so determined, the court may impose disqualification for a period of up to 5 years.]

[6. If at the hearing of the application the court, on the evidence then before it, is minded to impose, in the case of any defendant, disqualification for any period longer than 5 years, it will not make a disqualification order on the first hearing but will adjourn the application to be heard (with further evidence, if any) at a later date that will be notified to the defendant. At the second hearing, the court may impose disqualification period of more than 5 years without any further reference to you.]

7. Your attention is drawn to the possibility of resolving the claim by offering an undertaking pursuant to section 1A or 9B of the Company Directors Disqualification Act (as applicable) or pursuant to the summary procedure adopted in *Re Carecraft Construction Co. Ltd* [1994] 1 WLR 172 (as clarified by the decision of the Court of Appeal in *Secretary of State v Rogers* [1996] 1 WLR 1569).

Statement of Truth

*(I believe)(The claimant believes) that the facts stated in this claim form are true.
* I am duly authorised by the claimant to sign this statement.

Full name of claimant ....

Name of claimant's solicitor's firm ....

signed .... *(Claimant)(Claimant's solicitor)

position or office held .... (if signing on behalf of firm or company)

delete as appropriate

Claimant's or claimant's solicitor's address to which documents should be sent if different from overleaf. If you are prepared to accept service by DX, fax or e-mail, please add details.

Notes for claimant on completing claim form N500

Directors disqualification application

Please read all of these guidance notes before you begin completing the claim form. The notes follow the order in which information is required on the form.

- Court staff can help you fill in the claim form and give information about procedure once it has been issued. But they cannot give legal advice. If you need legal advice, for example, about the likely success of your claim or the evidence you need to prove it, you should contact a solicitor or a Citizens Advice Bureau.
- If you are filling in the claim form by hand, please use black ink and write in block capitals.
- You must file evidence to support your claim with the claim form in the form of an affidavit or affirmation or where permitted by rule 3(2) of the Insolvent Companies (Disqualification of Unfit Directors) Proceedings Rules 1986, a report by the Official Receiver.
- Copy the completed claim form, the defendant's notes for guidance and your written evidence so that you have one copy for yourself, one copy for the court and one copy for each defendant. Send or take the forms and evidence to the court office with the appropriate fee. The court will tell you how much this is.

Notes on completing the claim form

Heading
You must fill in the heading of the form to indicate whether you want the claim to be issued in a county court or in the High Court (The High Court means either a District Registry (attached to a county court) or the Companies Court at the Royal Courts of Justice in London).

Use whichever of the following is appropriate:

'In the .... county court'
(inserting the name of the court)

or

'In the High Court of Justice Chancery Division
.... District Registry'
(inserting the name of the District Registry)

or

'In the High Court of Justice Chancery Division, Companies Court'

A disqualification application under section 9A of the Company Directors Disqualification Act must be issued in the High Court, out of the office of the Companies Court Registrar at the Royal Courts of Justice.

The section of text beginning 'In the matter of...' is included to comply with paragraph 5.1 of the Directors Disqualification Proceedings Practice Direction. You should insert the name of the relevant company(ies) after this text.

Claimant and defendant details
As the person issuing the claim, you are called the 'claimant'; the person you are suing is called the 'defendant'. You must provide the following information about yourself **and** the defendant according to the capacity on which you are suing and in which the defendant is being sued. When suing or being sued as:-

an individual:
All known forenames and surname (whether Mr, Mrs, Miss, Ms or Other e.g. Dr) and residential address (**including** postcode and telephone and any fax or e-mail number) in England and Wales. Where the defendant is a proprietor of a business, a partner in a firm or an individual sued in the name of a club or other unincorporated association, the address for service should be the usual or last known place of residence or principal place of business of the company, firm or club or other unincorporated association.

Where the individual is:

a firm:
Enter the name of the firm followed by the words 'a firm' e.g. 'Bandbow - a firm' and an address for service which is either a partner's residential address or the principal or last known place of business.

a corporation (other than a company):
Enter the full name of the corporation and the address which is either its principal office or any other place where the corporation carries on activities and which has a real connection with the claim.

N500A Notes for claimant on completing a Part 8 claim form (06.05) HMCS

a company registered in England and Wales:
Enter the name of the company and an address which is either the company's registered office or any place of business that has a real, or the most, connection with the claim e.g. the shop where the goods were bought.

an oversea company (defined by s744 of the Companies Act 1985):
Enter the name of the company and either the address registered under s691 of the Act or the address of the place of business having a real, or the most, connection with the claim.

Hearing
Paragraph 4.3 of the Practice Direction states that 'When the claim form is issued, the claimant will be given a date for the first hearing of the disqualification application'. Court staff will complete these details when a date for a hearing is fixed, before the claim form is served. You should fill in the blanks in the sentence below the dates with the claimant's name and the section of the Company Directors Disqualification Act 1986 under which you are seeking the defendant's disqualification. You should then complete the empty section with the details of the order you wish the court to make, and delete the sections in the following sentence as appropriate.

Details of your claim
You should set out the details of your claim here, unless you have chosen to set them out only in an attached affidavit or report.

Evidence
The evidence in support of the claim must be set out in an attached affidavit or report, which must include a statement of the matters by reference to which it is alleged that a disqualification order should be made against the defendant.

Defendant's name and address
Enter in this box the full name and address of the defendant to be served with the claim form (i.e. one claim form for each defendant). If the defendant is to be served outside England and Wales, you may need to obtain the court's permission.

Endorsement
If the claim is not brought under section 7, 8 or 9A of the Company Directors Disqualification Act 1986, paragraphs 3, 5 and 6 of the endorsement should be deleted.

Statement of truth
This must be signed by you, by your solicitor or your litigation friend, as appropriate.

Where the claimant is a registered company or a corporation the claim must be signed by either the director, treasurer, secretary, chief executive, manager or other officer of the company or (in the case of a corporation) the mayor, chairman, president or town clerk.

Address for documents
Insert in this box the address at which you wish to receive documents, if different from the address you have already given under the heading 'Claimant'. The address you give must be either that of your solicitors or your residential or business address and must be in England or Wales. If you live or carry on business outside of England and Wales, you can give some other address within England and Wales.

Notes for defendant

Directors disqualification application

Please read these notes carefully - they will help you to decide what to do about this claim.

- You have 14 days from the date on which you were served with the claim form (see below) in which to respond to the claim by completing and returning the acknowledgment of service enclosed with this claim form. The acknowledgement of service should be completed and returned to the court office and a copy sent to the claimant named on the claim form.
- If you **do not return** the acknowledgment of service (Form N502), you will be allowed to attend any hearing of this claim but you will not be allowed to take part in the hearing unless the court gives you permission to do so.

Court staff can tell you about procedures but they cannot give legal advice. If you need legal advice, you should contact a solicitor or Citizens Advice Bureau immediately

Responding to this claim

Time for responding
The completed acknowledgment of service must be returned to the court office and a copy sent to the claimant named on the claim form within 14 days of the date on which the claim form was served on you. If the claim form was

- sent by post, the 14 days begins 7 days from the date of the postmark on the envelope.
- delivered or left at your address, the 14 days begins the day after it was delivered or left.
- handed to you personally, the 14 days begins on the day it was given to you.

Completing the acknowledgment of service (N502)
You should complete section A, B, or C as appropriate and all of section D.

Section A - contesting the claim
If you wish to contest the remedy sought by the claimant in the claim form, you should complete section A.

Section B - mitigation
If you do not wish to resist the claim for a disqualification order, but would like to offer evidence of mitigating circumstances with a view to justifying a shorter period of disqualification, you should complete section B.

Section C - disputing the court's jurisdiction
You should indicate your intention by completing section C and filing an application disputing the court's jurisdiction within 14 days of filing your acknowledgment of service at the court. The court will arrange a hearing date for the application and tell you and the claimant when and where to attend.

Section D - Statement of truth
This must be signed by you, by your solicitor or your litigation friend, as appropriate.

Where the defendant is a registered company or a corporation the claim must be signed by either the director, treasurer, secretary, chief executive, manager or other officer of the company or (in the case of a corporation) the mayor, chairman, president or town clerk.

Written evidence
Any evidence which you wish to be taken into consideration by the court must be filed in court within 28 days from the date of service of the claim form upon you. The evidence must be in the form of an affidavit.

Serving other parties
At the same time as you file your affidavit evidence with the court, you must also send copies of both the form and any written evidence to the claimant named on the claim form.

What happens next
The date of the first hearing of the claim is set out under 'Hearing'.

N500B Notes for defendant - Directors disqualification application (06.05) HMCS

Claim form

Directors disqualification section 8A application

In the	
Claim No.	

In the matter of a disqualification undertaking dated

and in the matter of the Company Directors Disqualification Act 1986.

SEAL

Name of Claimant

Name of Defendant(s)

The hearing

(This section will be completed by the court)

The defendant(s) must attend before the (Registrar/District Judge) on

Date   Time

Place

on the hearing of an application by ______________, the claimant, for an order under Section 8A of the Company Directors Disqualification Act 1986 that:

The grounds upon which the claimant seeks the order are set out (in the details of claim overleaf and) in the affidavit of (________) sworn on ________ a true copy of which is served herewith.

Note: If you do not attend, the court may make such order as it thinks fit

The court office at

is open between 10 am and 4 pm Monday to Friday. When corresponding with the court, please address forms or letters to the Court Manager and quote the claim number.

N501 Claim form - Directors disqualification section 8A application (06.05) HMCS

Claim No.	

Does your claim include any issues under the Human Rights Act 1998? ☐ Yes ☐ No

Details of your claim

Defendant's(s) name(s) and address(es)

	£
Court fee	
Solicitor's costs	
Issue date	

Endorsement

1. CPR Part 8 as modified by the Directors Disqualification Proceedings Pratice Direction applies to this claim.
2. Any evidence which the defendant wishes to be taken into consideration by the court must be filed in court within 28 days from the date of service of the claim form and copies must then be served forthwith on the claimant. The evidence must be in the form of one or more affidavits.

Statement of Truth

*(I believe)(The claimant believes) that the facts stated in this claim form are true.
* I am duly authorised by the claimant to sign this statement.

Full name of claimant ....

Name of claimant's solicitor's firm ....

signed .... position or office held ....
*(Claimant)(Litigation friend)(Claimant's solicitor) (if signing on behalf of firm or company)

delete as appropriate

Claimant's or claimant's solicitor's address to which documents should be sent if different from overleaf. If you are prepared to accept service by DX, fax or e-mail, please add details.

Notes for claimant on completing claim form N501

Directors disqualification section 8A application

Please read all of these guidance notes before you begin completing the claim form. The notes follow the order in which information is required on the form.

- Court staff can help you fill in the claim form and give information about procedure once it has been issued. But they cannot give legal advice. If you need legal advice for example, about the likely success of your claim or the evidence you need to prove it, you should contact a solicitor or a Citizens Advice Bureau.
- If you are filling in the claim form by hand, please use black ink and write in block capitals.
- You must file evidence to support your claim with the claim form in the form of an affidavit or affirmation.
- Copy the completed claim form, the defendant's notes for guidance and your written evidence so that you have one copy for yourself, one copy for the court and one copy for each defendant. Send or take the forms and evidence to the court office with the appropriate fee. The court will tell you how much this is.

Notes on completing the claim form

Heading
You must fill in the heading of the form to indicate whether you want the claim to be issued in a county court or in the High Court (The High Court means either a District Registry (attached to a county court) or the Royal Courts of Justice in London). Section 8A(3) of the Company Directors Disqualification Act 1986 identifies the courts which have jurisdiction to deal with Section 8A applications.

An application under section 8A of the Company Directors Disqualification Act which relates to a disqualification undertaking given under section 9B of the Act must be issued in the High Court, out of the office of the Companies Court Registrar at the Royal Courts of Justice.

Use whichever of the following is appropriate:

'In the ....county court'
(inserting the court name)

or

'In the High Court of Justice Chancery Division
....District Registry'
(inserting the name of the District Registry)

or

'In the High Court of Justice Chancery Division, Companies Court'

Claimant and defendant details
As the person issuing the claim, you are called the 'claimant'; the person you are suing is called the 'defendant'. You must provide the following information about yourself **and** the defendant according to the capacity on which you are suing and in which the defendant is being sued. When suing or being sued as:-

an individual:
All known forenames and surname (whether Mr, Mrs, Miss, Ms or Other e.g. Dr) and residential address (**including** postcode and telephone and any fax or e-mail number) in England and Wales. Where the defendant is a proprietor of a business, a partner in a firm or an individual sued in the name of a club or other unincorporated association, the address for service should be the usual or last known place of residence or principal place of business of the company, firm or club or other unincorporated association.

Where the individual is:

a firm:
Enter the name of the firm followed by the words 'a firm' e.g. 'Bandbow - a firm' and an address for service which is either a partner's residential address or the principal or last known place of business.

a corporation (other than a company):
Enter the full name of the corporation and the address which is either its principal office or any other place where the corporation carries on activities and which has a real connection with the claim.

N501A Notes for claimant on completing claim form N501 (06.05) HMCS

a company registered in England and Wales:
Enter the name of the company and an address which is either the company's registered office or any place of business that has a real, or the most, connection with the claim e.g. the shop where the goods were bought.

an oversea company (defined by s744 of the Companies Act 1985):
Enter the name of the company and either the address registered under s691 of the Act or the address of the place of business having a real, or the most, connection with the claim.

Hearing
Paragraph 30.3 of the Directors Disqualification Proceedings Practice Direction states that 'When the claim form is issued, the claimant will be given a date for the first hearing of the section 8A application'. Court staff will complete these details when a date for a hearing is fixed, before the claim form is served. However, you must complete the section below this with the details of the order you wish the court to make and fill in the details of your affidavit if you are attaching one to the form.

Details of your claim
You should set out the details of your claim here, unless you have chosen to set them out only in an attached affidavit.

Evidence
Evidence in section 8A applications must be by affidavit. The affidavit in support of the section 8A application must be filed in court at the same time as the claim form. Any exhibits to the affidavit must be lodged with the court at the same time. Copies of the affidavit and exhibits must be served with the claim form on the defendant.

Defendant's name and address
Enter in this box the full name and address of the defendant to be served with the claim form (i.e. one claim form for each defendant).

In the case of a disqualification undertaking given under section 9B of the Act, the defendant to the section 8A application shall be the Office of Fair Trading or specified regulator which accepted the undertaking. In all other cases, the defendant shall be the Secretary of State for Trade and Industry.

Addresses for service on government departments are set out in the List of Authorised government Departments issued by the Cabinet Office under section 17 of the Crown Proceedings Act 1947, which is annexed to the Practice Direction supplementing Part 66 of the Civil Procedure Rules.

Statement of truth
This must be signed by you, by your solicitor or your litigation friend, as appropriate.

Where the claimant is a registered company or a corporation the claim must be signed by either the director, treasurer, secretary, chief executive, manager or other officer of the company or (in the case of a corporation) the mayor, chairman, president or town clerk.

Address for documents
Insert in this box the address at which you wish to receive documents, if different from the address you have already given under the heading 'Claimant'. The address you give must be either that of your solicitors or your residential or business address and must be in England or Wales. If you live of carry on business outside of England and Wales, you can give some other address within England and Wales.

Notes for defendant
Directors disqualification section 8A application

Please read these notes carefully - they will help you to decide what to do about this claim.

- You have 14 days from the date on which you were served with the claim form (see below) in which to respond to the claim by completing and returning the acknowledgment of service enclosed with this claim form. The acknowledgement of service should be completed and returned to the court office and a copy sent to the claimant named on the claim form.
- If you **do not return** the acknowledgment of service (Form N503), you will be allowed to attend any hearing of this claim but you will not be allowed to take part in the hearing unless the court gives you permission to do so.

Court staff can tell you about procedures but they cannot give legal advice. If you need legal advice, you should contact a solicitor or Citizens Advice Bureau immediately

Responding to this claim

Time for responding
The completed acknowledgment of service must be returned to the court office (and a copy sent to the claimant named on the claim form) within 14 days of the date on which the claim form was served on you. If the claim form was:

- sent by post, the 14 days begins 7 days from the date of the postmark on the envelope.
- delivered or left at your address, the 14 days begins the day after it was delivered.
- handed to you personally, the 14 days begins on the day it was given to you.

If the claim form was issued in the High Court in London, the acknowledgment of service should be returned to the Companies Court, General Office, Room TM 2.09, Royal Courts of Justice, The Strand, London, WC2A 2LL

Completing the acknowledgment of service (N503)
You should complete section A or B as appropriate and all of section C.

Statement of truth
This must be signed by you, your solicitor or your litigation friend, as appropriate.

Written evidence
Any evidence which you wish to be taken into consideration by the court must be filed in court within 28 days from the date of service of the claim form upon you. The evidence must be in the form of an affidavit.

Serving other parties
At the same time as you file your affidavit evidence with the court, you must also send copies of both the form and any written evidence to the claimant named on the claim form.

What happens next
The date of the first hearing of the claim is set out under 'hearing'.

N501B Notes for defendant - Directors disqualification section 8A application (06.05) HMCS

Acknowledgment of service

Directors disqualification application

You should read the 'notes for defendant' (Form N500B) attached to the claim form which will tell you how to complete this form, and when and where to send it.

In the	
Claim No.	
Claimant (including ref)	
Defendant	

State the full name of the defendant

Section A

☐ I intend to contest the claim on the grounds that:

☐ I was not a director or shadow director of

at the time when my conduct, or the conduct of other persons, is in question.
(Please insert the name of each of the companies concerned in the box above)

☐ My conduct as a director or shadow director was not as alleged in support of the application for a disqualification order.

☐ I dispute the allegation that my conduct makes me unfit to be involved in the management of a company.

☐ I intend to contest the claim on the grounds that:
(Only complete this if the case has been brought under section 7 of the Company Directors Disqualification Act 1986. In the box below insert the name of any company listed on the claim form after the words 'In the matter of' to which this statement applies)

has at no time become insolvent within the meaning of section 6(2) of the Company Directors Disqualification Act 1986.

☐ I intend to contest the claim on the grounds that:
(Only complete this if the case has been brought under section 9A of the Company Directors Disqualification Act 1986. Please insert the name of any relevant company in the box below.)

has not committed a breach of competition law within the meaning of section 9A(4) of the Company Directors Disqualification Act 1986.

The court office at

is open between 10 am and 4 pm Monday to Friday. When corresponding with the court, please address forms or letters to the Court Manager and quote the claim number.

N502 Acknowledgment of service - Directors disqualification applications (06.05) HMCS

Section B

☐ I do not wish to dispute the claim for a disqualification order.

☐ I would like to offer evidence with a view to reducing the period of disqualification.

Section C

☐ The claim form was served outside England or Wales and I intend to dispute jurisdiction.
(You should file your application within 14 days of the date on which you file this acknowledgment of service with the court)

Section D

Statement of Truth

*(I believe)(The defendant believes) that the facts stated in this form are true.

*I am duly authorised by the defendant to sign this statement.

Full name ______________________

Name of defendant's solicitor's firm ______________________

Signed ______________ position or office held ______________

*(Defendant)(Litigation friend)(Defendant's solicitor) (if signing on behalf of firm or company)

Dated ______________

delete as appropriate

Give an address (including post code) to which notices about this case can be sent to you.

Telephone no.	

If applicable	
Ref no.	
Fax no.	
DX no.	
E-mail	

Acknowledgment of service

Directors disqualification section 8A application

You should read the 'notes for defendant' (Form N501B) attached to the claim form which will tell you how to complete this form, and when and where to send it.

In the	
Claim No.	
Claimant (including ref)	
Defendant	

Section A

☐ The defendant currently intends to appear at the hearing of the section 8A application.

☐ The defendant currently intends to file evidence on the section 8A application.

Section B

☐ The defendant intends to dispute jurisdiction

(You should file your application within 14 days of the date on which you file this acknowledgment of service with the court.)

Section C

Statement of Truth

*(I believe)(The defendant believes) that the facts stated in this form are true.

*I am duly authorised by the defendant to sign this statement.

Full name ____________________

Name of defendant's solicitor's firm ____________________

Signed ____________________ position or office held ____________________

*(Defendant)(Defendant's solicitor) (if signing on behalf of firm or company)

Dated ____________________ *delete as appropriate*

Give an address (including post code) to which notices about this case can be sent to you.

Telephone no.	

If applicable	
Ref no.	
Fax no.	
DX no.	
E-mail	

The court office at

is open between 10 am and 4 pm Monday to Friday. When corresponding with the court, please address forms or letters to the Court Manager and quote the claim number.

N503 Acknowledgment of service - Directors disqualification section 8A application (06.05) HMCS

Pre-trial checklist
Directors disqualification

To be completed by, or on behalf of,

who is [1st][2nd][3rd][   ][Claimant][Defendant] in this claim

Name of company to which claim relates

In the	
Claim no.	
Last date for filing with court office	
Date(s) fixed for trial or trial period	
Claimant	
Defendant	

This form must be **completed** and **returned** to the court no later than the date given above. If not, your evidence may be struck out or some other sanction imposed.

If the claim has settled, or settles before the trial date, you must let the court know immediately.

Legal representatives only: You must **attach** estimates of costs incurred to date, and of your likely overall costs. In substantial cases, these should be provided in compliance with CPR Part 43.

You must also **attach** a proposed timetable for the trial itself.

A Confirmation of compliance with directions

1. I confirm that I have complied with those directions already given which require action by me. ☐Yes ☐No

If you are unable to give confirmation, state which directions you have still to comply with and the date by which this will be done.

Directions	Date

2. I believe that additional directions are necessary before the trial takes place. ☐Yes ☐No

If Yes, you should attach an application and a draft order.

*Include in your application all directions needed to enable the claim **to be tried on the date, or within the trial period, already fixed.** These should include any issues relating to experts and their evidence, and any orders needed in respect of directions still requiring action by any other party.*

3. Have you agreed the additional directions you are seeking with the other party(ies)? ☐Yes ☐No

B Witnesses

1. How many witnesses (including yourself) will be giving evidence on your behalf at the trial? *(Do not include experts - see Section C)* ☐

Continued over ▯

Witnesses continued

2. If the trial date is not yet fixed, are there any days within the trial period you or your witnesses would wish to avoid if possible? *(Do not include experts - see Section C)*

Please give details

Name of witness	Dates to be avoided, if possible	Reason

Please specify any special facilities or arrangements needed at court for the party or any witness (e.g. witness with a disability).

3. Will you be providing an interpreter for any of your witnesses? ☐Yes ☐No

C Experts

You are reminded that you may not use an expert's report or have your expert give oral evidence unless the court has given permission. If you do not have permission, you must make an application (see section A2 above)

1. Please give the information requested for your expert(s)

Name	Field of expertise	Joint expert?	Is report agreed?	Has permission been given for oral evidence?
		☐Yes ☐No	☐Yes ☐No	☐Yes ☐No
		☐Yes ☐No	☐Yes ☐No	☐Yes ☐No
		☐Yes ☐No	☐Yes ☐No	☐Yes ☐No

2. Has there been discussion between experts? ☐Yes ☐No

3. Have the experts signed a joint statement? ☐Yes ☐No

4. If your expert is giving oral evidence and the trial date is not yet fixed, is there any day within the trial period which the expert would wish to avoid, if possible? ☐Yes ☐No

If Yes, please give details

Name	Dates to be avoided, if possible	Reason

2 of 4

D Legal representation

1. Who will be presenting your case at the trial? You ☐ Solicitor ☐ Counsel ☐

2. If the trial date is not yet fixed, is there any day within the trial period that the person presenting your case would wish to avoid, if possible? ☐Yes ☐No

If Yes, please give details

Name	Dates to be avoided, if possible	Reason

E Summary disposal under the Carecraft procedure or by disqualification undertaking

1. Have you considered the possibility of resolving this case by a disqualification undertaking or under the procedure adopted in *Re Carecraft Construction Co. Ltd* [1994] 1 WLR 172 ('a Carecraft application'). If not this should be considered as soon as possible. ☐ Yes ☐ No

2. Please state whether the case should be listed for a Carecraft disposal or full trial at a time and date to be fixed. ☐ Carecraft ☐ Full trial

3. If such a Carecraft application is to be made, the agreed written statement of facts must be submitted by the claimant as set out in the Practice Direction relating to disqualification proceedings and delivered to the court not later than 2 working days before the date upon which it is intended to make the application and in any event as soon as possible.

F The trial

1. Has the estimate of the time needed for trial changed? ☐ Yes ☐ No

If Yes, say how long you estimate the whole trial will take, including both parties' cross-examination and closing arguments ☐ days ☐ hours ☐ minutes

2. If different from original estimate have you agreed with the other party(ies) that this is now the **total** time needed? ☐ Yes ☐ No

3. Is the timetable for trial you have attached agreed with the other party(ies)? ☐ Yes ☐ No

3 of 4

G Document and fee checklist

Tick as appropriate

I attach to this questionnaire -

- ☐ An application and fee for additional directions
- ☐ A draft order
- ☐ Listing fee
- ☐ A proposed timetable for trial
- ☐ An estimate of costs

Signed

[Counsel][Solicitor][for the][1st][2nd][3rd][ ]
[Claimant][Defendant]

Date

Please enter your [firm's] name, reference number and full postal address including (if appropriate) details of DX, fax or e-mail

Postcode

Tel. no.		DX no.		E-mail	
Fax no.		Ref. no.			

4 of 4

Solicitor's Act: order for delivery of bill

DATED the [DATE]

IN THE HIGH COURT OF JUSTICE [Claim No]

[DIVISION]

[JUDGE TYPE][JUDGE NAME]

BETWEEN:

[CLAIMANT]

Claimant

- and -

[DEFENDANT]

Defendant

UPON THE APPLICATION OF THE [PARTY]

[the parties and their representatives who attended]

AND UPON HEARING

AND UPON READING the documents on the Court File

IT IS ORDERED THAT

(1) The [PARTY] must within [NUMBER OF DAYS] deliver to the [PARTY], or to his solicitor, a bill of costs in all causes and matters in which he has been concerned for the [PARTY]

(2) The [PARTY] must give credit in that bill for all money received by him from or on account of the [PARTY]

Order on Client's Application for Detailed Assessment of Solicitor's Bill

DATED the [DATE]

IN THE HIGH COURT OF JUSTICE [Claim No]

[DIVISION]

[JUDGE TYPE][JUDGE NAME]

BETWEEN:

[CLAIMANT]

Claimant

- and -

[DEFENDANT]

Defendant

UPON THE APPLICATION OF THE [PARTY]

[the parties and their representatives who attended]

AND UPON HEARING

AND UPON READING the documents on the Court File

IT IS ORDERED THAT

(1) A detailed assessment must be made of the bill dated [ ] delivered to the claimant by the defendant.

(2) On making the detailed assessment, the court must also assess the costs of these proceedings and certify what is due to or from either party in respect of the bill and the costs of these proceedings.

(3) Until these proceedings are concluded the defendant must not commence or continue any proceedings against the claimant in respect of the bill mentioned above.

(4) Upon payment by the claimant of any sum certified as due to the defendant in these proceedings the defendant must deliver to the claimant all the documentation in the defendant's possession or control which belong to the claimant.

Order on Solicitor's Application for Assessment Under the Solicitor's Act 1974 Part III

Upon hearing … upon reading …

IT IS ORDERED THAT

(1) A detailed assessment must be made of the bill dated [ ] delivered to the defendant by the claimant.

(2) If the defendant attends the detailed assessment the court making that assessment must also assess the costs of these proceedings and certify what is due to or from either party in respect of the bill and the costs of these proceedings.

(3) Until these proceedings are concluded the claimant must not commence or continue any proceedings against the defendant in respect of the bill mentioned above.

(4) Upon payment by the defendant of any sum certified as due to the claimant in these proceedings the claimant must deliver to the defendant all the documentation in the claimant's possession or control which belong to the defendant.

FORM EX80A

Legal aid/ Legal Services Commission assessment certificate

Claimant/Petitioner

Defendant/Respondent

In the	
Claim/Case No.	
Certificate No.	
Solicitors Ref.	

The costs in this matter have been assessed as set out in boxes A, B and C below and are claimed from the Community Legal Service Fund.

SEAL

The costs are those of the *(please tick)* ☐ Claimant ☐ Petitioner ☐ Defendant ☐ Respondent ☐ Other

They were assessed in the ☐ High Court ☐ County Court

Total pre-certificate costs, which are not being claimed, were £
(including disbursements, profit costs and VAT)

Dated ______________ Signed ______________________
(Solicitor)

A. Costs payable by another party as allowed or as in legal aid/LSC schedule if appropriate
(Do not include any pre-certificate costs, or the costs of assessment).

Profit costs	
VAT	
Counsel's Fees	
VAT	
Disbursements	
VAT (where appropriate)	
Total	£

B. Legal aid only/LSC only costs
(Do not include the costs of assessment)

Profit costs	
VAT	
Counsel's Fees	
VAT	
Disbursements	
VAT (where appropriate)	
Total	£

C. Costs of Assessment
(Allowed in respect of A and B above)

For Part A	
VAT	
Court fee (where appropriate)	
For Part B	
VAT	
Court fee (where appropriate)	
Total	£

D. Total Claimed
(Add totals A, B and C)

Total part A	
Total part B	
Total part C	
Total	£

Sealed by the court on ______________

EX80A Legal Aid /LSC Assessment Certificate (7.00)

Produced on behalf of The Court Service

Claim Form
(CPR Part 8)

DISQUALIFICATION PROCEEDINGS

In the	
Claim No.	

IN THE MATTER OF [INSERT NAME OF COMPANY:
SEE THE PRACTICE DIRECTION]

SEAL

AND IN THE MATTER OF COMPANY DIRECTORS
DISQUALIFICATION ACT 1986

Claimant

Defendant(s)

Name(s) and address(es) of Defendant(s)

	£
Court fee	
Solicitors costs	
Issue date	

The court office at

is open between 10 am and 4 pm Monday to Friday. When corresponding with the court, please address forms or letters to the Court Manager and quote the case number.

Claim form (CPR Part 8)

Claim No.	

Details of claim

LET the Defendant(s) attend before the Registrar/District Judge] on

Date ....
Time .... hours
Place ....

On the hearing of an application by [ ], the Claimant, for a disqualification order under section [ ] of the Company Directors Disqualification Act 1986 that:

The grounds upon which the Claimant seeks a Disqualification Order are [*set out below/summarised in the [affadavit/report] of [ ] [sworn/dated] [DATE] a true copy of which is served herewith.]

* delete as appropriate

NOTE: IF YOU DO NOT ATTEND, THE COURT MAY MAKE SUCH ORDER AS IT THINKS FIT

ENDORSEMENT

1. CPR Part 8 as modified by the Practice Direction relating to disqualification proceedings applies to this claim.

[2. This claim is made in accordance with the Insolvent Companies (Disqualification of Unfit Directors) Rules 1987 (SI 1987/2023).]

3. The court has power to impose a disqualification period as follows:-

where the application is under section 2 of the Company Directors Disqualification Act, for a period of up to 15 years;

where the application is under section 3 of the Company Directors Disqualification Act, for a period of up to 5 years;

where the application is under section 4 of the Company Directors Disqualification Act, for a period of up to 15 years;

where the application is under section 5 of the Company Directors Disqualification Act, for a period of up to 5 years;

where the application is under section 7 of the Company Directors Disqualification Act, for a period of not less than 2, and up to 15, years;

where the application is under section 8 of the Company Directors Disqualification Act, for a period of up to 15 years.

[4. On the first hearing of the claim, the court may hear and determine the claim summarily, without further or other notice to you, and, if it is so determined, the court may impose a disqualification for a period of up to 5 years.]

[5. If at the hearing of the application the court, on the evidence then before it, is minded to impose, in the case of any Defendant, disqualification for any period longer than 5 years, it will not make a disqualification order on the first hearing but will adjourn the application to be heard (with further evidence, if any) at a later date that will be notified to the Defendant. At the second hearing, the court may impose a disqualification period of more than 5 years without any further reference to you.]

6. Your attention is drawn to the possibility of resolving the claim pursuant to the summary procedure adopted in *Re Carecraft Construction Co. Ltd* [1994] 1 WLR 172 (as clarified by the decision of the Court of Appeal in *Secretary of State v Rogers* [1996] 1 WLR 1569).

Statement of Truth
*(I believe)(The Claimant believes) that the facts stated in this claim form are true.
* I am duly authorised by the claimant to sign this statement

Full name of the claimant ____________________

Name of claimant's solicitor's firm ____________________

Signed ____________________ position or office held ____________________

*(Claimant)(Litigation friend)(Claimant's solicitor) (if signing on behalf of firm or company)
*delete as appropriate

Claimant's or claimant's solicitor's address to which documents should be sent if different from overleaf. If you are prepared to accept service by DX, fax or e-mail, please add details.

Notes for claimant on completing a Part 8 claim form

- Please read all of these guidance notes before you begin completing the claim form. The notes follow the order in which information is required on the form.
- Court staff can help you fill in the claim form and give information about procedure once it has been issued. But they cannot give legal advice. If you need legal advice, for example, about the likely success of your claim or the evidence you need to prove it, you should contact a solicitor or a Citizens Advice Bureau.
- If you are filling in the claim form by hand, please use black ink and write in block capitals.
- You must file any evidence to support your claim either in or with the claim form in the form of an affidavit or affirmation.
- Copy the completed claim form, the defendant's notes for guidance and your written evidence so that you have one copy for yourself, one copy for the court and one copy for each defendant. Send or take the forms and evidence to the court office with the appropriate fee. The court will tell you how much this is.

Notes on completing the claim form

Heading

You must fill in the heading of the form to indicate whether you want the claim to be issued in a county court or in the High Court (The High Court means either a District Registry (attached to a county court) or the Royal Courts of Justice in London).

Use whichever of the following is appropriate:

'In the..........................county court'
(inserting the name of the court)

or

'In the High Court of Justice Chancery Division
and ....District Registry'
(inserting the name of the District Registry)

or

'In the High Court of Justice Chancery Division, Companies Court
Royal Courts of Justice'

Claimant and defendant details

As the person issuing the claim, you are called the 'claimant'; the person you are suing is called the 'defendant'. You must provide the following information about yourself **and** the defendant according to the capacity in which you are suing and in which the defendant is being sued. When suing or being sued as:-

an individual:
All known forenames and surname, (whether Mr, Mrs, Miss, Ms or Other e.g. Dr) and residential address (**including** postcode and telephone and any fax or e-mail number) in England and Wales. Where the defendant is a proprietor of a business, a partner in a firm or an individual sued in the name of a club or other unincorporated association, the address for service should be the usual or last known place of residence or principal place of business of the company, firm or club or other unincorporated association.

Where the individual is:

a firm:

Enter the name of the firm followed by the words 'a firm' e.g. 'Bandbox - a firm' and an address for service which is either a partner's residential address or the principal or last known place of business.

a corporation (other than a company):

Enter the full name of the corporation and the address which is either its principal office or any other place where the corporation carries on activities and which has a real connection with the claim.

a company registered in England and Wales:

Enter the name of the company and an address which is either the company's registered office or any place of business that has a real, or the most, connection with the claim e.g. the shop where the goods were bought.

an overseas company (defined by s744 of the Companies Act 1985):
Enter the name of the company and either the address registered under s69 1 of the Act or the address of the place of business having a real, or the most, connection with the claim.

Defendant's name and address
Enter in this box the full name and address of the defendant to be served with the claim form (ie. one claim form for each defendant). If the defendant is to be served outside England and Wales, you may need to obtain the court's permission.

Address for documents
Insert in this box the address at which you wish to receive documents, if different from the address you have already given under the heading 'Claimant'. The address you give must be either that of your solicitors or your residential or business address and must be in England or Wales. If you live or carry on business outside of England and Wales, you can give some other address within England and Wales.

Endorsement
If the claim is not brought under section 7 or section 8 of the Company Directors Disqualification Act 1986, paragraphs 2, 4 and 5 of the endorsement should be deleted.

Statement of truth
This must be signed by you, by your solicitor or your litigation friend, as appropriate.

Where the claimant is a registered company or a corporation the claim must be signed by either the director, treasurer, secretary, chief executive, manager or other officer of the company or (in the case of a corporation) the mayor, chairman, president or town clerk.

Written evidence

Any evidence which you wish to be taken into consideration by the Court must be filed in Court within 28 days from the date of service of the claim form upon you. The evidence must be in the form of an affidavit.

Serving other parties

At the same time as you file your affidavit evidence with the court, you must also send copies of both the form and any written evidence to the Claimant named on the claim form.

What happens next

The date of the first hearing of the claim is set out under "Details of Claim" above.

Statement of truth

This must be signed by you, by your solicitor or your litigation friend, as appropriate.
Where the claimant is a registered company or a corporation the claim must be signed by either the director, treasurer, secretary, chief executive, manager or other officer of the company or (in the case of a corporation) the mayor, chairman, president or town clerk.

Notes for defendant
(Part 8 Claim Form: Disqualification Proceedings)

Please read these notes carefully - they will help you to decide what to do about this claim.

- You have 14 days from the date on which you were served with the claim form (see below) in which to respond to the claim by completing and returning the acknowledgment of service enclosed with this claim form.
- If you **do not return** the acknowledgment of service, you will be allowed to attend any hearing of this claim but you will not be allowed to take part in the hearing unless the court gives you permission to do so.

Court staff can tell you about procedures but they cannot give legal advice. If you need legal advice, you should contact a solicitor or Citizens Advice Bureau immediately

Responding to this claim

Time for responding

The completed acknowledgment of service must be returned to the court office within 14 days of the date on which the claim form was served on you. If the claim form was

- sent by post, the 14 days begins 7 days from the date of the postmark on the envelope.
- delivered or left at your address, the 14 days begins the day after it was delivered.
- handed to you personally, the 14 days begins on the day it was given to you.

Completing the acknowledgment of service

You should complete section A, B, or C as appropriate **and all** of section D.

Section A - contesting the claim
If you wish to contest the remedy sought by the claimant in the claim form, you should complete section A.

Section B – mitigation
If you do not wish to resist the claim for a disqualification order, but would like to adduce mitigating circumstances with a view to justifying only a short period of disqualification, you should complete section B.

Section C - disputing the court's jurisdiction
You should indicate your intention by completing section C and filing an application disputing the court's jurisdiction within 14 days of filing of your acknowledgment of service at the court. The court will arrange a hearing date for the application and tell you and the claimant when and where to attend.

In the Supreme Court of the United Kingdom

Notice of appeal

(or application for permission to appeal)

On appeal from

V

Appeal number

Date of filing / /
D D M M M Y Y Y Y

Appellant's solicitors

Respondent's solicitors

SC001 Notice of appeal (04.09)

1. Appellant

Appellant's full name

Original status

☐ Claimant ☐ Defendant

☐ Petitioner ☐ Respondent

☐ Pursuer ☐ Defender

Solicitor

Name

Address

Telephone no.

Fax no.

DX no.

Postcode

Ref.

Email

How would you prefer us to communicate with you?

☐ DX ☐ Email

☐ Post ☐ Other *(please specify)*

Is the appellant in receipt of public funding/legal aid?

☐ Yes ☐ No

If Yes, please give the certificate number

Counsel

Name

Address

Telephone no.

Fax no.

DX no.

Postcode

Email

Page 2

SC001 Notice of appeal

Counsel

Name

Address | Telephone no.

Fax no.

DX no.

Postcode

Email

2. Respondent

Respondent's full name

Original status

- ☐ Claimant ☐ Defendant
- ☐ Petitioner ☐ Respondent
- ☐ Pursuer ☐ Defender

Solicitor

Name

Address | Telephone no.

Fax no.

DX no.

Postcode | Ref.

Email

How would you prefer us to communicate with you?

- ☐ DX ☐ Email
- ☐ Post ☐ Other *(please specify)*

Is the respondent in receipt of public funding/legal aid?

☐ Yes ☐ No

If Yes, please give the certificate number

Page 3

SC001 Notice of appeal

Counsel

Name

Address

Telephone no.

Fax no.

DX no.

Postcode

Email

Counsel

Name

Address

Telephone no.

Fax no.

DX no.

Postcode

Email

3. Decision being appealed

Name of Court

Names of Judges

Date of order/ interlocutor/decision

/ /
D D M M M Y Y Y Y

Page 4

SC001 Notice of appeal

4. Permission to appeal

If you have permission to appeal complete **Part A** or complete **Part B** if you require permission to appeal.

PART A

Name of Court granting permission

Date permission granted

[ ][ ] / [ ][ ][ ] / [ ][ ][ ][ ]
D D M M M Y Y Y Y

Conditions on which permission granted

PART B

☐ The appellant applies to the Supreme Court for permission to appeal.

Page 5

SC001 Notice of appeal

5. Information about the decision being appealed

Please set out

- Narrative of the facts
- Statutory framework
- Chronology of proceedings
- Orders made in the Courts below
- Issues before the Court appealed from
- Treatment of issues by the Court appealed from
- Issues in the appeal

6. Grounds of appeal

Counsel's name or signature:

7. Other information about the appeal

Are you applying for an extension of time?

☐ Yes ☐ No

If Yes, please explain why

What order are you asking the Supreme Court to make?

Order being appealed ☐ set aside ☐ vary

Original order ☐ set aside ☐ restore ☐ vary

Does the appeal raise issues under the:

Human Rights Act 1998? ☐ Yes ☐ No

Are you seeking a declaration of incompatibility?

☐ Yes ☐ No

Are you challenging an act of a public authority?

☐ Yes ☐ No

If you have answered Yes to any of the questions above please give details below:

Court's devolution jurisdiction? ☐ Yes ☐ No

If Yes, please give details below:

Page 8

SC001 Notice of appeal

Are you asking the Supreme Court to:

depart from one of its own decisions or from one made by the House of Lords?

☐ Yes ☐ No

If Yes, please give details below:

make a reference to the European Court of Justice of the European Communities?

☐ Yes ☐ No

If Yes, please give details below:

Will you or the respondent request an expedited hearing?

☐ Yes ☐ No

If Yes, please give details below:

8. Certificate of Service

Either complete this section or attach a separate certificate

The date on which this form was served on the

1st Respondent ☐☐ / ☐☐☐ / ☐☐☐☐
D D M M M Y Y Y Y

2nd Respondent ☐☐ / ☐☐☐ / ☐☐☐☐
D D M M M Y Y Y Y

I certify that this document was served on

by

by the following method

Signature

9. Other relevant information

Neutral citation of the judgment appealed against e.g. [2009] EWCA Civ 95

References to Law Report in which any relevant judgment is reported.

Subject matter catchwords for indexing.

Please return your completed form to:

The Supreme Court of the United Kingdom, Parliament Square, London SW1P 3BD
DX 157230 Parliament Square 4

Telephone: 020 7960 1991/1992 Fax: 020 7960 1901

email: registry@supremecourt.gsi.gov.uk

www.supremecourt.gov.uk

Page 10

SC001 Notice of appeal

Page 11

SC001 Notice of appeal

Page 12

SC001 Notice of appeal

Click here to reset form | Click here to print form

In the Supreme Court of the United Kingdom

Application form

On appeal from

——— V ———

Appeal number

Date of filing __ __ / __ __ __ / __ __ __ __
D D M M M Y Y Y Y

Applicant's solicitors

Appellant's solicitors

Respondent's solicitors

SC002 Application form (04.09)

1. Details of the applicant

Applicant's full name

Original status
- Claimant
- Defendant
- Intervener
- Petitioner
- Respondent
- Pursuer
- Defender

Solicitor

Name

Address

Telephone no.

Fax no.

DX no.

Postcode

Ref.

Email

How would you prefer us to communicate with you?
- DX
- Email
- Post
- Other *(please specify)*

Counsel

Name

Address

Telephone no.

Fax no.

DX no.

Postcode

Email

Page 2

SC002 Application form

Counsel

Name

Address

Telephone no.

Fax no.

DX no.

Postcode

Email

2. Nature of the application

The applicant applies for

- ☐ Extension of time
- ☐ Permission to intervene
- ☐ Security
- ☐ Order for substituted service
- ☐ Expedited hearing
- ☐ Review of Registrar's decision
- ☐ Other order *(please specify)*

3. Grounds on which application made

On what grounds are you making this application?

Page 4

SC002 Application form

4. Consent to application

The following parties **consent** to this application

See attached letter(s) dated

The following parties **object** to this application

See attached letter(s) dated

5. Other relevant information

Page 5

SC002 Application form

6. Details of the appellant

Appellant's full name

Original status

- Claimant
- Defendant
- Petitioner
- Respondent
- Pursuer
- Defender

Solicitor

Name

Address

Telephone no.

Fax no.

DX no.

Postcode

Ref.

Email

Counsel

Name

Address

Telephone no.

Fax no.

DX no.

Postcode

Email

Page 6

SC002 Application form

Counsel

Name

Address

Telephone no.

Fax no.

DX no.

Postcode

Email

7. Details of the respondent

Respondent's full name

Original status

- ☐ Claimant
- ☐ Defendant
- ☐ Petitioner
- ☐ Respondent
- ☐ Pursuer
- ☐ Defender

Solicitor

Name

Address

Telephone no.

Fax no.

DX no.

Postcode

Ref.

Email

Page 7

SC002 Application form

Counsel

Name

Address

Telephone no.

Fax no.

DX no.

Postcode

Email

Counsel

Name

Address

Telephone no.

Fax no.

DX no.

Postcode

Email

8. Certificate of Service

Either complete this section or attach a separate certificate

On what date was this form served on the

Appellant __ __ / __ __ __ / __ __ __ __
D D M M M Y Y Y Y

Respondent __ __ / __ __ __ / __ __ __ __
D D M M M Y Y Y Y

I certify that this document was served on

by

by the following method

Signature

Page 8

SC002 Application form

9. Details of Registrar's order/decision being appealed

Date of order/decision ☐☐/☐☐☐/☐☐☐☐
D D M M M Y Y Y Y

Click here to reset form | Click here to print form

Page 9

SC002 Application form

Page 10

SC002 Application form

Page 11

SC002 Application form

Please return your completed form to:

The Supreme Court of the United Kingdom, Parliament Square, London SW1P 3BD
DX 157230 Parliament Square 4

Telephone: 020 7960 1991/1992 Fax: 020 7960 1901
email: registry@supremecourt.gsi.gov.uk
www.supremecourt.gov.uk

Click here to reset form | Click here to print form

In the Supreme Court of the United Kingdom

Notice of objection/ Acknowledgement

— V —

Appeal number

Date of filing __ __ / __ __ __ / __ __ __ __
D D M M M Y Y Y Y

Name of respondent

Respondent's solicitors

Name of appellant

Appellant's solicitors

SC003 Notice of objection/Acknowledgement (04.09)

1. Respondent

Respondent's full name

The respondent was served with the

- ☐ application for permission to appeal
- ☐ notice of appeal
- ☐ application

On date ☐☐ / ☐☐☐ / ☐☐☐☐
D D M M M Y Y Y Y

The respondent intends to ask the Court to:

- ☐ refuse to grant permission to appeal
- ☐ order the appellant to give security for costs if permission to appeal is granted
- ☐ dismiss the appeal
- ☐ give the respondent permission to cross-appeal
- ☐ allow the appeal for reasons which are different from, or additional to, those given by the court below
- ☐ Other *(please specify)*

The respondent wishes to receive notice of any hearing date and to be advised of progress. The respondent's details are:

Solicitor

Name

Address

Telephone no.

Fax no.

DX no.

Postcode

Ref.

Email

How would you prefer us to communicate with you?

- ☐ DX
- ☐ Email
- ☐ Post
- ☐ Other *(please specify)*

Page 2

SC003 Notice of objection/Acknowledgement

Counsel

Name

Address

Telephone no.

Fax no.

DX no.

Postcode

Email

Counsel

Name

Address

Telephone no.

Fax no.

DX no.

Postcode

Email

2. Certificate of Service

Either complete this section or attach a separate certificate

On what date was this form served on the

Appellant D D / M M M / Y Y Y Y

Other D D / M M M / Y Y Y Y

I certify that this document was served on

by

by the following method

Signature

Page 3

SC003 Notice of objection/Acknowledgement

3. Other information about the respondent

☐ The respondent is in receipt of public funding/legal aid

Certificate number

☐ The respondent is applying for public funding/legal aid

Information about the respondent's case

Set out here the respondent's grounds of appeal, reasons why permission to appeal should be refused or why the appeal should be allowed. Include information to explain what the respondent intends to ask the Court to do.

Is the respondent seeking a declaration of incompatibility?

☐ Yes ☐ No

☐ The respondent will seek to raise issues under the Human Rights Act 1998 *(please give brief details)*

☐ The respondent will ask the court to make a reference to the European Court of Justice *(please give brief details)*

Click here to reset form | Click here to print form

Page 5

SC003 Notice of objection/Acknowledgement

Please return your completed form to:

The Supreme Court of the United Kingdom, Parliament Square, London SW1P 3BD
DX 157230 Parliament Square 4

Telephone: 020 7960 1991/1992 Fax: 020 7960 1901
email: registry@supremecourt.gsi.gov.uk
www.supremecourt.gov.uk

ADDRESSES

I ROYAL COURTS OF JUSTICE

ADD 1

Royal Courts of Justice	*Telephone*
Strand	
London, WC2A 2LL	
DX: 44450 Strand	020 7947 6000

COURT OF APPEAL

Civil Appeals General Inquiries	020 7947 6409
Civil Appeals Listing	
Appeals and Full Court Applications	020 7947 6917/6195
Applications to a single Lord Justice	020 7947 6409
Applications to the Master	020 7947 6917

ADMIRALTY & COMMERCIAL REGISTRY

Admiralty & Commercial Listing	020 7947 6112
Commercial	020 7947 6826

APPEALS TO THE HIGH COURT

Clerk of the Lists Appeals Office Room WG7	020 7947 7354

QUEEN'S BENCH DIVISION

Actions Department	
Claim forms	020 7947 6528
Judgments & Orders	020 7947 6221
Clerk of the Lists	020 7947 6010
Setting Down	020 7947 6806
Associates Department	020 7947 6298
Masters' Secretary's Department	020 7947 6474
Injunctions outside Court Office hours	020 7947 6260

CHANCERY DIVISION

Bankruptcy	
Registrars Listing	020 7947 6444
Issue Room	020 7947 6448
Chancery Chambers	
Masters Listings	020 7947 7391/6702
Registry	020 7947 6167/6148
Chancery Orders and Accounts	020 7947 7393
Companies Court: winding up, searches and listing	020 7947 7328

General Office	020 7947 6294
Fees Office	020 7947 6527
Injunctions outside Court Office hours	020 7947 6260

FAMILY DIVISION

Principal Registry of the Family Division
First Avenue House
London, WC1V 6NP

DX: 396 Chancery Lane	020 7947 6000
Clerk of the Rules (General Inquiries & listings)	020 7947 6543
Children	
Adoptions	020 7947 7102/6936
Children Section	020 7947 6937/6214/6980
Children's Listing Office	020 7947 7400
Divorce	
Section A, issue of petitions and pleadings	020 7947 6954/6972/7510
Section B, direction for trial and decrees absolute	020 7947 7013/7015/7080
Section C, applications and enforcement	020 7947 6913/6951/7088
Section 5 (Decree Absolute Searches)	020 7947 7016/7017/6051
Probate	
Forms	020 7947 6983
Will and Probate	020 7947 7574/7191
Personal applications	020 7947 7462/6953/7414
Solicitor's applications only	020 7947 7431
Listing	
Clerk of the Rules (Applications to High Court Judges and Circuit Judges sitting in the Royal Courts of Justice)	020 7947 6540/6543
Children's Branch Listing Officer (Applications to District Judges sitting at First Avenue)	020 7947 7400/6069

COURT FUNDS OFFICE

22 Kingsway
London, WC2B 6LE
DX: 44455 Strand — 020 7947 6844

OFFICIAL RECEIVERS' DEPARTMENT

21 Bloomsbury Street
London, WC1B 3SS — 020 7637 1110

PUBLIC GUARDIANSHIP OFFICE

Archway Tower
2 Junction Road
London, N19 5SZ

Funds	020 7947 6654
Statutory Wills and Gifts	020 7664 7000
Other proceedings in the Public Guardianship Office	020 7664 7000
Court Welfare Office	020 7947 6054
Criminal Appeal Office	020 7947 6011/7388
Administrative Court Office (Crown Office)	020 7947 6556/6569
Mechanical Recording Department	020 7947 6154

TECHNOLOGY AND CONSTRUCTION COURT

St Dunstan's House
133–137 Fetter Lane
London, EC4A 1HD
DX: 44450 Strand — 020 7947 6022/7427

COSTS OFFICE & FAMILY PROCEEDINGS DEPARTMENT TAXING BRANCH

Cliffords Inn
Fetter Lane
London, EC4A 1BT
DX: 44454 Strand — 020 7947 6404/7314
020 7947 7493

OFFICIAL SOLICITOR

81 Chancery Lane
London WC2A 1DD
DX: 0012 Chancery Lane — 020 7911 7127

II DISTRICT REGISTRIES AND COUNTY COURTS

ADD 2

The Directory below provides comprehensive information relating to district registries of the High Court, district probate registries and county courts and includes their addresses, telephone, fax and DX numbers, and in the case of district registries and county courts also details of their jurisdiction.

Column 1 gives the name of the court and indicates the type or types of court there, namely: district registry (DR), chancery district registry (CDR), mercantile court (MC), district probate registry (DPR), appeal centre (AC) (where an appeal to the High Court may be managed), hearing only centre (HOC) (where such an appeal may be heard) and county court (CC).

Column 2 gives details of any additional jurisdiction conferred on the local county court by the Civil Courts Order 1983, SI 1983/713 (as amended).

Column 3 gives the address and telephone number and in most cases the fax and document exchange numbers of the court. The fax process may be used for filing at court in accordance with para 5.3 of the Practice Direction supplementing CPR Part 5 (see **CPR PD 5**).

Court, Circuit, Group	Jurisdiction of County Court	Address, Tel, Fax, DX	County Courts within High Court District	County Court Trial Centre and for special jurisdiction	Court to which the district is attached for company and limited liability partnership matters for those courts excluded from that jurisdiction
ABERDARE CC Wales and Chester Circuit South Wales Group	Bankruptcy Company or LLP	The Court House Cwmbach Road Aberdare CF44 0JE Tel: 01685 888575 Fax: 01685 883413 DX: 99600 Aberdare 2		T: Swansea B: Aberdare R: Cardiff	
ABERYSTWYTH DR CC Wales and Chester Circuit South Wales Group	Bankruptcy Company or LLP Divorce Family Hearing Centre	Edleston House Queens Road Aberystwyth SY23 2HP Tel: 01970 617597 Fax: 01970 625985 DX: 99560 Aberystwyth 2	Aberystwyth	T: Swansea B: Aberystwyth R: Cardiff	
ACCRINGTON CC Northern Circuit Preston Group	Divorce	Bradshawgate House 1 Oak Street Accrington Lancashire BB5 1EQ Tel: 01254 237490 Fax: 01254 393869 DX: 702645 Accrington 2		T: Burnley B: Blackburn R: Manchester	Blackburn
ALDERSHOT AND FARNHAM CC Western Circuit – East Group	Divorce	78–82 Victoria Road Aldershot Hampshire GU11 1SS Tel: 01252 321639 Fax: 01252 345705 DX: 98530 Aldershot 2		T: Winchester B: Guildford R: Central London	Guildford

Court, Circuit, Group	Jurisdiction of County Court	Address, Tel, Fax, DX	County Courts within High Court District	County Court Trial Centre and for special jurisdiction	Court to which the district is attached for company and limited liability partnership matters for those courts excluded from that jurisdiction
ALTRINCHAM CC Northern Circuit Outer Manchester Group	Divorce	PO Box 240 Trafford Courthouse Ashton Lane Sale M33 7WX Tel: 0161 975 4760 Fax: 0161 975 4761 DX: 708292 Sale 6		T: Manchester B: Manchester R: Manchester	Manchester
ASHFORD CC South Eastern Circuit (Provincial) Maidstone Group		Ground Floor The Court House Tufton Street Ashford Kent TN23 1QQ Tel: 01233 632464 Fax: 01233 612786 DX: 98060 Ashford (Kent) 3		T: Canterbury B: Canterbury R: Canterbury	Canterbury
AYLESBURY CC South Eastern Circuit (Provincial) Luton Group	Bankruptcy Company or LLP	Aylesbury Magistrates' Court Walton Street Aylesbury Buckinghamshire HP21 7QZ Tel: 01296 554350 Fax: 01296 554320 DX: 149920 Aylesbury 10		T: Luton B: Aylesbury R: Oxford	

Court, Circuit, Group	Jurisdiction of County Court	Address, Tel, Fax, DX	County Courts within High Court District	County Court Trial Centre and for special jurisdiction	Court to which the district is attached for company and limited liability partnership matters for those courts excluded from that jurisdiction
BANBURY CC South Eastern Circuit (Provincial) Kingston & Oxford Group	Bankruptcy Company or LLP	Banbury County Court The Courthouse Warwick Road Banbury Oxfordshire OX16 8BW Tel: 01295 265799 Fax: 01295 277025 DX: 701967 Banbury 2		T: Oxford B: Banbury R: Oxford	
BARNET CC Supreme Court Circuit London County Court Group	Divorce Family Hearing Centre	St Mary's Court Regent's Park Road Finchley London N3 1BQ Tel: 020 8343 4272 Fax: 020 8343 1324 DX: 122570 Finchley (Church End)		T: Central London B: High Court R: Central London	High Court
BARNSLEY DR CC North Eastern Circuit Sheffield Group	Bankruptcy Company or LLP Divorce Family Hearing Centre	12 Regent Street Barnsley S70 2EW Tel: 01226 203471 Fax: 01226 779126 DX: 702080 Barnsley 3	Barnsley	T: Sheffield B: Barnsley R: Leeds	
BARNSTAPLE DR CC Western Circuit – West Group	Bankruptcy Company or LLP Divorce Family Hearing Centre	7th Floor The Civic Centre North Walk Barnstaple Devon EX31 1DY Tel: 01271 372252 Fax: 01271 322968 DX: 98560 Barnstaple 2	Barnstaple	T: Exeter B: Barnstaple R: Exeter	

Court, Circuit, Group	Jurisdiction of County Court	Address, Tel, Fax, DX	County Courts within High Court District	County Court Trial Centre and for special jurisdiction	Court to which the district is attached for company and limited liability partnership matters for those courts excluded from that jurisdiction
BARROW-IN-FURNESS DR CC Northern Circuit Preston Group	Bankruptcy Company or LLP Divorce	County Courthouse Abbey Road Barrow-in-Furness Cumbria LA14 5QX Tel: 01229 840370 Fax: 01229 840371 DX: 63909 Barrow-in-Furness	Barrow-in-Furness	T: Barrow-in-Furness B: Barrow-in-Furness R: Carlisle	
BASILDON CC South Eastern Circuit (Provincial) Chelmsford Group		The Gore Basildon Essex SS14 2EU Tel: 01268 458000 Fax: 01268 458100 DX: 97633 Basildon 5		T: Southend B: Southend R: Central London	
BASINGSTOKE DR CC Western Circuit – East Group	Divorce Family Hearing Centre	3rd Floor Grosvenor House Basing View Basingstoke RG21 4HG Tel: 01256 318200 Fax: 01256 357131 DX: 98570 Basingstoke 3	Basingstoke	T: Winchester B: Reading R: Southampton	Reading
BATH DR CC Western Circuit – West Group	Bankruptcy Company or LLP Divorce Family Hearing Centre	Cambridge House Henry Street Bath BA1 1DJ Tel: 01225 310282 Fax: 01225 480915 DX: 98580 Bath 2	Bath Trowbridge	T: Bristol B: Bath R: Bristol	

Court, Circuit, Group	Jurisdiction of County Court	Address, Tel, Fax, DX	County Courts within High Court District	County Court Trial Centre and for special jurisdiction	Court to which the district is attached for company and limited liability partnership matters for those courts excluded from that jurisdiction
BEDFORD DR CC South Eastern Circuit (Provincial) Luton Group	Bankruptcy Company or LLP Divorce Family Hearing Centre	PO Box 1405 Bedford MK40 9DN Tel: 01234 319001 Fax: 01234 327431 DX: 97590 Bedford 11	Bedford	T: Luton B: Bedford R: Central London	
BIRKENHEAD DR CC Northern Circuit Liverpool Group	Bankruptcy Company or LLP Divorce	76 Hamilton Street Birkenhead Merseyside CH41 5EN Tel: 0151 666 5800 Fax: 0151 666 5873 DX: 725000 Birkenhead 10	Birkenhead	T: Liverpool B: Birkenhead R: Manchester	
BIRMINGHAM CIVIL JUSTICE CENTRE CDR DR MC AC CC Midland Circuit	Appeal Centre Bankruptcy Company or LLP Divorce Care Centre Race Relations Family Hearing Centre	The Priory Courts 33 Bull Street Birmingham B4 6DS Tel: 0121 681 4441 Fax: 0121 681 3001 DX: 701987 Birmingham 7	Birmingham Redditch	T: Birmingham B: Birmingham R: Birmingham	
BIRMINGHAM DPR		5th Floor Priory Street Bull Street Birmingham B4 6JX Tel: 0121 250 6189 Fax: 0121 250 6183 DX: 715208 Birmingham 39			

Court, Circuit, Group	Jurisdiction of County Court	Address, Tel, Fax, DX	County Courts within High Court District	County Court Trial Centre and for special jurisdiction	Court to which the district is attached for company and limited liability partnership matters for those courts excluded from that jurisdiction
BISHOP AUCKLAND CC North Eastern Circuit Teesside Group	Divorce	Woodhouse Close Bishop Auckland County Durham DL14 6LD Tel: 01388 660251 Fax: 01388 660264 DX: 65100 Bishop Auckland 2		T: Teesside B: Durham R: Newcastle-upon-Tyne	Durham
BLACKBURN DR CC Northern Circuit Preston Group	Bankruptcy Divorce Care Centre Family Hearing Centre	64 Victoria Street Blackburn Lancashire BB1 6DJ Tel: 01254 680640 Fax: 01254 692712 DX: 702650 Blackburn 4	Blackburn	T: Preston B: Blackburn	
BLACKPOOL DR CC Northern Circuit Preston Group	Bankruptcy Company or LLP Divorce	The Law Courts Chapel Street Blackpool FY1 5RJ Tel: 01253 754020 Fax: 01253 295255 DX: 724900 Blackpool 10	Blackpool	T: Blackpool B: Blackpool R: Manchester	
BLACKWOOD DR CC Wales and Chester Circuit South Wales Group	Bankruptcy Company or LLP Divorce	Blackwood Road Blackwood South Wales NP12 2XB Tel: 01495 223197 Fax: 01495 220289 DX: 99470 Blackwood 2	Blackwood	T: Cardiff B: Blackwood R: Cardiff	

Court, Circuit, Group	Jurisdiction of County Court	Address, Tel, Fax, DX	County Courts within High Court District	County Court Trial Centre and for special jurisdiction	Court to which the district is attached for company and limited liability partnership matters for those courts excluded from that jurisdiction
BODMIN CC Western Circuit Western Circuit – West Group	Divorce	The Law Courts Launceston Road Bodmin Cornwall PL31 1XQ Tel: 01208 261580 Fax: 01208 77255 DX: 136846 Bodmin 2		T: Truro B: Truro R: Plymouth	Truro
BOLTON COMBINED COURT CENTRE DR CC Northern Circuit Central Manchester Group	Bankruptcy Company or LLP Divorce Family Hearing Centre	The Law Courts Blackhorse Street Bolton BL1 1SU Tel: 01204 392881 Fax: 01204 363204 DX: 702610 Bolton 3	Bolton	T: Bury B: Bolton R: Manchester	
BOSTON DR CC Midland Circuit Notts/Lincs/Derbys Group	Bankruptcy Company or LLP Divorce	The Sessions House Church Close Boston Lincolnshire PE21 6LZ Tel: 01205 366080 Fax: 01205 311692 DX: 701922 Boston 2	Boston Skegness	T: Lincoln B: Boston R: Nottingham	
BOURNEMOUTH COMBINED COURT CENTRE DR CC Western Circuit – East Group	Bankruptcy Company or LLP Divorce Care Centre Family Hearing Centre	Courts of Justice Deansleigh Road Bournemouth Dorset BH7 7DS Tel: 01202 502800 Fax: 01202 502801 DX: 98420 Bournemouth 4	Bournemouth Poole	T: Bournemouth B: Bournemouth R: Southampton	

Court, Circuit, Group	Jurisdiction of County Court	Address, Tel, Fax, DX	County Courts within High Court District	County Court Trial Centre and for special jurisdiction	Court to which the district is attached for company and limited liability partnership matters for those courts excluded from that jurisdiction
BOW CC Supreme Court Circuit London County Court Group	Divorce Family Hearing Centre	96 Romford Road Stratford London E15 4EG Tel: 020 8555 3421 Fax: 020 8503 1152 DX: 97490 Stratford (London) 2		T: Central London B: High Court R: Central London	High Court
BRADFORD COMBINED COURT CENTRE DR CC North Eastern Circuit North & West Yorkshire Group	Bankruptcy Company or LLP Divorce Family Hearing Centre	Bradford Law Courts Exchange Square Drake Street Bradford BD1 1JA Tel: 01274 840274 Fax: 01274 840275 DX: 702083 Bradford 3	Bradford	T: Bradford B: Bradford R: Leeds	
BRECKNOCK DR CC Wales and Chester Circuit South Wales Group	Divorce	Brecon Law Courts Cambrian Way Brecon Powys LD3 7HR Tel: 01685 358206 Fax: 01685 358211 DX: 124340 Brecon 2	Brecknock	T: Swansea B: Merthyr Tydfil R: Cardiff	Merthyr Tydfil
BRENTFORD CC Supreme Court Circuit London County Court Group	Divorce Family Hearing Centre	Alexandra Road Brentford Middlesex TW8 0JJ Tel: 020 8231 8940 Fax: 020 8568 2401 DX: 97840 Brentford 2		T: Central London B: High Court R: Central London	High Court

Court, Circuit, Group	Jurisdiction of County Court	Address, Tel, Fax, DX	County Courts within High Court District	County Court Trial Centre and for special jurisdiction	Court to which the district is attached for company and limited liability partnership matters for those courts excluded from that jurisdiction
BRIDGEND DR CC Wales and Chester Circuit South Wales Group	Bankruptcy Company or LLP Divorce	The Law Courts Sunnyside Bridgend CF31 4AJ Tel: 01656 673833 Fax: 01656 647124 DX: 99750 Bridgend 2	Bridgend Neath and Port Talbot	T: Cardiff B: Bridgend R: Cardiff	
BRIGHTON DR CC South Eastern Circuit (Provincial) Lewes Group	Bankruptcy Company or LLP Divorce Care Centre Family Hearing Centre	William Street Brighton BN2 2RF Tel: 01273 674421 Fax: 01273 602138 DX: 98070 Brighton 3	Brighton Haywards Heath Lewes	T: Brighton B: Brighton R: Central London	
BRIGHTON DPR		William Street Brighton BN2 2LG Tel: 01273 684071 Fax: 01273 625845 DX: 98073 Brighton 3			
BRISTOL DR CDR MC AC CC Western Circuit – West Group	Appeal Centre Bankruptcy Company or LLP Race Relations Divorce Care Centre Family Hearing Centre	Lewins Place Lewins Mead Bristol BS1 2NR Tel: 0117 9106700 Fax: 0117 9106729 DX: 95903 Bristol 3	Bristol Weston super Mare	T: Bristol B: Bristol R: Bristol	

Court, Circuit, Group	Jurisdiction of County Court	Address, Tel, Fax, DX	County Courts within High Court District	County Court Trial Centre and for special jurisdiction	Court to which the district is attached for company and limited liability partnership matters for those courts excluded from that jurisdiction
BRISTOL DPR		Ground Floor The Crescent Centre Temple Back Bristol BS1 6EP Tel: 0117 9273915 Fax: 0117 9253549 DX: 94400 Bristol 5			
BROMLEY CC South Eastern Circuit (Provincial) Maidstone Group	Divorce Family Hearing Centre	Court House College Road Bromley Kent BR1 3PX Tel: 020 8464 9727 Fax: 020 8313 9624 DX: 98080 Bromley 2		T: Croydon B: Croydon R: Central London	Croydon
BURNLEY COMBINED COURT CENTRE DR CC Northern Circuit Preston Group	Bankruptcy Company or LLP Divorce	The Law Courts Hammerton Street Burnley BB11 1XD Tel: 01282 416899 Fax: 01282 414911 DX: 724940 Burnley 4	Accrington Burnley Nelson Rawtenstall	T: Burnley B: Burnley R: Manchester	
BURTON-UPON-TRENT CC Midland Circuit Notts/Lincs/Derbys Group	Bankruptcy Company or LLP Divorce	165 Station Street Burton-upon-Trent Staffordshire DE14 1BP Tel: 01283 568241 Fax: 01283 517245 DX: 702044 Burton-upon-Trent 3		T: Derby B: Burton-upon-Trent R: Birmingham	

Court, Circuit, Group	Jurisdiction of County Court	Address, Tel, Fax, DX	County Courts within High Court District	County Court Trial Centre and for special jurisdiction	Court to which the district is attached for company and limited liability partnership matters for those courts excluded from that jurisdiction
BURY CC Northern Circuit Outer Manchester Group	Bankruptcy Company or LLP Divorce Insolvency	The Court House Tenters Street Bury Lancashire BL9 0HX Tel: 0161 447 8699 Fax: 0161 7634995 DX: 702615 Bury 2	Bury	T: Bury B: Bolton R: Manchester	
BURY ST EDMUNDS DR CC South Eastern Circuit (Provincial) Chelmsford Group	Bankruptcy Company or LLP Divorce	Triton House Entrance B St Andrews Street North Bury St Edmunds IP33 1TR Tel: 01284 753254 Fax: 01284 702687 DX: 97640 Bury St Edmunds 3	Bury St Edmunds	T: Cambridge B: Bury St Edmunds R: Cambridge	
BUXTON CC Midland Circuit Notts/Lincs/Derbys Group		From 1 February 2010, all admin will be processed at: Derby County Court Morledge Derbyshire DE1 2XE Tel: 013 3262 2600 Fax: 013 3262 2543 DX: 724060 Derby 21 Hearings will continue to be held at Peak Buildings, Terrace Road, Buxton, Derbyshire SK17 6DY		T: Derby B: Stockport R: Nottingham	Stockport

Court, Circuit, Group	Jurisdiction of County Court	Address, Tel, Fax, DX	County Courts within High Court District	County Court Trial Centre and for special jurisdiction	Court to which the district is attached for company and limited liability partnership matters for those courts excluded from that jurisdiction
CAERNARFON DR CC Wales and Chester Circuit North Wales & Chester Group	Bankruptcy Company or LLP Divorce Care Centre Family Hearing Centre	Court House Llanberis Road Caernarfon Gwynedd LL55 2DF Tel: 01286 678911 Fax: 01286 678965 DX: 702483 Caernarfon 2	Caernarfon Conwy and Colwyn	T: Chester B: Caernarfon R: Wrexham	
CAMBRIDGE DR CC South Eastern Circuit (Provincial) Chelmsford Group	Bankruptcy Company or LLP Race Relations Divorce Family Hearing Centre	Bridge House Bridge Street Cambridge CB2 1UA Tel: 01223 224500 Fax: 01223 224590 DX: 97650 Cambridge 3	Cambridge	T: Cambridge B: Cambridge R: Cambridge	
CANTERBURY COMBINED COURT CENTRE DR CC South Eastern Circuit (Provincial) Maidstone Group	Bankruptcy Company or LLP Race Relations Divorce Care Centre Family Hearing Centre	The Law Courts Chaucer Road Canterbury Kent CT1 1ZA Tel: 01227 819200 Fax: 01227 819283 DX: 99710 Canterbury 3	Ashford Canterbury	T: Canterbury B: Canterbury R: Canterbury	
CARDIFF CIVIL JUSTICE CENTRE CDR DR AC CC Wales and Chester Circuit South Wales Group	Appeal Centre Bankruptcy Company or LLP Race Relations Divorce Care Centre Family Hearing Centre	2 Park Street Cardiff CF10 1ET Tel: 02920 376400 Fax: 02920 376475 DX: 99500 Cardiff 6	Cardiff	T: Cardiff B: Cardiff R: Cardiff	

Court, Circuit, Group	Jurisdiction of County Court	Address, Tel, Fax, DX	County Courts within High Court District	County Court Trial Centre and for special jurisdiction	Court to which the district is attached for company and limited liability partnership matters for those courts excluded from that jurisdiction
CARDIFF DPR		Probate Registry of Wales PO Box 474 2 Park Street Cardiff CF10 1TB Tel: 02920 376479 Fax: 02920 229855 DX: 122782 Cardiff 13			
CARLISLE COMBINED COURT CENTRE DR HOC CC Northern Circuit Preston Group	Bankruptcy Company or LLP Race Relations Divorce Care Centre Family Hearing Centre Hearing Only Centre	Courts of Justice Earl Street Carlisle Cumbria CA1 1DJ Tel: 01228 520619 Fax: 01228 590588 DX: 65331 Carlisle 2	Carlisle Penrith	T: Carlisle B: Carlisle R: Carlisle	
CARMARTHEN DR CC Wales and Chester Circuit South Wales Group	Bankruptcy Company or LLP Divorce Family Hearing Centre	The Old Vicarage Picton Terrace Carmarthen SA31 1BJ Tel: 01267 242560 Fax: 01267 221844 DX: 99570 Carmarthen 2	Ammanford Carmarthen Llanelli	T: Swansea B: Carmarthen R: Cardiff	
CENTRAL LONDON CIVIL JUSTICE CENTRE CC (See notes) Supreme Court Circuit London County Court Group	Patents Race Relations	13–14 Park Crescent London W1N 4HT Tel: 020 7917 5000 Fax: 020 7917 5014 Fax (for documents needed in court urgently): 020 7917 7940 DX: 97325 Regents Park 2		T: Central London B: High Court R: Central London	

Court, Circuit, Group	Jurisdiction of County Court	Address, Tel, Fax, DX	County Courts within High Court District	County Court Trial Centre and for special jurisdiction	Court to which the district is attached for company and limited liability partnership matters for those courts excluded from that jurisdiction
CHELMSFORD DR HOC CC South Eastern Circuit (Provincial) Chelmsford Group	Bankruptcy Company or LLP Divorce Care Centre Family Hearing Centre Hearing Only Centre	London House New London Road Chelmsford Essex CM2 0QR Tel: 01245 264670 Fax: 01245 496216 DX: 97660 Chelmsford 4	Chelmsford	T: Colchester B: Chelmsford R: Central London	
CHELTENHAM DR CC Western Circuit – West Group	Bankruptcy Company or LLP	The Court House County Court Road Cheltenham GL50 1HB Tel: 01242 519983 Fax: 01242 252741 DX: 98630 Cheltenham 4	Cheltenham	T: Gloucester B: Cheltenham R: Bristol	
CHESTER DR AC CC Wales and Chester Circuit North Wales & Chester Group	Appeal Centre Bankruptcy Company or LLP Divorce Care Centre Family Hearing Centre	Trident House Little St John Street Chester CH1 1SN Tel: 01244 404200 Fax: 01244 404300 DX: 702460 Chester 4	Chester Runcorn	T: Chester B: Chester R: Manchester	
CHESTERFIELD DR CC Midland Circuit Notts/Lincs/Derbys Group	Bankruptcy Company or LLP Divorce	St Mary's Gate Chesterfield Derbyshire S41 7ED Tel: 01246 501200 Fax: 01246 501205 DX: 703160 Chesterfield 3	Chesterfield Worksop	T: Derby B: Chesterfield R: Nottingham	

Court, Circuit, Group	Jurisdiction of County Court	Address, Tel, Fax, DX	County Courts within High Court District	County Court Trial Centre and for special jurisdiction	Court to which the district is attached for company and limited liability partnership matters for those courts excluded from that jurisdiction
CHICHESTER COMBINED COURT CENTRE DR CC South Eastern Circuit (Provincial) Lewes Group	Divorce Family Hearing Centre	Southgate Chichester West Sussex PO19 1SX Tel: 01243 520700 Fax: 01243 533756 DX: 97460 Chichester 2	Chichester	T: Brighton B: Brighton R: Southampton	Brighton
CHORLEY CC Northern Circuit Preston Group	Divorce	59 St Thomas's Road Chorley Lancashire PR7 1JE Tel: 01257 262778 Fax: 01257 232843 DX: 702655 Chorley 3		T: Preston B: Preston R: Manchester	Perston
CLERKENWELL AND SHOREDITCH CC Supreme Court Circuit London County Court Group	Divorce	The Gee Street Courthouse 29-41 Gee Street London EC1V 3RE Tel: 020 7250 7200 Fax: 020 7250 7250 DX: 121000 Shoreditch 2		T: Central London B: High Court R: Central London	High Court
COLCHESTER DR CC South Eastern Circuit (Provincial) Chelmsford Group	Bankruptcy Company or LLP Divorce Family Hearing Centre	Falkland House 25 Southway Colchester Essex CO3 3EG Tel: 01206 572743 Fax: 01206 369610 DX: 97670 Colchester 3	Colchester Clacton	T: Colchester B: Colchester R: Central London	

Court, Circuit, Group	Jurisdiction of County Court	Address, Tel, Fax, DX	County Courts within High Court District	County Court Trial Centre and for special jurisdiction	Court to which the district is attached for company and limited liability partnership matters for those courts excluded from that jurisdiction
CONSETT CC North Eastern Circuit Newcastle Group	Divorce	Victoria Road Consett County Durham DH8 5AU Tel: 01207 502854 Fax: 01207 582626 DX: 65106 Consett 2		T: Newcastle-upon-Tyne B: Newcastle-upon-Tyne R: Newcastle-upon-Tyne	Newcastle-upon-Tyne
CONWY AND COLWYN CC Wales and Chester Circuit North Wales & Chester Group		36 Princes Drive Colwyn Bay North Wales LL29 8LA Tel: 01492 530807 Fax: 01492 533591 DX: 702492 Colwyn Bay		T: Chester B: Caernarfon R: Wrexham	Caernarfon
COVENTRY COMBINED COURT CENTRE DR CC Midland Circuit West Mids/Warks Group	Bankruptcy Company or LLP Divorce Care Centre Family Hearing Centre	140 Much Park Street Coventry CV1 2SN Tel: 02476 536166 Fax: 02476 520443 DX: 701580 Coventry 5	Banbury Coventry Nuneaton Stratford on Avon Warwick	T: Coventry B: Coventry R: Birmingham	
CREWE DR CC Wales and Chester Circuit North Wales & Chester Group	Bankruptcy Company or LLP Divorce Family Hearing Centre	The Law Courts Civic Centre Crewe Cheshire CW1 2DP Tel: 01270 539310 Fax: 01270 216344 DX: 702504 Crewe 2	Crewe Northwich	T: Chester B: Crewe R: Manchester	

Court, Circuit, Group	Jurisdiction of County Court	Address, Tel, Fax, DX	County Courts within High Court District	County Court Trial Centre and for special jurisdiction	Court to which the district is attached for company and limited liability partnership matters for those courts excluded from that jurisdiction
CROYDON COMBINED COURT DR CC South Eastern Circuit (Provincial) Maidstone Group	Bankruptcy Company or LLP Divorce Family Hearing Centre	The Law Courts Altyre Road Croydon Surrey CR9 5AB Tel: 020 8410 4700 Fax: 020 8781 1007 DX: 97473 Croydon 6	Bromley Croydon	T: Croydon B: Croydon R: Central London	
DARLINGTON DR CC North Eastern Circuit Teesside Group	Bankruptcy Company or LLP Divorce Family Hearing Centre	4 Coniscliffe Road Darlington County Durham DL3 7RL Tel: 01325 463224 Fax: 01325 362829 DX: 65109 Darlington 3	Darlington	T: Teesside B: Darlington R: Newcastle-upon-Tyne	
DARTFORD CC South Eastern Circuit (Provincial) Maidstone Group	Family Hearing Centre	Court House Home Gardens Dartford Kent DA1 1DX Tel: 01322 629820 Fax: 01322 270902 DX: 98090 Dartford 2		T: Croydon B: Medway R: Central London	Medway
DERBY COMBINED COURT CENTRE DR CC Midland Circuit Notts/Lincs/Derbys Group	Bankruptcy Company or LLP Divorce Care Centre Family Hearing Centre	Morledge Derby Derbyshire DE1 2XE Tel: 01332 622600 Fax: 01332 622543 DX: 724060 Derby 21	Burton upon Trent Buxton Derby	T: Derby B: Derby R: Nottingham	

Court, Circuit, Group	Jurisdiction of County Court	Address, Tel, Fax, DX	County Courts within High Court District	County Court Trial Centre and for special jurisdiction	Court to which the district is attached for company and limited liability partnership matters for those courts excluded from that jurisdiction
DEWSBURY DR CC North Eastern Circuit North & West Yorkshire Group	Bankruptcy Company or LLP Divorce Family Hearing Centre	Eightlands Road Dewsbury West Yorkshire WF13 2PE Tel: 01924 466135 Fax: 01924 456419 DX: 702086 Dewsbury 2	Dewsbury	T: Huddersfield B: Dewsbury R: Leeds	
DONCASTER DR CC North Eastern Circuit Sheffield Group	Bankruptcy Company or LLP Divorce Family Hearing Centre	74 Waterdale Doncaster South Yorkshire DN1 3BT Tel: 01302 381730 Fax: 01302 768090 DX: 702089 Doncaster 4	Doncaster Rotherham	T: Doncaster B: Doncaster R: Leeds	
DUDLEY DR CC Midland Circuit West Mids/Warks Group	Bankruptcy Company or LLP Divorce Family Hearing Centre	Harbour Buildings Waterfront West Brierley Hill Dudley DY5 1LN Tel: 01384 480799 Fax: 01384 482799 DX: 701949 Dudley 2	Dudley Kidderminster Stourbridge	T: Birmingham B: Dudley R: Birmingham	
DURHAM DR CC North Eastern Circuit Newcastle Group	Bankruptcy Company or LLP Divorce Family Hearing Centre	Hallgarth Street Durham DH1 3RG Tel: 0191 386 5941 Fax: 0191 386 1328 DX: 65115 Durham 5	Bishop Auckland Durham	T: Newcastle-upon-Tyne B: Durham R: Newcastle-upon-Tyne	
EASTBOURNE DR CC South Eastern Circuit (Provincial) Lewes Group	Bankruptcy Company or LLP Divorce	4 The Avenue Eastbourne East Sussex BN21 3SZ Tel: 01323 735195 Fax: 01323 638829 DX: 98110 Eastbourne 2	Eastbourne	T: Brighton B: Eastbourne R: Central London	

Court, Circuit, Group	Jurisdiction of County Court	Address, Tel, Fax, DX	County Courts within High Court District	County Court Trial Centre and for special jurisdiction	Court to which the district is attached for company and limited liability partnership matters for those courts excluded from that jurisdiction
EDMONTON CC Supreme Court Circuit London County Court Group	Divorce Family Hearing Centre	59 Fore Street Edmonton London N18 2TN Tel: 020 8884 6500 Fax: 020 8803 0564 DX: 136686 Edmonton 3		T: Central London B: High Court R: Central London	High Court
EPSOM CC South Eastern Circuit (Provincial) Kingston & Oxford Group	Divorce	The Parade Epsom Surrey KT18 5DN Tel: 01372 721801 Fax: 01372 726588 DX: 97850 Epsom 3		T: Kingston-upon-Thames B: Croydon R: Central London	Croydon
EVESHAM CC Midland Circuit Staff/West Mercia Group		1st Floor 87 High Street Evesham Worcestershire WR11 4EE Tel 01386 442287 Fax: 01386 49203 DX: 701910 Evesham 3		T: Worcester B: Worcester R: Birmingham	Worcester
EXETER CROWN AND COUNTY COURTS DR AC CC Western Circuit – West Group	Appeal Centre Bankruptcy Company or LLP Divorce Family Hearing Centre Race Relations	The Castle Exeter Devon EX4 3PS Tel: 01392 415300 Fax: 01392 415642 DX: 98440 Exeter 2	Exeter	T: Exeter B: Exeter R: Exeter	

Court, Circuit, Group	Jurisdiction of County Court	Address, Tel, Fax, DX	County Courts within High Court District	County Court Trial Centre and for special jurisdiction	Court to which the district is attached for company and limited liability partnership matters for those courts excluded from that jurisdiction
GATESHEAD CC North Eastern Circuit Newcastle Group	Divorce	5th Floor Chad House Tynegate Precinct Gateshead NE8 3HZ Tel: 0191 477 2445 Fax: 0191 477 8562 DX: 65118 Gateshead 2		T: Newcastle-upon-Tyne B: Newcastle-upon-Tyne R: Newcastle-upon-Tyne	Newcastle-upon-Tyne
GLOUCESTER CROWN AND COUNTY COURT DR CC Western Circuit – West Group	Bankruptcy Company or LLP Divorce Family Hearing Centre	Kimbrose Way Gloucester GL1 2DE Tel: 01452 529351 Fax: 01452 386309 DX: 98660 Gloucester 5	Gloucester Chepstow Monmouth	T: Gloucester B: Gloucester R: Bristol	
GOOLE CC		This is now a caller office. It is open to the public from 10am to 4pm every Friday and on District Judge hearing days which are held every other Wednesday. Post and telephone calls relating to Goole County Court matters should be directed to Doncaster County Court			
GRANTHAM CC Midland Circuit Notts/Lincs/Derbys Group		Harlaxton Road Grantham Lincolnshire NG31 7SB Tel: 01476 5390308 Fax: 01476 539040 DX: 701931 Grantham 2		T: Lincoln B: Lincoln R: Nottingham	Lincoln

Court, Circuit, Group	Jurisdiction of County Court	Address, Tel, Fax, DX	County Courts within High Court District	County Court Trial Centre and for special jurisdiction	Court to which the district is attached for company and limited liability partnership matters for those courts excluded from that jurisdiction
GRAVESEND CC South Eastern Circuit (Provincial) Maidstone Group		26 King Street Gravesend Kent DA12 2DU Tel: 01474 321771 Fax: 01474 534811 DX: 98140 Gravesend 2		T: Croydon B: Medway R: Central London	
GREAT GRIMSBY COMBINED COURT CENTRE DR CC North Eastern Circuit Sheffield Group	Bankruptcy Company or LLP Divorce Family Hearing Centre	Town Hall Square Grimsby Lincolnshire DN31 1HX Tel: 01472 265200 Fax: 01472 265201 DX: 702007 Grimsby 3	Great Grimsby	T: Great Grimsby B: Great Grimsby R: Nottingham	
GUILDFORD DR CC South Eastern Circuit (Provincial) Kingston & Oxford Group	Bankruptcy Company or LLP Divorce Care Centre Family Hearing Centre	The Law Courts Mary Road Guildford Surrey GU1 4PS Tel: 01483 595200 Fax: 01483 300031 DX: 97860 Guildford 5	Aldershot & Farnham Epsom Guildford Reigate	T: Kingston-upon-Thames B: Guildford R: Central London	
HALIFAX DR CC North Eastern Circuit North & West Yorkshire Group	Bankruptcy Company or LLP Divorce Family Hearing Centre	Prescott Street Halifax HX1 2JJ Tel: 01422 344700 Fax: 01422 360132 DX: 702095 Halifax 2	Halifax	T: Huddersfield B: Halifax R: Leeds	

Court, Circuit, Group	Jurisdiction of County Court	Address, Tel, Fax, DX	County Courts within High Court District	County Court Trial Centre and for special jurisdiction	Court to which the district is attached for company and limited liability partnership matters for those courts excluded from that jurisdiction
HARLOW DR CC South Eastern Circuit (Provincial) Chelmsford Group	Divorce	Gate House The High Harlow Essex CM20 1UW Tel: 01279 443291 Fax: 01279 451110 DX: 97700 Harlow 2	Harlow Hertford	T: Cambridge B: Hertford R: Central London	Hertford
HARROGATE DR CC North Eastern Circuit North & West Yorkshire Group	Bankruptcy Company or LLP Divorce Family Hearing Centre	2 Victoria Avenue Harrogate HG1 1EL Tel: 01423 503921 Fax: 01423 528679 DX: 702098 Harrogate 3	Harrogate	T: York B: Harrogate	
HARTLEPOOL DR CC North Eastern Circuit Teesside Group	Divorce	The Law Courts Victoria Road Hartlepool TS24 8BS Tel: 01429 268198 Fax: 01429 862550 DX: 65121 Hartlepool 2	Hartlepool	T: Teesside B: Middlesbrough R: Newcastle-upon-Tyne	Middlesbrough
HASTINGS DR CC South Eastern Circuit (Provincial) Lewes Group	Bankruptcy Company or LLP Divorce	The Law Courts Bohemia Road Hastings East Sussex TN34 1QX Tel: 01424 435128 Fax: 01424 421585 DX: 98150 Hastings 2	Hastings	T: Brighton B: Hastings R: Central London	

Court, Circuit, Group	Jurisdiction of County Court	Address, Tel, Fax, DX	County Courts within High Court District	County Court Trial Centre and for special jurisdiction	Court to which the district is attached for company and limited liability partnership matters for those courts excluded from that jurisdiction
HAVERFORDWEST DR CC Wales and Chester Circuit South Wales Group	Bankruptcy Company or LLP Divorce Family Hearing Centre	Penffynnon Hawthorn Rise Haverfordwest SA61 2AZ Tel: 01437 772060 Fax: 01437 769222 DX: 99610 Haverfordwest 2	Haverfordwest	T: Swansea B: Haverfordwest R: Cardiff	
HAYWARDS HEATH CC South Eastern Circuit (Provincial) Lewes Group		Haywards Heath Law Courts Bolnore Road Haywards Heath West Sussex RH16 4BA Tel: 01444 417611 Fax: 01444 472639 DX: 135596 Haywards Heath 6		T: Brighton B: Brighton R: Central London	Brighton
HEREFORD DR CC Midland Circuit Staff/West Mercia Group	Bankruptcy Company or LLP Divorce	First Floor Barclays Bank Chambers 1–3 Broad Street Hereford HR4 9BA Tel: 01432 357233 Fax: 01432 352593 DX: 701904 Hereford 2	Hereford Ludlow Monmouth	T: Worcester B: Hereford R: Birmingham	

Court, Circuit, Group	Jurisdiction of County Court	Address, Tel, Fax, DX	County Courts within High Court District	County Court Trial Centre and for special jurisdiction	Court to which the district is attached for company and limited liability partnership matters for those courts excluded from that jurisdiction
HERTFORD CC South Eastern Circuit (Provincial) Luton Group	Bankruptcy Company or LLP Divorce	4th Floor Sovereign House Hale Road Hertford Hertfordshire SG13 8DY Tel: 01992 503954 Fax: 01992 501274 DX: 97710 Hertford 2		T: Luton B: Hertford R: Central London	
HIGH WYCOMBE CC South Eastern Circuit (Provincial) Kingston & Oxford Group		The Law Courts Ground Floor Easton Street High Wycombe HP11 1LR Tel: 0118 987 0508 Fax: 01494 651030 DX: 98010 Reading 6		T: Reading B: Aylesbury R: Central London	Aylesbury
HITCHIN CC South Eastern Circuit (Provincial) Luton Group	Divorce Family Hearing Centre	Park House 1–12 Old Park Road Hitchin Hertfordshire SG5 1LX Tel: 01462 443750 Fax: 01462 443758 DX: 97720 Hitchin 2		T: Luton B: Luton R: Cambridge	Luton
HORSHAM CC South Eastern Circuit (Provincial) Lewes Group	Divorce	The Law Courts Hurst Road Horsham West Sussex RH12 2EU Tel: 01403 252474 Fax: 01403 258844 DX: 98170 Horsham 2		T: Brighton B: Brighton R: Central London	Brighton

Court, Circuit, Group	Jurisdiction of County Court	Address, Tel, Fax, DX	County Courts within High Court District	County Court Trial Centre and for special jurisdiction	Court to which the district is attached for company and limited liability partnership matters for those courts excluded from that jurisdiction
HUDDERSFIELD DR CC North Eastern Circuit North & West Yorkshire Group	Bankruptcy Company or LLP Divorce Family Hearing Centre	Queensgate House Queensgate Huddersfield HD1 2RR Tel: 01484 421 043 Fax: 01484 426 366 DX: 703013 Huddersfield 2	Huddersfield	T: Huddersfield B: Huddersfield R: Leeds	
HUNTINGDON CC South Eastern Circuit (Provincial) Chelmsford Group		Ground Floor Godwin House George Street Huntingdon PE29 3BD Tel: 01480 450932 Fax: 01480 438397 DX: 96550 Huntingdon 2		T: Northampton B: Peterborough R: Cambridge	Peterborough
ILFORD CC Supreme Court Circuit London County Court Group	Divorce Family Hearing Centre	Buckingham Road Ilford IG1 1TP Tel: 020 8477 1920 Fax: 020 8553 2824 DX: 97510 Ilford 3		T: Central London B: Romford R: Central London	Romford
IPSWICH DR CC DPR South Eastern Circuit (Provincial) Chelmsford Group	Bankruptcy Company or LLP Divorce Care Centre Family Hearing Centre	8 Arcade Street Ipswich Suffolk IP1 1EJ Tel: 01473 214256 Fax: 01473 251797 DX: 97730 Ipswich 3	Ipswich	T: Colchester B: Ipswich R: Cambridge	

Court, Circuit, Group	Jurisdiction of County Court	Address, Tel, Fax, DX	County Courts within High Court District	County Court Trial Centre and for special jurisdiction	Court to which the district is attached for company and limited liability partnership matters for those courts excluded from that jurisdiction
KEIGHLEY DR CC North Eastern Circuit North & West Yorkshire Group	Divorce Family Hearing Centre	Yorkshire Bank Chambers Keighley West Yorkshire BD21 3SH Tel: 01535 602803 Fax: 01535 610549 DX: 703007 Keighley 2	Keighley Skipton	T: Bradford B: Bradford R: Leeds	Bradford
KENDAL DR CC Northern Circuit Preston Group	Bankruptcy Company or LLP Divorce	Burneside Road Kendal Cumbria LA9 4NF Tel: 01539 721218 Fax: 01539 733840 DX: 63450 Kendal 2	Kendal	T: Lancaster B: Kendal R: Carlisle	
KETTERING CC Midland Circuit Leics/Northants Group		Dryland Street Kettering Northamptonshire NN16 0BE Tel: 01536 512471 Fax: 01536 416857 DX: 701886 Kettering 2		T: Northampton B: Northampton R: Birmingham	Northampton
KIDDERMINSTER CC Midland Circuit Staff/West Mercia Group	Bankruptcy Company or LLP	10 Comberton Place Kidderminster DY10 1QR Tel: 01562 822480 Fax: 01562 827809 DX: 701946 Kidderminster 2		T: Birmingham B: Kidderminster R: Birmingham	

Court, Circuit, Group	Jurisdiction of County Court	Address, Tel, Fax, DX	County Courts within High Court District	County Court Trial Centre and for special jurisdiction	Court to which the district is attached for company and limited liability partnership matters for those courts excluded from that jurisdiction
KING'S LYNN DR CC South Eastern Circuit (Provincial) Chelmsford Group	Bankruptcy Company or LLP Divorce Family Hearing Centre	Chequer House 12 King Street King's Lynn Norfolk PE30 1ES Tel: 01553 772067 Fax: 01553 769824 DX: 97740 King's Lynn 2	King's Lynn	T: Norwich B: King's Lynn R: Cambridge	
KINGSTON UPON HULL COMBINED COURT CENTRE DR CC North Eastern Circuit Sheffield Group	Bankruptcy Company or LLP Divorce Care Centre Family Hearing Centre	Lowgate Kingston Upon Hull HU1 2EZ Tel: 01482 586161 Fax: 01482 588527 DX: 703010 Hull 5	Goole Kingston-upon-Hull	T: Kingston-upon-Hull B: Kingston-upon-Hull R: Leeds	
KINGSTON-UPON-THAMES CC South Eastern Circuit (Provincial) Kingston & Oxford Group	Bankruptcy Company or LLP Divorce Family Hearing Centre	St James Road Kingston-Upon-Thames Surrey KT1 2AD Tel: 020 8546 8843 Fax: 020 8547 1426 DX: 97890 Kingston-Upon-Thames 3		T: Kingston-upon-Thames B: Kingston-upon-Thames R: Central London	
LAMBETH CC Supreme Court Circuit London County Court Group		Cleaver Street Kennington Road London SE11 4DZ Tel: 020 7091 4410 Fax: 020 7735 8147 DX: 145020 Kennington 2		T: Central London B: High Court R: Central London	High Court

Court, Circuit, Group	Jurisdiction of County Court	Address, Tel, Fax, DX	County Courts within High Court District	County Court Trial Centre and for special jurisdiction	Court to which the district is attached for company and limited liability partnership matters for those courts excluded from that jurisdiction
LANCASTER DR CC Northern Circuit Preston Group	Bankruptcy Company or LLP Divorce Care Centre	2nd Floor Mitre House Church Street Lancaster LA1 1UZ Tel: 01524 68112 Fax: 01524 846478 DX: 145880 Lancaster 2	Lancaster	T: Lancaster B: Lancaster R: Manchester	
LEEDS COMBINED COURT CENTRE DR CDR MC AC CC North Eastern Circuit North & West Yorkshire Group	Appeal Centre Bankruptcy Company or LLP Divorce Care Centre Family Hearing Centre Race Relations	The Court House 1 Oxford Row Leeds LS1 3BG Tel: 0113 306 2800 Fax: 0113 2452305 DX: 703016 Leeds 6	Leeds	T: Leeds B: Leeds R: Leeds	
LEEDS DPR	Bankruptcy Company or LLP	3rd Floor Coronet House Queen Street Leeds LS1 2BA Tel: 0113 386 3540 Fax: 0113 247 1893 DX: 26451 Leeds Park Square			
LEICESTER DR HOC CC Midland Circuit Leics/Northants Group	Bankruptcy Company or LLP Divorce Care Centre Family Hearing Centre Hearing Only Centre	90 Wellington Street Leicester LE1 6ZZ Tel: 0116 222 5700 Fax: 0116 222 5763 DX: 17401 Leicester 3	Leicester Melton Mowbray	T: Leicester B: Leicester R: Nottingham	

Court, Circuit, Group	Jurisdiction of County Court	Address, Tel, Fax, DX	County Courts within High Court District	County Court Trial Centre and for special jurisdiction	Court to which the district is attached for company and limited liability partnership matters for those courts excluded from that jurisdiction
LEIGH CC Northern Circuit Outer Manchester Group	Divorce	22 Walmesley Road Leigh Greater Manchester WN7 1YF Tel: 01942 673639 Fax: 01942 681216 DX: 702555 Leigh 2		T: Liverpool B: Wigan R: Manchester	Wigan
LEWES COMBINED COURT AC CC South Eastern Circuit (Provincial) Lewes Group	Appeals Centre	The Law Courts High Street Lewes East Sussex BN7 1YB Tel: 01273 480400 Fax: 01273 485269 DX: 97395 Lewes 4		T: Brighton B: Brighton R: Central London	Brighton
LINCOLN COMBINED COURT CENTRE DR HOC CC Midland Circuit Notts/Lincs/Derbys Group	Bankruptcy Company or LLP Divorce Care Centre Family Hearing Centre Hearing Only Centre	360 High Street Lincoln LN5 7PS Tel: 01522 883000 Fax: 01522 883003 DX: 703231 Lincoln 6	Grantham Lincoln Newark	T: Lincoln B: Lincoln R: Nottingham	
LIVERPOOL CIVIL AND FAMILY COURTS DR CDR MC AC CC Northern Circuit Liverpool Group	Bankruptcy Company or LLP Civil Divorce Care Centre Family Hearing Centre	35 Vernon Street Liverpool L2 2BX Tel: 0151 296 2200 Fax: 0151 296 2201 DX: 702600 Liverpool 5	Liverpool	T: Liverpool B: Liverpool R: Manchester	

Court, Circuit, Group	Jurisdiction of County Court	Address, Tel, Fax, DX	County Courts within High Court District	County Court Trial Centre and for special jurisdiction	Court to which the district is attached for company and limited liability partnership matters for those courts excluded from that jurisdiction
LIVERPOOL DPR		Queen Elizabeth II Law Courts Derby Square Liverpool L2 1XA Tel: 0151 236 8264 Fax: 0151 227 4634 DX: 14246 Liverpool 1			
LLANELLI CC Wales and Chester Circuit South Wales Group	Divorce	2nd Floor Court Buildings Town Hall Square Llanelli SA15 3AL Tel: 01554 757171 Fax: 01554 758079 DX: 99510 Llanelli 2		T: Swansea B: Swansea R: Cardiff	
LLANGEFNI DR CC Wales and Chester Circuit North Wales & Chester Group	Bankruptcy Divorce Family Hearing Centre	County Court Buildings Glanhwfa Road Llangefni Anglesey LL77 7EN Tel: 01248 750225 Fax: 01248 750778 DX: 702480 Llangefni 2	Llangefni	T: Chester B: Llangefni R: Wrexham	Swansea
LOWESTOFT DR CC South Eastern Circuit (Provincial) Chelmsford Group	Divorce	Old Nelson Street Lowestoft Suffolk NR32 1HJ Tel: 01502 501060 Fax: 01502 513875 DX: 41219 Lowestoft	Norwich	T: Norwich B: Norwich R: Cambridge	Norwich

Court, Circuit, Group	Jurisdiction of County Court	Address, Tel, Fax, DX	County Courts within High Court District	County Court Trial Centre and for special jurisdiction	Court to which the district is attached for company and limited liability partnership matters for those courts excluded from that jurisdiction
LUDLOW CC Midland Circuit Staff/West Mercia Group		The Guild Hall Mill Street Ludlow Shropshire SY8 1BB Tel: 01584 872091 Fax: 01584 877606 DX: 702013 Ludlow 2	Hereford	T: Telford B: Hereford R: Birmingham	Hereford
LUTON DR AC CC South Eastern Circuit (Provincial) Luton Group	Appeals Centre Bankruptcy Company or LLP Divorce Care Centre Family Hearing Centre	2nd Floor Cresta House Alma Street Luton Bedfordshire LU1 2PU Tel: 01582 506700 Fax: 01582 506701 DX: 97760 Luton 4	Hitchin Luton	T: Luton B: Luton R: Central London	
MACCLESFIELD DR CC Wales and Chester Circuit North Wales & Chester Group	Bankruptcy Company or LLP Divorce Family Hearing Centre	2nd Floor Silk House Park Green Macclesfield SK11 7NA Tel: 01625 412800 Fax: 01625 501262 DX: 702498 Macclesfield 3	Macclesfield	T: Chester B: Macclesfield R: Manchester	
MAIDSTONE COMBINED COURT CENTRE DR HOC CC DPR South Eastern Circuit (Provincial) Maidstone Group	Bankruptcy Company or LLP Divorce Family Hearing Centre Hearing Only Centre	The Law Courts Barker Road Maidstone Kent ME16 8EQ Tel: 01622 202000 Fax: 01622 202001 DX: 130065 Maidstone 7	Maidstone	T: Canterbury B: Maidstone R: Central London	

Court, Circuit, Group	Jurisdiction of County Court	Address, Tel, Fax, DX	County Courts within High Court District	County Court Trial Centre and for special jurisdiction	Court to which the district is attached for company and limited liability partnership matters for those courts excluded from that jurisdiction
MANCHESTER DR CDR MC AC CC Northern Circuit Central Manchester Group	Appeal Centre Bankruptcy Company or LLP Race Relations Divorce Care Centre Family Hearing Centre	The Court House 184-186 Deansgate Manchester M3 3WB Tel: 0161 954 1800 Fax: 0161 954 1661 DX: 702541 Manchester 11	Altrincham Manchester	T: Manchester B: Manchester R: Manchester	
MANCHESTER DPR	Bankruptcy Company or LLP Civil Partnership	9th Floor Astley House 23 Quay Street Manchester M3 4AT Tel: 0161 837 6070 Fax: 0161 832 2690 DX: 14387 Manchester 1			
MANSFIELD DR CC Midland Circuit Notts/Lincs/Derbys Group	Divorce Family Hearing Centre	Mansfield Magistrates' Court Rosemary Street Mansfield Nottingham NG19 6EE Tel: 01623 656406 Fax: 01623 626561 DX: 702180 Mansfield 3	Mansfield	T: Nottingham B: Nottingham R: Nottingham	Nottingham
MAYOR'S AND CITY OF LONDON CC Supreme Court Circuit London County Court Group		Guildhall Buildings Basinghall Street London EC2V 5AR Tel: 020 7796 5400 Fax: 020 7796 5424 DX: 97520 Moorgate EC2		T: Mayor's & City B: High Court R: Central London	

Court, Circuit, Group	Jurisdiction of County Court	Address, Tel, Fax, DX	County Courts within High Court District	County Court Trial Centre and for special jurisdiction	Court to which the district is attached for company and limited liability partnership matters for those courts excluded from that jurisdiction
MEDWAY DR CC South Eastern Circuit (Provincial) Maidstone Group	Bankruptcy Company or LLP Divorce Care Centre Family Hearing Centre	Anchorage House 47–67 High Street Chatham Kent ME4 4DW Tel: 01634 810720 Fax: 01634 811332 DX: 98180 Chatham 4	Dartford Gravesend Medway	T: Canterbury B: Medway R: Central London	
MELTON MOWBRAY CC Midland Circuit Leics/Northants Group		The Court House Norman Way Melton Mowbray Leicestershire LE13 1NH Tel: 01664 485100 Fax: 01664 501869 DX: 701937 Melton Mowbray 2		T: Leicester B: Leicester R: Nottingham	Leicester
MERTHYR TYDFIL COMBINED COURT CENTRE DR CC Wales and Chester Circuit South Wales Group	Bankruptcy Company or LLP Divorce Family Hearing Centre	The Law Courts Glebeland Place Merthyr Tydfil Mid Glamorgan CF47 8BU Tel: 01685 358200 Fax: 01685 359727 DX: 99582 Merthyr Tydfil 2	Merthyr Tydfil	T: Swansea B: Merthyr Tydfil R: Cardiff	
MIDDLESBROUGH (See Teesside)					

Court, Circuit, Group	Jurisdiction of County Court	Address, Tel, Fax, DX	County Courts within High Court District	County Court Trial Centre and for special jurisdiction	Court to which the district is attached for company and limited liability partnership matters for those courts excluded from that jurisdiction
MILTON KEYNES DR CC South Eastern Circuit (Provincial) Luton Group	Bankruptcy Company or LLP Care Centre Family Hearing Centre	351 Silbury Boulevard (Rear) Witan Gate East Milton Keynes MK9 2DT Tel: 01908 668855 Fax: 01908 230063 DX: 136266 Milton Keynes 6	Aylesbury Milton Keynes	T: Luton B: Milton Keynes R: Oxford	
MOLD CC Wales and Chester Circuit North Wales & Chester Group	Bankruptcy Company or LLP	Law Courts Civic Centre Mold Clwyd CH7 1AE Tel: 01352 707330 Fax: 01352 707333 DX: 702521 Mold 2		T: Chester B: Chester R: Wrexham	
MORPETH AND BERWICK CC North Eastern Circuit Newcastle Group	Divorce	Fountain House Newmarket Morpeth NE6 1LA Tel: 01670 512221 Fax: 01670 504188 DX: 65124 Morpeth 2		T: Newcastle-upon-Tyne B: Newcastle-upon-Tyne R: Newcastle-upon-Tyne	Newcastle-uopn-Tyne
NEATH AND PORT TALBOT CC Wales and Chester Circuit South Wales Group	Bankruptcy Company or LLP Divorce	Forster Road Neath West Glamorgan SA11 3BN Tel: 01639 642267/8 Fax: 01639 633505 DX: 99550 Neath 2		T: Swansea B: Neath R: Cardiff	

Court, Circuit, Group	Jurisdiction of County Court	Address, Tel, Fax, DX	County Courts within High Court District	County Court Trial Centre and for special jurisdiction	Court to which the district is attached for company and limited liability partnership matters for those courts excluded from that jurisdiction
NELSON CC Northern Circuit Preston Group	Divorce	Burnley Combined Court The Law Courts Hammerton Street Burnley Lancashire BB11 1XD Tel: 01282 855300 Fax: 01282 414911 DX: 702560 Nelson 2		T: Burnley B: Burnley R: Manchester	
NEWARK CC Midland Circuit Notts/Lincs/Derbys Group		Crown Building 41 Lombard Street Newark Nottinghamshire NG24 1EF Tel: 01636 703607 Fax: 01636 613726 DX: 701928 Newark 2		T: Lincoln B: Nottingham R: Nottingham	Nottingham
NEWBURY CC South Eastern Circuit (Provincial) Kingston & Oxford Group	Bankruptcy Company or LLP	The Court House Mill Lane Newbury Berkshire RG14 5AQS Tel: 01635 40928 Fax: 01635 37704 DX: 30816 Newbury		T: Reading B: Newbury R: Oxford	
NEWCASTLE-UPON-TYNE DR CDR MC AC CC North Eastern Circuit Newcastle Group	Appeals Centre Bankruptcy Company or LLP Race Relations Divorce Care Centre Family Hearing Centre	The Law Courts Quayside Newcastle-upon-Tyne NE1 3LA Tel: 0191 201 2000 Fax: 0191 201 2001 DX: 65128 Newcastle-upon-Tyne 2	Morpeth and Berwick Newcastle-upon-Tyne	T: Newcastle-upon-Tyne B: Newcastle-upon-Tyne R: Newcastle-upon-Tyne	

Court, Circuit, Group	Jurisdiction of County Court	Address, Tel, Fax, DX	County Courts within High Court District	County Court Trial Centre and for special jurisdiction	Court to which the district is attached for company and limited liability partnership matters for those courts excluded from that jurisdiction
NEWCASTLE-UPON-TYNE DPR		2nd Floor Plummer House Croft Street Newcastle-upon-Tyne NE1 6NP Tel: 0191 261 8383 Fax: 0191 230 4868 DX: 601181 Newcastle 1			
NEWPORT (Gwent) DR CC Wales and Chester Circuit South Wales Group	Bankruptcy Company or LLP Divorce Care Centre Family Hearing Centre	5th Floor Clarence House Clarence PLace Newport Gwent NP19 7AA Tel: 01633 245040 Fax: 01633 245041/245043 DX: 99480 Newport (South Wales) 4	Chepstow Monmouth Newport (Gwent) Pontypool	T: Cardiff B: Newport (Gwent) R: Cardiff	
NEWPORT (Isle of Wight) DR CC Western Circuit – East Group	Bankruptcy Company or LLP Divorce	1 Quay Street Newport Isle of Wight PO30 5YT Tel: 01983 526821 Fax: 01983 821039 DX: 98460 Newport (I.o.W.) 2	Newport (I O W)	T: Portsmouth B: Newport (I O W) R: Newport (I O W)	

Court, Circuit, Group	Jurisdiction of County Court	Address, Tel, Fax, DX	County Courts within High Court District	County Court Trial Centre and for special jurisdiction	Court to which the district is attached for company and limited liability partnership matters for those courts excluded from that jurisdiction
NORTHAMPTON DR HOC CC Midland Circuit Leics/Northants Group	Bankruptcy Company or LLP Divorce Care Centre Family Hearing Centre Hearing Only Centre	Combined Court 85–87 Lady's Lane Northampton NN1 3HQ Tel: 01604 470452 Fax: 01604 631853 DX: 725380 Northampton 21	Kettering Northampton Rugby Wellingborough	T: Northampton B: Northampton R: Oxford	
NORTH SHIELDS DR CC North Eastern Circuit Newcastle Group	Divorce	Northumbria House Norfolk Street North Shields Tyne & Wear NE30 1E Tel: 0191 298 2339 Fax: 0191 298 2337 DX: 65137 North Shields 2		T: Newcastle-upon-Tyne B: Newcastle-upon-Tyne R: Newcastle-upon-Tyne	Newcastle-upon-Tyne
NORTHWICH CC Wales and Chester Circuit North Wales & Chester Group		The Court House Chester Way Northwich Cheshire CW9 5ES Tel: 01606 338508 Fax: 01606 48760 DX:702515 Northwich 3		T: Chester B: Crewe R: Manchester	Crewe
NORWICH COMBINED COURT CENTRE DR AC CC South Eastern Circuit (Provincial) Chelmsford Group	Appeals Centre Bankruptcy Company or LLP Divorce Care Centre Family Hearing Centre	The Law Courts Bishopgate Norwich NR3 1UR Tel: 01603 728200 Fax: 01603 760863 DX: 97385 Norwich 5	Norwich	T: Norwich B: Norwich R: Cambridge	

Court, Circuit, Group	Jurisdiction of County Court	Address, Tel, Fax, DX	County Courts within High Court District	County Court Trial Centre and for special jurisdiction	Court to which the district is attached for company and limited liability partnership matters for those courts excluded from that jurisdiction
NOTTINGHAM COMBINED COURT CENTRE DR AC CC Midland Circuit Notts/Lincs/Derbys Group	Appeals Centre Bankruptcy Company or LLP Race Relations Divorce Care Centre Family Hearing Centre	60 Canal Street Nottingham NG1 7EJ Tel: 0115 9103500 Fax: 0115 9103524 DX: 702380 Nottingham 7	Nottingham	T: Nottingham B: Nottingham R: Nottingham	
NUNEATON CC Midland Circuit West Mids/Warks Group		Warwickshire Justice Centre PO Box 3878 Vicarage Street Nuneaton CV11 4WX Tel: 02476 482970 Fax: 02476 352835 DX: 701940 Nuneaton 2		T: Coventry B: Coventry R: Birmingham	Coventry
OLDHAM DR CC Northern Circuit Outer Manchester Group	Bankruptcy Company or LLP Divorce Family Hearing Centre	New Radcliffe Street Oldham OL1 1NL Tel: 0161 290 4200 Fax: 0161 2904222 DX: 702595 Oldham 2	Oldham Tameside	T: Oldham B: Oldham R: Manchester	
OSWESTRY CC Midland Circuit Staff/West Mercia Group		2nd Floor The Guildhall Bailey Head Oswestry Shropshire SY11 1PZ Tel: 01691 652127 Fax: 01691 671239 DX: 701958 Oswestry 2		T: Telford B: Wrexham R: Wrexham	Wrexham

Court, Circuit, Group	Jurisdiction of County Court	Address, Tel, Fax, DX	County Courts within High Court District	County Court Trial Centre and for special jurisdiction	Court to which the district is attached for company and limited liability partnership matters for those courts excluded from that jurisdiction
OXFORD COMBINED COURT CENTRE DR HOC CC South Eastern Cicuit (Provincial) Kingston & Oxford Group	Bankruptcy Company or LLP Race Relations Divorce Care Centre Family Hearing Centre Hearing Only Centre	St Aldates Oxford Oxfordshire OX1 1TL Tel: 01865 264200 Fax: 01865 790773 DX: 96450 Oxford 4	Oxford	T: Oxford B: Oxford R: Oxford	
PENRITH CC Northern Circuit Preston Group	Divorce	The Court Manager The Courts of Justice Earl Street Carlisle Cumbria CA1 1DJ Tel: 01228 882140 Fax: 01228 590588 DX: 65331 Carlisle 2		T: Carlisle B: Carlisle R: Carlisle	Carlisle
PENZANCE CC Western Circuit – West Group	Divorce	Trevear Alverton Terrace Penzance Cornwall TR18 4JH Tel: 01736 362987 Fax: 01736 330595 DX: 136900 Penzance 2		T: Truro B: Truro R: Plymouth	Truro
PETERBOROUGH COMBINED COURT CENTRE DR CC South Eastern Circuit (Provincial) Chelmsford Group	Bankruptcy Company or LLP Divorce Care Centre Family Hearing Centre	Crown Buildings Rivergate Peterborough PE1 1EJ Tel: 01733 349161 Fax: 01733 557348 DX: 702302 Peterborough 8	Huntingdon Peterborough	T: Northampton B: Peterborough R: Cambridge	

Court, Circuit, Group	Jurisdiction of County Court	Address, Tel, Fax, DX	County Courts within High Court District	County Court Trial Centre and for special jurisdiction	Court to which the district is attached for company and limited liability partnership matters for those courts excluded from that jurisdiction
PLYMOUTH COMBINED COURT CENTRE DR HOC CC Western Circuit – West Group	Bankruptcy Company or LLP Race Relations Divorce Care Centre Family Hearing Centre Hearing Only Centre	The Law Courts 10 Armada Way Plymouth Devon PL1 2ER Tel: 01752 208284 Fax: 01752 208286 DX: 98470 Plymouth 7	Plymouth	T: Plymouth B: Plymouth R: Plymouth	
PONTEFRACT DR CC North Eastern Circuit North & West Yorkshire Group	Divorce Family Hearing Centre	Horsefair House Horsefair Pontefract WF8 1RJ Tel: 01977 702357 Fax: 01977 600204 DX: 703022 Pontefract 2	Pontefract	T: Leeds B: Wakefield R: Leeds	Wakefield
PONTYPOOL CC Wales and Chester Circuit South Wales Group		The Court Manager Blackwood Civil and Family Court 8 Hall Street Blackwood Gwent NP12 1NY Tel: 01495 238215 Fax: 01495 238203 DX: 99470 Blackwood 2		T: Cardiff B: Newport (Gwent) R: Cardiff	Newport (Gwent)
PONTYPRIDD DR CC Wales and Chester Circuit Swansea Group	Bankruptcy Company or LLP Divorce Care Centre Family Hearing Centre	The Courthouse Courthouse Street Pontypridd CF37 1JW Tel: 01443 490800 Fax: 01443 480305 DX: 99620 Pontypridd 2	Aberdare Caerphilly Pontypridd	T: Swansea B: Pontypridd R: Cardiff	

Court, Circuit, Group	Jurisdiction of County Court	Address, Tel, Fax, DX	County Courts within High Court District	County Court Trial Centre and for special jurisdiction	Court to which the district is attached for company and limited liability partnership matters for those courts excluded from that jurisdiction
POOLE CC Western Circuit – East Group		The Law Courts Civic Centre Park Road Poole Dorset BH15 2NS Tel: 01202 741150 Fax: 01202 747245 DX: 98700 Poole 4		T: Bournemouth B: Bournemouth R: Southampton	Bournemouth
PORTSMOUTH COMBINED COURT DR CC Western Circuit Western Circuit – East Group	Bankruptcy Company or LLP Divorce Care Centre Family Hearing Centre	The Courts of Justice Winston Churchill Avenue Portsmouth Hampshire PO1 2EB Tel: 023 9289 3000 Fax: 023 9282 6385 DX: 98490 Portsmouth 5	Portsmouth	T: Portsmouth B: Portsmouth R: Southampton	
PRESTON COMBINED COURT CENTRE DR CDR AC CC Northern Circuit Preston Group	Appeals Centre Bankruptcy Company or LLP Divorce	The Law Courts Ringway Preston PR1 2LL Tel: 01772 844700 Fax: 01772 844710 DX: 702660 Preston 5	Chorley Preston	T: Preston B: Preston R: Manchester	
RAWTENSTALL CC Northern Circuit Preston Group	Divorce	1 Grange Street Rawtenstall Lancashire BB4 7RT Tel: 01706 214614 Fax: 01706 219814 DX: 702565 Rawtenstall 1		T: Burnley B: Burnley R: Manchester	Burnley

Court, Circuit, Group	Jurisdiction of County Court	Address, Tel, Fax, DX	County Courts within High Court District	County Court Trial Centre and for special jurisdiction	Court to which the district is attached for company and limited liability partnership matters for those courts excluded from that jurisdiction
READING DR AC CC South Eastern Circuit (Provincial) Kingston & Oxford Group	Appeals Centre Bankruptcy Company or LLP Divorce Care Centre Family Hearing Centre	160–163 Friar Street Reading Berkshire RG1 1HE Tel: 0118 9870500 Fax: 0118 9599827 DX: 98010 Reading 6	Newbury Reading Slough	T: Reading B: Reading R: Oxford	
REDDITCH CC Midland Circuit Staff/West Mercia Group		13 Church Road Redditch Worcestershire B97 4AB Tel: 01527 67822 Fax: 01527 65791 DX: 701880 Redditch 2		T: Worcester B: Birmingham R: Birmingham	Birmingham
REIGATE CC South Eastern Circuit (Provincial) Kingston & Oxford Group	Divorce	The Law Courts Hatchlands Road Redhill RH1 6BL Tel: 01737 763637 Fax: 01737 766917 DX: 98020 Redhill West		T: Kingston-upon-Thames B: Croydon R: Central London	
RHYL DR CC Wales and Chester Circuit North Wales & Chester Group	Bankruptcy Company or LLP Divorce Care Centre Family Hearing Centre	The Court House Clwyd Street Rhyl Denbighshire LL18 3LA Tel: 01745 352940 Fax: 01745 336726 DX: 702489 Rhyl 2	Rhyl	T: Chester B: Rhyl R: Wrexham	

Court, Circuit, Group	Jurisdiction of County Court	Address, Tel, Fax, DX	County Courts within High Court District	County Court Trial Centre and for special jurisdiction	Court to which the district is attached for company and limited liability partnership matters for those courts excluded from that jurisdiction
ROMFORD DR CC Supreme Court Circuit London County Court Group	Bankruptcy Company or LLP Divorce Family Hearing Centre	2a Oaklands Avenue Romford Essex RM1 4DP Tel: 01708 775353 Fax: 01708 756653 DX: 97530 Romford 2	Basildon Gray's Thurrock Ilford Romford	B: Romford R: Central London	
ROTHERHAM CC North Eastern Circuit Sheffield Group	Divorce Family Hearing Centre	Portland House Mansfield Road Rotherham S60 2BX Tel: 01709 364786 Fax: 01709 838044 DX: 703025 Rotherham 4		T: Sheffield B: Sheffield R: Leeds	Sheffield
RUGBY CC Midland Circuit West Mids/Warks Group		5 Newbold Road Rugby CV21 2RN Tel: 01788 542543 Fax: 01788 550212 DX: 701934 Rugby 2		T: Coventry B: Coventry R: Birmingham	Coventry
RUNCORN CC Wales and Chester Circuit North Wales & Chester Group	Divorce	The Law Courts Halton Lea Runcorn Cheshire WA7 2HA Tel: 01925 256703 Fax: 01925 413335 DX: 702501 Warrington 3		T: Chester B: Warrington R: Manchester	Warrington

Court, Circuit, Group	Jurisdiction of County Court	Address, Tel, Fax, DX	County Courts within High Court District	County Court Trial Centre and for special jurisdiction	Court to which the district is attached for company and limited liability partnership matters for those courts excluded from that jurisdiction
ST ALBANS HOC CC South Eastern Circuit (Provincial) Luton Group	Bankruptcy Company or LLP Hearing Only Centre	Victoria House Victoria Street St Albans Hertfordshire AL1 3TJ Tel: 0844 892 0550 Fax: 01462 445444 DX: 97770 St Albans 2		T: Luton B: St Albans R: Central London	
ST HELENS DR CC Northern Circuit Liverpool Group	Divorce	1st Floor Rexmore House Cotham Street St Helens Merseyside WA10 1SE Tel: 01744 27544 Fax: 01744 20484 DX: 725020 St Helens 2	St Helens	T: Liverpool B: Liverpool R: Manchester	Liverpool
SALFORD DR CC Northern Circuit Outer Manchester Group	Bankruptcy Company or LLP Divorce	Prince William House Peel Cross Road Salford M5 2RR Tel: 0161 745 7511 Fax: 0161 745 7202 DX: 702630 Salford 5	Salford	T: Manchester B: Salford R: Manchester	
SALISBURY COMBINED COURT CENTRE DR CC Western Circuit – East Group	Bankruptcy Company or LLP Divorce Family Hearing Centre	The Courts of Justice Alexandra House St John Street Salisbury Wiltshire SP1 2PN Tel: 01722 325444 Fax: 01722 412991 DX: 98500 Salisbury 2	Salisbury	T: Swindon B: Salisbury R: Southampton	

Court, Circuit, Group	Jurisdiction of County Court	Address, Tel, Fax, DX	County Courts within High Court District	County Court Trial Centre and for special jurisdiction	Court to which the district is attached for company and limited liability partnership matters for those courts excluded from that jurisdiction
SCARBOROUGH DR CC North Eastern Circuit North & West Yorkshire Group	Bankruptcy Company or LLP Divorce Family Hearing Centre	Pavilion House Valley Bridge Road Scarborough North Yorkshire YO11 2JS Tel: 01723 366361 Fax: 01723 501992 DX: 65140 Scarborough 2	Scarborough	T: York B: Scarborough R: Leeds	
SCUNTHORPE DR CC North Eastern Circuit Sheffield Group	Bankruptcy Company or LLP Divorce	Crown Buildings Comforts Avenue Scunthorpe DN15 6PR Tel: 01724 289111 Fax: 01724 291119 DX: 702010 Scunthorpe 3	Scunthorpe	T: Great Grimsby B: Scunthorpe R: Nottingham	
SHEFFIELD COMBINED COURT CENTRE DR AC CC North Eastern Circuit Sheffield Group	Appeals Centre Bankruptcy Company or LLP Divorce Care Centre Family Hearing Centre	The Law Courts 50 West Bar Sheffield S3 8PH Tel: 0114 281 2400 Fax: 0114 281 2425 DX: 703028 Sheffield 6	Sheffield	T: Sheffield B: Sheffield R: Leeds	
SHREWSBURY DR CC Midland Circuit Staff/West Mercia Group	Bankruptcy Company or LLP Divorce	4th Floor Cambrian Business Centre Chester Street Shrewsbury Shropshire SY1 1NA Tel: 01743 289069 Fax: 01743 237954 DX: 702047 Shrewsbury 3	Shrewsbury Telford	T: Telford B: Shrewsbury R: Birmingham	

Court, Circuit, Group	Jurisdiction of County Court	Address, Tel, Fax, DX	County Courts within High Court District	County Court Trial Centre and for special jurisdiction	Court to which the district is attached for company and limited liability partnership matters for those courts excluded from that jurisdiction
SKEGNESS CC Midland Circuit Notts/Lincs/Derbys Group		55 Norfolk Street Boston Lincolnshire PE21 6PE Tel: 01205 366080 Fax: 01205 311692 DX: 701922 Boston 2		T: Lincoln B: Boston R: Nottingham	Boston
SKIPTON CC North Eastern Circuit North & West Yorkshire Group	Divorce Family Hearing Centre	The Old Court House Otley Street Skipton North Yorkshire BD23 1EH Tel: 01756 692650 Fax: 01756 799989 DX: 703031 Skipton 2		T: Bradford B: Bradford R: Leeds	Bradford
SLOUGH CC South Eastern Circuit (Provincial) Kingston & Oxford Group	Bankruptcy Company or LLP Divorce Family Hearing Centre	The Law Courts Windsor Road Slough Berkshire SL1 2HE Tel: 01753 690300 Fax: 01753 575990 DX: 98030 Slough 3		T: Reading B: Slough R: Central London	
SOUTHAMPTON COMBINED COURT CENTRE DR CC Western Circuit Western Circuit – East Group	Admiralty Bankruptcy Company or LLP Race Relations Divorce Family Hearing Centre	The Courts of Justice London Road Southampton Hampshire SO15 2XQ Tel: 023 8021 3200 Fax: 023 8021 3222 DX: 111000 Southampton 11	Southampton	T: Southampton B: Southampton R: Southampton	

Court, Circuit, Group	Jurisdiction of County Court	Address, Tel, Fax, DX	County Courts within High Court District	County Court Trial Centre and for special jurisdiction	Court to which the district is attached for company and limited liability partnership matters for those courts excluded from that jurisdiction
SOUTHEND DR CC South Eastern Circuit (Provincial) Chelmsford Group	Bankruptcy Company or LLP Divorce Family Hearing Centre	Tylers House Tylers Avenue Southend Essex SS1 2AW Tel: 01702 601991 Fax: 01702 603090 DX: 97780 Southend on Sea 2	Southend-on-Sea	T: Southend B: Southend R: Central London	
SOUTHPORT DR CC Northern Circuit Liverpool Group	Divorce	Dukes House 34 Hoghton Street Southport Merseyside PR9 0PU Tel: 01704 531541 Fax: 01704 542487 DX: 702580 Southport 2	Southport	T: Liverpool B: Liverpool R: Manchester	Liverpool
SOUTH TYNESIDE MAGISTRATES' COURT DR CC North Eastern Circuit Newcastle Group	Divorce	Secretan Way South Shields Tyne and Wear NE33 Tel: 0191 456 3343 Fax: 0191 427 9503 DX: 65143 South Shields 3	North Shields South Shields	T: Newcastle-upon-Tyne B: Sunderland R: Newcastle-upon-Tyne	
STAFFORD COMBINED COURT CENTRE DR HOC CC Midland Circuit Staff/West Mercia Group	Bankruptcy Company or LLP Divorce Family Hearing Centre Hearing Only Centre	Victoria Square Stafford ST16 2QQ Tel: 01785 610730 Fax: 01785 213250 DX: 703190 Stafford 4	Stafford	T: Stoke-on-Trent B: Stafford R: Birmingham	

Court, Circuit, Group	Jurisdiction of County Court	Address, Tel, Fax, DX	County Courts within High Court District	County Court Trial Centre and for special jurisdiction	Court to which the district is attached for company and limited liability partnership matters for those courts excluded from that jurisdiction
STAINES CC South Eastern Circuit (Provincial) Kingston & Oxford Group	Divorce	The Law Courts Knowle Green Staines Middlesex TW18 1XH Tel: 01784 459175 Fax: 01784 460176 DX: 98040 Staines 2		T: Kingston-upon-Thames B: Kingston-upon-Thames R: Central London	Kingston-upon-Thames
STOCKPORT DR CC Northern Circuit Outer Manchester Group	Bankruptcy Company or LLP Divorce Family Hearing Centre	5th Floor Heron House Wellington Street Stockport SK1 3OJ Tel: 0161 747707 Fax: 0161 763129 DX: 702620 Stockport 4	Stockport	T: Oldham B: Stockport R: Manchester	
STOKE-ON-TRENT COMBINED COURT CENTRE DR CC Midland Circuit Staff/West Mercia Group	Bankruptcy Company or LLP Divorce Care Centre Family Hearing Centre	Bethesda Street Hanley Stoke-on-Trent Staffordshire ST1 3BP Tel: 01782 854000 Fax: 01782 854046 DX: 703363 Hanley 3	Stoke-on-Trent	T: Stoke-on-Trent B: Stoke-on-Trent R: Birmingham	
STOURBRIDGE CC Midland Circuit West Mids/Warks Group	Bankruptcy Company or LLP	7 Hagley Road Stourbridge West Midlands DY8 1QL Tel: 01384 394232 Fax: 01384 441736 DX: 701889 Stourbridge 2		T: Birmingham B: Stourbridge R: Birmingham	

Court, Circuit, Group	Jurisdiction of County Court	Address, Tel, Fax, DX	County Courts within High Court District	County Court Trial Centre and for special jurisdiction	Court to which the district is attached for company and limited liability partnership matters for those courts excluded from that jurisdiction
STRATFORD-UPON-AVON CC Midland Circuit West Mids/Warks Group		5 Elm Court Arden Street Stratford-upon-Avon CV37 6PA Tel: 01789 293056 Fax: 01789 293056 DX: 701998 Stratford-upon-Avon 3		T: Coventry B: Warwick R: Birmingham	Warwick
SUNDERLAND DR CC North Eastern Circuit Newcastle Group	Bankruptcy Company or LLP Divorce Care Centre Family Hearing Centre	44 John Street Sunderland Tyne and Wear SR1 1RB Tel: 0191 568 0750 Fax: 0191 514 3028 DX: 65149 Sunderland 2	Consett Gateshead Sunderland	T: Newcastle-upon-Tyne B: Sunderland R: Newcastle-upon-Tyne	
SWANSEA CIVIL JUSTICE CENTRE DR AC CC Wales and Chester Circuit South Wales Group	Appeals Centre Bankruptcy Company or LLP Divorce Care Centre Family Hearing Centre	Caravella House Quay West Quay Street Swansea West Glamorgan SA1 1SP Tel: 01792 510350 Fax: 01792 473520 DX: 99740 Swansea 5	Swansea	T: Swansea B: Swansea R: Cardiff	
SWINDON COMBINED COURT CENTRE DR CC Western Circuit – East Group	Bankruptcy Company or LLP Divorce Care Centre Family Hearing Centre	The Law Courts Islington Street Swindon Wiltshire SN1 2HG Tel: 01793 690500 Fax: 01793 690555 DX: 98430 Swindon 5	Swindon	T: Swindon B: Swindon R: Bristol	

Court, Circuit, Group	Jurisdiction of County Court	Address, Tel, Fax, DX	County Courts within High Court District	County Court Trial Centre and for special jurisdiction	Court to which the district is attached for company and limited liability partnership matters for those courts excluded from that jurisdiction
TAMESIDE CC Northern Circuit Outer Manchester Group	Bankruptcy Company or LLP Divorce	PO Box 166 Henry Square Ashton-under-Lyme Lancashire OL6 7TP Tel: 0161 339 1711 Fax: 0161 339 1645 DX: 702625 Ashton-under-Lyne 2		T: Oldham B: Tameside R: Manchester	
TAMWORTH CC Midland Circuit Staff/West Mercia Group		1st Floor, The Court House Spinning School Lane Tamworth Staffordshire B79 7AP Tel: 01827 305910 Fax: 01827 303823 DX: 702016 Tamworth 2		T: Stoke-on-Trent B: Birmingham R: Birmingham	Birmingham
TAUNTON COMBINED COURT CENTRE DR CC Western Circuit – West Group	Bankruptcy Company or LLP Divorce Care Centre Family Hearing Centre	The Shire Hall Taunton Somerset TA1 4EU Tel: 01823 335972 Fax: 01823 351337 DX: 98410 Taunton 2	Taunton	T: Taunton B: Taunton R: Bristol	
TEESSIDE COMBINED COURT CENTRE DR HOC CC North Eastern Circuit Teesside Group	Bankruptcy Company or LLP Divorce Care Centre Family Hearing Centre Hearing Only Centre	The Law Courts Russell Street Middlesbrough Cleveland TS1 2AE Tel: 01642 340000 Fax: 01642 340002 DX: 65152 Middlesbrough 2	Middlesbrough	T: Teesside B: Teesside R: Newcastle-upon-Tyne	

Court, Circuit, Group	Jurisdiction of County Court	Address, Tel, Fax, DX	County Courts within High Court District	County Court Trial Centre and for special jurisdiction	Court to which the district is attached for company and limited liability partnership matters for those courts excluded from that jurisdiction
TELFORD CC Midland Circuit Staff/West Mercia Group	Divorce Care Centre Family Hearing Centre	Telford Square Malinsgate Town Centre Telford Shropshire TF3 4JP Tel: 01952 291045 Fax: 01952 291601 DX: 701976 Telford 3		T: Telford B: Shrewsbury R: Birmingham	Shrewsbury
THANET DR CC South Eastern Circuit (Provincial) Maidstone Group	Divorce	The Court House 2nd Floor Cecil Square Margate Kent CT9 1RL Tel: 01843 221722 Fax: 01843 222730 DX: 98210 Cliftonville 2	Thanet	T: Canterbury B: Canterbury R: Canterbury	
TORQUAY AND NEWTON ABBOTT Western Circuit – West Group	Bankruptcy Company or LLP Divorce	The Willows Nicholson Road Torquay Devon TQ2 7AZ Tel: 01803 616 791 Fax: 01803 616 795 DX: 98740 Torquay 4	Torquay	T: Exeter B: Torquay R: Exeter	
TROWBRIDGE CC Western Circuit – East Group	Divorce	Ground Floor Clarks Mill Stallard Street Trowbridge Wiltshire BA14 8DB Tel: 01225 752101 Fax: 01225 776638 DX: 98750 Trowbridge 2		T: Swindon B: Bath R: Bristol	Bath

Court, Circuit, Group	Jurisdiction of County Court	Address, Tel, Fax, DX	County Courts within High Court District	County Court Trial Centre and for special jurisdiction	Court to which the district is attached for company and limited liability partnership matters for those courts excluded from that jurisdiction
TRURO DR HOC CC Western Circuit – West Group	Bankruptcy Company or LLP Divorce Care Centre Family Hearing Centre Hearing Only Centre	Courts of Justice Edward Street Truro TR1 2PB Tel: 01872 222340 Fax: 01872 222348 DX: 135396 Truro 2	Bodmin Penzance Truro	T: Truro B: Truro R: Plymouth	
TUNBRIDGE WELLS DR CC South Eastern Circuit (Provincial) Maidstone Group	Bankruptcy Company or LLP Divorce	Merevale House 42–46 London Road Tunbridge Wells Kent TN1 1DP Tel: 01892 515515 Fax: 01892 513676 DX: 98220 Tunbridge Wells 3	Tunbridge Wells	T: Croydon B: Tunbridge Wells R: Central London	
UXBRIDGE CC South Eastern Circuit (Provincial) Kingston & Oxford Group	Divorce	501 Uxbridge Road Hayes Middlesex UB4 8HL Tel: 020 8561 8562 Fax: 020 8561 2020 DX: 44658 Hayes (Middlesex)		T: Reading B: Slough R: Central London	Slough
WAKEFIELD DR CC North Eastern Circuit North & West Yorkshire Group	Bankruptcy Company or LLP Divorce Family Hearing Centre	Crown House 127 Kirkgate Wakefield WF1 1JW Tel: 01924 370268 Fax: 01924 200818 DX: 703040 Wakefield 3	Wakefield	T: Leeds B: Wakefield R: Leeds	

Court, Circuit, Group	Jurisdiction of County Court	Address, Tel, Fax, DX	County Courts within High Court District	County Court Trial Centre and for special jurisdiction	Court to which the district is attached for company and limited liability partnership matters for those courts excluded from that jurisdiction
WALSALL DR CC Midland Circuit West Mids/Warks Group	Bankruptcy Company or LLP Divorce Family Hearing Centre	Bridge House Bridge Street Walsall WS1 1JQ Tel: 01922 728855 Fax: 01922 728891 DX: 701943 Walsall 2	Tamworth Walsall	T: Stoke-on-Trent B: Walsall R: Birmingham	
WANDSWORTH CC Supreme Court Circuit London County Court Group	Divorce Family Hearing Centre	76–78 Upper Richmond Road Putney London SW15 2SU Tel: 020 8333 4351 Fax: 020 8877 9854 DX: 97540 Putney 2		T: Central London B: High Court R: Central London	High Court
WARRINGTON COMBINED COURT CENTRE DR CC Wales and Chester Circuit North Wales & Chester Group	Bankruptcy Company or LLP Divorce Care Centre Family Hearing Centre	The Law Courts Legh Street Warrington WA1 1UR Tel: 01925 256700 Fax: 01925 413335 DX: 702501 Warrington 3	Warrington	T: Chester B: Warrington R: Manchester	
WARWICK COMBINED COURT CENTRE CC Midland Circuit West Mids/Warks Group	Bankruptcy Company or LLP	Northgate Southside Warwick Warwickshire CV34 4RB Tel: 01926 495428 Fax: 01926 401266 DX: 701964 Warwick 2		T: Coventry B: Warwick R: Birmingham	

Court, Circuit, Group	Jurisdiction of County Court	Address, Tel, Fax, DX	County Courts within High Court District	County Court Trial Centre and for special jurisdiction	Court to which the district is attached for company and limited liability partnership matters for those courts excluded from that jurisdiction
WATFORD CC South Eastern Circuit (Provincial) Luton Group	Divorce Care Centre Family Hearing Centre	Cassiobury House 11–19 Station Road Watford Hertfordshire WD17 1EZ Tel: 0844 892 0550 Fax: 01923 251317 DX: 122740 Watford 5		T: Luton B: St Albans R: Central London	St Albans
WELLINGBOROUGH CC Midland Circuit Leics/Northants Group		Lothersdale House West Villa Road Wellingborough NN8 4NF Tel: 01933 226168 Fax: 01933 272977 DX: 701883 Wellingborough 2		T: Northampton B: Northampton R: Birmingham	Northampton
WELSHPOOL AND NEWTOWN DR CC Wales and Chester Circuit North Wales & Chester Group	Bankruptcy Company or LLP Divorce Family Hearing Centre	Town Hall Broad Street Welshpool Powys SY2 7TX Tel: 01938 552004 Fax: 01938 555395 DX: 702524 Welshpool 2	Welshpool	T: Chester B: Welshpool R: Wrexham	
WEST LONDON CC Supreme Court Circuit London County Court Group		West London Courthouse Magistrates, County and Youth Courts 181 Talgarth Road Hammersmith London W6 8DN Tel: 020 8600 6868 Fax: 020 8600 6860 DX: 97550 Hammersmith 8		T: Central London B: High Court R: Central London	High Court

Court, Circuit, Group	Jurisdiction of County Court	Address, Tel, Fax, DX	County Courts within High Court District	County Court Trial Centre and for special jurisdiction	Court to which the district is attached for company and limited liability partnership matters for those courts excluded from that jurisdiction
WESTON-SUPER-MARE CC Western Circuit – West Group	Divorce	North Somerset Courthouse The Hedges St Georges Weston-super-Mare BS22 7BB Tel: 01934 528686 Fax: 01934 528594 DX: 152361 Weston-super-Mare 5		T: Bristol B: Bristol R: Bristol	Bristol
WEYMOUTH AND DORCHESTER COMBINED COURT CENTRE DR CC Western Circuit – East Group	Bankruptcy Company or LLP Divorce Family Hearing Centre	2nd Floor Westwey House Westwey Road Weymouth Dorset DT4 8TE Tel: 01305 778684 Fax: 01305 788293 DX: 98820 Weymouth 3	Weymouth	T: Bournemouth B: Weymouth R: Southampton	
WHITEHAVEN CC Northern Circuit Preston Group	Bankruptcy Company or LLP Divorce	Old Town Hall Duke Street Whitehaven Cumbria CA28 7NU Tel: 01946 67788 Fax: 01946 691219 DX: 63990 Whitehaven 2		T: Carlisle R: Carlisle	

Court, Circuit, Group	Jurisdiction of County Court	Address, Tel, Fax, DX	County Courts within High Court District	County Court Trial Centre and for special jurisdiction	Court to which the district is attached for company and limited liability partnership matters for those courts excluded from that jurisdiction
WIGAN DR CC Northern Circuit Outer Manchester Group	Bankruptcy Company or LLP Divorce	Wigan & Leigh Courthouse Darlington Street Wigan WN1 1DW Tel: 01942 405405 Fax: 01942 405499 DX: 724820 Wigan 9	Leigh Wigan	R: Manchester T: Liverpool B: Wigan	
WILLESDEN CC Supreme Court Circuit London County Court Group	Divorce Family Hearing Centre	9 Acton Lane Harlesden London NW10 8SB Tel: 020 8963 8200 Fax: 020 8453 0946 DX: 97560 Harlesden 2		T: Central London B: High Court R: Central London	
WINCHESTER COMBINED COURT CENTRE DR AC CC Western Circuit – East Group	Appeals Centre Bankruptcy Company or LLP Divorce	The Law Courts Winchester Hampshire SO23 9EL Tel: 01962 814100 Fax: 01962 853821 DX: 98520 Winchester 3	Winchester	T: Winchester B: Winchester R: Southampton	

Court, Circuit, Group	Jurisdiction of County Court	Address, Tel, Fax, DX	County Courts within High Court District	County Court Trial Centre and for special jurisdiction	Court to which the district is attached for company and limited liability partnership matters for those courts excluded from that jurisdiction
WINCHESTER DPR		4th Floor Cromwell House Andover Road Winchester SO23 7EW Tel: 01962 897024 Fax: 01962 840796 DX: 96900 Winchester 2			
WOLVERHAMPTON COMBINED COURT CENTRE DR CC Midland Circuit West Mids/Warks Group	Bankruptcy Company or LLP Divorce Care Centre Family Hearing Centre	Pipers Row Wolverhampton WV1 3LQ Tel: 01902 481000 Fax: 01902 481076 DX: 702019 Wolverhampton 4	Wolverhampton	T: Telford B: Wolverhampton R: Birmingham	
WOOLWICH CC Supreme Court Circuit London County Court Group		165 Powis Street Woolwich London SE18 8JW Tel: 020 8854 2127 Fax: 020 8316 4842 DX: 123450 Woolwich 8		T: Central London B: Croydon R: Central London	Croydon
WORCESTER DR CC Midland Circuit Staff/West Mercia Group	Bankruptcy Company or LLP Divorce Care Centre Family Hearing Centre	The Shirehall Foregate Street Worcester WR1 1EQ Tel: 01905 730807 Fax: 01905 730801 DX: 721120 Worcester 1	Evesham Worcester	T: Worcester B: Worcester R: Birmingham	

Court, Circuit, Group	Jurisdiction of County Court	Address, Tel, Fax, DX	County Courts within High Court District	County Court Trial Centre and for special jurisdiction	Court to which the district is attached for company and limited liability partnership matters for those courts excluded from that jurisdiction
WORKINGTON DR CC Northern Circuit Preston Group	Bankruptcy Company or LLP Divorce	Langdale House Gray Street Workington Cumbria CA14 2PA Tel: 01900 603967 Fax: 01900 68001 DX: 63650 Workington 2	Whitehaven Workington	T: Carlisle B: Workington R: Carlisle	
WORKSOP CC Midland Circuit Notts/Lincs/Derbys Group		Worksop Magistrates' Court 30 Potter Street Worksop Nottinghamshire S80 2AJ Tel: 01623 656406 Fax: 01623 626561 DX: 743240 Worksop 4 This court is administered by Mansfield County Court.		T: Lincoln B: Sheffield R: Nottingham	Sheffield
WORTHING DR CC South Eastern Circuit (Provincial) Lewes Group	Divorce	The Law Courts Christchurch Road Worthing West Sussex BN11 1JD Tel: 01903 206721 Fax: 01903 235559 DX: 98230 Worthing 4	Horsham Worthing	T: Brighton B: Brighton R: Central London	Brighton
WREXHAM DR CC Wales and Chester Circuit North Wales & Chester Group	Bankruptcy Company or LLP Race Relations Divorce Family Hearing Centre	2nd Floor Crown Buildings 31 Chester Street Wrexham LL13 8XN Tel: 01978 351738 Fax: 01978 290677 DX: 721921 Wrexham 4	Mold Oswestry Wrexham	T: Chester B: Wrexham R: Wrexham	

Court, Circuit, Group	Jurisdiction of County Court	Address, Tel, Fax, DX	County Courts within High Court District	County Court Trial Centre and for special jurisdiction	Court to which the district is attached for company and limited liability partnership matters for those courts excluded from that jurisdiction
YEOVIL DR CC Western Circuit – West Group	Bankruptcy Company or LLP Divorce Family Hearing Centre	22 Hendford Yeovil Somerset BA20 2QD Tel: 01935 382150 Fax: 01935 410004 DX: 98830 Yeovil 2	Yeovil	T: Taunton B: Yeovil R: Bristol	
YORK DR CC North Eastern Circuit North & West Yorkshire Group	Bankruptcy Company or LLP Divorce Care Centre Family Hearing Centre	Piccadilly House 55 Piccadilly York YO1 9WL Tel: 01904 629935 Fax: 01904 679963 DX: 65165 York 4	York	T: York B: York R: Leeds	

KEY: DR: District Registry; CDR: Chancery District Registry; DPR: District Probate Registry; MC: Mercantile Court; CC: County Court; AC: Appeal Court; HOC: Hearing Only Centre; B: Bankruptcy; R: Race Relations; T: Trial Centre.

1. The offices, chambers and court rooms of the Patents County Court are on the third floor of the Central London Courthouse are at 26–29 Park Crescent, London W1 4HT but all correspondence should be addressed to the Patents County Court, 13–14 Park Crescent, London W1N 3PD.
2. Cases may be referred for trial by London county courts to the Central London Courthouse, 26–29 Park Crescent, London W1N 4HT.

III ENFORCEMENT OFFICERS

ADD 3

ADD 3 [1]

Introduction As from 1 April 2004, a new regime for High Court enforcement came into effect in England and Wales.

Prior to this date, enforcement of High Court Writs of Execution, such as Writs of Fieri Facias and Writs of Possession was carried out in the name of the High Sheriff for each bailiwick. (A 'bailiwick' being the area under the jurisdiction of the High Sheriff, these areas being roughly equivalent to the pre-1974 county boundaries).

From 1 April 2004, incoming High Sheriffs who take office are relieved of their obligation to enforce these High Court writs.

Instead, High Court writs of execution are now enforced by High Court Enforcement Officers appointed and assigned to districts by the Lord Chancellor or his nominated delegate (see generally **RSC 45**). The following directory contains a list of all those appointed as High Court Enforcement Officers, and the postal districts to which they have been assigned. It also contains their contact details.

An enforcement officer is obliged to accept any Writ of Execution forwarded to him or her for the postal districts to which they have been assigned. They also have the discretion to accept writs for any other district in England and Wales, but may decline to accept the writ if it is for an area to which they have not sought assignment.

Many court users may already have regular dealings with High Court enforcement officers, and may know whom they wish to approach to enforce their writs. However, many creditors may be unfamiliar with the system of High Court enforcement, and not know whom they wish to enforce their writs on their behalf. The directory contains details of all those appointed and to which areas they have been assigned. It also contains the address of the National Information Centre for Enforcement, where the writ may be sent for automatic allocation to a High Court enforcement officer for the relevant postal district, using the "cab rank" principle.

The address is:

National Information Centre for Enforcement

Westwood Park

London Road

Little Horkesley

Colchester

Essex

CO6 4BS

(DX number: DX 3654 Colchester)

ADD 3 [2]

This is a list of districts for writs of execution enforceable by enforcement officers. Directories containing details of all current enforcement officers, the districts to which they have been assigned and the addresses to which writs of execution issued from the High Court to enforcement officers are to be sent shall are available for inspection at—

(a) the Royal Courts of Justice;

(b) district registries of the High Court; and

(c) county courts,

during the hours when the offices of such courts are open, and are printed after the following table.

DIRECTORY OF HIGH COURT ENFORCEMENT OFFICERS

LISTED ALPHABETICALLY BY POSTAL DISTRICT

District	Code	Name
Bath	BA	ANDERSON, Michael
	BA	ASKER, David
	BA	BARNETT, Simon
	BA	BASTIN, Simon
	BA	BULLOCK, Richard
	BA	DUNCAN, Andrew
	BA	EGMORE, Angela
	BA	EVANS, Philip
	BA	FARRINGTON, Patrick
	BA	GATER, Jonathan
	BA	GRIFFITHS, Richard
	BA	HARGROVE, John
	BA	HATHAWAY, John
	BA	HORNER, Nigel
	BA	JAMES, John
	BA	KIMBER, Michael
	BA	LEYSHON, Martin
	BA	PEPPER, Nigel
	BA	SANDBROOK, Claire
	BA	SMITH, Alan
	BA	TRICKEY, David
Birmingham	B	ANDERSON, Michael
	B	ASKER, David
	B	BULLOCK, Richard
	B	BUTLER, Malcolm
	B	DEAN, Paul
	B	DUNCAN, Andrew
	B	EVANS, Philip
	B	FARRINGTON, Patrick
	B	GATER, Jonathan
	B	GRIFFITHS, Richard
	B	HARGROVE, John
	B	HARRISON, Karl
	B	HATHAWAY, John
	B	HORNER, Nigel
	B	JACKSON, Michael
	B	JAMES, John
	B	KIMBER, Michael
	B	LEYSHON, Martin
	B	MARSTON, John
	B	MORGAN, Ian
	B	PEPPER, Nigel
	B	SANDBROOK, Claire
	B	SMITH, Alan
	B	THOMSON, Patricia
	B	WILSON, Andrew
Blackburn	BB	ASKER, David
	BB	BOVAN, Gary
	BB	DEAN, Derek
	BB	DEAN, Gordon
	BB	DEAN, Paul
	BB	HARGROVE, John
	BB	HARRISON, Karl
	BB	LAING, John
	BB	SANDBROOK, Claire
	BB	SMITH, Alan
	BB	THOMSON, Patricia
	BB	WILSON, Andrew

District	Code	Name
Bolton	BL	ASKER, David
	BL	DEAN, Derek
	BL	DEAN, Gordon
	BL	DEAN, Paul
	BL	HARGROVE, John
	BL	HARRISON, Karl
	BL	SANDBROOK, Claire
	BL	SMITH, Alan
	BL	THOMSON, Patricia
	BL	VANN, Edward
	BL	WILSON, Andrew
Bournemouth	BH	ASKER, David
	BH	BARNETT, Simon
	BH	BASTIN, Simon
	BH	EGMORE, Angela
	BH	GATER, Jonathan
	BH	GRIFFITHS, Richard
	BH	HARGROVE, John
	BH	SANDBROOK, Claire
	BH	SMITH, Alan
	BH	TRICKEY, David
Bradford	BD	ASKER, David
	BD	BOVAN, Gary
	BD	HARGROVE, John
	BD	HARRISON, Dion
	BD	HARRISON, Karl
	BD	LAING, John
	BD	SANDBROOK, Claire
	BD	SMITH, Alan
	BD	THOMSON, Patricia
	BD	WHITWORTH, Frank
	BD	WILSON, Andrew
Brighton	BN	ASKER, David
	BN	GATER, Jonathan
	BN	GRIFFITHS, Richard
	BN	HARGROVE, John
	BN	SANDBROOK, Claire
	BN	SMITH, Alan
Bristol	BS	ALEXANDER, Nicholas
	BS	ANDERSON, Michael
	BS	ASKER, David
	BS	BULLOCK, Richard
	BS	DUNCAN, Andrew
	BS	EVANS, Philip
	BS	EWART-JAMES, Andrew
	BS	FARRINGTON, Patrick
	BS	GATER, Jonathan
	BS	GRIFFITHS, Richard
	BS	HARGROVE, John
	BS	HATHAWAY, John
	BS	HORNER, Nigel
	BS	JAMES, John
	BS	KIMBER, Michael
	BS	LEYSHON, Martin
	BS	PEPPER, Nigel
	BS	SANDBROOK, Claire
	BS	SMITH, Alan
Bromley	BR	ASKER, David
	BR	BUTLER, Malcolm
	BR	GATER, Jonathan

District	Code	Name
	BR	GRIFFITHS, Richard
	BR	HARGROVE, John
	BR	JACKSON, Michael
	BR	MARSTON, John
	BR	MORGAN, Ian
	BR	SANDBROOK, Claire
	BR	SMITH, Alan
Cambridge	CB	ASKER, David
	CB	CONSTANT, Bryan
	CB	HALL, Brian
	CB	HARGROVE, John
	CB	SANDBROOK, Claire
	CB	SILLS, Tim
	CB	SMITH, Alan
	CB	STEPHENS, Martin
	CB	WATT, Peter
Canterbury	CT	ASKER, David
	CT	GATER, Jonathan
	CT	GRIFFITHS, Richard
	CT	HARGROVE, John
	CT	SANDBROOK, Claire
	CT	SMITH, Alan
Cardiff	CF	ANDERSON, Michael
	CF	ASKER, David
	CF	BOWEN, David
	CF	BULLOCK, Richard
	CF	DUNCAN, Andrew
	CF	EVANS, Philip
	CF	FARRINGTON, Patrick
	CF	GATER, Jonathan
	CF	GRIFFITHS, Richard
	CF	HARGROVE, John
	CF	HATHAWAY, John
	CF	HORNER, Nigel
	CF	JAMES, John
	CF	KIMBER, Michael
	CF	LEYSHON, Martin
	CF	PEPPER, Nigel
	CF	SANDBROOK, Claire
	CF	SMITH, Alan
Carlisle	CA	ASKER, David
	CA	DEAN, Derek
	CA	DEAN, Gordon
	CA	DEAN, Paul
	CA	FITZGERALD, Hugh
	CA	HARGROVE, John
	CA	HARRISON, Karl
	CA	SANDBROOK, Claire
	CA	SMITH, Alan
	CA	THOMSON, Patricia
	CA	WILSON, Andrew
Chelmsford	CM	ASKER, David
	CM	BUTLER, Malcolm
	CM	HARGROVE, John
	CM	JACKSON, Michael
	CM	MARSTON, John
	CM	MORGAN, Ian
	CM	SANDBROOK, Claire
	CM	SMITH, Alan
	CM	TUNSTILL, Peter
	CM	WILLIAMS, James

District	Code	Name
Chester	CH	ANDERSON, Michael
	CH	ARNOLD, John
	CH	ASKER, David
	CH	BOVAN, Gary
	CH	BULLOCK, Richard
	CH	DEAN, Derek
	CH	DEAN, Gordon
	CH	DEAN, Paul
	CH	DUNCAN, Andrew
	CH	EVANS, Philip
	CH	FARRINGTON, Patrick
	CH	GATER, Jonathan
	CH	GREGORY, John
	CH	GRIFFITHS, Richard
	CH	GUEST, Robin
	CH	HARGROVE, John
	CH	HARRISON, Karl
	CH	HATHAWAY, John
	CH	HORNER, Nigel
	CH	JAMES, John
	CH	KIMBER, Michael
	CH	LEYSHON, Martin
	CH	MASON, David
	CH	MORRIS-JONES, Gareth
	CH	PARRY, Anthony
	CH	PEPPER, Nigel
	CH	SANDBROOK, Claire
	CH	SMITH, Alan
	CH	SOUTHERN, Norman
	CH	THOMSON, Patricia
	CH	WILSON, Andrew
Cleveland (Teeside)	TS	ASKER, David
	TS	DAVIES, Malcolm
	TS	ELLIOTT, Chris
	TS	FELLOWS, Kathleen
	TS	HARGROVE, John
	TS	HARRISON, Karl
	TS	SANDBROOK, Claire
	TS	SMITH, Alan
	TS	STOREY, Roy
	TS	THOMSON, Patricia
	TS	WILSON, Andrew
Colchester	CO	ASKER, David
	CO	HARGROVE, John
	CO	SANDBROOK, Claire
	CO	SMITH, Alan
	CO	STEPHENS, Martin
Coventry	CV	ANDERSON, Michael
	CV	ASKER, David
	CV	BULLOCK, Richard
	CV	BUTLER, Malcolm
	CV	DUNCAN, Andrew
	CV	EVANS, Philip
	CV	FARRINGTON, Patrick
	CV	GATER, Jonathan
	CV	GRIFFITHS, Richard
	CV	HARGROVE, John
	CV	HARRISON, Karl
	CV	HATHAWAY, John
	CV	HORNER, Nigel
	CV	JACKSON, Michael

District	Code	Name
	CV	JAMES, John
	CV	KIMBER, Michael
	CV	LEYSHON, Martin
	CV	MARSTON, John
	CV	MORGAN, Ian
	CV	PEPPER, Nigel
	CV	SANDBROOK, Claire
	CV	SMITH, Alan
	CV	THOMSON, Patricia
	CV	WILSON, Andrew
Crewe	CW	ANDERSON, Michael
	CW	ARNOLD, John
	CW	ASKER, David
	CW	BOVAN, Gary
	CW	BULLOCK, Richard
	CW	DEAN, Gordon
	CW	DEAN, Paul
	CW	DUNCAN, Andrew
	CW	EVANS, Philip
	CW	FARRINGTON, Patrick
	CW	GATER, Jonathan
	CW	GRIFFITHS, Richard
	CW	HARGROVE, John
	CW	HARRISON, Karl
	CW	HATHAWAY, John
	CW	HORNER, Nigel
	CW	JAMES, John
	CW	KIMBER, Michael
	CW	LEYSHON, Martin
	CW	MASON, David
	CW	PEPPER, Nigel
	CW	SANDBROOK, Claire
	CW	SMITH, Alan
	CW	SOUTHERN, Norman
	CW	THOMSON, Patricia
	CW	WILSON, Andrew
Croydon	CR	ASKER, David
	CR	BUTLER, Malcolm
	CR	GATER, Jonathan
	CR	GRIFFITHS, Richard
	CR	HARGROVE, John
	CR	JACKSON, Michael
	CR	MARSTON, John
	CR	MORGAN, Ian
	CR	SANDBROOK, Claire
	CR	SMITH, Alan
Darlington	DL	ASKER, David
	DL	DAVIES, Malcolm
	DL	ELLIOTT, Chris
	DL	FELLOWS, Kathleen
	DL	HARGROVE, John
	DL	HARRISON, Karl
	DL	SANDBROOK, Claire
	DL	SMITH, Alan
	DL	STOREY, Roy
	DL	THOMSON, Patricia
	DL	WILSON, Andrew
Dartford	DA	ASKER, David
	DA	BUTLER, Malcolm
	DA	GATER, Jonathan

District	Code	Name
	DA	GRIFFITHS, Richard
	DA	HARGROVE, John
	DA	JACKSON, Michael
	DA	MARSTON, John
	DA	MORGAN, Ian
	DA	SANDBROOK, Claire
	DA	SMITH, Alan
Derby	DE	ANDERSON, Michael
	DE	ASKER, David
	DE	BULLOCK, Richard
	DE	BUTLER, Malcolm
	DE	DEAN, Paul
	DE	DUNCAN, Andrew
	DE	EVANS, Philip
	DE	FARRINGTON, Patrick
	DE	GATER, Jonathan
	DE	GRIFFITHS, Richard
	DE	HARGROVE, John
	DE	HARRISON, Karl
	DE	HATHAWAY, John
	DE	HORNER, Nigel
	DE	JACKSON, Michael
	DE	JAMES, John
	DE	KIMBER, Michael
	DE	LEYSHON, Martin
	DE	MARSTON, John
	DE	MORGAN, Ian
	DE	PEPPER, Nigel
	DE	SANDBROOK, Claire
	DE	SMITH, Alan
	DE	THOMSON, Patricia
	DE	WILSON, Andrew
Doncaster	DN	ASKER, David
	DN	BAITSON, Helen
	DN	BAITSON, Michael
	DN	BUTLER, Malcolm
	DN	DEAN, Paul
	DN	HARGROVE, John
	DN	HARRISON, Dion
	DN	HARRISON, Karl
	DN	JACKSON, Michael
	DN	MARSTON, John
	DN	McGARRAGH, Robert
	DN	MORGAN, Ian
	DN	SANDBROOK, Claire
	DN	SMITH, Alan
	DN	THOMSON, Patricia
	DN	WILSON, Andrew
Dorchester	DT	ASKER, David
	DT	BARNETT, Simon
	DT	BASTIN, Simon
	DT	EGMORE, Angela
	DT	HARGROVE, John
	DT	SANDBROOK, Claire
	DT	SMITH, Alan
	DT	TRICKEY, David
Dudley	DY	ANDERSON, Michael
	DY	ASKER, David
	DY	BULLOCK, Richard
	DY	BUTLER, Malcolm
	DY	DUNCAN, Andrew

District	Code	Name
	DY	EVANS, Philip
	DY	FARRINGTON, Patrick
	DY	GATER, Jonathan
	DY	GRIFFITHS, Richard
	DY	HARGROVE, John
	DY	HARRISON, Karl
	DY	HATHAWAY, John
	DY	HORNER, Nigel
	DY	JACKSON, Michael
	DY	JAMES, John
	DY	KIMBER, Michael
	DY	LEYSHON, Martin
	DY	MARSTON, John
	DY	MORGAN, Ian
	DY	PEPPER, Nigel
	DY	SANDBROOK, Claire
	DY	SMITH, Alan
	DY	THOMSON, Patricia
	DY	WILSON, Andrew
Durham	DH	ASKER, David
	DH	DAVIES, Malcolm
	DH	ELLIOTT, Chris
	DH	FELLOWS, Kathleen
	DH	HARGROVE, John
	DH	HARRISON, Karl
	DH	SANDBROOK, Claire
	DH	SMITH, Alan
	DH	STOREY, Roy
	DH	THOMSON, Patricia
	DH	WILSON, Andrew
Enfield	EN	ASKER, David
	EN	BUTLER, Malcolm
	EN	HARGROVE, John
	EN	JACKSON, Michael
	EN	MARSTON, John
	EN	MORGAN, Ian
	EN	SANDBROOK, Claire
	EN	SMITH, Alan
	EN	TUNSTILL, Peter
	EN	WILLIAMS, James
Exeter	EX	ASKER, David
	EX	BARNETT, Simon
	EX	BASTIN, Simon
	EX	EGMORE, Angela
	EX	HARGROVE, John
	EX	SANDBROOK, Claire
	EX	SMITH, Alan
	EX	TRICKEY, David
Fylde (Blackpool)	FY	ASKER, David
	FY	DEAN, Derek
	FY	DEAN, Gordon
	FY	DEAN, Paul
	FY	HARGROVE, John
	FY	HARRISON, Karl
	FY	SANDBROOK, Claire
	FY	SMITH, Alan
	FY	THOMSON, Patricia
	FY	WILSON, Andrew
Gloucester	GL	ALEXANDER, Nicholas
	GL	ANDERSON, Michael
	GL	ASKER, David

District	Code	Name
	GL	BOWEN, David
	GL	BULLOCK, Richard
	GL	DUNCAN, Andrew
	GL	EVANS, Philip
	GL	EWART-JAMES, Andrew
	GL	FARRINGTON, Patrick
	GL	GATER, Jonathan
	GL	GRIFFITHS, Richard
	GL	HARGROVE, John
	GL	HATHAWAY, John
	GL	HORNER, Nigel
	GL	JAMES, John
	GL	KIMBER, Michael
	GL	LEYSHON, Martin
	GL	PEPPER, Nigel
	GL	SANDBROOK, Claire
	GL	SMITH, Alan
Guildford	GU	ANDERSON, Michael
	GU	ASKER, David
	GU	BUTLER, Malcolm
	GU	DUNCAN, Andrew
	GU	EVANS, Philip
	GU	FARRINGTON, Patrick
	GU	GATER, Jonathan
	GU	GRIFFITHS, Richard
	GU	HARGROVE, John
	GU	HATHAWAY, John
	GU	HORNER, Nigel
	GU	JACKSON, Michael
	GU	JAMES, John
	GU	KIMBER, Michael
	GU	LEYSHON, Martin
	GU	MARSTON, John
	GU	MORGAN, Ian
	GU	PEPPER, Nigel
	GU	SANDBROOK, Claire
	GU	SMITH, Alan
Halifax	HX	ASKER, David
	HX	BOVAN, Gary
	HX	HARGROVE, John
	HX	HARRISON, Dion
	HX	HARRISON, Karl
	HX	LAING, John
	HX	SANDBROOK, Claire
	HX	SMITH, Alan
	HX	THOMSON, Patricia
	HX	WHITWORTH, Frank
	HX	WILSON, Andrew
Harrogate	HG	ASKER, David
	HG	BOVAN, Gary
	HG	HARGROVE, John
	HG	HARRISON, Dion
	HG	HARRISON, Karl
	HG	LAING, John
	HG	SANDBROOK, Claire
	HG	SMITH, Alan
	HG	THOMSON, Patricia
	HG	WHITWORTH, Frank
	HG	WILSON, Andrew
Harrow	HA	ASKER, David
	HA	BUTLER, Malcolm

District	Code	Name
	HA	GATER, Jonathan
	HA	GRIFFITHS, Richard
	HA	HARGROVE, John
	HA	JACKSON, Michael
	HA	KIMBER, Michael
	HA	MARSTON, John
	HA	MORGAN, Ian
	HA	SANDBROOK, Claire
	HA	SMITH, Alan
Hemel Hempstead	HP	ANDERSON, Michael
	HP	ASKER, David
	HP	BULLOCK, Richard
	HP	BUTLER, Malcolm
	HP	DUNCAN, Andrew
	HP	EVANS, Philip
	HP	FARRINGTON, Patrick
	HP	GATER, Jonathan
	HP	GRIFFITHS, Richard
	HP	HARGROVE, John
	HP	HATHAWAY, John
	HP	HORNER, Nigel
	HP	JACKSON, Michael
	HP	JAMES, John
	HP	KIMBER, Michael
	HP	LEYSHON, Martin
	HP	MARSTON, John
	HP	MORGAN, Ian
	HP	PEPPER, Nigel
	HP	SANDBROOK, Claire
	HP	SMITH, Alan
	HP	TUNSTILL, Peter
	HP	WILLIAMS, James
Hereford	HR	ALEXANDER, Nicholas
	HR	ANDERSON, Michael
	HR	ASKER, David
	HR	BOWEN, David
	HR	BULLOCK, Richard
	HR	BUTLER, Malcolm
	HR	DUNCAN, Andrew
	HR	EVANS, Philip
	HR	EWART-JAMES, Andrew
	HR	FARRINGTON, Patrick
	HR	GATER, Jonathan
	HR	GRIFFITHS, Richard
	HR	HARGROVE, John
	HR	HATHAWAY, John
	HR	HORNER, Nigel
	HR	JACKSON, Michael
	HR	JAMES, John
	HR	KIMBER, Michael
	HR	LEYSHON, Martin
	HR	MARSTON, John
	HR	MORGAN, Ian
	HR	PEPPER, Nigel
	HR	SANDBROOK, Claire
	HR	SMITH, Alan
Huddersfield	HD	ASKER, David
	HD	BOVAN, Gary
	HD	DEAN, Paul
	HD	HARGROVE, John
	HD	HARRISON, Dion

District	Code	Name
	HD	HARRISON, Karl
	HD	LAING, John
	HD	SANDBROOK, Claire
	HD	SMITH, Alan
	HD	THOMSON, Patricia
	HD	WHITWORTH, Frank
	HD	WILSON, Andrew
Hull	HU	ASKER, David
	HU	BAITSON, Helen
	HU	BAITSON, Michael
	HU	HARGROVE, John
	HU	HARRISON, Dion
	HU	HARRISON, Karl
	HU	McGARRAGH, Robert
	HU	SANDBROOK, Claire
	HU	SMITH, Alan
	HU	THOMSON, Patricia
	HU	WILSON, Andrew
Ilford	IG	ASKER, David
	IG	BUTLER, Malcolm
	IG	GATER, Jonathan
	IG	GRIFFITHS, Richard
	IG	HARGROVE, John
	IG	JACKSON, Michael
	IG	MARSTON, John
	IG	MORGAN, Ian
	IG	SANDBROOK, Claire
	IG	SMITH, Alan
Ipswich	IP	ASKER, David
	IP	CONSTANT, Bryan
	IP	HALL, Brian
	IP	HARGROVE, John
	IP	SANDBROOK, Claire
	IP	SILLS, Tim
	IP	SMITH, Alan
	IP	STEPHENS, Martin
	IP	WATT, Peter
Kingston upon thames	KT	ASKER, David
	KT	BUTLER, Malcolm
	KT	GATER, Jonathan
	KT	GRIFFITHS, Richard
	KT	HARGROVE, John
	KT	JACKSON, Michael
	KT	KIMBER, Michael
	KT	MARSTON, John
	KT	MORGAN, Ian
	KT	SANDBROOK, Claire
	KT	SMITH, Alan
Lancaster	LA	ASKER, David
	LA	DEAN, Derek
	LA	DEAN, Gordon
	LA	DEAN, Paul
	LA	FITZGERALD, Hugh
	LA	HARGROVE, John
	LA	HARRISON, Karl
	LA	SANDBROOK, Claire
	LA	SMITH, Alan
	LA	THOMSON, Patricia
	LA	WILSON, Andrew

District	Code	Name
Leeds	LS	ASKER, David
	LS	BOVAN, Gary
	LS	HARGROVE, John
	LS	HARRISON, Dion
	LS	LAING, John
	LS	SANDBROOK, Claire
	LS	SMITH, Alan
	LS	THOMSON, Patricia
	LS	WHITWORTH, Frank
	LS	WILSON, Andrew
Leicester	LE	ANDERSON, Michael
	LE	ASKER, David
	LE	BULLOCK, Richard
	LE	BUTLER, Malcolm
	LE	DUNCAN, Andrew
	LE	EVANS, Philip
	LE	FARRINGTON, Patrick
	LE	GATER, Jonathan
	LE	GRIFFITHS, Richard
	LE	HARGROVE, John
	LE	HARRISON, Karl
	LE	HATHAWAY, John
	LE	HORNER, Nigel
	LE	JACKSON, Michael
	LE	JAMES, John
	LE	KIMBER, Michael
	LE	LEYSHON, Martin
	LE	MARSTON, John
	LE	MORGAN, Ian
	LE	PEPPER, Nigel
	LE	SANDBROOK, Claire
	LE	SMITH, Alan
	LE	STEPHENS, Martin
	LE	WATT, Peter
Lincoln	LN	ASKER, David
	LN	BAITSON, Helen
	LN	BAITSON, Michael
	LN	BULLOCK, Richard
	LN	BUTLER, Malcolm
	LN	HARGROVE, John
	LN	HARRISON, Karl
	LN	JACKSON, Michael
	LN	MARSTON, John
	LN	McGARRAGH, Robert
	LN	MORGAN, Ian
	LN	SANDBROOK, Claire
	LN	SMITH, Alan
	LN	THOMSON, Patricia
	LN	WILSON, Andrew
Liverpool	L	ARNOLD, John
	L	ASKER, David
	L	BOVAN, Gary
	L	DEAN, Derek
	L	DEAN, Gordon
	L	DEAN, Paul
	L	HARGROVE, John
	L	HARRISON, Karl
	L	MASON, David
	L	SANDBROOK, Claire
	L	SMITH, Alan
	L	THOMSON, Patricia
	L	WILSON, Andrew

District	Code	Name
Llandridnod Wells	LD	ANDERSON, Michael
	LD	ASKER, David
	LD	BOWEN, David
	LD	BULLOCK, Richard
	LD	DUNCAN, Andrew
	LD	EVANS, Philip
	LD	FARRINGTON, Patrick
	LD	GATER, Jonathan
	LD	GRIFFITHS, Richard
	LD	HARGROVE, John
	LD	HATHAWAY, John
	LD	HORNER, Nigel
	LD	JAMES, John
	LD	KIMBER, Michael
	LD	LEYSHON, Martin
	LD	PEPPER, Nigel
	LD	SANDBROOK, Claire
	LD	SMITH, Alan
Llandudno	LL	ANDERSON, Michael
	LL	ASKER, David
	LL	BULLOCK, Richard
	LL	DEAN, Derek
	LL	DEAN, Gordon
	LL	DEAN, Paul
	LL	DUNCAN, Andrew
	LL	EVANS, Philip
	LL	FARRINGTON, Patrick
	LL	GATER, Jonathan
	LL	GREGORY, John
	LL	GRIFFITHS, Richard
	LL	GUEST, Robin
	LL	HARGROVE, John
	LL	HARRISON, Karl
	LL	HATHAWAY, John
	LL	HORNER, Nigel
	LL	JAMES, John
	LL	KIMBER, Michael
	LL	LEYSHON, Martin
	LL	MORRIS-JONES, Gareth
	LL	OWEN, William
	LL	PARRY, Anthony
	LL	PEPPER, Nigel
	LL	SANDBROOK, Claire
	LL	SMITH, Alan
	LL	THOMSON, Patricia
	LL	WILSON, Andrew
London East	E	ASKER, David
	E	BUTLER, Malcolm
	E	GATER, Jonathan
	E	GRIFFITHS, Richard
	E	HARGROVE, John
	E	JACKSON, Michael
	E	MARSTON, John
	E	MORGAN, Ian
	E	SANDBROOK, Claire
	E	SMITH, Alan
London East Central	EC	ASKER, David
	EC	BUTLER, Malcolm
	EC	GATER, Jonathan
	EC	GRIFFITHS, Richard
	EC	HARGROVE, John

District	Code	Name
	EC	HENTY, Charles
	EC	JACKSON, Michael
	EC	MARSTON, John
	EC	MORGAN, Ian
	EC	SANDBROOK, Claire
	EC	SMITH, Alan
London North	N	ASKER, David
	N	BUTLER, Malcolm
	N	GATER, Jonathan
	N	GRIFFITHS, Richard
	N	HARGROVE, John
	N	JACKSON, Michael
	N	MARSTON, John
	N	MORGAN, Ian
	N	SANDBROOK, Claire
	N	SMITH, Alan
London North West	NW	ASKER, David
	NW	BUTLER, Malcolm
	NW	GATER, Jonathan
	NW	GRIFFITHS, Richard
	NW	HARGROVE, John
	NW	JACKSON, Michael
	NW	KIMBER, Michael
	NW	MARSTON, John
	NW	MORGAN, Ian
	NW	SANDBROOK, Claire
	NW	SMITH, Alan
London South East	SE	ASKER, David
	SE	BUTLER, Malcolm
	SE	GATER, Jonathan
	SE	GRIFFITHS, Richard
	SE	HARGROVE, John
	SE	JACKSON, Michael
	SE	MARSTON, John
	SE	MORGAN, Ian
	SE	SANDBROOK, Claire
	SE	SMITH, Alan
London South West	SW	ASKER, David
	SW	BUTLER, Malcolm
	SW	GATER, Jonathan
	SW	GRIFFITHS, Richard
	SW	HARGROVE, John
	SW	JACKSON, Michael
	SW	MARSTON, John
	SW	MORGAN, Ian
	SW	SANDBROOK, Claire
	SW	SMITH, Alan
London West	W	ASKER, David
	W	BUTLER, Malcolm
	W	GATER, Jonathan
	W	GRIFFITHS, Richard
	W	HARGROVE, John
	W	JACKSON, Michael
	W	KIMBER, Michael
	W	MARSTON, John
	W	MORGAN, Ian
	W	SANDBROOK, Claire
	W	SMITH, Alan
London West Central	WC	ASKER, David
	WC	BUTLER, Malcolm

District	Code	Name
	WC	GATER, Jonathan
	WC	GRIFFITHS, Richard
	WC	HARGROVE, John
	WC	JACKSON, Michael
	WC	KIMBER, Michael
	WC	MARSTON, John
	WC	MORGAN, Ian
	WC	SANDBROOK, Claire
	WC	SMITH, Alan
Luton	LU	ASKER, David
	LU	CONSTANT, Bryan
	LU	HALL, Brian
	LU	HARGROVE, John
	LU	HATHAWAY, John
	LU	SANDBROOK, Claire
	LU	SILLS, Tim
	LU	SMITH, Alan
	LU	STEPHENS, Martin
	LU	WATT, Peter
Manchester	M	ARNOLD, John
	M	ASKER, David
	M	DEAN, Derek
	M	DEAN, Gordon
	M	DEAN, Paul
	M	HARGROVE, John
	M	HARRISON, Karl
	M	MASON, David
	M	SANDBROOK, Claire
	M	SMITH, Alan
	M	THOMSON, Patricia
	M	VANN, Edward
	M	WILSON, Andrew
Medway	ME	ASKER, David
	ME	BUTLER, Malcolm
	ME	GATER, Jonathan
	ME	GRIFFITHS, Richard
	ME	HARGROVE, John
	ME	JACKSON, Michael
	ME	MARSTON, John
	ME	MORGAN, Ian
	ME	SANDBROOK, Claire
	ME	SMITH, Alan
Milton Keynes	MK	ASKER, David
	MK	CONSTANT, Bryan
	MK	HALL, Brian
	MK	HARGROVE, John
	MK	SANDBROOK, Claire
	MK	SILLS, Tim
	MK	SMITH, Alan
	MK	STEPHENS, Martin
	MK	WATT, Peter
Newcastle	NE	ASKER, David
	NE	DAVIES, Malcolm
	NE	ELLIOTT, Chris
	NE	FELLOWS, Kathleen
	NE	HARGROVE, John
	NE	HARRISON, Karl
	NE	SANDBROOK, Claire
	NE	SMITH, Alan
	NE	STOREY, Roy

District	Code	Name
	NE	THOMSON, Patricia
	NE	WILSON, Andrew
Newport	NP	ALEXANDER, Nicholas
	NP	ANDERSON, Michael
	NP	ASKER, David
	NP	BOWEN, David
	NP	BULLOCK, Richard
	NP	DUNCAN, Andrew
	NP	EVANS, Philip
	NP	EWART-JAMES, Andrew
	NP	FARRINGTON, Patrick
	NP	GATER, Jonathan
	NP	GRIFFITHS, Richard
	NP	HARGROVE, John
	NP	HATHAWAY, John
	NP	HORNER, Nigel
	NP	JAMES, John
	NP	KIMBER, Michael
	NP	LEYSHON, Martin
	NP	PEPPER, Nigel
	NP	SANDBROOK, Claire
	NP	SMITH, Alan
Northampton	NN	ASKER, David
	NN	CONSTANT, Bryan
	NN	HALL, Brian
	NN	HARGROVE, John
	NN	SANDBROOK, Claire
	NN	SILLS, Tim
	NN	SMITH, Alan
	NN	STEPHENS, Martin
	NN	WATT, Peter
Norwich	NR	ASKER, David
	NR	CONSTANT, Bryan
	NR	HALL, Brian
	NR	HARGROVE, John
	NR	SANDBROOK, Claire
	NR	SILLS, Tim
	NR	SMITH, Alan
	NR	STEPHENS, Martin
	NR	WATT, Peter
Nottingham	NG	ANDERSON, Michael
	NG	ASKER, David
	NG	BULLOCK, Richard
	NG	BUTLER, Malcolm
	NG	DEAN, Paul
	NG	DUNCAN, Andrew
	NG	EVANS, Philip
	NG	FARRINGTON, Patrick
	NG	GATER, Jonathan
	NG	GRIFFITHS, Richard
	NG	HARGROVE, John
	NG	HARRISON, Karl
	NG	HATHAWAY, John
	NG	HORNER, Nigel
	NG	JACKSON, Michael
	NG	JAMES, John
	NG	KIMBER, Michael
	NG	LEYSHON, Martin
	NG	MARSTON, John
	NG	MORGAN, Ian
	NG	PEPPER, Nigel

District	Code	Name
	NG	SANDBROOK, Claire
	NG	SMITH, Alan
	NG	THOMSON, Patricia
	NG	WILSON, Andrew
Oldham	OL	ASKER, David
	OL	BOVAN, Gary
	OL	DEAN, Gordon
	OL	DEAN, Paul
	OL	HARGROVE, John
	OL	HARRISON, Karl
	OL	LAING, John
	OL	SANDBROOK, Claire
	OL	SMITH, Alan
	OL	THOMSON, Patricia
	OL	VANN, Edward
	OL	WHITWORTH, Frank
	OL	WILSON, Andrew
Oxford	OX	ALEXANDER, Nicholas
	OX	ANDERSON, Michael
	OX	ASKER, David
	OX	BULLOCK, Richard
	OX	DUNCAN, Andrew
	OX	EVANS, Philip
	OX	EWART-JAMES, Andrew
	OX	FARRINGTON, Patrick
	OX	GATER, Jonathan
	OX	GRIFFITHS, Richard
	OX	HARGROVE, John
	OX	HATHAWAY, John
	OX	HORNER, Nigel
	OX	JAMES, John
	OX	KIMBER, Michael
	OX	LEYSHON, Martin
	OX	PEPPER, Nigel
	OX	SANDBROOK, Claire
	OX	SMITH, Alan
Peterborough	PE	ASKER, David
	PE	CONSTANT, Bryan
	PE	HALL, Brian
	PE	HARGROVE, John
	PE	SANDBROOK, Claire
	PE	SILLS, Tim
	PE	SMITH, Alan
	PE	STEPHENS, Martin
	PE	WATT, Peter
Plymouth	PL	ASKER, David
	PL	BARNETT, Simon
	PL	BASTIN, Simon
	PL	EGMORE, Angela
	PL	HARGROVE, John
	PL	HUGHES, David
	PL	POTE, David
	PL	REED, Philip
	PL	SANDBROOK, Claire
	PL	SMITH, Alan
	PL	TRICKEY, David
Portsmouth	PO	ANDERSON, Michael
	PO	ASKER, David
	PO	DUNCAN, Andrew
	PO	EVANS, Philip

District	Code	Name
	PO	FARRINGTON, Patrick
	PO	GATER, Jonathan
	PO	GRIFFITHS, Richard
	PO	HARGROVE, John
	PO	HORNER, Nigel
	PO	JAMES, John
	PO	KIMBER, Michael
	PO	LEYSHON, Martin
	PO	PEPPER, Nigel
	PO	SANDBROOK, Claire
	PO	SMITH, Alan
Preston	PR	ASKER, David
	PR	BOVAN, Gary
	PR	DEAN, Derek
	PR	DEAN, Gordon
	PR	DEAN, Paul
	PR	HARGROVE, John
	PR	HARRISON, Karl
	PR	LAING, John
	PR	SANDBROOK, Claire
	PR	SMITH, Alan
	PR	THOMSON, Patricia
	PR	WILSON, Andrew
Reading	RG	ANDERSON, Michael
	RG	ASKER, David
	RG	BULLOCK, Richard
	RG	DUNCAN, Andrew
	RG	EVANS, Philip
	RG	FARRINGTON, Patrick
	RG	GATER, Jonathan
	RG	GRIFFITHS, Richard
	RG	HARGROVE, John
	RG	HATHAWAY, John
	RG	HORNER, Nigel
	RG	JAMES, John
	RG	KIMBER, Michael
	RG	LEYSHON, Martin
	RG	PEPPER, Nigel
	RG	SANDBROOK, Claire
	RG	SMITH, Alan
Redhill	RH	ASKER, David
	RH	BUTLER, Malcolm
	RH	GATER, Jonathan
	RH	GRIFFITHS, Richard
	RH	HARGROVE, John
	RH	JACKSON, Michael
	RH	MARSTON, John
	RH	MORGAN, Ian
	RH	SANDBROOK, Claire
	RH	SMITH, Alan
Romford	RM	ASKER, David
	RM	BUTLER, Malcolm
	RM	GATER, Jonathan
	RM	GRIFFITHS, Richard
	RM	HARGROVE, John
	RM	JACKSON, Michael
	RM	MARSTON, John
	RM	MORGAN, Ian
	RM	SANDBROOK, Claire
	RM	SMITH, Alan

District	Code	Name
Salisbury	SP	ASKER, David
	SP	BARNETT, Simon
	SP	BASTIN, Simon
	SP	EGMORE, Angela
	SP	GATER, Jonathan
	SP	GRIFFITHS, Richard
	SP	HARGROVE, John
	SP	HATHAWAY, John
	SP	SANDBROOK, Claire
	SP	SMITH, Alan
	SP	TRICKEY, David
Sheffield	S	ASKER, David
	S	BOVAN, Gary
	S	BULLOCK, Richard
	S	BUTLER, Malcolm
	S	DEAN, Paul
	S	HARGROVE, John
	S	HARRISON, Dion
	S	HARRISON, Karl
	S	JACKSON, Michael
	S	LAING, John
	S	MARSTON, John
	S	MORGAN, Ian
	S	SANDBROOK, Claire
	S	SMITH, Alan
	S	THOMSON, Patricia
	S	TODD, Nicholas
	S	WILSON, Andrew
Shrewsbury	SY	ANDERSON, Michael
	SY	ARNOLD, John
	SY	ASKER, David
	SY	BULLOCK, Richard
	SY	DUNCAN, Andrew
	SY	EVANS, Philip
	SY	FARRINGTON, Patrick
	SY	GATER, Jonathan
	SY	GRIFFITHS, Richard
	SY	HARGROVE, John
	SY	HARRISON, Karl
	SY	HATHAWAY, John
	SY	HORNER, Nigel
	SY	JAMES, John
	SY	KIMBER, Michael
	SY	LEYSHON, Martin
	SY	MASON, David
	SY	PEPPER, Nigel
	SY	SANDBROOK, Claire
	SY	SMITH, Alan
	SY	THOMSON, Patricia
	SY	WILSON, Andrew
Slough	SL	ANDERSON, Michael
	SL	ASKER, David
	SL	BULLOCK, Richard
	SL	DUNCAN, Andrew
	SL	EVANS, Philip
	SL	FARRINGTON, Patrick
	SL	GATER, Jonathan
	SL	GRIFFITHS, Richard
	SL	HARGROVE, John
	SL	HATHAWAY, John
	SL	HORNER, Nigel

District	Code	Name
	SL	JAMES, John
	SL	KIMBER, Michael
	SL	LEYSHON, Martin
	SL	PEPPER, Nigel
	SL	SANDBROOK, Claire
	SL	SMITH, Alan
Southall (Uxbridge)	UB	ASKER, David
	UB	BUTLER, Malcolm
	UB	GATER, Jonathan
	UB	GRIFFITHS, Richard
	UB	HARGROVE, John
	UB	JACKSON, Michael
	UB	KIMBER, Michael
	UB	MARSTON, John
	UB	MORGAN, Ian
	UB	SANDBROOK, Claire
	UB	SMITH, Alan
Southampton	SO	ANDERSON, Michael
	SO	ASKER, David
	SO	DUNCAN, Andrew
	SO	EVANS, Philip
	SO	FARRINGTON, Patrick
	SO	GATER, Jonathan
	SO	GRIFFITHS, Richard
	SO	HARGROVE, John
	SO	HATHAWAY, John
	SO	HORNER, Nigel
	SO	JAMES, John
	SO	KIMBER, Michael
	SO	LEYSHON, Martin
	SO	PEPPER, Nigel
	SO	SANDBROOK, Claire
	SO	SMITH, Alan
Southend on Sea	SS	ASKER, David
	SS	BUTLER, Malcolm
	SS	HARGROVE, John
	SS	JACKSON, Michael
	SS	MARSTON, John
	SS	MORGAN, Ian
	SS	SANDBROOK, Claire
	SS	SMITH, Alan
St. Albans	AL	ASKER, David
	AL	BUTLER, Malcolm
	AL	HARGROVE, John
	AL	JACKSON, Michael
	AL	MARSTON, John
	AL	MORGAN, Ian
	AL	SANDBROOK, Claire
	AL	SMITH, Alan
	AL	TUNSTILL, Peter
	AL	WILLIAMS, James
Stevenage	SG	ASKER, David
	SG	BUTLER, Malcolm
	SG	CONSTANT, Bryan
	SG	HALL, Brian
	SG	HARGROVE, John
	SG	JACKSON, Michael
	SG	MARSTON, John
	SG	MORGAN, Ian
	SG	SANDBROOK, Claire
	SG	SILLS, Tim

District	Code	Name
	SG	SMITH, Alan
	SG	STEPHENS, Martin
	SG	TUNSTILL, Peter
	SG	WATT, Peter
	SG	WILLIAMS, James
Stockport	SK	ARNOLD, John
	SK	ASKER, David
	SK	BUTLER, Malcolm
	SK	DEAN, Derek
	SK	DEAN, Gordon
	SK	DEAN, Paul
	SK	HARGROVE, John
	SK	HARRISON, Dion
	SK	HARRISON, Karl
	SK	JACKSON, Michael
	SK	MARSTON, John
	SK	MASON, David
	SK	MORGAN, Ian
	SK	SANDBROOK, Claire
	SK	SMITH, Alan
	SK	THOMSON, Patricia
	SK	VANN, Edward
	SK	WILSON, Andrew
Stoke on Trent	ST	ANDERSON, Michael
	ST	ASKER, David
	ST	BULLOCK, Richard
	ST	BUTLER, Malcolm
	ST	DEAN, Paul
	ST	DUNCAN, Andrew
	ST	EVANS, Philip
	ST	FARRINGTON, Patrick
	ST	GATER, Jonathan
	ST	GRIFFITHS, Richard
	ST	HARGROVE, John
	ST	HARRISON, Karl
	ST	HATHAWAY, John
	ST	HORNER, Nigel
	ST	JACKSON, Michael
	ST	JAMES, John
	ST	KIMBER, Michael
	ST	LEYSHON, Martin
	ST	MARSTON, John
	ST	MORGAN, Ian
	ST	PEPPER, Nigel
	ST	SANDBROOK, Claire
	ST	SMITH, Alan
	ST	THOMSON, Patricia
	ST	WILSON, Andrew
Sunderland	SR	ASKER, David
	SR	DAVIES, Malcolm
	SR	ELLIOTT, Chris
	SR	FELLOWS, Kathleen
	SR	HARGROVE, John
	SR	HARRISON, Karl
	SR	SANDBROOK, Claire
	SR	SMITH, Alan
	SR	STOREY, Roy
	SR	THOMSON, Patricia
	SR	WILSON, Andrew
Sutton	SM	ASKER, David
	SM	BUTLER, Malcolm

District	Code	Name
	SM	GATER, Jonathan
	SM	GRIFFITHS, Richard
	SM	HARGROVE, John
	SM	JACKSON, Michael
	SM	MARSTON, John
	SM	MORGAN, Ian
	SM	SANDBROOK, Claire
	SM	SMITH, Alan
Swansea	SA	ANDERSON, Michael
	SA	ASKER, David
	SA	BULLOCK, Richard
	SA	DUNCAN, Andrew
	SA	EVANS, Philip
	SA	FARRINGTON, Patrick
	SA	GATER, Jonathan
	SA	GRIFFITHS, Richard
	SA	HARGROVE, John
	SA	HATHAWAY, John
	SA	HORNER, Nigel
	SA	JAMES, John
	SA	JENKINS, Anthony
	SA	KIMBER, Michael
	SA	LEYSHON, Martin
	SA	PEPPER, Nigel
	SA	SANDBROOK, Claire
	SA	SMITH, Alan
Swindon	SN	ALEXANDER, Nicholas
	SN	ANDERSON, Michael
	SN	ASKER, David
	SN	BULLOCK, Richard
	SN	DUNCAN, Andrew
	SN	EVANS, Philip
	SN	EWART-JAMES, Andrew
	SN	FARRINGTON, Patrick
	SN	GATER, Jonathan
	SN	GRIFFITHS, Richard
	SN	HARGROVE, John
	SN	HATHAWAY, John
	SN	HORNER, Nigel
	SN	JAMES, John
	SN	KIMBER, Michael
	SN	LEYSHON, Martin
	SN	PEPPER, Nigel
	SN	SANDBROOK, Claire
	SN	SMITH, Alan
Taunton	TA	ASKER, David
	TA	BARNETT, Simon
	TA	BASTIN, Simon
	TA	EGMORE, Angela
	TA	HARGROVE, John
	TA	HATHAWAY, John
	TA	SANDBROOK, Claire
	TA	SMITH, Alan
	TA	TRICKEY, David
Telford	TF	ANDERSON, Michael
	TF	ASKER, David
	TF	BULLOCK, Richard
	TF	DUNCAN, Andrew
	TF	EVANS, Philip
	TF	FARRINGTON, Patrick
	TF	GATER, Jonathan

District	Code	Name
	TF	GRIFFITHS, Richard
	TF	HARGROVE, John
	TF	HARRISON, Karl
	TF	HATHAWAY, John
	TF	HORNER, Nigel
	TF	JAMES, John
	TF	KIMBER, Michael
	TF	LEYSHON, Martin
	TF	PEPPER, Nigel
	TF	SANDBROOK, Claire
	TF	SMITH, Alan
	TF	THOMSON, Patricia
	TF	WILSON, Andrew
Tonbridge	TN	ASKER, David
	TN	BUTLER, Malcolm
	TN	GATER, Jonathan
	TN	GRIFFITHS, Richard
	TN	HARGROVE, John
	TN	JACKSON, Michael
	TN	MARSTON, John
	TN	MORGAN, Ian
	TN	SANDBROOK, Claire
	TN	SMITH, Alan
Torquay	TQ	ASKER, David
	TQ	BARNETT, Simon
	TQ	BASTIN, Simon
	TQ	EGMORE, Angela
	TQ	HARGROVE, John
	TQ	SANDBROOK, Claire
	TQ	SMITH, Alan
	TQ	TRICKEY, David
Truro	TR	ASKER, David
	TR	BARNETT, Simon
	TR	BASTIN, Simon
	TR	EGMORE, Angela
	TR	HARGROVE, John
	TR	HUGHES, David
	TR	POTE, David
	TR	REED, Philip
	TR	SANDBROOK, Claire
	TR	SMITH, Alan
	TR	TRICKEY, David
Tweeddale (Berwick upon Tweed)	TD	ASKER, David
	TD	DAVIES, Malcolm
	TD	ELLIOTT, Chris
	TD	HARGROVE, John
	TD	HARRISON, Karl
	TD	SANDBROOK, Claire
	TD	SMITH, Alan
	TD	THOMSON, Patricia
	TD	WILSON, Andrew
Twickenham	TW	ASKER, David
	TW	BUTLER, Malcolm
	TW	GATER, Jonathan
	TW	GRIFFITHS, Richard
	TW	HARGROVE, John
	TW	JACKSON, Michael
	TW	KIMBER, Michael
	TW	MARSTON, John
	TW	MORGAN, Ian

District	Code	Name
	TW	SANDBROOK, Claire
	TW	SMITH, Alan
Wakefield	WF	ASKER, David
	WF	BOVAN, Gary
	WF	DEAN, Paul
	WF	HARGROVE, John
	WF	HARRISON, Dion
	WF	HARRISON, Karl
	WF	LAING, John
	WF	SANDBROOK, Claire
	WF	SMITH, Alan
	WF	THOMSON, Patricia
	WF	WHITWORTH, Frank
	WF	WILSON, Andrew
Walsall	WS	ANDERSON, Michael
	WS	ASKER, David
	WS	BULLOCK, Richard
	WS	BUTLER, Malcolm
	WS	DUNCAN, Andrew
	WS	EVANS, Philip
	WS	FARRINGTON, Patrick
	WS	GATER, Jonathan
	WS	GRIFFITHS, Richard
	WS	HARGROVE, John
	WS	HARRISON, Karl
	WS	HATHAWAY, John
	WS	HORNER, Nigel
	WS	JACKSON, Michael
	WS	JAMES, John
	WS	KIMBER, Michael
	WS	LEYSHON, Martin
	WS	MARSTON, John
	WS	MORGAN, Ian
	WS	PEPPER, Nigel
	WS	SANDBROOK, Claire
	WS	SMITH, Alan
	WS	THOMSON, Patricia
	WS	WILSON, Andrew
Warrington	WA	ARNOLD, John
	WA	ASKER, David
	WA	DEAN, Derek
	WA	DEAN, Gordon
	WA	DEAN, Paul
	WA	HARGROVE, John
	WA	HARRISON, Karl
	WA	MASON, David
	WA	SANDBROOK, Claire
	WA	SMITH, Alan
	WA	SOUTHERN, Norman
	WA	THOMSON, Patricia
	WA	WILSON, Andrew
Walford	WD	ASKER, David
	WD	BUTLER, Malcolm
	WD	HARGROVE, John
	WD	JACKSON, Michael
	WD	MARSTON, John
	WD	MORGAN, Ian
	WD	SANDBROOK, Claire
	WD	SMITH, Alan
	WD	TUNSTILL, Peter
	WD	WILLIAMS, James

District	Code	Name
Wigan	WN	ARNOLD, John
	WN	ASKER, David
	WN	DEAN, Derek
	WN	DEAN, Gordon
	WN	DEAN, Paul
	WN	HARGROVE, John
	WN	HARRISON, Karl
	WN	MASON, David
	WN	SANDBROOK, Claire
	WN	SMITH, Alan
	WN	THOMSON, Patricia
	WN	WILSON, Andrew
Wolverhampton	WV	ANDERSON, Michael
	WV	ASKER, David
	WV	BULLOCK, Richard
	WV	BUTLER, Malcolm
	WV	DUNCAN, Andrew
	WV	EVANS, Philip
	WV	FARRINGTON, Patrick
	WV	GATER, Jonathan
	WV	GRIFFITHS, Richard
	WV	HARGROVE, John
	WV	HATHAWAY, John
	WV	HORNER, Nigel
	WV	JACKSON, Michael
	WV	JAMES, John
	WV	KIMBER, Michael
	WV	LEYSHON, Martin
	WV	MARSTON, John
	WV	MORGAN, Ian
	WV	PEPPER, Nigel
	WV	SANDBROOK, Claire
	WV	SMITH, Alan
Worcester	WR	ALEXANDER, Nicholas
	WR	ANDERSON, Michael
	WR	ASKER, David
	WR	BULLOCK, Richard
	WR	BUTLER, Malcolm
	WR	DUNCAN, Andrew
	WR	EVANS, Philip
	WR	EWART-JAMES, Andrew
	WR	FARRINGTON, Patrick
	WR	GATER, Jonathan
	WR	GRIFFITHS, Richard
	WR	HARGROVE, John
	WR	HARRISON, Karl
	WR	HATHAWAY, John
	WR	HORNER, Nigel
	WR	JACKSON, Michael
	WR	JAMES, John
	WR	KIMBER, Michael
	WR	LEYSHON, Martin
	WR	MARSTON, John
	WR	MORGAN, Ian
	WR	PEPPER, Nigel
	WR	SANDBROOK, Claire
	WR	SMITH, Alan
	WR	THOMSON, Patricia
	WR	WILSON, Andrew
York	YO	ASKER, David
	YO	BAITSON, Helen

District	Code	Name
	YO	BAITSON, Michael
	YO	BOVAN, Gary
	YO	FELLOWS, Kathleen
	YO	HARGROVE, John
	YO	HARRISON, Dion
	YO	HARRISON, Karl
	YO	LAING, John
	YO	SANDBROOK, Claire
	YO	SMITH, Alan
	YO	STOREY, Roy
	YO	THOMSON, Patricia
	YO	WILSON, Andrew

LISTED ALPHABETICALLY BY ENFORCEMENT OFFICER

Name	**District**	**Code**
ALEXANDER, Nicholas	Bristol	BS
	Gloucester	GL
	Hereford	HR
	Newport	NP
	Oxford	OX
	Swindon	SN
	Worcester	WR
ANDERSON, Michael	Bath	BA
	Birmingham	B
	Bristol	BS
	Cardiff	CF
	Chester	CH
	Coventry	CV
	Crewe	CW
	Derby	DE
	Dudley	DY
	Gloucester	GL
	Guildford	GU
	Hemel Hempstead	HP
	Hereford	HR
	Leicester	LE
	Llandridnod Wells	LD
	Llandudno	LL
	Newport	NP
	Nottingham	NG
	Oxford	OX
	Portsmouth	PO
	Reading	RG
	Shrewsbury	SY
	Slough	SL
	Southampton	SO
	Stoke on Trent	ST
	Swansea	SA
	Swindon	SN
	Telford	TF
	Walsall	WS
	Wolverhampton	WV
	Worcester	WR
ARNOLD, John	Chester	CH
	Crewe	CW
	Liverpool	L
	Manchester	M
	Shrewsbury	SY
	Stockport	SK

Name	District	Code
	Warrington	WA
	Wigan	WN
ASKER, David	Bath	BA
	Birmingham	B
	Blackburn	BB
	Bolton	BL
	Bournemouth	BH
	Bradford	BD
	Brighton	BN
	Bristol	BS
	Bromley	BR
	Cambridge	CB
	Canterbury	CT
	Cardiff	CF
	Carlisle	CA
	Chelmsford	CM
	Chester	CH
	Cleveland (Teeside)	TS
	Colchester	CO
	Coventry	CV
	Crewe	CW
	Croydon	CR
	Darlington	DL
	Dartford	DA
	Derby	DE
	Doncaster	DN
	Dorchester	DT
	Dudley	DY
	Durham	DH
	Enfield	EN
	Exeter	EX
	Fylde (Blackpool)	FY
	Gloucester	GL
	Guildford	GU
	Halifax	HX
	Harrogate	HG
	Harrow	HA
	Hemel Hempstead	HP
	Hereford	HR
	Huddersfield	HD
	Hull	HU
	Ilford	IG
	Ipswich	IP
	Kingston upon Thames	KT
	Lancaster	LA
	Leeds	LS
	Leicester	LE
	Lincoln	LN
	Liverpool	L
	Llandridnod Wells	LD
	Llandudno	LL
	London East	E
	London East Central	EC
	London North	N
	London North West	NW
	London South East	SE
	London South West	SW
	London West	W
	London West Central	WC
	Luton	LU
	Manchester	M
	Medway	ME

Name	District	Code
	Milton Keynes	MK
	Newcastle	NE
	Newport	NP
	Northampton	NN
	Norwich	NR
	Nottingham	NG
	Oldham	OL
	Oxford	OX
	Peterborough	PE
	Plymouth	PL
	Portsmouth	PO
	Preston	PR
	Reading	RG
	Redhill	RH
	Romford	RM
	Salisbury	SP
	Sheffield	S
	Shrewsbury	SY
	Slough	SL
	Southall (Uxbridge)	UB
	Southampton	SO
	Southend on Sea	SS
	St. Albans	AL
	Stevenage	SG
	Stockport	SK
	Stoke on Trent	ST
	Sunderland	SR
	Sutton	SM
	Swansea	SA
	Swindon	SN
	Taunton	TA
	Telford	TF
	Tonbridge	TN
	Torquay	TQ
	Truro	TR
	Tweeddale (Berwick upon Tweed)	TD
	Twickenham	TW
	Wakefield	WF
	Walford	WD
	Walsall	WS
	Warrington	WA
	Wigan	WN
	Wolverhampton	WV
	Worcester	WR
	York	YO
BAITSON, Helen	Doncaster	DN
	Hull	HU
	Lincoln	LN
	York	YO
BAITSON, Michael	Doncaster	DN
	Hull	HU
	Lincoln	LN
	York	YO
BARNETT, Simon	Bath	BA
	Bournemouth	BH
	Dorchester	DT
	Exeter	EX
	Plymouth	PL
	Salisbury	SP
	Taunton	TA
	Torquay	TQ
	Truro	TR

Name	District	Code
BASTIN, Simon	Bath	BA
	Bournemouth	BH
	Dorchester	DT
	Exeter	EX
	Plymouth	PL
	Salisbury	SP
	Taunton	TA
	Torquay	TQ
	Truro	TR
BOVAN, Gary	Chester	CH
	Crewe	CW
	Blackburn	BB
	Bradford	BD
	Halifax	HX
	Harrogate	HG
	Huddersfield	HD
	Leeds	LS
	Liverpool	L
	Oldham	OL
	Preston	PR
	Sheffield	S
	Wakefield	WF
	York	YO
BOWEN, David	Cardiff	CF
	Gloucester	GL
	Hereford	HR
	Llandridnod Wells	LD
	Newport	NP
BULLOCK, Richard	Bath	BA
	Birmingham	B
	Bristol	BS
	Cardiff	CF
	Chester	CH
	Coventry	CV
	Crewe	CW
	Derby	DE
	Dudley	DY
	Gloucester	GL
	Hemel Hempstead	HP
	Hereford	HR
	Leicester	LE
	Lincoln	LN
	Llandridnod Wells	LD
	Llandudno	LL
	Newport	NP
	Nottingham	NG
	Oxford	OX
	Reading	RG
	Sheffield	S
	Shrewsbury	SY
	Slough	SL
	Stoke on Trent	ST
	Swansea	SA
	Swindon	SN
	Telford	TF
	Walsall	WS
	Wolverhampton	WV
	Worcester	WR
BUTLER, Malcolm	Birmingham	B
	Bromley	BR
	Chelmsford	CM

Name	District	Code
	Coventry	CV
	Croydon	CR
	Dartford	DA
	Derby	DE
	Doncaster	DN
	Dudley	DY
	Enfield	EN
	Guildford	GU
	Harrow	HA
	Hemel Hempstead	HP
	Hereford	HR
	Ilford	IG
	Kingston upon Thames	KT
	Leicester	LE
	Lincoln	LN
	London East	E
	London East Central	EC
	London North	N
	London North West	NW
	London South East	SE
	London South West	SW
	London West	W
	London West Central	WC
	Medway	ME
	Nottingham	NG
	Redhill	RH
	Romford	RM
	Sheffield	S
	Southall (Uxbridge)	UB
	Southend on Sea	SS
	St. Albans	AL
	Stevenage	SG
	Stockport	SK
	Stoke on Trent	ST
	Sutton	SM
	Tonbridge	TN
	Twickenham	TW
	Walford	WD
	Walsall	WS
	Wolverhampton	WV
	Worcester	WR
CONSTANT, Bryan	Cambridge	CB
	Ipswich	IP
	Luton	LU
	Milton Keynes	MK
	Northampton	NN
	Norwich	NR
	Peterborough	PE
	Stevenage	SG
DAVIES, Malcolm	Cleveland (Teeside)	TS
	Darlington	DL
	Durham	DH
	Newcastle	NE
	Sunderland	SR
	Tweeddale (Berwick upon Tweed)	TD
DEAN, Derek	Blackburn	BB
	Bolton	BL
	Carlisle	CA
	Chester	CH
	Fylde (Blackpool)	FY
	Lancaster	LA

Name	District	Code
	Liverpool	L
	Llandudno	LL
	Manchester	M
	Preston	PR
	Stockport	SK
	Warrington	WA
	Wigan	WN
DEAN, Gordon	Blackburn	BB
	Bolton	BL
	Carlisle	CA
	Chester	CH
	Crewe	CW
	Fylde (Blackpool)	FY
	Lancaster	LA
	Liverpool	L
	Llandudno	LL
	Manchester	M
	Oldham	OL
	Preston	PR
	Stockport	SK
	Warrington	WA
	Wigan	WN
DEAN, Paul	Birmingham	B
	Blackburn	BB
	Bolton	BL
	Carlisle	CA
	Chester	CH
	Crewe	CW
	Derby	DE
	Doncaster	DN
	Fylde (Blackpool)	FY
	Huddersfield	HD
	Lancaster	LA
	Liverpool	L
	Llandudno	LL
	Manchester	M
	Nottingham	NG
	Oldham	OL
	Preston	PR
	Sheffield	S
	Stockport	SK
	Stoke on Trent	ST
	Wakefield	WF
	Warrington	WA
	Wigan	WN
DUNCAN, Andrew	Bath	BA
	Birmingham	B
	Bristol	BS
	Cardiff	CF
	Chester	CH
	Coventry	CV
	Crewe	CW
	Derby	DE
	Dudley	DY
	Gloucester	GL
	Guildford	GU
	Hemel Hempstead	HP
	Hereford	HR
	Leicester	LE
	Llandridnod Wells	LD
	Llandudno	LL

Name	District	Code
	Newport	NP
	Nottingham	NG
	Oxford	OX
	Portsmouth	PO
	Reading	RG
	Shrewsbury	SY
	Slough	SL
	Southampton	SO
	Stoke on Trent	ST
	Swansea	SA
	Swindon	SN
	Telford	TF
	Walsall	WS
	Wolverhampton	WV
	Worcester	WR
EGMORE, Angela	Bath	BA
	Bournemouth	BH
	Dorchester	DT
	Exeter	EX
	Plymouth	PL
	Salisbury	SP
	Taunton	TA
	Torquay	TQ
	Truro	TR
ELLIOTT, Chris	Cleveland (Teeside)	TS
	Darlington	DL
	Durham	DH
	Newcastle	NE
	Sunderland	SR
	Tweeddale (Berwick upon Tweed)	TD
EVANS, Philip	Bath	BA
	Birmingham	B
	Bristol	BS
	Cardiff	CF
	Chester	CH
	Coventry	CV
	Crewe	CW
	Derby	DE
	Dudley	DY
	Gloucester	GL
	Guildford	GU
	Hemel Hempstead	HP
	Hereford	HR
	Leicester	LE
	Llandridnod Wells	LD
	Llandudno	LL
	Newport	NP
	Nottingham	NG
	Oxford	OX
	Portsmouth	PO
	Reading	RG
	Shrewsbury	SY
	Slough	SL
	Southampton	SO
	Stoke on Trent	ST
	Swansea	SA
	Swindon	SN
	Telford	TF
	Walsall	WS
	Wolverhampton	WV
	Worcester	WR

Name	District	Code
EWART-JAMES, Andrew	Bristol	BS
	Gloucester	GL
	Hereford	HR
	Newport	NP
	Oxford	OX
	Swindon	SN
	Worcester	WR
FARRINGTON, Patrick	Bath	BA
	Birmingham	B
	Bristol	BS
	Cardiff	CF
	Chester	CH
	Coventry	CV
	Crewe	CW
	Derby	DE
	Dudley	DY
	Gloucester	GL
	Guildford	GU
	Hemel Hempstead	HP
	Hereford	HR
	Leicester	LE
	Llandridnod Wells	LD
	Llandudno	LL
	Newport	NP
	Nottingham	NG
	Oxford	OX
	Portsmouth	PO
	Reading	RG
	Shrewsbury	SY
	Slough	SL
	Southampton	SO
	Stoke on Trent	ST
	Swansea	SA
	Swindon	SN
	Telford	TF
	Walsall	WS
	Wolverhampton	WV
	Worcester	WR
FELLOWS, Kathleen	Cleveland (Teeside)	TS
	Darlington	DL
	Durham	DH
	Newcastle	NE
	Sunderland	SR
	York	YO
FITZGERALD, Hugh	Carlisle	CA
	Lancaster	LA
GATER, Jonathan	Bath	BA
	Birmingham	B
	Bournemouth	BH
	Brighton	BN
	Bristol	BS
	Bromley	BR
	Canterbury	CT
	Cardiff	CF
	Chester	CH
	Coventry	CV
	Crewe	CW
	Croydon	CR
	Dartford	DA
	Derby	DE

Name	District	Code
	Dudley	DY
	Gloucester	GL
	Guildford	GU
	Harrow	HA
	Hemel Hempstead	HP
	Hereford	HR
	Ilford	IG
	Kingston upon Thames	KT
	Leicester	LE
	Llandridnod Wells	LD
	Llandudno	LL
	London East	E
	London East Central	EC
	London North	N
	London North West	NW
	London South East	SE
	London South West	SW
	London West	W
	London West Central	WC
	Medway	ME
	Newport	NP
	Nottingham	NG
	Oxford	OX
	Portsmouth	PO
	Reading	RG
	Redhill	RH
	Romford	RM
	Salisbury	SP
	Shrewsbury	SY
	Slough	SL
	Southall (Uxbridge)	UB
	Southampton	SO
	Stoke on Trent	ST
	Sutton	SM
	Swansea	SA
	Swindon	SN
	Telford	TF
	Tonbridge	TN
	Twickenham	TW
	Walsall	WS
	Wolverhampton	WV
	Worcester	WR
GREGORY, John	Chester	CH
	Llandudno	LL
GRIFFITHS, Richard	Bath	BA
	Birmingham	B
	Bournemouth	BH
	Brighton	BN
	Bristol	BS
	Bromley	BR
	Canterbury	CT
	Cardiff	CF
	Chester	CH
	Coventry	CV
	Crewe	CW
	Croydon	CR
	Dartford	DA
	Derby	DE
	Dudley	DY
	Gloucester	GL
	Guildford	GU

Name	District	Code
GRIFFITHS, Richard	Harrow	HA
	Hemel Hempstead	HP
	Hereford	HR
	Ilford	IG
	Kingston upon Thames	KT
	Leicester	LE
	Llandridnod Wells	LD
	Llandudno	LL
	London East	E
	London East Central	EC
	London North	N
	London North West	NW
	London South East	SE
	London South West	SW
	London West	W
	London West Central	WC
	Medway	ME
	Newport	NP
	Nottingham	NG
	Oxford	OX
	Portsmouth	PO
	Reading	RG
	Redhill	RH
	Romford	RM
	Salisbury	SP
	Shrewsbury	SY
	Slough	SL
	Southall (Uxbridge)	UB
	Southampton	SO
	Stoke on Trent	ST
	Sutton	SM
	Swansea	SA
	Swindon	SN
	Telford	TF
	Tonbridge	TN
	Twickenham	TW
	Walsall	WS
	Wolverhampton	WV
	Worcester	WR
GUEST, Robin	Chester	CH
	Llandudno	LL
HALL, Brian	Cambridge	CB
	Ipswich	IP
	Luton	LU
	Milton Keynes	MK
	Northampton	NN
	Norwich	NR
	Peterborough	PE
	Stevenage	SG
HARGROVE, John	Bath	BA
	Birmingham	B
	Blackburn	BB
	Bolton	BL
	Bournemouth	BH
	Bradford	BD
	Brighton	BN
	Bristol	BS
	Bromley	BR
	Cambridge	CB
	Canterbury	CT
	Cardiff	CF

Name	District	Code
	Carlisle	CA
	Chelmsford	CM
	Chester	CH
	Cleveland (Teeside)	TS
	Colchester	CO
	Coventry	CV
	Crewe	CW
	Croydon	CR
	Darlington	DL
	Dartford	DA
	Derby	DE
	Doncaster	DN
	Dorchester	DT
	Dudley	DY
	Durham	DH
	Enfield	EN
	Exeter	EX
	Fylde (Blackpool)	FY
	Gloucester	GL
	Guildford	GU
	Halifax	HX
	Harrogate	HG
	Harrow	HA
	Hemel Hempstead	HP
	Hereford	HR
	Huddersfield	HD
	Hull	HU
	Ilford	IG
	Ipswich	IP
	Kingston upon Thames	KT
	Lancaster	LA
	Leeds	LS
	Leicester	LE
	Lincoln	LN
	Liverpool	L
	Llandridnod Wells	LD
	Llandudno	LL
	London East	E
	London East Central	EC
	London North	N
	London North West	NW
	London South East	SE
	London South West	SW
	London West	W
	London West Central	WC
	Luton	LU
	Manchester	M
	Medway	ME
	Milton Keynes	MK
	Newcastle	NE
	Newport	NP
	Northampton	NN
	Norwich	NR
	Nottingham	NG
	Oldham	OL
	Oxford	OX
	Peterborough	PE
	Plymouth	PL
	Portsmouth	PO
	Preston	PR
	Reading	RG
	Redhill	RH

Name	District	Code
	Romford	RM
	Salisbury	SP
	Sheffield	S
	Shrewsbury	SY
	Slough	SL
	Southall (Uxbridge)	UB
	Southampton	SO
	Southend on Sea	SS
	St. Albans	AL
	Stevenage	SG
	Stockport	SK
	Stoke on Trent	ST
	Sunderland	SR
	Sutton	SM
	Swansea	SA
	Swindon	SN
	Taunton	TA
	Telford	TF
	Tonbridge	TN
	Torquay	TQ
	Truro	TR
	Tweeddale (Berwick upon Tweed)	TD
	Twickenham	TW
	Wakefield	WF
	Walford	WD
	Walsall	WS
	Warrington	WA
	Wigan	WN
	Wolverhampton	WV
	Worcester	WR
	York	YO
HARRISON, Dion	Bradford	BD
	Doncaster	DN
	Halifax	HX
	Harrogate	HG
	Huddersfield	HD
	Hull	HU
	Leeds	LS
	Sheffield	S
	Stockport	SK
	Wakefield	WF
	York	YO
HARRISON, Karl	Birmingham	B
	Blackburn	BB
	Bolton	BL
	Bradford	BD
	Carlisle	CA
	Chester	CH
	Cleveland (Teeside)	TS
	Coventry	CV
	Crewe	CW
	Darlington	DL
	Derby	DE
	Doncaster	DN
	Dudley	DY
	Durham	DH
	Fylde (Blackpool)	FY
	Halifax	HX
	Harrogate	HG
	Huddersfield	HD
	Hull	HU

Name	District	Code
	Lancaster	LA
	Leicester	LE
	Lincoln	LN
	Liverpool	L
	Llandudno	LL
	Manchester	M
	Newcastle	NE
	Nottingham	NG
	Oldham	OL
	Preston	PR
	Sheffield	S
	Shrewsbury	SY
	Stockport	SK
	Stoke on Trent	ST
	Sunderland	SR
	Telford	TF
	Tweeddale (Berwick upon Tweed)	TD
	Wakefield	WF
	Walsall	WS
	Warrington	WA
	Wigan	WN
	Worcester	WR
	York	YO
HATHAWAY, John	Bath	BA
	Birmingham	B
	Bristol	BS
	Cardiff	CF
	Chester	CH
	Coventry	CV
	Crewe	CW
	Derby	DE
	Dudley	DY
	Gloucester	GL
	Guildford	GU
	Hemel Hempstead	HP
	Hereford	HR
	Leicester	LE
	Llandridnod Wells	LD
	Llandudno	LL
	Luton	LU
	Newport	NP
	Nottingham	NG
	Oxford	OX
	Reading	RG
	Salisbury	SP
	Shrewsbury	SY
	Slough	SL
	Southampton	SO
	Stoke on Trent	ST
	Swansea	SA
	Swindon	SN
	Taunton	TA
	Telford	TF
	Walsall	WS
	Wolverhampton	WV
	Worcester	WR
HENTY, Charles	London East Central	EC
HORNER, Nigel	Bath	BA
	Birmingham	B
	Bristol	BS
	Cardiff	CF

Name	District	Code
	Chester	CH
	Coventry	CV
	Crewe	CW
	Derby	DE
	Dudley	DY
	Gloucester	GL
	Guildford	GU
	Hemel Hempstead	HP
	Hereford	HR
	Leicester	LE
	Llandridnod Wells	LD
	Llandudno	LL
	Newport	NP
	Nottingham	NG
	Oxford	OX
	Portsmouth	PO
	Reading	RG
	Shrewsbury	SY
	Slough	SL
	Southampton	SO
	Stoke on Trent	ST
	Swansea	SA
	Swindon	SN
	Telford	TF
	Walsall	WS
	Wolverhampton	WV
	Worcester	WR
HUGHES, David	Plymouth	PL
	Truro	TR
JACKSON, Michael	Birmingham	B
	Bromley	BR
	Chelmsford	CM
	Coventry	CV
	Croydon	CR
	Dartford	DA
	Derby	DE
	Doncaster	DN
	Dudley	DY
	Enfield	EN
	Guildford	GU
	Harrow	HA
	Hemel Hempstead	HP
	Hereford	HR
	Ilford	IG
	Kingston upon Thames	KT
	Leicester	LE
	Lincoln	LN
	London East	E
	London East Central	EC
	London North	N
	London North West	NW
	London South East	SE
	London South West	SW
	London West	W
	London West Central	WC
	Medway	ME
	Nottingham	NG
	Redhill	RH
	Romford	RM
	Sheffield	S
	Southall (Uxbridge)	UB

Name	District	Code
	Southend on Sea	SS
	St. Albans	AL
	Stevenage	SG
	Stockport	SK
	Stoke on Trent	ST
	Sutton	SM
	Tonbridge	TN
	Twickenham	TW
	Walford	WD
	Walsall	WS
	Wolverhampton	WV
	Worcester	WR
JAMES, John	Bath	BA
	Birmingham	B
	Bristol	BS
	Cardiff	CF
	Chester	CH
	Coventry	CV
	Crewe	CW
	Derby	DE
	Dudley	DY
	Gloucester	GL
	Guildford	GU
	Hemel Hempstead	HP
	Hereford	HR
	Leicester	LE
	Llandridnod Wells	LD
	Llandudno	LL
	Newport	NP
	Nottingham	NG
	Oxford	OX
	Portsmouth	PO
	Reading	RG
	Shrewsbury	SY
	Slough	SL
	Southampton	SO
	Stoke on Trent	ST
	Swansea	SA
	Swindon	SN
	Telford	TF
	Walsall	WS
	Wolverhampton	WV
	Worcester	WR
JENKINS, Anthony	Swansea	SA
KIMBER, Michael	Bath	BA
	Birmingham	B
	Bristol	BS
	Cardiff	CF
	Chester	CH
	Coventry	CV
	Crewe	CW
	Derby	DE
	Dudley	DY
	Gloucester	GL
	Guildford	GU
	Harrow	HA
	Hemel Hempstead	HP
	Hereford	HR
	Kingston upon Thames	KT
	Leicester	LE
	Llandridnod Wells	LD

Name	District	Code
	Llandudno	LL
	London North West	NW
	London West	W
	London West Central	WC
	Newport	NP
	Nottingham	NG
	Oxford	OX
	Portsmouth	PO
	Reading	RG
	Shrewsbury	SY
	Slough	SL
	Southall (Uxbridge)	UB
	Southampton	SO
	Stoke on Trent	ST
	Swansea	SA
	Swindon	SN
	Telford	TF
	Twickenham	TW
	Walsall	WS
	Wolverhampton	WV
	Worcester	WR
LAING, John	Blackburn	BB
	Bradford	BD
	Halifax	HX
	Harrogate	HG
	Huddersfield	HD
	Leeds	LS
	Oldham	OL
	Preston	PR
	Sheffield	S
	Wakefield	WF
	York	YO
LEYSHON, Martin	Bath	BA
	Birmingham	B
	Bristol	BS
	Cardiff	CF
	Chester	CH
	Coventry	CV
	Crewe	CW
	Derby	DE
	Dudley	DY
	Gloucester	GL
	Guildford	GU
	Hemel Hempstead	HP
	Hereford	HR
	Leicester	LE
	Llandridnod Wells	LD
	Llandudno	LL
	Newport	NP
	Nottingham	NG
	Oxford	OX
	Portsmouth	PO
	Reading	RG
	Shrewsbury	SY
	Slough	SL
	Southampton	SO
	Stoke on Trent	ST
	Swansea	SA
	Swindon	SN
	Telford	TF
	Walsall	WS

Name	District	Code
	Wolverhampton	WV
	Worcester	WR
MARSTON, John	Birmingham	B
	Bromley	BR
	Chelmsford	CM
	Coventry	CV
	Croydon	CR
	Dartford	DA
	Derby	DE
	Doncaster	DN
	Dudley	DY
	Enfield	EN
	Guildford	GU
	Harrow	HA
	Hemel Hempstead	HP
	Hereford	HR
	Ilford	IG
	Kingston upon Thames	KT
	Leicester	LE
	Lincoln	LN
	London East	E
	London East Central	EC
	London North	N
	London North West	NW
	London South East	SE
	London South West	SW
	London West	W
	London West Central	WC
	Medway	ME
	Nottingham	NG
	Redhill	RH
	Romford	RM
	Sheffield	S
	Southall (Uxbridge)	UB
	Southend on Sea	SS
	St. Albans	AL
	Stevenage	SG
	Stockport	SK
	Stoke on Trent	ST
	Sutton	SM
	Tonbridge	TN
	Twickenham	TW
	Walford	WD
	Walsall	WS
	Wolverhampton	WV
	Worcester	WR
MASON, David	Chester	CH
	Crewe	CW
	Liverpool	L
	Manchester	M
	Shrewsbury	SY
	Stockport	SK
	Warrington	WA
	Wigan	WN
McGARRAGH, Robert	Doncaster	DN
	Hull	HU
	Lincoln	LN
MORGAN, Ian	Birmingham	B
	Bromley	BR
	Chelmsford	CM

Name	District	Code
	Coventry	CV
	Croydon	CR
	Dartford	DA
	Derby	DE
	Doncaster	DN
	Dudley	DY
	Enfield	EN
	Guildford	GU
	Harrow	HA
	Hemel Hempstead	HP
	Hereford	HR
	Ilford	IG
	Kingston upon Thames	KT
	Leicester	LE
	Lincoln	LN
	London East	E
	London East Central	EC
	London North	N
	London North West	NW
	London South East	SE
	London South West	SW
	London West	W
	London West Central	WC
	Medway	ME
	Nottingham	NG
	Redhill	RH
	Romford	RM
	Sheffield	S
	Southall (Uxbridge)	UB
	Southend on Sea	SS
	St. Albans	AL
	Stevenage	SG
	Stockport	SK
	Stoke on Trent	ST
	Sutton	SM
	Tonbridge	TN
	Twickenham	TW
	Walford	WD
	Walsall	WS
	Wolverhampton	WV
	Worcester	WR
MORRIS-JONES, Gareth	Chester	CH
	Llandudno	LL
OWEN, William	Llandudno	LL
PARRY, Anthony	Chester	CH
	Llandudno	LL
PEPPER, Nigel	Bath	BA
	Birmingham	B
	Bristol	BS
	Cardiff	CF
	Chester	CH
	Coventry	CV
	Crewe	CW
	Derby	DE
	Dudley	DY
	Gloucester	GL
	Guildford	GU
	Hemel Hempstead	HP
	Hereford	HR
	Leicester	LE

Name	District	Code
	Llandridnod Wells	LD
	Llandudno	LL
	Newport	NP
	Nottingham	NG
	Oxford	OX
	Portsmouth	PO
	Reading	RG
	Shrewsbury	SY
	Slough	SL
	Southampton	SO
	Stoke on Trent	ST
	Swansea	SA
	Swindon	SN
	Telford	TF
	Walsall	WS
	Wolverhampton	WV
	Worcester	WR
POTE, David	Plymouth	PL
	Truro	TR
REED, Philip	Plymouth	PL
	Truro	TR
SANDBROOK, Claire	Bath	BA
	Birmingham	B
	Blackburn	BB
	Bolton	BL
	Bournemouth	BH
	Bradford	BD
	Brighton	BN
	Bristol	BS
	Bromley	BR
	Cambridge	CB
	Canterbury	CT
	Cardiff	CF
	Carlisle	CA
	Chelmsford	CM
	Chester	CH
	Cleveland (Teeside)	TS
	Colchester	CO
	Coventry	CV
	Crewe	CW
	Croydon	CR
	Darlington	DL
	Dartford	DA
	Derby	DE
	Doncaster	DN
	Dorchester	DT
	Dudley	DY
	Durham	DH
	Enfield	EN
	Exeter	EX
	Fylde (Blackpool)	FY
	Gloucester	GL
	Guildford	GU
	Halifax	HX
	Harrogate	HG
	Harrow	HA
	Hemel Hempstead	HP
	Hereford	HR
	Huddersfield	HD
	Hull	HU
	Ilford	IG

Name	District	Code
	Ipswich	IP
	Kingston upon Thames	KT
	Lancaster	LA
	Leeds	LS
	Leicester	LE
	Lincoln	LN
	Liverpool	L
	Llandridnod Wells	LD
	Llandudno	LL
	London East	E
	London East Central	EC
	London North	N
	London North West	NW
	London South East	SE
	London South West	SW
	London West	W
	London West Central	WC
	Luton	LU
	Manchester	M
	Medway	ME
	Milton Keynes	MK
	Newcastle	NE
	Newport	NP
	Northampton	NN
	Norwich	NR
	Nottingham	NG
	Oldham	OL
	Oxford	OX
	Peterborough	PE
	Plymouth	PL
	Portsmouth	PO
	Preston	PR
	Reading	RG
	Redhill	RH
	Romford	RM
	Salisbury	SP
	Sheffield	S
	Shrewsbury	SY
	Slough	SL
	Southall (Uxbridge)	UB
	Southampton	SO
	Southend on Sea	SS
	St. Albans	AL
	Stevenage	SG
	Stockport	SK
	Stoke on Trent	ST
	Sunderland	SR
	Sutton	SM
	Swansea	SA
	Swindon	SN
	Taunton	TA
	Telford	TF
	Tonbridge	TN
	Torquay	TQ
	Truro	TR
	Tweeddale (Berwick upon Tweed)	TD
	Twickenham	TW
	Wakefield	WF
	Walford	WD
	Walsall	WS
	Warrington	WA
	Wigan	WN

Name	District	Code
	Wolverhampton	WV
	Worcester	WR
	York	YO
SILLS, Tim	Cambridge	CB
	Ipswich	IP
	Luton	LU
	Milton Keynes	MK
	Northampton	NN
	Norwich	NR
	Peterborough	PE
	Stevenage	SG
SMITH, Alan	Bath	BA
	Birmingham	B
	Blackburn	BB
	Bolton	BL
	Bournemouth	BH
	Bradford	BD
	Brighton	BN
	Bristol	BS
	Bromley	BR
	Cambridge	CB
	Canterbury	CT
	Cardiff	CF
	Carlisle	CA
	Chelmsford	CM
	Chester	CH
	Cleveland (Teeside)	TS
	Colchester	CO
	Coventry	CV
	Crewe	CW
	Croydon	CR
	Darlington	DL
	Dartford	DA
	Derby	DE
	Doncaster	DN
	Dorchester	DT
	Dudley	DY
	Durham	DH
	Enfield	EN
	Exeter	EX
	Fylde (Blackpool)	FY
	Gloucester	GL
	Guildford	GU
	Halifax	HX
	Harrogate	HG
	Harrow	HA
	Hemel Hempstead	HP
	Hereford	HR
	Huddersfield	HD
	Hull	HU
	Ilford	IG
	Ipswich	IP
	Kingston upon Thames	KT
	Lancaster	LA
	Leeds	LS
	Leicester	LE
	Lincoln	LN
	Liverpool	L
	Llandridnod Wells	LD
	Llandudno	LL
	London East	E

Name	District	Code
	London East Central	EC
	London North	N
	London North West	NW
	London South East	SE
	London South West	SW
	London West	W
	London West Central	WC
	Luton	LU
	Manchester	M
	Medway	ME
	Milton Keynes	MK
	Newcastle	NE
	Newport	NP
	Northampton	NN
	Norwich	NR
	Nottingham	NG
	Oldham	OL
	Oxford	OX
	Peterborough	PE
	Plymouth	PL
	Portsmouth	PO
	Preston	PR
	Reading	RG
	Redhill	RH
	Romford	RM
	Salisbury	SP
	Sheffield	S
	Shrewsbury	SY
	Slough	SL
	Southall (Uxbridge)	UB
	Southampton	SO
	Southend on Sea	SS
	St. Albans	AL
	Stevenage	SG
	Stockport	SK
	Stoke on Trent	ST
	Sunderland	SR
	Sutton	SM
	Swansea	SA
	Swindon	SN
	Taunton	TA
	Telford	TF
	Tonbridge	TN
	Torquay	TQ
	Truro	TR
	Tweeddale (Berwick upon Tweed)	TD
	Twickenham	TW
	Wakefield	WF
	Walford	WD
	Walsall	WS
	Warrington	WA
	Wigan	WN
	Wolverhampton	WV
	Worcester	WR
	York	YO
SOUTHERN, Norman	Chester	CH
	Crewe	CW
	Warrington	WA
STEPHENS, Martin	Cambridge	CB
	Colchester	CO
	Ipswich	IP
	Leicester	LE

Name	District	Code
	Luton	LU
	Milton Keynes	MK
	Northampton	NN
	Norwich	NR
	Peterborough	PE
	Stevenage	SG
STOREY, Roy	Cleveland (Teeside)	TS
	Darlington	DL
	Durham	DH
	Newcastle	NE
	Sunderland	SR
	York	YO
THOMSON, Patricia	Birmingham	B
	Blackburn	BB
	Bolton	BL
	Bradford	BD
	Carlisle	CA
	Chester	CH
	Cleveland (Teeside)	TS
	Coventry	CV
	Crewe	CW
	Darlington	DL
	Derby	DE
	Doncaster	DN
	Dudley	DY
	Durham	DH
	Fylde (Blackpool)	FY
	Halifax	HX
	Harrogate	HG
	Huddersfield	HD
	Hull	HU
	Lancaster	LA
	Leeds	LS
	Lincoln	LN
	Liverpool	L
	Llandudno	LL
	Manchester	M
	Newcastle	NE
	Nottingham	NG
	Oldham	OL
	Preston	PR
	Sheffield	S
	Shrewsbury	SY
	Stockport	SK
	Stoke on Trent	ST
	Sunderland	SR
	Telford	TF
	Tweeddale (Berwick upon Tweed)	TD
	Wakefield	WF
	Walsall	WS
	Warrington	WA
	Wigan	WN
	Worcester	WR
	York	YO
TODD, Nicholas	Sheffield	S
TRICKEY, David	Bath	BA
	Bournemouth	BH
	Dorchester	DT
	Exeter	EX
	Plymouth	PL

Name	District	Code
	Salisbury	SP
	Taunton	TA
	Torquay	TQ
	Truro	TR
TUNSTILL, Peter	Chelmsford	CM
	Enfield	EN
	Hemel Hempstead	HP
	St. Albans	AL
	Stevenage	SG
	Walford	WD
VANN, Edward	Bolton	BL
	Manchester	M
	Oldham	OL
	Stockport	SK
WATT, Peter	Cambridge	CB
	Ipswich	IP
	Leicester	LE
	Luton	LU
	Milton Keynes	MK
	Northampton	NN
	Norwich	NR
	Peterborough	PE
	Stevenage	SG
WHITWORTH, Frank	Bradford	BD
	Halifax	HX
	Harrogate	HG
	Huddersfield	HD
	Leeds	LS
	Oldham	OL
	Wakefield	WF
WILLIAMS, James	Chelmsford	CM
	Enfield	EN
	Hemel Hempstead	HP
	St. Albans	AL
	Stevenage	SG
	Walford	WD
WILSON, Andrew	Birmingham	B
	Blackburn	BB
	Bolton	BL
	Bradford	BD
	Carlisle	CA
	Chester	CH
	Cleveland (Teeside)	TS
	Coventry	CV
	Crewe	CW
	Darlington	DL
	Derby	DE
	Doncaster	DN
	Dudley	DY
	Durham	DH
	Fylde (Blackpool)	FY
	Halifax	HX
	Harrogate	HG
	Huddersfield	HD
	Hull	HU
	Lancaster	LA
	Leeds	LS
	Lincoln	LN
	Liverpool	L
	Llandudno	LL

Name	District	Code
	Manchester	M
	Newcastle	NE
	Nottingham	NG
	Oldham	OL
	Preston	PR
	Sheffield	S
	Shrewsbury	SY
	Stockport	SK
	Stoke on Trent	ST
	Sunderland	SR
	Telford	TF
	Tweeddale (Berwick upon Tweed)	TD
	Wakefield	WF
	Walsall	WS
	Warrington	WA
	Wigan	WN
	Worcester	WR
	York	YO

ADDRESSES AND CONTACT DETAILS FOR APPOINTED ENFORCEMENT OFFICERS

Name	Postal Address *(DX Address in italics)*	Phone Number(s) *(Mobile or out of hours numbers in italics)*	Fax Number	Email address *(Web address in italics)*
ALEXANDER, Nicholas	2nd Floor 65 London Road Gloucester Gloucestershire GL1 3HF *Dx 7514 Gloucester*	01452 429883 *01531 636108*	01452 300922	nalexander@whitemans.com
ANDERSON, Michael	141 Walter Road Swansea SA1 5RW *DX 52966 Swansea*	01792 466771	01792 455755	mike@mleyshon.co.uk *www. mleyshon.co.uk*
ARNOLD, John	Birch Cullimore, Solicitors Friars White Friars Chester CH11XS *DX 19985 Chester*	01244 321066	01244 312582	john.arnold@bclaw.co.uk
ASKER, David	20-21 Tooks Court London EC4A1LB *DX 70 LONDON/CHANCERY LANE WC2*	020 7025 2550 *07775 590469*	020 7025 2556	sysman@sheriffs.co.uk *www.sherforce. co. uk*
BAITSON, Helen	The Edwardian Auction Galleries Wiltshire Road Hull HU4 6PG	01482 500500 *07860 649230*	01482 500501	info@gilbert-baitson.co.uk *www.gilbert-baitson.co.uk*
BAITSON, Michael	The Edwardian Auction Galleries Wiltshire Road Hull HU4 6PG	01482 500500 *07860 674714*	01482 500501	info@gilbert-baitson.co.uk *www. gilbert-baitson. co. uk*

Name	Postal Address *(DX Address in italics)*	Phone Number(s) *(Mobile or out of hours numbers in italics)*	Fax Number	Email address *(Web address in italics)*
BARNETT, Simon	High Court Enforcement Group Limited 2nd Floor Lloyds Bank Chambers 30 High Street Crediton Devon EX17 3AH *DX 54207 Crediton*	01363 775118	01363 773009	shb@hceo.fsbusiness.co.uk
BASTIN, Simon	High Court Enforcement Group Limited 2nd Floor Lloyds Bank Chambers 30 High Street Crediton Devon EX17 3AH *DX 54207 Crediton*	01363 775118	01363 773009	scb@hceo.fsbusiness.co.uk
BOVAN, Gary	C N Gaunt & Son 12 New John Street Bradford West Yorkshire BD1 2QZ *DX 11701 Bradford*	01274 391929/ 01274 721711	01274 734773	post@cngaunt.co.uk
BOWEN, David	Victoria Chambers 11 Clythia Park Road Newport South Wales NP20 4PB *DX 33204 Newport (South Wales)*	01633 264194	01633 841146	bowen@colbornes.demon.co.uk

Name	Postal Address *(DX Address in italics)*	Phone Number(s) *(Mobile or out of hours numbers in italics)*	Fax Number	Email address *(Web address in italics)*
BULLOCK, Richard	Freethcartwright LLP Cumberland Court 80 Mount Street Nottingham NG16HH *DX 10039 Nottingham*	0115 9369396	0115 8599617	richard.bullock@freethcartwright.co.uk
BUTLER, Malcolm	John Marston & Co 24/26 Broadway North Walsall West Midlands WS1 2AJ *DX 12143 Walsall*	01922 720 777	01922 647 222	post@johnmarston.co.uk *www.hceo.co.uk*
CONSTANT, Bryan	Invicta House 71 High Street Riseley Bedford MK44 1DD *DX 5641 Bedford*	01234 708044/ 01234 708688	01234 708177	sheriffsofficer@kbnet.net
DAVIES, Malcolm	32 Front Street Whickham Tyne & Wear NE16 4DT *DX 60414 Whickham*	0191 4888800	0191 4888811	info@elliottdavies.com
DEAN, Derek	A & D Dean Trident House 31/33 Dale Street Liverpool L2 2DA *DX 14104 Liverpool*	0151 236 4751 0151 236 6406	0151 236 8071	sheriff@a-d-dean.co.uk

Name	Postal Address *(DX Address in italics)*	Phone Number(s) *(Mobile or out of hours numbers in italics)*	Fax Number	Email address *(Web address in italics)*
DEAN, Gordon	A & D Dean Trident House 31/33 Dale Street Liverpool L2 2DA *DX 14104 Liverpool*	0151 236 4751 0151 236 6406	0151 236 8071	sheriff@a-d-dean.co.uk
DEAN, Paul	A & D Dean Trident House 31/33 Dale Street Liverpool L2 2DA *DX 14104 Liverpool*	0151 236 4751 0151 236 6406	0151 236 8071	sheriff@a-d-dean.co.uk
DUNCAN, Andrew	16 TheTything Worcester WR1 1HD *DX 716264 Worcester*	01905 732881	01905 22347	a.duncan@wwf.co.uk
EGMORE, Angela	High Court Enforcement Group Limited 2nd Floor Lloyds Bank Chambers 30 High Street Crediton Devon EX17 3AH *DX 54207 Crediton*	01363 775118	01363 773009	are@hceo.fsbusiness.co.uk
ELLIOTT, Chris	32 Front Street Whickham Tyne & Wear NE16 4DT *DX 60414 Whickham*	0191 4888800	0191 4888811	info@elliottdavies.com
EVANS, Philip	22 St Andrews Crescent Cardiff CF10 3DD *DX 50752 Cardiff 2*	029 20229716	029 20377761	pevans@cardiff-law.co.uk

Name	Postal Address *(DX Address in italics)*	Phone Number(s) *(Mobile or out of hours numbers in italics)*	Fax Number	Email address *(Web address in italics)*
EWART-JAMES, Andrew	2nd Floor 65 London Road Gloucester Gloucestershire GL1 3HF *DX 7514 Gloucester*	01452 429883 *01453 872470*	01452 300922	aewartjames@whitemans.com
FARRINGTON, Patrick	17 Martin Street Stafford ST16 2LF *DX 14554 Stafford 1*	01785 211411	01785 248573	pfarrington@hmo.co.uk
FELLOWS, Kathleen	Storey & Fellows Albert Chambers 50 Albert Road Middlesbrough TS11QD *DX 60534 Middlesbrough*	01642 218819	01642 246456	k.fellows@virgin.net
FITZGERALD, Hugh	39 High Street Wigton Cumbria CA7 9PE *DX 714666 Wigton*	016973 43241	016973 44820	hugh_f@atkinsonritson.co.uk
GATER, Jonathan	Blandy & Blandy 1 Friar Street Reading Berkshire RG11DA *DX 4008 Reading*	0118 951 6947	0118 958 3032	hceo@blandy.co.uk
GREGORY, John	95 High Street Mold CH7 1BJ *DX 26556 Mold*	01352 753882	01352 758927	office@keeneandkelly.fsnet.co.uk

Name	Postal Address *(DX Address in italics)*	Phone Number(s) *(Mobile or out of hours numbers in italics)*	Fax Number	Email address *(Web address in italics)*
GRIFFITHS, Richard	Blandy & Blandy 1 Friar Street Reading Berkshire RG11DA *DX 4008 Reading*	0118 951 6947	0118 958 3032	hceo@blandy.co.uk
GUEST, Robin	95 High Street Mold CH7 1BJ *DX 26556 Mold*	01352 753882	01352 758927	office@keeneandkelly.fsnet.co.uk
HALL, Brian	6 Bedford Road Sandy Bedfordshire SG19 1EN *DX 47801 Sandy*	01767 680251	01767 691775	brian.hall@leedssmith.co.uk *www. leedssmith. co. uk*
HARGROVE, John	20-21 Tooks Court London EC4A1LB *DX 70 LONDON/CHANCERY LANE WC2*	020 7025 2551 *07775 590475*	020 7025 2556	j-hargrove@sheriffs.co.uk *www. sherforce. co. uk*
HARRISON, Dion	Ashfield House Illingworth Street Ossett West Yorkshire WF5 8AL *DX 707162, Ossett 2*	01924 279005	01924 280114	sheriffs@cwharrison.net

Name	Postal Address *(DX Address in italics)*	Phone Number(s) *(Mobile or out of hours numbers in italics)*	Fax Number	Email address *(Web address in italics)*
HARRISON, Karl	The Sheriffs Office 26 Missouri Avenue Salford Manchester M50 2NP *DX 710252 Manchester 3*	0161 925 1800	0161 925 1801	karl.harrison@northernsheriffs.com *www. northernsheriffs. com*
HATHAWAY, John	42 Brook Street Warwick Warwickshire CV34 4BL *DX 18109 Warwick*	01926 492407	01926 401424	heath.blenkinsop@btopenworld.com
HENTY, Charles	Office of the Secondary Central Criminal Court Old Bailey London EC4M 7EH	020 7248 3277 ext 2326/2323/2338	020 7192 2444	charles.henty@corpoflondon.gov.uk
HORNER, Nigel	16 TheTything Worcester WR1 1HD *DX 716264 Worcester*	01905 732881	01905 22347	n.horner@wwf.co.uk
HUGHES, David	Cornwall High Court Recovery Graham & Graham Solicitors High Cross House St Austell PL25 4AE *DX 81253 St Austell*	01726 75565	01726 61484	sheriff@graham-graham.co.uk

Name	Postal Address *(DX Address in italics)*	Phone Number(s) *(Mobile or out of hours numbers in italics)*	Fax Number	Email address *(Web address in italics)*
JACKSON, Michael	John Marston & Co 24/26 Broadway North Walsall West Midlands WS1 2AJ *DX 12143 Walsall*	01922 720 777	01922 647 222	post@johnmarston.co.uk *www.hceo.co.uk*
JAMES, John	17 Martin Street Stafford ST16 2LF *DX 14554 Stafford 1*	01785 211411	01785 248573	info@hmo.co.uk *www.hmo.co.uk*
JENKINS, Anthony	Messrs Ungoes Thomas and King Gwynne House Quay Street Carmarthen SA33 3JX	01267 237441 (Switchboard) 01267 239192 (Direct Line) *07974 071739*	01267 238317	ajenkins@utk.co.uk
KIMBER, Michael	6 Bellman Court Great Knollys Street Reading RG17HU *DX 40135 Castle Street, Reading*	0118 939 1816 *07831 436112*	0118 958 8258	sheriff@berksandoxon.co.uk michael. kimber@thimbleby-shorland.co.uk
LAING, John	C N Gaunt & Son 12 New John Street Bradford West Yorkshire BD1 2QZ *DX 11701 Bradford*	01274 391929/ 01274 721711	01274 734773	post@cngaunt.co.uk
LEYSHON, Martin	141 Walter Road Swansea SA1 5RW *DX 52966 Swansea*	01792 466771	01792 455755	martin@mleyshon.co.uk *www. mleyshon .co.uk*

Name	Postal Address *(DX Address in italics)*	Phone Number(s) *(Mobile or out of hours numbers in italics)*	Fax Number	Email address *(Web address in italics)*
McGARRAGH, Robert	PO Box 654 Lincoln LN2 2XP	01673 862899 *07785 902352*	01673 862899	r.mcgarragh@tiscali.co.uk
MARSTON, John	John Marston & Co 24/26 Broadway North Walsall West Midlands WS1 2AJ *DX 12143 Walsall*	01922 720 777	01922 647 222	post@hceo.co.uk *www.hceo.co.uk*
MASON, David	Birch Cullimore, Solicitors Friars White Friars Chester CH11XS *DX 19985 Chester*	01244 321066	01244 312582	david.mason@bclaw.co.uk
MORGAN, Ian	John Marston & Co 24/26 Broadway North Walsall West Midlands WS1 2AJ *DX 12143 Walsall*	01922 720 777	01922 647 222	post@johnmarston.co.uk *www.hceo.co.uk*
MORRIS-JONES, Gareth	95 High Street Mold CH7 1BJ *DX 26556 Mold*	01352 753882	01352 758927	office@keeneandkelly.fsnet.co.uk
OWEN, William	314 High Street Bangor Gwynedd LL57 1YA	01248 353357	01248 372272	wowenestate@yahoo.co.uk

Name	Postal Address *(DX Address in italics)*	Phone Number(s) *(Mobile or out of hours numbers in italics)*	Fax Number	Email address *(Web address in italics)*
PARRY, Anthony	9 Chester Street Mold CH7 1EG *DX 26556 Mold*	01352 752552	01352 752542	auctions.dodds@tesco.net dodds@ door_key.com
PEPPER, Nigel	17 Martin Street Stafford ST16 2LF *DX 14554 Stafford 1*	01785 211411	01785 248573	npepper@hmo.co.uk
POTE, David	Cornwall High Court Recovery Graham & Graham Solicitors High Cross House St Austell PL25 4AE *DX 81253 St Austell*	01726 75565	01726 61484	sheriff@graham-graham.co.uk
REED, Philip	Cornwall High Court Recovery Graham & Graham Solicitors High Cross House St Austell PL25 4AE *DX 81253 St Austell*	01726 75565	01726 61484	sheriff@graham-graham.co.uk
SANDBROOK, Claire	Shergroup Westwood Park London Road Little Horkesley Colchester Essex CO6 4BS *DX3654 COLCHESTER*	01206 274255 *07775 590454*	01206 274176	c-sandbrook@sheriffs.co.uk *www.sherforce. co. uk*

Name	Postal Address *(DX Address in italics)*	Phone Number(s) *(Mobile or out of hours numbers in italics)*	Fax Number	Email address *(Web address in italics)*
SILLS, Tim	6 Bedford Road Sandy Bedfordshire SG19 1EN *DX 47801 Sandy*	01767 680251	01767 691775	tim.sills@leedssmith.co.uk *www.leedssmith.co. uk*
SMITH, Alan	12 Greek Street Leeds LS1 5RU *DX 26416 LEEDS PARK SQUARE*	0113 2855979 *07717 508105*	0113 2855977	asmith@sheriffs.co.uk *www.sherforce.co.uk*
SOUTHERN, Norman	A & D Dean Trident House 31/33 Dale Street Liverpool L2 2DA *DX 14104 Liverpool*	0151 236 4751 0151 236 6406	0151 236 8071	sheriff@a-d-dean.co.uk
STEPHENS, Martin	Beattie Son & Leslie 35 Palmerston Road Northampton NN15EU	01604 605400 *07860 762736*	01604 605069	sheriffs@supanet.com
STOREY, Roy	Storey & Fellows Albert Chambers 50 Albert Road Middlesbrough TS11QD *DX 60534 Middlesbrough*	01642 218819	01642 246456	k.fellows@virgin.net

Name	Postal Address *(DX Address in italics)*	Phone Number(s) *(Mobile or out of hours numbers in italics)*	Fax Number	Email address *(Web address in italics)*
THOMSON, Patricia	The Sheriffs Office 26 Missouri Avenue Salford Manchester M50 2NP *DX 710252 Manchester 3*	0161 925 1800	0161 925 1801	tricia.thomson@northernsheriffs.com *www. northernsheriffs. com*
TODD, Nicholas	The Old Bull's Head Dun Street Sheffield S3 8SL DX *10531 Sheffield*	0114 2729667 *07764 559748*	0114 276160	info@ewbauctions.co.uk
TRICKEY, David	High Court Enforcement Group Limited 2nd Floor Lloyds Bank Chambers 30 High Street Crediton Devon EX17 3AH *DX 54207 Crediton*	01363 775118	01363 773009	dt@hceo.fsbusiness.co.uk
TUNSTILL, Peter	Breeze & Wyles 114 Fore Street Hertford Hertfordshire SG14 1AG *DX 57901 Hertford*	01992 558411	01992 503889	peter.tunstill@breezeandwyles.co.uk

IV OTHER USEFUL ADDRESSES

ADD 4

The Bar Council
289-293 High Holborn
London, WC1V 7HZ
DX: 240 LDE
Tel 020 7242 0082

LexisNexis Butterworths
Halsbury House
35 Chancery Lane
London, WC2A 1EL
DX: London Chancery Lane 1023
Tel 020 7400 2500

Court Service
Customer Service Unit
6th Floor Southside
105 Victoria Street
London SW1E 6QT
Tel 020 7210 1775/2009
Fax 020 7210 1797

Ministry of Justice
102 Petty France
London SW1H 9AJ
DX 152380 Westminster 8
Tel 020 3334 3555

Intellectual Property Office
Concept House,
Cardiff Road,
Newport, South Wales NP10 8QQ
Tel 01633 814000

The Law Society
113 Chancery Lane
London, WC2A 1PL
DX: 56 Chancery Lane
Tel 020 7242 1222

Companies House
Crown Way
Cardiff CF4 3UZ
DX: 33050
Tel 029 2038 8588

Legal Aid Board
85 Gray's Inn Road
London WC1X 8AA
DX: 450 Chancery Lane
Tel 020 7813 1000

Solicitors Regulation Authority
Ipsley Court
Berrington Close
Redditch
B98 0TD
DX: 19114 Redditch
Tel 0870 606 2555

Solicitor's Indemnity Fund Ltd
2nd Floor
28 Threadneedle Street
London EC2R 8AY
Tel 020 7621 3900

INDEX

This index covers material in the Forms supplement only.
References in **bold** *are to page numbers.*